BLACK THEOLOGY

A Documentary History
Volume I
1966–1979

BLACK THEOLOGY

A Documentary History

Volume I
1966–1979

Edited by
James H. Cone and Gayraud S. Wilmore

Second Edition, Revised

ORBIS BOOKS

Maryknoll, New York 10545

Third Printing, November 1999

The Catholic Foreign Mission Society of America (Maryknoll) recruits and trains people for overseas missionary service. Through Orbis Books, Maryknoll aims to foster the international dialogue that is essential to mission. The books published, however, reflect the opinions of their authors and are not meant to represent the official position of the society.

Acknowledgment is gratefully extended for permission to reprint the following: "The Religion of Black Power" by Vincent Harding, reprinted from *The Religious Situation: 1968*, ed. Donald R. Cutler. Copyright 1968 by Beacon Press. Used by permission. "Are American Negro Churches Christian?" by Joseph R. Washington, Jr. Reprinted with permission from *Theology Today* 20 (April 1963-January 1964). "The Black Messiah" by Albert B. Cleage, Jr. from *The Black Messiah*, Copyright 1968 by Albert B. Cleage. Used with permission of Sheed and Ward. "Black Theology and Black Liberation" by James H. Cone. Copyright 1970 by Christian Century Foundation. Reprinted with permission from the September 16, 1970 issue of *Christian Century*. "Black Theology in the Making" by J. Deotis Roberts, reprinted with permission from *Review and Expositor* 70, no. 3 (Summer 1973). "Theodicy and Methodology in Black Theology" by William R. Jones, reprinted with permission from *Harvard Theological Review* 64 (1971). "Biblical Revelation and Social Existence" by James Cone, reprinted with permission from *Interpretation* 28 (October 1974). "Biblical Theology and Black Theology" by Robert A. Bennett, reprinted with permission from *The Journal of the Interdenominational Theological Center* 3 (Spring 1976). "Double Jeopardy: To Be Black and Female" by Frances Beale, reprinted with permission of Signet Books from *The Black Woman*, edited by Toni Cade, Copyright 1970. "Black Women and the Churches: Triple Jeopardy" by Theressa Hoover, from *Sexist Religion and Women in the Church*, ed. by A. Hageman, copyright 1974. Used by permission of Follet Publishing Company. "Black Theology and Feminist Theology: A Comparative View" by Pauli Murray, from the January 1978 *Anglican Theological Review*, used by permission. "In Search of Our Mothers' Gardens" by Alice Walker, from *Ms.* magazine, vol. 2, no. 11, May 1974. Reprinted with permission. "Black Theology and African Theology" by James H. Cone and Gayraud S. Wilmore, reprinted by permission of Friendship Press from *Black Faith and Black Solidarity*, ed. by Priscilla Massie, copyright 1973. "An African Views American Black Theology" by John Mbiti, reprinted with permission from *Worldview* 17 (August 1974). "Black Theology/African Theology—Soul Mates or Antagonists" by Desmond M. Tutu, reprinted with permission from *Journal of Religious Thought* 32, no. 1 (Fall-Winter, 1975).

Library of Congress Cataloging-in-Publication Data

Black theology : a documentary history / edited by Jamas H. Cone and
   Gayraud S. Wilmore.—2nd ed., rev.
      p. cm.
   Includes bibliographical references and index.
   Contents: v. 1. 1966–1979.
   ISBN 0-88344-853-X (v. 1 : paper)
   1. Black theology. 2. Afro-Americans—Religion. 3. Black power.
I. Cone, James H. II. Wilmore, Gayraud S.
BT82.7.B56   1993
230'.089'96—dc20   92-44927
                                                                         CIP

To Verna and Jack Frost, my aunt and uncle,
remembering their loving kindness.

James H. Cone

To my father and mother,
Gayraud Stephen Wilmore, Sr., and Patricia Gardner Wilmore
—watching over us from the realm of the Ancestors.

Gayraud S. Wilmore

CONTENTS

General Introduction   1

PART I
BLACK POWER AND BLACK THEOLOGY

Introduction   15
1. **Black Power**   19
   Statement by the National Committee of Negro Churchmen
2. **The Black Manifesto**   27
3. **Black Theology**   37
   Statement by the National Committee of Black Churchmen
4. **The Religion of Black Power**   40
   Vincent Harding
5. **The White Church and Black Power**   66
   James H. Cone

PART II
FOUNDATIONAL VOICES BEFORE 1980

Introduction   89
6. **Are American Negro Churches Christian?**   92
   Joseph R. Washington, Jr.
7. **The Black Messiah**   101
   Albert B. Cleage, Jr.
8. **Black Theology and Black Liberation**   106
   James H. Cone
9. **Black Theology in the Making**   114
   J. Deotis Roberts
10. **Black Power, Black People, Theological Renewal**   125
    Gayraud S. Wilmore
11. **Theodicy and Methodology in Black Theology: A Critique
    of Washington, Cone, and Cleage**   141
    William R. Jones

PART III
BLACK THEOLOGY AND THE BIBLE

Introduction	155
12. **Biblical Revelation and Social Existence**	159
    James H. Cone
13. **Biblical Theology and Black Theology**	177
    Robert A. Bennett
14. **The Courage To Be Black**	193
    Allan Boesak
15. **Jesus, The Liberator**	203
    Joseph A. Johnson, Jr.

PART IV
BLACK THEOLOGY AND THE BLACK CHURCH

Introduction	217
16. **The Black Paper, 1968**	224
    Statement by Black Methodists for Church Renewal
17. **A Statement of the Black Catholic Clergy Caucus**	230
18. **Factors in the Origin and Focus of the National Black Evangelical Association**	233
    William H. Bentley
19. **The Basic Theological Position of the National Baptist Convention, U.S.A., Inc.**	245
    Joseph H. Jackson
20. **Liberation Movements: A Critical Assessment and a Reaffirmation**	250
    Position Paper of the African Methodist Episcopal Church
21. **The Episcopal Address to the 40th Quadrennial General Conference of the African Methodist Episcopal Zion Church**	257
    Herbert Bell Shaw
22. **What Black Christian Nationalism Teaches and Its Program**	263
    Statement from the Black Christian Nationalist Church, Inc.
23. **Black Theology and the Black Church: Where Do We Go from Here?**	266
    James H. Cone

PART V
BLACK THEOLOGY AND BLACK WOMEN

Introduction	279
24. **Double Jeopardy: To Be Black and Female**	284
    Frances Beale
25. **Black Women and the Churches: Triple Jeopardy**	293
    Theressa Hoover

26. Black Theology and Feminist Theology: A Comparative View 304
   Pauli Murray
27. Black Theology and the Black Woman 323
   Jacquelyn Grant
28. In Search of Our Mothers' Gardens 339
   Alice Walker

PART VI
BLACK THEOLOGY AND THIRD WORLD THEOLOGIES

Introduction 349
29. Black Theology and African Theology: Considerations for Dialogue,
   Critique, and Integration 366
   James H. Cone and Gayraud S. Wilmore
30. An African Views American Black Theology 379
   John Mbiti
31. Black Theology/African Theology—Soul Mates or Antagonists? 385
   Desmond M. Tutu
32. A Black American Perspective on the Future of African Theology 393
   James H. Cone
33. Black Theology and Latin American Liberation Theology 404
   Excerpts from a Symposium of the World Council of Churches
34. Black Theology and Marxist Thought 409
   Cornel West
Epilogue: An Interpretation of the Debate among Black Theologians 425
   James H. Cone
Annotated Bibliography of Black Theology, 1966–1979 441
   Mark L. Chapman

Index 455

GENERAL INTRODUCTION

Orbis Books agreed to publish the first edition of *Black Theology: A Documentary History, 1966–1979* shortly after the first national conference of the Black Theology Project of "Theology in the Americas," which met in Atlanta, Georgia, August 3-7, 1977. This was an historic gathering of church people and street people, academics and nonacademics, nationalists and Marxists. And it was clear that unless someone collected and published in one volume the major pronouncements, critical analyses, and interpretations that were piling up in libraries, intelligent lay people, theological students, and pastors would be unduly frustrated trying to make sense of what had obviously been an unprecedented movement of theological restlessness and dissent in the Black community since the mid-sixties.

Thus, the first edition of this volume was one of the key literary outgrowths of the 1970s. African-American scholars in religion had made an unmistakable declaration of independence from White theology as early as 1970 with the founding of the Society for the Study of Black Religion (SSBR), but by the end of the decade a growing maturity was taking the place of early precociousness.[1]

By 1979 African-American theological thought in the United States had attained a critical mass of literature, and although it was marked by unevenness and a lack of clarity about what Black theology actually was, it seemed highly useful for a systematic theologian and an historian of Black religion to collaborate on a book that would place a representative selection of essays and documents before the reading public.

It is now 1993. Most of what was said in the dawning days of Black theology in the United States and South Africa has been forgotten and much of what was written is now out of print. But the beat goes on in the African-American churches and neither Blacks nor Whites can ignore it. Pastors and lay people, Black feminists and womanists, Black and White theological students and their professors, are still wrestling with the ideas and interpretations of Christianity that poured from the minds and souls of Black women and men who tried to make a new faith-stand on ground that had been seized by the assaults of Malcolm X and Martin Luther King, Jr., on conventional American religion. Because many people today continue to discover that common ground existed between those two great Black religious thinkers of the twentieth century, and because younger people are still debating the issues we raised in the early years of Black theology, what we compiled and published on the subject in 1979 deserves to be revised and enlarged today.

1

Readers who are familiar with the first edition will immediately notice that in planning this new two-volume work we decided to eliminate many of the documents that appeared in the 1979 edition. This should not be interpreted as our judgment that those documents no longer have historical significance. In order to make room for a second volume, covering the period of 1979 to 1992, we were obliged to be more selective about what was retained from the earlier single volume. We were, therefore, anxious to republish only the landmark documents of the movement, statements of church leaders and assemblies, and examples of the theological writings of the formative period of Black theology.

We were also more sensitive this time to the needs of the classroom. Today courses in Black theology are taught in more than a hundred schools of theology in North America, Europe, and the Third World. Works by Black theologians are being used in seminaries and universities all over the world, not to mention in a variety of church study conferences and institutes in the United States and abroad. The selections in both new volumes have been tailored to the needs of instructors and students who will want to consult the key statements and articles that shaped the movement and to do so in the sequence we are recommending for optimum comprehension of the discourse that has taken place over the past twenty-six or twenty-seven years.

An important demurrer should be entered here. Those who require a more comprehensive grasp of the ethos and tone of the formative period should go back to the original Orbis Books edition of 1979. That edition not only contains many useful statements and essays we found it necessary to drop from this one, but also introductory essays that represented in 1979 what we viewed from our different perspectives as essential for understanding Black theology. We have continued in the present volumes the practice of identifying who wrote what by initialing the introductory essays, retaining most of the material from the first edition, but in some instances revising and shortening the text in the interest of space. Some readers may want, therefore, to compare the revised Introductions preceding each part of the present Volume I with those we wrote for the 1979 edition. Our minds have not changed about most things, but points of view and insights that have come to each of us over the years could not be denied in the process of republishing this work.

It is still useful to approach Black theology from an interdisciplinary perspective.[2] At the very least, systematic theology, Christian ethics, and church history are indispensable aids for unpacking the meaning of the debate and events that accompanied the emergence of this way of doing theology. The cognitive background for this assertion is the well-known partnership between liberation theologies and the social sciences. There have been undeniable strains of antiintellectualism in Black religion in the United States, but as a general rule, modern Black Christians have welcomed the insights of the social sciences in clarifying the meaning and demands of the gospel in the hurly-burly of what was going on either to impel or impede their struggle for justice.

In the African-American community news about Jesus is habitually read "between the lines" of the public media, or through the transparent overlay that history places over daily events. From the beginning, Black theology and Black history have been inseparable. Karl Barth, who is reputed to have said that the Christian strides into the world with the Bible in one hand and the newspaper in the other, recognized how essential this reading together of the Word of God and the signs of the times was for developing "a theology of freedom" that we believed was the peculiar task of American Christians.[3] Almost everything that has been good or bad about America has come to its most relentless and enduring expression in the African-American community where Christianity has provided a bridge over the troubled waters between God's design and the willfulness of human disorder, between biblical faith and secular history, between theology and sociology. As Charles Long says in his discussion of Barth and Black religion:

> The locus of these congeries of the American experience is now situated in the black community in this land, and no American theology or theology of freedom can come about without dealing with the existence of this community. To be sure, the recognition of the visibility of the black community in America will prompt many to confront the new situation as simply an ethical-moral problem. It is certainly this; but it is more. The visibility of this community raises critical and constructive issues on the intellectual and theological levels of our work.[4]

It is on these two levels that Black Christians have erected a historical project for freedom that reads the world through the Bible and the Bible through the world. Our interpretation of history, its tragedies and its triumphs, has come out of our encounter with God, and our understanding of God has come out of our historical struggle. The world has been a stage, and the slaves and masters, the Black underclass and the White establishment, have supplied the *dramatis personae* for God's mission in behalf of God's oppressed Black children. Black History, therefore, must be understood as sacred history and Black theological thought must be understood as eventful theology.

To speak of "eventful theology" is not to suggest that Black Christians are obsessed with inventing knee-jerk theological reactions to the flux of circumstance. Black Theology is not some impulsive, egotistical reaction to whatever happens to be transpiring at every moment of time — a kind of ready-made balm, a mixture of florid emotionalism and pious propaganda we carry around in our religious first-aid kits. It is, rather, a hardheaded, practical, and passionate reading of the most meaningful signs of times in the White community as well as the Black. It is an elucidation of what we have understood God to be doing, particularly in the history of our struggle against racism.

Karl Barth, when he came to Chicago in 1963, did not know enough about Black people to appreciate how Martin Luther King, Jr. and Malcolm X laid the groundwork for a new American theology. If Barth had lived through that momentous decade he would have celebrated Black Theology as the answer to

Parts or Sections 3 Explanation

his question: "Will such a specific American theology one day arise?" The documents and essays in Volume I will demonstrate that Black theology did indeed arise as just such a "theology of freedom." A theology of liberation in response to critical events—events that had the unmistakable sign that God was saying and doing something unprecedented about oppressed minorities and freedom in White America.

Part I, Black Power and Black Theology, deals with the evolution of Black theological reflection out of the quasi-religious movement of Black Power in the late 1960s. Today we see more clearly that although Martin Luther King rejected the early definitions of Black Power that supported and legitimated Malcolm's separatism, King came to invest the phrase with positive content, and to relate it to what he considered a healthy movement toward "black consciousness" (the term adopted later in South Africa).[5] We begin this book with five crucial documents and essays from the earliest period that show how some Black church leaders and theologians interpreted Black Power, and how their interpretations opened the floodgates for a new Black theology that was indebted to both King and Malcolm.

Most of what we have included in Part II, Foundational Voices Before 1980, is new material. Our purpose this time is to lift up the contributions of a few of the thinkers who first articulated a Black theology of liberation that was both old and new. These "foundational voices" before 1980 grounded theology in the religion of the early Black churches, but revitalized and radicalized it in the mid-twentieth century in order to raise new questions and new answers for African-American Christians.

Part III, Black Theology and the Bible, introduces an aspect of the early development of Black theology to which we gave scant attention in the first edition: the relationship between Black theology and Biblical Studies. The number of Black scholars who have received advanced degrees in the Old and New Testaments since 1979 made us more sensitive to the critical role the Bible has always played in Black religious thought. We have also become more alert to the hermeneutical proposals that were put forth by a few scholars, beginning with Charles B. Copher, emeritus professor of Old Testament at the Interdenominational Theological Center in Atlanta, and Robert Bennett of the Episcopal Theological School in Cambridge, Massachusetts. Here we concentrate on Black Theology and the Bible during the formative period. Volume II will deal with this important development since 1980 in greater detail.

In the first edition we included a section entitled "Black Theology and the Response of White Theologians." At that time it was important to present essays reflecting the critical rejoinders White American and European theologians were making to the rumblings of dissent in Black religious circles. In 1979 the importance of an engagement on the field of battle between Black and White theologians could not be gainsaid. The early meetings of the Society for the Study of Black Religion (SSBR), which brought together most of the Black men and women who were teaching in theological seminaries and a few university departments of religion, were full of news from the campuses about how White colleagues were either indifferent or scornfully opposed to what we were saying about the need for breaking the silence of European-American neoorthodoxy concerning the significance of the Black religious experience. Only a few prominent theologians, like Helmut Gollwitzer in Germany and John Bennett in the United States, were willing to admit the blind spots in mainstream Christian theology and open themselves to the writings of African-American scholars. We thought it illuminating to include their reflections in the first anthology on Black theology. If we were collecting such responses today we would probably include sample writings of White colleagues like Peter C. Hodgson of Vanderbilt University Divinity School, Frederick Herzog of Duke Divinity School, Benjamin Reist of San Francisco Theological Seminary, and Georges Casalis of Paris, France, all of whom made early and positive acknowledgments of the place of Black theology at the round table of theological discussion in the White academy.[6]

Today it does not seem so necessary to prove that Black theology was both condemned and applauded by White scholars. Most reputable seminaries and university departments of religion are making an effort, some enthusiastically and some grudgingly, to deal with it somewhere in their curriculums. Moreover, we are no longer shouting at each other, or pretending that we cannot hear each other's pained voices over the transom. The dialogue does and should continue, but in order to conserve space for new material we decided to excise the section on White responses that appeared in the first edition.

The responses of White theologians are, however, an important part of the journey of Black theology from the strident cries of activist pastors like Calvin Marshall and Lawrence Lucas,[7] and the early writings of James H. Cone and J. Deotis Roberts,[8] to the more modest and moderate theological agenda of African-American religious thinkers today. Anyone who wants to revisit the first discussions between Black and White theologians will need to go back to the earlier edition of this book (Wilmore & Cone 1979, Part III).

In the first General Introduction, I placed the documents on the response of the Black churches to Black theology in what I called the "second stage while the discussion of . . . Black theology went begging for an audience in the Black churches" (Wilmore & Cone 1979, 5). From the vantage point of thirteen years later there seems to be reason to consider the second stage, when Black theology became the most progressive and consolidated form of liberation theology available in North America, as coming a little later—perhaps after 1980. The reaction of the Black denominations and the Black caucuses of the predominantly White denominations to what we were writing came earlier—in the formative period. It was coterminous with the founding of the National Committee of Black Churchmen (NCBC) and its Theological Commission in Dallas, Texas, in 1967. The first statements from the denominations, both positive and negative, were issued between 1967 and 1969.

Richard M. Nixon assumed the presidency of the United States on January 20, 1969. He was just in time to counter the new militancy in the Black community. Immediately his Southern strategy of law and order and "benign

continued

neglect" of the poor disparaged people in the ghetto. He set about to turn the so-called War on Poverty declared by President Lyndon Johnson, with a viciousness bordering sometimes on genocide, into a systematic and clandestine war on Black radicalism. Soon after, the White churches and denominations broke away from their disaffected Black caucuses, and the Interreligious Foundation for Community Organization (IFCO), an interracial, interfaith coalition for funding grassroots movements, floundered in disuse. Local congregations and judicatories fumed over such improprieties as Black support for Angela Davis, a Black woman Marxist who was implicated in a courtroom shoot-out in Marin County, California, in 1970. Contributions to denominational budgets fell off precipitously as Whites complained that their money was being misused by being funneled to the Angela Davis Defense Fund and other militant causes. By the time of the humiliating denouement of Nixon's Watergate administration in August 1974, what had been known as the "church civil rights movement," the response of America's religious leaders to Martin Luther King, Jr., was practically dead. From that time on, the Black theology movement was regarded with grim dismay by the White religious community: Protestant, Catholic, and Jewish.

The material in Part IV, Black Theology and the Black Church, will show that these national developments actually helped to push the official leadership of the Black Church, whether as part of the predominantly White denominations or in the historic Black denominations, toward the militancy of Black Theology, even though many people in the pew were still ignorant of the term. With, however, one notable exception—the position taken in 1971 by the late Joseph H. Jackson, president of the National Baptist Convention, U.S.A., Inc., and pastor of the Olivet Baptist Church of Chicago—almost all of the other major Black denominations responded positively, if timidly, to Black theology in various public statements and position papers.

The end of the formative stage of Black theology was more complex than its beginning. The first annual meeting of the Society for the Study of Black Religion in conjunction with the annual meeting of the American Academy of Religion in 1971,[9] indicated that new interests and concerns were edging the movement toward the academic community and away from the local congregations and the people in the streets. By 1976 the reformulation of the NCBC statement on Black theology (Wilmore & Cone 1979, 340–344) made it clear that a complex transition was in process. But nothing marks this transition more than the stirring of theological repudiation of the patriarchism of Black theology on the part of Black women. The numerical predominance of women in African-American churches and the phenomenal increase of Black female seminarians during the 1970s, made it inevitable that the next high-water mark in African-American religious thought would come from the women.[10]

We have retained Part V, Black Theology and Black Women, essentially as it appeared in the first edition. Nothing in the intervening years has changed our minds about the critical importance of the five essays originally published in this section. But no aspect of Black theology has developed more rapidly.

Womanist Theology

The reader will be able to mark the progress from 1979 of theological work among African-American women by essays contained in Volume II, Part IV, entitled Womanist Theology.

We come finally to Part VI, Black Theology and Third World Theologies, and the relationship between Black Theology in the United States and theological work going on in the Third World. The National Committee of Black Churchmen, from whose conferences and commissions this way of doing theology issued, began a dialogue with African theologians in 1969. This conversation ripened during the 1970s, mainly due to the efforts of the Society for the Study of Black Religion, and then was expanded in the second period to include a wider range of dialogue partners from other parts of the so-called Third World. In the first edition, this section on Black and Third World theologies was the longest because we included articles dealing with Latin America and Asia. The discussions that first opened up Black Theology to global considerations, however, began between North American Black and African theologians. In this revision we decided to retain only the key documents from the early history of African and African-American discussions and an important document about the early discussions with Latin America.

Accordingly, Volume I ends with documentation on the international development of Black liberation theology before the end of the decade of the 1970s. African-American theologians and church leaders were looking abroad for partnership in what was understood as a struggle of Black people for justice and liberation all over the world. The situation at home only served to remind us that our fortunes were tied to other poor and oppressed people who were similarly disabled by a relentless and greedy system of international capitalism. When President Jimmy Carter took office in January 1977, the bleak statistics on the economic condition of African Americans was his unwelcome legacy from the Nixon-Ford years. The unemployment rate was 13.2 percent in the Black community as compared with 6.1 percent for Whites. Black teenagers were experiencing 39 percent joblessness, with figures running as high as 45 percent in some inner-city areas. Although African Americans were earning their highest wages in history, almost a third of all families were beneath the poverty line of $5,500 for an urban family of four. Only 8.9 percent of White families were in that category. In the meantime, the cities were stagnating after the loss of more than a million jobs to the suburbs since 1969. They festered with widespread physical decay, inferior, segregated public schools, and crime.[11] Black people looked expectantly toward Washington where Jimmy Carter, who would not have been elected without huge Black majorities, faced the challenge of an apathetic Congress and a conservative Supreme Court.

The appointment of Andrew Young and Patricia Harris to high offices in the Carter administration should not be permitted to obscure the fact of Carter's failure to move quickly and decisively to amend the disastrous situation of Black people at the end of the decade. The coincidence of a presidential election with the national bicentennial celebration made patriotic rhetoric a common commodity among both politicians and church leaders for several tedious months. But when all the shibboleths about God and the "Rights of Man" faded, White America returned to its customary indifference about the plight of the poor. The gap continued to widen between the rising middle class of all colors and the eight to ten million destitute Americans, predominantly Black, Native American, and Hispanic. Monsignor Geno Baroni, the erstwhile champion of the "White ethnics," warned that this unmeltable underclass that crossed the boundaries of ethnicity "presents our most dangerous crisis, more dangerous than the Depression of 1929, and more complex."[12]

An equally dangerous situation existed in southern Africa. Since the late 1960s it had become a matter of urgent concern for African Americans. The stalemate in Zimbabwe and Namibia had grown steadily more explosive under the communist-baiting policies of U. S. Republican administrations and a feckless United Nations. In June 1976 a rebellion broke out between thousands of Black students and the police in the segregated township of Soweto, South Africa. This precipitated the most serious crisis for the Vorster government since Sharpeville.

Carter dispatched Andrew Young, his ambassador to the United Nations and ended a long-standing American estrangement from the front-line African states by inviting President Julius K. Nyerere of socialist Tanzania to Washington. It was an uncertain gesture. Many African Americans regarded these motions toward Africa as insincere, a calculated move to prevent Soviet incursion and to mollify the outrage of Black citizens who were becoming aware of the linkages between the struggle against racism at home in the United States and U. S. supported racism in South Africa.

It was in this charged atmosphere of disappointments at home and anxieties about the situation in southern Africa that the first national conference on Black theology met in Atlanta in August 1977. It was, perhaps, the most important meeting in the latter half of the formative period and was planned as a revitalization of the movement that was showing signs of being in decline. Unlike any previous gathering since the Detroit IFCO conference in 1969, which produced the Black Manifesto, the Atlanta conference included not only prominent church officials and theologians, but the so-called "street people" and representatives of left-wing political organizations. The discussion was less dominated by members of the academically oriented Society for the Study of Black Religion and less inclined simply to react to the attitudes of the White churches. The Atlanta meeting was more political and international than any that preceded it. Its initiative had come from Theology in the Americas (TIA), a new interracial agency that sponsored the first conversations between North American and Latin American theologians in Detroit in 1975. TIA's intention was to promote a North American theology of liberation and it saw clearly that the theological activity that accompanied the civil rights movement and the subsequent eruption of Black Power was the vanguard for something comparable to Latin American Liberation Theology that might issue from Christians in North America.

The paper of James H. Cone, which opened the conference (Document 23), defined the basic issues, pointed toward the future, and marked the beginning of what we now call the second stage of Black theology, which is the subject of Volume II. Cone was critical of conservative tendencies in the Black denominations and called for the application of "the most severe scientific analysis to our church communities in terms of economics and politics." He stressed the need for the churches to deal with their "credibility problem" and questioned whether their dreams of a new heaven and a new earth embraced the injustices and deficiencies of Western capitalism, or a radically new polity that employed a Marxist analysis of history. Cone's challenge injected new life into the veins of Black theology in the United States and opened the way for the contribution of younger thinkers such as Cornel West whose essay on "Black Theology and Marxist Thought" (Document 34) is the last selection in this volume. Volume II will show whether or not this inclination toward radical politics was to be the distinguishing feature of Black Theology in the eighties and nineties, or whether the "second generation" of Black theologians was to take the movement in another direction.

In planning this revision it seemed necessary to retain the Epilogue that ended the first edition. Throughout the formative period Black theologians debated among themselves about the nature and function of Black religion, God and the problem of suffering, the place of Scripture and Tradition in Black Christianity, the meaning and significance of the African heritage and the religion of the slaves, the revision of church history and the role of the Black Church in the liberation struggle, and the relevance of a critique of Western capitalism in the formulation of a politically relevant Black theology. In the Epilogue, James H. Cone assesses the debate of Black theologians around these topics after the civil rights movement.

The new annotated bibliography by Mark Chapman that closes this volume is a further help for understanding the ebb and flow of controversy in the literature and the various organizations that made up what was called the Black theology movement during the first ten or twelve years of its existence.

One of the advantages of revising a text is the opportunity to correct that which would have otherwise gone down in history as presumed fact or settled opinion. We have welcomed this opportunity and have taken advantage of it to the best of our knowledge. The reader will have to be the judge. One of the pains and pleasures of revision more than a decade later, depending upon how kind or unkind history has been, is the discovery of how accurate one's analyses and how flawless one's predictions were. In this regard we think that we have more reason to be pleased than sorry. We believe that the first edition was a fairly accurate picture of the movement up to 1979, but that this revised edition in two volumes is a necessary improvement. We trust that the reader will find it a leaner, more concise record, better grounded in the foundational literature and, therefore, better fitted for the broader and deeper stream of movement history than the resource we compiled prior to 1980.

Hindsight has made it necessary to adjust our lenses on the past and we certainly see more clearly today where the movement may have faltered when it should have plowed straight ahead, and where it made wrong turns to the right or left, as the case may be. But on the whole, we are still convinced that in terms of methodology and content, Black liberation theology is today the most fruitful and exciting theological development in North America since the rise of neoorthodoxy. It is all the more noteworthy because it drew its sustenance from a community of slaves who were treated no better than beasts of burden and it came into full bloom among their descendants who were segregated, ignored, neglected, and patronized, by people who considered themselves the custodians and arbiters of Christian theology in the West.

Black theology, like all movements of the mind and spirit, will doubtless have its day and fade into oblivion. But for our time and place God has used it for the shaking of the foundations of both the church and the academy. We believe that that disruptive work is not yet over and is still imperative if the constructive development of a more faithful and obedient church, and a more learned and liberating academic community, is to continue into the future. We believe that the content of these two volumes will help pastors and lay people, students and teachers, to catch the spirit of the movement and, if God so wills, take it into the twenty-first century with courage and hope.

G.S.W.

NOTES

1. There were signs of a transition from the first statement of James H. Cone in *Black Theology and Black Power* (Seabury Press, 1969), to his more contemplative assessment in 1982, *My Soul Looks Back* (Abingdon Press). In 1979 we saw Olin P. Moyd's efforts at systematization in *Redemption in Black Theology* (Judson Press, 1979); in 1982 — with the ultimacy of a *coup de grâce* — Cornel West's shocking *Prophesy Deliverance! An Afro-American Revolutionary Christianity* (Westminster Press); and as if for good measure, J. Deotis Roberts' *Black Theology Today: Liberation and Contextualization* (Edwin Mellen Press), in 1983.

2. See parts III and IV of Gayraud Wilmore, ed., *African American Religious Studies: An Interdisciplinary Anthology* (Durham, N.C.: Duke University Press, 1989).

3. Charles H. Long recalls this opinion expressed by Barth in a lecture at the University of Chicago. See Long's *Significations: Signs, Symbols, and Images in the Interpretation of Religion* (Philadelphia: Fortress Press, 1986), 133–134.

4. Ibid., 135.

5. James H. Cone, *Martin & Malcolm & America: A Dream or a Nightmare* (Maryknoll, N.Y.: Orbis Books, 1991), 227–229.

6. See Peter C. Hodgson, *Children of Freedom* (Philadelphia: Fortress Press, 1974), Frederick Herzog, *Liberation Theology: Liberation in the Light of the Fourth Gospel* (New York: Seabury Press, 1972), Benjamin Reist, *Theology in Red, White, and Black* (Philadelphia: Westminster Press, 1975), and Georges Casalis, "Un Colloque insolite ou: 'la non-communication,'" in *Parole et Societe* (Paris, 1973).

7. Calvin Marshall, pastor of the Varick Memorial African Methodist Episcopal Zion Church in Brooklyn, New York, was one of the founders of the National Committee of Black Churchmen and the second chairman, after James Forman, of the Black Economic Development Conference that sponsored the Black Manifesto in 1969 — roles that made him influential in the shaping of a Black theological response to the White Church. Lawrence Lucas, Roman Catholic pastor of Harlem's Church of the Resurrection in the Archdiocese of New York, was also a founder of NCBC and author of the controversial *Black Priest/White Church: Catholics and Racism* (New York: Random House, 1970).

8. James H. Cone, *Black Theology and Black Power* (New York: Seabury Press, 1969), and J. Deotis Roberts, *Liberation and Reconciliation: A Black Theology* (Philadelphia: Westminster Press, 1971).

9. See an extended discussion of the role and significance of the Society for the Study of Black Religion in Charles Shelby Rooks, *Revolution in Zion: Reshaping African American Ministry, 1960–1974* (New York: Pilgrim Press, 1990), 134–147.

10. Statistics on predominance of women in the Black Church and the numbers of Black women seminarians in 1960 compared to 1980.

11. See *The State of Black America, 1969* (New York: National Urban League, 1970).

12. *Time* magazine, 12 August 1977, 15.

PART I

BLACK POWER
AND
BLACK THEOLOGY

INTRODUCTION

The documents in this first section of this book represent the earliest attempt of Black theologians and church leaders in the 1960s to explain why they felt constrained to break with the tentative coalition that existed between the civil rights movement led by Martin Luther King, Jr., and the mainstream of American liberal and neoorthodox Christianity. But most Black theologians were more comfortable with Dr. King than they were with the White Protestant theological establishment. As the late Bishop Joseph A. Johnson, Jr., of the Christian Methodist Episcopal Church, wrote in 1971:

> We had passed our courses in the four major fields of study; we knew our Barth, Brunner, and Niebuhr. We had entered deeply into a serious study of Bonhoeffer and Tillich, but we discovered that these white theologians had described the substance and had elucidated a contemporary faith for the white man. These white scholars knew nothing about the black experience, and to many of them this black experience was illegitimate and inauthentic.[1]

Black theology emerged from the need of Black people to think theologically for themselves and from the theological implications of the Black Power movement of the 1960s. The clergy who gathered in July 1966, during one of the "long, hot summers" of rebellion against the crushing despotism of White Power, rejected Dr. King's early judgment, applauded by many mainstream White church leaders, that Black Power was "a nihilistic philosophy born out of the conviction that the Negro can't win."[2] The northern Black clergy were not about to repudiate the leader of the most important church-related campaign since Black abolitionism. As much as they may have disagreed with King, they felt themselves bound to him and the Southern Christian Leadership Conference (SCLC) as a loyal but dissenting northern phalanx of the movement. But they were prepared, as King was not, to repudiate White Christian objections to the idea of an oppressed minority using coercive power to advance what Blacks had decided for themselves was a "necessary means" for achieving justice and liberation for the masses.

The pioneers of early Black theology were determined to extrapolate from the concept of Black Power a theological referent that would not only vindicate the young civil rights workers laboring in the rural South, who wanted to apply more severe sanctions against white die-hards, but would also galvanize the left

15

wing of the Southern-based civil rights movement and reassemble it within the province of Black Christians who lived in the urban North.

Under the leadership of a Harvard-educated Baptist preacher, Benjamin F. Payton, then executive director of the Commission of Religion and Race of the National Council of Churches of Christ in the U.S.A., a meeting was called that brought together a small group of Harlem pastors and denominational staff who worked at The Interchurch Center in New York City. The purpose was to defy the White churches by drafting a moderate, but ringing affirmation of Black Power. Few who attended that meeting in Payton's office realized that their theological analysis and justification of secular Black Power would set the stage for a new religio-political perspective called Black theology.

The first document in Part I, "Black Power" (statement by the National Committee of Negro Churchmen) was the product of that historic meeting chaired by Payton. The final version was written by a small committee that met two or three times. It was then circulated for signatures among some of the most influential clergy in the nation and published on July 31, 1966 as a full-page advertisement in the *New York Times*. A study of the names that appear at the end of the statement will indicate the wide support it received from Black Church leadership across the country. Despite its essentially integrationist tone, it nevertheless represents the beginning of Black independence from White theologians and ethicists of the time who were either silent about or critical of the Black Power movement. The statement was also the banner around which a new organization was formed: the National Committee of Negro Churchmen (later to become the National Committee of Black Churchmen and still later the National Conference of Black Christians). Predictably, Benjamin F. Payton was elected its first president.

Coming out of a different context but, in terms of making a generative contribution to early Black theology, of no less importance, is Document 2, "The Black Manifesto." A brief explanation of that context is necessary if the reader is to understand what led to James Forman's highly controversial challenge to Christian churches and Jewish synagogues in the United States, and how that challenge affected the early development of Black theology.

In September 1967 the Interreligious Foundation for Community Organization (IFCO) was founded as an agency of Protestants, Catholics, and Jews that would allow them to fund radical inner-city organizations without, it was hoped, getting the denominations and synagogues into difficulty with their more conservative lay constituencies. Under the inspiration of the Reverend Lucius Walker, an Alinski-trained community organizer who became IFCO's executive director, a National Black Economic Development Conference was called at Wayne State University in Detroit in late April 1969. Although IFCO was financed almost entirely by money from wealthy White sources, its board of directors was controlled by Black grassroots community organizers and northern Black church leaders. When the funding sources sought to assert their ultimate control of the resources by diverting most of it to their own "designated projects" rather than directly funding ghetto organizations with "no strings attached," there was rebellion in the ranks. Lucius Walker, Albert B. Cleage, Jr., Earl Allen, Anna Arnold Hedgeman, and others, welcomed the Wayne State conference as a way of hearing from the people. The conference was thrown wide open to encourage proposals and suggestions from the poor people of the decaying and violence-torn urban areas. What were their most urgent needs and how should the churches and synagogues of the nation really assist them in their struggle?

It was from this conference, on April 26, 1969, that the "Black Manifesto," was issued. The strategy of direct funding was, in fact, its main burden. Its controversial preamble concentrated on the complicity of America's religious establishment in the oppression of the Black masses and used Marxist rhetoric to call for the empowerment of Black social, economic, and political institutions along nationalist lines. The "Black Manifesto," although written by an outsider to the churches, was more or less endorsed by the church leaders and Black bureaucrats at The Interchurch Center who controlled IFCO. The Manifesto's emphasis upon social revolution and the self-determination of Black institutions was not incompatible with their views and gave impetus to the fledgling theological movement that had begun two years earlier.

The reader may want to consult the first edition of this book to delve more deeply into the complexities of the emergence of the National Committee of Black Churchmen and the Black Manifesto. Parts I and II of the 1979 edition include important documents that were left out of this edition in order to make space for material that we felt would be needed to clarify the development of Black theology from 1979 to the present. We would recommend particularly "The Church and the Urban Crisis" (Wilmore & Cone 1979, 43–47), three short statements from the first conference of the National Council of Churches, held September 27–30, 1967, in Washington, D.C., at which national church leaders made what was then an unprecedented and momentous decision to break up into separate Black and White caucuses to express their concern about the effect of racism on what was happening in the cities of the nation. Also, for the serious student of this period, we recommend NCBC's "Response to the Black Manifesto," issued in 1969 by its board of directors (Wilmore and Cone 1979, 90–92).

Document 3, the statement on "Black Theology," written by the NCBC Committee on Theological Prospectus on June 13, 1969, was the culmination of three years of tension between Black and White churches over Black Power. It expressed the growing theological consensus that was developing—in the heat generated by the Manifesto crisis—among Black church leaders and academics. The key drafter of this document was James H. Cone, then a newly appointed professor of systematic theology at Union Theological Seminary in New York. His first book, *Black Theology and Black Power* (Seabury, 1969. Reprint, Harper & Row, 1989), preceded the Atlanta meeting of the Theological Prospectus Committee by a matter of weeks. The book had caused such a sensation in the academic world that its author was bound to exercise extraordinary influence on this first official attempt to define the scope and substance of Black theology.

Although Black theology has been shaped and reshaped by many events and perspectives since 1969, this brief statement, hammered out at the Interdenominational Theological Center in Atlanta, still expresses the essentials of doing theology out of the African-American religious experience.

The decision to eliminate some documents that appeared in the earlier edition gave us sufficient space to include this time an important essay by Vincent Harding that belongs to the early assessment of the spiritual and cultural forces that prompted Black lay people to think theologically about the meaning of the events that were swirling around them during the 1960s. Document 4, "The Religion of Black Power," is a remarkably prophetic and lucid analysis of the spiritual content and intensity of Black Power. It is no accident that a social historian and lay theologian like Vincent Harding, now a professor at Iliff Theological Seminary in Denver, would have anticipated as early as 1968, some of the lineaments of a theology that originated in the Black ghetto—from the bottom up, rather than from the top down.

We conclude Part I with a reprint of the third chapter of Cone's *Black Theology and Black Power*. It is entitled "The White Church and Black Power." No documentary history of the Black theology movement would be complete without a sample of this ground-breaking work that articulated the profound meaning of Black people's rebellion against White Christianity and the theological and political significance of their quest for power with which to exorcise the demon of racism.

G.S.W.

NOTES

1. Joseph A. Johnson, "Jesus, the Liberator," in J. Deotis Roberts and James J. Gardiner, eds., *Quest for a Black Theology* (Philadelphia: United Church Press, 1971), 100.

2. Martin Luther King, Jr., *Where Do We Go From Here: Chaos or Community?* (New York: Harper & Row, 1967), 44.

[Handwritten at top:] The distortion in the Controversy about "black power" is rooted in a gross imbalance of power & consciousness between Negroes + white Americans

[Handwritten:] * Assumption that white **1**Americans can get what they want thru use of power ———— Negro Americans must make their appeal only thru ~~consciousness~~ Conscience.

BLACK POWER

Statement by the National Committee
of Negro Churchmen,
July 31, 1966

We, an informal group of Negro churchmen in America, are deeply disturbed about the crisis brought upon our country by historic distortions of important human realities in the controversy about "black power." What we see shining through the variety of rhetoric is not anything new but the same old problem of power and race which has faced our beloved country since 1619.

We realize that neither the term "power" nor the term "Christian conscience" is an easy matter to talk about, especially in the context of race relations in America. The fundamental distortion facing us in the controversy about "black power" is rooted in a gross imbalance of power and conscience between Negroes and white Americans. It is this distortion, mainly, which is responsible for the widespread, though often inarticulate, assumption that white people are justified in getting what they want through the use of power, but that Negro Americans must, either by nature or by circumstance, make their appeal only through conscience. As a result, the power of white men and the conscience of black men have both been corrupted. The power of white men is corrupted because it meets little meaningful resistance from Negroes to temper it and keep white men from aping God. The conscience of black men is corrupted because, having no power to implement the demands of conscience, the concern for justice is transmuted into a distorted form of love, which, in the absence of justice, becomes chaotic self-surrender. Powerlessness breeds a race of beggars. We are faced now with a situation where conscienceless power meets powerless conscience, threatening the very foundations of our nation.

This statement was first published in the *New York Times*, July 31, 1966. At the time the organization was known as the National Committee of Negro Churchmen with headquarters in New York City. The name was changed to the National Committee of Black Churchmen in 1967, and then to the National Conference of Black Christians.

Therefore, we are impelled by conscience to address at least four groups of people in areas where clarification of the controversy is of the most urgent necessity. We do not claim to present the final word. It is our hope, however, to communicate meanings from our experience regarding power and certain elements of conscience to help interpret more adequately the dilemma in which we are all involved.

I. To the Leaders of America: Power and Freedom

It is of critical importance that the leaders of this nation listen also to a voice which says that the principal source of the threat to our nation comes neither from the riots erupting in our big cities, nor from the disagreements among the leaders of the civil rights movement, nor even from mere raising of the cry for "black power." These events, we believe, are but the expression of the judgment of God upon our nation for its failure to use its abundant resources to serve the real well-being of people, at home and abroad.

We give our full support to all civil rights leaders as they seek for basically American goals, for we are not convinced that their mutual reinforcement of one another in the past is bound to end in the future. We would hope that the public power of our nation will be used to strengthen the civil rights movement and not to manipulate or further fracture it.

We deplore the overt violence of riots, but we believe it is more important to focus on the real sources of the eruptions. These sources may be abetted inside the ghetto, but their basic causes lie in the silent and covert violence which white middle-class America inflicts upon the victims of the inner city. The hidden, smooth and often smiling decisions of American leaders which tie a white noose of suburbia around their necks, and which pin the backs of the masses of Negroes against the steaming ghetto walls—without jobs in a booming economy; with dilapidated and segregated educational systems in the full view of unenforced laws against it; in short: the failure of American leaders to use American power to create equal opportunity *in life* as well as *in law*—this is the real problem and not the anguished cry for "black power."

From the point of view of the Christian faith, there is nothing necessarily wrong with concern for power. At the heart of the Protestant reformation is the belief that ultimate power belongs to God alone and that men become most inhuman when concentrations of power lead to the conviction—overt or covert—that any nation, race or organization can rival God in this regard. At issue in the relations between whites and Negroes in America is the problem of inequality of power. Out of this imbalance grows the disrespect of white men for the Negro personality and community, and the disrespect of Negroes for themselves. This is a fundamental root of human injustice in America. In one sense, the concept of "black power" reminds us of the need for and the possibility of authentic democracy in America.

We do *not* agree with those who say that we must cease expressing concern for the acquisition of power lest we endanger the "gains" already made by the civil rights movement. The fact of the matter is, there have been few substantive gains since about 1950 in this area. The gap has constantly widened between the incomes of non-whites relative to the whites. Since the Supreme Court decision of 1954, de facto segregation in every major city in our land has increased rather than decreased. Since the middle of the 1950s unemployment among Negroes has gone up rather than down while unemployment has decreased in the white community.

While there has been some progress in some areas for equality for Negroes, this progress has been limited mainly to middle-class Negroes who represent only a small minority of the larger Negro community.

These are the hard facts that we must all face together. Therefore we must not take the position that we can continue in the same old paths.

When American leaders decide to serve the real welfare of people instead of war and destruction; when American leaders are forced to make the rebuilding of our cities first priority on the nation's agenda; when American leaders are forced by the American people to quit misusing and abusing American power; then will the cry for "black power" become inaudible, for the framework in which all power in America operates would include the power and experience of black men as well as those of white men. In that way, the fear of the power of each group would be removed. America is our beloved homeland. But, America is not God. Only God can do everything. America and the other nations of the world must decide which among a number of alternatives they will choose.

II. To White Churchmen: Power and Love

As black men who were long ago forced out of the white church to create and to wield "black power," we fail to understand the emotional quality of the outcry of some clergy against the use of the term today. It is not enough to answer that "integration" is the solution. For it is precisely the nature of the operation of power under some forms of integration which is being challenged. The Negro Church was created as a result of the refusal to submit to the indignities of a false kind of "integration" in which all power was in the hands of white people. A more equal sharing of power is precisely what is required as the precondition of authentic human interaction. We understand the growing demand of Negro and white youth for a more honest kind of integration; one which increases rather than decreases the capacity of the disinherited to participate with power in all of the structures of our common life. Without this capacity to *participate with power*—i.e., to have some organized political and economic strength to really influence people with whom one interacts—integration is not meaningful. For the issue is not one of racial balance but of honest interracial interaction.

For this kind of interaction to take place, all people need power, whether black or white. We regard as sheer hypocrisy or as a blind and dangerous illusion the view that opposes love to power. Love should be a controlling element in power, not power itself. So long as white churchmen continue to moralize and misinterpret Christian love, so long will justice continue to be subverted in this land.

III. To Negro Citizens: Power and Justice

Both the anguished cry for "black power" and the confused emotional response to it can be understood if the whole controversy is put in the context of American history. Especially must we understand the irony involved in the pride of Americans regarding their ability to act as individuals on the one hand, and their tendency to act as members of ethnic groups on the other hand. In the tensions of this part of our history is revealed both the tragedy and the hope of human redemption in America.

America has asked its Negro citizens to fight for opportunity *as individuals* whereas at certain points in our history what we have needed most has been opportunity for the whole group, not just for selected and approved Negroes. Thus in 1863, the slaves were made legally free, as individuals, but the real question regarding personal and group power to maintain that freedom was pushed aside. Power at that time for a mainly rural people meant land and tools to work the land. In the words of Thaddeus Stevens, power meant "40 acres and a mule." But this power was not made available to the slaves and we see the results today in the pushing of a landless peasantry off the farms into big cities where they come in search mainly of the power to be free. What they find are only the formalities of unenforced legal freedom. So we must ask, "What is the nature of the power which we seek and need today?" Power today is essentially organizational power. It is not a thing lying about in the streets to be fought over. It is a thing which, in some measure, already belongs to Negroes and which must be developed by Negroes in relationship with the great resources of this nation.

Getting power necessarily involves reconciliation. We must first be reconciled to ourselves lest we fail to recognize the resources we already have and upon which we can build. We must be reconciled to ourselves as persons and to ourselves as an historical group. This means we must find our way to a new self-image in which we can feel a normal sense of pride in self, including our variety of skin color and the manifold textures of our hair. As long as we are filled with hatred for ourselves we will be unable to respect others.

At the same time, if we are seriously concerned about power then we must build upon that which we already have. "Black power" is already present to some extent in the Negro church, in Negro fraternities and sororities, in our professional associations, and in the opportunities afforded to Negroes who make decisions in some of the integrated organizations of our society.

We understand the reasons by which these limited forms of "black power" have been rejected by some of our people. Too often the Negro church has stirred its members away from the reign of God in *this world* to a distorted and complacent view of *an otherworldly* conception of God's power. We commit ourselves as churchmen to make more meaningful in the life of our institution our conviction that Jesus Christ reigns in the "here" and "now" as well as in the future he brings in upon us. We shall, therefore, use more of the resources of our churches in working for human justice in the places of social change and upheaval where our Master is already at work.

At the same time, we would urge that Negro social and professional organizations develop new roles for engaging the problem of equal opportunity and put less time into the frivolity of idle chatter and social waste.

We must not apologize for the existence of this form of group power, for we have been oppressed as a group, not as individuals. We will not find our way out of that oppression until both we and America accept the need for Negro Americans as well as for Jews, Italians, Poles and white Anglo-Saxon Protestants, among others, to have and to wield group power.

However, if power is sought merely as an end in itself, it tends to turn upon those who seek it. Negroes need power in order to participate more effectively at all levels of the life of our nation. We are glad that none of those civil rights leaders who have asked for "black power" has suggested that it means a new form of isolationism or a foolish effort at domination. But we must be clear about why we need to be reconciled with the white majority. It is *not* because we are only one-tenth of the population in America; for we do not need to be reminded of the awesome power wielded by the 90% majority. We see and feel that power every day in the destructions heaped upon our families and upon the nation's cities. We do not need to be threatened by such cold and heartless statements. For we are men, not children, and we are growing out of our fear of that power, which can hardly hurt us any more in the future than it does in the present or has in the past. Moreover, those bare figures conceal the potential political strength which is ours if we organize properly in the big cities and establish effective alliances.

Neither must we rest our concern for reconciliation with our white brothers on the fear that failure to do so would damage gains already made by the civil rights movement. If those gains are in fact real, they will withstand the claims of our people for power and justice, not just for a few select Negroes here and there, but for the masses of our citizens. We must rather rest our concern for reconciliation on the firm ground that we and all other Americans *are* one. Our history and destiny are indissolubly linked. If the future is to belong to any of us, it must be prepared for all of us whatever our racial or religious background. For in the final analysis, we are *persons* and the power of all groups must be wielded to make visible our common humanity.

The future of America will belong to neither white nor black unless all Americans work together at the task of rebuilding our cities. We must organize not only among ourselves but with other groups in order that we can, together, gain power sufficient to change this nation's sense of what is *now* important and what must be done *now*. We must work with the remainder of the nation to organize whole cities for the task of making the rebuilding of our cities first priority in the use of our resources. This is more important than who gets to the moon first or the war in Vietnam.

To accomplish this task we cannot expend our energies in spastic or ill-tempered explosions without meaningful goals. We must move from the politics of philanthropy to the politics of metropolitan development for equal opportunity. We must relate all groups of the city together in new ways in order that the truth of our cities might be laid bare and in order that, together, we can lay claim to the great resources of our nation to make truth more human.

IV. To the Mass Media: Power and Truth

The ability or inability of all people in America to understand the upheavals of our day depends greatly on the way power and truth operate in the mass media. During the Southern demonstrations for civil rights, you men of the communications industry performed an invaluable service for the entire country by revealing plainly to all ears and eyes, the ugly truth of a brutalizing system of overt discrimination and segregation. Many of you were mauled and injured, and it took courage for you to stick with the task. You were instruments of change and not merely purveyors of unrelated facts. You were able to do this by dint of personal courage and by reason of the power of national news agencies which supported you.

Today, however, your task and ours is more difficult. The truth that needs revealing today is not so clear-cut in its outlines, nor is there a national consensus to help you form relevant points of view. Therefore, nothing is now more important than that you look for a variety of sources of truth in order that the limited perspectives of all of us might be corrected. Just as you related to a broad spectrum of people in Mississippi instead of relying only on police records and establishment figures, so must you operate in New York City, Chicago and Cleveland.

The power to support you in this endeavor *is present* in our country. It must be searched out. We desire to use our limited influence to help relate you to the variety of experience in the Negro community so that limited controversies are not blown up into the final truth about us. The fate of this country is, to no small extent, dependent upon how you interpret the crises upon us, so that human truth is disclosed and human needs are met.

Signatories:

Bishop John D. Bright, Sr., A.M.E. Church, First Episcopal District, Philadelphia, Pennsylvania

The Rev. John Bryant, Connecticut Council of Churches, Hartford, Connecticut

Suffragan Bishop John M. Burgess, The Episcopal Church, Boston, Massachusetts

The Rev. W. Sterling Cary, Grace Congregational Church, New York, New York

The Rev. Charles E. Cobb, St. John Church (UCC), Springfield, Massachusetts

The Rev. Caesar D. Coleman, Christian Methodist Episcopal Church, Memphis, Tennessee

The Rev. Joseph C. Coles, Williams Institutional CME Church, New York, New York

The Rev. George A. Crawley, Jr., St. Paul Baptist Church, Baltimore, Maryland

The Rev. O. Herbert Edwards, Trinity Baptist Church, Baltimore, Maryland

The Rev. Bryant George, United Presbyterian Church in the U.S.A., New York, New York

Bishop Charles F. Golden, The Methodist Church, Nashville, Tennessee

The Rev. Quinland R. Gordon, The Episcopal Church, New York, New York

The Rev. James Hargett, Church of Christian Fellowship, U.C.C., Los Angeles, California

The Rev. Edler Hawkins, St. Augustine Presbyterian Church, New York, New York

The Rev. Reginald Hawkins, United Presbyterian Church, Charlotte, North Carolina

Dr. Anna Arnold Hedgeman, Commission on Religion and Race, National Council of Churches, New York, New York

The Rev. R. E. Hodd, Gary, Indiana

The Rev. H. R. Hughes, Bethel A.M.E. Church, New York, New York

The Rev. Kenneth Hughes, St. Bartholomew's Episcopal Church, Cambridge, Massachusetts

The Rev. Donald G. Jacobs, St. James A.M.E. Church, Cleveland, Ohio

The Rev. J. L. Joiner, Emanuel A.M.E. Church, New York, New York

The Rev. Arthur A. Jones, Metropolitan A.M.E. Church, Philadelphia, Pennsylvania

The Rev. Stanley King, Sabathini Baptist Church, Minneapolis, Minnesota

The Rev. Earl Wesley Lawson, Emanuel Baptist Church, Malden, Massachusetts

The Rev. David Licorish, Abyssinian Baptist Church, New York, New York

The Rev. Arthur B. Mack, St. Thomas A.M.E.Z. Church, Haverstraw, New York

The Rev. James W. Mack, South United Church of Christ, Chicago, Illinois

The Rev. O. Clay Maxwell, Jr., Baptist Ministers Conference of New York City and Vicinity, New York, New York

The Rev. Leon Modeste, The Episcopal Church, New York, New York

Bishop Noah W. Moore, Jr., The Methodist Church, Southwestern Area, Houston, Texas

The Rev. David Nikerson, Episcopal Society for Cultural and Racial Unity, Atlanta, Georgia

The Rev. LeRoy Patrick, Bethesda United Presbyterian Church, Pittsburgh, Pennsylvania

The Rev. Benjamin F. Payton, Commission on Religion and Race, National Council of Churches, New York, New York

The Rev. Isaiah P. Pogue, St. Mark's Presbyterian Church, Cleveland, Ohio

The Rev. Sandy F. Ra, Empire Baptist State Convention, Brooklyn, New York

Bishop Herbert B. Shaw, Presiding Bishop, Third Episcopal District, A.M.E.Z. Church, Wilmington, North Carolina

The Rev. Stephen P. Spottswood, Commission on Race and Cultural Relations, Detroit Council of Churches, Detroit, Michigan

The Rev. Henri A. Stines, Church of the Atonement, Washington. D.C.

Bishop James S. Thomas, Resident Bishop, Iowa Area, The Methodist Church, Des Moines, Iowa

The Rev. V. Simpson Turner, Mt. Carmel Baptist Church, Brooklyn, New York

The Rev. Edgar Ward, Grace Presbyterian Church, Chicago, Illinois

The Rev. Paul M. Washington, Church of the Advocate, Philadelphia, Pennsylvania

The Rev. Frank L. Williams, Methodist Church, Baltimore, Maryland

The Rev. John W. Williams, St. Stephen's Baptist Church, Kansas City, Missouri

The Rev. Gayraud Wilmore, United Presbyterian Church U.S.A., New York, New York

The Rev. M. L. Wilson, Covenant Baptist Church, New York, New York

The Rev. Robert H. Wilson, Corresponding Secretary, National Baptist Convention of America, Dallas, Texas

The Rev. Nathan Wright, Episcopal Diocese of Newark, Newark, New Jersey

2

THE BLACK MANIFESTO

Introduction: Total Control as the Only Solution to the Economic Problems of Black People

Brothers and Sisters:

We have come from all over the country burning with anger and despair not only with the miserable economic plight of our people but fully aware that the racism on which the Western World was built dominates our lives. There can be no separation of the problems of racism from the problems of our economic, political, and cultural degradation. To any black man, this is clear.

But there are still some of our people who are clinging to the rhetoric of the Negro, and we must separate ourselves from these Negroes who go around the country promoting all types of schemes for black capitalism.

Ironically, some of the most militant Black Nationalists, as they call themselves, have been the first to jump on the bandwagon of black capitalism. They are pimps, black power pimps and fraudulent leaders, and the people must be educated to understand that any black man or Negro who is advocating a perpetuation of capitalism inside the United States is in fact seeking not only his ultimate destruction and death but is contributing to the continuous exploitation of black people all around the world. For it is the power of the United States Government, this racist, imperialist government, that is choking the life of all people around the world.

We are an African people. We sit back and watch the Jews in this country make Israel a powerful conservative state in the Middle East, but we are concerned actively about the plight of our brothers in Africa. We are the most advanced technological group of black people in the world, and there are many skills that could be offered to Africa. At the same time, it must be publicly stated that many African leaders are in disarray themselves, having been duped into following the lines as laid out by the western imperialist governments.

This document was presented by James Forman to the National Black Economic Development Conference in Detroit, Michigan, and adopted on April 26, 1969. On May 4, 1969, Forman presented it to the congregation of Riverside Church, New York City.

Africans themselves succumbed to and are victims of the power of the United States. For instance, during the summer of 1967, as the representatives of SNCC, Howard Moore and I traveled extensively in Tanzania and Zambia. We talked to high, very high, government officials. We told them there were many black people in the United States who were willing to come and work in Africa. All these government officials, who were part of the leadership in their respective governments, said they wanted us to send as many skilled people as we could contact. But this program never came into fruition, and we do not know the exact reasons, for I assure you that we talked and were committed to making this a successful program. It is our guess that the United States put the squeeze on these countries, for such a program directed by SNCC would have been too dangerous to the international prestige of the United States. It is also possible that some of the wild statements by some black leaders frightened the Africans.

In Africa today there is a great suspicion of black people in this country. This is a correct suspicion since most of the Negroes who have left the States for work in Africa usually work for the Central Intelligence Agency (CIA) or the State Department. But the respect for us as a people continues to mount, and the day will come when we can return to our homeland as brothers and sisters. But we should not think of going back to Africa today, for we are located in a strategic position. We live inside the United States, which is the most barbaric country in the world, and we have a chance to help bring this government down.

Time is short, and we do not have much time and it is time we stop mincing words. Caution is fine, but no oppressed people ever gained their liberation until they were ready to fight, to use whatever means necessary, including the use of force and power of the gun to bring down the colonizer.

We have heard the rhetoric, but we have not heard the rhetoric which says that black people in this country must understand that we are the vanguard force. We shall liberate all the people in the United States, and we will be instrumental in the liberation of colored people the world around. We must understand this point very clearly so that we are not trapped into diversionary and reactionary movements. Any class analysis of the United States shows very clearly that black people are the most oppressed group of people inside the United States. We have suffered the most from racism and exploitation, cultural degradation and lack of political power. It follows from the laws of revolution that the most oppressed will make the revolution, but we are not talking about just making the revolution. All the parties on the left who consider themselves revolutionary will say that blacks are the vanguard, but we are saying that not only are we the vanguard, but we must assume leadership, total control, and we must exercise the humanity which is inherent in us. We are the most humane people within the United States. We have suffered and we understand suffering. Our hearts go out to the Vietnamese, for we know what it is to suffer under the domination of racist America. Our hearts, our soul and all the compassion we can mount go out to our brothers in Africa, Santo Domingo, Latin America and Asia who are being tricked by the power structure of the United States which is dominating the world today. These ruthless, barbaric men have systematically tried to kill all people and organizations opposed to its imperialism. We no longer can just get by with the use of the word "capitalism" to describe the United States, for it is an imperial power sending money, missionaries and the army throughout the world to protect this government and the few rich whites who control it. General Motors and all the major auto industries are operating in South Africa, yet the white dominated leadership of the United Auto Workers sees no relationship to the exploitation of the black people in South Africa and the exploitation of black people in the United States. If they understand it, they certainly do not put it into practice, which is the actual test. We as black people must be concerned with the total conditions of all black people in the world.

But while we talk of revolution, which will be an armed confrontation and long years of sustained guerrilla warfare inside this country, we must also talk of the type of world we want to live in. We must commit ourselves to a society where the total means of production are taken from the rich and placed into the hands of the state for the welfare of all the people. This is what we mean when we say total control. And we mean that black people who have suffered the most from exploitation and racism must move to protect their black interest by assuming leadership inside of the United States of everything that exists. The time has ceased when we are second in command and the white boy stands on top. This is especially true of the welfare agencies in this country, but it is not enough to say that a black man is on top. He must be committed to building the new society, to taking the wealth away from the rich people, such as General Motors, Ford, Chrysler, the DuPonts, the Rockefellers, the Mellons, and all the other rich white exploiters and racists who run this world.

Where do we begin? We have already started. We started the moment we were brought to this country. In fact, we started on the shores of Africa, for we have always resisted attempts to make us slaves, and now we must resist the attempts to make us capitalists. It is in the financial interest of the United States to make us capitalist, for this will be the same line as that of integration into the mainstream of American life. Therefore, brothers and sisters, there is no need to fall into the trap that we have to get an ideology. We HAVE an ideology. Our fight is against racism, capitalism and imperialism, and we are dedicated to building a socialist society inside the United States where the total means of production and distribution are in the hands of the State, and that must be led by black people, by revolutionary blacks who are concerned about the total humanity of this world. And, therefore, we obviously are different from some of those who seek a black nation in the United States, for there is no way for that nation to be viable if in fact the United States remains in the hands of white racists. Then too, let us deal with some arguments that we should share power with whites. We say that there must be a revolutionary black vanguard, and that white people in this country must be willing to accept black leadership, for that is the only protection that black people have to protect ourselves from racism rising again in this country.

Racism in the United States is so pervasive in the mentality of whites that only an armed, well-disciplined, black-controlled government can insure the stamping out of racism in this country. And that is why we plead with black people not to be talking about a few crumbs, a few thousand dollars for this cooperative, or a thousand dollars which splits black people into fighting over the dollar. That is the intention of the government. We say . . . think in terms of total control of the United States. Prepare ourselves to seize state power. Do not hedge, for time is short, and all around the world the forces of liberation are directing their attacks against the United States. It is a powerful country, but that power is not greater than that of black people. We work the chief industries in this country, and could cripple the economy while the brothers fought guerrilla warfare in the streets. This will take some long range planning, but whether it happens in a thousand years is of no consequence. It cannot happen unless we start. How then is all of this related to this conference?

First of all, this conference is called by a set of religious people, Christians, who have been involved in the exploitation and rape of black people since the country was founded. The missionary goes hand in hand with the power of the states. We must begin seizing power wherever we are, and we must say to the planners of this conference that you are no longer in charge. We the people who have assembled here thank you for getting us here, but we are going to assume power over the conference and determine from this moment on the direction which we want it to go. We are not saying that the conference was planned badly. The staff of the conference has worked hard and has done a magnificent job in bringing all of us together, and we must include them in the new membership which must surface from this point on. The conference is now the property of the people who are assembled here. This we proclaim as fact and not rhetoric, and there are demands that we are going to make and we insist that the planners of this conference help us implement them.

We maintain we have the revolutionary right to do this. We have the same rights, if you will, as the Christians had in going into Africa and raping our Motherland and bringing us away from our continent of peace and into this hostile and alien environment where we have been living in perpetual warfare since 1619.

Our seizure of power at this conference is based on a program, and our program is contained in the following Manifesto:

We the black people assembled in Detroit, Michigan, for the National Black Economic Development Conference are fully aware that we have been forced to come together because racist white America has exploited our resources, our minds, our bodies, our labor. For centuries we have been forced to live as colonized people inside the United States, victimized by the most vicious, racist system in the world. We have helped to build the most industrial country in the world.

We are therefore demanding of the white Christian churches and Jewish synagogues, which are part and parcel of the system of capitalism, that they begin to pay reparations to black people in this country. We are demanding $500,000,000 from the Christian white churches and the Jewish synagogues. This total comes to 15 dollars per nigger. This is a low estimate for we maintain there are probably more than 30,000,000 black people in this country. $15 a nigger is not a large sum of money and we know that the churches and synagogues have a tremendous wealth, and its membership, white America, has profited and still exploits black people. We are also not unaware that the exploitation of colored peoples around the world is aided and abetted by the white Christian churches and synagogues. This demand for $500,000,000 is not an idle resolution or empty words. Fifteen dollars for every black brother and sister in the United States is only a beginning of the reparations due us as people who have been exploited and degraded, brutalized, killed and persecuted. Underneath all of this exploitation, the racism of this country has produced a psychological effect upon us that we are beginning to shake off. We are no longer afraid to demand our full rights as a people in this decadent society.

We are demanding $500,000,000 to be spent in the following way:

1. We call for the establishment of a Southern land bank to help our brothers and sisters who have to leave their land because of racist pressure on people who want to establish cooperative farms, but who have no funds. We have seen too many farmers evicted from their homes because they have dared to defy the white racism of this country. We need money for land. We must fight for massive sums of money for this Southern Land Bank. We call for $200,000,000 to implement this program.

2. We call for the establishment of four major publishing and printing industries in the United States to be funded with ten million dollars each. These publishing houses are to be located in Detroit, Atlanta, Los Angeles, and New York. They will help to generate capital for further cooperative investments in the black community, provide jobs and an alternative to the white-dominated and -controlled printing field.

3. We call for the establishment of four of the most advanced scientific and futuristic audio-visual networks to be located in Detroit, Chicago, Cleveland, and Washington, D.C. These TV networks will provide an alternative to the racist propaganda that fills the current television networks. Each of these TV networks will be funded by ten million dollars each.

4. We call for a research skills center which will provide research on the problems of black people. This center must be funded with no less than 30 million dollars.

5. We call for the establishment of a training center for the teaching of skills in community organization, photography, movie making, television making and repair, radio building and repair and all other skills needed in communication. This training center shall be funded with no less than ten million dollars.

6. We recognize the role of the National Welfare Rights Organization and we intend to work with them. We call for ten million dollars to assist in the organization of welfare recipients. We want to organize the welfare workers in

this country so that they may demand more money from the government and better administration of the welfare system of this country.

7. We call for $20,000,000 to establish a National Black Labor Strike and Defense Fund. This is necessary for the protection of black workers and their families who are fighting racist working conditions in this country.

*8. We call for the establishment of the International Black Appeal (IBA). This International Black Appeal will be funded with no less than $20,000,000. The IBA is charged with producing more capital for the establishment of cooperative businesses in the United States and in Africa, our Motherland. The International Black Appeal is one of the most important demands that we are making for we know that it can generate and raise funds throughout the United States and help our African brothers. The IBA is charged with three functions and shall be headed by James Forman:

    (a) Raising money for the program of the National Black Economic Development Conference.

    (b) The development of cooperatives in African countries and support of African Liberation movements.

    (c) Establishment of a Black Anti-Defamation League which will protect our African image.

9. We call for the establishment of a Black University to be funded with $130,000,000 to be located in the South. Negotiations are presently under way with a Southern University.

10. We demand that IFCO allocate all unused funds in the planning budget to implement the demands of this conference.

In order to win our demands we are aware that we will have to have massive support, therefore:

(1) We call upon all black people throughout the United States to consider themselves as members of the National Black Economic Development Conference and to act in unity to help force the racist white Christian churches and Jewish synagogues to implement these demands.

(2) We call upon all the concerned black people across the country to contact black workers, black women, black students and the black unemployed, community groups, welfare organization, teacher organizations, church leaders and organizations explaining how these demands are vital to the black community of the U.S.

Pressure by whatever means necessary should be applied to the white power structure of the racist white Christian churches and Jewish synagogues. All black people should act boldly in confronting our white oppressors and demanding this modest reparation of 15 dollars per black man.

(3) Delegates and members of the National Black Economic Development Conference are urged to call press conferences in the cities and to attempt to

---

*Revised and approved by Steering Committee.

get as many black organizations as possible to support the demands of the conference. The quick use of the press in the local areas will heighten the tension and these demands must be attempted to be won in a short period of time, although we are prepared for protracted and long-range struggle.

(4) We call for the total disruption of selected church-sponsored agencies operating anywhere in the U.S. and the world. Black workers, black women, black students, and the black unemployed are encouraged to seize the offices, telephones, and printing apparatus of all church-sponsored agencies and to hold these in trusteeship until our demands are met.

(5) We call upon all delegates and members of the National Black Economic Development Conference to stage sit-in demonstrations at selected black and white churches. This is not to be interpreted as a continuation of the sit-in movement of the early sixties but we know that active confrontation inside white churches is possible and will strengthen the possibility of meeting our demands. Such confrontation can take the form of reading the Black Manifesto instead of a sermon or passing it out to church members. The principle of self-defense should be applied if attacked.

(6) On May 4, 1969, or a date thereafter, depending upon local conditions, we call upon black people to commence the disruption of the racist churches and synagogues throughout the United States.

(7) We call upon IFCO to serve as a central staff to coordinate the mandate of the conference and to reproduce and distribute en masse literature, leaflets, news items, press releases, and other material.

(8) We call upon all delegates to find within the white community those forces which will work under the leadership of blacks to implement these demands by whatever means necessary. By taking such actions, white Americans will demonstrate concretely that they are willing to fight the white skin privilege and the white supremacy and racism which have forced us as black people to make these demands.

(9) We call upon all white Christians and Jews to practice patience, tolerance, understanding, and nonviolence as they have encouraged, advised, and demanded that we as black people should do throughout our entire enforced slavery in the United States. The true test of their faith and belief in the Cross and the words of the prophets will certainly be put to a test as we seek legitimate and extremely modest reparations for our role in developing the industrial base of the Western world through our slave labor. But we are no longer slaves, we are men and women, proud of our African heritage, determined to have our dignity.

(10) We are so proud of our African heritage and realize concretely that our struggle is not only to make revolution in the United States, but to protect our brothers and sisters in Africa and to help them rid themselves of racism, capitalism, and imperialism by whatever means necessary, including armed struggle. We are and must be willing to fight the defamation of our African image wherever it rears its ugly head. We are therefore charging the Steering

Committee to create a Black Anti-Defamation League to be funded by money raised from the International Black Appeal.

(11) We fully recognize that revolution in the United States and Africa, our Motherland, is more than a one-dimensional operation. It will require the total integration of the political, economic, and military components and therefore, we call upon all our brothers and sisters who have acquired training and expertise in the fields of engineering, electronics, research, community organization, physics, biology, chemistry, mathematics, medicine, military science, and warfare to assist the National Black Economic Development Conference in the implementation of its program.

(12) To implement these demands we must have a fearless leadership. We must have a leadership which is willing to battle the church establishment to implement these demands. To win our demands we will have to declare war on the white Christian churches and synagogues and this means we may have to fight the total government structure of this country. Let no one here think that these demands will be met by our mere stating of them. For the sake of the churches and synagogues, we hope that they have the wisdom to understand that these demands are modest and reasonable. But if the white Christians and Jews are not willing to meet our demands through peace and good will, then we declare war and we are prepared to fight by whatever means necessary. We are, therefore, proposing the election of the following Steering Committee:

Lucius Walker	Mark Comfort
Renny Freeman	Earl Allen
Luke Tripp	Robert Browne
Howard Fuller	Vincent Harding
James Forman	Mike Hamlin
John Watson	Len Holt
Dan Aldridge	Peter Bernard
John Williams	Michael Wright
Ken Cockrel	Muhammad Kenyatta
Chuck Wooten	Mel Jackson
Fannie Lou Hamer	Howard Moore
Julian Bond	Harold Holmes

Brothers and sisters, we no longer are shuffling our feet and scratching our heads. We are tall, black and proud.

And we say to the white Christian churches and Jewish synagogues, to the government of this country, and to all the white racist imperialists who compose it, there is only one thing left that you can do to further degrade black people and that is to kill us. But we have been dying too long for this country. We have died in every war. We are dying in Vietnam today fighting the wrong enemy.

The new black man wants to live and to live means that we must not become static or merely believe in self-defense. We must boldly go out and attack the white Western world at its power centers. The white Christian churches are another form of government in this country and they are used by the government of this country to exploit the people of Latin America, Asia, and Africa, but the day is soon coming to an end. Therefore, brothers and sisters, the demands we make upon the white Christian churches and the Jewish synagogues are small demands. They represent 15 dollars per black person in these United States. We can legitimately demand this from the church power structure. We must demand more from the United States Government.

But to win our demands from the church which is linked up with the United States Government, we must not forget that it will ultimately be by force and power that we will win.

We are not threatening the churches. We are saying that we know the churches came with the military might of the colonizers and have been sustained by the military might of the colonizers. Hence, if the churches in colonial territories were established by military might, we know deep within our hearts that we must be prepared to use force to get our demands. We are not saying that this is the road we want to take. It is not, but let us be very clear that we are not opposed to force and we are not opposed to violence. We were captured in Africa by violence. We were kept in bondage and political servitude and forced to work as slaves by the military machinery and the Christian church working hand in hand.

We recognize that in issuing this Manifesto we must prepare for a long range educational campaign in all communities of this country, but we know that the Christian churches have contributed to our oppression in white America. We do not intend to abuse our black brothers and sisters in black churches who have uncritically accepted Christianity. We want them to understand how the racist white Christian church with its hypocritical declarations and doctrines of brotherhood has abused our trust and faith. An attack on the religious beliefs of black people is not our major objective, even though we know that we were not Christians when we were brought to this country, but that Christianity was used to help enslave us. Our objective in issuing this Manifesto is to force the racist white Christian church to begin the payment of reparations which are due to all black people, not only by the Church but also by private business and the U.S. government. We see this focus on the Christian church as an effort around which all black people can unite.

Our demands are negotiable, but they cannot be minimized; they can only be increased and the Church is asked to come up with larger sums of money than we are asking. Our slogans are:

ALL ROADS MUST LEAD TO REVOLUTION
UNITE WITH WHOMEVER YOU CAN UNITE
NEUTRALIZE WHEREVER POSSIBLE
FIGHT OUR ENEMIES RELENTLESSLY
VICTORY TO THE PEOPLE

LIFE AND GOOD HEALTH TO MANKIND
RESISTANCE TO DOMINATION BY THE WHITE CHRISTIAN CHURCHES AND THE
  JEWISH SYNAGOGUES
REVOLUTIONARY BLACK POWER
WE SHALL WIN WITHOUT A DOUBT

3

BLACK THEOLOGY

Statement by the National Committee of Black Churchmen, June 13, 1969

Why Black Theology?

Black people affirm their being. This affirmation is made in the whole experience of being black in the hostile American society. Black Theology is not a gift of the Christian gospel dispensed to slaves; rather it is an *appropriation* which black slaves made of the gospel given by their white oppressors. Black Theology has been nurtured, sustained and passed on in the black churches in their various ways of expression. Black Theology has dealt with all the ultimate and violent issues of life and death for a people despised and degraded.

The black church has not only nurtured black people but enabled them to survive brutalities that ought not to have been inflicted on any community of men. Black Theology is the product of black Christian experience and reflection. It comes out of the past. It is strong in the present. And we believe it is redemptive for the future.

This indigenous theological formation of faith emerged from the stark need of the fragmented black community to affirm itself as a part of the kingdom of God. White theology sustained the American slave system and negated the humanity of blacks. This indigenous Black Theology, based on the imaginative black experience, was the best hope for the survival of black people. This is a way of saying that Black Theology was already present in the spirituals and slave songs and exhortations of slave preachers and their descendants.

All theologies arise out of communal experience with God. At this moment in time, the black community seeks to express its theology in language that speaks to the contemporary mood of black people.

This statement, produced by the Committee on Theological Prospectus, NCBC, was issued at the Interdenominational Theological Center, Atlanta, Georgia. It was adopted at the NCBC 1969 annual convocation in Oakland, California.

What Is Black Theology?

Black Theology is a theology of black liberation. It seeks to plumb the black condition in the light of God's revelation in Jesus Christ, so that the black community can see that the gospel is commensurate with the achievement of black humanity. Black Theology is a theology of "blackness." It is the affirmation of black humanity that emancipates black people from white racism, thus providing authentic freedom for both white and black people. It affirms the humanity of white people in that it says No to the encroachment of white oppression.

The message of liberation is the revelation of God as revealed in the incarnation of Jesus Christ. Freedom IS the gospel. Jesus is the Liberator! "He . . . hath sent me to preach deliverance to the captives" (Luke 4:18). Thus the black patriarchs and we ourselves know this reality despite all attempts of the white church to obscure it and to utilize Christianity as a means of enslaving blacks. The demand that Christ the Liberator imposes on all men *requires* all blacks to affirm their full dignity as persons and all whites to surrender their presumptions of superiority and abuses of power.

What Does This Mean?

It means that Black Theology must confront the issues which are a part of the reality of black oppression. We cannot ignore the powerlessness of the black community. Despite the *repeated requests* for significant programs of social change, the American people have refused to appropriate adequate sums of money for social reconstruction. White church bodies have often made promises only to follow with default. We must, therefore, once again call the attention of the nation and the church to the need for providing adequate resources of power (reparation).

Reparation is a part of the Gospel message. Zacchaeus knew well the necessity for repayment as an essential ingredient in repentance. "If I have taken anything from any man by false accusation, I restore him fourfold" (Luke 19:8). The church which calls itself the servant church must, like its Lord, be willing to strip itself of possessions in order to build and restore that which has been destroyed by the compromising bureaucrats and conscienceless rich. While reparation cannot remove the guilt created by the despicable deed of slavery, it is, nonetheless, a positive response to the need for power in the black community. This nation, and, a people who have always related the value of the person to his possession of property, must recognize the necessity of restoring property in order to reconstitute personhood.

What Is the Cost?

Living is risk. We take it in confidence. The black community has been brutalized and victimized over the centuries. The recognition that comes from seeing Jesus as Liberator and the Gospel as freedom empowers black men to risk themselves for freedom and for faith. This faith we affirm in the midst of a hostile, disbelieving society. We intend to exist by this faith at all times and in all places.

In spite of brutal deprivation and denial the black community has appropriated the spurious form of Christianity imposed upon it and made it into an instrument for resisting the extreme demands of oppression. It has enabled the black community to live through unfulfilled promises, unnecessary risks, and inhuman relationships.

As black theologians address themselves to the issues of the black revolution, it is incumbent upon them to say that the black community will not be turned from its course, but will seek complete fulfillment of the promises of the Gospel. Black people have survived the terror. We now commit ourselves to the risks of affirming the dignity of black personhood. We do this as men and as black Christians. This is the message of Black Theology. In the words of Eldridge Cleaver:

We shall have our manhood.
We shall have it or the earth will be leveled by our efforts to gain it.

4

THE RELIGION OF BLACK POWER

Vincent Harding

For scholars and ordinary citizens standing near the edges of the latest stage of America's perennial racial crisis, certain conclusions are easy to come by, especially when they are formed against the glare of burning buildings, the staccato reports of weapons and a certain malaise verging on fear. To the observers who are at all concerned with what might be called religious phenomena, there is an especially deceptive set of circumstances and deductions surrounding the newest expression of Black Power as a force within the ancient struggle. For if movements are judged primarily by their public rhetoric and other obvious manifestations, it seems abrasively apparent that the time of singing, of preaching, and of nonviolent concern for the redemption of American society is rapidly passing, if not gone. More black love for whites evidently burns in every ghetto-shaped inferno. By certain standards, the religious elements of the struggle are to be studied only as historical manifestations from a recent and lamented past.

Such an interpretation of the present black moment is encouraged by the words of an anonymous spokesman for the current mood: "Man, the people are too busy getting ready to fight to bother with singing any more." When a song does burst forth it often proclaims.

> Too much love,
> Too much love,
> Nothing kills a nigger like
> Too much love [13:25].*

Vincent Harding is Professor of Religion and Social Transformation at the Iliff School of Theology. This essay originally appeared in *The Religious Situation: 1968*, ed. Donald R. Cutler. Boston: Beacon Press, 1968. Reprinted with permission of the publisher.

*Citations refer to reference and page number of works listed at the end of this chapter.

Even in the presence of such compelling testimony against the adequacy of the older, more comforting religious symbols, rituals, and words, it would be myopic to miss the central issues of human life and destiny which course through the current expression of blackness. Issues of anthropology, incarnation, the nature of the universe and of God, issues of hope and faith, questions of eschatology and of the nature of the kingdom, problems concerning love and its functions — all these and more are at stake in the present situation. That they are usually disguised, often submerged, and sometimes denied does not lessen the power of their reality. Indeed the inherent power of the issues may be heightened by such camouflaging pressures. (One may even conjecture that the current black mood is in surprising harmony with much of the American trend towards a secular religion or a religionless church which, though it often overreacts to older explicit orthodox formulations is shaped unmistakably by the life of the streets.)

Black Power and the New Man

In spite of the tendency among Black Power advocates to repress any reference to the earlier Afro-American religious expressions — especially as they were found in the nonviolent movement — the most familiar word from the past remains available to set the stage for an exploration of the religious implication of the current themes. At a forum on Black Power in Atlanta during the fall of 1966, while discussing "love," a spokesman for Black Power was heard to say, "Martin King was trying to get us to love white folks before we learned to love ourselves, and that ain't no good."

When there is serious reflection upon these words, a meaningful examination of the religious elements of Black Power may properly begin, for here is an issue which, if not the heart of the affair, is certainly very near the center of things. In spite of some public images to the contrary, it is likely that no element is so constant in the gospel of Blackness — at least as it is encountered in its native communities — as the necessity of self-love. One writer tells much that is crucial to the story when she refers to "the inner power that comes with self-esteem, the power to develop to full stature as human beings" [4:29].

Healthy self-esteem has been seen in many traditions as a prerequisite to the establishment of community — whether with a spouse, a society, or a God. It has most often been the bedrock of love. It is surely this that comes through in the teaching of Jesus to love the neighbor as oneself. Black Power is a calling for black self-love, but it is not an unambiguous summons. Its clearest implications on this level are suggested by John Oliver Killens, one of the major literary spokesmen for the movement, when he writes,

[Black Power] does not teach hatred; it teaches love. But it teaches us that love, like charity, must begin at home; that it must begin with ourselves, our beautiful black selves [11:36].

Stokely Carmichael has put this love in the context of the building of a black society "in which the spirit of community and humanistic love prevail" [2:8]. So in spite of "too much love" and in spite of the fact that Carmichael also admitted that the word was "suspect," no writer in the newest black state fails to refer to a need for this love among black people.

Such an emphasis grows partly out of historical necessity, for all who make it are actively aware of the crushing psychological effects American life has had on the self-image of black men and women. However it may also rise out of an intuitive recognition that a call to love cuts across the deepest grain of man's being when it is addressed to an individual who is without some clear ground of self-respect.

It is precisely at this point that the ambiguity of the new black love becomes most evident, especially as it is exemplified in the writing of Killens. In the essay cited above he goes on to say that the love taught by Black Power is

> so powerful that it will settle for nothing short of love in return. Therefore it does not advocate unrequited love, which is a sick bit under any guise or circumstance. Most black folk have no need to love those who would spit on them or practice genocide against them. ... Profound love can only exist between equals [11].

Killens' point of view represents much of the thinking on this subject in Black Power circles, and it is obviously a retort to what is understood to be nonviolence and to what is thought to be the teaching of Christian churches, especially black ones. However, it may be an overreaction, for, while one is eminently wise to realize that love flows out of self-esteem, one may be less than wise in demanding a predetermined response to black love. In a sense this is an interesting variation on one of the basic pitfalls of the rhetoric of nonviolence. For while the nonviolent movement promised that black love would bring predictable, favorable white responses, Killens says that, unless whites respond as they ought, love will stop. Much of the world's religion teaches that love demands nothing more than the freedom of the other to respond. Perhaps it takes the strongest love of all to continue in the path while realizing that such freedom can never be coerced.

Perhaps, however, it is even more pertinent to note that Killens speaks of love and hate as being totally irrelevant until black and white men are equals. This is the even stronger frame of mind in the ghettos today. Love for Black Power is, as Carmichael puts it, a love "within the black community, the only American community where men call each other 'brother' when they meet. We can build a community of love," he says, "only where we have the ability and power to do so among blacks" [2:8]. At this juncture white persons are simply not considered as valid objects of black love. Such love (or, more accurately, its outward appearance) has been forced from blacks for too long; now, as one of the movement's most sensitive authors puts it, for many of the present black generation, the white man no longer exists. He is not to be lived with and he is not to be destroyed. He is simply to be ignored. . . .

If whites consider this relegation to nonexistence as hatred, Julius Lester says, such an interpretation "is only a reflection of [their] own fears and anxieties. . . . " As for blacks, he says, "There is too much to do to waste time and energy hating white people" [13:24].

This powerful strand of Black Power thinking raises a long series of religiously oriented issues. First among many is the recurring issue regarding the control and direction of love. If it is assumed—as it surely must be—that black love must begin among black people and find its nurture there, can it be quarantined? What shall be said of a love that is willed towards some men and not towards others? Is this goal in any way related to the deadly disease that has afflicted so much of American life for so many generations?

An interim goal is now to make white men "invisible" while black men are brought into the light. Can it be brought off by blacks with any less poisoning of the spirit than occurred in whites who invented "tuning out"? If it is true that white men dream long dreams of the dark brothers they have rejected, what are the dreams in black beds? Such an exploration must also ask whether it is enough not to hate. Does our recent experience suggest that hatred might well be preferable to the creation of a new breed of nonexistent nonblack men?

The answers do not come with ease. Perhaps refusal to hate is enough to begin with when one considers the deep sources of human justification for black hatred and revenge against whites. Perhaps those who can rise out of such carefully poisoned wells of human experience with the strength not to hate their oppressors have made a major beginning, whatever their dreams may be. Of course, if anyone should dare to press on and raise the most disturbing religious issue of even loving enemies, there may be two initial responses. It must first be acknowledged that the American religious communities have offered no consistent examples of this love for enemies, especially in times of war. (Black people consider themselves at war, and they have imbibed more of American religion than they know.) Second it is essential that all questioners should examine the possibility that men may need the freedom to hate their enemies before love can become an authentic response. It may be that black freedom offers no less dangerous a path than any other variety.

Black Power and the New Community

In part, an answer to our questions must await the further development of the black pilgrimage in this hostile land. Now it is sufficient to note another major thrust of the Black Power movement that has deep religious moorings, a sharing in men's constant search for community. As black exiles search in an often alien world for the ground of their being, the movement is increasingly towards the building of community. Love is recognized as a necessary foundation for this structure—whatever its form.

There was a time when the vision of the community to be built was as large as America, but that is no longer the case. At least that seems no longer a task that black men can set themselves to. Julius Lester put it this way:

At one time black people desperately wanted to be American, to communicate with whites, to live in the Beloved Community. Now that is irrelevant. They know that it can't be until whites want it to be, and it is obvious now that whites don't want it [13:25].

Now black men must build their own beloved black community, Lester concludes. Does such a statement indicate a recoil from the religious search for the fully inclusive community, or is it a more sober and therefore a more faithful estimate of the world and of the power of race?

Those persons who think of such a withdrawal into blackness as a racist or nationalist retreat from universalism would likely find comfort in the thoughts of one of the Afro-American leaders who said, "The fact that we are Black is our ultimate reality. We were black before we were born" [8:3]. When one considers some of the basic "realities" of American life, there is a certain soundness in this view, and it is supplemented by Lester's call for black men to recognize and celebrate "those things uniquely theirs which separate them from the white man."

Those who see goals of black community as falling short of the goal of universal community must recognize the fact that black men in America have long been encouraged to disdain their community no less than themselves. Therefore, such a call may be the beginning of true corporate health and integrity for black people. It is surely a significant change from the major direction of Afro-American movement toward the larger society during the past generation, for that has been largely a movement away from the ghettos, away from the ground out of which we sprang. "Integration" has most often been the call to escape. (At least it was so interpreted until hard white rocks made clear the nature of its siren sounds.) Now a Karenga teaches that "Our purpose in life should be to leave the Black Community more beautiful than we inherited it" [8:27]. Now Carmichael and others like him plead with black college students to train themselves not to be siphoned out of the ghettos, but to pour themselves back into it. This direction of Black Power is one of its surest words of judgment upon the black churches of the Afro-American communities. It is the same judgment that the Nation of Islam and Malcolm X brought, for it speaks to congregations and pastors who usually have no more use for the black depths than their white Christian counterparts.

The call for communal identification among the black outcasts of America has had observable impact and will probably increase in force. It is the closest thing to a sense of religious vocation that some of the current black college and graduate students know. It is surely significant that one of them spoke in the image of John Donne's human land mass when he voiced the response of a growing proportion of his generation. In a recent article in *Ebony* magazine,

Stanley Saunders, a Rhodes Scholar now in Yale's law school, confessed his former attempts to hide from his white friends the truth of his origins in the blackness of Watts. Saunders said this attempt was for him a means of gaining acceptance and assimilation into the American society. Now, with the coming of the new black consciousness, that has changed. He can say instead,

> If there is no future for the black ghetto, the future of all Negroes is diminished. What affects it, affects me, for I am a child of the ghetto. When they do it to Watts, they do it to me, too. I'll never escape from the ghetto. I have staked my all on its future. Watts is my home [17:36].

There is probably a message in these words for all who see the call for solidarity with the black community as a call away from universalism. For it is quite possible that the earlier liberal invitations to highly selected black men—calls into the Party or into the Church, or into some other wing of the idol of Integration—were really deceptive, or at least premature. Perhaps we were urged towards an identification with mankind-at-large (often meaning white mankind) before we had learned to identify with our black neighbors. It is likely that our humanity really begins in the black ghetto and cannot be rejected there for an easier, sentimental, white-oriented acceptance elsewhere. So it may be that the question of "who is my neighbor?" is answered for us.

Of paramount importance is the fact that these questions are being answered for persons in the ghettos who will never see Yale. Many of the burgeoning black-oriented groups—organized in varying degrees of structural sophistication—are manned primarily by young men who have been cast out of the restless bowels of a technological society. Now in their teens and early twenties, with little prospect of any meaningful work in the larger society as it now stands, these black youths have begun to find themselves as members of groups dedicated to the protection and development of the ghetto that has so long been their prison. The new vision that Black Power has brought to them may be one of the most important of all its consequences. These were the rejected stones of integration. They had neither the skills nor the graces demanded. They may well become the cornerstones of a renewed black community.

Such a transformation may suggest that if black men are ever to achieve to the larger universal calling, we must, like Paul, clearly apprehend the things which are a part of our own racial and cultural heritage. Perhaps we must be able to glory in that past as a gift of God before we will be prepared to count it as garbage for the sake of the new family of man [16]. For if we begin with a conception of our ancestral community as garbage, of our heritage as worthless, we shall be guilty of irresponsible escapism and not growth when we move to transcend them. Isn't it taught in some circles that Jesus of Nazareth had first to explore the most profound levels of his own culture—both physically and spiritually—before he was eligible to transcend it?

So Black Power holds a healthy possibility for the coming of true religious community. It suggests the destruction of ugly and ironic caste distinctions within the Afro-American community. It encourages the discovery of roots long buried and rejected. It insists that men be true to themselves. It calls a broken people to see its own black section of the mainland. It reveals the gifts of those who were once the scorned members of the black body. Karenga may therefore be most accurate when he writes, "Until Blacks develop themselves, they can do nothing for humanity" [8:2]. Obviously, what is being suggested is that men must not only love themselves in order to love their neighbor, but they must love their communities in order to love the world.

Actually, many sections of the world are already included in the concerns of Black Power, and one has the feeling that there is intimated in these concerns a universalism that is at least as broad as that known by most western religious traditions. Black Power calls for an identification between black people here and all the wretched nonwhites of the earth. (Some leaders, like Carmichael, now expand this to the poor and oppressed of every color.) This is certainly the meaning of Lester's statement that, while a black man must now live his life in the United States

> only within the framework of his own blackness [that] blackness links him with the Indians of Peru, the miner in Bolivia, the African and the free-dom fighters of Vietnam. What they fight for is what the American black man fights for—the right to govern his own life [13:25].

(Is it possible that a universalism based on suffering, struggle, and hope is more vital than some vague identification based on common links to a possible dead Creator-Father?)

Such breadth of concern for "the broken victims" in their struggle to be free is surely another of Black Power's judgments upon American religion, especially the faith of those persons who claim a great tradition of prophetic concern for social justice, and those who claim a master who came to set all broken victims free. For while such religious respectables stand silently or march weakly pro-testing, the devotees of Black Power identify themselves unambiguously with the oppressed and with the revolutions made by the oppressed. So if only by sheer numbers—the numbers of the earth's humiliated people—such identifi-cation actually brings Black Power into the orbit of a universality more authentic than the largely parochial sentiments of a "Judeo-Christian" western commit-ment.

Nor are the righteous delivered by pointing accurately to the fact that Black Power makes no effort to identify with the oppressors who, according to the teachings of many traditions, are also theoretically eligible for concern. The example of American religion has been poor (perhaps it will eventually prove poisonous), for its identification has been largely with the exploiters or with those who live comfortably because of the action of exploitation. Therefore black men may well sense a need to redress this imbalance, this "crookedness" that is prevalent throughout the western world—no matter how many times the

Messiah is sung, which refers to making the crooked become straight (Isaiah 40:3-4, e.g.).

Perhaps, too, black rebels remember the example of Jesus, the focus of much of western religion. For while he evidently was filled with ultimate concern for both oppressed and oppressor, he reserved his sharpest words of judgment for the politico-religious leaders and oppressors within the Jewish community, and his death came outside the gates of respectability. Black Power may well suggest that religious concern for both sides does not mean neutrality in the face of injustice. Indeed, it reminds us that the world most often will not permit that questionable luxury even should it be desirable.

(This identification with the wretched of the earth is especially significant for the incipient struggle for leadership between Black Power adherents and the traditional spokesmen of the Negro masses—their ministers. For though there have been important exceptions, the public stance of most of the respectable pastors has been in accord with the dominant American attitudes towards modern, radical revolution. By and large, the black church hierarchy has been no more Christian than its white counterpart on such issues, except where the accident of race has forced it to certain stances. Should the sense of solidarity with the exploited peoples grow to major proportions in the Afro-American communities, it may well prove impossible for such religious leaders to hold on to their already shaky grounds.)

Black Messiahs and Marching Saints

The qualified universalism of Black Power is also streaked with vivid suggestions of Messianism at many points. Indeed, Afro-American intellectual history has long been filled with images of Black messiahs, either individually or en masse, rising up to deliver Black America from its bondage and White America from its lethal folly. Though the first event was always guaranteed the second did not necessarily follow from it in every case [9]. In our own century the theme was first voiced fully in the fascinating and significant movement led by Marcus Garvey. It was this audacious black genius who sent a Messianic promise to the black world from his cell in the Atlanta Federal Penitentiary. In 1925, Garvey said,

> If I die in Atlanta my work shall then only begin, but I shall live, in the physical or spiritual to see the day of Africa's glory. When I am dead wrap the mantle of the Red, Black, and Green around me, for in the new life I shall rise with God's grace and blessing to lead the millions up the heights of triumph with the colors that you well know. Look for me in the whirlwind or the storm, look for me all around you, for, with God's grace, I shall come and bring with me countless millions of black slaves who have died in America and the West Indies and the millions in Africa to aid you in the fight for Liberty, Freedom and Life [7:136-137].

There are still Afro-Americans in this country, the West Indies, and Africa who attribute every movement towards black liberation to the living, vibrant spirit of Marcus Garvey.

It was so, too, with Malcolm X, and after his death there came a resurgence of the Messianic theme. The visions of an anointed leader and a Messianic people have been most recently joined in the work of a black novelist, Ronald Fair. Writing in *Negro Digest* about the meaning of Black Power Fair moved quickly to the issue of ultimate hope, and said,

> we are the ones who will right all the wrongs perpetrated against us and our ancestors and we are the ones who will save the world and bring a new day, a brilliantly alive society that swings and sings and rings out the world over for decency and honesty and sincerity and understanding and beauty and love. . . . [5:30, 94].

Again the chosen people are black and promise a new day out of the matrix of their sufferings. Fair was not specific about the means by which the newness would come, but he said, "we fight on and we spread the love we have been told we cannot feel for ourselves to each and every black man we meet."

Finally the novelist tied the Messianic people to its leader and invoked the revered name when he said,

> We look about us and wait because somewhere, somewhere in the ten-ements in Harlem, or from the west side of Chicago, or from Watts, there *will* be another Malcolm and this one won't be murdered.

As Ronald Fair read the moment, "every black man in this country is aware that our time has come" [5:94].

Now is the fullness of time in many black minds; and though traditional religion is often denied, the deeper symbols and myths are appropriated to express the sense of expectation that stirs within the black communities, focused now in the ideology of Black Power. As might be predicted, the black Messianic hope expands beyond America's shores, and this aspect of it was also expressed by Killens. He wrote,

> we black Americans are no longer a "minority" but a part of that vast majority of humanity yearning to be free and struggling with every ounce of their strength to throw off the blackman's burden and the yoke of white supremacy. We are a part of that fellowship of the disinherited which will surely inherit the earth in this century [11:37].

The ambiguities of Fair's "fight" are largely discarded in Killens' vision of the way ahead. It is those who were forced to be meek (as some count meekness) who now enter into armed struggle to inherit the earth.

Another spokesman for Black Power is even less ambiguous, for Nathan

Hare speaks of a "Black Judgment Day around the corner" for America. He envisions it as a possible "black *blitzkrieg* ... making America a giant, mushrooming Watts, in which this country will either solve its problems or get the destruction it deserves" [10:01]. It is surely not presumptuous to suggest that elements of the same vision impel an H. Rap Brown to demand from the nation that it either "straighten up" or face the fire of judgment.

Within the heart of Black Power stands the perennial tension between a salvation leading to swinging and singing and love, and a day of destruction demanded by a just God. Throughout the history of black American radicalism run the themes of repentance and atonement or judgment [18:62–147]. Always there is the memory of bloodshed being connected to the remission of sins. But when the chosen, sinned-against people become both armed and anointed, when the saints march with guns, then the issues are mooted, and the day of the Lord is clouded indeed. For it may be that armed and marching black saints in Harlem are not likely to conceive of their task any differently than those who killed infidel Indians in New England, cut off unrepentant heads in old England, or now burn "suspected" children in Vietnam. Is it given to black men any more than to whites to be self-commissioned executors of Divine judgment on evil-doers? Easy replies must not suffice, for what if the Divine Judge has retired from his bench, leaving all things in the hands of men? What then? Does evil for evil become mandatory?

Black Resurrection: The Power and the Glory

What are the means to be used in building new black men, new black communities and a renewed, black-oriented world? Already certain pathways have been suggested. The new men must come partly from a new vision of themselves. Indeed the image that has been constantly used in this century involves more than new self-image, it presumes resurrection. Ever since Marcus Garvey preached an Easter sermon on "The Resurrection of the Negro" in 1922, the theme has been constantly renewed. For Garvey, self-knowledge was a key to this resurrection.

On the occasion of his sermon he said, "We are about to live a new life—a risen life—a life of knowing ourselves" [6:88]. His central passage in the discourse was an anticipation of so much that was to come on the black scene that it merits another temporary movement back into the first quarter of the century. Continuing the crucial image of resurrection, Garvey said,

> I trust there will be a spiritual and material resurrection among Negroes everywhere; that you will lift yourselves from the doubts of the past; that you will lift yourselves from the slumbers of the past; that you will lift yourselves from the lethargy of the past, and strike out in this new life— in this resurrected life—to see things as they are [6:90].

The theme was continued faithfully in the Nation of Islam where Elijah Muhammad constantly spoke of "dead, so-called Negroes" who needed to be resurrected to their true life as black men [14]. At the current juncture the same concept finds various expressions among those who seek to build new black men. Thus Ron Karenga insists that "We must not be so busy calling the Negro dead that we can't work out methods to resurrect him" [8:17]. One of the methods is obviously the love and concern that other black men show for the "dead" brother. Another, related, path to new life is suggested by Carmichael who speaks of "the necessity to reclaim our history and our identity from the cultural terrorism and depredation of self-justifying white guilt" [3:639]. The process of teaching becomes crucial. History becomes a balm for healing and a hope for new beginnings.

The pages of recent black history are thus filled with testimonies of Afro-Americans who saw themselves as "dead" or "sick" before their contact with the healing and resurrecting power of black concern and black self-knowledge. One of Karenga's own disciples (and the word is used intentionally) recently wrote,

> I can remember myself before Maulana ["Great Leader," the title assumed by Karenga] showed me the "Path of Blackness." I was so sick no one but Maulana could have saved me. Running around with no identity, purpose or direction. Maulana gave me an alternative to this white system. . . . I say, "all praises due to Maulana" [8:iii].

Such dependence upon new or previously hidden knowledge for salvation is at least as old as Gnosticism and most of the mystery religions, and perhaps one also hardly needs to comment about the significance of love as a conqueror of death. Nevertheless it might be well to note that in a world where God's absence is more evident than his presence to large numbers of men, an individual's worth may no longer be sufficiently affirmed in terms of his worthiness before a Divine being. Or could one say that black love and resurrection are simply ways of speaking about and discovering incarnation where it is most needed today?

Some persons are nevertheless disturbed by what they consider a "glorification of blackness" in the healing process under discussion. In a significant sense, this is exactly what is involved with the relationship of Black Power to black and broken men who have been made ashamed of their blackness. It is indeed glorified; and a perceptive theological interpreter of this aspect of the issue offers a most helpful understanding of the action when he writes,

> The glorification of blackness implicit in the term Black Power is a conscious or unconscious effort to stake a claim for the Worth of those in our nation who are termed nonwhite. Essentially it is a clarification. The root meaning of the term "glorify" is to clarify, to make clear and plain and straight [19:139].

Nor does Nathan Wright confine the issue to the human sphere with this highly suggestive description of black glorification. He goes on to say,

All of life must be clarified in this sense. It must be given and seen in that dimension which sets it forth in terms of glory—now and forever. To see life as it truly is means to see it as God sees it, in its eternal dimension, in the glory appropriate to its involvement with and in the life of God [19:139-140].

If one follows this invaluable line of thought, it is obvious that Black Power has within it the possibility of setting black men in an entirely new light—the light of their Creator. They are called upon to see themselves as they were meant to be. This glorification has the potential of setting them at peace with themselves and—with the creative purposes of the universe; they no longer need to curse God and die. For their blackness is now—like the rest of their createdness—a sign of His love and not His anger.

At its best, such glorification sets black men at peace whether or not the white world recognizes the reality of their dark blessedness; such clarity makes it unnecessary for them to prove to whites the facts of that glory or even to demand that they be recognized. For men at peace with the universe are at once profoundly at peace with themselves and with all others who participate in that universe. Unfortunately, such a time is not yet with us, and black men have been forced to live in shameful dependency and self-negation for too long. So the process of resurrection may well be more like three generations than three days for some of the black dead. But it is also possible that the coming forth may be unlike the quiet stories of the Gospels and more like the volcanic eruptions of the Old Testament or the fire-framed bursting of the graves in the vision of John.

One difficult aspect of the rebuilding task urged by Black Power is the break with white leadership. This has long been a subject of furious discussion among blacks, and in this century it began when several Negro members of W. E. B. Du Bois' radical, black Niagara Movement, refused in 1909 to join the newly created white-dominated National Association for the Advancement of Colored People [I: vol 2, 927]. In our own time the issue was perhaps raised most sharply by SNCC, partly as a result of its Mississippi Summer experience of 1964. Even before the experiment of bringing large numbers of whites into the state had begun, it was reported that some black staff members of the organization "felt that it would destroy everything which they had accomplished." According to Julius Lester's account, the objectors were convinced that

Whites, no matter how well meaning, could not relate to the Negro community. A Negro would follow a white person to the courthouse, not because he'd been convinced he should register to vote, but simply because he had been trained to say Yes to whatever a white person wanted [13:23].

Therefore it was determined that the resurrection of black people required decisive breaks with the old patterns of life, patterns of constant dependence on whites which had been begun in slavery and then encouraged ever since. By 1966, Stokely Carmichael had put the new dictum into words, using "psychological equality" as a synonym for black mental resurrection. He wrote, "The need for psychological equality is the reason why SNCC today believes that blacks must organize in the black community. Only black people can convey the revolutionary idea that black people are able to do things themselves" [2:6].

While this decision on the part of Black Power advocates has been one of the most difficult for well-intentioned whites to abide, there is much logic in its direction if one is primarily concerned with the building of men and communities which have been shattered, threatened, or used by forces with white faces. It is difficult for white men and women to be told to go and organize in white communities "where the racism really is," but such words are certainly worthy of serious consideration, especially if one's deepest concern is with the healing of shattered black egos more than with the bolstering of relatively intact white ones.

Even though the logic is powerful, the implications of the moment towards separation and the questions it raises are no less significant. How shall the black and white victims of American racism best find their healing before the last night settles in? What is the nature of the binding process and under what conditions shall it best take place? One wonders, for instance, if the restoration of broken, embittered spirits can take place apart from the presence—at some point—of the offending, denying, guilt-dominated brother. Or is it impossible for black men to build the necessary strength to love themselves—which must precede all else—except through studied alienation from their former oppressors, even the truly repentant ones? Perhaps an even more sobering and "practical" question is whether or not a white community without inner quietness will allow the black workers time and space to build a unique (and thereby threatening) set of structures and beings.

The models for guidance are difficult to discover, but it is evident that the ancient issue of means and ends is involved in the discussion, if one takes seriously the stated goals of some of the Black Power advocates. For instance, few members of the younger, enraged generation have any program of separate states or of Zionism on another continent. Therefore most seek to find some *modus vivendi* on the American scene. At the heart of the matter under discussion is the issue of how we can prepare black people to live with integrity on the scene of our former enslavement and our present estrangement. In examining this matter, Karenga says, "We're not for isolation but interdependence—but we can't become interdependent unless we have something to offer." In other words, he says, "We can live with whites interdependently once we have Black Power" [8:3]. So the summary response to the central question seems to be that it is only a temporary withdrawing of the black community into itself which will prepare it for interdependence, and therefore the end appears threatened by the seemingly unavoidable means.

(Somehow the black-white dilemma is often suggestive of an unhealthy and mutually destructive marriage which may require at least a period of separation for the mutual benefit of the two partners. At other times America seems to be the forever unfaithful lover of the Blues, the lover who is always lamented but never left—until the last, inevitably bloody scene. The same unclarity that marks the religious response to unhealthy love affairs and destructive marriages is likely present when one searches for guidance here. Is divorce preferable to the kitchen knife? But what would divorce mean?)

A question no less difficult arises in another step that Black Power takes towards the building of black men and the black community—the emphasis on self-defense. Speaking for his organization in 1966, Carmichael set the most obvious theme: "SNCC reaffirms the right of black men everywhere to defend themselves when threatened or attacked" [2:5]. Moving the idea from a right to an authentication of black freedom, Killens wrote, "Men are not free unless they affirm the right to defend themselves" [11:33]. But for those who would intelligently explore Black Power, even these explanations are insufficient. It was Killens who set out—largely by implication—the fuller and more profound psychological significance of self-defense for black men. He wrote in the same revealing article,

> We black folk have a deep need to defend ourselves. Indeed we have an obligation. We must teach the brutalizers how it feels to be brutalized. We must teach them that it hurts. They'll never know unless we teach them [11:34].

The issues raised by this series of statements are worthy of thoughtful consideration, for they eventually move to a level of profound moment. On the surface they seem to be nothing more than an affirmation of the somewhat disreputable "American right" to self-defense. (A right, incidentally, which most Americans have no sound moral grounds for questioning when it suddenly appears among angry black men.)

In some ways this affirmation of self-defense is an obvious response to a situation in which black people find that neither separation, respect, nor love is forthcoming from the dominant portion of the society. On another, related, level it is a repetition of the earlier theme of judgment at the hands of the injured. As we have mentioned, in a world in which God is at least obscure, and where no one else seems a dependable agent of justice for black people, black men should stand firmly on their responsibility to do the necessary work. There is, however, an even more profound issue involved in what Killens describes so sensitively as "a deep need" for black men to defend themselves. What he seems to be implying is this: when men have long been forced to accept the wanton attacks of their oppressors, when they have had to stand by, and watch their women prostituted, it is crucial to their own sense of self-esteem that they affirm and be able to implement their affirmation of a right to strike back.

The basic human search for a definition of manhood is here set out in significant black lineaments. Does manhood indeed depend upon the capacity to defend one's life? Is this American shibboleth really the source of freedom for men? Is it possible that a man simply becomes a slave to another man's initiative when he feels obliged to answer his opponent on the opponent's terms? Is there perhaps a certain kind of bondage involved when men are so anxious about keeping themselves alive that they are ready to take the lives of others to prevent that occurrence? The question is really one of the image man was meant to reflect; what is it? Certain ways of looking at the world would suggest that such questions are pointless before they come from the lips. Other religious perspectives might suggest that manhood can be discussed, but only in terms of the capacity to create new grounds for response to danger, and in the act of bringing new life into being, rather than in the animal capacity to strike back.

In his characteristically vivid way, Karenga allows no circumventing of the issue. He writes, "If we fight we might be killed. But it is better to die as a man than to live like a slave" [8:19]. In the midst of a hostile, threatening environment the Zealot pathway is often chosen by those who are in honest search of their manhood, by those who seek to protect and avenge their oppressed community. Most persons who claim to be followers of the Man who introduced Zealots to a new way of response have chosen not to follow him at this point. And here is one of the most telling witnesses to the possibility that Black Power may be more fully bound to the traditions of the western Christian world than its proponents would ever dare believe.

Now, if it is possible that the fullest stature of man was found in one who honestly and sharply opposed his enemies but finally faced them with his cross, then Black Power may have chosen far less than the best available way. If it has chosen a bondage to death, the mistake is completely understandable. It is understandable not only because retaliatory violence is deeply etched into the American grain, but also because men who have been forced up against crosses all of their lives find it difficult to take one up when the choice is fully theirs. It is understandable, too, because western society now seems unable to offer any normative response to the question, "What is man?" Moreover it appears totally without courage to experiment with possibilities beyond the old, "heroic," destructive replies.

Perhaps one possibility yet stands in the future, and Black Powers' immediate choice must not be counted as its last. For who knows where the inner quest will lead black men if they are honestly in search of true manhood, true community, and true humanity? Are there not grounds for hope wherever men are soberly and devotedly engaged in the quest for new light?

Old White Models and New Black Hopes

If the relationship of self-defense to the building of black manhood is crucial on the personal level, then it is likely that the kinds of power by the black community is the focal question on the broader scale. Not only is it crucial, but it faces us with another set of religious issues of considerable force. Initially one must ask: what is the power necessary to build the new black community? Perhaps Stokely Carmichael best summarized the normative Black Power response when he wrote,

Almost from its beginning, SNCC sought to [build] a program aimed at winning political power for impoverished Southern blacks. We had to begin with politics because black Americans are a propertyless people in a country where property is valued above all. We had to work for power, because this country does not function by morality, love, and nonviolence, but by power [2:5].

Political, economic and social power with a final recourse to armed self-defense are at the heart of the black search, even though Carmichael has since gone on to espouse aggressive guerrilla warfare. Ron Karenga, who feels the movement is not yet ready for such warfare, put the issues of power for the black community more colorfully, but no less directly when he said,

Like it or not, we don't live in a spiritual or moral world and the white boys got enough H-bombs, missiles, T.V.'s, firehoses and dogs to prove it.

Therefore, he concluded, "we must move not spiritually but politically, i.e., with power" [8:19].

In some ways it is understandable to hear the avowed revolutionaries among Black Power forces refer to political, economic, and military realities as the ultimate forces in life. It is even more interesting to note that same direction in the forceful statement of an impressive group of black churchmen who wrote on the subject of black and white power in 1966. In the midst of the national furor over the newly discovered term, the churchmen published a full page advertisement in the *New York Times* which said, in part, "The fundamental distortion facing us in the controversy about 'black power' is rooted in a gross imbalance of power and conscience between Negroes and white Americans." After setting out this basic introduction to their thesis, the statement continued,

It is this distortion, mainly, which is responsible for the widespread though often inarticulate, assumption that white people are justified in getting what they want through the use of power, but that Negro Americans must, either by nature or by circumstances, make their appeal only through conscience. As a result, the power of white men and the conscience of black men have both been corrupted. The power of white men is corrupted because it meets little meaningful resistance from Negroes to temper it and keep white men from aping God.

Tracing the corruption of the black conscience, the churchmen attributed it to a condition in which, having no power to implement the demands of conscience, the concern for justice is transmuted into a distorted form of love, which, in the absence of justice, becomes chaotic self-surrender. Powerlessness breeds a race of beggars. We are faced now with a situation where conscienceless power meets powerless conscience, threatening the very foundations of our nation [15:187].

It was evident that the churchmen were convinced that "conscience," or "love" as they later referred to it, was "powerless" without the coercive forces of the society. They appeared no less disturbed than John Killens about "unrequited love," and in a sophisticated adumbration, the group simply gave religious expression to the political views of Carmichael, Karenga and a host of other black spokesmen. Though it is not fully stated they seem to be saying that the ultimate weapons necessary for the building of the new black community are those now monopolized by white power leaders. Blacks have to get their hands on some of these weapons and perhaps depend upon their own consciences to "temper" black uses of the same instruments whites had used for such destructive purposes. But when blacks begin getting their proper share of the power, it would appear that they might be less dependent upon the development of "conscience" — unless it was theirs in large supplies "by nature" rather than "by circumstance." How then would Black Power be tempered?

A question at least as compelling is this: Does the theological position implicit in the churchmen's statement carry a doctrine of two kingdoms with it? Do these leaders seek the Kingdom of the weaponless, defenseless, homeless King at certain times, and the Kingdom of the armed, propertied, politically powerful, American, white (soon to be technicolored) King at another time? Where do the kingdoms meet? Are the guidelines to the nature of human community as blurred as those for the nature of man? On issues of ultimate power, are the insights of Christian ministers only accidentally the same as Stokely Carmichael's and Ron Karenga's?

The implications of the churchmen's statement are numerous and provocative but it is important to supplement that statement with an even more theologically astute brief for Black Power by one of the individual senators, Nathan Wright. Dr. Wright, who is also chairman of the National Conference on Black Power, recently wrote of the image of God and its relationship to power among black men. He said,

In religious terms, a God of power, of majesty and of might, who has made men to be in His own image and likeness, must will that His creation reflect in the immediacies of life His power, His majesty and His might. Black Power raises . . . the far too long overcooked need for power, if life is to become what in the mind of its Creator it is destined to be [15:136].

In a fascinating way Karenga, one of the best trained and most thoughtful of the Black Power leaders, picks up the precise time set down by Wright. In all likelihood he does it independently, so it is even more significant and illuminating that his definition of Black Power should also find its basis in a powerful deity. He writes, "God is God who moves in power; God is God who moves in change and creates something out of nothing. If you want to be God just think about that" [8:26]. (Karenga's last sentence is not random rhetoric. Evidently he has so imbibed the homocentric orientation of the American society that he upstages the Mormons by telling men that they become Gods now by entering into Godlike action. Indeed, the emphasis on autonomous black action is another of the hallmarks of Black Power ideology, a hallmark that leaves little room for any dependence on what might be called grace—a hallmark that would stamp it as far more Protestant than one might desire.)

The difficulty with the analogy evoked by Wright and Karenga is its failure to recognize another aspect of the power of God within the biblical tradition. If Wright and the other black churchmen put any serious stock in the life and teachings of Jesus of Nazareth as the clearest possible window to the face of God, then one must at least examine another way of power. That is, one must see the power of God demonstrated in weakness and in humiliation. Is it not possible that the God who dies for his enemies, who rejects their terms and their weapons—and their kind of power—is also worthy of consideration as a model for the empowerment of the black community?

Though it is difficult to propound, it would appear that such a question may have some possible validity when one remembers some of the goals of Black Power. May not one properly ask if a new black community will be created by the appropriation of the old American weapons of power? More specifically, what of Karenga's insight into the nature of racism? He said at one point,

Racist minds created racist institutions. Therefore you must move against racism, not institutions. For even if you tear down the institutions that same mind will build them up again [8:14].

How does one "move against racism"? Surely not with "H-bombs, missiles, T.V.'s, firehoses . . . dogs" and all the other institutions of political power now possessed by "the white boy." And what of Stokely Carmichael's strangely religious metaphor: "For racism to die, a totally different America must be born" [2:61]? Will a black community in search of a new society really participate in the process of new birth by a reactionary fixation on all the kinds of power which have helped to corrupt the nation? How does new birth come?

Talk of weakness and death, quests for new birth, all tend to be at once sources of fascination and anathema for the current black breed. It is likely that the apparently contradictory references to such matters in their writings are largely unconscious, and that the conscious stance is one of opposition to Gods who die on crosses. As we have seen, black men have been chained to weakness for so long that any talk of voluntarily choosing a way that the society counts as weak is considered sheer madness.

Is this the scandal of the cross for the present black moment? Or is it all foolishness in the most irrelevant sense of the word? Perhaps Karenga was most true to himself and to the universe when he said, "We don't live in a spiritual or moral world." Somehow it sounds like the old black deacons who constantly joked behind the minister's back: "Praying is fine in a prayer meeting but it ain't no good in a bear meeting."

If the world is primarily a bear meeting, and if the only way to survive in such a gathering is by becoming a bear, then the way of Black Power is evident. (Even the preachers seem to agree with elements of Black Bear Power.) Nevertheless, in such a situation, the way of human beings remains cloudy.

Black Power and Religion: Beyond Implications

Reference to a black prayer meeting serves as a reminder that the discussion of religious issues in this essay has generally grown out of the intimations, suggestions, and tendencies one finds in the words and deeds of Black Power advocates. There has been almost no attempt to address the subject of the precise, institutionalized religious manifestations of Black Power, largely because such an attempt would be somewhat premature. It is evident, however, that if the ideology does institutionalize itself, a more clearly articulated religious message and ritual will likely develop, or rather a set of such phenomena will emerge.

Anticipation of this is present already throughout the black ghettos. Ever since the days of Garvey's African Orthodox Church, Black Nationalist groups have found religion to be one of their major modes of expression. The Nation of Islam's success is the best known indication of the power inherent in this direction. Recently—especially since Malcolm X's appearance on the national scene—there have been many Black Nationalist attempts to reestablish variations of African religious practices, and one can only speculate on the mutual transformations such attempts may bring about.

None of these developments should be surprising, of course. For instance, when the strongly nationalist Bandung Conference of Afro-Asian peoples gathered in 1955 a resolution was passed "to resurrect their old religions and cultures and modernize them. ... " Similarly at the world conference of black writers, artists, and intellectuals held in Paris in the following year, one of the participants said that "the main and only resolution called for the rehabilitation of their ancient cultures and religions" [20:22]. These were significant international prefigurings of Black Power in America, and they probably suggest the way that the Afro-American movements will increasingly take.

Besides the plethora of Black Nationalist religious experiments in the ghettos of the land, it is likely that Karenga's West Coast organization, US, has so far articulated the most clearly structured and self-consciously religious manifestos of all the Black Power groups. It is representative of much of the movement's concerns both in its rather humanistic, secular (in the most recent religious sense of that word) orientation and in its obvious reaction to the black Christian churches. Thus Karenga teaches that "We must concern ourselves more with the plans for this life, rather than the next life which has its own problems. For the next life across Jordan is much further away than the grawl [sic] of dogs and policemen and the pains of hunger and disease" [8:26].

In spite of the familiar reference to Jordan, groups like Karenga's tend to believe that men live on only through the lives of their children, and there is among them a strong emphasis on the rebuilding of the shattered black home. In such a home the role of the woman follows almost strictly Pauline lines, and some female believers in Black Power find it difficult to adjust their western indoctrination of equality to the old-new emphasis on the supremacy of the black man.

The New Testament stream that flows through their doctrine of the relationship of husband to wife does not prevent Black Power groups from engaging in constant attacks on the Christian churches. For instance, Karenga—in keeping with many other similar leaders who preceded him—says that "Christians do good because they fear—we do good because we love. They do good because God says so—we do good ... in response to need" [8].

The issue of religion is constantly before many of the young persons who are drawn back into the ghettos by the urgent logic of Black Power. As they return—from college or from prison—to struggle against what can be reasonably described as "principalities and powers" which seem anonymously but fiercely to control the life of their people, they find themselves often insufficient as autonomous sources of inner strength. They cannot return to the Christian churches they once knew, because these churches have so often appeared irrelevant to the real needs of the community and most often they are controlled by older men and women who seem unprepared for the competition from radical black youth. In here, strangely enough, a few black Christian churches have responded fully to the call of Black Power. In Detroit the pastor of one such congregation, the Reverend Albert B. Cleage, Jr., of the Central United Church of Christ, preaches of a black revolutionary Jesus who came to set the non-white peoples free. A Black Madonna is the focal point of worship and the church has probably attracted more persons committed to Black Power than any other single institution still connected to the Christian churches.

Even when they cannot find such havens, there is nevertheless something in the black religious tradition that continues to attract many racially conscious young people. For instance, it is most moving and revealing to watch a group of them respond totally with clapping and dancing to the gospel songs that continue to shape the tradition that spawned them. They are at home for a time. Ideologies aside, this is still "Soul."

On what may or may not be another level of their being, some of the group also sense a strange sense of attraction to Jesus of Nazareth. They are convinced that an encounter with the historical Jesus would likely be a meeting with a revolutionary, but they have been turned off by the whiteness infused into this Jesus by the western Christian tradition. They are also able and often accurate catalogers of the unfaithfulness of the churches—black and white. Sometimes they consider these churches as irrelevant as white persons are. A few of the seekers turn to Judaism, but often meet the reality of the Jewish middleman in the ghettos and find it an obstacle to faith. Others move towards Islamic variations of belief, often giving up their western, Christian names. This is partly another declaration of independence from slavery and its postreconstruction variations, but it is in some situations simply part of the ancient practice of men taking on new names when they find new faiths.

In the light of their search for the lineaments of a new societal order, it is surely significant that some black groups have now moved towards various forms of communitarianism. In locations like Los Angeles and Philadelphia attempts are made to find this style of life in the urban context. In upper New York state real estate has been set aside for such an experiment; while in Brooklyn a group of some sixty men and women now plan for moving back to the south, to the land. Is it likely that such actions represent more than exercises in anguished flight? Is it possible that they are really a challenge to the two settings which have been most destructive to black life — the city and the south? Are they expressions of hope in the power of resurrected black lives to conquer even these ancient foes?

There is a sense of religious ferment on the path to Black Power, a sense that is not easy to document. Mixtures of old and new approaches to the essential issues of life are being attempted. Allah and other gods of Africa enter into competition with Yahweh, Jesus, and Buddha. It is a joyously difficult time, but part of the affirmation of Black Power is "We are a spiritual people." The institutional manifestations of that affirmation are still being tested. A people separated from their past now attempt to build bridges, create new realities, or search among the ruins for whatever remains of value there may be.

So Afro-Americans enter the experience that many peoples have known before them, peoples who in time of national crisis have turned to the gods they knew before the coming of Christian missionaries, seeking for what seemed a more solid ground. For should it be forgotten that such searches have taken place in this century no less significantly in Ireland and Germany than in Kenya and the Congo.

As for the possible results here, one can only begin to speculate, for instance, on the impact of some African religions on a Black Power movement that is still more western oriented and Protestant than it can possibly admit. Will these religions which seek unity and harmony with the forces of God in the universe transform an ideology that is still determined to change the world around it? Can one accept the Yoruba dreams and dress without falling sway to its world-view? Only the questions are available now.

Meanwhile, few adherents of Black Power deny their need for religious moorings and, though no clear pattern has yet emerged, it must be evident by now that for many persons this movement is likely to become as full a "church" as the earlier phase was for others. Not only does it begin to fill the need for personal commitment and a sense of fellowship with other similarly committed black persons; it also embodies impressive social concern, a call for ultimate justice, and a search to be present with the sufferers of the society. Gladly identifying with the oppressed beyond national borders, this church increasingly seeks to glorify at least that part of God which may reside in black folk.

In the midst of such developments, one central question cries out for an answer, the kind of answer that is perhaps to be found most fully in the insight of true religion. Though often articulated only in parts, if put into words by Black Power adherents, it would be, "How shall we deal with an enemy who has more power than we do, who has long controlled and destroyed our lives that are even now more fully dependent upon him than we dare confess?" Whatever religion arises from the heart of Black Power will need to address itself to such a dilemma with more honesty than most black religion has ever done before. (One of the generally unrecognized religious blessings of this movement is the honesty it has already forced into the black-white dialogue in America. It has not produced hate; it has rather revealed hate and called upon both whites and blacks to admit its sorrowful depths. There are, of course, large segments of the society who still fear this radical honesty, but it is likely that they also fear true religion.)

Epilogue: Martin Luther King and Black Power

No discussion of black religion in America today can ignore the immensely important figure of Martin Luther King, Jr. In spite of statements to the contrary, he remains an individual of critical importance for anyone who would gain insights into the black experience here. Therefore it is crucial to examine King's response to a movement that has seemed to push him off the stage. The encounter may well provide unexpected illumination for some summary views.

In his most recent work, *Where Do We Go From Here?* [12] King attempts an assessment of Black Power that is significant and revealing, not for its originality or its challenge, but for the basic weakness of his response to the realities evoked and addressed by the ideology. There is in one chapter a favorable interpretation of the "positive" aspects of Black Power as a psychological healing force. Then as King attempts to define the elements which will bring the "necessary" power to the black community, he refers to power as "the strength required to bring about social, political or economic changes," and identifies this power in many of the same ways as the churchmen and the leading Black Power advocates. When the words come from King, however, they bear somewhat more powerful implications. He writes,

There is nothing essentially wrong with power. The problem is that in America power is unequally distributed. This has led Negro Americans in the past to seek their goals through love and moral suasion devoid of power and white Americans to seek their goals through power devoid of love and conscience. ... It is precisely this collision of immoral power with powerless morality which constitutes the major crisis of our times [12:37].

In religious (as well as political) terms, King's words constitute something of a crisis in themselves and raise many difficult issues. They tempt us, most importantly, to ask whether King was describing his own movement when he spoke of Negroes in the past who sought goals "through love and moral suasion" because no other way was available to them. If this identification is precise, then one must surely question the nature of such love and the motives of the moral suasion. And if the love was "powerless" why were there so many past references made to "the power of love and nonviolence"—references found even in King's current work?

Surely the talk of love and suasion that was a kind of last resort is not in keeping with the insights of the great teachers of nonviolence, who set out this way for men who were not cowards, who had other weapons available, but who chose to put them aside for the sake of a better way. King's statements cause one to ask if there was really a nonviolent movement at any point. Was "too much love" really the problem? Could it be that nonviolence was simply impossible for a people who had never had an opportunity to affirm their manhood or to choose violence as a way of response on a widespread scale? Perhaps the late, lamented nonviolent movement can really come only after the Malcolms, Stokelys, and Raps have offered another real choice to millions of black folk.

Even more significant for the present discussion is King's failure to deal clearly and precisely with the central black radical conviction concerning America. Its advocates believe (and they have a growing company of fellow believers) that this nation will not allow black men the freedom, opportunity, and restitution needful for meaningful lives without a total, violent disruption of the society. Like revolutionaries before them, they believe that the national fabric must be rent before white people will believe in the validity of black demands for life. Here is the price of three centuries of racism, they say. King does not really respond to this assumption. He warns against cynicism, but fails to set out in clarity his response to a situation in which even massive, disciplined nonviolent resistance will continue to meet increasingly violent (and/or sophisticated) repression.

Somehow the night of that terror seems too dark for King to enter. His only real attempt at an answer to the Black Power conviction is a vague statement of faith, but the object of the faith also remains vague. King writes,

> Our most fruitful course is to stand firm, move forward nonviolently, accept disappointments and cling to hope. Our determined refusal not to be stopped will eventually open the door to fulfillment. By recognizing the necessity of suffering in a righteous cause, we may achieve our humanity's full stature. To guard ourselves from bitterness, we need the vision to see in this generation's ordeals the opportunity to transfigure both ourselves and American society [12:46–47].

There are missing links and false notes apparent in any religiously focused examination of this central statement. Nowhere is there any explanation of why

King believes that the door "will eventually open." Is it faith in American goodness, in the power of a nonviolent movement that he hardly discusses, or faith in an abstract justice in the universe? (King's God often seems no less dead than anyone else's — at least if one judges life by appearance in the printed pages.) Without such clarification, his call could be dismissed as a Pollyanna voice attempting to challenge the whirlwind.

Even more important is his failure to discuss the possible reasons for an amorphous, variously motivated group of black people to suffer without retaliation the continued scorn and injury of people they consider at least fools and at most devils. When King referred to "powerless morality" and identified authentic power for black people with economic and political power, he was then likely obligated to ask who would be willing to live without such power once it became possible either to kill for it or to kill to protest its denial.

It would appear that, unless King is ready to face black men with the need to suffer without retaliation and also to live without the power he considered "necessary," much of his argument against violence falls apart. For the violence of revolutionaries comes not from "hatred," as he says, but from the insistence of the oppressed that they must have at least a proportionate share of the power which the oppressor insists upon keeping and defending by violent means. Leaders like Karenga say such power is absolutely necessary for black men. So does King. Black Power leaders are convinced that the country will not make such power available without armed struggle of one kind or another. What does a believer in religious nonviolence have to say to such a situation? Is it enough not to face it squarely? And if he does must King eventually choose between armed struggle and a powerless future for black people in the United States?

In a sense this dilemma is a reminder of how much the present black situation — especially in its religious dimensions — is a microcosmic expression of the main lines of the development of American Christian ethics in this century. Within the microcosm King stands for the liberal tradition, continuing to maintain faith in American goodness, in reason, in the ordered nature of the world. Such a stance seems to require his refusing to look directly into chaos, seems to demand that he fail to trace the deepest lineaments of the nation's racist core. In a sense King appears to hope that dark "principalities and powers" in massive array are only figments of overexercised religious imagination. In their place he substitutes an eloquent dream.

On the other hand stand the proponents of Black Power, like some dark blossoms of "realism" gone beyond control. They look with cynical but not dishonest eyes at the forces of evil in the society, at their depth and their extent. They see without flinching the possibility that power will not be shared voluntarily, that atonement cannot come without the shedding of blood, and they are determined that as little of the blood as possible will flow from them. They see the night and prepare men for its terror. They refuse to dream. But like much of the realist position, they also fail to acknowledge sufficiently (perhaps because of insensitivity on certain levels of their being) the reality of creative, healing forces in the situation. Somehow the power of resurrection is totally irrelevant to the struggles they outline, except in the most personal applications to individual "dead" black men.

Moved out of the metaphorical microcosm, these two perspectives are badly in need of each other for the mutual sharing and the possible mutual growth which may well be the nation's only visible hope in the racial crisis. The necessary, relentless determination of Black Power to look fully on the evil of American life must be informed by some hope even more solid than King's, some expectation of creative possibilities (even of Messiahs), some determination not to succumb to the enemy's disease. Even more soberly put, it may be that all who speak with any seriousness about addressing the profound social and psychological distortions brought by American racism must be prepared to experiment with totally new weapons, and be ready (how hard the words!) for complete defeat—at least as it is commonly counted.

For if racism rages as deep into American life as it appears and if violence is its closest brother, then a black revolution will no more solve the problem than a civil war did (even if Rap Brown gets his atomic bomb). So it may be most responsible to ask if it is more than despair to speak of a long, grueling battle with no victory—and no illusions—this side of the grave? Has it been important and necessary simply to learn that there are no large citizen armies of white deliverers? Was it not absolutely necessary that all trust in courts and troops and presidents be shattered? Is this part of a black coming of age, a coming which will eventually reveal that even the black God of the ghetto is dead?

Perhaps, though, he is not dead. Perhaps this new God has not lived long enough to die. Perhaps there is still a Beloved Community ahead. But if it is, it must be seen as the kingdom whose realization does not depend upon whether whites (or anyone else around) really want it or not. If it comes, it may come only for those who seek it for its own sake and for the sake of its Lord, recognizing that even if He is black, the final glory is not the glory of blackness, but a setting straight of all the broken men and communities of the earth. In some strange ways Black Power may be headed in that way, but it probably needs some new and stripped-down coming of Martin King's most fervent hopes to accompany its path.

On the other hand, if the night is already too dark for the way to be found, or if society should make it impossible for these two black tendencies to live and find each other, then there seems little to expect that is not apocalyptic. This has always been a religious implication of life, especially black life. It is certainly one of the deepest implications of a wishful liberalism and any inescapable possibility for a Black Power that finally accepts not America's weapons but also its ultimate definitions of manhood, power, majesty, and might.

Was it for this that we have come so painfully far together— and yet apart— in this strange land? Was it only for this? Is there no saving message from the drums of our homeland, or did all gods die at once?

REFERENCES

1. Herbert Aptheker, ed. *A Documentary History of the Negro People in the United States*, 2 vol. (New York: Citadel Press, 1965).
2. Stokely Carmichael, "What We Want," *New York Review of Books* 7, no. 4 (22 September 1966).
3. Stokely Carmichael, "Towards Black Liberation," *Massachusetts Review* (Autumn 1966).
4. Anita Cornwell, "Symposium on Black Power," *Negro Digest* 16, no. 1 (November 1966).
5. Ronald Fair, "Symposium on Black Power," *Negro Digest* 16, no. 1 (November 1966).
6. Amy Jacques Garvey, ed. *Philosophy and Opinions of Marcus Garvey* (New York: Universal Publishing House, 1923).
7. Marcus Garvey, in Edmund D. Cronon, *Black Moses* (Madison, Wis.: University of Wisconsin Press, 1964).
8. Clyde Halisi and James Mtume, eds. *The Quotable Karenga* (Los Angeles: US, 1967).
9. Vincent Harding, "Religion and Resistance Among Antebellum Negroes, 1800–1860" in *Making of Black America*, August Meier and Elliot Rudwick, eds. (New York: Atheneum, 1972).
10. Nathan Hare, "Symposium on Black Power," *Negro Digest* 16, no. 1 (November 1966).
11. John Oliver Killens, "Symposium on Black Power," *Negro Digest* 16, no. 1 (November 1966).
12. Martin Luther King, Jr., *Where Do We Go From Here?* (New York: Harper & Row, 1967).
13. Julius Lester, "The Angry Children of Malcolm X," *Sing Out* 16, no. 5 (November 1966), an important and eloquent contribution to our understanding of the coming of Black Power.
14. Elijah Muhammad, *Message to the Black Man*.
15. National Committee of Negro Churchmen, "Black Power," in Nathan Wright, Jr., *Black Power and Urban Unrest* (New York: Hawthorne Books, 1967).
16. Philippians 3.
17. Stanley Saunders, "I'll Never Leave the Ghetto," *Ebony* 20, no. 10 (August 1967).
18. David Walker, *Appeal* (1829); reprint in Herbert Aptheker, ed., *One Continual Cry* (New York: Humanities Press, 1965).
19. Wright, *Black Power*.
20. Richard Wright, *White Man, Listen!* (Garden City, N.Y.: Anchor Books/Doubleday, 1964).

5

THE WHITE CHURCH AND BLACK POWER

James H. Cone

Let the Church discover and identify itself with groups of people that suffer because of unjust situations, and who have no way of making themselves heard. The Church should be the voice of those who have no one. The Church must discover these groups and identify herself with them. Here is the modern Way of the Cross, the way of Christian responsibility.

Emilio Castro

The meaning of Black Power and its relationship to Christianity has been the focal point of our discussion thus far. It has been argued that Black Power is the spirit of Christ himself in the black-white dialogue which makes possible the emancipation of blacks from self-hatred and frees whites from their racism. Through Black Power, blacks are becoming men of worth, and whites are forced to confront them as human beings.

There is no other spirit in American life so challenging as the spirit of Black Power. We can see it affecting every major aspect of American life— economic, political, and social. In major white and black universities its spirit is manifested in the demand for more emphasis on "black studies." Black students have literally taken over some administration buildings in an effort to make white authorities recognize the importance of their demands. In politics, Stokely Carmichael and Charles Hamilton have given the political implications of Black Power.[1] For them Black Power in politics means blacks controlling their political destiny by voting for black people and perhaps eventually forming a coalition with poor whites against middle-class whites. For some others it means black nationalism. Economically it may mean boycotting, or building stores for black people. Religiously or philosophically it means an inner sense of freedom from

This essay is excerpted from *Black Theology and Black Power* by James H. Cone. New York: Seabury Press, 1969; San Francisco: HarperCollins, 1989. Reprinted with permission of the publisher.

the structures of white society which builds its economy on the labor of poor blacks and whites. It means that the slave now knows that he is a man, and thus resolves to make the enslaver recognize him. I contend that such a spirit is not merely compatible with Christianity; in America in the latter twentieth century it is Christianity.

Some critics of this thesis may ask about the place of the Church in my analysis. It may appear that its role as an agent of God in the world has been overlooked. This leads us to an investigation of the biblical understanding of the Church and its relationship to white denominational churches.

What Is the Church?

What is the Church and its relationship to Christ and Black Power? The Church is that people called into being by the power and love of God to share in his revolutionary activity for the liberation of man.

Mythically the interrelation of God, man, and the world is presented in the Genesis picture of the man and the woman in the garden. Man was created to share in God's creative (revolutionary) activity in the world (Gen. 1:27-28). But through sin man rejects his proper activity and destiny. He wants to be God, the creator of his destiny. This is the essence of sin, every man's desire to become "like God." But in his passion to become superhuman, man becomes subhuman, estranged from the source of his being, threatening and threatened by his neighbor, transforming a situation destined for intimate human fellowship into a spider web of conspiracy and violence. God, however, will not permit man thus to become less than the divine intention for him. He therefore undertakes a course of not-so-gentle persuasion for the liberation and restoration of his creatures.

The call of Abraham was the beginning of this revolutionary activity on behalf of man's liberation from his own sinful pride. This was followed by the exodus, the most significant revelatory act in the Old Testament, which demonstrated God's purposes for man. God showed thereby that he was the Lord of history, that his will for man is not to be thwarted by other human wills. And when Pharaoh said to Moses and Aaron, "The Lord is righteous, and I and my people are wicked" (Exod. 9:27), he was saying that even he recognized the righteousness of God in contrast to the wickedness of men.

The history of Israel is a history of God's election of a special, oppressed people to share in his creative involvement in the world on behalf of man. The call of this people at Sinai into a covenant relationship for a special task may be said to be the beginning of the Church.[2] In the Old Testament, Israel often refers to herself as the *qahal*, the assembly or people of God.[3] Israel is called into being as a people of the covenant in which Yahweh promises to be their God and they his people. Israel's task is to be a partner in God's revolutionary activity and thus to be an example to the whole world of what God intends for all men. By choosing Israel, the oppressed people among the nations, God reveals that his concern is not for the strong but for the weak, not for the enslaver but for the slave, not for whites but for blacks. To express the goal of her striving, Israel spoke of the Day of the Lord and the Kingdom of God, in which God would vindicate his people from oppression and the rule of his righteousness would be recognized by all. This would be the day when the lion would lie down with the lamb and men would beat their swords into plowshares.

In the New Testament, the coming of God in Christ means that the Kingdom of God expected in the Old Testament is now realized in Jesus of Nazareth. The Day of the Lord has come in the life, death, and resurrection of Jesus. This day is no longer future but present in the man Jesus. In him is embodied God's Kingdom in which men are liberated. He is, as Paul says, the "New Adam," who has done for man what man could not do for himself. His death and resurrection mean that the decisive battle has been fought and won, and man no longer has to be a slave to "principalities and powers."

With him also comes a new people which the New Testament calls the *ekklesia* (church). Like the people of Old Israel, they are called into being by God himself—to be his agent in this world until Christ's second coming. Like Old Israel, they are an oppressed people, created to cooperate in God's liberation of all men. Unlike Old Israel, their membership is not limited by ethnic or political boundaries, but includes all who respond in faith to the redemptive act of God in Christ with a willingness to share in God's creative activity in the world. Unlike Old Israel, they do not look forward to the coming of the Kingdom, but know that, in Christ, God's Kingdom has already come and their very existence is a manifestation of it. The Church merely waits for its full consummation in Christ's second coming. Therefore, its sole purpose for being is to be a visible manifestation of God's work in the affairs of men. The Church, then, consists of people who have been seized by the Holy Spirit and who have the determination to live as if all depends on God. It has no will of its own, only God's will; it has no duty of its own, only God's duty. Its existence is grounded in God.

The Church of Christ is not bounded by standards of race, class, or occupation. It is not a building or an institution. It is not determined by bishops, priests, or ministers as these terms are used in their contemporary sense. Rather, the Church is God's suffering people. It is that grouping of men who take seriously the words of Jesus: "Blessed are you when men revile you and persecute you and utter all kinds of evil against you falsely on my account" (Matt. 5:11). The call of God constitutes the Church, and it is a call to suffering. As Bonhoeffer put it:

Man is challenged to participate in the sufferings of God at the hands of a godless world.

He must plunge himself into the life of a godless world, without attempting to gloss over its ungodliness with a veneer of religion or trying to transfigure it. . . . To be a Christian does not mean to be religious in a particular way, to cultivate some particular form of asceticism, . . . but

to be a man. It is not some religious act which makes a Christian what
he is, but participation in the suffering of God in the life of the world.[4]

"Where Christ is, there is the Church." Christ is to be found, as always,
where men are enslaved and trampled under foot; Christ is found suffering
with the suffering; Christ is in the ghetto—there also is his Church.

The Church is not defined by those who faithfully attend and participate in
the 11:00 A.M. Sunday worship. As Harvey Cox says: "The insistence by the
Reformers that the church was 'where the word is rightly preached and the
sacraments rightly administered' will simply not do today."[5] It may have been
fine for distinguishing orthodoxy from heresy, but it is worthless as a vehicle
against modern racism. We must therefore be reminded that Christ was not
crucified on an altar between two candles, but on a cross between two thieves.
He is not in our peaceful, quiet, comfortable suburban "churches," but in the
ghetto fighting the racism of churchly white people.

In the New Testament perspective, the Church has essentially three functions: preaching *(kerygma),* service *(diakonia),* and fellowship *(koinonia).*
Preaching means proclaiming to the world what God has done for man in Jesus
Christ. The Church tells the world about Christ's victory over alien hostile
forces. If we compare Christ's work on the cross with warfare, as Oscar
Cullmann[6] and others do, then it is the task of the Church to tell the world
that the decisive battle in the war has been fought and won by Christ. Freedom
has come! The old tyrants have been displaced, and there is no need for anyone
to obey evil powers. The Church, then, is men and women running through the
streets announcing that freedom is a reality. This is easily translated into the
context of modern racism. God in Christ has set men free from white power,
and this means an end to ghettos and all they imply. The Church tells black
people to shape up and act like free men because the old powers of white
racism are writhing in final agony. The Good News of freedom is proclaimed
also to the oppressor, but since he mistakes his enslaving power for life and
health he does not easily recognize his own mortal illness or hear the healing
word. But the revolution is on, and there is no turning back.

Modern kerygmatic preaching has little to do with white ministers admon-
ishing their people to be nice to "Negroes" or "to obey the law of the land."
Nor does it involve inviting a "good Negro" preacher to preach about race
relations. Preaching in its truest sense tells the world about Christ's victory and
thus invites people to act as if God has won the battle over racism. To preach
in America today is to shout "Black Power! Black Freedom!"

It is important to remember that the preaching of the Word presents a crisis
situation. The hearing of the news of freedom through the preaching of the
Word always invites the hearer to take one of two sides: He must either side
with the old rulers or the new one. "He that is not for me is against me." There
is no neutral position in a war. Even in silence, one is automatically identified
as being on the side of the oppressor. There is no place in this war of liberation
for nice white people who want to avoid taking sides and remain friends with

both the racists and the Negro. To hear the Word is to decide: Are you with us or against us? There is no time for conferences or talk of any sort. If the hearing of the Word and the encounter with the Spirit do not convict you, then talk will be of little avail.

The Church not only preaches the Word of liberation, it joins Christ in his work of liberation. This is *diakonia*, "service." Though the decisive battle has been fought and won over racism, the war is not over. There is still left what G. P. Lewis calls the "mopping-up operations."[7] Just as the war in Europe continued for months after it was "won" at Stalingrad and El Alamein, so the war against the principalities and powers continues after the decisive battle on the cross.[8] We still have to fight racism. The evil forces have been defeated but refuse to admit it. "Although defeated," writes William Hordern, "evil still has sufficient strength to fight a stubborn rear-guard action."[9] It is the task of the Church to join Christ in this fight against evil. Thomas Wieser puts it this way:

> The way of the church is related to the fact that the Kyrios Lord himself is on his way in the world, . . . and the church has no choice but to follow him who precedes. Consequently obedience and witness to the Kyrios require the discernment of the opening which he provides and the willingness to step into this opening.[10]

The opening has been made and the Church must follow. To follow means that the Church is more than a talking or a resolution-passing community. Its talk is backed up with relevant involvement in the world as a witness, through action, that what it says is in fact true.

Where is "the opening" that Christ provides? Where does he lead his people? Where indeed, if not in the ghetto. He meets the blacks where they are and becomes one of them. We see him there with his black face and big black hands lounging on a streetcorner. "Oh, but surely Christ is above race." But society is not raceless, any more than when God became a despised Jew. White liberal preference for a raceless Christ serves only to make official and orthodox the centuries-old portrayal of Christ as white. The "raceless" American Christ has a light skin, wavy brown hair, and sometimes—wonder of wonders—blue eyes. For whites to find him with big lips and kinky hair is as offensive as it was for the Pharisees to find him partying with tax-collectors. But whether whites want to hear it or not, *Christ is black, baby*, with all of the features which are so detestable to white society.

To suggest that Christ has taken on a black skin is not theological emotionalism. If the Church is a continuation of the Incarnation, and if the Church and Christ are where the oppressed are, then Christ and his Church must identify totally with the oppressed to the extent that they too suffer for the same reasons persons are enslaved. In America, blacks are oppressed because of their blackness. It would seem, then, that emancipation could only be realized by Christ and his Church becoming black. Thinking of Christ as nonblack in the twentieth century is as theologically impossible as thinking of him as non-

Jewish in the first century. God's Word in Christ not only fulfills his purposes for man through his elected people, but also inaugurates a new age in which all oppressed people become his people. In America, that people is a black people. In order to remain faithful to his Word in Christ, his present manifestation must be the very essence of blackness.

It is the job of the Church to become black with him and accept the shame which white society places on blacks. But the Church knows that what is shame to the world is holiness to God. Black is holy, that is, it is a symbol of God's presence in history on behalf of the oppressed man. Where there is black, there is oppression; but blacks can be assured that where there is blackness, there is Christ who has taken on blackness so that what is evil in men's eyes might become good. Therefore Christ is black because he is oppressed, and oppressed because he is black. And if the Church is to join Christ by following his opening, it too must go where suffering is and become black also.

This is what the New Testament means by the service of reconciliation. It is not smoothing things over by ignoring the deep-seated racism in white society. It is freeing the racist of racism by making him confront blacks as men. Reconciliation has nothing to do with the "let's talk about it" attitude, or, "it takes time" attitude. It merely says, "Look man, the revolution is on. Whose side are you on."

The Church is also a fellowship *(koinonia)*. This means that the Church must be in its own community what it preaches and what it seeks to accomplish in the world. Through the preaching of the Word, the Church calls the world to be responsible to God's act in Christ, and through its service it seeks to bring it about. But the Church's preaching and service are meaningful only insofar as the Church itself is a manifestation of the preached Word. As Harvey Cox puts it, *koinonia* is "that aspect of the church's responsibility . . . which calls for a visible demonstration of what the church is saying in its kerygma and pointing to in its diakonia."[11] Thus the Church, by definition, contains no trace of racism. Christ "has broken down the dividing walls of hostility" (Eph. 2:14). That is why Karl Barth describes the Church as "God's subjective realization of the atonement."[12]

It is this need to be the sign of the Kingdom in the world which impels the Church continually to ask: "Who in the community does not live according to the spirit of Christ?" This is the kind of question which was so important to the sixteenth-century Anabaptists, and it must be vital for the Church of any age. Speaking to this question, Barth says: "The church which is not deeply disturbed by it is not a Christian church."[13] It cannot be "Christ existing as community" or "Christ's presence in history," as Bonhoeffer would put it, without being seriously concerned about the holiness of its members.

It is true that this concern may cause the community to ask the wrong questions. It may focus on irrelevancies (smoking, dancing, drinking, etc.) rather than on the essential (racism). But it is only through the asking of the question, "What makes men Christians?" that the true Church is able to be Christ in the world. The true Church of Christ must define clearly through its members the meaning of God's act in Christ so that all may know what the Church is up to. There can be no doubt in the minds of its members regarding the nature of its community and its purpose in the world. It must be a community that has accepted Christ's acceptance of us, and in this sense, it must be holy. At all times and in all situations holy members of the holy church, and therefore Christians, were and are the men assembled in it who are thereto elected by the Lord, called by His Word, and constituted by His Spirit: just so many, no more and no less, these men and no others.[14]

The White Church and Black Power

If the real Church is the people of God, whose primary task is that of being Christ to the world by proclaiming the message of the gospel *(kerygma),* by rendering services of liberation *(diakonia)* and by being itself a manifestation of the nature of the new society *(koinonia),* then the empirical institutionalized white church has failed on all counts. It certainly has not rendered services of reconciliation to the poor. Rather, it illustrates the values of a sick society which oppresses the poor. Some present-day theologians, like Hamilton and Altizer, taking their cue from Nietzsche and the present irrelevancy of the Church to modern man, have announced the death of God. It seems, however, that their chief mistake lies in their apparent identification of God's reality with the signed-up Christians. If we were to identify the work of God with the white church, then, like Altizer, we must "will the death of God with a passion of faith." Or as Camus would say, "If God *did* exist, we should have to abolish him."

The white church has not merely failed to render services to the poor, but has failed miserably in being a visible manifestation to the world of God's intention for humanity and in proclaiming the gospel to the world. It seems that the white church is not God's redemptive agent but, rather, an agent of the old society. It fails to create an atmosphere of radical obedience to Christ. Most church fellowships are more concerned about drinking or new buildings or Sunday closing than about children who die of rat bites or men who are killed because they want to be treated like men. The society is falling apart for want of moral leadership and moral example, but the white church passes innocuously pious resolutions and waits to be congratulated.

It is a sad fact that the white church's involvement in slavery and racism in America simply cannot be overstated. It not only failed to preach the kerygmatic Word but maliciously contributed to the doctrine of white supremacy. Even today all of the Church's institutions—including its colleges and universities— reveal its white racist character. Racism has been a part of the life of the Church so long that it is virtually impossible for even the "good" members to recognize the bigotry perpetuated by the Church. Its morals are so immoral that even its most sensitive minds are unable to detect the inhumanity of the Church on the black people of America. This is at least one of the suggestions by Kyle Has-elden, who was in most cases a very perceptive white southern churchman:

We must ask whether our morality is itself immoral, whether our codes of righteousness are, when applied to the Negro, a violation and distortion of the Christian ethic. Do we not judge what is right and what is wrong in racial relationships by a righteousness which is itself unrighteous, by codes and creeds which are themselves immoral?[15]

The question is asked and the answer is obvious to the astute observer. The Church has been guilty of the gravest sin of all — "the enshrining of that which is immoral as the highest morality."[16] Jesus called this the sin against the Holy Spirit. It is unforgivable because it is never recognized.

Pierre Berton puts it mildly:

In . . . the racial struggle, there is revealed the same pattern of tardiness, apathy, non-commitment, and outright opposition by the church. . . . Indeed, the history of the race struggle in the United States has been to a considerable extent the history of the Protestant rapport with the status quo. From the beginning, it was the church that put its blessing on slavery and sanctioned a caste system that continues to this day.[17]

As much as white churchmen may want to hedge on this issue, it is not possible. The issue is clear: Racism is a complete denial of the Incarnation and thus of Christianity. Therefore, the white denominational churches are unchristian. They are a manifestation of both a willingness to tolerate it and a desire to perpetuate it.

The old philosophical distinction between the primary and secondary qualities of objects provides an analogy here, where only the primary qualities pertain to the essence of the thing. Regarding the Church, are not fellowship and service primary qualities, without which the "church" is not the Church? Can we still speak of a community as being Christian if that body is racist through and through? It is my contention that the racism implies the absence of fellowship and service, which are primary qualities, indispensable marks of the Church. To be racist is to fall outside the definition of the Church. In our time, the issue of racism is analogous to the Arian Controversy of the fourth century. Athanasius perceived quite clearly that if Arius' views were tolerated, Christianity would be lost. But few white churchmen have questioned whether racism was a similar denial of Jesus Christ. Even Haselden, certainly one of the most sensitive of the white churchmen who have written on the subject, can speak of white Christian racists.

If there is any contemporary meaning of the Antichrist (or "the principalities and powers"), the white church seems to be a manifestation of it. It is the enemy of Christ. It was the white "Christian" church which took the lead in establishing slavery as an institution and segregation as a pattern in society by sanctioning all-white congregations. As Frank Loescher pointed out, its very existence as an institution is a symbol of the "philosophy of white supremacy."[18] "Long before the little signs — 'White Only' and 'Colored' — appeared in the public utilities they had appeared in the church."[19] Haselden shows clearly the work of the Church in setting the pattern which later became general law for all of America:

> First came the segregation of the Negro within the church; then followed the separation of the churches by the "spontaneous" withdrawal of the Negro Christians; much later, the elaborate patterns of segregation were to arise in the church and in secular society.[20]

With its all-white congregations, it makes racism a respectable attitude. By remaining silent it creates an ethos which dehumanizes blacks. It is the Church which preaches that blacks are inferior to whites—if not by *word* certainly by "moral" example.

In the old slavery days, the Church preached that slavery was a divine decree, and it used the Bible as the basis of its authority.

> Not only did the Christianity fail to offer the Negro hope of freedom in this world, but the manner in which Christianity was communicated to him tended to degrade him. The Negro was taught that his enslavement was due to the fact that he had been cursed by God. His very color was a sign of the curse which he had received as a descendant of Ham. Parts of the Bible were carefully selected to prove that God had intended that the Negro should be the servant of the white man and that he would always be a "hewer of wood and a drawer of water."[21]

Several ministers even wrote books justifying slavery. "It may be," wrote George D. Armstrong in *The Christian Doctrine of Slavery,* "that *Christian* slavery is God's solution of the problem [relation of labor and capital] about which the wisest statesmen of Europe confess themselves at fault."[22] In another book, *Slavery Ordained of God,* Fred A. Ross wrote that "slavery is ordained of God, ... to continue for the good of the slave, the good of the master, the good of the whole American family, until another and better destiny may be unfolded."[23]

Today that same Church sets the tone for the present inhumanity to blacks by remaining silent as blacks are killed for wanting to be treated like human beings. Like other segments of this society, the Church emphasizes obedience to the law of the land without asking whether the law is racist in character or without even questioning the everyday deadly violence which laws and law enforcers inflict on blacks in the ghetto. They are quick to condemn Black Power as a concept and the violence in the ghetto without saying a word about white power and its 350 years of constant violence against blacks. It was the Church which placed God's approval on slavery and today places his blessings on the racist structure of American society. As long as whites can be sure that God is on their side, there is potentially no limit to their violence against anyone who threatens the American racist way of life. Genocide is the logical conclusion of racism. It happened to the American Indian, and there is ample reason to believe that America is prepared to do the same to blacks.

Many writers have shown the Church's vested interest in slavery and racism in America.[24] At first the "white Christian" questioned the Christianizing of the slave because of the implications of equality in the Bible and because of the fear that education might cause the slave to fight for his freedom. Slave masters at first forbade the baptism of slaves on the ground that it was an invasion of their property rights. But the churchmen assured them that there was no relationship between Christianity and freedom in civil matters. In the words of the Bishop of London:

> Christianity, and the embracing of the Gospel, does not make the least Alteration in Civil property, or in any of the Duties which belong to Civil Relations; but in all these Respects, it continues Persons just in the same State as it found them. The Freedom which Christianity gives, is a Freedom from the Bondage of Sin and Satan, and from the Dominion of Men's Lust and Passions and inordinate Desires; but as to their outward Condition, whatever that was before, whether bond or free, their being baptized and becoming Christians, makes no matter of Change in it.[25]

In fact some churchmen argued that Christianity made blacks better slaves. When slaves began to get rebellious about their freedom, according to a Methodist missionary, "it was missionary influence that moderated their passions, kept them in the steady course of duty, and prevented them from sinning against God by offending against the laws of man. Whatever outbreaks or insurrections at any time occurred, no Methodist slave was ever proved guilty of incendiarism or rebellion for more than seventy years, namely from 1760 to 1833."[26]

Many ministers even owned slaves. In 1844, 200 Methodist traveling preachers owned 1,600 slaves, and 1,000 local preachers owned 10,000 slaves. This fact alone indicates the white Methodist Church's tolerance and propagation of the slave system. There is no evidence that it saw any real contradiction between slavery and essential Christianity.

Some northern white Methodist churchmen would probably remind me that the Church split precisely over that issue in 1844. This seems to suggest that at least the north was against slavery. If the north was against slavery, it nevertheless had no intention of viewing blacks as men. Northern churchmen are reminded that it was in their section of the country that "free Negroes" seceded from various white churches because of intolerable humiliation by whites. It was northerners who pulled Richard Allen and his companions from their knees as they knelt at prayer at St. George's Methodist Episcopal Church in Philadelphia. "We all went out of the church in a body," wrote Allen, "and they were no more plagued with us in the church."[27] There is no evidence at all that the north was more humane than the south in its treatment of blacks in the churches. The north could appear to be more concerned about the blacks because of their work toward the abolition of slavery. But the reason is clear: Slavery was not as vital to their economy as it was to the south's.

Some southern churchmen might argue that the Church in the pre-Civil War days was indeed a real expression of their concern for blacks. It was an integrated Church! Surprisingly, H. Richard Niebuhr suggests that the worship of white and black people together was an indication that the great revival and the democratic doctrines of the Revolution which fostered the sense of equality had "pricked the conscience of the churches on the subject of slavery."[28]

> White and black worshipped together and, at their best, sought to realize the brotherhood Jesus had practiced and Paul had preached. There were many significant exceptions, it is true. But the general rule was that the two races should be united in religion. ... In the Methodist and Baptist churches, ... it was the conviction of the essential equality of all souls before God which inspired the white missionary and an occasional master to share the benefits of the common gospel in a common church with members of the other race.[29]

Apparently, Niebuhr's identity with the oppressor got the best of his theological and sociological analysis. For it is clear that "integration" was a practice in the southern churches because, as Niebuhr himself says, it was "the less of two evils." It was dangerous to the slave system to allow slaves to have independent uncontrolled churches. The abolitionist activity in the northern black churches and the Nat Turner revolt of 1831 reaffirmed this fear. Laws were even passed which prevented the education of blacks and the assembly of more than five blacks without white supervision. Rather than being a demonstration of brotherhood or equality, the "integration" in the churches was a means of keeping a close watch on blacks. Haselden is right about the Church. It was and is the "mother of racial patterns," the "purveyor of arrant sedatives," and the "teacher of immoral moralities."

The Quakers were the only denominational group which showed any signs of radical obedience to Christ. Its leaders, George Fox and George Keith, declared clearly the contradiction between slavery and the gospel of Christ. An example of the Quaker view of slavery is illustrated by the resolution of 1688, passed in Germantown:

> Now tho' they are black, we cannot conceive there is more liberty to have them slaves, as it is to have other white ones. There is a saying, that we shall doe to all men, like as we will be done our selves: making no difference of what generation, descent, or Color they are. And those who steal or rob men, and those who buy or purchase them, are they not all alicke? Here is liberty of Conscience, which is right and reasonable, here ought to be lickewise liberty of the body, except of evildoers, which is an other case. But to bring men hither, or to rob and sell them against their will, we stand against.[30]

It is unfortunate that such men were in the minority even among the Quakers. There was the temptation to let economics, rather than religion, determine one's actions. The Quakers, like most groups who could afford it, owned slaves. But the spirit of freedom and liberty in civil matters was at least the concern of some Quakers, which is more than can be said of others.

In light of this history it is not surprising that the white churchmen have either condemned Black Power, or, as is more often the case, joined the other silent intellectuals in our colleges and universities. They have never championed black freedom. During the most fervent period of lynching,[31] the Church scarcely said a word against it. Loescher's study of the twenty-five major denominations comprising the Federal Council of Churches of Christ in America shows that until 1929 most churches scarcely uttered a word about white inhumanity toward blacks. In fact, Gunnar Myrdal pointed out, "Methodist and Baptist preachers were active in reviving the Ku Klux Klan after the First World War."[32] There is little question that the Church has been and is a racist institution, and there is little sign that she even cares about it.

> So far as the major denominations are concerned, it is the story of indifference, vacillation, and duplicity. . . . It is a history in which the church not only compromised its ethic to the mood and practice of the times but was itself actively unethical, sanctioning the enslavement of human beings, producing the patterns of segregation, urging upon the oppressed Negro the extracted sedatives of the Gospel, and promulgating a doctrine of interracial morality which is itself immoral.[33]

Some churchmen probably would want to point out their "unselfish involvement" in the civil rights struggle of the 1950's and 1960's. It was a black man, Martin Luther King, Jr., who challenged the conscience of this nation by his unselfish giving of his time and eventually his life for the poor blacks and whites of America. During the initial stages of his civil-disobedience campaign, most white churchmen stood silently by and criticized with their political cohorts. And most who eventually joined him in his work were "Johnnies-come-lately." Even here their participation reminds one of the white churchmen of the pre-Civil War era. As long as the south was the target, northern churchmen could assure themselves that it was a southern problem, totally unrelated to their own northern parishes. Most thus came to think of themselves as missionaries for Christ in a foreign land. But when King brought his work north, many retreated and complained that he was confusing politics with religion. King only regained his popularity among northern churchmen after the emergence of the concept of Black Power. They came to view King's nonviolence as the lesser of two evils. I am convinced that King's death was due to an ethos created by the white church, which permits whites to kill blacks at will without any fear of reprisal. Few white men have been convicted and imprisoned for slaying a black or a white involved in civil rights.

Since the emergence of the recent rebellion in the cities, it seems that the most the white churches do is to tell blacks to obey the law of the land. Occasionally, a church body passes a harmless resolution. Imagine, men dying of hunger, children maimed from rat bites, women dying of despair—and the Church passes a resolution. Perhaps it is impossible to prevent riots, but one can fight against the conditions which cause them. The white church is placed in question because of its contribution to a structure which produces riots. Some churchmen may reply: "We do condemn the deplorable conditions which produce urban riots. We do condemn racism and all the evils arising from it." But to the extent that this is true, the Church, with the exception of a few isolated individuals, voices its condemnation in the style of resolutions that are usually equivocal and almost totally unproductive. If the condemnation was voiced, it was not understood! The Church should speak in a style which avoids abstractions. Its language must be backed up with relevant involvement in the affairs of people who suffer. It must be a grouping whose community life and personal involvement are coherent with its language about the gospel.

The Church does not appear to be a community willing to pay up personally. It is not a community which views every command of Jesus as a call to the cross. It appears, instead, as an institution whose existence depends on the evils which produce the riots in the cities. With this in mind, we must say that when a minister condemns the rioters and blesses by silence the conditions which produce the riots, he gives up his credentials as a Christian minister and becomes inhuman. He is an animal, just like those who, backed by an ideology of racism, order the structure of this society on the basis of white supremacy. We need men who refuse to be animals and are resolved to pay the price, so that all men can be something more than animals.

Whether Black Power advocates are that grouping, we will have to wait and see. But the Church has shown many times that it loves life and is not prepared to die for others. It has not really gone where the action is with a willingness to die for the neighbor, but has remained aloof from the sufferings of men. It is a chaplaincy to sick middle-class egos. It stands (or sits) condemned by its very whiteness.

This leads one to conclude that Christ is operating outside the denominational white church. The real Church of Christ is that grouping which identifies with the suffering of the poor by becoming one with them. While we should be careful in drawing the line, the line must nevertheless be drawn. The Church includes not only the Black Power community but all men who view their humanity as inextricably related to every man. It is that grouping with a demonstrated willingness to die for the prevention of the torture of others, saying with Bonhoeffer, "When Christ calls a man, he bids him come and die."

Is there any hope for the white church? Hope is dependent upon whether it will ask from the depths of its being with God: "What must I do to be saved?" The person who seriously asks that question is a person capable of receiving God's forgiveness. It is time for the white church to ask that question with a willingness to do all for Christ. Like the Philippian jailers who put the question to St. Paul, the answer is the same for the white church as it was to them: *Repent*, and believe in the Lord and Saviour Jesus Christ! There is no other way. It must own that it has been and is a racist institution whose primary purpose is the perpetuation of white supremacy. But it is not enough to be sorry or to admit wrong. To repent involves change in one's whole being. In the Christian perspective, it means conversion.

Speaking of Jesus' understanding of repentance, Bornkamm says: It means "to lay hold on the salvation which is already at hand, and to give up everything for it."[34] This involves a willingness to renounce self and the world and to grasp the gift of salvation now here in Jesus Christ. But there is no repentance without obedience and there is no obedience without action. And this is always action in the world with Christ fighting the evils which hold men captive.

For the white churches this means a radical reorientation of their style in the world toward blacks. It means that they must change sides, giving up all claims to lofty neutrality. It means that they will identify utterly with the oppressed, thus inevitably tasting the sting of oppression themselves. It means that they will no longer "stand silently or march weakly protesting" but will join the advocates of Black Power in their unambiguous identification "with the oppressed and with the revolutions made by the oppressed."[35] A racist pattern has been set, and the Church has been a contributor to the pattern. Now it must break that pattern by placing its life at stake.

Black Power and American Theology

In a culture which rewards "patriots" and punishes "dissenters," it is difficult to be prophetic and easy to perform one's duties in the light of the objectives of the nation as a whole. This was true for the state church of Germany during the Third Reich, and it is true now of the white church in America as blacks begin to question seriously their place in this society. It is always much easier to point to the good amid the evil as a means of rationalizing one's failure to call into question the evil itself. It is easier to identify with the oppressor as he throws sops to the poor than to align oneself with the problems of the poor as he endures oppression. Moreover, the moral and religious implications of any act of risk are always sufficiently cloudy to make it impossible to be certain of right action. Because man is finite, he can never reach that state of security in which he is free of anxiety when he makes moral decisions. This allows the irresponsible religious man to grasp a false kind of religious and political security by equating law and order with Christian morality. If someone calls his attention to the inhumanity of the political system toward others, he can always explain his loyalty to the state by suggesting that this system is the least evil of any other existing political state. He can also point to the lack of clarity regarding the issues, whether they concern race relations or the war in Vietnam. This will enable him to compartmentalize the various segments of the societal powers so that he can rely on other disciplines to give the word on the appropriate course of action. This seems to characterize the style of many religious thinkers as they respond to the race problem in America.

Therefore, it is not surprising that the sickness of the Church in America is also found in the main stream of American religious thought. As with the

Church as a whole, theology remains conspicuously silent regarding the place of the black man in American society. In the history of modern American theology, there are few dissenters on black slavery and the current black oppression among the teachers and writers of theology. And those who do speak are usually unclear. Too often their comments are but a replica of the current cultural ethos, drawing frequently from nontheological disciplines for the right word on race relations.

More often, however, theologians simply ignore the problem of color in America. Any theologian involved in professional societies can observe that few have attempted to deal seriously with the problem of racism in America. It is much easier to deal with the textual problems associated with some biblical book or to deal "objectively" with a religious phenomenon than it is to ask about the task of theology in the current disintegration of society. It would seem that it is time for theology to make a radical break with its identity with the world by seeking to bring to the problem of color the revolutionary implications of the gospel of Christ. It is time for theology to leave its ivory tower and join the real issues, which deal with dehumanization of blacks in America. It is time for theologians to relate their work to life-and-death issues, and in so doing to execute its function of bringing the Church to a recognition of its task in the world.

For the sickness of the Church in America is intimately involved with the bankruptcy of American theology. When the Church fails to live up to its appointed mission, it means that theology is partly responsible. Therefore, it is impossible to criticize the Church and its lack of relevancy without criticizing theology for its failure to perform its function.

Theology functions within the Church. Its task is to make sure that the "church" is the Church. The mission of the Church is to announce and to act out the gospel it has received. When the Church fails in its appointed task by seeking to glorify itself rather than Jesus Christ, it is the job of theology to remind her what the true Church is, for theology is that discipline which has the responsibility of continually examining the proclamation of the Church in the light of Jesus Christ. "Dogmatic theology is the scientific test to which the Christian church puts herself regarding the language about God which is peculiar to her."[36] The task of theology, then, is to criticize and revise the language of the Church. This includes not only language as uttered speech but the language of radical involvement in the world. The Church not only speaks of God in "worship" but as it encounters the world with the gospel of Jesus Christ. It is the task of theology to make sure that the Church's thoroughly human speech, whether word or deed, agrees with the essence of the Church, that is, with Jesus Christ who is "God in his gracious approach to man in revelation and reconciliation."[37]

The Church cannot remain aloof from the world because Christ is in the world. Theology, then, if it is to serve the need of the Church must become "worldly theology." This means that it must make sure that the Church is in the world and that its word and deed are harmonious with Jesus Christ. It must make sure that the Church's language about God is relevant to every new generation and its problems. It is for this reason that the definitive theological treatise can never be written. Every generation has its own problems, as does every nation. Theology is not, then, an intellectual exercise but a worldly risk.

American theology has failed to take that worldly risk. It has largely ignored its domestic problems on race. It has not called the Church to be involved in confronting this society with the meaning of the Kingdom in the light of Christ. Even though it says, with Tillich, that theology "is supposed to satisfy two basic needs: the statement of the truth of the Christian message and the interpretation of this truth for every new generation,"[38] it has virtually ignored the task of relating the truth of the gospel to the problem of race in America. The lack of a relevant, risky theological statement suggests that theologians, like others, are unable to free themselves from the structures of this society.

The close identity of American theology with the structures of society may also account for the failure to produce theologians comparable in stature to Europeans like Bultmann, Barth, and Bonhoeffer. Some try to account for this by pointing to the youth of America; but that seems an insufficient explanation, since other disciplines appear to hold their own. The real reasons are immensely complex. But one cogent explanation is that most American theologians are too closely tied to the American structure to respond creatively to the life situation of the Church in this society. Instead of seeking to respond to the problems which are unique to this country, most Americans look to Europe for the newest word worth theologizing about. Most graduate students in theology feel that they must go to Germany or somewhere else in Europe because that is where things are happening in the area of theology. Little wonder that American theology is predominantly "footnotes on the Germans." Theology here is largely an intellectual game unrelated to the issues of life and death. It is impossible to respond creatively and prophetically to the life-situational problems of society without identifying with the problems of the disinherited and unwanted in society. Few American theologians have made that identification with the poor blacks in America but have themselves contributed to the system which enslaves black people. The seminaries in America are probably the most obvious sign of the irrelevance of theology to life. Their initiative in responding to the crisis of black people in America is virtually unnoticeable. Their curriculum generally is designed for young white men and women who are preparing to serve all-white churches. Only recently have seminaries sought to respond to the black revolution by reorganizing their curriculum to include courses in "black studies" and inner-city involvements; and this is due almost exclusively to the insistence of black students. Most seminaries still have no courses in black church history and their faculties and administrators are largely white. This alone gives support to the racist assumption that blacks are unimportant.

In Europe the situation seems to be somewhat different. Karl Barth's theology was born in response to the political and economic crisis of Germany. He began his career as a liberal theologian; he believed that the Kingdom of God would soon be achieved through the establishment of a socialist society. He put his confidence in the latent resources of humanity; and this meant that Barth, along with many liberal theologians of his day, believed in the adequacy of the religious man, the adequacy of religion, and the security of the culture and civilization. The First World War shattered his hope of the Kingdom of God on earth. The "civilized man" who was supposed to be moving steadily, even rapidly, toward perfection had cast himself into an orgy of destruction. In the wake of the war came Communism and Fascism, both of which denied Christian values. As a result of the war and its aftermath, Barth felt that the problem of man was much more desperate than most people realized and would not be solved simply by changing the economic structure. For a while Barth was in a state of shock. In particular he was burdened with the task of declaring the Christian message to his congregation every Sunday. What could he say? People did not want to hear, he was quite sure, his own man-made philosophy or his own opinions.

In due time Barth was led from his anthropocentric conception of Christianity to a thoroughgoing theocentric conception. He was led from trust in man to complete trust in God alone. He was convinced that he could not identify God's Word with man's word. No human righteousness can be equated with divine righteousness; no human act can be synonymous with God's act. Even the so-called good which man does in this world counts as nothing in God's eyes. To identify God's righteousness with human righteousness is to fail to see the "infinite qualitative distinction" between God and man, the distinction between what is human and what is divine.

This radical change in Barth's theological perspective had nothing to do with abstract theological thinking but with his confrontation with the political, economic, and social situation of Germany. It was the rise of a new political order that caused Barth to launch a devastating and relentless attack on natural theology. When American theologians picked up the problem, they apparently did so without really knowing that for Barth and his sympathizers the natural theology issue was not merely an intellectual debate but an event, an event about the life and death of men. Observing the rise of Hitler during the 1930s, Barth saw clearly the danger of identifying man's word with God's Word. To say that God's Word is wholly unlike man's word means that God stands in judgment against all political systems. The work of the state can never be identified or confused with God's Word. In Hitler's campaign against the Jews, an alien god dominated Germany; men were being slaughtered on his altar. It was no time for caution or lofty "objectivity." When Barth said "Nein!"—no natural theology, no blending of the Word of God and the word of man—the *political* implication was clear: Hitler is the Antichrist; God has set his face against the Third Reich.

Americans have generally agreed that Barth's rejection of natural theology was a mistake. Is that because American theologians still see a close relationship between the structures of this society and Christianity? As long as there is no absolute difference between God and man, it is possible to view America as the "land of the free and the home of the brave," despite the oppression of blacks. As long as theology is identified with the system, it is impossible to criticize it by bringing the judgment of God's righteousness upon it.

Barth's theology may serve as an example of how to relate theology to life. The whole of his theology represents a constant attempt to engage the Church in life situations. Its notable development (compare *Romans* with *The Humanity of God*) is clearly a response to the new problems which men face in worldly involvement.

If American theology is going to serve the needs of the Church by relating the gospel to the political, economic, and social situation of America, it must cut its adoring dependence upon Europe as the place to tell us what theology ought to be talking about. Some European theologians, like Barth and Bonhoeffer, may serve as examples of how to relate theology to life, but not in defining *our* major issues.

There is a need for a theology of revolution, a theology which radically encounters the problems of the disinherited black people in America in particular and the oppressed people of color throughout the world in general. As Joseph Washington puts it:

> In the twentieth century white Protestantism has concentrated its personnel, time, energy, and finances on issues that it has deemed more significant than the "American Dilemma": pacifism, politics, liberal versus conservative controversies, prohibition, socialism, Marxism, labor and management aspects of economic justice, civil liberties, totalitarianism, overseas mission, fascism, war and peace, reorganization of ecclesiastical structures, and ecumenical issues.[39]

It has overlooked the unique problem of the powerless blacks.

In this new era of Black Power, the era in which blacks are sick of white power and are prepared to do anything and give everything for freedom now, theology cannot afford to be silent. Not to speak, not to "do theology" around this critical problem, is to say that the black predicament is not crucial to Christian faith. At a moment when blacks are determined to stand up as human beings even if they are shot down, the Word of the cross certainly is focused upon them. Will no one speak that Word to the dead and dying? Theologians confronted by this question may distinguish three possible responses. Some will, timidly or passionately, continue to appeal (mistakenly) to Paul's dictum about the "powers that be." We will have law-and-order theologians as we have law-and-order pastors and laymen. Others will insist that theology as such is necessarily unrelated to social upheaval. These men will continue as in a vacuum, writing footnotes on the Aramaic substratum of Mark's Gospel or on the authorship of the *Theologia Germanica* or on the "phenomenon" of faith. Could a black man hope that there are still others who, *as theologians*, will join the oppressed in their fight for freedom? These theologians will speak unequivocally of revelation, Scripture, God, Christ, grace, faith, Church, ministry, and hope, so that the message comes through loud and clear: *The black revolution is the work of Christ.*

If theology fails to re-evaluate its task in the light of Black Power, the emphasis on the death of God will not add the needed dimension. This will mean that the white church and white theology are dead, not God. It will mean that God will choose another means of implementing his word of righteousness in the world. It will mean also that the burden of the gospel is placed solely on the shoulders of the oppressed, without any clear word from the "church." This leads us to our last concern, the black church. It is indeed possible that the only redemptive forces left in the denominational churches are to be found in the segregated black churches.

The white response so far, in and out of the Church, is, "Not yet," which in the twisted rhetoric of the land of the free means, "Never!" "Law and order" is the sacred incantation of the priests of the old order; and the faithful respond with votes, higher police budgets, and Gestapo legislation. Private and public arsenals of incredible destructive force testify to the determination of a sick and brutal people to put an end to black revolution and indeed to black people. The black man has violated the conditions under which he is permitted to breathe, and the air is heavy with the potential for genocide. The confrontation of black people as real persons is so strange and out of harmony with the normal pattern of white behavior that most whites cannot even begin to understand the meaning of black humanity.

In this situation of revolution and reaction, the Church must decide where its identity lies. Will it continue its chaplaincy to the forces of oppression, or will it embrace the cause of liberation, proclaiming in word and deed the gospel of Christ?

NOTES

1. See their *Black Power. The Politics of Liberation in America* (New York: Random House, 1967).

2. Some biblical scholars identify the call of Abraham as the beginning of the Church, but this involves critical-historical problems that are not pertinent here. As far as Israel's awareness of herself as an elect people is concerned, few authorities would fail to place the beginning at the exodus and wilderness experiences.

3. For an analysis of the relationship between *qahal* and *ekklesia* see J. Robert Nelson, *The Realm of Redemption* (New York: Seabury Press, 1951), pp. 3-19.

4. Bonhoeffer, *Prisoner of God*, ed. Eberhard Bethge, trans. R. H. Fuller (New York: Macmillan Co., 1953) pp. 166-167. Used with permission.

5. Cox, *The Secular City* (New York: Macmillan Co., 1965), p. 145.

6. Cullmann, *Christ and Time,* trans. F. V. Filson (Philadelphia: Westminster Press, 1949).

7. Lewis, *The Johannine Epistles* (London: Epworth Press, 1961), p. 84

8. Ibid.

9. Hordern, *Christianity, Communism and History* (London: Lutterworth Press, 1957), p. 27.

10. Quoted in Cox, *Secular City*, p. 126.

11. Ibid., p. 144.

12. Barth, *Church Dogmatics*, Vol . IV, Part I, trans. G. Bromiley (Edinburgh: T. & T. Clark, 1956), p. 643.

13. Ibid., p. 695.

14. Ibid., p. 696.

15. Haselden, *The Racial Problem in Christian Perspective* (New York: Harper & Row, 1959), p. 48.

16. Ibid.

17. Berton, *The Comfortable Pew* (Philadelphia: J. B. Lippincott Co., 1965), pp. 28-29.

18. Loescher, *The Protestant Church and the Negro, A Pattern of Segregation* (New York: Association Press, 1948), p. 9.

19. Haselden, *The Racial Problem,* p. 29.

20. Ibid.

21. E. Franklin Frazier, *Black Bourgeoisie* (New York: Collier Books, 1965), p. 115. Used with permission.

22. Quoted in ibid., p. 115.

23. Ibid.

24. See Washington, *Black Religion* (1964) and *Politics of God* (1967), both published by Beacon Press; H. Richard Niebuhr, *The Social Sources of Denominationalism* (Cleveland: Mendian Books, 1929); Haselden, *The Racial Problem*; E. Franklin Frazier, *The Negro Church in America* (New York: Schocken Books, 1963).

25. Quoted in Niebuhr, *Social Sources of Denominationalism*, p. 249.

26. Ibid., p. 251.

27. Ibid., p. 260.

28. Ibid., p. 244.

29. Ibid., pp. 247-248.

30. Shelton Smith, Robert Handy, and Lefferts Loetscher, *American Christianity*, Vol. I (New York: Charles Scribner's Sons, 1960), p. 181.

31. See Ralph Ginzburg, *One Hundred Years of Lynching* (New York: Lancer Books, 1962).

32. Myrdal, *An American Dilemma. The Negro Problem and Modern Democracy* (New York: Harper & Brothers, 1944), p. 563.

33. Haselden, *The Racial Problem,* p. 63. Used with permission.

34. Bornkamm, *Jesus of Nazareth,* p. 82.

35. Harding, "The Religion of Black Power," in *Religious Situation,* p. 12.

36. Barth, *Church Dogmatics*, Vol. 1, Part 1, p. 1.

37. Ibid., p. 3.

38. Tillich, *Systematic Theology*, Vol. I (Chicago: University of Chicago Press, 1951).

39. J. Washington, *Black Religion*, p. 228.

PART II

FOUNDATIONAL VOICES
BEFORE 1980

INTRODUCTION

The rise of Black theology in the 1960s and early 1970s represented the first self-conscious attempt by African American ministers and scholars of religion to define the faith of Black churches differently from White American Protestantism. When Blacks separated themselves from White denominations and organized their own churches in the late eighteenth and early nineteenth centuries, they did not perceive their actions as being motivated by theological differences. They accepted without alteration the church doctrines and polities of the White denominations from which they separated. For Blacks their separation was based, as Bishop R. R. Wright of the African Methodist Episcopal (A.M.E.) Church said in 1947, "entirely upon sociological grounds: to promote brotherhood and equality across racial lines."

The first person to claim that the separated existence of Black churches created a different faith from the Christianity of White churches was Joseph R. Washington, author of the well-known text, *Black Religion: The Negro and Christianity in the United States* (Beacon Press, 1964). Washington's negative answer to the question, "Are American Negro Churches Christian?" (Document 6), made him the most talked about and controversial Black scholar of religion during that time. Black church leaders were incensed that a scholar of their own race could be so negative in his evaluation of the Christian identity of Black churches, and so positive about White churches whose racist behavior made the former's existence necessary. Most Black ministers were not theologically sophisticated enough to debate the fine points of Washington's argument. But they were firmly convinced that his theological judgment was incorrect, even though they could not demonstrate it to the satisfaction of seminary professors. "If God is no respecter of persons," they asked, "how could racists be more Christian than their victims?"

While Black ministers rejected Washington's book, Whites seemed delighted by it. Martin E. Marty wrote a glowing review of it for the *New York Herald Tribune*, which was also published in the 1966 paperback edition. Washington became a popular lecturer for church conferences, community groups, seminaries, universities, and colleges. Contrary to his intentions, Washington's book reinforced a theological arrogance among White churches and their theologians, and thereby made it difficult for Black ministers to relate the religion of Jesus to the Black struggle for justice in the churches and the society.

Albert B. Cleage, Jr., a clergyman of the United Church of Christ and pastor of the Shrine of the Black Madonna in Detroit, published a widely influential collection of sermons under the provocative title, *The Black Messiah* (Seabury, 1969). The idea that Jesus was a Black man created a heated debate in both Black and White churches, with Whites dismissing the idea as absurd and Blacks arguing the pros and cons of it. Some Blacks praised Cleage's attempt to "dehonkify" Christianity and others called his Christology a "religiously illiterate position."

The debate became more widespread when the Black artist Devon Cunningham's image of the Black Christ adorned the cover of the March 1969 issue of *Ebony* magazine. On the inside, Cunningham's Christ was placed beside Warner Sallman's White Christ under the title, "The Quest For A Black Messiah: Radical Clerics Reject 'Honky Christ' created by American Culture-Religion." An interpretation of Albert Cleage's views was the main focus of the essay by *Ebony* editor Alex Poinsett.

Like Joseph Washington, Cleage contended that Black religion was unique and thus could not be subsumed under the general rubric of Protestantism. But unlike Washington, Cleage claimed that original Christianity was a Black religion. The key event that separated the publications of Washington's *Black Religion* and Cleage's *Black Messiah* was the dramatic irruption of the Black Power slogan in June 1966, transforming the consciousness of African Americans in every sphere of their existence. After Black Power, integrationism began to lose ground to Black separatism, as Blacks everywhere began to celebrate their own cultural heritage and political power. While not rejecting completely the integrationist philosophy of Martin Luther King, Jr., Blacks began to take another look at the Black nationalist philosophy of Malcolm X, especially his radical critique of Christianity as the White people's religion.

Albert Cleage, a one-time close friend of Malcolm, tailored his preaching and teaching to prevent the exodus of radical young Black nationalists out of the church. The titles of his sermons included: "An Epistle to Stokely," "Brother Malcolm," "Not Peace But A Sword," "He Stirs Up The People," and "The Resurrection of the Nation." Cleage's primary aim was to show how Whites corrupted Christianity, teaching Blacks to love their enemies when in fact Jesus commanded Blacks to love their own kind and to fight their oppressors. In the essay for this volume (Document 7), taken from the Introduction of *The Black Messiah*, Cleage outlined his basic theological position.

It was one thing to proclaim the need for a Christian theology for Black churches and to preach sermons about the Black Christ and quite another to create a theology that was both *Black* and *Christian* and also one that the churches and seminaries would take seriously. James H. Cone's *Black Theology and Black Power* (1969) was the first effort in that direction. The second effort was his 1970 publication, *A Black Theology of Liberation*, which was as controversial as the first. Both appeared during the time Black students were demanding that White professors take seriously the Black experience as a source for doing theology. Using liberation as the defining center of his theological perspective, Cone's books made it more difficult for White seminary professors to dismiss Black theology as nothing but the rhetoric of radical Black clergy.

"Black Theology and Black Liberation" (Document 8) was presented at a consultation on Black theology and was later published in *The Christian Century* (16 September 1970).

J. Deotis Roberts, long-time professor of Christian theology at Howard University School of Religion and author of several books in theology, played an important role in the development of Black theology. In his first essay on the subject, "Black Consciousness in Theological Perspective" (presented at a "Black Church/Black Theology" conference in Washington, D.C., May 1969), liberation and reconciliation emerged as the center of his theological perspective. In 1971, Roberts published his most influential text, *Liberation and Reconciliation: A Black Theology*. Some people welcomed his accent on reconciliation as a much needed complement and corrective to James Cone's more militant view of Black theology. In a 1973 essay, "Black Theology in the Making" (Document 9), Roberts outlined his perspective on Black theology, showing how his program differed from Washington, Cleage, and Cone.

No one contributed more to the early development of Black theology, especially in the churches, than Gayraud S. Wilmore who served as the executive director of the Council on Church and Race of the United Presbyterian Church. One of the founding members of the NCBC, he was selected as the first chairman of its Theological Commission and thereby provided the theological vision of the newly created organization. Wilmore was one of the writers of NCBC's influential "Black Power" statement, and his theological hand is also found on most of the statements that followed it. Black theology's link with militant Black political and cultural groups, like the Black Panthers, Maulana Karenga's US Organization, and James Forman's "Black Manifesto," was largely due to his influence. For Wilmore, Black theology is more than Christian discourse about the God of the mainline denominational Black churches; it is discourse about the religious dimensions in the total Black community—past and present, Christian and non-Christian, militant and conservative, and in the Diaspora and on the African continent. A detailed analysis of his perspective on Black theology and its relationship to the history of Black religion is found in his influential book, *Black Religion and Black Radicalism* (1972).

William R. Jones wrote the most important critique of Black liberation theology. It caught most Black theologians off-guard, stunned by the cogency of his analysis of the limitations of their perspectives on liberation. His essay, "Theodicy and Methodology in Black Theology" (Document 11), was one of the earliest (1971) of his critiques. A more detailed presentation of it is found in his book, published under the provocative title, *Is God a White Racist?* (1973).

J.H.C.

6

ARE AMERICAN NEGRO CHURCHES CHRISTIAN?

Joseph R. Washington, Jr.

Thesis: Negro religious institutions have developed a pattern of life totally irrelevant to the Christian faith. The historical conditions which severed Negro religio-socio-theological life from mainstream Christianity have issued in religious compartmentalization. Rooted in racial concerns and emerging through response to social questions the Negro has little basis for renewal. The hope for the Negro in religion, as in every other aspect of life, lies in full participation within the mainline congregations whose errors are under the judgment of a dynamic theology which seeks to interpret the contemporary mission and message of the church. But, there is no present possibility for the inclusion of Negro religion within the Christian faith; only a few Negroes are accepted in Christian communities outside the bond of color. On the way to the inclusion of Negroes into the mainstream the present may best serve as a period of preparation for the future when Negro (qua Negro) institutions will no longer be the only alternative for the Negro who is also a Christian.

The current insistence which demands the entrance of Negro Americans into the political, economic, and social mainstream has not left unaffected the religious communions. It is evident, for the first time in American history, that full participation of the Negro is the pervasive mood of the influential forces which determine the future of the nation—however deliberate and void of enthusiasm. This new fact of seeing the Negro as a responsible participant in all areas of our structural life may be realistically recognized as a future rather than a present fulfillment.

Joseph R. Washington, Jr., is Professor of Religious Studies and director of Afro-American Studies at the University of Pennsylvania. This essay originally appeared in *Theology Today* 20 (April 1963-January 1964). Reprinted with permission of the publisher.

I

It is clear that a universally-geared technological economy operated by a comparable bureaucratic administration of organization men cannot permit racial conflicts which tend to disrupt a well-oiled organized society or rob it of necessary though colored cogs.

It is also clear that one does not need to be a functionalist to perceive the truth that the church mirrors the culture. The natural drive towards merging denominations inherent in the growing movement called ecumenicity can hardly be passed off as a mere occurrence accidentally emerging in the same climate of a world-wide technological revolution. To the degree that the economy seeks to integrate persons regardless of color, we can expect a similar response within the church. The fiction of the church as a sphere of private life not unlike the local country club will easily submit to reality when the very economy which supports it institutes the inclusion of hitherto unacceptable demands and equal access to the leisure-time activities for all employees as an insurance of operational efficiency.

There is a noticeable absence of tension between Protestantism and the culture in which its religious life is nurtured because the persons involved in both are one and the same. Few split loyalties or personalities are engendered by either Negro or white Protestantism at the point of the exclusive nature of these various denominations. But tension of a less heroic nature does persist. It is the tension between those limited Protestant voices who urge the churches to become an accessory before the fact in the sphere of race relations and their numberless opponents who insist that the churches became an accessory after the fact. This tension points up the ethical dimension of Protestantism beyond the realm of functionalism. The two positions ultimately agree concerning the outcome which does not depend upon their efforts; the disagreement concerns the minor question of timing. To those who have perceived the historical responses of Protestant churchmen to ethical issues of social consequences there is little doubt but that the vast majority who approve of following the society will have their way.

The major non-Roman religious bodies in America are best described as middle class in their life and mission. The extension of the middle class expands with each fiscal year, drawing within its bulge Negro white-collar employees and blue-collar workers inspired by middle-class values. In this light, the tension between before- and after-the-fact Protestants appears less irrelevant though no less inconsequential. In this historical period white Protestant dominance is more fiction than fact and pluralism is more fact than fiction. As white Protestants commence to adjust to playing the minority role in politics, they do so in religion as well. Simultaneously, the political power of Negroes who may be described as primarily Protestant in religious heritage has just begun to display itself in the realm of economics which augurs well for improvement of their monetary well being, even if their social status will improve ever so minutely if at all.

The significance of this direction is in its turn or opportunity for Protestantism to steady its ranks with the rising Negro whose inclination to Protestant forms is undeniable, but who may turn to uniquely Negro or no religious loyalties insofar as he achieves participation in the economic mainstream of American life. The argument of the before-the-fact Protestants tends to this advantage — the growth of Protestantism as an inclusive community of faith.

It is worth noting the liberal awareness which views the future as one of diminishing returns for Protestantism. This is heightened by the tendency of the previously Protestant if segregated Negro to participate in the middle class without his traditional religious perspective. Thus beyond the theological and ethical question threatens the practical problem due to numerical losses of an increasing number of Negroes who prefer identification with Protestantism per se and are denied this opportunity of commitment within an inclusive faith. This double problem of a pluralistic America in which the dominance of Protestantism no longer rides and the loss of the Negro who is turning to other or no theistic religions urges before-the-fact liberals not to be deterred by the majority of their fellow churchmen.

Presently, working-class Negroes are being influenced by forces such as the Black Muslims, and middle-class Negroes are either turning increasingly to rigid Negro churches or away from Protestantism. The latter trend is unhappily viewed by some liberals as ingratitude for the favors extended by the various Protestant denominations in the past. It is pointed out that only Protestants have granted Negro clergymen and laymen places of leadership in the churches.

The interesting result of this tension may be seen as a defensive posture which seeks in the past performance of Protestantism the reason why Negroes should gratefully adhere to these various denominations. It is not that the failures of Protestantism are ignored but that their deeds of kindness and penance ought to be honored.

II

A thorough historical search clarifies the claim of Protestantism that from 1619 to the beginning of the nineteenth century, no other American institution openly and consistently expressed such indubitable interest in the Negro. No less real were the churches' gain in outlets for missionary fervor which generated an incalculable amount of enthusiasm and gave purpose and meaning beyond the cost in personnel and money.

Of course the institutional approach to the virgin territory of the slave was prompted by the missionary zeal to spread the gospel. At the same time it was necessary to counteract the general opinion that slaves should not be introduced to the gospel since the obvious result would mean openness to the Christian doctrine of freedom. The earliest opposition to proclaiming the Christian faith among Negroes was profoundly theological in nature: the Christian faith is inseparable from the doctrine of freedom. Though this doctrine cannot be severed from ultimate moral values, moral ideals are the fruit and not the root of theology. From the commencement of the missionary endeavor to bring the good news to the slave Negroes, it was necessary to face the theological edge of the Christian faith. Theology was quickly by-passed in favor of telling the Negro a simple story. (Here, in this decision, not only were the roots of the Christian faith expendable and of spurious value, but the real meaning of the Christian faith was distorted.) Negroes have yet to recover from this indifference to theology taught to them by missionaries.

The way around the theological question, particularly the doctrine of freedom, was to require slaves to take an oath prior to baptism to the effect that they presented themselves for the sacrament merely for the health of their souls and not as a means to seek freedom from their duty—obedience to their masters, in this world. From the beginning slaves were taught to seek their good in the life beyond, not in this world. The absence of a rounded theology was instrumental in the development of those spirituals, which centered on the world beyond to the exclusion of a meaningful existence in this life. However provocative and accurate this eschatological theme, it suffered from the non-development of other equally significant theological concerns.

Popular opinion suggests that the lack of theological grounding given to the Negro was simply due to his total illiteracy as a slave. This half-truth fails to identify the fact that any experiment in teaching Christian doctrines was ruled out a priori, by and large, and never because a general ingredient for the religious foundations of the Negro. Moreover, there were a limited number of Negroes who were not only introduced to Christian doctrines but which gave evidence of real comprehension. However, the religious communions in America have in each generation been so overwhelmed with other problems that they never expended the energy necessary to do a thorough job of religious education among Negroes.

The initial and pervasive failure of Protestantism was theological. This error may prove to be far more disrupting to the Protestant mission than its social impotence which merely reflects the culture. The lack of a theological perspective among Negroes remains the critical and sole irresponsibility of Protestant churchmen.

It is not enough to plead that one can be a Christian and a slave without contradiction—this is too narrow a concept of the Christian doctrine of freedom. If the price of reaching slaves with the gospel was de-emphasis of theology, the claim of spreading the Christian understanding of God, the world, and man is at least suspect. It is less true that doctrines were not within the grasp of slaves who early expressed real critical abilities. What is certain is this: the essence of Protestantism as autonomous self-criticism was regrettably withheld from the Negro.

Under the discipline of missionaries, slaves were kept busy in the evenings in catechism classes and revivals both of which were drills in the moralities of a substandard religion. Ethical issues were not raised. Moreover, the view of salvation was misconstrued as faithful following of morality codes. It is widely recognized that the religious services of scriptural memorization and recitation, prayers, and lessons in etiquette drawn from the Bible provided a most effective means of social control. While there were obvious exceptions to this general effectiveness, Protestant missionaries were in great demand. These enthusiastic evangelicals served to reinforce the institution of slavery; they were invaluable to the plantation lords and no less a welcome diversion for the slaves. And it is this conception of religion as diversion which continues to rear its ubiquitous head among Negroes today.

Missionaries compromised their own theological insights in order to evangelize the slaves. This was true of the Baptists and Methodists whose theological dimensions were less systematic than their Episcopal and Presbyterian brethren. The fact that Methodists and Baptists were more successful than other communions with slaves does not simply imply that Negroes were more receptive to a non-critical approach; it does indicate that limited time and funds were allocated to developments of the slaves.

III

The contention that this initial, limited Christian outlook, originated by Protestant evangelicals, provides the basis for the misunderstanding of the Christian faith by American Negroes finds corroboration in the common knowledge that the religious congregation among Negroes is not essentially different in theological awareness from that of their slave ancestors. In fact, the Negro congregation is better known for its role as the spearhead of social protest than for its contribution to the tension between faith and culture. Indeed, the social protests of religious congregations are hardly rooted in the theological depths of faith. Social protests have an ethical thrust born of political and social thought which only vaguely resemble theological perspectives. To protest that the social impact of Negro congregations basically results from the gospel teachings of missionaries is to foster a misconception which borders on illusion. However glib the use of Christian terminology, Negro protests have been rooted for the most part outside the Christian faith. Indeed, the radical protest which finds its expression in some Negro congregations even today is based upon influences external to the Christian faith, if not in contradiction with the faith.

With the unconscious and uncritical acceptance of simplified Christian abridgments equated with spurious moral values, Negroes were early introduced to religion without theology—Christianity divorced from the mainstream of the Christian faith.

This virtually complete omission of the doctrines of classic Christian theology, not only as dogmas but also as guidelines, resulted in an impoverished version of the gospel for the faithful slave. Missionaries waived theology in favor of biblical literalism, an approach which ignored the history of the Christian church. The caste system in religion put the lid on the psychological identity with the European heritage of Protestantism. The religion of Protestant expression was accepted without its source and authority, this side of the early Christian community.

With the radical separation of Negro congregations from their white sponsors, in response to the psychological and social forces following the first quarter of the nineteenth century, Negro Protestantism was left to develop on its own. Negro religious communions were set adrift, for the most part at their own request, from a historical tie with Protestantism, possessing a deeply embedded simple equation between New Testament literalism and cultural morality — without any doctrines of the faith or historical tie with the church as guides to relevance and meaning.

When the socioeconomic forces eliminated Negro and white Protestant communication in the life of the church, the opportunity for identification with the white man's historical ties was lost. Thus the Negro religious bodies became the instruments for salvation, moral guidance, and social protest. The core of these activities found direction outside the historical community of faith, in the majority of instances. And in times of crisis Negro religious bodies recalled the biblical stories and related them to the catechetical teachings. There was no way out of slavery or second-class citizenship through the Christian faith, conspicuously stripped of its inherent social protests, an unknown history to the Negro. It is no surprise to find that the religious perspective provided no support for radical protests prior to the 1850s and that the roots of protest did not find their beginnings in the religious teachings of the missionaries. In fact, the sole reason for protests being centered in churches is due to the fact that these buildings were singular in their ownership by Negroes and thus provided the one place where Negroes were able to gather in mass.

IV

A gulf of intimacy continues to divide Negro and white Americans, so much so that it is meaningless to speak of religious communities in America except as Negro and white. Moreover, if Protestantism involves identification with the Reformers and their post-Reformation interpreters, it is not helpful to call Negroes Protestants in this historical and theological sense. The fact that Negroes form congregations called by the same denominational nomenclature as white Americans remains the extent of their common ground. There have been divisions of Negro congregations on every conceivable issue except that of the usual theological schisms because there is little theology in Negro Protestantism.

Past alienation from the theological roots of Protestantism, social separation from white Protestants and their historical and cultural extensions of the European tradition, addiction to religion as personal salvation by means of moral purity, worship as the primary means of release and the occasion for class identification — these are the bases for the religion of the Negro.

In this regard, a distinction is necessary between the Negro religion and the Negro church. Negro communities do not constitute churches in the theological

sense, but religious congregations. Religion initiated and perpetuated in irrelevance can persist in response to whatever social, political, or economic needs
are dominant. Concern with the ultimate or God and what is required of those
who are called to live responsibly in his world may easily be less than primary
for a segregated minority without a theology. There is a crass materialism which
pervades the Negro congregations, overlaid with theological terminology and a
feeling for religion which when analyzed may now be more liberally this-worldly
than other-worldly. But the theological basis for this liberal perspective is missing; also missing is a theological point of view or justification for existence. The
theological center continues to be a vacuum because its potential as the point
of departure is yet to be discovered. This lack of awareness not only means
that the theological void emits no tension or anxiety; it also means that the
dictates of society and class values go unchallenged as the center and not the
periphery of Negro Protestantism.

In the perversion of the religious community, for the non-authentic if understandable purposes of ostentation and personal gratification the Negro religious
community takes its cue and then exaggerates it beyond recognition from the
white community who are the bearers of the Protestant doctrine of vocation
and who have status partly as a result of this doctrine's socio-economic rather
than theological implications. Precisely at this point there is a significant difference between Negro and white Protestants. At least white Protestantism in
its turn to cultural religion does so under the judgment of a theology which
declares there is a tension between faith and culture and calls attention to the
conflict between spurious religious concerns and the Christian faith. In this
difference lies the seeds of renewal, however far white Protestantism may stray
from its roots. In seeking economic and social status under the guise of religious
affiliation and class congregations, the Negro is not only imitative but has no
theology which judges his response in the sphere of culture. Negro congregations are free (or perhaps damned is equally theological) to treat economic
values and class symbols as sanctions of religion.

These are the factors which support the hypothesis that Negro congregations
are best understood as religious communities rather than Christian churches.

The judgment that the absence of theology prevents the Negro congregations
from bearing a corrective which distinguishes between participation in economic
well-being and seeking economic values as ends in themselves discloses the
Negro community as the most materialistic religious group in America. The
truth that this absence of a theological dimension was not the result of failure
or deliberation on the part of the Negro, historically and primarily, does not
alter the fact. Those who join a religious community in search of meaning and
relevance are thwarted in this quest, not because there is no ultimate belief in
God, but because there are no middle guidelines on the way.

The question of Negro religious communities being Christian or even Protestant is not finally reflected by this poverty of perspective, though the quality
of authenticity and dynamism is in question. Whether or not this suicidal trend
can be reversed or redirected is the basic question which faces the Christian

who is also a Negro. There is no doubt that Negro communions are losing creative participants and that the only thing they have going for them is color which forces some kind of identity. It is this fact, that Negro congregations will exist for the foreseeable future because of the bond of color, which also is the reason why a new direction must be experimented with if the religion of the Negro is to have ultimate value.

V

The lack of theology or the critical understanding of the Christian faith is a serious defect which has been neglected at an extraordinarily high cost. If this perspective has validity, these congregations are at a point in history where it is imperative that they decide in which direction they are heading. Either movement into the mainstream of the Christian church or the general stream of religion is the authentic choice before Negro congregations who wish to be responsible. The urgency of this decision is the increasing loss of college-trained men and women to the church. To be sure, the Roman Catholic Church is making significant in-roads here, but this is indicative of the needs of Negroes and their inability to find a meaningful response within Protestantism.

Negro laymen and clergymen might helpfully begin at the most sensitive, and yet live, distinction between Christian principles and the Christian faith. This is a sensitive area because Negroes have been indoctrinated for better than three centuries with the simple equation of Christian living with the teachings of Jesus.

The teachings of Jesus are readily available to anyone who wishes to live by them as a basis for principles to spark action in the realm of civil liberties or rights. Commitment to the Christian faith is not required for response to Christian principles. To say, for example, the nonviolent movements are based upon Christian principles is no more significant than to say that pacifism stems from the same source. It is quite possible to be involved in either or both of these movements without loyalty to the Christian faith, however loyal one may be to Christian principles.

The Christian faith is indeed quite different. Christian principles take on a new and different meaning within the household of faith. The Christian faith begins with the crucifixion and resurrection of Jesus Christ. It is only from the vantage point of these events that the Christian claims with the disciples that Jesus Christ is Lord. The Christian claims that these events give meaning to human existence and clarify the nature of God and the response he intends for man. Because God acted in Christ, the Christian is committed to the extension of the love of God between man and neighbor. In this way, the teachings of Jesus are not merely universal principles but the expression of a man who revealed himself as the Son of God and in whom the Christian has faith.

In this sense the Christian is not motivated by principles, even the Sermon on the Mount. He is committed to respond to God in the best interest of himself and his neighbor which is without principle—save that of the love relationship between man and God which is the force that calls forth a favorable response, though a different one in each situation. The Christian understands that the imitation of Jesus is valid only in the form of Christ who submitted his will to God, and that the content of his response is necessarily distinctive for he is called to contribute in situations in a condition which is unique because he is unique.

Of course the Christian lives Christonomously, insofar as his faith is in God who revealed himself in Jesus Christ. In this order of existence the Christian seeks to be guided by God who is the Creator, Judge, and Redeemer of the universe. In everything the faithful Christian does, he sees his action as an affirmation of the will of God.

Against this background is readily seen the distortion of Christianity in the Negro community. The Negro has grounded his belief in Christianity in an ethical code, the principles of which are not founded in an enduring faith and therefore devoid of content and the refreshment of a critical dimension. The principles he esteems are not relevant to his contemporary needs. Thus the Negro is forced to depend upon civil rights, religious feeling, sentiment, and color as substitutes for faith. It is the absence of historical loyalty to the Christian faith which expresses itself as religious sentiment. This feeling for religion is not inherent but nurtured, and to make virtue of necessity does not justify the title of Christian faith.

If Negro laymen and clergymen can begin to take seriously the theological disciplines so necessary for a meaningful faith, their contribution to the lives of their constituents and the future of Protestantism will be rich indeed. The time for a fully-integrated Protestant community is not yet, but on the way to this inevitability Negro adherents would do well to sharpen their perspective through communication with their white brethren at every possible level. An early target for both white and Negro sources of influence might well be the discovery and cultivation of promising young Negro leadership, nurturing them in either or both communities. The spirit and freedom which the Negro offers to a truly ecumenical fellowship will be met with a disciplined understanding, for the health of the church and to the glory of God. But the Negro cannot do this alone—he needs the wise counsel of his white brethren. The growth and vitality of Protestantism, in part, depends upon whether or not Negroes will become participants with an indigenous understanding of the Christian faith and church.

7

THE BLACK MESSIAH

Albert B. Cleage, Jr.

For nearly 500 years the illusion that Jesus was white dominated the world
only because white Europeans dominated the world. Now, with the emergence
of the nationalist movements of the world's colored majority, the historic truth
is finally beginning to emerge — that Jesus was the nonwhite leader of a non-
white people struggling for national liberation against the rule of a white nation,
Rome. The intermingling of the races in Africa and the Mediterranean area is
an established fact. The Nation Israel was a mixture of Chaldeans, Egyptians,
Midianites, Ethiopians, Kushites, Babylonians and other dark peoples, all of
whom were already mixed with the black people of Central Africa.

That white Americans continue to insist upon a white Christ in the face of
all historical evidence to the contrary and despite the hundreds of shrines to
Black Madonnas all over the world, is the crowning demonstration of their
white supremacist conviction that all things good and valuable must be white.
On the other hand, until black Christians are ready to challenge this lie, they
have not freed themselves from their spiritual bondage to the white man nor
established in their own minds their right to first-class citizenship in Christ's
kingdom on earth. Black people cannot build dignity on their knees worshiping
a white Christ. We must put down this white Jesus which the white man gave
us in slavery and which has been tearing us to pieces.

Black Americans need to know that the historic Jesus was a leader who went
about among the people of Israel, seeking to root out the individualism and
the identification with their oppressor which had corrupted them, and to give
them faith in their own power to rebuild the Nation. This was the real Jesus
whose life is most accurately reported in the first three Gospels of the New
Testament. On the other hand, there is the spiritualized Jesus, reconstructed

Albert B. Cleage, Jr. (Jaramogi Abebe Agyeman) is founder and Holy Patriarch of the Pan
African Orthodox Christian Church. This essay is a reprint of the introduction that appeared
in Albert B. Cleage, Jr., *The Black Messiah*. New York: Sheed and Ward, 1968. Reprinted
with permission of the publisher.

many years later by the Apostle Paul who never knew Jesus and who modified his teachings to conform to the pagan philosophies of the white gentiles. Considering himself an apostle to the gentiles, Paul preached individual salvation and life after death. We, as black Christians suffering oppression in a white man's land, do not need the individualistic and otherworldly doctrines of Paul and the white man. We need to recapture the faith in our power as a *people* and the concept of Nation, which are the foundation of the Old Testament and the prophets, and upon which Jesus built all of his teachings 2,000 years ago.

Jesus was a revolutionary black leader, a Zealot, seeking to lead a Black Nation to freedom, so the Black Church must carefully define the nature of the revolution.

What do we mean when we speak of the Black Revolution? I can remember an incident at the beginning of the Harlem Rebellion only a few short years ago when a news reporter snapped an unforgettable picture of a black girl who was present when a black boy was brutally killed by a white apartment house caretaker. She stood there on the sidewalk, her face contorted with anger and frustration, tears streaming down her cheeks, and she screamed at the cops who had rushed to the scene to keep their kind of law and order, "Kill me too! Kill me too!"

This was the absolute in frustration. "The problem of being black in a white man's world is just too big. I don't know what to do with it. So just kill me too and get it over with." That was what she was saying.

Black brothers and sisters all over the country felt a spontaneous identification with that girl because every black person has felt just this kind of frustration. We feel it every day. At every meeting some young black man jumps to his feet screaming, "I can't stand it any longer. Let's take to the streets and get it over with!" We all know how he feels and why he feels that way. Sometimes we go home and say it was a very "nervous" meeting, and everyone knows what we are talking about because each of us has felt that same sense of powerlessness that makes us ache with helplessness and hopelessness and drives us to seek death as an easy way out. Those of us who cry out think of ourselves as revolutionists and participants in the Black Revolution. But a revolution seeks to change conditions. So each day we must decide. Either we are trying to achieve the power to change conditions or we have turned from the struggle and are seeking an heroic moment when we can die in the streets.

As black people, we have entered a revolution rather than the evolution or gradual change which white folks would like us to accept. We want to move fast enough to be able to see that we are moving. And four hundred years of standing still is a long time. We are trying to make the world over so that our children and our children's children can have power and live like human beings. We look at the world in which we live today and we are determined to turn the world upside down.

But when I hear cries of "Kill me too!" I know that that individual no longer has any hope. When he screams, "Let's get together and die in the streets," I know that in his desperate hopelessness this individual has put aside the revolution. Dying in the streets is not revolution. This is escapism. This is suicide. But it is not revolution. As long as there is the slightest possibility of victory, we are still engaged in a revolution. But when an individual sees no way to achieve power to change conditions, then the revolution is over. It doesn't make any difference how he spends his remaining time, singing hymns, getting drunk or buying guns. For him the revolution is over.

The Black Church has not always been revolutionary, but it has always been relevant to the everyday needs of black people. The old down-home black preacher who "shouted" congregation on Sunday morning was realistically ministering to the needs of a black people who could not yet conceive of changing the conditions which oppressed them. If you can't solve your problems, you can at least escape from them! So we had Saturday night to escape in one way, and Sunday morning to pray for repentance and to escape in another way. The Church was performing a valuable and real function. However uneducated the old-time preacher was, he was relevant and significant. What he offered was an ingenious interpretation of a slave Christianity to meet the needs of an oppressed and suffering people. He took it and used it so that black people could go to church on Sunday morning and find the strength to endure white folks for another six days. You could go to church and "shout" and feel that God was just, even though the world in which you lived was unjust. Implicit in every ignorant black preacher's sermon was the faith that God must eventually shake white people over hell-fire, and that after death black people were going to heaven. White people were the oppressors. They were the sinners, they were guilty. Black people were innocent and suffered oppression through no fault of their own. Therefore, they were going to heaven and walk on golden streets, and white people were going to hell. There is still profound truth in this simple message of the primitive Black Church.

But today the Church must reinterpret its message in terms of the needs of a Black Revolution. We no longer feel helpless as black people. We do not feel that we must sit and wait for God to intervene and settle our problems for us. We waited for four hundred years and he didn't do much of anything, so for the next four hundred years we're going to be fighting to change conditions for ourselves. This is merely a new theological position. We have come to understand how God works in the world. Now we know that God is going to give us strength for our struggle. As black preachers we must tell our people that we are God's chosen people and that God is fighting with us as we fight. When we march, when we take it to the streets in open conflict, we must understand that in the stamping feet and the thunder of violence we can hear the voice of God. When the Black Church accepts its role in the Black Revolution, it is able to understand and interpret revolutionary Christianity, and the revolution becomes a part of our Christian faith. Every Sunday morning when we preach from the Old Testament, or when we preach about Jesus, we seek to help black people understand that the struggle in which we are engaged is a cosmic struggle, that the very universe struggles with us when we fight to throw off the oppression of white people. We want black people to understand that they are coming to church to get the strength and direction to go out and fight oppression all week. We don't pray for the strength to endure any more. We pray for the strength to fight heroically.

Basic to our struggle and the revitalization of the Black Church is the simple fact that we are building a totally new self-image. Our rediscovery of the Black Messiah is a part of our rediscovery of ourselves. We could not worship a Black Jesus until we had thrown off the shackles of self-hate. We could not follow a Black Messiah in the tasks of building a Black Nation until we had found the courage to look back beyond the slave block and the slave ship without shame.

In recent years the contradiction inherent in the worship of a white Christ by black people oppressed by whites has become increasingly acute. In the Negro Renaissance after World War I the anguish of this contradiction was voiced by poet Countee Cullen in his famous lines:

> My conversion came high-priced;
> I belong to Jesus Christ, . . .
> Lamb of God, although I speak
> With my mouth thus, in my heart
> Do I play a double part. . . .
> Wishing he I served were black . . .?*

The widespread repudiation by many black Americans of a white Christ has added to the attractiveness of the Black Muslim movement. But many more black Americans, race conscious enough to reject a white Christ, have been reluctant to embrace Islam in view of the role played by the Arabs in fostering and carrying on the slave trade in Africa. The result has been the self-exclusion of most black militants from any religious affiliations whatsoever.

The only black leader in this country to meet this problem head-on was Marcus Garvey who organized the African Orthodox Church with a black hierarchy, including a Black God, a Black Jesus, a Black Madonna, and black angels. Forty years ago black Americans apparently were not yet ready for Garvey's religious ideas, although to this day, in every major city, individual Garveyites continue to circulate portraits of a Black Jesus. In Africa, however, Garvey's religious ideas played a key role in founding the African Independent Churches which in many countries acted as the center of the liberation movement. As Roosevelt University professor and writer St. Clair Drake has pointed out, the Kenya Africans invited one of Garvey's bishops to train and ordain their preachers and to help form the African independent schools and churches out of which the Mau Mau eventually grew.

The Black Church in America has served as the heart and center of the life of black communities everywhere, but, for the most part, without a conscious-

---

*Abridgement from fifth and sixth stanzas of "Heritage" in *On These I Stand* by Countee Cullen, Copyright 1925 by Harper & Brothers; Renewed 1953 by Ida M. Cullen. By permission of Harper & Row Publishers.

ness of its responsibility and potential power to give a lost people a sense of earthly purpose and direction. During the Black Revolt following the 1954 Supreme Court desegregation decision, the Southern Black Church found that involvement in the struggle of black people for freedom was inescapable. Without a theology to support its actions (actions almost in contradiction to its otherworldly preachings), it provided spokesmen and served as a meeting place and source of emotional inspiration. In the North, where the black man's problems at one time seemed less pressing, the Black Church has failed miserably to relate itself to the seething ghetto rebellions and therefore has practically cut itself off from vast segments of the black community. The Northern Church has been black on the outside only, borrowing its theology, its orientation and its social ideology largely from the white Church and the white power structure.

The present crisis, involving as it does the black man's struggle for survival in America, demands the resurrection of a Black Church with its own Black Messiah. Only this kind of a Black Christian Church can serve as the unifying center for the totality of the black man's life and struggle. Only this kind of a Black Christian Church can force each individual black man to decide where he will stand—united with his own people and laboring and sacrificing in the spirit of the Black Messiah, or individualistically seeking his own advancement and maintaining his slave identification with the white oppressor.

8

BLACK THEOLOGY AND BLACK LIBERATION

James H. Cone

Black theology is relatively new to America. Though it has roots in the pre-Civil War black church which recognized that racism and Christianity were opposites, "black theology" is a phenomenon of the 1960s. One way of describing it is to say that it is the religious counterpart of the more secular movement called "black power." This means that black theology is a religious explication of black people's need to define the scope and meaning of black existence in a white racist society. Black power focuses on the political, social and economic condition of black people, seeking to define concretely the meaning of black self-determination in a society that has placed definite limits on black humanity. Black theology puts black identity into a theological context, showing that black power is not only *consistent* with the gospel of Jesus Christ: it *is* the gospel of Jesus Christ. My purpose is to investigate this thesis, analyzing black theology in relation to black history, black power, and the biblical message.

Black History

The black existential mood that expresses itself in black power and black theology stems from the recognition that black identity must be defined in terms of its African heritage rather than in terms of European enslavement. James Baldwin has put the case memorably:

> I was a kind of bastard of the West; when I followed my past, I did not find myself in Europe but in Africa. And this meant that in some subtle way, in a really profound way, I brought to Shakespeare, Bach, Rembrandt, to the stones of Paris, to the Cathedral at Chartres and to the Empire state building, a special attitude. These were really not my cre-

This essay originally appeared in *The Christian Century* (16 September 1970).

ations, they did not contain my history; I might search them in vain forever for any reflection of myself![1]

Baldwin's words epitomize the spiritual and intellectual anguish that black people experience when they try to find meaning amid historical categories that are white and not black. They summarize black existence that is condemned to *be* in an environment inimical to black being. Black history has established an authentic black past. Unlike Europeans who immigrated to this land to escape from tyranny, Africans came not by choice but as bonds-men, chained in ships. It was the slave-experience that shaped our idea of this land. Surely it should have been expected that the slave-event would not aid in our admiration of America, despite America's rhetoric about "equality" in "the land of the free and the home of the brave."

Unfortunately, our slavery was not limited to physical bondage. Added to physical domination was the mental enslavement of black people—the internalization of the values of slavemasters. We were required to deny our African past and to affirm the European values that were responsible for our enslavement. At worst, this meant accepting the slave condition as ordained of God; at best, it meant that Shakespeare and Bach provided the standards of literary and musical creativity. In either case, our true African identity was denied. That was why Malcolm said: "The worst crime the white man has committed has been to teach us to hate ourselves." The recovery of black history changes all this.

It is clear now (perhaps it has always been clear) that we are not Europeans, thus that George Washington, Thomas Jefferson and Abraham Lincoln are not our heroes. To accept them is to embrace Europe as the most significant cultural expression of our being. If, as President Havari Boumédienne of Algeria says, culture is that which "enables men to regulate their lives,"[2] then Richard Nixon and Spiro Agnew cannot be the embodiment of our culture. Affirming them is tantamount to accepting our place as defined by slavemasters and denying the significance of Africa in the definition of black being. It is like trying to reconcile being and nonbeing, blackness and whiteness. It is not possible to achieve a unified consciousness if we affirm two irreconcilable opposites. W. E. B. Du Bois spoke of the agony of this experience:

> It is a peculiar sensation, this double-consciousness, this sense of always looking at one's self through the eyes of others, of measuring one's soul by the tape of a world that looks on in amused contempt and pity. One ever feels his two-ness—an American, a Negro; two souls, two thoughts, two unreconciled strivings; two warring ideals in one dark body, whose dogged strength alone keeps it from being torn asunder.[3]

The only cure for this double-consciousness is to move toward the definition of blackness that is formed in the context of black liberation from white domination. Authentic black history is an investigation of the past through the eyes of black victims, a projection of our being into the unexplored depths of black consciousness—creating and affirming the *novum* of blackness in its undistorted African expression. In order to be free, we must be willing to move into unchartered dimensions of our being as defined by the need to create new value structures so that our understanding of blackness will not depend upon European misconceptions. It means realizing that our history did not begin with the fifteenth century European enslavement of Africans. Our origins lie further back—much further back!—in known and "unknown" history. Known in the sense that we were there in Egypt's Nile valley, traditionally called the cradle of civilization. "Unknown" in the sense that the meaning of our personhood is not dependent on the records of ancient history. The present reality of our encounter with blackness defines who we are. The new black consciousness arises from the need of black people to defend themselves against those who seek to destroy them. We know who we are in terms of doing what is necessary to protect ourselves and our families from rats and filth, police and government officials. Our defense is at the same time a definition, a way of moving in the world, and it is programed according to our need for liberation. The investigation of our past in the light of our liberation may be defined as black power taking on historical dimensions.

Black Power

Strictly speaking, black power appeared in the spring of 1966, when Stokely Carmichael verbalized the unwillingness of black people to live under white definitions of their humanity. It may be true that the actual content of the phrase was not clearly defined and the dynamic of its implications in black-white relations not clearly understood. Nevertheless this was the beginning of the will of black people to make public their utter distrust of white do-gooders and their displeasure with whites who try to tell them what their blackness ought to mean. Black power means that blacks are publicly declaring that whatever white people do, it will inevitably work against black freedom. Black people realize that they cannot change oppressors' attitudes by praying, singing gospel hymns and reading Scripture or preaching sermons. Neither can we change their attitude simply by peaceably disobeying laws and allowing the oppressors to beat our women and children with police clubs. It just isn't true that if we try hard enough and wait patiently, eventually the oppressors will feel ashamed of their conduct and thus relinquish their power to enslave. Oppressors have no conscience except that of defending their own interests. We wait in vain for the Holy Spirit on this matter! Men in power will never admit that the society rewards them far in excess of the service they render. Appeals to reason, religion, philosophy or sociology will not change their perspective. These disciplines are their tools and will inevitably serve as rationalizations of their own interest.

"There is, in fact, nothing in common between a master and a slave," writes Camus. "It is impossible to speak and communicate with a person who has been reduced to servitude."[4] In part, this means that the presumption of power insensitizes the master to the humanity of the slave, making him behave as if his own humanity is dependent upon the enslavement of his brother. There is an "infinite qualitative distinction" (to use a Kierkegaardian-Barthial phrase) between world views of master and slave; and if the slave intends to change his existence, his first task is to inform the master what the limits are. The slave must be willing to define himself in terms of the silence of the master, realizing that the latter's gibberish about life and happiness is a projection of his own ego, having nothing to do with authentic human existence. To silence the master is necessary because the oppressor will never conclude that he should not be the ruler. The slave must not delude himself; freedom is not easy. "Freedom," as Camus's Jean-Baptiste puts it, "is not a reward or a decoration that is celebrated with champagne. Nor yet a gift, a box of dainties designed to make you lick your chops. Oh, no! It's a chore . . . and a long distance race."[5]

Black power is the recognition that black freedom becomes a reality only when the victims of white racism declare that the oppressors have overstepped the bounds of human relations and that it is now incumbent upon black people to do what is necessary to bring to a halt the white encroachments on black dignity. The willingness to behave on the basis of this conclusion is nothing but reducing phraseology to action. It means that blacks accept the risk of defining themselves. Like our forefathers who rebelled against slavery, we know that life is not worth living unless we are fighting against its limits. This is what black power means.

Black Theology Defined

How are black history and black power related to black theology? Black history is recovering a past deliberately destroyed by slavemasters, an attempt to revive old survival symbols and create new ones. Black power is an attempt to shape our present economic, social and political existence according to those actions that destroy the oppressor's hold on black flesh. Black theology places our *past* and *present* actions toward black liberation in theological context, seeking to destroy alien gods; and to create value-structures according to the God of black freedom.

The significance of black theology then is found in the conviction that the content of the Christian gospel is liberation. This means that any talk about God that fails to take seriously the righteousness of God as revealed in the liberation of the weak and downtrodden is not Christian language. It may be "religious" or "churchly" and thus "patriotic," but it has nothing to do with him who has called us into being and who came to us in Jesus Christ and is present as Holy Spirit with us today. To speak of the God of Christianity is to speak of him who has defined himself according to the liberation of the oppressed. Christian theology, then, pursuing its church-function, is that discipline which analyzes the meaning of God's liberation in the light of Jesus Christ, showing that all actions that make for the freedom of man are indeed the actions of God. Herein lies the heart of black theology's perspective on the theological task.

Two Sources

The definition of theology as an explication of the meaning of God's liberation of the oppressed arises essentially from two sources: biblical history and black liberation.

Biblical history. According to the Bible, the God of Israel is known by what he is *doing* in history for the salvation of man. It is this critical dimension of divine activity that makes history and revelation inseparable in biblical religion. To see the revelation of God is to see the *action* of God in the historical affairs of men. God is not uninvolved in human history, as in the Greek philosophical tradition; the opposite is the case. He is participating in human history, *moving* in the direction of man's salvation which is the goal of divine activity.

Of course, we must be cautious in our use of the word salvation. Salvation means many things for different communities. For white oppressors, it seems to have acquired a "spiritual" connotation that is often identified with divine juice, squirted into the souls of believers, thereby making them better Christians and citizens. Understandably, salvation for them has little to do with the economic, political and social dimensions of human existence unless, however, there are those who wish to challenge societal injustice. Then men are called upon to *act* out their salvation not only through silent prayer but by faithfully protecting the existing laws. An attack upon the state is tantamount to an affront to God, and all "good" Christians must *show* their faith by protecting the sanctity of the nation. This view of the salvation of God is not only anti-biblical; it is *dangerous*, for it identifies God with oppressors, giving political and religious approval to the oppression of man.

The biblical view of salvation has an entirely different meaning. "In the Old Testament salvation is expressed by a word which has the root meaning of 'to be wide' or 'spacious,' 'to develop without hindrance' and thus ultimately 'to have victory in battle' (I Sam. 14:45)"—so F. J. Taylor declares.[6] To be saved means that one's enemies have been conquered, and the savior is he who has the power to gain victory. As Taylor says, again:

> He who needs salvation is one who has been threatened or oppressed, and his salvation consists in deliverance from danger and tyranny or rescue from imminent peril (I Sam. 4:3, 7:8, 9:16). To save another is to communicate to him one's own prevailing strength (Job 26:2), to give him the power to maintain necessary strength.[7]

In the Old Testament, Yahweh is the Savior par excellence because Israel's identity as a people is grounded in his liberating activity in the escape from Egypt. "You have seen what I did to the Egyptians, and how I bore you on eagles' wings and brought you to myself. Now therefore, if you will obey my voice and keep my covenant, you shall be my own possession among all peoples" (Exod. 19:4–5a). Through his election of this people God reveals that his right-eousness is for the poor and weak, and their salvation consists in his liberation of them from earthly bondage.

The same emphasis is found in the New Testament. Jesus is pictured as the oppressed one who views his own person and work as an identification with the humiliated condition of the poor. The poor were at the heart of his mission: "The last shall be first and the first last" (Matt. 20:16). That is why he was always kind to traitors, adulterers and sinners and why the Samaritan came out on top in the parable. Speaking of Pharisees (the religious oppressors of his day), he said: "Truly I say to you the tax collectors [traitors] and harlots go into the kingdom—but not you" (Matt. 21:31).[8] Jesus had little toleration for the middle- or upper-class religious snob whose attitude attempted to usurp the sovereignty of God and destroy the dignity of the poor. The kingdom is for the poor and not the rich because the former has nothing to expect from this world while the latter's entire existence is grounded in his commitment to worldly things. The weak and helpless may expect everything from God while the oppressor may expect nothing because of his own refusal to free himself from his pride. It is not that poverty is a precondition for salvation. But those who recognize their utter dependence on God and wait on his liberation despite the miserable absurdity of life are usually poor, according to our Lord.

Furthermore, it is not possible to be for Christ and also for the enslavement of men. For Christ, salvation is not an eschatological longing for escape to a transcendent reality; neither is it an inward serenity which eases unbearable suffering. Rather it is God in Christ encountering man in the depths of his existence in oppression, liberating him from all human evils (like racism) which hold him captive. The repentant man knows that though God's ultimate king-dom be in the future, yet Christ's resurrection means that even now God's salvation breaks through like a ray of "blackness" upon the "whiteness" of the condition of the oppressed, disclosing that oppressed man is not alone in the world. He who has called things into being is with the oppressed, and he guar-antees that man's liberation will become a reality of the land—and "all flesh shall see it together."

Black liberation. "Theology, as a function of the Christian church, must serve the needs of the church. A theological system is supposed to satisfy two basic needs: The statement of the truth of the Christian message and the interpre-tation of this truth for every new generation." So says Paul Tillich.[9] If the truth of the gospel is God's liberation that centers on the resurrection of Jesus Christ as the divine guarantee that he who is Father, Son and Holy Spirit has taken upon himself the oppressed condition of all people, then theology must ask: What is the significance of this message for our time? In what ways can we best explicate the meaning of God's liberating activity in the world so that the oppressed will be ready to risk all for earthly freedom? These questions are not easy, and they require willingness to discard long-standing oppressive values, facing the necessity to create new values as defined according to the reality of divine liberation.

Taking seriously the necessity to make the Christian message of liberation relevant to our time, we conclude that Christian theology in America must be black. In a society where men are defined on the basis of color for the purpose of humiliation, Christian theology takes on the color of the victims, proclaiming that the condition of the poor is incongruous with him who has come to liberate us. Soulful James Brown is right: Black is beautiful! It is beautiful because the white oppressors have made it ugly. Christians must glorify it because the oppressors despise it, must love it because the oppressors hate it. This is the new Christian way of saying, "To hell with your stinking white society and its middle-class ideas about the world. It has nothing to do with liberating deeds of God."

The Fallacy of Colorlessness

It is to be expected that white theologians, clinging to their own sense of worth as defined through identification with whiteness, will not endorse black theology enthusiastically. Some will ignore it while others will respond with the dictum: Theology is colorless! Such judgments are typical of those who have not experienced the concreteness of human suffering inflicted because of color, or who are very comfortable with a theology that is "colorless" only if "white" means absence of color.

To ignore black theology is the easy way out. It is analogous to whites' moving into suburbia because they cannot deal with the reality of the black ghetto in the city. More interesting, though not surprising, is the white insistence that theology does not come in colors. They who have made color the vehicle of dehumanization are now telling us that theology is raceless and "universal." This seems a bit late after nearly 400 years of silence on this issue. Why did we not hear this word when people were being enslaved in the name of God and democracy precisely on the basis of color? Where were these "colorless" theologians when people were being lynched because of the color of their skins? Everyone should know that whites and not blacks are responsible for the demarcation of community on the basis of color. We blacks are merely the victims. And to criticize the theology of the victims because it centers on the aspect that best defines the limits of their existence seems to miss the point entirely.

Of course, black theology cannot waste its time trying to demonstrate its legitimacy to oppressors. It is accountable only to its Lord as he makes himself known through the liberation of an oppressed community. It says: If Jesus Christ is in fact the Liberator whose resurrection is the guarantee that he is present with us today, then he too must be black, taking upon his person and work the blackness of our existence, and revealing to us what is necessary in our destruction of whiteness. This means therefore that authentic theological speech arises only from the community of the oppressed who realize that their humanity is inseparable from their liberation from earthly bondage. All other speech is at best irrelevant and at worst blasphemy.

NOTES

1. *Notes of a Native Son* (New York: Bantam, 1968), p. 4.
2. Cited by Stanislas Adoteri, *Black Scholar*, November 1969.
3. *The Souls of Black Folk* (New York: Fawcett, 1961), pp. 16-17.
4. *The Rebel* (New York: Vintage, 1946), p. 283.
5. *The Fall and Exile and the Kingdom* (New York: Modern Library, 1956), p. 132.
6. See "Save" in *Theological Word Book of the Bible* (New York: Macmillan, 1960).
7. Ibid.
8. For support of this translation see Günther Bornkamm: *Jesus of Nazareth* (New York: Harper, 1960), pp. 79, 203n29; and Joachim Jeremias: *The Parables of Jesus* (New York: Scribner's, 1955), p. 100n54.
9. Paul Tillich, *Systematic Theology* (Chicago: University of Chicago Press, 1951), p. 3.

9

BLACK THEOLOGY IN THE MAKING

J. Deotis Roberts

The Definitions

Theology is *logos* of *theos*—reasoning about God. Thinking about God includes God's *action* in creation and history. "God" implies creation, providence, and redemption. Man is God's creative masterpiece. God as love creates a being capable of an independent love-response. Among the creatures, man alone has the moral, intellectual, and spiritual capacity to fulfill a loving relationship with the "Maker of Heaven and Earth." He is co-creator with God, the Lord of All Creation.

MacQuarrie is correct. Theology may begin with the divine existence, or it may begin with human existence. Either way we have to do with God.[1]

William Temple called our attention to the necessity of bringing "nature" into theological discourse. He makes the point that Christianity is the most materialistic of all religions in that the center of our faith is the Incarnation, the Word made Flesh. This inhistorization of the Word, this enfleshment of the *Logos,* indicates that God has a high regard for his creation. It is in and through this order that He breaks through with the highest revelation of His redemptive purpose in the world.[2]

Theology is a discipline of interpretation. We are concerned with nature, man, and God—how God creates, sustains, and redeems in creation and history.

Revelation is the process of unveiling. Revelation is the divine self-manifestation or self-disclosure. God's word is for man. I agree with Brunner[3] that man is addressable. Revelation, in order to complete its process, must have a revealer and a revealee. Revelation is transcendent and immanent; it is ontological and existential; it is objective and subjective. Revelation comes to the human order

J. Deotis Roberts is Distinguished Professor of Philosophical Theology at Eastern Baptist Theological Seminary in Philadelphia. This essay originally appeared in *Review and Expositor* 70, no. 3 (Summer 1973).

from the divine order which is the Beyond within. The integrity of the self contains knowledge and freedom. Man is free to respond to God's revelation in terms of obedience or disobedience.

Experience is the receptacle and the repository of revelation. God reveals His mind and will to men in the situation where they exist — their *Sitz im Leben.* Experience is the context of decision, action, and life. Experience determines to a great extent the understanding and the appropriation of revelation. In the case of the Israel of the Old Testament and of Blacks, we have happily not merely the experience of individuals but of a people. We have a collective or ethnic body experience as the context for decision, action, and living. We will pursue this matter in a moment, but now we wish merely to establish the importance of experience in theology. Experience determines the need, the meaning, and the effectiveness of revelation in the human situation.

We need to distinguish between universal and private revelations. Revelation always moves between the particular and the universal. The reason Blacks need to abide by the Ten Commandments is that they are universal. It would be a mistake to accept or reject them according to whether the White man obeys or disobeys them. The fact is he *ought* and we *ought.* The justification is our common humanity. In this sense revelation is universal. On the other hand, God speaks to *each* man and *each* people as well as to *every* man and to *every* people. God who reveals Himself as Creator, Provider, and Redeemer is aware of the special needs and cares of *each* man and of *each* people. God is aware of centuries of undeserved Black suffering. He is aware of our experience of oppression. God cares concerning the "wretched of the earth." Black hope stems from the assurance that God seeks the liberation of the oppressed.

Theology is reflection upon the experience of revelation. Theology is concerned about God, man, world, and history. Revelation is both an objective and a subjective experience. God speaks from beyond, but He also speaks within our human experience, both personal and social. Revelation is universal and particular.

The Heritage

We are African and American. Blacks are Afro-American. In terms of language, total culture, and experience, we are not thorough Africans. We cannot recover 350 years of history, however tragic the circumstances. We are not unlike Indians in East Africa who have never seen India. While in Nairobi, I met several Indians who had less personal knowledge of the land of their fathers than I, who had been there, did. They partook of much of the Indian culture through their family life and religious practices, but they knew only Africa as their homeland. They were Indian-Africans and not thoroughly Indians.

Our heritage is African and it is American. We may learn to know and respect our long heritage through study, travel, and cultural activities, but we cannot be African only. We are also American. Our world-view is essentially Western. We have absorbed much of the Graeco-Roman, Judeo-Christian environment. Du Bois was keenly perceptive when he spoke of our "two-ness," of "two souls . . . in one dark body."[4] This fact is the basis of the personal and ethnic identity-crisis which is the meaning of black awareness.

My assumption from the outset is based upon a cultural nationalism. We are learning to appreciate "the Africanism" in our culture which we once denied and rejected. We now glory in an ancient and rich heritage that is our past, our present, and our future. The quest for these roots in "our Afro-American Past" is described by Vincent Harding as "the quest for the new land."[5]

Now that black theologians have begun to do their own reflection upon experience, they will find a rich heritage to support their work. What Jim Cone has done on the history of the black church and, more recently, the blues and spirituals, is a giant step in the right direction.[6] My own writings have been concerned with the contribution of "black religious thinkers," past and present. Our heritage is more unitive and regards the sacred and the secular. Therefore, non-theological investigation in history, literature, and the arts will be useful. The more we learn of the black experience in general the more we will understand the meaning of the peculiar religious experience which forms the base for our theology.

Our heritage is rich in folk tale, sermon, literature, and art. Undergirding all forms of black expression, oral, written, or dramatic is the quality of "soul." Whether one listens to James Cleveland sing Gospel or to James Brown, Soul Brother No. 1, what one hears is "soul." For weeks during summers my family and I live in a small town in western North Carolina. A railroad runs straight through the Black community. A musician friend of mine from Washington, D.C., picked up on the sounds on the train whistle one evening. He inquired if there were any Black engineers on the line. It was discovered that the engineer of the particular train was black. We are a rhythm people. Soul is black, as Joseph Washington so well describes it in an essay entitled "How Black is Black Religion?"

I have recently been moved by the insights of the writings of French-speaking Africans of the Negritude movement. Men like Aime Cesaire of Martinique and Leopold Senghor of Senegal. Senghor, in an essay on "Aesthetics," describes imagery and rhythm as the main characteristic of African-Negro style. He goes on to say that he does not think that he feels, but he feels that he feels. Lerone Bennett refers to our experience in *Black Mood* as "sorrow-joy" and goes on to exalt the triumph of sensitivity in the Black experience. In the midst of a tragic Diaspora, we have acquired a gift of laughter in the midst of tears. The blues chronicle the bittersweet experience of Black life and the facing up to life's disappointments. Soul is for Blacks a way of coping with life, whether in the African forests or in the asphalt jungles of major western cities. Black theology must, therefore, be "soul" theology. It is at this point that Black theology resembles existential theology. I am aware of this affinity and I am stepping up my investigations in existential philosophy and theology as I deepen my knowledge of the Black heritage. It is, however, the Black experience which is to be interpreted. Existentialism is a means only.

If Black theology based upon our heritage is existential, it is likewise political. Just as the sacred and secular coalesce in the Black experience, even so do the priestly and the prophetic. Here I will not go into a tirade regarding the confusion and omissions of White scholars. I am pro-Black and not merely anti-White. James Cone has done the demolition work. Now we must assume the task of theological construction based upon the Black religious experience.

Because of Black suffering, we have always seen the need to wed faith to ethics. Long before Rauschenbusch and the Niebuhrs, Black preachers were proclaiming a message of deliverance from the shackles of social, political, and economic oppression. Our fathers in the ministry were often in the forefront of the battle for freedom. They were urged forth by the prophetic word. They knew the gospel as a gospel of Power. For Blacks the gospel has sometimes been like aspirin, but it has often been like dynamite as well. Long before Bloch, Moltmann, and others of the hope movement, Black religion has been a means to liberation. Our circumstances have led us to the conclusion that Christian faith and social action go together. This is the reason why the oppressor did not want us to read. He feared that we might read the Bible and, if we read the Bible, we might use it to challenge the existing order of injustice.

The Program

The goal of Black theology determines its means. If the Black theologian addresses only Black people, he is limited by that end. His concern will be liberation. Whites will be considered only in a negative frame of reference — they are the oppressors. We can then juxtapose "we" to "they." We have Black saints and White sinners. This may be an overstatement, but it is intended to illustrate the logical direction such a program might take. James Cone and Albert Cleage move in this direction. Cleage is a folk theologian who goes further in this direction than Cone, who is an academic theologian. Cone hesitates because he wishes to maintain credibility with the disciplines of theology which is still controlled by the White mind. I get the impression that Cone is conscious that Paul Lehmann is looking over his shoulder. Joseph Jackson charged that James Cone was a Black racist theologian to the members of the National Baptist Convention in its annual session. It is doubtful that Jackson attempted to understand Cone's books. Cleage, who operates with more heat than light, can hardly be defended against this charge, but Cone is in an overall sense more pro-Black than anti-White. Even when Cone is angry, there is evidence of profound reflection. Cone's program is Black liberation from White oppression. All of his reflection moves between the oppression /liberation poles. This is obviously one way of doing Black theology.

We must understand the nature of Cone's program in order to appreciate the passion and overstatement characteristic of his writing. He is one-sided; he proclaims half-truths and he takes the offensive against all forms of White oppression—and especially in the church and among theologians. He is a pioneer writing a revolutionary theology. A theologian has to become an evangelist or a flaming prophet to start a new theological movement. This is the reason why Luther rather than Erasmus started the Reformation. This is why Karl Barth rather than Emil Brunner fathered the theology of crisis. Reason alone will not do it. Reason has to be mixed with pardon. In order for Black theology to come to birth, much underbrush had to be cleared away, demons had to be exorcised, critics had to be silenced. The work done by LeRoi Jones Amir Baraka on Black art needed to be done on Black religious experience and its theological interpretation. While we cannot gainsay the importance of Joseph Washington's controversial volume, *Black Religion,* I do not personally consider him as the real pioneer of Black theology. Without Al Cleage's *Black Messiah* and especially Jim Cone's *Black Theology and Black Power,* American theology in black would not have been born. In these words the necessary demolition work was done. The anger of the Black Christian against racism in religious institutions was expressed and the necessary justification for a new departure in theology based upon the Black experience was given.

Every theological movement has its innovators and its scholastics. Black theology will not escape this either. But it is not yet time for scholasticism to settle in upon us.

There are going to be several Black theologies. At Gary, at the first Black political convention in this century, the theme was "unity without uniformity." This is what we must be after in Black theology. We need all our creative minds at work on the Black religious experience. During the fall of 1971, I spent several exciting hours in dialogue with Bill Jones at Yale Divinity School. His mind had seized upon Black suffering centering in theodicy as a departure for a Black theology. Bill is a young scholar having just completed his Ph.D. thesis at Brown on Sartre. He taught philosophy at Howard briefly before his appointment at Yale. As a philosopher of religion, Bill Jones is very critical of all existing programs in Black theology. He has made telling criticisms of Cone, Cleage, and Washington on theodicy. He has raised serious questions regarding my program also. Oddly enough, Bill was wondering whether he should expose his fellow Black scholars, but he could not really get into his creative role without doing so. My observation was immediate. No scholar has the right to escape constructive criticism for his own sake as well as for the sake of his program. Our consensus on liberation must not allow us to be so kind to each other that we will not criticize deficiencies in our programs. Those of us who wrote in the early sixties and before were subject to severe criticism by everyone. I look back with great appreciation to this period.

My program combines liberation and reconciliation. Many feel that I am neither fish nor fowl. Some have observed that it is too soon to talk of reconciliation. Others rule reconciliation out altogether. Still others insist that only Whites should be concerned about reconciliation since they are the oppressors. These are mainly reactions from Blacks. Many Whites overlook *liberation* altogether and embrace *reconciliation* as my only concern. They seek a kind of "cheap grace" approach to race relations. Some pietistic, otherworldly Christians believe that I have made a blanket endorsement of their religious perspective. There have been times when being aware of the misunderstanding inherent in the use of reconciliation, I have spoken only of liberation. In other words, I have refused to allow do-nothing oppressors to be comforted by what I have to say. In most cases those who have reacted to my program as outlined have not really read my book.[7]

In the first instance, I have presented liberation as a primary goal. This means that I have been very affirmative in my use of much that Cone, Cleage, and others have said. This does not mean that I have always been in basic agreement with everything they have said. But liberation from oppression is the heart and center of my program. What I have to say about reconciliation has first to come to terms with my message of liberation. A second point as regards liberation is this: I use liberation more comprehensively and in a different context. Liberation is personal and social. It is particular and it is universal. I do not accept Black liberation versus White oppression as an adequate formula to cover the human condition of estrangement. Therefore, I do not hesitate to suggest liberation between Blacks and Blacks as well as between Blacks and Whites. It is unwise to make these structures too ironclad, for suppose the oppressed became the liberated? What happens to our theology then? Or again, because of our experience of oppression, we identify easily with Fanon's "wretched of the earth."[8] This means that we can write a theological outline for two-thirds of the human race, among whom are Reds, Browns, Whites, as well as Blacks. Liberation, conceived as personal and social, particular and universal, can address "all sorts and conditions of men."

Reconciliation is a theological way of seeing the essential nature of this interracial society. We must not only co-exist; we must in-exist in a pluralistic society. We are a pleasure-loving, consuming people. Our portion of the Gross National Product is greater than any group of colored people in the world, and yet we are dependent on others for our very existence. Every working day in every major city in this country, Whites invade the center city where they earn top salaries and then are shuttled by rapid transportation back to their bedroom communities. At the same time Blacks are herded by buses out into the suburbs, as maids and janitors, to clean houses, mow lawns and the like for the Whites who work downtown. The Blacks return from these mansions to the dark ghetto—to rats and roaches and all the social ills of the Black subculture. A small percentage of Blacks have escaped this nightmare, but masses of Blacks must face this dismal existence.

Few Blacks want to return to Africa. Most African countries are underdeveloped and do not need or desire a bumper crop of unskilled and uneducated Blacks. We must find a way to interracial togetherness in this country. Baldwin points to the White man's dependence upon the Black man as well as the Black man's dependence upon the White man as a basis for cooperation.[9] If this is so, enlightened self-interest is on our side. Samuel Yevette, in *Choice,* sees the Black man as completely expendable. I am not yet ready to buy this. On a purely pragmatic level I am not yet willing to concede that guerilla warfare, genocide, or mutual suicide are the only options available in the racial struggle. Once you embrace the ethic of expediency and accept the violent syndrome, there are few options left.

Reconciliation is the more excellent way. Christ the Liberator is likewise Christ the Reconciler. God was in Christ setting us free and God was in Christ reconciling the world unto Himself. We are called forth as agents of reconciliation. Reconciliation has to do with overcoming estrangement, mending fences, breaking down walls of separation between men. Reconciliation is "costly grace"—it is beyond liberation, beyond confrontation. It is not based upon sentimental love. Reconciliation includes cross-bearing for Whites as well as for Blacks. It is not so much concerned with taming Black power as it is with humanizing White power. Reconciliation can take place only between equals. It cannot co-exist with a situation of Whites over Blacks. The cross in reconciliation for Whites is repentance. The cross in reconciliation for Blacks is forgiveness. Whites participate in and benefit from the fact of institutional racism whether they sponsor racism as individuals or not. There is a need for the awareness of guilt based upon the collective sin of racism. Whites who are aware of the widespread and all-embracing effects of White racism have the responsibility to awaken and activate other Whites to the end that racism may be overcome, root and branch. This reconciling work is much more difficult than charitable deeds in the inner city. Reconciliation is a "costly grace." This is true because confrontations and liberation are on the road to reconciliation.

Moltmann is correct when he asserts that we must now be liberated in time rather than in space. The frontiers have been pushed back. One does not win his freedom by self-imposed exile. In our own country the West has now been won and the influx of people to the West Coast has now passed the crest and is on the decline. Drifters are finding less and less excitement in their craft. James Baldwin, Richard Wright, and Eldridge Cleaver have convinced many that there is no escape from blackness and one has to overcome his identity-crisis wherever he is. We seek inner freedom. If one is not free in time, he cannot be liberated in space. Finding one's way to inner freedom in this country requires co-existence under conditions of interdependence in a pluralistic society. This is another way of indicating that Blacks as well as Whites need to seek reconciliation as an ultimate goal. But reconciliation on a different basis and on a higher level than ever known in this society before.

"Integration" as we have experienced it was a farce. It was mainly "tokenism" and "gradualism." It did not challenge the superiority-inferiority syndrome operating in race relations. The worship of White-skin was not questioned. The pride and self-glory associated with the established order of Whites over Blacks remained status quo. Through "integration" Blacks could never have obtained self-respect. They could never have known inner freedom and they would not have felt truly equal. The self-hatred and the rejection of their heritage in favor of the majority culture would have prevented that. The very failure of "integration" opened the way for the triumph of reconciliation emerging out of liberation. My program seeks liberation and reconciliation. It is my belief that true freedom overcomes estrangement and heals the brokenness between peoples.

The Credo

What I have to say about God, man, salvation, Christ, Church, and Kingdom must be understood against the joint concerns of liberation and reconciliation.

God reveals Himself within the Black experience. To the Black man God reveals Himself as the God of the Exodus, of restoration, of prophecy, of the cross-resurrection event. God is a God of liberation. Christ is the liberator. The God who participates in the "scandal of particularity" is also the universal word. Israel's God is the "desire of all nations." The God of *each* people is the God of *every* people. As we look at Black suffering, we become aware that divine providence rather than divine existence is our main concern. We want to know, "Does God care?" We do not question *en masse* His existence. We have made it on a faith in the "if not." Like the Hebrew boys in the furnace of fire, we have asserted that the God we serve is able to deliver us—but "if not" we will still trust Him. Black suffering has produced a strong doctrine of providence.

Our concern is with the dignity of man. By *dignity* we do not imply the self-sufficiency of man apart from God. The dignity of man is not a robust humanism. For the Black man, dignity is the departure for a doctrine of man, for it is our dignity which has been denied. All men have equal status before God. Racism is a gross sin because it exalts the creature to the level of the Creator. It is self-glory, the worship of White-skin and the disdain of the brother in Black-skin. All men are one in the creative purpose of God—we are made in the image of God. This is the basis of human dignity and equality. We must treat the dignity of man before moving on to discuss his nature and destiny.

Man is a sinner. This means all men, Black as well as White. We are not only a people sinned against; we are a sinning people. Sin is self-glory. All have sinned. All men are self-centered. They are guilty of sensuality, pride, and estrangement. There is a broken relationship between man and himself, man and his brother, and man and God. All men are in need of grace to overcome this separation. All men need to be set free from sin and all men need to experience reconciliation.

This is a realistic humanism. Man is a free, rational, moral agent. But he can be angel or demon. He can ascend lofty heights, but he can sink to diabolical depths. I do not hold an optimistic or a pessimistic view of man. Only a realism is adequate; for we must live with "men of flesh and bone." This realism concerning man obtains within the Black community. We need to be liberated within and among each other. If we do not experience this inner freedom, we may not be liberated or reconciled with others outside our ethnic group.

For me the Jesus of history is the Christ of Faith. The Incarnation is the Atonement. Jesus is concerned about this life as well as the next. He saves us body, mind, and spirit. Salvation is an experience of wholeness. Jesus is the Savior of *each* people and *every* people. The particularism and the universalism of the gospel merge in His saving mission. He is prophet, priest, and king. As the Black messiah he liberates us. We overcome our identity-crisis through the symbol of the Black messiah. In His presence we cry out, "My lord and my God." As the universal word, He reconciles us with all humans. The Black messiah liberates; the universal Christ reconciles. The one who sets us free brings us together.

The Holy Spirit is God within to strengthen, to comfort and to guide. We suffer not from the absence of the Spirit but from the presence of too many spirits. This is the reason why the spirits must be "tried" to see if they be of God. A good rule of thumb is to observe whether the character of the Incarnate Lord is manifested whenever the Spirit is present. Jesus is said in scripture to be the bearer of the Spirit. The Lord is the Spirit.

The Church is the extension of the Incarnation. It is a Spirit-filled fellowship. It is the family of God, the household of faith. It is the body of Christ. The Black theologian can make use of such symbols as "family," "household," and "body" in treating the "unity without uniformity" character of the Christian community. The Church was a family for us when we had no family life. It is still a haven for the lonely and the fatherless. The Black church should be a place where everybody is somebody. We suffer at once a personal and an ethnic identity crisis. The Black church is perhaps the one place where we can overcome these crises and be accepted. The Lord of the Church, its head, is gracious. He accepts us even though we are unacceptable. His reconciling love has claimed us and transformed us into agents of reconciliation.

The Kingdom is present and future. Belief in the future life gives drive and hope to the present life. They cannot be separated. Both are part of the Christian hope. Our heritage from Africa has maintained a holistic and unitive view of all existence. Fellowship is believed to exist between the living and the dead. Furthermore, the fellowships of the invisible Church consist of saints and martyrs and all the faithful through the ages of faith. Death is an experience within life and not the cessation of existence. The social, political, and economic involvement of the Black Christian here and now is undergirded by an eternal hope.

The Future

The constructive phase of Black theology has just begun. Black theology has been caught within the crossfire of the Black rage, White backlash syndrome. We have also expended a lot of energy striving to be respectable in the eyes of White scholars and several of our Black brothers who have hangups from Harvard and Yale. But now the more important and more difficult task is upon us. The task of the Black scholar writing Black theology is a plus rather than a *minus*. He must plug into his discipline as a theologian, but at the same time he must develop a new program of theological reflection. His departure is the

Black religious heritage which is both African and Afro-American. The personal experience of the Black theologian is grounded in this context of life and thought. The task ahead is to build a viable interpretation of the Christian faith for masses of Blacks.

We are in need of a Church theology. Black theology must be concerned with peoplehood as well as with personhood. The pietistic and activistic, the priestly and the prophetic, the sacred and the secular are to be brought together. In essence, Black theology must be an ethical and political theology. There is a need for a multidisciplinary and team approach to Black theology with more reliance upon the social and behavioral science than upon philosophy as basic tools of interpretation. This new venture in theology will imply a new program of theological education. It will imply an investigation into our heritage requiring considerable non-theological sources of information — e.g., the history, art, literature of the Black cultural heritage. It will require cooperation and sharing between Black scholars. A real responsibility rests upon those of us who are involved in theological education in Black institutions. Between us there is no room for competition. There is room only for cooperation. Black theology must be ecumenical in a different sense. It will be ethnocentric, but not as an end in itself. It will be particular in a conscious sense, but it will make the particular important in face of the universal. Henceforth, the experience of blackness will by necessity enrich all theological reflection.

A final word needs to be said about the unity-in-diversity of the Black experience and, therefore, of Black theology. We must be sufficiently tolerant of each other to enable creative minds to do their best work. We need to encourage our best thinkers. We need to provide opportunities for research and writing for our most creative minds at work. It should not be that White scholars or Black scholars operating out of White institutions will always be in the forefront. I just said recently in a faculty meeting that if we know of a Black scholar we need who is now located at a major White institution, we should not hesitate to invite him to join us. It is often true that the glamour has already worn thin and the brother is ready to come home anyway.

We need unity without uniformity to enable each Black scholar to do what he can do best. We need serious but creative scholarship. Some will be interested in a biblical theology; others will major in the historical or the philosophical approaches. Some will major in methodology, others in content. We will have our Bultmanns, Tillichs, Niebuhrs, and Barths. The problem of Black suffering will challenge some. The nature and mission of the Church will urge others on, while still others will pursue the Black Messiah. Black theology is a theology in the making and only the Lord of the Church knows at this moment the ultimate direction it will take. "The harvest is plentiful, but the laborers are few; pray therefore the Lord of the harvest to send out laborers into his harvest" (Luke 10:2, RSV).

NOTES

1. John MacQuarrie, *Principles of Christian Theology* (New York: Charles Scribner's Sons, 1966), 51.

2. William Temple, *Nature, Man and God* (London: Macmillan, 1956), 478.

3. Emil Brunner, *Revelation and Reason,* tr. Olive Wyon (Philadelphia: Westminster Press, c. 1946), 32ff.

4. W. E. B. Du Bois, *The Souls of Black Folk* (Chicago: A. C. McCluug & Co., 1907), 3.

5. Vincent Harding, *Must Walls Divide?* (New York: Friendship Press, 1965).

6. James H. Cone, *Black Theology and Black Power* (New York: Seabury Press, 1969); *A Black Theology of Liberation* (New York: Lippincott, 1970); *The Spirituals and the Blues* (New York: Seabury Press, 1972).

7. *Liberation and Reconciliation* (Philadelphia: Westminster Press, 1971).

8. Frantz Fanon, *The Wretched of the Earth* (New York: Globe, 1966).

9. James Baldwin, *Go Tell It on the Mountain* (New York: Dell, 1969).

10

BLACK POWER, BLACK PEOPLE, THEOLOGICAL RENEWAL

Gayraud S. Wilmore

The Black Manifesto controversy illuminated, more than the King-led church freedom movement, the contours of America's civil religion and spurred the development of the Black Theology which had laid dormant within the amalgam of Black religion and Black radicalism for more than a half century. Even before 1966, a few Black churchmen within and on the fringes of the Southern Christian Leadership Conference had begun to explore prospects for the revitalization of the Black church and the renewal of its distinctive theological perception of the relationship between redemption and liberation. The publication of Joseph R. Washington's *Black Religion* in 1964, almost by way of negative reaction rather than positive response, accelerated this development. But it was the groundswell of political activity, ideological reflection and cultural education among the masses of the ghetto, induced by the Black Power movement, which provided the incentive for a genuine theological renewal within the Black church.

The Black Manifesto served as the final booster stage for a development which was adumbrated in the 1966 Statement on Black Power of the National Committee of Negro Churchmen. When the organization met in its first convocation in Dallas in 1967, there was unanimous agreement that further theological work needed to be done, and a Theological Commission was created and instructed to report to the St. Louis convocation in November 1968.

The discussion in Dallas generated excitement and enthusiasm for a "prospective" theology, building upon militant Black preachers of the past, which would break new ground in the dialogue between religionists and secular radicals in the Black Power movement—a dialogue which had become stultified

This essay is excerpted from Gayraud S. Wilmore, *Black Religion and Black Radicalism.* Garden City, N.Y.: Anchor Press/Doubleday, 1973; rev. ed., Maryknoll, N.Y.: Orbis Books, 1983.

by the domination of the nonviolence, redemptive suffering ethics of Martin Luther King, Jr. Moreover, the charge by Joseph R. Washington that the Black church was bereft of an authentic theology was regarded by many as an obsequious imitation of E. Franklin Frazier's sociological reductionism regarding the Black church.[1] The work group on theology rejected both of these analyses and recommended that the new Commission conduct a survey among Black seminary professors and "scholarly pastors" to determine what might be the ingredients of a basic theological position paper which would clarify the growing interest in "Black Theology" and provide churchmen with a conceptual framework for "a new dialogue and confrontation with both conservative 'whitenized' black Christians and liberal, but paralyzed white Christians, whose accommodation to the religious and secular status quo has all but robbed American Christianity of its vitality and credibility—especially among the poor, the black and the young."[2]

The publication of Washington's *The Politics of God* in 1967 pointed toward a revision of certain previous assumptions and, despite its essentially integrationist flavor, provided a new context for reflection on the theological basis for involvement with the Black masses in community organization and political action. Washington's theology was a defensive polemic against the "ghettoization" of the Negro, and the reconstruction of his folk-religion thesis moved toward a conception of the Negro's "suffering servant" role as a divine vocation to release white Christianity from its Puritan ethno-centrism.[3] He did, nevertheless, indicate the possibilities of a radical theology within the Black church that would incorporate the passion and experience of the Black masses for a new expression of the Kingdom of God within the structures and institutions of a white-dominated society. He writes:

> In order to meet the needs of the Negro, which are the demands of the Kingdom of God, Negro ministers, laymen and denominational institutions require a conscious rejection of white theological and ecclesiastical double talk and a conscious acceptance of their black promise. .... The inclusion of the Negro in the society is the demand of the Kingdom for the health of whites and blacks, but is dependent for extensity upon black cohesion in the present for the fullness of black dispersion throughout the society with equality in the future and as a whole.[4]

Between 1966 and 1970 a spate of articles by Black writers in the national religious press heralded the beginning of a new era of Black theological reflection and began to sound the themes and motifs which have been developed in depth by a few scholars scattered in a half-dozen Black and predominantly white seminaries. The venerable interdenomination journal *The Christian Century* published articles by C. Eric Lincoln and Vincent Harding on Black Power from a theological perspective. Harding's "Black Power and the American Christ" came to the defense of Carmichael and McKissick and declared that for Black Christians, "Christ is the Lord of this too."[5] A Mennonite churchman who was chairman of the History Department of Spellman College in Atlanta, Harding brought an impressionist but keenly insightful view of what Nathan Wright called "the dehonkification of black Christianity." His famous essay, "The Religion of Black Power," which appeared in 1968, caused a flurry of excitement in both Black and white theological circles and brought to the fore the mixture of old and new Black folk traditions in the religious ferment swirling around the Black Power movement. Harding, whose penchant has been to raise questions rather than suggest answers, boldly affirmed in "The Religion of Black Power" that "Allah and other gods of Africa enter into competition with Yahweh, Jesus and Buddha" in the ideological and theological winds rising in the Black community. "It is," he wrote, "joyously difficult, but part of the affirmation of Black Power is 'We are a spiritual people.' "[6]

Harding's equation of Black religion with the eclectic religiosity of Black Power was the contribution of an academician whose major interests were outside of organized Black religion in the United States. As such, it lacked the practical realism and authority of a Black churchman who could view the function of Black theology from within the church and would be obliged to test its validity in the sanctuary and on the streets. Such a man was Albert B. Cleage, Jr., a minister of the United Church of Christ and pastor of the Shrine of the Black Madonna in Detroit, a Black nationalist congregation which experienced a new birth during the rise of the Black Power fervor in the mid-sixties. Cleage's *The Black Messiah* was a collection of sermons preached during the tumultuous years in the Detroit ghetto, where one of the most devastating riots in the nation occurred during the summer of 1967.

No Black theologian has been more controversial than Cleage. His thesis, drawn from the radical Black preachers of the nineteenth century and the religious cults of the urban ghetto, was that Jesus is the Black Messiah, the descendant of the Nation of Israel, which became Black during its sojourn in Babylon and Egypt, and that he was part of a small underground movement, a Zealot, whose revolutionary message of separation and liberation from Rome was corrupted by the Apostle Paul and the theologians of white, Western civilization. Cleage told his Detroit congregation, once heavily infiltrated by movement people:

> So then, I would say to you, you are Christian, and the things you believe are the teachings of a Black Messiah named Jesus, and the things you do are the will of a black God called Jehovah; and almost everything you have heard about Christianity is essentially a lie.[7]

Like other Black theologians, Cleage attacked the traditional Christian concept of love and redemptive suffering. He also declared that only the Old Testament was canonical for the Black Nation. He pressed the idea of Blacks as God's Chosen People called to purify the authentic religion of Israel, which the white man had despoiled, and to undertake revolutionary political action "to build one Black community, one Black Nation, all stemming from the hub which is the Shrine of the Black Madonna."[8] Deeply involved in the Black Power movement in Detroit and much sought for as a spokesman and organizer for Black nationalist causes, he worked to assimilate the radical, anticlerical element of the movement into a reconstructed Black church which had divested itself of the norms of white Christianity. A recurring proposition in his work is the brotherhood of Black people who prefer one another to the white enemy and who rebuilt the ghetto by self-help and mutual aid—a familiar theme in the history of the Black community. "Jesus was black," he writes, "and he did *not* preach universal love . . . God is working with us every day, helping us find a way to freedom. Jesus tried to teach the Nation Israel how to come together as black people, to be brothers one with another and to stand against their white oppressors."[9] Harding is similarly emphatic about the pastoral care of Blacks for one another. Commenting on the alienation of Black youth from the church and the need of the Black church to address itself to them, he writes:

> The issue of religion is constantly before many of the young persons who are drawn back into the ghettos by the urgent logic of Black Power. As they return—from college or from prison—to struggle against what can be reasonably described as "principalities and powers" which seem anonymously but fiercely to control the life of their people, they find themselves often insufficient as autonomous sources of inner strength . . . a few black Christian churches have responded fully to the call of Black Power. In Detroit, the pastor of one such congregation, the Reverend Albert B. Cleage, Jr., of the Central United Church of Christ, preaches of a black revolutionary Jesus who came to set the nonwhite peoples free. A Black Madonna is the focal point of worship, and the church has probably attracted more persons committed to Black Power than any single institution still connected to the Christian churches.[10]

It is, perhaps, a matter of speculation whether James Forman, who spent considerable time in Detroit, was influenced by Cleage. But it is certainly true that he and other young Blacks, who were drawn into the orbit of IFCO and BEDC, were among those who returned to the northern ghetto with the highest humanitarian motives and sought, in the loneliness and anguish of their struggle, a greater sense of mission and a more profound resource of spirit than the crass secularism of the white Left.

The Manifesto incident and the involvement of Black churchmen in Forman's confrontation of the white religious establishment underscored the alienation of young Blacks from the doctrinaire politics of Marxism. It also indicated the alienation of Black religious thought from white theology and the quasi-fundamentalism of much of the historic Black church. In the midst of the struggle a little-known scholar with a doctorate in systematic theology from Northwestern University joined the faculty of Union Theological Seminary in New York City. James H. Cone's first book, *Black Theology and Black Power,* was published during the Manifesto controversy. Even before its publication date advance notices made it a sensation among Black religionists. Cone, the youngest of the new theologians, was the first to suggest the broad outlines of a Black theology based upon an essentially classical interpretation of the Christian faith. Calling upon Protestant theologians, from Karl Barth to Jürgen Moltmann, Cone showed how a radical, but historically accurate, interpretation of the Biblical story and a thorough reading of Paul Tillich, Albert Camus and Frantz Fanon leads to the indisputable conclusion that Black Power is the affirmation of Black being and humanity against the nonbeing and dehumanization of white racism. Not only is it a correlative of Black theology, but it is essential to a Christian understanding of freedom. He writes:

> It would seem that Black Power and Christianity have this in common: the liberation of man! If the work of Christ is that of liberating men from alien loyalties, and if racism is, as George Kelsey[11] says, an alien faith, then there must be some correlation between Black Power and Christianity ... Black Power is the power to say No; it is the power of Blacks to refuse to cooperate in their own dehumanization. If Blacks can trust the message of Christ, if they can take him at his word, this power to say No to white power and domination is derived from him.[12]

Cone attended the Theological Commission of NCBC meeting at the Interdenominational Theological Center in Atlanta on June 13, 1969. The first public statement of the Commission on the nature and meaning of Black theology unmistakably shows his influence, and its opening paragraph reflects one of the principal motifs of his work:

> Black people affirm their being. This affirmation is made in the whole experience of being black in the hostile American society. Black theology is not a gift of the Christian gospel dispensed to slaves; rather it is an *appropriation* which black slaves made of the gospel given by their white oppressors. Black theology has been nurtured, sustained and passed on in the black churches in their various ways of expression. Black theology has dealt with all the ultimate and violent issues of life and death for a people despised and degraded.[13]

It is again the influence of Cone, supported by Preston N. Williams, Henry Mitchell and Deotis Roberts—all seminary professors—which comes through in the key section of the statement, which has become almost standardized as the main line of the NCBC. This concept of Black theology provided a guideline for the NCBC debates with white churchmen during the Manifesto crisis:

> Black Theology is a theology of black liberation. It seeks to plumb the black condition in the light of God's revelation in Jesus Christ, so that the black community can see that the gospel is commensurate with the achievement of black humanity ... The message of liberation is the rev-

elation of God as revealed in the incarnation of Jesus Christ. Freedom IS the gospel. Jesus is the Liberator![14]

The NCBC understanding of Black theology issued out of the existential situation the organization faced in its attempt to make the white church acknowledge what Black churchmen believed to be God's judgment upon the American church and society as stated in the Black Manifesto. "Black Theology," said the statement, "must confront the issues which are a part of the reality of Black oppression." A basic reality was the refusal of the American people, after years of tokenism in state and federal programs, to make massive funds available for the social and economic reconstruction of the Black community. The Theological Statement, therefore, eschewed the abstractions of the debate among white theologians about the possibility of a self-consciously *Black* theology which could, at the same time, be a *Christian* theology. The issue at Atlanta was not whether Black theology could be authenticated to white colleagues and churchmen as having universal applicability, apart from immediate and self-serving contingencies, for oppressed people everywhere and in every circumstance, but whether or not it could serve the needs of Black people who were caught up in a struggle for manhood and self-determination with the structures of White Power. At the heart of the Theological Statement was the issue of reparations and the Black Manifesto. Thus it reads:

> Reparation is a part of the gospel message. Zacchaeus knew well the necessity for repayment as an essential ingredient in repentance. "If I have taken anything from any man by false accusation, I restore him fourfold" (Luke 19:8). The church which calls itself the servant church must, like its Lord, be willing to strip itself of possessions in order to build and restore that which has been destroyed by the compromising bureaucrats and conscienceless rich. While reparation cannot remove the guilt created by the despicable deed of slavery, it is, nonetheless, a positive response to the need for power in the black community . . . As black theologians address themselves to the issues of the black revolution, it is incumbent upon them to say that the black community will not be turned from its course . . . This is the message of black theology. In the words of Eldridge Cleaver: "We shall have our manhood. We shall have it or the earth will be leveled by our efforts to gain it."

Since the Black theology statement of NCBC, an unpublicized, quiet controversy has raged in theological circles over the justification of a "Black Theology." The warrant for Black theology is Black oppression. The religion of Israel depended solely upon Israel's need for deliverance from Egyptian bondage. Thus, Yahweh was not the object of philosophical speculation, but the subject of a subjugated and yearning people. He refused to give Moses ontological and epistemological answers to the question, "What shall I say to the people when they ask me, 'Who is this God who has sent you to summon us?' "

The answer: "I AM WHO I AM. I AM has sent you," terminates the discussion. Any further inquiry is not only irrelevant but blasphemous. The fundamental explication of Jewish theophany and the warrant for both Judaism and for Black theology are the words of Exodus 3:16–17.

> I have observed you and what has been done to you in Egypt; and I promise that I will bring you up and out of the affliction of Egypt, to the land of the Canaanites, the Hittites, the Amorites, the Perizzites, the Hivites, and the Jebusites, a land flowing with milk and honey.

James Cone, as the leading exponent of Black theology, has taken the brunt of the criticism that Blackness is an illegitimate basis for a Christian theology. The argument has been that there is nothing unique in the historical experience of Black people that justifies the particularity of the claim that the whole of Biblical revelation points to what is being called Black theology.[15] In his first book Cone states that "Black Theology is Christian theology precisely *because* it has the black predicament as its point of departure."[16] White Christians, therefore, must become Black in order to be Christians. But in his effort to lay the groundwork for a systematic theology of the Black experience which meets the requirement of universality, Cone adds:

> Being black in America has very little to do with skin color. To be black means that your heart, your soul, your mind, and your body are where the dispossessed are ... Therefore, being reconciled to God does not mean that one's skin is physically black. It essentially depends on the color of your heart, soul and mind.[17]

In *A Black Theology of Liberation,* Cone further develops this position by a reference to Paul Tillich's description of the symbolic nature of all theological speech. He writes:

> The focus on blackness does not mean that *only* blacks suffer as victims in a racist society, but that blackness is an ontological symbol and a visible reality which best describes what oppression means in America ... Blackness, then, stands for all victims of oppression who realize that their humanity is inseparable from man's liberation from whiteness.[18]

Cone's struggle with the legitimation of a Black theology, as such, is commendable and he satisfies the norm of universality, which he sometimes seems to believe is necessary for an acceptable systematic. The question is whether the Black religious experience requires such validation by the norms of white systematic theology, and whether the strain toward universality does not, *ipso facto,* rob Black religion of its freedom as one approach to the knowledge of God and, thereby, of its existential singularity. As J. V. L. Casserley reminds us:

The advent of Christianity forced a new problem upon the attention of
the ancient world—the problem of the singular ... There is a profound
distinction between the term "particular" and the term "singular." The
"particular" is the individual as seen by the man who is looking for the
universal, and who will feel baffled intellectually until he finds it; the
"singular," on the other hand, is the individual seen from the point of
view of the man who is out to capture and enjoy the full flavor of its
individuality.[19]

Is Black theology simply the Blackenization of the whole spectrum of traditional Christian theology, with particular emphasis upon the liberation of the
oppressed, or does it find in the experience of the oppression of Black people,
as *black*, a singular religiosity, identified not only with Christianity, but with
other religions as well? To say that being Black in America has little to do with
skin color is, at best, only half true. It is possible to argue that in a world
dominated by white power that has been inextricable from white Christianity,
being Black, or identifiably "Negroid," is a unique experience and has produced
a unique religion, closely related to, but not exclusively bound by, the Christian
tradition. Simply being oppressed or psychologically and politically in sympathy
with the dispossessed does not deliver one into the experience of Blackness any
more than putting on a blindfold delivers one into the experience of being
blind.

There is no attempt here to denigrate the sensitivity to divine revelation of
other oppressed peoples or even to invalidate the provisional authenticity of
white Christianity as a true religion—one of several valid approaches to the
One Eternal God. It is simply to affirm that Black theology authenticates itself
in the unique religious experience of Black people in the particular circumstance of white, Western civilization since the beginning of slavery in the New
World. That Cone himself also recognizes this difference is seen in his statement that:

Black Theology seeks to create a theological norm which is in harmony
with the black condition and the biblical revelation ... Theology cannot
be indifferent to the importance of blackness by making some kind of
existential leap beyond blackness to an undefined universalism.[20]

He can even speak of "Jesus as the Black Christ who provides the necessary
soul for black liberation."[21] In so doing he opens up the possibility of a Black
theology which is neither Protestant nor Catholic, but the way Black people
think, feel and *act* with the intensity of ultimate concern about their liberation
from oppression and racism. Such a theology is rooted in the resistance of the
historic Black church, but it extends beyond organized religion. It embraces
also the attempt of Black secular and non-Christian groups to express verbally
and to act out the meanings and values of the Black experience in America
and Africa.

Black theology expresses both affirmation and negation. It affirms the real possibility of freedom and manhood for Black people, and it negates every power that seeks to demean and rob Black people for the determination of their own destiny. Black theology's contribution to the universal knowledge of God does not lie in its being only the reverse side of traditional Christian theology—white theology in Black vesture. In this, Leon E. Wright is correct to say that a judgment and protest against white Christianity is not enough. Rather, in its illumination of the religious meaning of Black liberation, Black theology breaks with the determinative norms of white theology and unveils the deepest meaning of human freedom for all men.

The informal, unsystematic and, to a large degree, inarticulate "theology" of the Black folk has spoken, and still speaks, to their distinctive, singular needs. That theology, confirmed and nurtured not only in the church, but in every institution of the Black community, was oriented toward an indestructible belief in freedom. Although political emancipation was the concrete expression of that freedom, it did not exhaust its meaning. The freedom toward which the Afro-American religious experience and early Black theology tended was freedom as existential deliverance, as liberation from every power or force that restrains the full, spontaneous release of body, mind and spirit from every bondage which does not contribute to the proper development of the whole person in community. Not simply political freedom, but the freedom of the human being as a child of God, to be himself; to realize the deepest and highest potentialities of his psychosomatic nature. In short, the freedom to be a man or a woman, rather than a brain, a muscle, or a subhuman appendage to an IBM computer.

The first source of Black theology is in the existing Black community, where the tradition of Black folk religion is still extant and continues to stand over against the institutional church—merging with it at times in the ministry of such men as Henry M. Turner, Adam Clayton Powell, Jr., and Martin Luther King, Jr. This Black folk religion has never ceased providing the resources for radical movements in the Black community while the organized church receded into white evangelical pietism. Movements of Black nationalism, from the Moorish Science Temple to the Shrine of the Black Madonna, have their roots in a tradition which maintained a tenuous but persistent connection with Voodoo-ism and the spirituality of the religions of Africa. It continues to be represented in the sects and cults of the Black ghetto and has periodically been enlisted as the base of contemporary movements led by such men as Imamu Amiri Baraka, Maulana Ron Karenga, and Brother Imari of the Republic of New Africa. It is reflected in the National Negro Evangelical Association. It breaks out in Black music, Black drama, and the writing of the new Black "alienation" poets. The Black middle class has generally sought to evade these influences, but even they are too deeply rooted in the masses, of whom Langston Hughes wrote:

But then there are the low-down folks, the so-called common element, and they are the majority—may the Lord be praised! The people who have their nip of gin on Saturday nights and are not too important to themselves or the community, or too well fed, or too learned to watch the lazy world go round. They live on 7th Street in Washington, or State Street in Chicago and they do not particularly care whether they are like white folks or anybody else. Their joy runs, bang! into ecstasy. Their religion soars to a shout. Work maybe a little today, rest a little tomorrow. Play awhile. Sing awhile. O, let's dance! These common people are not afraid of spirituals, as for a long time their more intellectual brethren were, and jazz is their child. They furnish a wealth of colorful, distinctive material for any artist because they still hold their own individuality in the face of American standardization.[22]

This spirit is still the soul of Black religion and Black culture. Black theology must begin to understand and interpret it before it turns to white theologians for the substance of its reflection. The ebb and flow of Black folk religion is a constituent factor in every important crisis and development in the Black community. When the community is relatively integrated with the white society it recedes from Black institutions to form a hard core of unassimilable Black nationalism in an obscure corner of the social system—biding its time. When the community is hard-pressed, when hopes fade and the glimmer of light at the end of the tunnel is blocked out by resurgent white racism, then the essential folk element in Black religion exhibits itself again and begins anew to infiltrate the institutions which had neglected it. That is the meaning of the religion of Black Power today and the renewal of a radical Black theology within the contemporary Black church.

The second source of Black theology is in the writings and addresses of the Black preachers and public men of the past. As white theology has its Augustine, its John Calvin, Martin Luther, Ulrich Zwingli, and John Wesley, Black theology has its Nat Turner, its Richard Allen, Martin Delany, Edward Blyden, and W. E. Burghardt Du Bois. Not all Black thinkers were ministers, but all of them were greatly influenced by Black religion. One cannot understand the genius of Black spirituality or the work of charismatic leaders like Martin King, Malcolm X or James Forman, without understanding how their interpretations of the Black experience were conditioned by great Black men of the past. Forman and Malcolm X belong as much to this theological tradition as Powell or King. In an important and neglected article written in 1964 Carleton Lee indicated the significance of prophecy in the Black community as spiritual vision, as a way of "forth-telling" the transcendent meaning of history revealed to the inspired imagination.[23] To the extent that secular prophets draw upon the history of suffering and struggle in the Black community and point to its destiny as the fulfillment of the faith and hope of a stolen and oppressed people, they deal with insights, themes and motifs of the Black religious consciousness and interpret Black reality in ways that are either religious or are readily incorporated into a basically religious view of life.

As we have seen in the earlier chapters of this book the writings of the nineteenth-century Black philosophers and preachers lift up some of the seminal ideas of a Black Theology—liberation, self-help, elevation, chosenness, emigration and unity. These are some of the major themes, charged with religious significance, with which men like Payne, Crummell, Turner and Grimke were obsessed. The broad vistas of Black reality which these concepts encompass need to be prospected for the rich veins of theological insight they contain. Cone has made a beginning of this development of a theology rooted and grounded in the Black experience, but even in *A Black Theology of Liberation* he retains the traditional categories, and in so doing finds it necessary to use the arguments of white theologians to buttress his position. This is certainly not prohibited, but neither is it the only option available to Black theologians whose ancestors have not produced a systematic theology.

Black theology's interests lie in another direction. What is needed to think theologically about the corpus of Black opinion—both written and oral—is a "new consciousness," a new way of perceiving and ordering religious, cultural and political data from the Black community. This, of course, requires a new set of interpretative tools, a new hermeneutic. Henry H. Mitchell recognizes the need for the Black theologian to break the interpretative strictures of white theology when he observes:

> Just as the new hermeneutic of Ebeling and others has sought to recapture the vital message of Luther and the Reformation Fathers for the benefit of their sons, so must the Black hermeneutic seek to look into the message of the Black past and see what the Black Father could be saying to Black people today.[24]

Mitchell has not, however, developed that hermeneutic in his two propositions of communicating in the argot of the uneducated Black Baptist preacher, and "Putting the gospel on a tell-it-like-it-is, nitty-gritty basis."[25] The problem is infinitely more difficult than that. It has to do with unpacking the mythology, folklore and norms of the Black community as reflected in its verbal tradition and literature, in order to discover the ways in which Black people have acted out and linguistically communicated their provisional and ultimate concerns under an exploitative system. What Frantz Fanon has done for the native people of Algeria and the Antilles, must yet be done for the oppressed Blacks of the United States.[26]

Although Fanon would not agree with its utility, such a Black hermeneutic will deal with the morphology of Black language, the meaning of Black music, poetry, the dance, and, as Mitchell himself has suggested, not only the content, but the accent and cadences of Black preaching. In other words, if the God of justice and liberation has identified himself with the struggle of Black humanity and has manifested himself, in special ways, in the Black subcommunity of the United States, then theologians need to know much more about the lifestyle of that community and look at it through the eyes of its formal and informal leaders of the past and present. Only so will they be able to unlock the secrets of understanding and communicating the gospel of freedom in a new and meaningful way.

Black people, as Du Bois continually reminded us, are "a spiritual people." The theology of the Black community is developed not in theological seminaries, but on the streets, in the taverns and pool halls, as well as in the churches. The evolution of the first African Societies into the African Methodist Church or a group of Black youths from a fighting gang to a Black nationalist club, reforming ex-convicts and fighting dope pushers, will suggest more about the operative religion and ethics of the Black community than a study of the literature of the neighborhood Sunday schools. It is out of this welter of knowledge of the thought, feeling and action of the Black fathers and the contemporary Black ghetto that a hermeneutic can be constructed which will make it possible for Black theologians to read back to the community an interpretation of its indigenous religion that will clarify its basic commitments and integrate Black values and institutions around the core of liberation.

The third source of Black theology is the traditional religions of Africa, the way those religions encountered and assimilated, or were assimilated by, Christianity, and the process by which African theologians are seeking to make the Christian faith indigenous and relevant to Africa today. Black people are not only a spiritual people—they are also an African people. The dispute about African survivals in Negro culture and religion will go on, but it is clear that Black people did not begin on the auction blocks of Charlestown and New Orleans, nor did their religious consciousness commence with the preaching of Christianity to the slaves. It is still possible to recover some of the major beliefs of the traditional religions of Nigeria, Dahomey, Ghana, and other parts of Africa from which our ancestors came. Their development and alteration may be traced to the islands of the Caribbean and, to a lesser extent, to the mainland. It may be true that the contributions of African religion have all but evaporated from Black Christianity in the United States, but we do not know enough about the psychic structure of Black people, about what the Jungian psychologists call "the collective unconscious," of Black Americans to be able to say with absolute assurance that nothing of African spirituality lies deeply impregnated in "the souls of black folk." In any event, Black people who have struggled for their humanity against the suffocating domination of a racist, Anglo-Saxon culture, need to examine in much greater detail the religious contributions of their ancient homeland, which arise out of a vastly different cultural matrix than Europe and America. Professor Charles Long of the University of Chicago has written:

> Our colleague Mircea Eliade said long ago that the West was in danger of provincialism through a lack of attention to the orientations and solutions of non-Western man. It would be difficult, if not impossible, to make the case for the non-Western identity of the black community in America, though several make this claim. The element of truth in this claim is that though we are Westerners, we are not Western in the same way as our

compatriots, and thus we afford within America an entree to the *otherness* of America and the otherness of mankind.[27]

Those contributions, among others, are: a deep sense of the pervasive reality of the spirit world, the blotting out of the line between the sacred and the profane, the practical use of religion in all of life; reverence for ancestors and their real or symbolic presence with us, the corporateness of social life, the source of evil in the consequences of an act rather than in the act itself, and the imaginative and creative use of rhythm—singing and dancing—in the celebration of life and the worship of God. All of these aspects of African religions were found in some form, however attenuated, in the Black religion of the eighteenth and nineteenth centuries and were absorbed into Black Christianity in the Caribbean, South America and the United States. The feeling, spontaneity and freedom in Black religion and life had much to do with their resistance to complete whitenization, but this is also related to the intrinsic discontinuity between African and European religiosity. Black theology must be concerned about the recovery of those values, particularly the recovery of the achievement of freedom, the freedom to be *Muntu*—a man or a woman—in the most profound meaning of that profound Bantu word.

The theological program of African scholars for the Africanization of Christianity in modern Africa has much to say to Black theology's "ghettoization" of the Christian faith in the United States. In either case, the purpose is not to impose the sterile thought-forms and traditions of Western Christianity upon the Black community, but by a new approach to general revelation to discover a new and creative *Theologia Africana* that can unveil the reality of the Eternal Christ in the life and destiny of his Black people. Related to this quest are the urgent political issues of liberation in southern Africa and the United States, social justice and development, the relationship of Christianity to the separatist and independent churches on both sides of the Atlantic, and the contribution of Africa and Black America to the great social revolution of the Third World. Only by a sympathetic and intensive dialogue between the new younger theologians of Africa and Black theologians in the United States and the Caribbean will it be possible to uncover the harmonies and disharmonies in Black religion and forge the theological and ideological links which can bind modern Africa and Black America together for the unimaginable possibilities of the future.

What of that future? Perhaps the most that can be said is that the reformation and revivification of the faith that has come down to us from Jesus of Nazareth awaits the unhindered contribution of the nonwhite peoples of the world and that Black people of Africa and America will play a crucial role in that development. It will be preceded by the end of divisive sectarianism and the beginning of ecumenism in the institution of Black religion in the United States, by increasing communication and emigration between African and Black American churchmen, and by the development of an incisively relevant theology—on both continents—that will free itself from the false consciousness and impiety of white Christianity and bind Black people together, inside and outside of churches, in the solidarity of a new faith in God and humanity.

It can only be a matter of judgment, based upon the history of the Black race, and faith in the grace of a God who does not reward us according to our iniquities, to affirm that the Black world will not repeat the inhumanities of the white world. And if this judgment and faith are vindicated, mankind will be the beneficiary and the reconciliation for which the whole Church of Christ prays will become a realized eschatological event.

Until that time, too remote to deflect Black people from the revolutionary tasks which lie at hand today, white men must take, with utmost seriousness, the words of the National Committee of Black Churchmen in its "Message to the Churches from Oakland" in 1969—the year of the Black Manifesto:

> We black people are a religious people. From the earliest time we have acknowledged a Supreme Being. With the fullness of our physical bodies and emotions we have unabashedly worshipped Him with shouts of joy and tears of pain and anguish. We neither believe that God is dead, white, nor captive to some rationalistic and dogmatic formulation of the Christian faith which relates Him exclusively to the canons of the Old and New Testaments, and accommodate Him to the reigning spirits of a socio-technical age. Rather, we affirm that God is Liberator in the man Jesus Christ, that His message is Freedom, and that today He calls all men to be what they are in themselves, and among their own people, in the context of a pluralistic world society of dignity and self-determination for all. We believe that in a special way God's favor rests today upon the poor and oppressed peoples of the world and that He calls them to be the ministering angels of His judgment and grace, as His Kingdom of freedom and peace breaks in from the future upon a world shackled to ancient sins and virtues.

That 1969 "Message to the Churches from Oakland" of the National Committee of Black Churchmen and the "Black Manifesto" of the Black Economic Development Conference are, one must concede, merely words on paper, not ideas that have been actualized nor deeds performed. But they are prophecies of things to come and to be worked for. They belong together, and in the course of events they sought each other out. These two documents represent, each in its own way and together, the basic theme we have explored throughout this book, namely, that Black religion and Black radicalism are historic and complementary aspects of an essential characteristic of the Black experience in America—a pervasive "pragmatic spirituality" which, in a world dominated by the peculiar racism and oppression of Anglo-Saxon or Euro-American civilization, has always expressed itself in terms of a religio-political struggle for humanization and liberation. Black nationalism and pan-Africanism, hard-pressed and poverty-stricken, may surrender to the rising forces of political repression non-white people and white radicals are now experiencing in the United States, and the mainline Black churches, piously complacent, may yet succumb to the temptation of solemn assemblies and bourgeois captivity. If that happens in our time, it will be a retreat in a long history of retreats, but not a decisive repudiation of the fundamental meaning of our striving. That is to say, we will never give up the right to be what we are. We are a spiritual people. We are an African people. And we are determined, by the power of God or of Satan, to be free.

NOTES

1. E. Franklin Frazier, *The Negro Church in America* (New York, Schocken, 1962), pp. 44-46, 85-86, and Joseph R. Washington, Jr., *Black Religion: The Negro & Christianity in the United States* (Boston, Beacon Press, 1964), pp. 140-43.

2. *NCBC Theological Commission Project: A Summary Report*, November 1968, p. 4.

3. Joseph R. Washington, Jr., *The Politics of God* (Boston, Beacon Press, 1967), pp. 170-71.

4. Ibid., p. 185. For the further development of his thought toward the Black Power position, with an obvious Fanon influence, see his *Black and White Power Subreption* (Boston, Beacon Press, 1969), pp. 124-27.

5. Vincent Harding, "Black Power and the American Christ," *Christian Century*, January 4, 1967, p. 10.

6. Harding, "The Religion of Black Power," Donald R. Cutler, ed., *The Religious Situation: 1968* (Boston, Beacon Press, 1968), p. 31.

7. Albert B. Cleage, Jr., *The Black Messiah* (New York, Sheed and Ward, 1968), p. 37.

8. Ibid., p. 277.

9. Ibid., p. 111.

10. Cutler, *op. cit.*, pp. 29-30.

11. George D. Kelsey was one of the first Black Christian ethicists to teach at a major white seminary. A professor at Drew in New Jersey, his principal work, *Racism and the Christian Understanding of Man* (New York, Charles Scribner's Sons, 1965), antedates the Black theology movement.

12. James H. Cone, *Black Theology and Black Power* (New York, Seabury Press, 1969), pp. 39-40.

13. "Black Theology—A Statement of the National Committee of Black Churchmen," *Christian Century*, October 15, 1969, p. 1310. See in the same issue commentary on the statement by Preston N. Williams, chairman of the NCBC Theological Commission.

14. Ibid.

15. Leon E. Wright writes: "It would be hazardous to insist . . . that one has made a case for a uniquely oriented world-view—'Black Theology'—whose posture consists essentially in judgment and protest of 'White Christianity' and/or 'racist' society. Though such judgment can be shown to be supremely righteous and just and the protest seen to stem from deep prophetic depths, there is involved in all this no distinctive alternative to the traditional approaches to 'God-talk' and man's self-understanding." Howard University, *Journal of Religious Thought*, Summer 1969, p. 54.

16. Cone, *op. cit.*, p. 118. Italics added.

17. Ibid., p. 151.

18. James H. Cone, *A Black Theology of Liberation* (Philadelphia, J. B. Lippincott Co., 1970), pp. 27-28.

19. J. V. Langmead Casserley, *The Christian in Philosophy* (New York, Charles Scribner's Sons, 1951), p. 31. Perhaps more to the point is Fanon, who writes: "The natives' challenge to the colonial world is not a rational confrontation of points of view. It is not a treatise on the universal, but the untidy affirmation of an original idea propounded as an absolute." Frantz Fanon, *The Wretched of the Earth* (New York, Grove Press 1963), p. 41.

20. Cone, *Black Theology of Liberation*, p. 76. Cf. pp. 120-23; 156-57.

21. Ibid., p. 80.

22. Langston Hughes in *Black Protest Thought in the Twentieth Century* (New York, Bobbs-Merrill Co., 1970), ed. by Francis Broderick, et al., p. 92.

23. Carleton L. Lee, "Religious Roots of the Negro Protest" in *Assuring Freedom to the Free*, Arnold Rose, ed. (Detroit, Wayne State Univ. Press, 1964).

24. Henry H. Mitchell, *Black Preaching* (Philadelphia, J. B. Lippincott Co., 1970), p. 27.

25. Ibid., pp. 29-30.

26. Frantz Fanon, *Black Skin, White Masks* (New York, Grove Press, 1967).

27. Charles H. Long, "The Black Reality: Toward a Theology of Freedom," *Criterion*, Univ. of Chicago Divinity School, September 1969.

11

THEODICY AND METHODOLOGY IN BLACK THEOLOGY: A CRITIQUE OF WASHINGTON, CONE, AND CLEAGE

William R. Jones

Our study criticizes the respective theodicies and methodologies of Joseph Washington, James Cone, and Albert Cleage. Our argument is reducible to the following propositions. (1) On the basis of their own presuppositions, the point of departure for black theology must be the question: Is God a white racist? (2) Accordingly, a viable theodicy, one which refutes the charge of divine racism, must be the foundation for the edifice of black theology. (3) The theodicies of the above theologians leave the issue of God's racism essentially unresolved. Consequently, the remainder of the theological system lacks adequate support.

I

The argument of Richard Rubenstein[1] provides the initial framework for our analysis. The oppression and slaughter of the Jews in World War II led him to conclude that two key elements of his theological tradition must be scrapped: God as active in *and* sovereign over history, i.e., the politics of God, and the Jews as God's chosen people. Though he does not use the following language, his argument raises the question: Is God an anti-Semite? And to raise the latter question is, as Moltmann correctly suggests,[2] to revive the theodicy question.

The implications for black theology are clear. In the light of black suffering— a suffering which may exceed that of the Jews—[3] the unsavory and, some will say, blasphemous question must be put at the outset: is God a white racist?

William R. Jones is Director of Black Studies at Florida State University. This essay originally appeared in the *Harvard Theological Review* 64 (1971): 541-557. Reprinted with permission of the publisher.

Once raised, the methodological consequences are equally clear; a viable theodicy must be the first order of business before construction of the rest of the theological system can begin. This is not to say that a theodicy must, numerically, be the first chapter. We suggest, rather, that the theodicy question must control the theological enterprise. Christological and eschatological options, for instance, must be weighed in terms of their value to the theodicy problem. Black theology, we purport to show, must be an extended theodicy.

One should not conclude that Rubenstein's argument makes the theodicy question central for black theologians. To be exact, the methodological position they adopt, in part, forces the issue to center stage. If black suffering is in any way crucial for the black theologian, if reflection upon black suffering is the starting point for his theology, then the theodicy question must precede all others. For each of the figures in our study, black suffering, explicitly or implicitly, is central.

Explicitly: "The point of departure for black theology," according to Cone, "is the question: How do we *dare* speak of God in a suffering world . . . in which blacks are humiliated because they are black? This question . . . occupies the central place in our theological perspective."[4] Implicitly: if black liberation is the goal of black theology, black suffering, in the final analysis, is its starting point. To regard liberation as the *summum bonum* necessitates that its opposite, suffering as oppression, is an aspect of the *summum malum.* The precondition for black liberation as the objective for black theology is the prior affirmation of black suffering as oppressive.

Because of the nature of suffering in general *and* black suffering in particular, the question of divine racism cannot be avoided. Suffering is multievidential; it can express a relation of *favor* or *disfavor* between man and ultimate reality. Consequently, in the face of suffering, whatever its character, one must at least entertain the possibility that the relation of disfavor obtains.

The peculiar character of black suffering points to the same possibility. There is, first, its maldistribution. It is suffering confined to a specific ethnic group; it is not spread, more or less impartially, upon mankind as a whole. Black suffering, then, manifests the scandal of particularity to the degree that it is balanced by white *non*-suffering instead of white suffering. There is, second, its enormity. If we accept the statistics of Davidson, the issue is more acute for blacks than for Jews. Finally, black suffering is not catastrophic but extends over long periods of history. One is tempted, accordingly, to interpret its causal nexus in terms of purpose and thereby person—not the operation of some indifferent natural law. Actually, the same observation could be made for each characteristic of black suffering.

We contend that the peculiar nature of black suffering raises the *question* of divine racism; we do not conclude that it *answers* the question. We do insist that black theology, precisely because of the fact of black suffering, cannot proceed as if the goodness of God for *all* mankind were a theological axiom. The black religionist must press the issue at the outset, and, most important, he must demonstrate—not assume—its falsity.

Our argument is strengthened when we show that there are determining factors besides suffering that oblige black theologians to ponder the issue of transcendent racism. We purport to show that black theology is committed to a *de novo* approach, and in the latter context divine racism is a genuine option. The implications of the concept of black consciousness for theological method establish our point.

Black religionists, today, identify black consciousness with a specific theological method. Because it recognizes the Negro's inauthentic attraction and commitment to white theology – a theology of racism and oppression – black consciousness fosters the development of a counter theology, a black theology, a theology of liberation. Black consciousness requires, in short, a theological movement not simply beyond white theology, but in conscious opposition to it.

This means in general methodological terms that the black experience must control the theological enterprise. More specifically, it means (1) that black theology must adopt a method of correlation. The starting point for theological reflection must be the issues and questions that emerge from the black experience, and the answers, i.e., the black theology, must be consistent with that experience. (2) The black experience must function as the theological singular. As the theological Supreme Court, it passes final judgment upon the functional or dysfunctional quality of each part of the theological tradition. (3) A theological concept is functional if and only if it advances the cause of black liberation. (4) As a consequence of the foregoing – and here we come to the significant point for our analysis – black theology is methodologically obliged to conduct a radical and comprehensive appraisal of classical theological concepts to determine if each possesses sufficient "soul" to be included in the emerging black theology. The appraisal must be total – not even God or Jesus Christ can *a priori* be regarded sacrosanct; they, too, must be jettisoned if they flunk the test. Because black theology suspects that the norms of the Christian tradition are racist, it must proceed, as it were, *de novo*. The entire tradition must be placed under a strict theological ban until each part demonstrates its orthodoxy, the enhancement of black liberation. And since from a *de novo* perspective, the claims, God is a racist and God is a "soul" brother, are on equal footing, can consideration of the former claim, we ask, be avoided? Indeed, our previous discussion permits us to say that black theology methodologically contradicts itself if it both adopts a *de novo* approach and emphasizes black suffering, but fails to ask the troublesome question of divine racism. Once the issue is broached, the mandatory next step for black theology is to refute the charge, i.e., formulate a viable theodicy.[5]

That a viable theodicy is crucial to the methodological consistency of black theology can be supported on other grounds, and again, in terms of the black theologians' presuppositions. Central to each is the doctrine of the politics of God; man must discover where God is at work in human history and join His effort of human liberation. But the politics of God, in the context of black theology, presupposes that God is, in fact, for the liberation of blacks. He is not, in other words, a racist. It is obvious, however, that a politics of God approach presupposes a prior demonstration that God is not a racist or else it begs the question. Is it possible to construct a black theology with the politics of God as the second story without a foundational theodicy which refutes the charge of divine racism? And what has just been argued for relative to the politics of God holds as well for another crucial category in black theology: blacks as God's chosen people. This is particularly the case if one makes vicarious suffering, as Washington does, defining for the elect.

Finally, if black theology defines itself as a theology of liberation or revolution, the theodicy question is again controlling. For if the impulse to liberation is to obtain, the suffering implicit in the present situation of blacks must be interpreted as oppressive. Clearly, not every theodicy provides the requisite interpretation. Indeed, certain ones, e.g., a theodicy which entails quietism, must be labeled counter-revolutionary. Our point is this: a theology of liberation must formulate not just a theodicy, but one with a specific character. Moreover, to clear the field for itself, it must spell out the deficiencies of alternative theodicies.

Our summary can be brief: the foundation the black theologian constructs for his system must be a theodicy which refutes the claim, God is a white racist. Whether Washington, Cone, and Cleage supply the indispensable rebuttal must now be determined by critically analyzing their respective answers to the theodicy question.

II

Washington's theodicy is an elaboration of the suffering servant theme. God is engaged in human history for a purpose which will not be frustrated. He fulfills his plan, totally or in part, through the vicarious suffering of an elect group. Black suffering, which must be the suffering of the entire group, is the means by which God's plan is realized.

Washington moves between two different but related soteriological roles for blacks. There is, on the one hand, a universal mission to the total human family which parallels the saving role of another chosen people, the Jews. Their task is "to witness to the one God," while the mission of blacks "is to witness to the one humanity of the one God."[6] The realization of the universal mission of blacks both begins with and hinges upon the successful completion of a more particular assignment: the concrete salvation of the white oppressor in America from the shackles of his own racism and white folk religion, i.e., irreligion.

Blacks should not seek to evade the suffering inherent in their roles; actually, they could not, even if they hoped for release. Since one's status as suffering servant-chosen people is rooted in God's choice, a choice consequently that cannot be nullified, one cannot choose not to be the suffering servant-chosen people. One can choose not to be obedient to the demands of one's mission — but only at the peril of rebelling against God himself. Washington is willing to affirm that, ultimately, the only hope for the success of black liberation is to follow the path he describes — through the valley and shadow of vicarious suffering. For it is this path alone which God demands and therefore nurtures.

The deficiencies of Washington's theodicy, in our view, are severe if not fatal. Before describing them, it is necessary to isolate the structure of his argument and thus provide a framework for our criticism.

The argument appears to have the following structure: (a) If blacks are the suffering servant-chosen people, then the charge of divine racism is refuted. (b) Blacks are the suffering servant-chosen people. (c) Therefore, the charge of divine racism is refuted. To round out the argument it is necessary to show that the category of the suffering servant-chosen people, the cornerstone of his theodicy, carries two meanings for Washington, and each constitutes a refutation of divine racism. To be chosen means that one has found favor in God's sight. Chosenness is also essentially related to one's salvation.

Clearly the validity of his argument is contingent upon his establishing (b). We question whether the label of suffering servant-chosen people is justified on the basis of Washington's evidence.

An analysis of Isaiah 53:5–12, the section Washington cites as support for his classification, is our point of departure. Our reading concludes that *two* conditions are required to index an individual or group in the category of suffering-servant. (1) There is the fact of suffering, but suffering as a necessary condition. (2) There is a radical shift in the status of the suffering individual or group which we will name the *liberation event* or factor. The shift comprises something similar to the principle of "from last to first." If we call (1) the situation of humiliation, then (2) would designate exaltation or reward. The references, "I will divide him a portion with the great" and "He shall divide the spoil with the strong," supply the general sense of (2) that is intended. Even where the liberation event is interpreted eschatologically, i.e., the change in status is yet to come, it is on the basis of the eschatological event that the present suffering, for instance, is alleged to be unjustified. Two rhetorical questions summarize our point. Can we speak of Jesus as Lord if we speak only of the cross and omit the resurrection? Can we speak of blacks as suffering servant-chosen people if the only evidence given is their suffering?

The point can be put in another way. Without the liberation event how can we differentiate between two mutually exclusive alternatives, vicarious suffering and suffering as deserved punishment? Is it not premature to classify someone as suffering servant-chosen people *prior* to the occurrence of the liberation event?[7] Is it not incumbent upon Washington, from the methodological standpoint, to designate the liberation event(s) for blacks which justifies the label, chosen people-suffering servant?

One might argue that the eschatological option is available for black theology; the liberation event is yet to come. This option, from our vantage point, is a theological dead end, for, in the final analysis, it leaves the issue of God's racism unresolved until the eschaton. Prior to the actual eschatological event, and in the face of black suffering, God's favor and disfavor relative to blacks remain equally probable.

Moreover, it would appear that Washington further undercuts the strength of his theodicy when he acknowledges that the reason for God's choice of blacks as suffering servant-chosen people "is no more fathomable than His choice of Israel to be His 'suffering servant.' "[8] Does not the uncertainty regarding the reason for the election make problematical Washington's stipulation of a specific purpose for the selection?

Washington's theodicy is even more questionable when we consider that it appears to entail a consequence which is clearly consistent with the concept of a racist God: the *perpetuity* of black suffering. He appears to establish an either/or situation in which both alternatives involve suffering. There is, on the one hand, the inevitable suffering associated with blacks as suffering servant; on the other, blacks suffer because "Negroes will always be black and objectionable to whites."[9] The former cannot be evaded because it expresses the will of ultimate reality, the latter because blacks are powerless in a racist society. Consequently, the Negro has the choice either "to be what he is, 'suffering servant' the source of power, or fatalistically acquiesce in suffering. . . ."[10]

Black suffering will be terminated, according to Washington, only when their soteriological mission is complete, and this may not occur until the eschaton. In a similar vein he concludes: "The continuing chastisement of the Jews may be to the end of time."[11] If I understand Washington correctly, he is affirming that blacks will not be liberated until their assignment is *successfully* concluded. "The Negro will receive no reward until all are healed."[12] In reading Washington, we have the nagging suspicion that black suffering is intended as much for white liberation as for black freedom. In fact, one could argue that the position is weighted in favor of white freedom since black reward is contingent upon the success of their soteriological assignment. The suspicion grows even stronger when we note that slavery, for Washington, is a necessary part of God's purpose and, moreover, less "bruising" than the present mission.[13] If this were not sufficient to make one distrust the God he represents, Washington further asserts that though God's purpose demanded the exodus of the Jews from bondage in Egypt, the will of God for the Negro does not include a similar exodus. We do not think it unfair to suggest that blacks should at least ponder over God's purpose and motive if it involves the type of suffering Washington describes — particularly without a corresponding suffering for whites. Washington's theodicy, we submit, does not disprove the charge of divine racism, rather it has the net effect of reaffirming the charge.

III

It is to Cone's merit that he avoids a theodicy which implies the perpetuity of black suffering. Indeed, the opposite impulse informs his approach. The elect are not chosen to suffer for the other, not even indirectly; their election entails, instead, their release from suffering and bondage. Yet his theodicy, in our view, is also a failure since it does not falsify the assertion, God is a white racist.

The logical structure of Cone's argument parallels that of Washington. Three steps can be indicated. (1) A class is posited that involves a special and favored relation to deity. For Washington, as we saw, this class was the suffering servant-chosen people; for Cone, the *oppressed*. (2) It is argued that blacks are members of the class in question. (3) The conclusion follows: God is not a racist.

The major support for Cone's argument boils down to an exegetical demonstration that the liberation of the oppressed is the core of the biblical *Heilsgeschichte*. This, in turn, is the ground for the other pillar of his theodicy: "The *liberation* of the oppressed is a part of the innermost nature of God."[14] Making liberation the essence of God serves a dual purpose. It links blacks to the biblical acts of liberation, and, consequently, it answers, at the same time, the question of divine racism. If "liberation is . . . the essence of divine activity,"[15] racism, by definition, is not possible. Thus, God's acts of liberation in the past, which are the clue to his character, purpose, and motive, are sufficient grounds for blacks to rest assured that he has made their liberation his concern and is in their midst as they struggle towards freedom. Cone is willing to conclude that if God is not "identified totally" with the goals of blacks, he is a murderer, i.e., a racist, and the only appropriate response for blacks is deicide.[16]

One other feature of Cone's theodicy deserves special attention. His approach does not explain the "why" of black suffering; nor does he seek to harmonize it with God's will or purpose. He is content to see white racism as the cause. The weight of his argument falls upon what God has done for the oppressed in the *past* and, thus by implication, what he is now doing about black oppression. Black suffering does not imply divine racism, because God is presently participating in the black struggle for freedom.

If our analysis is correct,[17] Cone's position is vulnerable at crucial points. The first crucial issue is whether the first step of his argument begs the question; the same question can also be put to Washington. To posit a class that presupposes a favored relation to God — and the term *oppressed* carries this stipulative meaning for Cone — is to exclude the alternative of God's disfavor by definition.

Of equal importance is whether Cone has substantiated the claim that the liberation of *blacks* is essential to God's being. We wish to show that, on his own terms, the claim can be corroborated only by pointing to concrete acts of God in behalf of *black* liberation — not acts for some other group. That is, once the issue of God's racism is raised, the fact of his liberating activity for non-blacks, e.g., the Israelites, is irrelevant to the charge, God is a white racist. The exodus may refute the accusation of anti-Semitism but not racism.

Our criticism gains clarity when we consider Albert Cleage's response to the same issue. That God is liberating blacks is established by Cleage at the outset in terms of his concepts of the blackness of God, Jesus, and the Jews. The *physical* blackness of God and Jesus — not their symbolic blackness — partially confirms their status as "soul" brother and assures their active participation in the struggle for black freedom. By regarding the Jews as black, he guarantees, again at the outset, the fact of God's liberating effort in behalf of the *particular* group at issue. In summary, the scandal of particularity, which is raised by virtue of the nature of black suffering, can only be answered by reference to the particularity of God's liberating activity, e.g., an exodus for *blacks*.

Let us consider some decisive statements from Cone himself to show that they support our interpretation. "There is no revelation of God without a condition of oppression *which develops into a situation of liberation.*"[18] What can this statement mean except that revelation presupposes the two conditions we detailed in the previous section: suffering and the liberation event? Must we not conclude that in the absence of the latter, there is no revelation, and consequently, no knowledge of God's nature? In the absence of the liberation event *for blacks*, is it possible to speak of the liberation of blacks as implicit in God's innermost nature?

Other statements yield the same conclusion. He rejects the suggestion that knowledge of God "as he is in himself" is possible and also the view that we can know God "independently of his liberating work."[19] When we combine these with another claim, our criticism is justified. "Black theology," he claims, "cannot accept a view of God which does not represent him as being for blacks and thus against whites . . . We must know where God is and what he is doing in the revolution. There is no use for a God who loves whites the *same* as blacks."[20] Does not Cone's position here push him to the conclusion that blacks can know God as for them, as liberator, only if there are concrete acts of black liberation where the hand of God is detected? To conclude that God is on the side of blacks because he has participated in the liberation of non-blacks is to assign a character to God which, in Cone's own terms, has not been established. It is to speak of God "independently of his liberating acts." Is it not comparable to arguing that since Huey Long was on the side of the oppressed, i.e., Southern whites, he was also on the side of blacks?

Finally, can we fail to give full weight to this point? The conditions Cone cites as the basis for saying blacks are oppressed and thereby the beneficiary of God's liberating work — "blacks are humiliated because they are black" — are, in fact, the same conditions one would expect if God were a racist.

We submit that Cone has not substantiated the one fact which his own position asserts must be shown if God is not a murderer, namely, that black liberation is a part of his innermost nature. If this is the case, the remainder of the system is without a sturdy foundation. Obviously, the equation between black theology and the Gospel he advocates becomes suspect. Further, the black factor of his theology would lose its support. It is on the basis of God's identification with the oppressed, i.e., blacks, and his assumption of their condition that he is able to speak of a black Christ. But if the issue of God's relation to blacks remains unresolved, there is no basis for speaking of a black Christ.

What options are available to Cone to authenticate the liberation event for blacks? He can adopt Cleage's approach which makes the exodus, for instance, an act of black liberation since the Jews, in Cleage's system, are black. Another possibility is to isolate the liberation factor or progress of events through a survey of black history, but his own position makes this option unattractive. His claim, previously considered, that God must be for blacks and against whites, has this methodological consequence: he can prove that God is on the side of blacks only if he also marshals empirical warrant for God's opposition to whites.

It is embarrassing even to mention that whites have been on top for centuries. Moreover, he could not legitimately speak of a progressive improvement for blacks if their status *relative to whites* did not measurably improve. An appeal to white racism as the cause of black suffering would simply shift the issue to another level. The central question would then be to account for white racism in the context of God's sovereignty and his alleged opposition to whites.

The option of eschatological confirmation, the liberation event(s) is yet to come, also appears to be closed by Cone's own position, though his thought may be inconsistent here. It should be clear that an eschatological verification would not fit with his argument that blacks must know here and now whose side God is on, for, as we have already argued, the actual effect of eschatological confirmation is to leave the issue of divine racism unresolved until the eschaton.

Moreover, Cone rejects the concept of eschatological compensation for this-worldly suffering, but curiously, he introduces something strikingly similar in content and intent. He finds it necessary to postulate "the future reality of life after death"[21] for various reasons: to substantiate that God is on the side of blacks, to insure that fear of death will not lead to defeatism and thus diminish one's total commitment to the struggle, to assure that the death of the black freedom fighter is not meaningless, etc. One wonders, however, what the real difference is between the eschatological perspective he accepts and the one he rejects. The slave eschatology promised compensation for those who suffer patiently here; while Cone's eschatology guarantees reward and meaning for those who die valiantly here. Though the difference reflects a much needed corrective for black ethics, is it an improvement on black theodicy? I raise this question because the following possibility sticks in my mind. Consider: the promise of a future reality after death motivates blacks to make the ultimate sacrifice for their liberation, and this is the means by which a racist God beckons blacks to suicidal efforts and thus accomplishes black genocide.

IV

The core of Cleage's position seems to be a complex of categories which he does not explicitly relate to the theodicy issue. As we suggested above, the concepts of the blackness of God, Jesus, and the Jews, along with the view of the particularity of the divine action for liberation, constitute an answer to the question of divine racism. Since these categories also form the core of Cleage's total system, their description and criticism would require another article. Our admittedly incomplete analysis must, accordingly, be an outline of the argument we would present if space and time permitted.

Cleage's refutation of God's racism is reducible to two points. (1) To be on the side of blacks requires that one be like them, i.e., physically black; thus the necessity of a black God and a black Jesus. (2) Since not everyone who is black is also a "soul" brother, there must be concrete evidence of God's activity in their behalf. Here the major evidential materials are the exodus and the revolutionary ministry of Jesus, the black messiah, to the black nation, Israel. The same point is affirmed when blacks are considered as the chosen people which means that God is working for their emancipation.

It is important for purposes of criticism, to recognize the logical connection between (1) and (2). In the final analysis (2) is dependent upon the demonstration of (1). It is only on the basis of the blackness of God, Jesus, and the Jews that the Exodus, for instance, becomes an event of black liberation. Thus, it becomes necessary to consider how he defends the particularity of God's saving activity based on an identity of pigmentation with the specific group in question.

The concept of the *imago dei* is the ground for claiming that God is black. Specifically, according to Cleage, we must describe God as some "combination" of the actual characteristics of the human family considered in terms of their numerical representation. Since an empirical analysis indicates that there are black men, red men, yellow men, and "a few, a mighty few, white men," it can be concluded that God must be some combination of red, yellow, and black, "with just a little touch of white, and (hence) we must think of God as a black God."[22] To reach the latter conclusion Cleage emphasizes the American view that one drop of black blood makes one black.

Though Cleage's argument refutes the charge of divine racism, it must be noted that he depends upon an interpretation of the *imago dei* concept which leads to very dubious consequences, and these undercut the value of his refutation. It is obvious that the "combination" interpretation of the *imago dei* can be applied to other features of the divine nature as well. If we conclude that God is a combination of the various hues represented in the human family, must we not also apply the combination interpretation to the category of weight, size, sex, intelligence, etc. The logical consequence, it appears, would be total anthropomorphism. Moreover, since Cleage utilizes the combination interpretation in an exclusive way—"Certainly thou must understand that as black people, it would be impossible for us to kneel before thee, believing thee to be a white God—"[23] would not a plurality of gods, each with a different color, be necessary to accommodate the human family of worshipers?

Special note, moreover, should be made of the fact that Cleage does not establish that God is black but only *non-white.* Accordingly, it is also appropriate to speak of a yellow messiah or a red messiah.

We turn now to Cleage's explicit treatment of black suffering, and here he utilizes the category of *deserved punishment.* This interpretive framework, at first glance, seems odd, for it would appear to entail quietism. If the suffering is deserved, then evasion is inappropriate. Further, if it is the result of God's disfavor, then it is futile, as Father Paneloux observes in *The Plague,* to try to escape the full brunt of the punishment. Cleage avoids the albatross of quietism by making quietism itself the sin which is being punished. Blacks are being punished because of their failure to affirm their manhood by challenging every dehumanizing act of the oppressor.

To round out this side of the theodicy other features must be described. God's nature, i.e., the morality of the universe, requires an atoning act for each sin. The atonement must be man's work, and the act of atonement must be the antithesis of the sin under question. "For every moment of cowardice, there must be a moment of courage."[24] In sum, our suffering will continue until we have made total restitution for our past sins, and it is presupposed that the sins of the father are visited upon the son.

We would question whether the category of deserved punishment can carry the weight Cleage places upon it. We find it difficult to describe the nature of the sin that requires the degree of suffering blacks have experienced since coming to America. Is the sin to be traced to an African past? It would seem that the character of black suffering in Cleage's analysis raises the issue of the commensurability of sin and punishment. To make our point another way. We argued that the crucial issue for Washington and Cone was the identification of the liberating event for blacks; for Cleage, it is the identification of the sin for which black suffering is the restitution.

What we are suggesting, indirectly, is that Cleage's position carries within it a hint of the perpetuity of black suffering. His argument that every sin must be matched by an antithetical act is open-ended to the extent that one can never know when full satisfaction has been made. And one wonders why God insists upon parity between sin and suffering when it is allowed that God was willing to "break the very laws of the universe"[25] for his chosen people.

Nor is it apparent that his position can accommodate white non-suffering. In the light of continued black suffering and white non-suffering, what are we to conclude about whites, particularly when we invoke the rigid principle of equal satisfaction for each sin? Has another people replaced blacks as God's chosen? Must we conclude that God has broken the rules of the universe in their favor by nullifying the necessity of punishment for their crime of white racism? In general terms, Cleage must explain how it is that blacks are God's chosen people in light of the fact that whites were allowed to get on top and stay there. Cleage's framework would allow him to conclude that black suffering is due to black sin, therefore the issue of the status of whites is irrelevant. We admit this, but such a line of argumentation would also sever, it appears, any causal connection between white racism and black suffering.

In sum, we find Cleage's theodicy to be an unsure answer to the question of divine racism.

V

A description of our positions falls beyond the scope of this article, but we must emphasize that it does not enlist the position of divine racism. We would see black suffering in particular and suffering in general as simply a matter of powerlessness. We would also find the framework of humanistic existentialism to be a more viable framework for black theology than the scaffolding we find in Washington, Cone, and Cleage. We hope to have more to say on these themes in the near future.[26]

NOTES

1. *After Auschwitz* (Bobbs-Merrill Co., 1966).

2. "Since we experience reality as history and no longer as cosmos, the fundamental theodicy question is still with us and is more pressing than before. For us it has no longer only its old naturalistic form, as in the earthquake of Lisbon in 1755. It appears today in a political form, as in the question of Auschwitz. . . . We ask the question: *An Deus sit?* ('Whether God is?') on grounds of history and its crimes. . . ." *Religion, Revolution and the Future* (Charles Scribner's Sons, 1969), 205.

3. Basil Davidson estimates that slavery, "before and after embarkation," cost Africa fifty million blacks. *Black Mother* (Atlantic-Little, Brown Co., 1961), 80.

4. James H. Cone, *A Black Theology of Liberation* (Philadelphia: Lippincott, 1970), 115.

5. It is not our intent to establish deductive requirements for a viable theodicy. We contend that the issue of divine racism emerges from the events and crimes of history. The answer, likewise, must appeal to historical data and not a mere rational or theoretical formulation unsubstantiated by the actual history of blacks. It will become clear that the presuppositions of the black theologians—the politics of God, the priority of the black experience, etc.—dictate that the actual black experience, past, present, or future, must be the arena for debate, and not abstract possibilities.

6. Joseph Washington, *The Politics of God* (Boston: Beacon Press, 1969), 158.

7. Though the category of deserved punishment stands in essential contradiction to Washington's position, he gives it only scant attention. The following seems to be his only "refutation" of the alternative of deserved punishment. "Historically, the systematic victimization of the African and the American Negro has been accepted as the punishment of the will of God. But this very belief sparks the reality so opposite, the truth of hope; these victims bear the marks of those blessed of God to do his work of love . . . ," 176.

8. Washington, 173.

9. Washington, 173.

10. Washington, 166.

11. Washington, 158.

12. Washington, 160.

13. "Slavery was but the means for inextricably binding the Negro and the Caucasian. Without this binding the immeasurably more bruising work of releasing whites from their blasphemous bondage to whiteness and racial superiority cannot be done," 157.

14. Cone, 121.

15. Cone, 121.

16. Cone, 59-60.

17. We have not included Cone's treatment of theodicy in *Black Theology and Black Power* on the assumption that his later work presents his definitive position.

18. Cone, 91. Emphasis supplied.

19. Cone, 133.

20. Cone, 131-32.

21. Cone, 247.

22. Albert B. Cleage, Jr., *The Black Messiah* (New York: Sheed and Ward, 1969), 42-43.

23. Cleage, 46-47.

24. Cleage, 271.

25. Cleage, 242.

26. Cf. my work, *Is God a White Racist? Prolegomenon to Black Theology* (Garden City, N.Y.: Anchor Press/Doubleday, 1973).

PART III

BLACK THEOLOGY
AND
THE BIBLE

INTRODUCTION

A peculiar situation existed relative to Black theology and the Bible in 1969. On the one hand, there were less than a half-dozen African-American scholars who had doctorates in the Old or New Testament, and even fewer so credentialed who expressed any interest in the emerging Black theology. On the other hand, for many generations Black preachers had relied heavily upon Scripture in both their priestly and prophetic offices. Even during slavery, when few Black preachers could read well and many had to memorize large portions of the text, the Bible played a central role in the Black Church and it was almost unthinkable that any new school of theology would attract Black people without having a strong biblical foundation.

Although it is difficult to find any examples of exegetical or expository writings by Black biblical scholars on what became the major themes of Black theology, it is nevertheless true that ordinary Black ministers and laity who attempted to articulate a theology of liberation from an African-American perspective, did so with the help of a few familiar texts from both testaments that deal with the judgment of the great prophets against the rich and powerful who crush the poor; justice for the widow and orphan; liberation for the captive and the slave; the ministry of Jesus to the poor and those outside the precincts of conventional piety; the fact that God is no respecter of people and that at the judgment the last shall be first and the first last.

Such themes, basic to all schools of Black theology, were thundered from the pulpits of Black congregations throughout the civil rights period as they were since the early nineteenth century. What preachers may have lacked in sophisticated, scholarly interpretation was made up for by their powerful proclamation, accompanied by marching feet, old gospel hymns, and cries of "Freedom now," "we shall overcome someday" and, after 1965, "Black Power!" Most Black Christians who were radicalized during the late sixties and early seventies simply assumed that Scripture eminently supported their repudiation of and resistance to American racism and the half-stepping, reluctant response of the White churches. They didn't need biblical scholars to provide intricate exegetical studies that would confirm their belief that God was on the side of the oppressed and that the gospel of Jesus Christ means freedom from every form of bondage and the recovery of self-esteem and dignity for every human being.

For the Black Church the credibility of Scripture has generally been pneumatological rather than canonical. The Bible is authenticated not because scholars can demonstrate that it contains the inspired Word of God, "the unique

155

and authoritative witness to Jesus Christ in the Church," and "the only rule of faith and practice," but because of its spiritual power. It is authenticated in life, rather than by legal fiat or theological abstraction, when the Holy Spirit gives the believer the power to "overcome," to transcend the brutality, despair, and resignation of ordinary, worldly existence while living in and through it day by day. Hence most Black theologians of the period between 1966 and 1979 did not turn to the few biblical scholars in the academy or the church to provide them with scriptural authorization and confirmation for what they were saying and doing. They felt instinctively that they had sound, biblical support for "the blackenization of the gospel," without attempting to prove it by citing Scripture chapter and verse. If those who were shaping a Black theology in the waning days of the civil rights movement used the Bible as a primary resource, it was selectively—in the way that John Lovell, Jr., says the slave poets who created the spirituals used biblical material—for

> symbolization of the deliverer or overcoming the oppressors; inspiration from notable accomplishments under almost impossible circumstances (the slave considered himself a potential accomplisher in a universe where he had little or no real hope but great expectation); and exemplification of the workings of faith and power.[1]

Among the first Black biblical scholars to take note of Black theology was Charles B. Copher, emeritus professor of Old Testament at the Interdenominational Theological Center (ITC) in Atlanta. As early as 1972 Professor Copher presented a brief report of a study he had made to a theological conference held at the ITC. In this study he claimed that there were four distinguishable views about the Bible among the Black theologians whose writings were then available. He wrote:

> I am prepared . . . to identify four classifications of Black theology in terms of its biblical perspectives, with apologies to those persons I will mention who may wish to disavow the pigeonholes into which I have placed them. I classify these four points of view under the following headings: (1) Traditional, (2) Moderately Traditional, (3) Radical, and (4) Revolutionary.
>
> It is to be noted and emphasized that these labels are narrowly focused. They are based upon the relative degree to which these Black theologians seem to adhere to the belief that the canonical Scriptures, Bible, is normative for Christian theology.[2]

James H. Cone, whom Charles Copher identified as Traditional, however, presents what is almost a special case.[3] As a student of Karl Barth, "the theologian of the Word of God," it was inevitable that Cone's effort to articulate a Black theology of liberation would be rooted in Scripture. In his first book, *Black Theology and Black Power*, he refers to Barth more frequently than to any other theologian and leans heavily upon Barth's insistence that God has an exclusive partiality for the poor and lowly against the rich and powerful. Here Cone, like Barth, takes his stand not on reason or tradition, but on the Bible. He writes:

> This is certainly the message of the eighth-century prophets—Amos, Hosea, Isaiah, and Micah. Being ethical prophets, concerned with social justice, they proclaimed Yahweh's intolerance with the rich, who, as Amos says, "trample the head of the poor into the dust of the earth" (2:7) and "sell the righteous for silver, and the needy for a pair of shoes" (2:6). God unquestionably will vindicate the poor.
>
> And if we can trust the New Testament, God became man in Jesus Christ in order that the poor might have the gospel preached to them; that the poor might have the Kingdom of God (Luke 6:20); that those who hunger might be satisfied; that those who weep might laugh.[4]

But Cone went much further in his early work. In "Biblical Revelation and Social Existence" (Document 12), he not only shows that his theological speech is rooted in the traditions of the Old Testament, contending that God meets us in history, in the social context of existence, but also that the hermeneutical principle for any true exegesis is the revelation of Jesus Christ as the liberator of humankind from social oppression. By considering any other exegesis of the Scripture from a Christian perspective invalid, Cone began his work with an unequivocal affirmation of the biblical basis of Black theology.

One of the early criticisms of Black theology was that it had a decided bias toward the Old Testament. That is not surprising in view of the fact that Christian slaves in both Africa and the New World had a strong affinity to the story of Israel's encounter with God and the heroes and heroines of the faith from Abraham and Sarah to the birth of Jesus. Robert A. Bennett, who wrote "Biblical Theology and Black Theology" (Document 13), was perhaps the second Black biblical scholar to apply his skill and training to an analysis of Black theology's claim to be based on a hermeneutic of liberation rooted in Scripture. We include his article here because, in a way that Copher's report does not, it represents the faint beginning of a dialogue between Black theologians and Black biblical scholars that did not come into its own until the 1980s with the publication of Cain Hope Felder's *Troubling Biblical Waters: Race, Class, and Family.*[5]

Allan Boesak, a doctoral student in systematic theology in the Netherlands, was laying out a theological platform for the Black revolution in his homeland of South Africa as early as 1974, drawing from the firm biblical roots of Reformed Theology and his reading of Cone and other African-American theologians. Boesak's essay "The Courage To Be Black" (Document 14) is excerpted from an article that first appeared in the Dutch journal *Wereld en zending* in 1974. Here Boesak, who was to become the leading liberation theologian of South Africa, exegetes the Old Testament concept of justice and righteousness. He then goes on to show how the image of Jesus in the New Testament identifies him as the Black Messiah to men and women of color under assault by systemic poverty and oppression.

"Jesus, the Liberator" (Document 15) is the last essay in Part III. The late Bishop Joseph A. Johnson, Jr. was a biblical scholar par excellence who held doctoral degrees in both theology and the New Testament. This chapter from his book, *The Soul of the Black Preacher* (1971), does not deal explicitly with exegetical issues in New Testament texts used by Black theologians, but is such a powerful christological statement that focuses on the picture Black Christians have of Jesus, and the inability of White theologians to understand and mediate that picture to the Black Church, that we include it as a biblical-theological addendum to the other essays in Part III. Bishop Johnson's statement is one of the most quoted in the literature of Black theology. It was presented to an enthusiastic and receptive audience at the Twenty-Seventh General Conference of the Christian Methodist Episcopal Church in 1970. It represents, therefore, one of the earliest endorsements of Black theology at a major convocation of a historic African-American denomination.

G.S.W.

NOTES

1. John Lovell, Jr., *Black Song: The Forge and the Flame* (New York: Macmillan Co., 1972), 257.

2. Charles B. Copher, "Biblical Perspectives on Black Theology," an unpublished report in possession of the editors.

3. Copher also places in this category Joseph R. Washington, Jr., J. Deotis Roberts, and Rosemary Ruether, who, as a White woman theologian then teaching at Howard University Divinity School, had written perceptively on Black Theology by 1972.

4. James H. Cone, *Black Theology and Black Power*, 20th Anniversary Edition (San Francisco: Harper & Row, 1989) 45.

5. Felder's work and his important role in the flowering of African-American biblical studies in the United States as it relates to the second generation of Black theologians are dealt with in Volume II, Part III.

12

BIBLICAL REVELATION AND
SOCIAL EXISTENCE

James H. Cone

*Any point of departure for exegesis which ignores God in Christ as the
liberator of the oppressed or makes salvation as liberation secondary is
invalid. The test of validity lies not only in the particularity of the
oppressed culture, but in the One who freely grants us freedom when we
were doomed to slavery.*

Theologians are becoming increasingly aware of the influence of social context upon their work. The sociologists of knowledge, such as Karl Mannheim,
Werner Stark, Thomas Luckmann, and Peter Berger, have persuaded us that
all theology, past and present, is shaped by socially determined values. Werner
Stark speaks of an "axiological grid," which every person develops in childhood
before the age of reflection.

> We see the broad and deep acres of history through a mental grid . . .
> through a system of values which is established in our minds *before* we
> look out on to it—and it is this grid which decides . . . what will fall into
> our field of perception.[1]

Stark and the others were not contending for social determinism but for the
reciprocity between ideas and social existence. Thought is not pure and autonomous; it is an expression of life. Accordingly, the consideration of any system
of ideas is not complete without an investigation of the social context in which
the system arose.

This essay originally appeared in *Interpretation* 28 (October 1974). Reprinted with permission
of the publisher. Scripture quotations marked NEB are from *The New English Bible.* © The
Delegates of the Oxford University Press and The Syndics of the Cambridge University Press,
1961, 1970. Used by permission.

While all this may bring sorrow to some who would elevate ideas to an ethereal realm, it is a fact of life and, I contend, not a regrettable fact. In fact, for those who take seriously the doctrine of creation, it has a friendly, earthy feel. Furthermore, because creation entails revelation, we recognize that revelation itself, the radiant point of contact between God and people, has its own social context or (since it occurred at different times) contexts. Unlike the God of Greek philosophy, who is removed from history, the God of the Bible is involved in history. His revelation is inseparable from the social and political affairs of Israel. The God of Peter, James, and John is not an eternal idea nor an absolute ethical principle. Yahweh is known and worshipped as the Lord who brought Israel out of Egypt and raised Jesus from the dead. He is the active God, the political God, the Protector of the poor and the Establisher of right for those who are oppressed. To know him is to experience his acts in the concrete affairs and relationships of people, liberating the weak and helpless from pain and humiliation.

Theological language, therefore, is necessarily social language, not only because of what people are but also because of who God is. The purpose of this article is to examine the social context of divine revelation and to set forth the implications of that context for the theologian's task.

The Social Context of Divine Revelation in the Old Testament

The Old Testament is a history book. To understand it and the divine revelation to which it testifies, we must think of the Old Testament as the drama of God's mighty acts in history. It tells the story of God's acts of grace and of judgment as he calls the people of Israel into a free, liberated existence.

Historically, the story began with the Exodus. The Exodus was the decisive event in Israel's history, because through it Yahweh revealed himself as the Savior of an oppressed people. The Israelites were slaves in Egypt; thus, their future was closed. But Yahweh "heard their groaning, and remembered his covenant with Abraham, Isaac and Jacob; he saw the plight of Israel, he took heed of it" (Exodus 2:24–25 NEB). Yahweh, therefore, took Israel's history into his own hands, and gave this people a divine future, thereby doing for Israel what she could not do for herself. "With arm outstretched and with mighty acts of judgments" (Exodus 6:6 NEB), he delivered Israel out of Egypt and across the Red Sea. And "when Israel saw the great power which the Lord had put forth against Egypt, . . . they put their faith in him," responding with a song to the Lord:

> I will sing to the Lord, for he has risen up in triumph;
> the horse and his rider he has hurled into the sea.
> (Exodus 15:1 NEB)

In the Exodus-event, God is revealed by means of his acts on behalf of a weak and defenseless people. He is the God of power and of strength, able to destroy the enslaving power of the mighty Pharaoh.

> The Lord is my refuge and my defence,
> he has shown himself my deliverer.
> (Exodus 15:2 NEB)

The centrality of the Exodus for Israel's consciousness, seen first through the people's recognition of deliverance, was further developed at Sinai, as the Exodus became the basis for Israel's covenant with Yahweh.

> You have seen with your own eyes what I did to Egypt, and how I carried you on eagles' wings and brought you here to me. If only you will now listen to me and keep my covenant, then out of all peoples you shall become my special possession; for the whole earth is mine. You shall be my kingdom of priests, my holy nation.
> (Exodus 19:4–5 NEB)

This passage connects the Exodus, the revelation of Yahweh through his acts ("You have seen . . . what I did"), with the covenant, which is the foundation of Yahweh's revelation through his Word ("If only you will listen to me and keep my covenant"). The Exodus is the point of departure of Israel's existence, the foundation of her peoplehood established at Sinai. This is the meaning of the preface to the Ten Commandments in Exodus 20:2: "I am the Lord your God who brought you out of Egypt, out of the land of slavery." *Therefore,* "you shall have no other god to set against me" (20:3 NEB).

The covenant is an invitation to Israel to enter into a responsible relationship with the God of the Exodus wherein he will be her God and she his "special possession." This invitation places Israel in a situation of decision, because the covenant requires obedience to the will of Yahweh. To accept the covenant means that Israel must now live as Yahweh's liberated people, becoming the embodiment of freedom made possible through his freeing presence. The covenant not only places upon Israel the responsibility of accepting the absolute sovereignty of Yahweh as defined in the first commandment; it also requires Israel to treat the weak in her midst as Yahweh has treated her. This is the significance of the apodictic laws in the Covenant Code:

> You shall not wrong a stranger or oppress him;
> for you were strangers in the land of Egypt.
> (Exodus 22:21; see also 23:9 RSV)

> You shall not ill-treat any widow or fatherless child.
> If you do, be sure that I will listen if they appeal to me;
> My anger will be roused and I will kill you with the
> sword.
> (Exodus 22:23–24 NEB)

In the Exodus-Sinai tradition Yahweh is disclosed as the God of history, whose revelation is identical with his power to liberate the oppressed. There is no knowledge of Yahweh except through his political activity on behalf of the weak and helpless of the land. This is the significance of Yahweh's contest with Pharaoh, the plagues against Egypt, and the "hardening" of Pharaoh's heart. The biblical writer wishes to emphasize that Israel's liberation came not from her own strength but solely from the power of Yahweh, who completely controls history.

God's election of oppressed Israelites has unavoidable implications for the doing of theology. If God had chosen as his "holy nation" the Egyptian slave-masters instead of the Israelite slaves, then a completely different kind of God would have been revealed. Thus Israel's election cannot be separated from her servitude and liberation. Here God discloses that he is the God of history whose will is identical with the liberation of the oppressed from social and political bondage. The doing of theology, therefore, on the basis of the revelation of Yahweh, must involve the politics which takes its stand with the poor and against the rich. Indeed, theology ceases to be a theology of the Exodus-Sinai tradition when it fails to see Yahweh as unquestionably in control of history, vindicating the weak against the strong.

The Old Testament story does not end with the Exodus and the gift of the covenant. Yahweh does not withdraw from his people's history. On the contrary, the covenant means that Yahweh's liberating presence continues to sustain the people through the wilderness to the Promised Land. And when Israel failed to keep her side of the covenant by running after the gods of Canaan, Yahweh did not reject his people. His will to save and to make them free was a constituent of his being with them. God's grace could not be destroyed by Israel's disobedience.

The conflict between grace and disobedience was escalated when Israel became a monarchy, for the rulers often forgot the Exodus-Sinai experience and the function of the King in Israel. It is within this social and political context that we ought to understand the rise of prophecy. The prophets were messengers of Yahweh who gave God's Word to the people, reminding them of God's deliverance and covenant which brought the community into existence. They also proclaimed Yahweh's future activity of judgment and renewal that was about to burst into the present.

The prophets gave a large measure of their addresses to proclaiming the emptiness and tragedy of Israel's present existence. The tragedy of Israel is due to her failure to remember the Exodus-Sinai tradition. As Amos said,

> It was I who brought you up from the land of Egypt,
> I who led you in the wilderness forty years,
>   to take possession of the land of the Amorites.
>
> (2:10 NEB)

Because Israel often failed to live on the basis of God's saving-event of the Exodus, she also failed to understand the significance of Yahweh's imminent eschatological judgment. Amos proclaimed the connection between the past and the future as they both invaded Israel's present moment.

> For you alone have I cared
> among all the nations of the world;
> therefore I will punish you
> for all your iniquities.
>
> (Amos 3:2 NEB)

What was Israel's sin? What did the people do to rouse the anger of their Lord? The prophets were almost unanimous in their contention that Israel disobeyed the first commandment. The people failed to recognize Yahweh's sovereignty in history, and thus began to trust their own power and the power of political alliances with other nations (Isa. 31:1). But that was not all! The disobedience of the first commandment always has consequences in the social life of the community. Israel, therefore, began to oppress the weak and the poor in their own community. That was why Amos said that "the Lord has sworn by his holiness that your time is coming," because you "grind the destitute and plunder the humble" (4:2; 8:4 NEB). Even though Yahweh "cared for you in the wilderness, in a land of burning heat, as if you were in a pasture," you "forgot [him]," becoming "an oppressor trampling on justice, doggedly pursuing what is worthless" (Hosea 13:5–6; 5:11 NEB). Because Yahweh will not permit the triumph of evil, Israelites must be punished for their wrong doings.

According to Amos and Hosea, Israel will be punished because the people do not "practice loyalty and justice" (Hosea 12:6 NEB), but rather "have turned into venom the process of the law and justice itself into poison" (Amos 6:12 NEB). They " 'buy the poor for silver and the destitute for a pair of shoes[.]' The Lord has sworn by the pride of Jacob: I will never forget any of their doings."

> Shall not the earth shake for this?
> Shall not all who live on it grieve?
> All earth shall surge and seethe like the Nile
> and subside like the river of Egypt.
>
> Did I not bring Israel up from Egypt,
> the Philistines from Captor, the Aramaeans from Kir?
> Behold, I, the Lord God,
> have my eyes on this sinful kingdom,
> and I will wipe it off the face of the earth.
>
> (Amos 8:6–8; 9:7–8 NEB)

We may shudder at the anger of Yahweh as voiced in the prophecy of Amos and say that the latter lacks tender mercy found in Hosea. Nevertheless God's mercy can never invalidate his will for justice. There is no divine grace in the

Old Testament (or in the New Testament) that is bestowed on oppressors at
the expense of the suffering of the poor. The theme of justice and Yahweh's
special concern for the poor and the widows have a central place in Israelite
prophecy. Thus Jeremiah:

> For among my people there are wicked men, . . .
> Their houses are full of fraud,
>   as a cage is full of birds.
> They grow rich and grand,
>   bloated and rancorous;
> their thoughts are all of evil,
>   and they refuse to do justice,
> the claims of the orphan they do not put right
> nor do they grant justice to the poor.
>
> (5:26–28 NEB)

And Micah:

> God has told you what is good;
>   and what is it that the Lord asks of you?
> Only to act justly, to love loyalty,
> to walk wisely before your God.
>
> (6:8 NEB)

The emphasis upon justice for the poor is present even in a prophet like
Isaiah of Jerusalem, for whom David's reign, rather than the Exodus, is the
significant act of deliverance. According to Isaiah, "Yahweh bound himself by
a covenant oath to David, promising to preserve the Davidic line to spare the
Davidic kingdom 'for the sake of my servant David' . . . (Isaiah 37:35; see 2
Sam. 7)."[2] Isaiah thus represents what scholars designate as the David-Zion
tradition. Yet Isaiah, in perfect solidarity with the prophets of the Mosaic
tradition, proclaimed that Yahweh is the God of justice who sides with the
weak against the strong.

> Put away the evil of your deeds,
>   away out of my sight.
> Cease to do evil and learn to do right,
> pursue justice and champion the oppressed;
> give the orphan his rights, plead the
>   widow's cause.
>
> (1:16–17 NEB)

In Israel, only Yahweh is King:

> For the Lord our judge, the Lord our law-giver,
> the Lord our king—he himself will save us.
>> (Isaiah 33:22 NEB)

The function of the human king in Israel is to be Yahweh's servant, executing justice in his name. "The King is God's son . . . He is commissioned to rule by God himself, he governs with perfect justice and wisdom, he is the great benefactor and shepherd of his people. . . ."[3] As Yahweh's son by adoption (Ps. 2:7), the king is enthroned to rescue the needy from their rich oppressors, the distressed who have no protector.

> May he have pity on the needy and the poor,
> deliver the poor from death;
> may he redeem them from oppression and violence
> and may their blood be precious in his eyes.
>> (Psalm 72:12–14 NEB)

The poor are Yahweh's own, his special possession. These are the people the divine has called into being for freedom. Therefore as the sovereign King of Israel whose existence is dependent upon God's saving power, Yahweh judges Israel in the light of their treatment of the poor. The indictment is severe.

> The Lord comes forward to argue his case
> and stands to judge his people.
> The Lord opens the indictment
> against the elders of his people and their officers:
>
> They have ravaged the vineyard,
> and the spoils of the poor are in your houses.
> Is it nothing to you that you crush my people
> and grind the faces of the poor?
>> (Isaiah 3:13–15 NEB)

It is a fact: In almost every scene of the Old Testament drama of salvation, the poor are defended against the rich, the weak against the strong. Yahweh is the God of the oppressed whose revelation is identical with their liberation from bondage. Even in the wisdom literature where the sages seem to be unaware of Israel's saving history, God's concern for the poor is nonetheless emphasized.

> He who is generous to the poor lends to the Lord.
>> (Proverbs 19:17 NEB)

> He who oppresses the poor insults his Maker;
> he who is generous to the needy honors him.
>> (Proverbs 14:13 NEB)

Like Moses and the prophets, the wise man is concerned for the orphan:

> Do not move the ancient boundary-stone
> or encroach on the land of orphans:
> they have a powerful guardian
> who will take their cause against you.
>
> (Proverbs 23:10–11 NEB)

If theological speech is based on the traditions of the Old Testament, then it must heed their unanimous testimony to Yahweh's commitment to justice for the poor and the weak. Accordingly it cannot avoid the risk of taking sides in politics, and the side that theology must take is disclosed in the side that Yahweh has already taken. Any other side, whether it be with the oppressors or the side of neutrality (which is nothing but a camouflaged identification with the rulers), is unbiblical. If theology does not side with the poor, then it cannot speak for Yahweh who is the God of the poor.

As the Old Testament story continues, we see that the people of Israel did not listen to the voice of prophecy. Thus they went into exile—the Northern Kingdom in 722 B.C. and the Southern Kingdom of Judah in 597 B.C. and 587 B.C. The experience of exile was a shattering event for Israel. "They believed that Yahweh had manifested his lordship in Palestine; but could he be worshiped in a strange land where other gods seemed to be in control?"[4]

> By the rivers of Babylon we sat down and wept
> when we remembered Zion.
> There on the willow-trees
> we hung up our harps,
> for there those who carried us off
> demanded music and singing,
> and our captors called on us to be merry:
> 'Sing us one of the songs of Zion.'
> How could we sing the Lord's song
> in a foreign land?
>
> (Psalm 137 NEB)

It was in the midst of Israel's despair that prophecy began to strike a new note. Jeremiah began to speak of the new covenant (31:31–34) and Ezekiel of a new heart and a new spirit (36:26). And then there was the voice of the unknown prophet who began by proclaiming:

> Comfort, comfort my people;
> —it is the voice of your God;
> speak tenderly to Jerusalem
> and tell her this,
> that she has fulfilled her term of bondage,

and that her penalty is paid;
she has received at the Lord's hand
double measure for all her sins.
(Isaiah 40:1–2 NEB)

Again Yahweh revealed himself as the deliverer of the weak and defenseless Israel. This was Israel's second Exodus, and like the first it was due exclusively to the power of Yahweh overwhelming those who asserted their power against his people.

On the people's return to their homeland there was the rebuilding of the Temple and the rededication of the community to the obedience of the Law. But Israel's story logically does not end with the Old Testament. If Yahweh is to keep his promise to bring freedom, then the Old Testament cannot be the end of Yahweh's drama with Israel. The Old Testament pushes beyond itself to an expected future event which Christians say happened in Jesus Christ.

The Social Context of Divine Revelation in the New Testament

Christians believe that the Old Testament story of salvation is continued in the New Testament. Indeed, they affirm that the New Testament is the witness to the fulfillment of God's drama of salvation begun with Israel's liberation from Egypt. This view is expressed in the New Testament itself: "Do not suppose that I have come to abolish the Law and the prophets," says the Matthean Jesus. "I did not come to abolish, but to complete" (5:17 NEB). Without exception, the New Testament writers believe that the God present in Jesus is none other than the God of Abraham, Isaac, and Jacob, and that through the divine act in the man from Nazareth something radically new has happened. On the one hand, Jesus is the continuation of the Law and the prophets; but on the other, he is the inauguration of a completely new age, and his words and deeds are signs of its imminent coming.

The Gospels according to Matthew and Luke begin the Jesus-story with his birth in Bethlehem. Although most New Testament scholars rightly question the historicity of these two apparently independent accounts, both sources (often designated "L" and "M") nonetheless reflect accurately the character of the early church's memory of the historical Jesus. Continuing the Exodus-Sinai and David-Zion traditions in which there is a special connection between divine revelation and the poor, the early church remembered Jesus' historical person as exemplifying the same character. That character, they concluded, must have been present in his birth. This is the significance of the birth stories in Matthew and Luke, the Son of God Christology in Mark, and the Fourth Gospel's contention that "When all things began, the Word already was" (1:1 NEB). The four Gospels intend to express divine purpose; and the content of the purpose is disclosed clearly in the Magnificat:

His name is Holy;
his mercy sure from generation to generation
   toward those who fear him;
the deeds his own right arm has done
   disclose his might:
the arrogant of heart and mind he has put to rout,
he has brought down monarchs from their thrones,
   but the humble have been lifted high.
The hungry he has satisfied with good things,
   the rich sent empty away.

(Luke 1:49–53 NEB)

From the outset, the Gospels wish to convey that the Jesus-story is not simply a story about a good man who met an unfortunate fate. Rather, in Jesus, God is at work, telling his story and disclosing the divine plan of salvation.

The first historical reference to Jesus is his baptism by John the Baptist.[5] Whatever may be said about the messianic consciousness of Jesus at this stage in his ministry, it seems clear from the evidence of the Synoptic Gospels that something happened between Jesus and God wherein the former became aware of a special calling. The clue to the meaning of his divine election is found in "the Spirit . . . descending upon him" (Mark 1:10 NEB; cf. Matt. 3:16f.; Luke 3:21f.) and the much discussed proclamation: "Thou art my Son, my Beloved; on thee my favor rests" (Mark 1:11 NEB; cf. Matt. 3:17; Luke 3:22). The saying about the descent of the Spirit suggests Jesus' awareness of the prophetic character of his vocation as well as the presence of something entirely new in his person. This new thing was Jesus' recognition that the dawn of the time of salvation, inaugurated by the return of the Spirit, was inseparable from his person and also that this new age was identical with the liberation of the poor and the afflicted. Apparently Jesus in his own eyes was not merely a prophetic messenger like John the Baptist, who, proclaiming the advent of the coming age, stood between the old age and the new.[6] Rather through his words and deeds he became the *inaugurator* of the Kingdom, which is bound up with his person as disclosed in his identification with the poor.

The proclamation (Mark 1:11; Matt. 3:17; Luke 3:22) following the baptism supports the contention that Jesus saw a connection between his person and the dawning of the Kingdom. This proclamation is reminiscent of Psalm 2:7 and Isaiah 42:1, and it suggests Jesus' awareness of a kingship role in the context of servanthood.

'You are my son,' he said;
'this day I become your father.'

(Psalm 2:7 NEB)

Here is my servant, whom I upheld,
my chosen one in whom I delight,

I have bestowed my spirit upon him,
and he will make justice shine on the nations.

(Isaiah 42:1 NEB)

If we take this echo of Psalm 2:7 and Isaiah 42:1 as a clue to Jesus' self-understanding at baptism, then his subsequent words and deeds also become clearer. Psalm 2:7, a coronation hymn, emphasizes his role as King, who is God's representative to bring justice to the nation. Here the political note emerges in Jesus' consciousness. Isaiah 42:1 refers to the Servant of Yahweh, who brings justice by his own suffering. Jesus' synthesis of these two themes produced a new messianic image. Servanthood provides the context for exercising kingship or lordship. The King is a *Servant* who suffers on behalf of the people. He takes their pain and affliction upon himself, thereby redeeming them *from* oppression and *for* freedom. Here, then, we have the key to Jesus' understanding of his mission: *Lordship and Servanthood together, that is, the establishment of justice through suffering.*

This same theme is connected with the temptation story which follows (Luke 4:1f.; Matt. 4:1f.; cf. also Mark 1:12–13). The chief point in this narrative is not so much Jesus' rejection of the role of a "political," revolutionary messiahship (as defined by the Zealots), though that may be partly involved. Most New Testament interpreters are so quick to make that point that they miss the heart of the matter,[7] namely, *Jesus' rejection of any role that would separate him from the poor.* This story affirms that Jesus rejected such roles as wonder worker or political king, because they would separate him from the suffering of the poor, the very people he had come to liberate.

The theme of God's liberation of the poor is continued in the story of Jesus' reading in the Nazareth synagogue from the Book of Isaiah.

> The spirit of the Lord is upon me because he has anointed me,
> he has sent me to announce good news to the poor,
> to proclaim release for prisoners and recovery of sight for the
>   blind;
> to let the broken victims go free,
> to proclaim the year of the Lord's favour.
>
> (Luke 4:18–19, Isaiah 61:1–2 NEB)

After the reading, Jesus commented, "Today in your very hearing this text has come true," thus tying the promised deliverance to his own mission.

The theme appears again when John the Baptist sent his disciples to Jesus to ask of him, "Are you the one who is to come, or shall we expect another." And Jesus replied: "Go and tell John what you have seen and heard: how the blind recover their sight, the lame walk, the lepers are made clean, the deaf hear, the dead are raised to life, the poor are hearing the good news . . ." (Luke 7:22f. NEB; cf. Matt. 11:5f.). This reply echoes Isaiah 61:1–2 (the passage read at Nazareth) in combination with Isaiah 35:5ff. and 29:18f., which depict the day of salvation.[8]

> Then shall blind men's eyes be opened,
>   and the ears of the deaf unstopped.
> Then shall the lame man leap like a deer,
>   and the tongue of the dumb shout aloud;
> for water springs up in the wilderness,
> and torrents flow in dry land.
> The mirage becomes a pool,
>   the thirsty land bubbling springs . . .
>
>   (Isaiah 35:5f. NEB)

> On that day deaf men shall hear
>   when a book is read,
>   and the eyes of the blind shall see
>   out of impenetrable darkness.
> The lowly shall once again rejoice in the Lord,
>   and the poorest of men exult in the Holy One of Israel.
> The ruthless shall be no more, the arrogant shall cease to
>   be;
>   those who are quick to see mischief,
>   those who charge others with a sin
> or lay traps for him who brings the wrongdoer into court
> or by falsehood deny justice to the righteous —
>   all these shall be exterminated.
>
>   (Isaiah 29:18–21 NEB)

The reply to John's disciples, like the saying in the Nazareth synagogue, shows that Jesus understood his person and work as the inauguration of the new age, which is identical with the freedom for the oppressed and health for the sick. Accordingly any understanding of the Kingdom in Jesus' teachings that fails to make the poor and their liberation its point of departure is a contradiction of Jesus' presence.

Jesus' conquest of Satan and the demons also carries out the theme of the liberation of the poor. "If it is by the finger of God that I drive out the devils, then be sure that the kingdom of God has already come upon you" (Luke 11:20 NEB). Jesus' power to exorcise demons is the sine qua non of the appearance of the Kingdom, because freedom for the oppressed can come about only by overcoming the forces of evil. Jesus saw this victory already in hand after his disciples returned from the mission of the Seventy: "I watched how Satan fell, like lightning, out of the sky" (Luke 10:18 NEB).

The reference to Satan and demons is not simply an outmoded first-century worldview that is objectionable to twentieth-century science. The issue is much more complex than that! Bultmann and his program of demythologization notwithstanding, the *offense* of the gospel is and ought to be located precisely at the point where our confidence in modern knowledge encounters the New Testament message, namely, in Jesus' liberating exorcisms. Unlike the fundamentalists, I am not contending that the biblical cosmology ought to replace contemporary science in college classrooms. Rather I intend to make the *theological* point that the "scandal" (*skandalon,* stumbling-block) is no different for us today than for the people who encountered Jesus in the first century. It is that the exorcisms disclose that God in Jesus has brought liberation to the poor and the wretched of the land, and that liberation is none other than the overthrow of everything that is against the fulfillment of their humanity. The scandal is that the gospel means liberation, that this liberation comes to the poor, and that it gives them the strength and the courage to break the conditions of servitude. This is what the Incarnation means. God in Christ comes to the weak and helpless, and becomes one with them, taking their condition of oppression as his own and thus transforms their slave-existence into a liberated existence.

To locate the scandal of the Jesus-story at the point of God's liberation of the poor and in opposition to Rudolf Bultmann's emphasis on human self-understanding, means that the gospel comes not only as a gift but that the acceptance of the gift of freedom transforms our perception of our social and political existence. The New Testament gospel of liberation turns our priority system upside down and demands that we fight for the freedom of those in captivity. This message of liberation cannot appeal to those who profit from the imprisonment of others but only to slaves who strive against unauthorized power. The gospel of liberation is *bad news* to all oppressors, because they have defined their "freedom" in terms of the slavery of others. Only the poor and the wretched who have been victims of evil and injustice can understand what Jesus meant when he said: "Come to me, all whose work is hard, whose load is heavy; and I will give you relief. Bend your neck to my yoke, and learn from me, for I am gentle and humble-hearted; and your souls will find relief. For my yoke is good to bear, my load is light" (Matt. 11:28–30 NEB).

The gospel will always be an offense to the rich and the powerful, because it is the death of their riches and power. That was why the man from the ruling class could not follow Jesus. The price was too high: "Sell everything you have and distribute it to the poor, and you will have riches in heaven; and come, follow me" (Luke 18:22 NEB). This man was incapable of separating himself from his commitment to his possessions. There were others who had similar problems. They could not follow Jesus because they had priorities higher than the gospel of liberation for the poor. There was the person who wanted to bury his father and another who wanted to say good-bye to the people at home (Luke 9:59f.). They, like the five foolish girls in the parable of Matthew 25:1f., did not recognize the *urgency* of the hour nor the *priority* inherent in the acceptance of the coming kingdom. Jesus expressed the claim of the kingdom in radical terms: "If anyone comes to me and does not hate his father and mother,

Baptisms
Beatitudes
Parables
Prayers
Law
Grace

James H. Cone

wife and children, brothers and sisters, even his own life, he cannot be a disciple of mine" (Luke 1:26 NEB).

Because most biblical scholars are the descendants of the advantaged class, it is to be expected that they would minimize Jesus' gospel of liberation for the poor by interpreting poverty as a spiritual condition unrelated to social and political phenomena. But a careful reading of the New Testament shows that the poor of whom Jesus spoke were not primarily (if at all) those who are spiritually poor as suggested in Matthew 5:3. Rather, as the Lukan tradition shows, these people are "those who are really poor, . . . those who are really hungry, who really weep and are persecuted."9 The poor are the oppressed and the afflicted, those who cannot defend themselves against the powerful. They are the least and the last, the hungry and the thirsty, the unclothed and the strangers, the sick and the captives. It is for these little ones that the gospel is preached and for whom liberation has come in the words and deeds of Jesus.

It is important to point out that Jesus does not promise to include the poor in the kingdom *along with* others who may be rich and learned. His promise is that the kingdom belongs to the poor *alone*. This is the significance of his baptism with and life among the poor, and his contention that he "did not come to invite virtuous people, but sinners" (Mark 2:17 NEB). The first beatitude has the same emphasis: "How blest are you who are in need; the kingdom of God is yours" (Luke 6:20 NEB). Another dimension of the same theme is stressed in Luke 10:21 (cf. Matt. 11:25 NEB): "I thank thee, Father, Lord of heaven and earth, for hiding these things from the learned and wise and revealing them to the simple." In the words of Joachim Jeremias, "God does not give his revelation to learned theologians, but to the uneducated . . . ; he opens the *basileia* (kingdom) to children (Mark 10:14) and to those who can say '*Abbā*' like a child (Matthew 10:3)."10 God's kingdom is for the bad characters, the outcasts, and the weak, but not for the self-designated righteous people. "Publicans and prostitutes will enter the *basileia* of God, and not you" (Matt. 21:31).11 Here the gospel, by the very definition of its liberating character, *excludes* those who stand outside the social existence of the poor.

The centrality of the New Testament emphasis on God's liberation of the poor is the key to its continuity and discontinuity with the Old Testament message. The continuity is obvious: Just as the Mosaic and David-Zion traditions, the prophetic and the wisdom literature focus on the divine right of the poor to be free, Jesus also defines himself as the helper and the healer of the oppressed. "Never despise one of these little ones; I tell you, they have their guardian angels in heaven, who look continually on the face of my heavenly Father" (Matt. 18:10 NEB). Jesus' life was a historical demonstration that the God of Israel wills salvation for the weak and the helpless. God hates injustice and will not tolerate the humiliation of the outcasts.

If Jesus' life with the poor reveals that the continuity between the Old and New Testaments is found in the divine will to liberate the oppressed from sociopolitical slavery, what then is the discontinuity? Or, more appropriately, in what sense does the New Testament witness take us beyond the Old and fulfill it? The new element is this: The divine freedom revealed in Jesus, as that freedom is disclosed in the cross and resurrection, is more than the freedom made possible in history. While God's freedom for the poor is not *less than* the liberation of slaves from bondage (Exodus), yet it is *more than* that historical freedom. And it is this *more* which separates the exodus from the Incarnation, the Old Testament view of the Savior as the victor in the battle and the New Testament view of the Savior as the One who "give[s] up his life as a ransom for many" (Mark 10:45 NEB). While both stress the historical freedom of the unfree, the latter transcends history and affirms a freedom not dependent on sociopolitical limitations.

Amen!

The cross and the resurrection of Jesus stand at the center of the New Testament story, without which nothing is revealed that was not already known in the Old Testament. In the light of Jesus' death and resurrection, his earthly life achieves a radical significance not otherwise possible. The cross-resurrection events mean that we now know that Jesus' ministry with the poor and the wretched was God himself effecting his will to liberate the oppressed. The Jesus story is the poor person's story, because God in Christ becomes poor and weak in order that the oppressed might become liberated from poverty and powerlessness. God becomes the victim in their place and thus transforms the condition of slavery into the battleground for the struggle of freedom. This is what Christ's resurrection means. The oppressed are freed for struggle, for battle in the pursuit of humanity.

Jesus was not simply a nice fellow who happened to like the poor. Rather his actions have their origin in God's eternal being. They represent a new vision of divine freedom, climaxed with the cross and the resurrection, wherein God breaks into history for the liberation of slaves from societal oppression. Jesus' actions represent God's will not to let his creation be destroyed by noncreative powers. The cross and the resurrection show that the freedom promised is now fully available in Jesus Christ. This is the essence of the New Testament story without which Christian theology is impossible.

Amen

Christian Theology and the Biblical Story

If, as suggested above, Christian theology exists only as its language arises out of an encounter with the biblical story, what then is the meaning of this encounter? Since the Bible consists of many traditions woven together, how does a theologian use the Bible as a source for the expression of truth without being arbitrary in selecting some traditions while ignoring others? Some critics have accused Black Theology of just that: a decided bias towards the Mosaic tradition in contrast to the David-Zion tradition, towards the Old Testament in relation to the New, and towards the prophets with little reference to the sages of Israel. These critics have a right to ask what is the hermeneutical principle of selection involved here, and how is its validity tested. What is valid and invalid hermeneutics, and how is one distinguishable from the other?

Black Theology's answer to the question of hermeneutics can be stated briefly: *The hermeneutical principle for an exegesis of the scriptures is the revelation of God in Christ as the liberator of the oppressed from social oppression and to political struggle, wherein the poor recognize that their fight against poverty and injustice is not only consistent with the gospel but is the gospel of Jesus Christ.* Jesus Christ the liberator, the helper and the healer of the wounded, is the point of departure for valid exegesis of the scriptures from a Christian perspective. Any starting point that ignores God in Christ as the liberator of the oppressed or that makes salvation as liberation secondary is ipso facto invalid and thus heretical. The test of the validity of this starting point, although dialectically related to Black cultural experience, is not found in the particularity of the oppressed culture alone. It is found in the one who freely grants us freedom when we were doomed to slavery. In God's revelation in Scripture we come to the recognition that the divine liberation of the oppressed is not determined by our perceptions but by the God of the Exodus, the prophets, and Jesus Christ who calls the oppressed into a liberated existence. Divine revelation *alone* is the test of the validity of this starting point. And if it can be shown that God as witnessed in the Scriptures is not the liberator of the oppressed, then Black Theology would have to either drop the "Christian" designation or choose another starting point.

The biblical emphasis on the social and the political character of God's revelation in history for the weak and the helpless has important implications for the task of theology today. (1) There can be no Christian theology that is not social and political. If theology is to speak about the God of Jesus who reveals himself in the struggle of the oppressed for freedom, then theology *must* also become political, speaking for the God of the poor and the oppressed.

(2) The biblical emphasis on God's continuing act of liberation in the present and future means that theology cannot merely repeat what the Bible says or what is found in a particular theological tradition. Theology must be prophetic, recognizing the *relativity* of human speech, but also that God can use human speech at a particular time for the proclamation of his Word to the suffering poor. As theologians, therefore, we must take the risk to be prophetic by doing theology in the light of those who are helpless and voiceless in the society.

(3) Theology cannot ignore the tradition. While the tradition is not the gospel, it is the bearer of an interpretation of the gospel at a particular point in time. By studying the tradition, we not only gain insight into a particular time but also into our time as the past and present meet dialectically. For only through this dialectical encounter with the tradition are we given the freedom to move beyond it.

(4) Theology is always a word about the liberation of the oppressed and the humiliated. It is a word of judgment for the oppressors and the rulers. Whenever theologians fail to make this point unmistakably clear, they are not doing Christian theology but the theology of the antichrist.

NOTES

1. *The Sociology of Knowledge* (London: Routledge and Kegan Paul, 1958), 16, 7-8. For other important works in the field see Mannheim, *Ideology and Utopia*, trans. Louis

Wirth and E. Shils (New York: Harcourt Brace and World, 1936); Berger and Luckmann, *The Social Construction of Reality* (New York: Doubleday Anchor Books, 1967); and Berger, *The Sacred Canopy* (New York: Doubleday Anchor Books, 1969).

2. Bernhard W. Anderson, *Understanding the Old Testament* (Englewood Cliffs, N. J.: Prentice-Hall, 1957), 289f.

3. Gerhard von Rad, *Old Testament Theology*, vol. 1, trans. by D. M. G. Stalker (New York: Harper & Row, 1962), 41.

4. Anderson, *Understanding the Old Testament,* 377.

5. Although few New Testament scholars question the historical validity of Jesus' baptism by John, yet the question of the accessibility of the historical Jesus has undergone much discussion in the 20th century. Since the publication of Albert Schweitzer's *The Quest of the Historical Jesus* (1906) and the rise of Form Criticism shortly thereafter, it was commonplace to hear distinctions drawn between the Jesus of history and the Christ of faith. The former referred to the person accessible to the tools of historical scholarship, and the latter to the proclamation and teachings of the early church. It was generally assumed by Rudolf Bultmann that practically nothing can be known of the Jesus of history (cf. his *Jesus and the Word,* trans. by L. P. Smith and E. H. Lantera [New York: Charles Scribner's Sons, 1934], where he says: "I do indeed think that we can now know almost nothing concerning the personality of Jesus" [p. 8].). That view tended to dominate New Testament scholarship in Germany until the 1950's when many of Bultmann's followers began to speak of the new quest for the historical Jesus. These persons (who included Ernst Käsemann, Gunther Bornkamm, Hans Conzelmann and Ernst Fuchs) recognized that Bultmann's historical skepticism not only had scientific flaws but also, and more importantly, threatened the foundation of the faith itself. Käsemann expressed it well: "Only if Jesus' proclamation decisively coincides with the proclamation about Jesus is it understandable, reasonable, and necessary that the Christian kerygma in the New Testament conceals the message of Jesus; only then is the resurrected Jesus the historical Jesus. From this perspective we are required, precisely as theologians, to inquire behind Easter. ... By this means we shall learn whether he stands behind the word of his church or not, whether the Christian kerygma is a myth that can be detached from his word and from himself or whether it binds us historically and insolubly to him" (cited in Wolfhart Pannenberg, *Jesus — God and Man,* trans. by L. L. Wilkins and D. A. Priebe [Philadelphia: Westminster Press, 1968], p. 56). For a detailed discussion of this problem, see James Robinson, *The New Quest of the Historical Jesus* (London: SCM Press, Ltd., 1959); also Hugh Anderson, *Jesus and Christian Origins* (New York: Oxford University Press, 1964).

It should be made clear that this essay is being written on the assumption that there is no radical distinction between the Jesus of history and the Christ of faith. I have discussed elsewhere this issue and have located the indispensable historical datum (without which the gospel is no longer valid) as Jesus' identification with the oppressed (*A Black Theology of Liberation,* Chapter VI). The key, therefore, to the baptism incident (and with others reported in the Gospels) for our purposes is not only "Did it really happen?" but rather "What is the theological meaning embedded in it?" Although history *qua* is the place where revelation happens, it is not revelation. Revelation is the disclosure of God in the social context of history but is not identical with it. Since I contend that the Jesus of the Gospels cannot be separated from the "real" Jesus and have discussed the reasons for this conclusion elsewhere, there is no need here to enter into the critical discussion about the old and new quests for the historical Jesus. The text of the New Testament serves not only as a theological check on what we theologians are permitted to do with Jesus; but it also serves as a *historical* check against contemporary historians.

6. There has been much discussion about Jesus' probable attitude toward John the Baptist. Jesus certainly saw his ministry connected with John's, and there is evidence from the Fourth Gospel that he received his first disciples from John (1:35-39). For a discussion of John's relation to Jesus, see Joachim Jeremias, *New Testament Theology,* trans. by John Bowden (New York: Charles Scribner's Sons, 1971), 43ff.

7. One of the few exceptions is Ernst Käsemann whose writings disclose an unusual sensitivity to the use of the gospel as an opiate of the oppressed. "Every word, every deed, every demonstration is a denial of our Lord and ourselves, unless we test them from the point of view of whether they are opium of the people, or can be regarded and abused as such." *Jesus Means Freedom,* trans. by Frank Clarke (London: SCM Press, 1969), 13. See also his *New Testament Questions of Today,* trans. by W. J. Montague (Philadelphia: Fortress Press, 1969); *Perspectives On Paul,* trans. by Margaret Kohl (Philadelphia: Fortress Press, 1971.)

8. See Jeremias, *New Testament Theology,* 103f.

9. Ibid., 112.

10. Ibid., 116.

11. For the exegetical support of the exclusive interpretation of Matthew 21:31, see Jeremias, *New Testament Theology,* 117. "The *proagousin 'umas* . . . does not denote a priority in time, but an exclusive displacement of the others."

13

BIBLICAL THEOLOGY AND BLACK THEOLOGY

Robert A. Bennett

I. Introduction

It is to the credit of black theologians such as James Cone and J. Deotis Roberts that the black religious experience is beginning to receive a serious hearing within the theological curriculum. In some sense it is incorrect to equate black studies in seminaries with black studies programs in the university, for this investigation has a more pervasive role within the theological curriculum than in the university. A college black studies program can be contained within a given department, no matter how diverse the offerings within that department, but black studies within theological education cannot be so contained. Rightly understood as being revelatory the black religious experience must pervade Bible and church history no less than ethics, theology, and practical theology.[1] Therefore, this paper has as its special concern the place of black theology within the area of scripture and vice-versa. Furthermore, of the two major exponents of this emerging discipline a profitable dialogue can take place with James Cone, who has more explicitly tackled the matter of Bible content and interpretation for his theological position than has J. Deotis Roberts.

No doubt because of criticism of aspects of *Black Theology of Liberation* (1970), Cone has made a fuller statement of his approach to scripture in "Biblical Revelation and Social Existence," chapter 4 of his *God of the Oppressed* (1975). Here he states his position with regard to an interpretative principle for the Bible:

Robert A. Bennett is Professor of Old Testament at Episcopal Divinity School in Cambridge. This essay originally appeared in *The Journal of the Interdenominational Theological Center* 3 (Spring 1976).

The hermeneutical principle for an exegesis of the scriptures is the revelation of God in Christ as the liberator of the oppressed from social
oppression and to political struggle. . . .[2]

It is clear in this chapter that Cone is laying out his case for a *Heilsgeschichte*
pointing toward liberation of the oppressed, while at the same time broadening
his biblical base to include other elements such as those found in wisdom and
messianic texts that also support this hermeneutic of liberation. Thus, not only
the parade examples of Moses-Exodus and prophetic texts speaking of God's
will toward justice but also David-Zion and Psalter hymnic and even wisdom
sayings on demands for societal justice are marshaled (Ps. 72:12–14, Isa. 33:22,
Prov. 14:13 and 23:10–11). Great emphasis is placed on "The Social Context
of Divine Revelation in the New Testament," in which section the case is made
for Jesus' plan for the Kingdom as including liberation of the poor and afflicted.
A very long footnote restates Cone's refusal to separate the Jesus of history
from the Christ of faith, no doubt in rebuttal of the charge of being overly
Barthian and indifferent to history.[3] In any event, Cone's is the fullest explication of an identifiable biblical stance of the black theologians.

William Jones, *Is God a White Racist?* (1973), in what he calls a "Preamble
to Black Theology," takes the problem of theodicy, namely the why of black
suffering, as a controlling category for any black theology. His use of scripture
is limited to the issue of apparently unmerited suffering and clearly shows his
own humanistic bent or bias. Albert Cleage, *The Black Messiah* (1969), handles
numerous passages but with the aim of establishing that the Hebrews were
black. Major Jones, *Black Awareness* (1971), emphasizing the relevance of the
theology of hope for a discouraged black community, and J. Deotis Roberts,
Liberation and Reconciliation (1971) and *A Black Political Theology* (1974),
emphasizing black personhood and reconciliation, both focus on New Testament calls to love and to be reconciled. In none of these leading representatives
of black theology is there as conscious a dealing with principles of scripture
and its interpretation. The Bible is used, is indeed vital to the presentation of
argument, but no real effort is given to stating a stance for interpretation as
Cone has done in his writings, particularly now in *God of the Oppressed*. For
this reason Cone will loom larger in this effort to establish a more incisive
dialogue between biblical theology and black theology.

The disciplines of biblical theology and black theology are both at critical
positions in their development. Black theology has emerged to the point where
it can truly be in dialogue with itself and with other kindred efforts, as in South
American liberation theology, African theology (both in the name of indigenization and liberation), and feminist perspectives in theology.[4] As for within
black theology, there is internal debate on questions such as the place of scripture, the politically aggressive versus the more theologically reflective emphasis,
or the place of blackness as a racial or theological symbol, the narrower definition or the more universally applicable one. Biblical theology itself has passed
from a stage of confidence, as reflected in Krister Stendahl's classic statement

in behalf of the descriptive approach (*IDB*, 1962), to one of reappraisal after the trenchant criticism of James Barr, from *Old and New in Interpretation* (1966) to *The Bible in the Modern World* (1973), and Brevard Childs, *Biblical Theology in Crisis* (1970). The major thrust of the critique concerns hermeneutics and the forging of links between what the Bible meant then (descriptive approach) and what it means today (contemporary proclamation), the latter of which is too often ignored or given too little attention. It is at this point, where biblical theology seeks to be able to deal with biblical interpretation and even proclamation, that it must engage and be engaged by black theology whose avowed purpose is to do "God talk" from a contemporary (black) perspective. It is overly simplistic to say that biblical theology needs issues and that black theology needs biblical sophistication, but it is not too far from the mark to suggest that each can learn from the other at this critical juncture of their careers.

II. Issues in Biblical Theology Today

It is possible for a particularly fruitful and mutually beneficial dialogue to take place. In biblical theology the search seems to be shifting from efforts to find the "center of biblical theology" to that of bridging the gap between what the text "meant" then and what it "means" today. At the same time black theology is beginning to examine more closely the relevance of the scripture for its agenda of interpreting the reality of God for black Americans today. What is particularly interesting is the quest within both disciplines to recognize the dialectical relationship between the contemporary community of faith and the text, that is, an increasing recognition of the validity of later generations' appropriation and interpretation of scripture with regard to their own needs and understanding of God's will in their time. In biblical theology this is apparently the thrust of scholars such as James Sanders in a call for canonical criticism or even midrash criticism and the provocative exegesis and comment of Brevard Childs, which give new import to the subsequent interpretations of the text up to the present hearers of the word.[5] Similarly, the debate between Cone and Roberts over the value of christological proclamation for the contemporary black struggle focuses on how the word is most potently communicated to that community of faith called the black church. An attendant discussion, closely related to that over canon, is also being carried out as to whether the biblical text is the sole vehicle for discerning the divine will for black folk today. Here J. Deotis Roberts is joined by those with a more historical and sociological interest such as Charles Long, Gayraud Wilmore, and Vincent Harding, who argue for a broader theological agenda than James Cone is ready to allow.[6] Within both disciplines the discussion centers on the text or the texts and the validity of later interpretations given them by the faithful.

Surveys of the history and recent developments within biblical theology are readily available, such as those given by Robert Dentan, *Preface to Old Testament Theology* (rev. ed., 1961), Norman Porteous, "Old Testament Theology," in H. H. Rowley, ed., *The Old Testament and Modern Study* (1951), and both

Otto Betz and Krister Stendahl articles on "Biblical Theology" in *Interpreter's Dictionary of the Bible* (1962). What emerges from these studies is the fact of the uneasy merging of biblical study and theological discourse into a discipline committed to exposition of scripture in theological categories. The marriage is between content of the Bible and the fitting of the same into the structures of dogmatic theology—which includes philosophical and cultural matter—aimed at the church's contemporary needs. It was the late eighteenth-century theologian, Johann Philipp Gabler, who called for the clear distinction between biblical theology which was historical in character, setting forth what the biblical writers said about God, and dogmatic theology which was more didactic and concerned with what the contemporary age thought about God. Yet even in this distinction, which holds sway to the present, it is clear that a dialectic relationship exists between the two. Each is in dialogue with and exerting some influence upon the other. We are only lately aware of the reciprocal nature of the dialogue, namely, how our thought is shaped by scripture and how our perceptions of what the sacred writers thought reflect so much more of our own perspective than we had acknowledged. It is this new awareness of an inability to fully disrobe when, in the historical-critical process, we would rethink the thought of the ancient writer that has undermined some of the earlier confidence in the objectivity of the descriptive approach in biblical analysis. In a sense Stendahl's statement of a descriptive biblical theology repeats that of Gabler nearly two centuries earlier, for Gabler spoke of three steps which both separate and link the historical-critical task and the interpretative one: first, individual passages of scripture are examined using grammatical-historical principles; second, these texts are to be compared and contrasted with one another; third, certain general principles are formulated on the basis of this analysis. Only then, after the work of the biblical theologian is done, can the systematic theologian begin to erect his system to meet the needs of his contemporary situation. Stendahl would have the exegete (1) describe, (2) interpret, and then (3) relate the results of his historical-critical analysis of the text to his own time.[7]

How then shall biblical theology be defined once its descriptive character has been set and placed in contra-distinction to the contemporary cultural demands of dogmatic theology? While it is clear that the term does not refer to the use of scripture within theology, it continues to be debated how it refers to the theological part of biblical study. At a very minimum this discipline can be said to be "the study of the religious ideas of the Bible in their historical context."[8]

Yet even this basic definition points to a continuing discussion of the distinctiveness of biblical theology, as against a history of religion's or comparative religion's approach. Is biblical theology simply a survey of religious concepts and institutions of Israel old and new, judged vis-à-vis the ancient Near Eastern setting? Or is it something else, say, the isolation of key elements in the classic period of religious development? Dentan refers to Eichrodt's expression for this further distinction, namely, that biblical theology is concerned not with "lengthwise section" of history of religion's interest in the grasp of generic elements in the growth of a religious system but with the "cross section" in the more systematic task of describing the key, central, or most persistent elements within the religion.[9] In a sense this distinction marks the difference between the two major Old Testament theologies of this era, Eichrodt's concern for the covenant idea as central (the cross-cut) and von Rad's more lengthwise history of traditions survey. This holds for von Rad's Volume 2 analysis of the prophetic tradition as a trenchant critique of previous tradition, making that movement normative for Old Testament interpretation. Note the titles of von Rad's volumes, *The Theology of the Historical Traditions of Israel* and *The Theology of the Prophetic Traditions of Israel.*[10] In a sense we live with a dual definition of biblical theology. One definition is more concerned with a systematic treatment of key religious ideas of the scripture, often borrowing the God-Man-Sin-Redemption schema of dogmatics. Ludwig Kohler, *Old Testament Theology* (1957), is typical of this point of view. The other definition, represented by von Rad and in G. E. Wright, *The God Who Acts: Biblical Theology as Recital* (1952), interprets biblical theology more out of the matrix of Israel's historical development, tracing and highlighting the vital traditions of the people. Both views are wedded to the descriptive historical approach, but one sets forth its results in logical categories, while the other is more reportorial.[11]

The crisis in biblical theology of which Brevard Childs speaks comes not at the point of the descriptive, historical-critical approach to scripture but at the point of bridging the gap between what the text meant then and what it means for us today. The crisis is not at the point of exposition, whether one takes the cross-cut of biblical ideas using the terminology of systematics or the long-cut, being wedded to the *Heilsgeschichte* and retelling the story of God's mighty acts, but at the point of proclamation—of interpreting the text as divine command for today. The crisis comes at the point of treating the biblical passage as kerygma. The problem is hermeneutical. By what mode or what interpretative principle can the word be effectively preached? The gap between the seminary classroom and the pulpit is not readily closed by exhortation to think things through with the mind of Christ or contemplate what Jesus would do. The focusing of the biblical word on contemporary issues is not achieved by asserting that the God of scripture is active today in the church, that the salvation events are still working themselves out within the community of faith.[12] The linguistic efforts of the New Hermeneutic movement would use the historical-critical approach to free the ancient word so it could audibly be proclaimed, so that with Ebeling, "proclamation that has taken place is to become proclamation that takes place."[13]

Yet in each of these approaches to bridging the gap, there is a forced quality of exhortation without real conviction. This refers of course to mainline "liberal" as against more narrowly conservative stances with regard to biblical interpretation. Nor is there agreement as to the essential validity of either the typological or christological mode of interpreting the word, let alone that of the much maligned allegorical method. These of course primarily refer to efforts to relate the testaments—the quest for the unity of scripture—and only to a lesser degree apply to linking the divine word to contemporary concerns. Yet in the end, if the three-fold definition and role of hermeneutics as mode of translation, interpretation, and transmission is to be met, then effective use of typological or christological—and why not even allegorical?—interpretation must be used. To say God and man are the same within the Old and New Testaments and that their histories are the same means that what holds there can be applied as a span over the chasm separating this witnessing community from the biblical one. The biblical witness to God's commitment to his people, often expressed in the promise/fulfillment or way of promise schema, provides a useful key to the continuity between the then and the now of proclamation.[14]

Closely related to the hermeneutical problem is that of identifying the central or unifying theme found in the Bible, especially within the realm of Old Testament theology, that is, the key to the message of proclamation which spans the there/then and here/now communication gap. The methodological approach to doing Old Testament theology can be said to consist of two basic types. The cross section or central biblical theme type, which is often expressed in the God-Man-Salvation categories of systematic theology, is represented in Eichrodt's focusing on covenant and the God-People, God-World, and God-Man schema. The long cut or salvation history (acts of God) type, which shuns external logical categories for a simple recital of events, is championed by von Rad, who can be said to be writing on the "theologies" of the Old Testament in his dependence on the tradition-history approach. These representative modes of approaching the text can also be characterized as defining the internal unity of scripture as either "word" (idea or concept of covenant) or as "event" (process of salvation history).

Gerhard Hasel calls attention to the fact that neither focus alone can encompass the breadth of the biblical witness, for as covenant or election ideology cannot adequately handle the testimony to God's universal lordship, neither can any event-centered schema permit the non-*Heilsgeschichte* (as Psalms, Wisdom) portion of scripture to speak. Hasel questions whether the manifold nature of the Old Testament testimony can be systematized, even in a dual use of word and event "center," for both modes of approach represent what he calls an "unconscious philosophical-speculative premise."[15]

Hasel argues against seeking any center superimposed on the dynamic of growth, as represented in the biblical witness to "diverse and manifold encounters between God and man" over such a long period. Hasel would break the impasse in the search for a single unifying "center" in Old Testament theology by focusing on the dynamic encounter between God and man, where God becomes the center of both word and event. The emphasis is on God as a dynamic, unifying core rather than on any form of static organizing principle. The critique of both Barr and Childs against OT theology as it is pursued today points to the lack of any agreed upon unity, and those which are proffered fail most noticeably to deal adequately with the wisdom tradition.[16] We shall return to this question as it affects black theology's use of the Old Testament, especially in the area of the scope of the divine-human encounter.

Particularly intriguing are recent suggestions by Childs and Sanders that more attention be given the process of reaction and selection of the biblical material by the initial communities of faith.[17] Tradition criticism, which traces the process of selecting and linking traditions, and canonical criticism—if such can be looked upon as a distinct discipline, which focuses on the final selection process giving us our scripture, both acknowledge a dialectic process at work between inspired word and community of faith. Could not the reciprocal relationship apparently at work in the midrashic and canonical process give some hint of a vital relationship which continues to be at work between church and scripture? Instead of looking for an elusive central unifying message in scripture and then in dismay being brought to a concept such as that of a canon within a canon in order to separate wheat from chaff, cannot the dynamic process of scripture's growth itself be instructive of the biblical message? As in earlier debates over the nature of revelation as to whether it concerned propositional truth about God or was a process of divine self-revelation, so in this area of discussion it would be useful to shift emphasis away from unifying principle(s) toward the dynamic of the divine-human encounter itself. The focus then would be on the formation of scripture and the community's relationship to it throughout the total process. This is also to say that despite the passage of time, later generations such as ours would continue to stand in a dynamic relationship with the sacred text. Tradition-history points up the very long process by which the received text emerged, the palimpsest idea of subsequent generations rearranging and adding to received traditions. A look at the evolution of canon reveals the criteria and motives for the final fixing of the sacred story. What emerges is a mixture of theological-political-existential motives and criteria for such significant shifts of emphasis as in the movement from

(a) Hexateuch (Exodus-Sinai-Conquest plus Promise to Fathers) to (b) Tetrateuch and Deuteronomic History (Promise-Exodus-Sinai plus Creation) now with Conquest-Kingdom(s) to (c) Pentateuch (Creation-Promise-Exodus-Sinai-Wilderness) and Prophets (Conquest-Kingdoms plus Prophets).

James Sanders, *Torah and Canon* (1972), addresses this issue, treating as well the Writings, that often neglected final portion of the tripartite canon of the Hebrew Bible. Crisis situations—all involving oppression from without—forced upon the community a new relationship vis-à-vis the traditions, a new reading and a new ordering of the story of God's dealing with his people.

E. A. Speiser has written cogently of Israel's election to be both "nation" (*goy/ethnos*) and "people" (*'am/laos*).[18] Thus, it is the threat to the socio-political configuration that poses the trauma of lost identity in the fall of the northern kingdom (impetus for Deuteronomic effort), the fall of Jerusalem and Exile (impetus for Priestly and Prophetic work), and the Restoration adjustment within the Persian empire (formation of incipient Law-Prophets-Writings canon). This is to say that canonical process reflected both political and spiritual realities of the day and, further, that this ought not to be viewed as mere historical accident or contingency but rather as itself part and parcel of the divine-human encounter that makes up the scripture. Saving word and saving event that emerge from Sinai covenant and exodus liberation (also prophetic word and Zion—"Day of Yahweh" event) must also be expanded to include these moments of trauma when a still newer and deeper awareness of God's self-revelation led to re-readings and adjustments of the sacred traditions, to say nothing of several additions to the text from Restoration literature. The discovery and interpretation of the literature at Qumran points not only to the fluid nature of canon near the turn of the millennium but also to the role of questions of identity during oppression in determining what is held to be "sacred," whether ancient or newly created.[19] Though the person of Jesus is central to the New Testament canonical process, similar factors seem to have given impetus to gathering the Epistles and the creation of the Apocalypse of John, the latter of which parallels Daniel as a punctuation mark for the canon. Though the question of adding to or subtracting from the received canon has not been argued with success, it is clear that subsequent generations of the church (and synagogue) have approached the scripture with different questions from age to age; and they have been rewarded with direction and power appropriate to that age or situation. The Patristic era was shaped by its reading of the text but also brought new ideas to it in its use of philosophical concepts. Protestant Reformation and Bible are yoked together, with subsequent interpretation being marked by questions put to the text by Calvin and Luther. Today two groups profoundly shaped by a new encounter with the Bible are the Catholic Church and the black church, the one more recently after the freeing encyclical *Divino Afflante Spiritu* (1943), the other in its recaption of the word in bondage.[20]

III. The Bible in Black Theology Today

It is at this point where Bible and people encounter one another, the hermeneutical nexus, that biblical theology and black theology must begin their dialogue. Begin is the word because the ensuing interchange will pass beyond hermeneutics to touch the manner in which the exegete performs his descriptive task and the theologian forms his statement on the reality of God in life today. As stated at the beginning, this paper more directly concerns the black theologian, particularly as he engages the theological community. This is because the black religious experience seen as revelatory has a pervasive role within the theological curriculum and hence cannot be relegated to a few electives in church history and perhaps homiletics or pastoral theology. The subject matter of black theology rightfully touches on the entire curriculum—Bible, history, theology, ethics, pastoral theology—and is of consequence for black and white alike. The black theologian will also be touched by biblical theology because his special constituency, the black church, has a unique relationship with holy scripture. Like the biblical community, this community of faith met its lord in a very long moment of crisis. A very special link was forged during bondage between the God of scripture and the African slave bereft of every other form of identity—homeland, language, religion, kinship. His new life became marked by hope and a profound trust that the God of his enslaver would bring deliverance. The Bible for the slave ancestors was both holy book and primer; and like the African who received the Gospel from missionaries during colonialism, the new religion was a way both to salvation and to a new socio-political existence. Thus biblical and black theologians have parallel tasks, with one moving from the past to the present meaning of scripture and the other moving between that word and the realities of the modern situation. The point is that the cultural awareness and perceptions of the black religious community, as in the Tillichian method of correlation, pose vital questions to scripture and also bring with the question some new insights (revelations) in the encounter.

Since this effort is directed more toward the black theologian than the biblical theologian, it gives more attention to what is happening in biblical theology than in black theology. Since of the theologians, James Cone is more dependent upon and more articulate about his use of scripture, most of the comment about the discourse between the disciplines will focus on his presentation. In that important chapter, "Biblical Revelation and Social Existence," in his latest work, *God of the Oppressed* (1975), Cone asserts that liberation is the key to biblical interpretation and is the (sole?) hermeneutical principle. While he has not committed himself as clearly as Cone has to a hermeneutical position, J. Deotis Roberts attacks Cone for his Barthian christological stance, which doubtlessly refers to (a) disparagement of history in the great stress on transcendence and (b) firm denial of any form of natural revelation.[21] The former puts total emphasis on kerygmatic proclamation and the crucial encounter with God's word where personal decision is required, and the latter rejects any source for revelation save that in the risen Lord. Roberts acknowledges Cone's concern for history and recognition of other forms of revelation but rejects the exclusivity of Cone's stance on blackness and salvation-liberation as limited to the oppressed. Roberts opts for a more universalistic approach and owns up to the influence of his teachers in the British neo-liberal school, John Baille and Herbert Farmer, plus his own black experience in shaping his christological statement.[22] His *A Black Political Theology* (1974) speaks of the special place of scripture in black theology but seems to take an "anthropological" approach in emphasizing the significant concepts for black selfhood, e.g., "The Bible speaks existentially to the individual black man, but it also addresses black people."[23]

There is a more than subtle shift in emphasis when Cone speaks of the Bible among the sources of black theology in *A Black Theology of Liberation* (1970): "The Bible is inspired because through reading it, a community can encounter the resurrected Christ and thus be placed in a state of freedom whereby it will be willing to risk all for earthly freedom."

In the same section of that volume, Cone argues that the link between then and now of proclamation is God as revealed in Jesus and that by reading of

God's activity in the biblical era, the black faithful can "experience" his work in the contemporary world. The meaning of scripture is not found in its words but "in its power to point beyond itself to the reality of God's revelation; and in America, that means black liberation."[24]

There is a hint of typology in this use of scripture to find patterns for God's behavior in present existence, but overriding this is Cone's emphasis on Jesus as the true revelation of God.

Using Cone as representative of black theology—not because he is typical but because he has given the clearest statement of his use of scripture—let us now have biblical and black theology converse one with the other. Some major issues within biblical theology have been exposed, so what now can be said about black theology à la James Cone? Cone takes the lengthwise view of scripture, reciting the saving acts of God for the elect community, emphasizing throughout the social context of God's decisions and activity. God chooses to free Hebrew slaves, not their oppressors; he punishes disobedient Israel for its divine and societal covenant infractions but again shows mercy toward the oppressed in the prophetic call for justice. Justice is for the poor and for the disobedient, each receiving his due. "There is no divine grace in the Old Testament (or in the New Testament) that is bestowed on oppressors at the expense of the suffering poor."[25]

Cone sees this theme as present in the royal theology and in wisdom tradition, namely, special concern and responsibility for the poor and helpless. Exile and return are seen as setting the stage for future events in Jesus Christ. Indeed the New Testament (Matthew 5:17) speaks of itself as the fulfillment of God's "drama of salvation." Cone spends some time on the Gospel accounts of Jesus and the question of history being especially careful to emphasize the historicity of Jesus and its importance in relation to the Christ of faith and the Lord's identification with the poor in his ministry.[26] The messianic role of Jesus, seen as a linking of royal and (suffering) servant themes, focuses on "the establishment of justice through suffering." It is upon this key affirmation that Cone interprets the divine mission as one of liberation for the poor and outcast. Furthermore, in this day and time the *scandal* of the Gospel is seen as just such a call for a radical transformation of our social and political existence. Cone places this at the heart of the Gospel and rejects Bultmann's emphasis on human self-understanding as emerging from the divine-human encounter. The Gospel is bad news for the privileged and good news for the oppressed. Jesus is contiguous with the Old Testament in that his life is the "historical demonstration that the God of Israel wills salvation for the weak and helpless"; he is discontiguous in that his saving grace is more than "historical freedom," that is, the incarnation goes beyond the exodus as a liberation event. The Christ event "transcends history and affirms a freedom not dependent on sociopolitical limitations."[27]

The essence of the New Testament story is that in the crucified-resurrected Lord the promised freedom is "now fully available."

Cone concludes this statement on scripture with an examination of the relationship between theology and the Bible in black theology. His statement of a hermeneutical position is made in face of a charge that black theology is too selective, ignoring vital traditions such as David-Zion and wisdom and placing one-sided emphasis on Moses and the prophets. Referring to black theology's use of scripture, he says,

> The hermeneutical principle for an exegesis of the scriptures is the revelation of God in Christ as the liberator of the oppressed from social oppression and to political struggle, wherein the poor recognize that their fight against poverty and injustice is not only consistent with the gospel but is the Gospel of Jesus Christ.[28]

Cone argues that the test of the validity of such a hermeneutic can only come from God; that is, it is to be found in revelation alone. This is to say that the principle of interpretation is given in scripture and is grasped by those for whom the liberation is intended. From this lengthwise survey of God's self-disclosure in event, Cone concludes that the Bible has a message for all of theology. Given the nature of God's self-revelation within history, theology must therefore (a) be itself social and political; (b) be prophetic, daring to speak up in behalf of the helpless; (c) be aware of and itself become a bearer of the tradition of interpretation; and (d) address a word of liberation directly to the oppressed and one of judgment to the oppressor. The encounter with scripture lays a heavy responsibility upon theology—one of reflecting the divine word in both its method and its message.

Is Cone right—some may even ask if he is serious—in such an appraisal of the theological task? Cone is here speaking about all Christian theology, not simply black theology. We will not presume to address the matter of his words to the theologian, except to wonder if his recital approach in biblical analysis can or even should be carried over into theology. Cone begins this concluding section of his paper with the statement, ". . . Christian theology exists only as its language arises out of an encounter with the biblical story. . . ."[29]

While he is aware that theology is more than simply repeating the Bible story, Cone seems to lay too heavy a weight here, to the exclusion of the task of communicating the story to the contemporary culture in the logical categories and schema through which it might fully grasp the message and begin to work out its directives.

What of the author's mode of biblical analysis and his hermeneutical principle? Here, let us venture comment and begin by saying the obvious. Cone stands squarely within the salvation-history, biblical-theology-as-recital school. But as noted above, some biblical critics are less confident today in the adequacy of such an approach for dealing with the breadth of the Bible witness. Yet it seems that Cone is sensitive to such an observation in that he has moved to include some royal and wisdom motifs in his presentation. These, however, cannot simply be added by title as it were, but must be worked into his system through an expansion of his view of the divine self-disclosure and the varied nature of the divine-human encounter. Yet just as Cone seems to be "event" oriented in his Old Testament analysis, so his New Testament survey shows more concern for a "word" orientation. Can there be such a shift from God-event in the Old to what might be called Jesus-word in the New Testament? Would not the consistent use of both word and event concepts for both testaments better describe the God-man encounter in both and provide a greater breadth of approach for the black theologian? Wisdom no less than royal-messianic themes augment the God-in-history emphasis in the whole of scripture. In any event, whether one continues the search for a "center" in biblical theology such as Cone's stance reflects or replaces this approach with one allowing for a greater diversity of the biblical encounter with God as Hasel suggests, the liberation note would continue to be essential in any resulting biblical theology. It would seem to me that the impact of black theology should be such as to prevent the liberation element being left out of any subsequent program.

The black theology of James Cone is a contemporary witness to the encounter which can take place between Bible and theology, between the then and the now of biblical meaning. Cone himself, avowedly addressing a black audience, has moved to a position calling for all of Christian theology to become so engaged. The implication is that in using the hermeneutic of liberation others will hear the same contemporary word of God now unfolding in black theology. This is an aspect of the revelatory nature of the black religious experience. The general context is that of faith addressing faith, of witness in dialogue with witness. The weakness of Cone's engagement with scripture is not so much a matter of substance as one of method. It does not follow that the "language" of theology must be that of the Bible, even if Cone agrees with von Rad's view that biblical theology is fundamentally "telling the story." The New Testament parables indicate that there are numerous ways of telling the story, the language need not in a narrow sense be the very words of the *Heilsgeschichte* or of the prophets or of the psalmist and sages. If we learn anything from Bultmann, it is that there must be a transposing of language for real communication to take place across the ages. Even for a biblically shaped and oriented community like the black community there must be a translation of the message into modern cultural and philosophical categories. One of the messages of biblical wisdom is that Israelites could communicate in what was the lingua franca of pervasive non-Yahwistic cultural forms. This is also testimony of the numerous borrowed forms within Israel's cultic corpus.

Another methodological weakness consists of the use of an assumed "center" within biblical meaning and its use as the basis of a hermeneutic approach to the whole of scripture. The question of whether there is or is not a single central concept or meaning adequate for the construction of a biblical theology is one of methodological approach. It does not affect the truth of the liberation motif and its centrality within the scriptural witness. But being conscious of methodology, of opting for a broader rather than a narrower principle for ordering the material does open up even more avenues for viewing the operation of the liberation theme within the Bible. By focusing on the variety of God's relationship with his creation, that is, with the broad scope of the divine-human encounter, the liberation concept is broadened and deepened and not limited to the *Heilsgeschichte.* Thus viewed it cannot be diluted or pushed aside for some other conceptual word or event. The cultic hymn and lament, the wisdom, prudential counsel or critique of orthodoxy, are now opened to be interpreted vis-à-vis God's will to save, and not merely as an appendage to his action in history or dim mirror image of the divine activity. Far from diverting attention from the salvation history, these otherwise non-event elements contribute both a humanizing and a mystical note to the divine-human encounter. The contribution of black theology toward a new sense of God's reality today will be enhanced by taking a broader view with regard to the core of biblical thought. In seeking a "center," such as the idea of covenant, Eichrodt's biblical theology has difficulty in speaking meaningfully about God and his world and that which falls outside the election tradition. Von Rad's theology is also marred by such an exclusive concern for credal affirmation of Yahweh-event and prophetic comment thereon that he must relegate the Writings of the Hebrew canon to a second-class status ("Israel's Response") of something less than revelation. These too narrowly drawn circles present pitfalls which black theology might well avoid, because so many elements testifying to God's liberating grace and to the mystery of that activity are lost in the quest for a central meaning-idea-concept in the Bible.

IV. Black Theology in the Theological Curriculum

A very brief statement reiterating the broad significance of black theology for theological education is necessary. The word of Childs and Sanders is that we have drawn our circles too closely with regard to the descriptive approach in biblical theology, that exegesis must move to contemporary meaning via the path of the history of meanings given to the text. Our canon is the result of the ongoing process of extended meaning of the text and tradition, and from this we should learn that the process of revelation does not end with the close of canon. Biblical theology, therefore, must not only give statement to that ever-widening circle of encounter with God within the textual tradition but also point to the ongoingness of the process. Black theology, like the great theologies of the past, gives testimony to the ongoing process of the human family's encounter with God within life. As such, biblical theologians as well as systematic theologians and church historians and ethicists should take up the challenge of black theology to examine and act upon its liberation theme. Rather than being seen as a low priority elective for black and some white students, black theology ought to have a regular place within the theological curriculum, and some of its concerns as regular elements within other course offerings.

If we rightly hear what black theology is trying to say, it is that its word is a word for all who would hear the gospel today. Though he does not mention black theology or the American urban unrest, I am sure that Brevard Childs' perceptive commentary of Exodus 2:11–25, Moses' slaying of an Egyptian, represents a digging into the text on the basis of new questions being put to the scripture as a result of pressing social issues.[30] From a very different corner of the intellectual sphere, we might do well to look at C. S. Lewis, *Reflections on the Psalms* (1961), especially the chapter on the imprecatory psalms, "The Cursings," for sensitive and fresh treatment of anger and its place in the divine scheme. In addition to putting questions to scripture out of contemporary concerns, black theology also points to the hymns and sermons of the black religious heritage as texts giving classic statement to black perceptions of God's saving activity in life. These affirmations are stamped out of the biblical mold, but bring such new perceptions with them as to be compared with that biblical palimpsest process of the new being inscribed upon the old. The black sermon, "Behold the rib," is more than comment on Genesis 2:21–25, for out of the black experience which forged a new relationship between black male and female, there is a profound new word on the man and woman belonging side by side in everything.[31] Many a black preacher was able to grasp the deepest meaning of Esther 4:14 despite its apparent silence (non-reference) regarding the source of deliverance.[32] Particularly valuable source material and interpretation is found in Howard Thurman, *The Negro Spiritual Speaks of Life and Death* (Ingersoll Lecture) (1947), and *Deep River* (1955), and also James Cone, *Spirituals and the Blues* (1972). These are simply hints of what has been done, recently and not so recently, relating interpretation of scripture to the existential situation of the contemporary culture.[33]

Perhaps the greatest challenge of black theology to the theological curriculum is in the biblical discipline, the one committed to searching for meaning and the means to the same for today. Thus, even as this study has been directed primarily to the black theologian, it is also a word to the biblical theologian. That word is that black theology is the most serious effort within the theological community today attempting to grapple with biblical meaning for today. Inasmuch as it is bridging that gap between what it meant then and what it means now, biblical theology can find no more worthy or profitable enterprise than to be in dialogue with black theology.

NOTES

1. Warner Traynham, "Black Studies in Theological Education," *Harvard Theological Review* 66/2 (April, 1973): 257-271.
2. Cone, *God of the Oppressed*, 81; also in *Interpretation* 28/4 (Oct., 1974): 439.
3. See J. Deotis Roberts, *A Black Political Theology*, 123.
4. Some representative works are: (African Theology) Kwesi Dickson and Paul Ellingworth, eds., *Biblical Revelation and African Beliefs*, Maryknoll, N. Y.: Orbis Books, 1971; Mark Glasswell and Edward Fashole-Luke, eds., *New Testament Christianity for Africa and the World*, London: SPCK, 1974; Basil Moore, ed., *The Challenge of Black Theology in South Africa*, Atlanta: John Knox, 1974; (Liberation Theology) Gustavo Gutierrez, *A Theology of Liberation*, Maryknoll, N. Y.: Orbis Books, 1973; Frederick Herzog, *Liberation Theology*, New York: Seabury, 1972; (Women's Perspective) Rosemary Ruether, ed., *Religion and Sexism*, New York: Simon & Schuster, 1974; Phyllis Trible

"Biblical Theology as Women's Work," *Religion in Life* 44/1 (Spring, 1975):7-13.

5. Brevard Childs, *The Book of Exodus: A Critical Theological Commentary* (Old Testament Library), Philadelphia: Westminster, 1974; James Sanders, *Torah and Canon*, Philadelphia: Fortress, 1972, and "The Dead Sea Scrolls: A Quarter Century of Study," *Biblical Archaeologist* 36/4 (December, 1973).

6. Vincent Harding, "Reflections and Meditations on the Training of Religious Leaders for the New Black Generation," *Theological Education* 4/3 (Spring, 1970): 189-201; Charles Long, "Perspectives for a Study of Afro-American Religion in the United States," *History of Religion* 2/1 (August, 1971): 54-66; Gayraud Wilmore, *Black Religion and Black Radicalism*, New York: Doubleday, 1972; rev. ed., Maryknoll, N.Y.: Orbis, 1983.

7. Robert Dentan, *Preface to Old Testament Theology*, rev. ed., New York: Seabury, 1963, 22-23. Cf. Krister Stendahl, "Biblical Theology, Contemporary," *Interpreter's Dictionary of the Bible* (1962), 422, 425. History and methodology are examined in Gerhard Hasel, *Old Testament Theology: Basic Issues in the Current Debate*, Grand Rapids: Eerdmans, 1972, 11-47.

8. Dentan, op. cit., 90.

9. Ibid., 64, 92.

10. Eichrodt and von Rad debate the relative merits of their positions: Walter Eichrodt, *Theology of the Old Testament* Vol. 1, Philadelphia: Westminster, 1961, 512-520; Gerhard von Rad, *Old Testament Theology*, Vol. 1, New York: Harper & Row, 1962, 105-128.

11. G. E. Wright, *Old Testament and Theology*, New York: Harper & Row, 1969, 62, shifts to a position more supportive of Eichrodt's covenant emphasis, and states in "The Theological Study of the Bible," *Interpreter's One-Volume Commentary on the Bible* (1971), 986, that the Mosaic covenant is the "primary structuring concept in the OT."

12. Brevard Childs, *Biblical Theology in Crisis*, 51-60.

13. Gerhard Ebeling, *Word and Faith*, Philadelphia: Fortress, 1963, 329.

14. So we may surmise from the arguments of Zimmerli, Westermann, von Rad, and Eichrodt in Claus Westermann, ed., *Essays on Old Testament Hermeneutics*, Richmond: John Knox Press, 1964, and especially in B. W. Anderson, "The New Covenant and the Old," in Bernhard W. Anderson, ed., *The Old Testament and Christian Faith*, New York: Harper & Row, 1963, 225-242.

15. Gerhard Hasel, "The Problem of the Center in the OT Theology Debate," *ZAW* 86/1 (1974): 79. Cf. his *Old Testament Theology: Basic Issues in the Current Debate*, 49-63.

16. Childs, *Biblical Theology in Crisis*, 66-70; James Barr, *Old and New in Interpretation*, London: SCM, 1966, 72-76.

17. See note 5 above.

18. E. A. Speiser, " 'People' and 'Nation' in Israel," *JBL* 79/2 (1960): 157-163. Cf. Robert Bennett, "Black Experience and the Bible," *New Theology* No. 9 (1972): 176-189.

19. James Sanders, "The Dead Sea Scrolls . . . ," *Biblical Archaeologist* 36/4 (December, 1973).

20. Robert Grant, *A Short History of the Interpretation of the Bible*, New York: Macmillan, 1963; and Robert Bennett, "Biblical Hermeneutics and the Black Preacher," *Journal of the ITC* 1/2 (1974): 38-53.

21. James Cone speaks of the Bible in black theology in *A Black Theology of Liberation*, New York: Lippincott, 1970, 66-69, passim, as well as in *God of the Oppressed*, New York: Seabury, 1975, 62-83, on the hermeneutical question. In the latter work he also speaks of: biblical revelation, 91-101; Bible and black suffering, 163-183; and of Jesus, 108-137. J. Deotis Roberts offers critique of Cone's biblical stance in *Black Political Theology*, Philadelphia: Westminster, 1974, 123, 181-182, and in "Theology of Religions . . . ," *Journal of ITC* 1/2 (1974): 54-68, esp. 65-66.

22. J. Deotis Roberts, *Liberation and Reconciliation*, Philadelphia: Westminster, 1971, pp. 142 ff., and in *Black Political Theology*, 127.

23. *Black Political Theology*, 38. Roberts states his view on scripture in pp. 36-42.

24. *Black Theology of Liberation*, 69.

25. *God of the Oppressed*, 68.

26. Ibid., 258-259, note 4; and 78-80.

27. Ibid., 80.

28. Ibid., 81-82. Cf. *Black Theology of Liberation*, 114-116.

29. Ibid., 81.

30. Childs, *Book of Exodus* (1974), 27-46; *Biblical Theology In Crisis*, 164-83.

31. Langston Hughes and Arna Bontemps, eds., *Book of Negro Folklore*, New York: Dodd, Mead & Co., 1958, 233-235. Cf. James Weldon Johnson's *God's Trombones,* New York: Viking, 1955. Also, James Cone, "The Content and Method of Black Theology" Consultation, Accra, Ghana, December 1974.

> "Behold de rib!
> Brothers, if God
> Had taken dat bone out of man's head
> He would have meant for woman to rule, hah
> If he has taken a bone out of his foot,
> He would have meant for us to dominize and rule.
> He could have made her out of back-bone
> And then she would have been behind us.
> But, no, God Almighty, he took de bone out of his side.
> So dat places the woman beside us.
> Hah! God knowed his own mind.
> Behold de rib!"

32. "And who knows whether you have not come to the kingdom for such a time as this?" Esther 4:14b (RSV). While the black preacher uses this text to inspire the favored of the community to aid the distressed, others such as Frederick Douglass speak of the broader black-white situation in America. In his journal, North Star (1849), Douglass interprets the black presence in America thus, "We shall never die out nor be driven out; but shall go with this people, either as testimony against them, or as evidence in their favor throughout their generations."

33. Julius Lester's review of C. Eric Lincoln, ed., *The Black Experience in Religion* in *Christianity and Crisis* 35/5 (March 31, 1975): 73-75, criticizes much of black theology for not making more of the "experience of faith" which he finds at the core of black religion. While this is not the last word on the subject, it is significant that one outside of the theological discipline should make such a comment on essays devoted to the black religious experience.

14

THE COURAGE TO BE BLACK

Allan Boesak

The right to live in God's world as a human being is not the sole right of whites that eventually, through the kindness of whites, can be extended to 'deserving' (obsequious?) Blacks as a 'special privilege.' Human dignity for all is a fundamental biblical right. Nevertheless, many whites seem to think that Blacks live by the grace of whites. Whites determine who and what we must be. Whites determine what our life shall be like. Whites determine where and how we may live. Whites determine who shall be our friends. Whites determine whom we may marry. Whites determine how we shall be educated. Whites determine—insofar as our children receive an education at all—what sort of education our children shall receive. Whites determine the possibilities and the boundaries of our humanity. In this process, *the* criterion always was and still is skin color: white.

Blacks now wish to make it clear to whites that this whole process is sinful. We can no longer continue to live in this manner without bringing God's consuming wrath upon us. How shall we correct this neglect, this evasion of our responsibility, to realize our humanity, the potential God has structured into us? How it must grieve the Holy Spirit that God's human creation is destroyed, is denigrated to a 'thing'—and this in the name of God! How it must, furthermore, grieve the Holy Spirit that *we* have *permitted* this to happen! We, therefore, shall not beg for the right to live as human beings. That we need not do. No one person has the right to take our life in their hands, and to exercise the power to give our life to us or to withhold it from us. As Adam Small says,

We do *not* live by the grace of the whites ... Even the 'best' whites have thought always that they hold our lives in their hands. Although, there-

Allan Boesak is a Black South African theologian, former president of the World Alliance of Reformed Churches and member of the Executive Committee of the African National Congress. This essay first appeared in *Wereld en zending* in the Netherlands, 3 (1974). This excerpt has been edited for inclusion in this volume by permission of the author.

fore, protest shall play a role in our future actions, we must realize, nevertheless, that protest is itself a form of begging. We shall not, I repeat, beg. The primary form of expression shall be the manifestation of our Blackness. Over and over again we shall make our Blackness visible. We do not exist for the benefit of the whites. We *exist*.[1]

The source of our certainty in this matter is not this or that white promise or, to use the modern idiom, necessary concession. The source of our certainty, rather, is God's righteousness, God's justice. The state that wishes to be respectable cannot permit justice to be negated. The state that wishes to be known as 'Christian' must be more careful than this. In the Bible there is a close connection among God's love, God's justice or righteousness, and human rights. Black theology maintains that you cannot talk about God's love without talking about God's righteousness or justice. These both assume concrete form in the relationship between God and humankind, and in our interpersonal relationships.

God's love for the people is active, concerned with providing justice for the people and with making the divine justice visible. God's love for Israel is never a romantic or sentimental feeling that may or may not have a focus. God's love for Israel, rather, is startlingly concrete. God hears the grievances of the people and sees the cruelty of its oppressors: 'I *know* their sufferings' (Exod. 3:7). God's love means that God chooses in favour of the people, and against the oppressor Pharaoh; that God makes the lost cause of the people God's own cause. Choosing one side means that it is impossible for God to maintain the status quo. God, in a wonderful manner, becomes involved completely in the liberation of the people.

God acts openly, not secretly. God does this as a challenge to the powers that be and to the powerful ones who think that they can manipulate God's justice, or that they can escape God's judgment. God acts openly so that the world may know that Israel's God lives—lives for the people of Israel; that Yahweh is the Liberator of the oppressed and the Warrior who fights for justice on behalf of the down trodden. God is not ashamed to be called 'the God of the oppressed.' 'You have seen what I did to the Egyptians, and that I have borne you up on eagle's wings and have brought you to me' (Exod. 19:4, 5). Of course! You have *seen!*

We can now state the following conclusion: God's righteousness is manifested in liberative deeds. We must add a further point: God's liberation is not an isolated deed, a blinding flash in history that we see today but of which no trace will be found tomorrow. God's liberation, rather, is a movement. It moves through history. Over and over again God is manifested as the warrior who fights for justice. God deals grimly—justly—with the pharaoh who oppresses Israel; but God deals no less grimly—justly—with the wealthy Israelites who offer no justice to their poor fellow Israelites. Israel knew God as earnest and supportive (Isaiah); biting, sarcastic, and angry (Amos); but always unrivaled in struggle for the people, even when unappreciative. God's justice or righteousness, therefore, is the liberation, the healing and salvation, that God wills to realize and actualize among us.

Something more, however, must be said about God's deeds. God performs mighty deeds *and* motivates people to do the divine will, to do justice. It is no accident that the text I have referred to (Exod. 19:4, 5) is followed by Exod. 20:1 – 'I am the Lord, your God, who led you out of the house of bondage, out of Egypt.' Liberation cannot be dissociated from love. When God uses Hosea to stimulate Israel to remember its liberation, it is God who proclaims a relationship between love and justice: 'When Israel was a child, I loved him, and I called my son out of Egypt' (Hosea 11:1).

H. M. Kuitert has demonstrated that in the Bible the terms 'justice,' 'righteousness,' and 'to do justice' are concepts that are operative in the framework of 'the covenantal partnership.'[2] You must act in justice vis-à-vis the other if you are to be an authentic covenantal partner of the other. 'To act in justice' contains in it the meaning 'to enable others to realize their potential,' 'to give recognition to the other's humanity.' It means 'to give recognition to the other's claim to justice.' God does not merely liberate; God liberates people from one situation so that they can live in a new, appropriate, situation. God liberated people so that they are able to do justice. This is the basis for the legitimate desire of everyone to live as a whole, real person.

God's justice is the source of Black humanity. God's tireless zeal for the liberation of the enslaved and needy is the inspiration for the struggle to liberate Blacks. We take the biblical message seriously and we accept it unconditionally! – that is, we have faith in, we *believe in* the God who is the liberator. We believe that God unconditionally establishes justice for the wretched; that God saves the poor; but that God shatters the oppressor (Ps. 72:4). We know that we have been called to freedom (liberation), and that we must persevere in the freedom that Christ has effected for us (Gal. 5:1).

True freedom never consists in fleeing from the world and its problems, in acting as if the only concern of the Christian were 'heaven.' Countless Blacks have been guilty of this in the past – with, I may add, the encouragement of white Christians.

True freedom is not the art of mere survival. This is still a well-known stunt of Blacks. South African Blacks for a long time, in both speech and action, gave the appearance of being cooperative, addressed meekly all whites as *baas,* said what the whites wanted to hear, and worked in harmony with the system for the purpose of 'getting out of the system what there was to get.' Behind the backs of whites, however, Blacks for a long time poked fun at them because whites were 'so very stupid.' In addition to being dangerous, this is also dishonest. Dishonest people, moreover, are never free people.

Black freedom should never be conceived of as a duplication of white, bourgeois individualism. The truly free are those who realize that God is the basis and the guarantee of their freedom. They therefore regard every curtailment of freedom as rebellion against God. They furthermore champion the cause of the oppressed and of freedom. They know, also, that freedom, as is true of justice and love, is not a passive state and status. It is, rather, a movement, an action. God liberates people, as was said above, so that they can enact and embody justice.

True justice can make covenant partners out of us because justice serves God's *shalom* and creates true community. In the situation in which we live at present, we are not covenant partners. We, rather, are enemies. Justice is not in effect. We are bribed with substitutes for justice. Among us 'fellowship' has come to mean, 'above all, do not tell the truth.' One must pay a price for honesty and real Christian obedience. The price is coercion, ostracism, and exile. Black theology, therefore, is indispensable if we are to penetrate all the sham and to discern the heart of the matter.

The Black Messiah and Black Humanity

True love and justice, as I have said, enable people to realize the full potential of their humanity. In this situation a person can be an authentic person. Humanity is extremely important; it is not a general and empty concept that can be given any content one desires. Humanity is an important concept: it functions in the context of God's activity among us. At the center of this activity of God is the Christ-event.

We confess that Jesus Christ embodies true divinity and true humanity. He was human as God intended humans to be. In him God was in the world. In him God was with humankind. In him our being 'like God,' of necessity, took a clear and distinct form. Subsequently there could be no misunderstanding about what God expects from us.

Our being 'like God' has nothing to do with the physical appearance of God. It is meant to indicate how God is God and how we must be what we are. Jesus of Nazareth was the concrete and living image of God. Israel recognized and knew God in God's deeds, in God's 'dealings' with and on behalf of the people. In his 'dealings' with people Jesus was the true and authentic reelection of the gracious God in action: 'The one who has seen me [in action] has seen the Father [in action]' (John 14:9).[3]

We must raise the following question: What is the meaning of this confession for Blacks who are the oppressed of the world? Do we see in Jesus the one to whom we have been introduced through the ages—the romantic preacher who declared a message of submissiveness which was oriented solely to the future, to heaven? Is Jesus really as 'Western' as the 'civilization' that claims him? Is the Jesus whom thousands of our ancestors learned to know while they worked on plantations as slaves identified with the power and the oppression of whites? If this picture of Jesus is true and real, then Jesus is white and he is unacceptable to Blacks. The Jesus who represented the God of the Bible cannot be the same one whose name was carved into bows of the Dutch slave ships in which Africans were transported to their death. For Black Christians, as James Cone has said, the only authentic confession in our age is the confession of Jesus Christ as the Black Messiah.[4]

The image of Jesus that the New Testament presents to us is one that identifies him to a remarkable degree with the Black experience. He was poor. At the time of his circumcision his poor parents were not able to bring the sacrifice prescribed in the law. They brought instead the sacrifice of the poor: two turtledoves in place of a year-old lamb (Lev. 12:6–8; Luke 2:21–24). He maintained the humble status of his birth throughout his life. He belonged to a poor dispossessed people, without rights in its own land, subjected daily to countless humiliations by foreign oppressors. Jesus lived and worked among the poor. His disciples and followers came from among the poor. He lived a life of solidarity with the poor. He felt at home with the 'have-nots' rather than with the 'haves.' All must admit that his message spoke to the condition of the people. His message generated hope and trust among them. And they felt at home with *him.* His message had an effect among the poor. It had little or no effect among the rich and the privileged.

Jesus made no secret of the fact that he had come for the lowly—the outcasts, the despised ones, those of whom the rich in their 'sophisticated' language would have said, they 'are very primitive. If they were to be given freedom in an amiable fashion, they would not live virtuously, and would not know how to govern themselves. But even if they live in wretched circumstances, nevertheless, one can expect them to serve one well.'[5] This is how the Reformed pastor from Coevorden, the Netherlands, Johan Picardt, wrote about the 'kaffirs' in South Africa. But Jesus came for them; not for those who had no need of a physician.

At the very beginning of his public ministry, Jesus made clear what his mission was: 'The Spirit of the Lord is upon me, because he has anointed me to bring the good news to the poor. He has sent me to proclaim release to the captives and recovery of sight to the blind, to set at liberty those who are oppressed, to proclaim the acceptable year of the Lord' (Luke 4:18ff). This programme is one in which there is solidarity between Jesus and those he has come to serve. Jesus, the oppressed one, came and took sides with the oppressed. He came as the forsaken one without form or appearance, a man of sorrows, bowed down with illness (Isa. 53). He knew what it was to live like a hunted animal. He knew what it was to speak with care at all times so as to evade the clutches of 'informers.' He lived on earth in a way familiar to us Blacks. He identified himself completely with us. He is the Black Messiah.

In spite of his humble position, however, he still is called Jesus the liberator. He brought a new message to his oppressed people and to everyone who will listen to it: a new message of hope and liberation. He lived among the oppressed with a heavenly radicalism. By so doing he set dynamite to the status quo and to 'law and order.' The people had been 'things.' They were without value except insofar as they were useful to the Romans and their accomplices. Jesus told them that he loved them; that they were of greater value than the birds and the flowers, even if it was true that Solomon in all his glory lacked their natural splendour. In a country where the Roman fist was the highest authority, Jesus enthroned the human value of the oppressed. Nor did Jesus practise a

'Christian sadism' among his followers. When he was alone with the woman who had been accused of adultery, he did not permit her to bow down on the ground to demonstrate her gratitude. She, rather, was able to assume a responsible role immediately: 'Go and from now on sin no more!' (John 8:11).

Jesus protected the people from the religious tyranny of the priests and scribes: the person is more important than the Sabbath; the law functions in the service of the people. Herod, the political tyrant and accomplice of the Romans, Jesus called a 'fox.' The self-centered Pharisees he called 'whited sepulchers,' 'hypocrites,' 'serpents,' 'a brood of adders.' Jesus calls the Pharisees by these names because they 'devoured the houses of widows,' but 'for the sake of appearance they prayed long prayers and because they ignored 'the weightier' matters of the law: judgment and mercy and fidelity (Matt. 23). He offers liberation to the people and establishes their humanity in a radical way. By his royal association with them, he summoned the people to claim and to strengthen their own humanity.

We have looked in vain for this Jesus in the preaching of whites. The message we heard there was a completely different message. The message was one of passivity, of glossing over white injustice — a message that assured their position always and unconditionally. You need only read the sermons and orations that have been given in South Africa on the 'Day of the Covenant' to understand why one of the issues of *Pro Veritate* speaks about an 'Afrikaner gospel' (i.e., a white gospel).[6]

I cannot omit reference to one more example of 'gospel proclamation,' to emphasize how the ground was prepared for both Blacks and whites to view black-white relations. This example comes from a report of the Dutch pastor M. C. Vos, who migrated to South Africa at the end of the eighteenth century. In his report he tells how he persuaded reformers to permit their slaves to be instructed in the gospel.[7] Keep in mind that he was neither ignorant nor blind to reality.

It is natural that your slaves will not become worse but, rather, better through education. Let me try to convince you of this. You have slaves, I have noticed, who originally came from a variety of lands. Put yourself in the place of one of them for a few minutes and think in the following way: I am a poor slave, but I was not born in this status. I was taken from my dear parents, my loving wife or husband, from my children, my brothers and sisters, by human thieves who kidnapped me and took me away from my own country. I have no hope that I shall ever see one of my family members again. I have been dragged here to this land by tyrants. On the ride to this place, if I had not been in chains and fetters I would have chosen death in preference to life. Here I was sold as an animal. Now I am a slave. I must do everything which is commanded me even to the point of doing very undesirable work. If I do not do this willingly, then I am beaten severely.

'Suppose for a few minutes,' the pastor continued in his conversation with the farmer, 'that this was the situation in which *you* found yourself. Tell me, if you were to be in that situation, would you have the desire to do your work? Would you not, rather, frequently be despondent, sorrowful, obstinate, and disobedient?'

The man was moved. He said, 'I had never thought about that. If I were in the place of one like the one you have described, who knows to what sort of acts of despair I would be driven?'

'Well,' I continued, 'if you permit them to remain stupid and ignorant, upon occasion thoughts of this type will arise and, at times, come to expression in terribly extreme actions. If they are instructed correctly as they should be, they will be instructed that God rules all things; that nothing happens apart from his rule; that God is a God of order; that in the same way in which they must serve their master and mistress, their master and mistress must serve those who are in positions of authority over them; that those who do not serve obediently are punished either on their body or in their pulse. You can make clear to them that which seems evil to us frequently turns out to our advantage. If they had remained by their friends in their own country, then they would have remained ignorant of the way of salvation until their death; and then, at death, because of this ignorance, they would have been lost forever. Now, however, since they have been brought to a Christian land, they have the opportunity of gaining knowledge of the only Saviour who can and shall make them happy through all eternity. When they begin to understand this a bit, the despondent and grieving thoughts will change. Then they will begin to think: if that is the way things are, then I shall be content with my lot and I shall attempt to do my work obediently and joyfully.'

The farmer cried out, 'Why weren't we told these things before? I must confess my ignorance. From now on I shall never dissuade anyone from educating his slaves. I, rather, shall persuade everyone to educate their slaves.'

Today, of course, different arguments are used. We are all more sophisticated. The heart of the matter, however, is unchanged. The calling and responsibility is of Black theology to liberate us from this undesirable 'whiteness.' Because our Blackness, and only our Blackness, is the cause of the oppression of the Black community. Cone says, 'the Christological importance of Jesus Christ must be found in his Blackness ... Taking our cue from the historical Jesus who is pictured in the New Testament as the Oppressed One, what else, except Blackness, could adequately tell us the meaning of his presence today?'[8] Today, just as yesterday, he has taken the sorrow of his people upon himself. He has become for them everything that is necessary for their liberation. For us Jesus is the Black Messiah and the irrevocable guarantee of our Black humanity.

Black Theology, Black Identity, and the Future

Black theology, as I have said, seeks a breakthrough so that it can expose the true human person, the authentic being of humanity. And, once more, *our* true humanity consists precisely in our creation as Blacks. We shall never be able to gain better human relations until whites have learned to accept Blacks as *Black people,* and to give themselves in service to them. Let me state the matter very clearly: when we speak about the affirmation of our Blackness, the affirmation of our creation as Black, it has nothing to do with *being resigned* to our Blackness. It is precisely what I indicated that it is: the affirmation of our Blackness, the affirmation of our creation as Black. *Black is Beautiful.*

We speak about a rebirth, a re-creation, a renewal, a reevaluation of our self. In this connection Black theology frequently uses the word *self-love.* Some interpret this to mean: 'love for the Black and hate for the white.' I offer no apology here, because we need not discuss every white absurdity, but I do wish to say one thing: Jesus did not prescribe a law when he gave his followers the commandment to love your neighbour 'as yourself.' He began with a fact that is universally accepted. Everyone values their own self. Everyone desires to live a life that has significance and value. Everyone is driven to preserve their own self.

There are, however, circumstances that work such destruction of one's self that even this fundamental human drive is lacking. People under severe pressure can build up a devastating contempt for their own self. This was the lot of Blacks. Slavery, domination by others, total dependence, lack of legal rights and the status of an alien whether in one's own or in another land, discrimination and humiliation—all have had a devastating influence on the spiritual life of Blacks. In the society dominated by whites, 'white' was the acme of all that was 'good'; 'Black' was the symbol of everything that was of little value or status.

In America, Blacks scarcely survived the assault on their traditions and history. In South Africa Blacks were said to have had no history. South Africa 'arose' first in 1652 and the only traditions that may continue to operate are the 'non dangerous' ones.

What whites, consciously or unconsciously, think about Blacks need not be repeated here. Martin Luther King, Jr., said that in *Roget's Thesaurus of English Words and Phrases,* a standard American reference work, there are no less than 120 synonyms for 'black,' and at least 60 of them are offensive. 'Black' is 'dirty,' 'demonic,' 'angry,' etc. The same dictionary, on the other hand, contains 134 synonyms for 'white,' and every one of them is favourable. The standard Afrikaans-English dictionary (*Die Groot Engels/Afrikaans Woordeboek*) still teaches students that the correct translation of 'black person' is *swartnerf* ('black hide') or *swartslang* ('black snake'). The last word, 'swartslang,' is a collective noun that translates the term 'natives.' Black child-children furthermore, must use the same dictionary and must learn that the English word 'gentleman' is translated into Afrikaans by the word 'white man' (*witman*). When you, furthermore, discover that 'gentle' is defined in terms of 'respectable,' 'civilized,' 'loving,' and 'skillful,' then both the meaning of the word and its implications are very clear. *Van Dale,* the standard Dutch dictionary, represents no improvement. It is no wonder then, is it, that the Blacks have learned to hate and despise themselves?

And I have said almost nothing about the systematic veneration of whites and the scorn for Blacks that are perpetuated by the countless apartheid laws.

South African Blacks are now searching for their true humanity: a 'decolonized' humanity free from the infection of white scorn and contempt. This does not mean, of course, that Blacks inevitably will hate whites. It means that Blacks simply shall not accept any longer a 'brotherhood' in which the one brother, the Black, must be a slave and the other brother, the white, must be the master. We find it intolerable that this hypocrisy, this inauthenticity, continues under the banner 'Christian.' Any form of white oppression is equally intolerable. White values shall no longer be thought of as 'the highest good.' Blacks shall no longer hate themselves and wish that they were white. No longer shall Blacks define themselves in terms of others. They shall, rather, move toward their own authentic Blackness out of their 'negroness' and 'non-white' character. In this way they shall force whites to see themselves in their whiteness and to perceive the consequences of this whiteness for others.

This is the meaning of Black self-love. We will hate no whites simply because they are white. We hate their oppression, their enslavement of others. As long as they desire to be oppressors they cannot be coequals. The choice is theirs. We will live without any apology or defence, and we will not make any excuse for our existence; or for what is our birthright. We are not eager to hate whites; we wish to treat them as human beings. If this causes whites to panic, that is their problem.

Black theology wishes to proclaim this message of authenticity to whites. Future generations of both Blacks and whites may not have to learn and embody a theology that is nothing other than an extension of cultural imperialism (Rubem Alves). Our theology must concern itself with authentic questions, with the true liberation of the unliberated. In our theology, we must dare to limit ourselves to that which is most urgent and most authentic. The criteria of urgency and authenticity make it all the foolish, even in the West, for Christians to run around making a great fuss and much ado about their love for their neighbours. In this connection, Cardonnel writes about the parable of the good Samaritan:

> The essential difference between, on the one hand, the Samaritan, the common man, the man of the people, the man who disappears in the crowd, and, on the other hand, the priests, the economists, the psychologists, and the experts in power and authority lies in this: the first-named needed no religion, no doctrine or precise definition of his field of labour, in order to love, in order to exercise empathy, in order to act in a loving fashion and to experience solidarity with the other.[9]

The man from Samaria, however, first appeared in the parable after the struggle was ended, when everything was over. At this point Cardonnel raises the real question that theology must raise: What will happen if love is expressed during the struggle, not after the struggle?[10]

In this situation Black theology wishes to be present in the role of a servant. Black theology wishes to cooperate in addressing urgent and authentic questions without any anxiety. Only in this way shall we achieve authentic community. Black theology wishes to make operative what was holy in the Black African community long before whites came on the scene: unity, mutual respect, community. It is alarming that this element of community has been virtually absent as long as we have known one another—that is, as long as Blacks have known the Christian faith. This community is not openly available to seize whenever one happens to desire it. Community, rather, lies on the far side of much struggle and doubt, of mutual trust and courage. For us this is the courage to be Black.

This community located on the far side of struggle is not to be regarded as an eschatological event, at present only an incomprehensible chimera; it is, rather, as real as Africa itself. There is a centuries-old proverb in the language of Tumbuka: *Muntu ni munta cifukwa cabanyake*—'A person is a person only because of others and on behalf of others.' This is the objective toward which we wish to move.

NOTES

1. Adam Small, 'Blackness vs. Nihilism,' in *Essays on Black Theology*, Motlhabi, ed. (Johannesburg, 1972), 14-15.
2. H. M. Kuitert, *De spelers en het spel* (Baarn; Ten Have, 5th ed., 1970).
3. Ibid., 52.
4. See James Cone, *A Black Theology of Liberation* (Philadelphia: Lippincott, 1970), 203-27; Albert Cleage, Jr., *The Black Messiah* (New York: Sheed & Ward, 1969).
5. Van Kaam, 'Arbeid,' 11.
6. Beyers Naudé and Roelf Meyer, 'Christusfees of Baalfees,' an Appendix to *Pro Veritate*, December 15, 1971.
7. J. T. Bakker wrote about this in *Gereformeerde Weekblad*, October 12, 1973. Comparing an article by J. D. Vorster on 'communal prayer,' published in the South African periodical *Die Kerkbode* in 1973, Bakker concludes in his article that white South Africans continue to state the gospel in ideological terms just as M. C. Vos stated the gospel in ideological terms in the eighteenth century.
8. Cone, *A Black Theology*, 214.
9. J. Cardonnel, 'Van konservatieve erfenis naar revolutionair traditie,' *Tijdschrift voor Theologie* (special number: *Religie van de Toekomst, Toekomst der Religie*): 116.
10. Ibid., 120.

15

JESUS, THE LIBERATOR

Joseph A. Johnson, Jr.

In 1 Corinthians 1:18–24 Paul speaks of the doctrine of the cross. To some this doctrine is sheer folly; to others, it is the power of God. Some think the doctrine of the cross is weakness, but to the believers it is a revelation of the power of God, the wisdom of God, and the love of God. Jesus Christ is the subject of the Gospel. Paul writes:

This doctrine of the cross is sheer folly to those on their way to ruin, but to us who are on the way to salvation it is the power of God. Scripture says, "I will destroy the wisdom of the wise, and bring to nothing the cleverness of the clever." Where is your wise man now, your man of learning, or your subtle debater—limited, all of them, to this passing age? God has made the wisdom of this world look foolish. As God in his wisdom ordained, the world failed to find him by its wisdom, and he chose to save those who have faith by the folly of the Gospel. Jews call for miracles, Greeks look for wisdom; but we proclaim Christ—yes, Christ nailed to the cross; and though this is a stumbling-block to Jews and folly to Greeks, yet to those who have heard his call, Jews and Greeks alike, he is the power of God and wisdom of God.

Jesus, the Liberator, is the power of God, the wisdom of God, and the love of God. Paul knew firsthand of the operation of these qualities: wisdom, power, and love. He could never quite understand this new wisdom, this new power, and this new love which he had experienced in Jesus, the Liberator. It was a queer kind of wisdom and love that had chosen him, one who had been a persecutor of the church and now summoned to be a messenger of the crucified-

The late Joseph A. Johnson, Jr., was a distinguished teacher, theologian, and bishop of the Christian Methodist Episcopal Church. This essay, now a classic in the field of Black theology, was taken from his *The Soul of the Black Preacher* (Philadelphia: United Church Press, 1971), and is reprinted by permission of the United Church Press.

risen Lord. He could never comprehend this kind of love that had permitted Jesus, God's only son, to die on the cross for the salvation of men. Paul is astonished and amazed at this new revelation of love: "While we were yet helpless, at the right time Christ died for the ungodly. Why, one will hardly die for a righteous man—though perhaps for a good man one will dare even to die. But God shows his love for us in that while we were yet sinners Christ died for us (Rom. 5:6–8)."

Paul's new life had been determined by this encounter with Jesus, the Liberator. This new life which was God-given was the life of grace, and he shouts, "By the grace of God, I am what I am." The experience of this wisdom, power, and love, Paul defines as "the power of God unto salvation." It was a new kind of power, a power that had granted him freedom to life, righteousness, peace, and joy, and also freedom from sin, from the law, and from death. The liberating power of Jesus had emancipated him and set him free. He exhorts his fellow Christians: "For freedom Christ has set us free; stand fast therefore, and do not submit again to a yoke of slavery (Gal. 5:1)."

Jesus, the Liberator, had given to Paul not only freedom but also a new self-understanding. This new self-understanding, according to Bultmann, is bestowed with faith and it is freedom through which the believer gains life and thereby his own self.[1] Paul discovered that he who belongs to Jesus, the Liberator, and thus to God has become master of everything. He declares to the Christians at Corinth that this grace-freedom event which they had experienced in Jesus, the Liberator, placed the whole world at their disposal: "So let no one boast of men. For all things are yours, whether Paul or Apollos or Cephas or the world or life or death or the present or the future, all are yours; and you are Christ's; and Christ is God's (1 Cor. 3:21–23)."

Jesus is the Liberator. He is the revelation of the wisdom, the power, and the love of God. This was the message which the early Christian preachers were commissioned to proclaim. This message was called the kerygma. We preach Christ, Paul shouts. At the heart of the kerygma lies this fundamental christological affirmation: Jesus is the Liberator! Jesus is the emancipator!

Nineteen hundred years have passed since these stirring words were written by Paul and various interpretations of Jesus, the Liberator, have been presented. These interpretations range all the way from Jesus as the Son of God, of Paul, the writers of the Synoptic Gospels, John, and Hebrews to the Jesus of Barth, Brunner, Bonhoeffer, Tillich, and Kierkegaard.

The tragedy of the interpretations of Jesus by the white American theologians during the last three hundred years is that Jesus has been too often identified with the oppressive structures and forces of the prevailing society. His teachings have been used to justify wars, exploitation of the poor and oppressed peoples of the world. In his name the most vicious form of racism has been condoned and advocated. In a more tragic sense this Jesus of the white church establishment has been white, straight-haired, blue-eyed, Anglo-Saxon; that is, presented in the image of the oppressor. This "whiteness" has prevailed to the extent that the black, brown, or red peoples of the world, who had accepted Jesus as Lord and Savior, were denied full Christian fellowship in his church and were not accepted as brothers for whom Jesus died.

I have been asked to address myself to the theme, "The Christian Faith in a Revolutionary Age" and to indicate the techniques by which this faith may be communicated. You should expect that we would first critically evaluate the existing understanding of the Christian faith as interpreted and presented by white theologians and as a black American reveal to you the thinking concerning this interpretation of the Christian faith in the black community. We begin with the premise that white theology is severely limited in its interpretation of the Christian faith insofar as the nonwhite peoples of the world are concerned. This limitation is one of the causes for the quest for a black Messiah.

The Limitations of White Theology

To be sure, during the past fifteen years we have entered, insofar as the black community is concerned, into one of the most exciting periods in the life of the black people of this country. For more than one hundred years black students have studied in predominantly white seminaries and have been served a theological diet, created, mixed, and dosed out by white theological technicians. The black seminarians took both the theological milk and meat and even when they had consumed these, their souls were still empty. Those of us who went through the white seminaries did not understand why then. We had passed the courses in the four major fields of studies; we knew our Barth, Brunner, and Niebuhr. We had entered deeply into a serious study of Bonhoeffer and Tillich, but we discovered that these white theologians had described the substance and had elucidated a contemporary faith for the white man. These white scholars knew nothing about the black experience, and to many of them this black experience was illegitimate and inauthentic.

The black man's religious style was considered subhuman by many of the white theological seminaries of this nation and the emotional nature of his religious experience was termed primitive. For the black seminary student to become a great preacher really meant that he had to *whitenize* himself. He had to suppress his naturalness and remake himself in the image of a Sockman, Fosdick, or Buttrick. You see, insofar as the white seminaries were concerned there were no great black preachers, and if a black preacher was fortunate to be called great by the white community, it meant that he was merely a pale reflection of the white ideal.

The young black seminary student today has been introduced into a whole new experience—one fashioned by the late Martin Luther King, Jr., but clarified and profoundly interpreted by Frantz Fanon, Malcolm X, Stokely Carmichael, and Ron Karenga. The young black seminary student today has been tried by every conceivable ordeal that sadistic racial minds can devise; from the fire hoses to vicious dogs, from tear gas to electric animal prods. They have matched wits with the white racist of the power structure and are helping to pull down the system of segregation and discrimination. They have no objection to the combination of such words as "black and power," "black and theology," "black and church," "black and Christ," "black and God." They believe Du Bois who wrote, "This assumption that of all the hues of God, whiteness is inherently and obviously better than brownness or tan leads to curious acts." They are not shocked nor are they discouraged if the term Black Power seems to offend or frighten white or black Americans. To these young Blacks, Black Power means consciousness and solidarity. It means the amassing by black people of the economic, political, and judicial control necessary to define their own goals and share in the decisions that determine their faith. Fanon, Malcolm, Carmichael, and Karenga forced the black seminary students to ask these questions: What do these white American and European theologians of a white racist-dominated religious establishment know about the soul of black folks? What do Barth, Brunner, and Tillich know about the realities of the black ghettos or the fate of black sharecroppers' families whose souls are crushed by the powerful forces of a society that considers everything black as evil? Could these white theologians see the image of the crucified Jesus in the mutilated face of a rat-bitten child, or a drug addict bleeding to death in a stinking alley?

We have learned that the interpretation of Christian theology and of Jesus expounded by white American theologians is severely limited. This is due to the simple reason that these white scholars have never been lowered into the murky depth of the black experience of reality. They never conceived the black Jesus walking the dark streets of the ghettos of the North and the sharecropper's farm in the Deep South without a job, busted, and emasculated. These white theologians could never hear the voice of Jesus speaking in the dialect of Blacks from the southern farms, or in the idiom of the Blacks of the ghetto. This severe limitation of the white theologians' inability to articulate the full meaning of the Christian faith has given rise to the development of black theology.

The Commission on Theology of the National Committee of Black Churchmen has issued a statement on black theology. In this document black theology is defined:

> For us, Black theology is the theology of black liberation. It seeks to plumb the black condition in the light of God's revelation in Jesus Christ, so that the black community can see the gospel is commensurate with the achievement of black humanity. Black theology is a theology of "blackness." It is the affirmation of black humanity that emancipates black people from white racism thus providing authentic freedom for both white and black people. It affirms the humanity of white people in that it says "No" to the encroachment of white oppression.[2]

The black scholars are indebted in a measure to white theologians. We have learned much from them. However, the white theologians in their interpretation of the Christian faith have ignored the black Christian experience. Many have felt that this black Christian experience was devoid of meaning and therefore could be omitted in their exposition and interpretation of the Christian faith. To be sure, this was a grievous error. The omission of the black Christian experience by white interpreters of the Christian faith meant that the message of the Christian faith thus interpreted was oriented toward the white community. Therefore this message had nothing significant to say to the black man who is now struggling for identity and dignity. The black theologians were forced to look at the black Christian experience and interpret this experience so as to ascertain what the black Christian experience has to say to the black man concerning the vital matters of the Christian faith. Black theology is a product of black Christian experience and reflection. It comes out of the past. It is strong in the present and we believe it is redemptive for the future.

The Quest for the Black Jesus

The reason for the quest for the black Jesus is deeply embedded in the black man's experience in this country. The black man's introduction to the white Jesus was a catastrophe! Vincent Harding reminds us that the Blacks encountered the American white Christ first on the slave ships that brought them to these shores. Blacks on the slave ship heard his name sung in hymns of praise while they died chained in stinky holes beneath the decks, locked in terror and disease. When the Blacks leaped from the decks of the slave ships they saw his name carved on the side of the ship. When the black women were raped in the cabins by white racists, they must have noticed the Holy Bible on the shelves. Vincent Harding declares, "The horrors continued on American soil. So all through the nation's history many black men have rejected this Christ— indeed the miracle is that so many accepted him. In past times our disdain often had to be stifled and sullen, our angers silent and self-destructive. But now we speak out."[3]

One white perceptive theologian, Kyle Haselden, has observed:

The white man cleaves Christian piety into two parts: the strong, virile virtues he applies exclusively to himself; the apparently weak, passive virtues he endorses especially for the Negro. "Whatsoever things are true, honest, just, pure, lovely" belong to the white man; "whatsoever things are of good report" belong to the Negro. The white man takes the active and positive Christian adjectives for himself: noble, manly, wise, strong, courageous; he recommends the passive and negative Christian adjectives to the Negro: patient, long-suffering, humble, self-effacing, considerate, submissive, childlike, meek.[4]

White theology has not presented us with good theological reasons why we should not speak out against this gross perversion of the Christian faith. White theology has not been able to reshape the life of the white church so as to cleanse it of its racism and to liberate it from the iron claws of the white racist establishment of this nation. White theology has presented the Blacks a religion of contentment in the state of life in which they find themselves. Such an interpretation of the Christian faith avoided questions about personal dignity, collective power, freedom, equality, and self-determination. The white church establishment presented to the black people a religion carefully tailored to fit the purposes of the white oppressors, corrupted in language, interpretation, and application by the conscious and unconscious racism of white Christians from the first plantation missionary down to Billy Graham.

The white Christ of the white church establishment is the enemy of the black man. The teachings of this white Christ are used to justify wars, exploitation, segregation, discrimination, prejudice, and racism. This white Christ is the oppressor of the black man and the black preacher and scholar were compelled to discover a Christ in his image of blackness. He was forced to look at the teachings of Jesus in the light of his own black experience and discover what this black Jesus said about the realities of his own life. The black preacher, seminary student, and scholar had their work cut out for them. If Bultmann's task was to demythologize the New Testament, the black preacher and scholar had to detheologize his mind of the racist ideas which had crept into interpretations of Jesus and to see him in the depth of his full humanity.

We remind you, we were asked to address ourselves "in the general area of understanding and communicating the Christian faith into today's revolutionary society." The first requirement is one of admitting the inadequacies of an understanding of the Christian faith which is used to support our contemporary racist society. Black and white scholars must read again the scriptures with new eyes and minds so as to hear the words of Jesus in their disturbing clarity.

The subject of all preaching is Jesus Christ. As Paul says, "We proclaim Christ—yes, Christ nailed to the cross; and though this is a stumbling-block to Jews and folly to Greeks, yet to those who have heard his call, Jews and Greeks alike, he is the power of God and the wisdom of God."

A Recovery of the Humanity of Jesus

Detheologizing demands that we recover the humanity of Jesus in all of its depth, length, breadth, and height. Jesus was born in a barn, wrapped in a blanket used for sick cattle, and placed in a stall. He died on a city dump outside Jerusalem.

The New Testament presents with disturbing clarity its record of the birth, ministry, and death of Jesus. There is no attempt to hide the stark realities which confronted Jesus from the barn of Bethlehem to the city dump of Jerusalem. The realism is naked and stark. Jesus was born in a barn. He died on a city dump. Even the place of the birth of Jesus is identified with the needs and the conditions of people. Where the need is the deepest, the situation most desperate, and the pain the sharpest, that is precisely where Jesus is. We repeat, even in the birth of Jesus, the Gospels of Matthew and Luke identify him with the needs, the suffering, the pain, and the anxieties of the world. You see, most of the world's babies are not born in the palaces of kings or the government houses of prime ministers, or the manses of bishops. Most of the world's babies are born in the ghettos of corrupt cities, in mud houses, in disintegrated cottages with cracked floors and stuffed walls where the muffled cries of unattended mothers mingle with the screams of newborn infants.

Bultmann writes about the offense of the incarnation of the word.[5] He contends that the revealer appears not as man in general; that is, not simply as a barrier of human nature but as a definite human being in history—Jesus of Nazareth—a Jew. The humanity of Jesus is genuine humanity. The writer of the Gospel of John has no theory about the preexistent miraculous entrance into the world or of the legend of the virgin birth. You know this legend or myth is presented to us in the Gospels of Matthew and Luke. The writer of the Gospel of Mark, the evangelist of the Fourth Gospel, and Paul teach a high Christology without reference to the virgin birth.

Permit us to make this suggestion: Suppose we would omit the phrase "of the Holy Spirit" from Matthew 1:18 where it is recorded that "Mary had been betrothed to Joseph, before they came together she was found to be with child," what would this teach us about the humanity of Jesus? The reaction of many would be instantaneous and we would be accused of teaching "a doctrine of the illegitimate birth of Jesus." These objectors would insist that the birth of Jesus was due to a special act of God in and through humanity and that since Jesus is who he is and has done what he has done, this requires that his entrance into the world through humanity must be unique. Those who advocate this position forget the teachings of Jesus in particular and the New Testament writers in general concerning all life. Jesus taught that all life comes from God and that the birth of every child embodies and expresses a unique act of God.

Who Jesus was, was determined not necessarily by the manner of his birth but rather by what he did. John Knox states that the first form of the christological question was, "What has God done through Jesus?"[6] The New Testament writers go to great length in presenting and discussing the saving deed of God through Jesus.

It was the belief of most writers of the New Testament that God was at work in the life and deeds of Jesus and that what God was doing in Jesus had both soteriological and eschatological significance. The conviction shared by most New Testament writers was to the effect that the last days had finally dawned and that God was acting decisively for man's salvation, renewal, and liberation. Again John Knox notes that the supreme importance of Jesus was determined more by his role and function than by his nature and further, "the christological question, which was originally a question about the eschatological and soteriological significance of an event, has become a question about the metaphysical nature of a person."[7] What must be done, therefore, if we are to understand the meaning and significance of Jesus, the Liberator, is to go behind the metaphysical speculation concerning him and ascertain and study those events which were foundational and believed by writers of the New Testament to possess saving and liberating significance. Men knew Jesus in terms of what he had done for them. J. K. Mozley states, "There is in the New Testament no speculative Christology divorced from the gospel of the Savior and the salvation he brings."[8] The early Christians were not seeking abstract definitions concerning the person of Jesus. The language of the early Christians was experimental, functional, and confessional. The foundation for the theology of Paul is the experience of what God had done for him in his own conversion, and he is basically interested in Jesus as the Redeemer, Revealer, and Liberator.

Brunner has argued that the titles given to Jesus in the New Testament are verbal in nature and character. They all describe an event, a work of God, or what God has done through Jesus in and for mankind. Further, Brunner writes, "Who and what Jesus is can only be stated at first at any rate by what God does and gives in him."[9]

Brunner insists that all christological titles must be understood not in terms of their substantive implications but in terms of their verbal functions. The term *Christos* may be interpreted as the one in whom and through whom God is to establish his sovereignty. The title *Son of God* is functional and it suggests an office and *the work* of the Liberator rather than a description of his metaphysical nature. Even the title *Immanuel* is defined in terms of its functional implications because this title means "God is with us." The title *Kyrios* describes the one who rules over the church. And finally, the title *Savior* points to the one who is to bring the healing, salvation, and liberation for which mankind yearns.[10]

The significance of Jesus for religious living is determined by what Jesus has done for mankind and all the christological titles applied to Jesus emphasize his gift of liberation to and for men.[11]

The divinity of Jesus is a divinity of service. His humanity was stretched in service so as to include the whole world of man in its miseries, slavery, frustration, and hopelessness. The New Testament word used to express this deep concern for men is *splagchnizesthai*. This word means to be moved with compassion, and it is used to describe an emotion which moved Jesus, the Liberator, at the very depth of his being. This word also indicates the depth of Jesus' concern and identification with others. Whenever the Gospel writers used this word *splagchnizesthai* in reference to Jesus, they were attempting to describe the manner and the way in which Jesus identified himself completely with others and how he entered into the world of their misery and suffering, their slavery and hopelessness and provided the means for liberation and renewal.

The men and women of the New Testament period who witness this ministry of service, love, and liberation reach the astounding conclusion that Jesus is the Revelation of a new kind of freedom and has made available to men the liberating power of God's love. Jesus is God acting in the service of men, thereby enabling them to realize their God-given potentials as human beings and as sons of God.

The Christians of the first century saw in Jesus, the Liberator, the answer to their most distressing problems. Jesus in his ministry identifies himself with all men. The early Christians believed that he provided the answer to their most disturbing problems and whatever their needs he was sufficient. The writers of the Four Gospels interpreted Jesus in the light of what they considered to be the greatest need of mankind. For the writer of the Gospel of Matthew, Jesus is the new Rabbi; for Luke, he is the great Physician; for Mark, he is the Stranger satisfying the deepest needs of men; and for John, Jesus is the Revealer.

The people of all races, because of his service, are able to identify with him and to see in his humanity, a reflection of their own images. Today the black man looks at Jesus, observes his ministry of love and liberation and considers him the black Messiah who fights oppression and sets the captive free.

Committed to the Message and Mission of Jesus

The radicalness of the humanity of Jesus is not only expressed in his service but also in his speech. We must permit his speech to address, probe, disturb, and challenge us. Professor Ernst Fuchs has called the rise of the gospel a speech event—an opening of a new dimension of man's awareness, a new break-through in language and symbolization. Professor Fuchs writes: "The early Church is itself a language phenomenon. It is precisely for this reason that it has created for itself a memorial in the new stylistic form of the Gospel. Even the Apocalypse of John, and more than ever the apostolic epistles, are creations of a new language that transforms everything with which it comes into contact."[12]

The words of Jesus have the rugged fiber of a cypress tree and the jagged edge of a crosscut saw. His language is extreme, extravagant, explosive as hand grenades which are tossed into the crowds that listened to him. A tremendous vigor and vitality surges through his words. In Jesus' words, "a man with a log in his eye tries to pick a cinder out of his brother's eye." In the words of Jesus, "a giant hand hangs a millstone around the neck of one who exploits a little child and hurls the sinner into the midst of the sea." In the words of Jesus, "a man asks for bread and is given a stone, another asks for fish and is given a snake." In the words of Jesus, "men strain at the little gnats and gulp down the camels." In the words of Jesus, "a mountain develops feet and casts itself into the sea." He attacks the religious establishment of his day—the religious leaders, the ordained ministers with such phrases as "you hypocrites," "you blind guides," "you blind Pharisees," "you brood of snakes," "you serpents," "you murderers."

Jesus spoke with authority and with power!

In the city of Nazareth where he was reared, this dark, long-haired, bearded ghetto lad took over the synagogue service and read his universal manifesto of liberation:

> The spirit of the Lord is upon me because he has
> anointed me;
> he has sent me to announce good news to the poor,
> to proclaim release for prisoners and recovery of sight
> for the blind;

to let the broken victims go free,
to proclaim the year of the Lord's favour.
                    —Luke 4:18–19, NEB

The reading of this liberation manifesto caused debates, rebuttals, accusations, counterrebuttals, wrath, anger, and hate. The Gospel of Luke is explicit in describing the reaction of the religious establishment to the manifesto of liberation of Jesus. "When they heard this, all in the synagogue were filled with wrath. And they rose up and put him out of the city, and led him to the brow of the hill on which their city was built, that they might throw him down headlong. But passing through the midst of them he went away (Luke 4:28–30)."

Liberation was the aim and the goal of the life of Jesus in the world. Liberation expresses the essential thrust of his ministry. The stage of his ministry was the streets. His congregation consisted of those who were written-off by the established church and the state. He ministered to those who needed him, "the nobodies of the world," the sick, the blind, the lame, and the demon-possessed. He invaded the chambers of sickness and death and hallowed these with the healing words of health and life. He invaded the minds of the demon-possessed and in those dark chambers of night he brought light, sanity, and order. Jesus ministered to men in their sorrow, sin, and degradation and offered them hope and light and courage and strength. He offered comfort to the poor who did not fit into the structure of the world. Jesus comforted the mourner and offered hope to the humble. He had a message for the men and women who had been pushed to the limits of human existence and on these he pronounced his blessing.

The people who received help from Jesus are throughout the Gospels on the fringe of society—men who because of fate, guilt, and prejudices were considered marked men; *sick people,* who had to bear their disease as punishment for crime or for some sin committed; *demoniacs,* that is those possessed of demons; *the lepers,* the first born of death to whom fellowship was denied; *gentiles,* women, and children who did not count for anything in the community; and *the really bad people,* the prostitutes, the thieves, the murderers, the robbers. When Jesus was pressed for an explanation of the radicalness of the thrust of his ministry, his answer was simple and direct. "Those who are well have no need of a physician, but those who are sick; I have not come to call the righteous, but sinners (Luke 5:31–32)."

The greatness of Jesus is to be found precisely in the way in which he makes himself accessible to those who need him, ignoring conventional limitations and issuing that grand and glorious welcome—"Come unto me all ye that labor and are heavy laden and I will give you rest."

The Gospel of Mark records the healing of Peter's mother-in-law. Please listen to this passage. "And immediately he left the synagogue, and entered the house of Simon and Andrew, with James and John. Now Simon's mother-in-law lay sick with a fever, and immediately they told him of her (Mark 1:29–30)." Now, verse 31 tells us what Jesus did: "And he came and took her by the hand and lifted her up, and the fever left her, and she served them."

Jesus is saying to his disciples the only way to lift is to touch. You cannot lift men without touching them. Jesus is saying to the church—the people of God—the church must not be locked in its stained-glass fortress with its multicolored windows, red-cushioned seats, crimson carpets, and temperature-controlled auditorium where according to Kierkegaard, "An anemic preacher preaches anemic gospel about an anemic Christ to an anemic congregation."[13]

The church building must be a point of departure, a departure into the world, into the dirty here and now.

We are challenged to continue in our world Jesus' ministry of love and liberation. We must recognize that to be a Christian is to be contemporaneous with Jesus, the Liberator. To be sure, to be a Christian is not to hold views about Jesus but rather to become a contemporary with Jesus in his ministry of suffering and humiliation and of love and liberation. To be a Christian is to be committed to the man Jesus in spite of the world's rejection of him, in spite of Christendom's betrayal of him, and in spite of the social and intellectual stigma involved in accepting and following him. To be a Christian is to stand with Jesus and participate in his ministry of love and liberation at the crossways of the world where men are crucified on the crosses of poverty, racism, war, and exploitation. To be a Christian is to try again to introduce Christianity into Christendom and to set free again the powers of the love and liberating ministry of Jesus, the Liberator.

NOTES

1. Rudolf Bultmann, *Theology of the New Testament,* trans. Kendrick Grobel (London: SCM Press, 1952), I, 330-31.

2. "Black Theology: A Statement of the National Committee of Black Churchmen," June 13, 1969. Reprinted in this volume, see Document 3.

3. Vincent Harding, "Black Power and the American Christ," *Black Power Revolt,* ed. Floyd B. Barbour (Boston: F. Porter Sargent, 1968), 86.

4. Kyle Haselden, *The Racial Problem in Christian Perspective* (New York: Harper & Bros., 1959), 42-43.

5. Bultmann, *Theology,* II, 40-41.

6. John Knox, *On the Meaning of Christ* (New York: Charles Scribner's Sons, 1947), 49.

7. Ibid., 55-56.

8. J. K. Mozley, "Jesus in Relation to Believing Man," *Interpretation, A Journal of Bible and Theology,* January 1958, 11.

9. Emil Brunner, *The Christian Doctrine of Creation and Redemption* (London: Lutterworth Press, 1952), 272.

10. Ibid., 273.

11. Ferdinand Hahn, *The Titles of Jesus in Christology* (New York: World Publishing Co., 1969), 347-50; Oscar Cullmann, *The Christology of the New Testament* (London: SCM Press, 1959), 3-6.

12. Ernst Fuchs, *Studies of the Historical Jesus* (Napervine Ill.: Alec R. Allenson, Inc., 1960), 68.

13. Soren Kierkegaard, *Attack upon Christianity,* trans. Walter Lowrie (Princeton: Princeton University Press, 1946), 30.

PART IV

BLACK THEOLOGY
AND
THE BLACK CHURCH

INTRODUCTION

An impressive literature on the Black Church has accumulated since the 1960s, but the term still carries a certain ambiguity. In their authoritative, *The Black Church in the African American Experience,* C. Eric Lincoln and Lawrence Mamiya limit their definition to "those independent, historic, and totally Black controlled denominations, which were founded after the Free African Society of 1787 and which constituted the core of Black Christians," while at the same time recognizing that, "any Black Christian person is included in 'the Black Church' if he or she is a member of a Black congregation."[1] On the other hand, one frequently hears in popular lectures and discussions the ploy that there is no such thing as *the* Black Church—there are only Black churches.

While clarifications are always necessary, most scholars recognize that what we usually mean when we use the term "Black Church" is the plurality of formal institutions and networks of ethnic caucuses and congregations of Black Christians that seek to preserve some historic continuity with African-American founders and forebears and some measure of separate identity, if not autonomy, from White controlled judicatories. The general term "Black Church," or "Greater Black Church" (Lincoln-Mamiya), therefore, can be taken to refer to from sixteen to eighteen million Christians in the United States who both claim and are recognized to have some degree of African ancestry and who are organized in congregations and other religious institutions in which the African-American membership numerically predominates and is in control on the local level.

The other definition of "Black Church" one hears is basically ideological and, some would even argue, theological. It is weighted toward cultural and social attitudinal factors. This use of the term came into vogue in the mid-1960s when the designations "Negro" and "Colored" were rejected by the majority of urban, middle-class Blacks and "Black" began to connote pride in dark skin, ethnic solidarity, affirmation of the history and culture of African Americans, and militancy in the struggle against all forms of White racism "by any means necessary." Applied to religious institutions Blackness means the renewal and enhancement of the most esteemed values of African-American spirituality. While a debate goes on about precisely what those values are, the continued search for distinctive norms and characteristics of African and African-American religion points to a de facto sense of separateness on the part of many Black Christians, even as they avow the universality of the Church that crosses all boundaries of race, color, class, and nationality.

One or the other, and sometimes both of these two meanings of the term "Black Church" should be borne in mind when it appears in this essay. The context should help clarify the degree of emphasis intended in one sense or another. The terminological ambiguity that usually arises in any discussion of the African Americans in the United States shows the significance of the problem of identity in every period of Black History and, in relationship to the study of Black theology, suggests why the issue of ethnicity cannot be separated from questions of religious faith, despite a general commitment among Christians to the ideal of a "church beyond racial and ethnic barriers."

Notwithstanding its "client" relationship to White denominations, the Black Church of the nineteenth century was clearer about its identity than many African-American churches are today. It thought of itself as God's judgment upon racism. Its Blackness, therefore, was an expression of its sense of cultural vocation—a calling to serve the *whole* Black person in the *whole* society. By every measure it was an amazing institution. Led for the most part by illiterate preachers, many of whom were slaves or recently freed, impoverished, and repressed by custom and law, this church converted thousands, stabilized the Black family, established insurance and burial societies, founded schools and colleges, commissioned missionaries to the far corners of the world when most Blacks had difficulty buying a ticket on a steamship, *and at the same time,* petitioned governments for the abolition of slavery, fomented slave uprisings, organized the Underground Railroad, promoted the Civil War, developed programs of political education and action on behalf of citizenship rights, and provided the social, cultural, economic, and political base of the entire African-American community in the United States.

This Black Church of the nineteenth century concerned itself with the broad range of needs in the African-American community. Its identity with its African origin and its sense of cultural vocation went hand in hand. The term "African," which had the same force as the term "Black" has today, was avowed by Baptists, Methodists, Presbyterians, Congregationalists, and Episcopalians alike as a badge of pride and a sign of the church's calling from God to vindicate the dignity of Black humanity through the power of the gospel of Jesus Christ.

Sometime between the end of Reconstruction and the beginning of the modern civil rights movement the identity of the Black Church, as an institution with the specific vocation of liberation for all facets of Black life, faded in the face of the enervating forces of northern migration and widespread racist repression. Black preachers and their followers wilted before principalities and powers they neither understood nor were able to control. Most of them shrank behind the walls of religious otherworldliness and distracted themselves with institutional maintenance and ecclesiastical politics. What one researcher discovered about the Black churches of Memphis, Tennessee, during the first half of the twentieth century could be said about most of them in many cities across the nation when the traditional institution shattered and splintered on the hard realities of the urban ghetto.

The ministry lagged so far behind black business and professional groups in supporting black labor unionism and civil rights, that by the end of the thirties a black scholar, Ralph Bunche, could profile the leadership in Memphis without mentioning the clergy, except to criticise their inertia. "The Negro preachers of Memphis as a whole have avoided social questions ... They have preached thunder and lightning, fire and brimstone, and Moses out of the bullrushes, but about the economic and political exploitation of the Negro of Memphis they have remained silent."[2]

There are, of course, exceptions to this melancholy picture of the Black Church of the early twentieth century, but it is close to the truth about the institution as a whole. It was not simply the triumph of Bookerite accommodationism that robbed the clergy of its nineteenth-century militancy. The identity of the church as an instrument of Black solidarity and liberation collapsed under the weight of a pathological and ghettoized version of Protestant Fundamentalism. Shorn of roots in the radical Black tradition of the mid-nineteenth century, Black Christians turned inward to worship a White, Americanized Jesus—the image of their own psychic void—and traditional Black spirituality that had always kept one eye open to the pragmatic requirements of existence under oppression became uncoupled from a sense of the church's historic cultural vocation to transform the whole of Black life.

The major purpose of the new Black Theology movement in the United States, as well as in the Caribbean and South Africa, was not to glorify Black skin color or promote a new form of Black racism. It was rather to impel a crisis of identity that would focus especially on Black Christians—forcing them to choose between assimilation into a conventional form of White Christianity, and commitment to their own sense of religious particularity and chosenness; to see their peoplehood as something providential that bound them to the vocation of cultural decolonization and political liberation for themselves and all oppressed people. The history of God's liberating acts, from the Exodus to the mission of Jesus, the Black Messiah, provided a paradigm of a gathered nation, a people "who were no people," often faithless and disobedient, but nevertheless summoned through their suffering and sacrifice to demonstrate that God delivers those who are oppressed and "to him who has no might increases strength" (Isa. 40:29 RSV).

Whether C. Eric Lincoln is correct in his allegation that "the Negro Church died in the 1960s" because its old self-image and norms are not those which prevail in the contemporary Black community,[3] it is certain that the ghost of the politically irrelevant, culturally obtuse, and religiously fundamentalistic "Negro" church of the early twentieth century still haunts the leadership of the Black Church today. If Emmanuel L. McCall is correct that Black theologians speak mostly to themselves and are mistaken if they assume "that black liberation theologians represent the thinking and attitudes of the 'rank and file,' "[4] it is not because they are obscure, unbiblical, or antichurch, but because the majority of Black preachers have not been trained by them and have been too greatly influenced by White televangelists and the most unenlightened forms of conservative Protestant evangelicalism. Because so many of Black clergy are willing to accept what Lincoln calls "Americanity"[5] as normative biblical faith, they are unable to see how their own ethnic experience in the United States authenticates God's revelation in Scripture and how the gospel then gives meaning to the most profound symbol of that experience—the symbol of Blackness.[6]

The first three documents in Part IV, from the Black Methodists for Church Renewal (Document 16), from the Black Catholic Clergy Caucus (Document 17), and from the National Black Evangelical Association (Document 18), represent the contributions of that part of the Black Church that since the 1960s we have identified as the "Black caucuses" of larger, predominantly White bodies. Most scholars of the Black Theology movement will acknowledge that it was from these embattled Black minorities "in the belly of the whale" that the first voices of protest and resistance against White theological imperialism were raised. During the period from which these documents come, caucuses were organized in at least ten of the largest predominantly White Protestant churches, and Black priests, nuns, and laity were organized within the Roman Catholic Church.[7]

There has been almost no scholarly investigation of this remarkable phenomenon in American church history of the twentieth century, but we will not fully understand the religious meaning of our times until this movement has been carefully studied and its impact upon White American denominations assessed. Within the space of a few years, roughly from about 1965 to 1970, African-American clergy and laity who were assumed to have been securely "integrated" within the White Church, reconstituted themselves into separate Black enclaves for the purpose of declaring war on the White religious establishment and its official theology.

It would be a gross error to assume that Document 19, "The Basic Theological Position of the National Baptist Convention, U.S.A., Inc.," represents the thinking of all the clergy and laity of that six-million member denomination. Its writer, the late Joseph H. Jackson, who was president of the Convention at that time, placed it before the delegates and it subsequently found its way into the record of the ninety-first annual session of the Convention in Cleveland, Ohio, September 3–8, 1971. As such, it comes as close as anything we have to an official position of our largest denomination on Black theology. We may regard it as the voice of that "Negro Church" that Lincoln says died in the 1960s, "but lives on in the Black Church that is born of its loins and is flesh of its flesh. . . ." Somewhat surprisingly, Jackson pays appreciative compliments to James H. Cone in several places. He speaks of his "brilliant theological work" and acknowledges that his interpretation stands upon biblical grounds. But in the end, Cone and Black Theology are denounced, not so much because they do not cohere with the evangelical tenets explicated in the first part of the document, but because Black Theology is understood as threatening the harmonious relationship between Blacks and Whites. It polarizes the races, gives comfort to those who prefer the tactics of confrontation to those of reconciliation, and neglects the experiences of Negroes who are not full of "bitterness and hatred against people of other races and groups."

It is appropriate to follow this negative appraisal of one historic Black denomination with the positive statement of another. Document 20, "Liberation Movements: A Critical Assessment and a Reaffirmation," is a position paper and study document of the African Methodist Episcopal Church. It was adopted at the fortieth General Conference of the A.M.E. Church, meeting June 16–27, 1976, in Atlanta, Georgia. It makes the assertion that "the Church of Allen" came into existence as a liberation movement, recounts some of the history of the denomination's resistance to White oppression, and cites with favor James H. Cone's second book, *A Black Theology of Liberation*. Although it barely uses the term Black theology, preferring to concentrate on liberation movements, it nevertheless should be construed as supportive of the general direction of Cone's work.

Document 21, an excerpt from "The Episcopal Address to the 40th Quadrennial General Conference of the African Methodist Episcopal Zion Church" in 1976, is of particular interest, not only because Zion has long held the reputation of being "the Freedom Church" of the antebellum period, but also because in recent years its clergy were in the forefront of the Black Theology movement. In the late 1960s a caucus of younger Zionite ministers, calling themselves the "Sons of Varick," began to challenge the church to take a more active role in the Black revolution. Among them was Leon Watts, then teaching at Yale Divinity School; Calvin Marshall, pastor of the Varick Memorial A.M.E. Zion Church in Brooklyn and successor to James Forman as chairman of the Black Economic Development Conference; and Vaughn Eason, the founder of the Philadelphia Council of Black Clergy and compiler of the bibliography for the first edition of this book (Wilmore & Cone 1979, 624–637). Moreover, Bishop Herbert Bell Shaw was chairman of the board of directors of NCBC. Shaw was more than a titular leader of that interdenominational coalition of militant church leaders. He attempted to build an institutional base for Black Theology within African Methodist Episcopal Zionism in the United States and Great Britain.

It was important to include here Document 22, "What Black Christian Nationalism Teaches and Its Program." By far the most radical development of Black Theology has occurred in the Black Christian Nationalist movement under the leadership of the Holy Patriarch Jarmogi Abebe Agyeman, formerly known as Albert B. Cleage, the Detroit pastor who founded it.[8] Albert B. Cleage was one of the leading figures in the early days of the Interreligious Foundation for Community Organization and the National Committee of Black Churchmen. He later broke with NCBC and most of the architects of the Black Theology movement because of their refusal to concur with his rejection of the New Testament canon and the institutional Black Church that he considered irrelevant. Still he has been a consistent proponent of a radical Black Christian theology and has successfully organized around its tenets a movement that continues to have a special appeal to African-American youth in Detroit, Atlanta, Houston, and other cities.

The final essay in Part IV is "Black Theology and the Black Church: Where Do We Go From Here?" (Document 23). This was the keynote address of James H. Cone to the National Conference of the Black Theology Project, Inc., that met in Atlanta in August 1977. It is a fitting conclusion for this series of statements reflecting the tenuous and sometimes ambivalent relationship between Black theology and the organized Black Church. In it Cone challenged the movement to "new concepts and new methods." This essay represents an important point of transition in the development of Black theology from a sometimes mystifying cultural focus to a nondogmatic, race-conscious Marxist social and political analysis; but at the same time, from a sometimes narrow orientation to African-American freedom from White racism to a more global vision of human liberation from every form of economic and political oppression.

Many students of Black theology in the period 1966 to 1979 may find it necessary to go back to the Introduction to Part IV, "Black Theology and the Black Church," in the first edition of this book (Wilmore & Cone 1979, 241–256) to find a more detailed analysis and twice as many documents illustrative of the relationship between the churches and the movement than are contained in the present volume. In this revised edition our intention was to present only a representative sample of the responses Black churches and caucuses made to Black theology in the early period in order to reserve space for the more critical investigation of its later impact upon one important aspect of Black church life—the pastoral ministry. That discussion appears in Volume II, Part II, entitled "Black Theology and Pastoral Ministry." The older members of the Black Church have experienced difficulty in appropriating the methodology and emphases of Black liberation theology, but its younger leadership has not been able, despite denominational inertia and conservatism, to ignore it in the practice of ministry and mission in the African-American community of the eighties and nineties.

G.S.W.

NOTES

1. C. Eric Lincoln and Lawrence H. Mamiya, *The Black Church in the African American Experience* (Durham: Duke University Press, 1990), 1.

2. David M. Tucker, *Black Pastors and Leaders: Memphis, 1819–1972* (Memphis: Memphis State University Press, 1975), 102.

3. C. Eric Lincoln, *The Black Church Since Frazier* (New York: Schocken Books, 1974), 106–107.

4. Emmanuel L. McCall, in a review of Allan Boesak's *Farewell to Innocence*, in *The Occasional Bulletin of Missionary Research*, 2, no. 3 (July 1978), 110.

5. C. Eric Lincoln, "Black Sects and Cults and Public Policy," in Joseph R. Washington, Jr., ed., *Black Religion and Public Policy: Ethical and Historical Perspectives*, a University of Pennsylvania Afro-American Studies Program publication (1978), 2.

6. My thinking about the symbolic meaning of Blackness and how its theological

significance comes to light under a mythico-historical interpretation has been greatly influenced by the writings of Charles H. Long. See, for example, his "Perspectives for a Study of Afro-American Religion in the United States," *History of Religions*, 2 (August 1971), especially pp. 58–61, and "Structural Similarities and Dissimilarities in Black and African Theologies," *Journal of Religious Thought*, 32, no. 2 (Fall-Winter 1975), 9–24. For a provocative discussion of the color symbolism of Western society and a transvaluation of Blackness in process terms, see also, Eulalio P. Balthazar, *The Dark Center, A Process Theology of Blackness* (New York: Paulist Press, 1973).

7. The Protestant denominations that experienced the emergence of new or revitalized Black caucuses in the sixties and seventies include the American Baptist Convention, the Christian Church (Disciples of Christ), the Episcopal Church, Lutheran (Missouri Synod) Church, the Presbyterian Church U.S., and United Presbyterian Church U.S.A., the United Church of Christ, United Methodist Church, Unitarian Universalists, and the Reformed Church in America.

8. The major writings of the Holy Patriarch under the name of Albert B. Cleage, Jr., are *The Black Messiah* (New York: Sheed & Ward, 1968), and *Black Christian Nationalism: New Directions for the Black Church* (New York: Morrow, 1972). See also, Hiley H. Ward, *Prophet of the Black Nation* (Philadelphia: n.p., 1969).

16

THE BLACK PAPER, 1968

Statement by Black Methodists for Church Renewal

I. Our Confession

We, a group of black Methodists in America, are deeply disturbed about the crisis of racism in America. We are equally concerned about the failure of a number of black people, including black Methodists to respond appropriately to the roots and forces of racism and the current Black Revolution.

We, as black Methodists, must first respond in a state of confession because it is only as we confront ourselves that we are able to deal with the evils and forces which seek to deny our humanity.

We confess our failure to be reconciled with ourselves as black men. We have too often denied our blackness (hair texture, color and other God-given physical characteristics) rather than embrace it in all its black beauty.

We confess that we have not always been relevant in service and ministry to our black brothers, and in so doing we have alienated ourselves from many of them.

We confess that we have not always been honest with ourselves and with our white brothers. We have not encountered them with truth but often with deception. We have not said in bold language and forceful action that, "You have used 'white power' in and outside of the church to keep us in a subordinate position." We have failed to tell our white brothers "like it is!" Instead, we have told our white brothers what we thought they would like to hear.

We confess that we have not become significantly involved in the Black Revolution because, for the most part, white men have defined it as "bad," for the other part, we have been too comfortable in our "little world," too pleased with our lot as second-class citizens and second-class members of The Methodist Church.

This document is a part of a report entitled "Findings of Black Methodists for Church Renewal" delivered to the United Methodist Church in February 1968 by the Black Methodists for Church Renewal Caucus.

We confess that we have accepted too long the philosophy of racism. This has created a relationship in which white people have always defined the "terms," and, in fact, defined when and how black people would exist.

We confess that we have accepted a "false kind of integration" in which all power remained in the hands of white men.

II. The Black Revolution

"The Black Revolution is a fact! It is a call for black people throughout the nation and the world to stand on their feet and declare their independence from white domination and exploitation. The mood of the day is for black people to throw off the crippling myths of white superiority and black inferiority. The old myths are being replaced by black pride, self-development, self-awareness, self-respect, self-determination and black solidarity."[1]

We are new men—the old man, "nigger," is dead. The "boy" is now a man!

We now stand as proud black men prepared to embrace our blackness and committed to address ourselves unequivocally and forcefully to racism wherever we find it, in and outside the church.

III. Black Power

How then do we respond forcefully and responsibly to racism in America and racism in The United Methodist Church?

"It is abundantly clear to many Americans that power is basic to all human dynamics. The fundamental distortion facing us in a controversy about 'black power' is rooted in a gross imbalance of power and conscience between Negroes and white Americans. It is this distortion, mainly, which is responsible for the widespread, though often inarticulate, assumption that white people are justified in getting what they want through the use of power, but that Negro Americans must, either by nature or by circumstance, make their appeal only through conscience. As a result, the power of white men and the conscience of black men have both been corrupted."[2]

Black power provides the means by which black people do for themselves that which no other group can do for them.

"... Black power speaks to the need for black people to move from the stands of humble, dependent and impotent beggars to the stature of men who will take again into their own hands, as all men must, the fashioning of their own destiny for their own growth into self-development and self-respect."[3]

Black power is a call for black people in this country to unite, to recognize their heritage, and to build a sense of community. It is a call for us to take the initiative, to build the kind of community which crosses all class lines and geographical lines, in order that the resources and leadership of all black people may be used.

Black power means the development and utilization of the gifts of black men for the good of black men and the whole nation.

Finally, it is a call for us to respond to God's action in history which is to make and keep human life human.

IV. Black Power and The United Methodist Church

We, as black Methodists, affirm the search for black identity. When we affirm and embrace our blackness we are acknowledging what God has done and we no longer wear our blackness as a stigma, but as a blessing.

"In religious terms, a God of power, of majesty and of might, who has made man to be in His own image and likeness, must will that His creation reflect in the immediacies of life His power, His majesty and His might. Black power raises, for the healing of humanity and for the renewal of commitment to the creative religious purpose of growth, the far too long overlooked need for power, if life is to become what in the mind of its Creator it is destined to be."[4]

Therefore, as black Methodists, if we are obedient to God's creation, we have a responsibility to ourselves, the white community and to white Methodists to relate from a position of power.

The Methodist Church has failed institutionally and spiritually to be the church. It has refused to take seriously its mission to redeem all mankind. It has denied the black man's right to self-determination because it has frustrated his quest for self-realization. It has failed in every respect to see the black man as a child of God. The reality has been that the black man is denied full membership in the institutional church.

We as black Methodists reaffirm our belief in God and His church. We believe that all men are brothers and that God is our Father. However, we see the possibility that "white" Christians in general, and white Methodists in particular, may not be seriously committed to the church or the concept of the brotherhood of man under the fatherhood of God. We therefore have a responsibility under God to bring about renewal in the church at all levels of its existence. The thrust of "black power" in this context is to awaken black and white Methodists so they might come to see and carry out the mission of the church as it relates to all men. The United Methodist Church ought to be sensitive to every segment of society. It should minister realistically and effectively to the total needs of men—especially those who have been dispossessed by society and the church. Black power seeks to be the moving force behind the black man's effort to get the church to see and recognize him. A second aim of black power in The United Methodist Church is to help the dispossessed, especially the black man, to establish his selfhood in society and in the church.

To do this we propose that black and white Methodists across the country mobilize their spiritual, intellectual, economic, social and political resources in order to exert the necessary influence and/or pressure upon the power structures of The United Methodist Church on all levels to bring about change and renewal in order that it might unconditionally include all Methodists in its total life. At the same time we propose to preach the Gospel of the "somebodiness" of the black man so that those who have not "identified" themselves as men might find that identity and exert their manhood.

We hope that this can be done within the new framework of the United Methodist Church. As for black Methodists, we are determined to serve God by redeeming our brothers, which in turn redeems us.

The Role of the Local Church

The local church in the black community must immediately redefine its own structure and life in terms of its ability to minister to the black community. If necessary, the local church should not hesitate to restructure itself in order to minister to its community, whether or not the restructuring reflects existing Methodist policy. In order that the totality of man's existence (for which the local church is concerned) may be seen as the arena for local church involvement, any redefinition plans should include an examination of all current movements and organizations such as those related to civil rights, social and economic justice, peace and general welfare.

I. Principles Regarding Local Church Staff Financing

A. It is necessary to have more direct "benevolent" giving from the black church to salaries of church staffs in order to compete effectively with agencies in and outside of the church for the best black leadership available.

B. Churches in a given area (parish, district, conference) should develop salary equalization plans, thus making it possible for church staffs to be assigned and utilized where need is apparent without undergoing financial jeopardy.

II. Local Church and Black Culture

The local church should undertake a program of creative teaching about the black man's contributions to the building of America, and nations throughout the world. This effort would include the collection of books and periodicals, contemporary and otherwise, written about African and Afro-American accomplishments, thus making the local church a resource and surveyor of black culture.

III. The Local Church Community

The local church must look upon its task in the black community to be so crucial that the church initiates plans to establish team ministries in every congregation in the community. Such teams composed of clergy and laity, should be organized on the task force basis, providing special functions as legal services, employment counseling, cooperative buying, extra-educational programs, and community organization.

IV. *Effective Educational Programming*

A. The following educational styles should be introduced to local congregations:

1. establish courses of study on the black church to be used in schools of mission and other educational settings (e.g., E. Franklin Frazier, *The Negro Church in America*; Joseph R. Washington, *Black Religion: The Negro and Christianity in the United States*).
2. educate churchmen relative to the role of the church in the midst of violence.
3. educate for the redefinition of ministry in the black community to include concern for the totality of man's existence and the community's needs.
4. establish programs of political action using pertinent community issues, such as inadequate schools, sanitation problems, elections, etc.

B. Educational innovations for local church staffs should include:

1. establishing training programs for effective staff efforts in the black community.
2. establishing courses in urban and rural sociology, each in its appropriate setting; and courses in administration for mission.
3. establishing programs linking pastors and laymen of different churches ("partners in learning") to utilize a variety of experiences and resources.
4. supporting mandatory "refresher-educational" opportunities for all local church staff, no less than one, opportunity each quadrennium.

V. *The Local Church — Creative Power*

A. Programs and policies of all general boards and agencies of The United Methodist Church must be designed and/or implemented to insure the placement of black men at all levels of involvement in those agencies. Local churches can indicate this concern to the Methodist Publishing House and its affiliates, for example, through their support and purchases of church school materials, hymnals, clerical vestments, etc.

B. Utilizing this purchasing power, local churches must also insist that Methodist literature present a more composite account of black people, especially of their participation in The United Methodist Church.

VI. *The Local Church and Economic Independence — "Action Toward the Transformation of the System" — Recommendations for Black Methodists*

A. Pooling of financial resources for specific tasks which take priority in the black community. Such action might involve the following methods:

1. channeling a percentage of, or all of, the benevolence apportionment of a local church to local communal projects undertaken in alliance with other black congregations in a local community.
2. establishing a national fund (a portion of the above to be channeled to a national fund) in order to assist in those communities where personal involvement in situations has been threatened; and in order to aid communal projects in any of the nation deemed in need of national support.

B. Establish the means of initiating and responding to measures employed by "the system." Insure communal responsibility by seeing that:

1. each local church assesses its own situation and undertakes such actions as suggested in VI, A, only after having communicated a declaration of intention to appropriate representatives of "the system," and to the continuing body, Black Methodists for Church Renewal.
2. each church agrees upon means of accountability. When action suggested in VI, A and B, is undertaken, each church should consent to answer for those actions in the name of the black community.
3. responses to measures employed by the system be developed out of the black community's self-interest and strengths. It is in the black community's self-interest to survive in and for its chosen purposes; to realize its own peace and order; to protect itself.

Therefore, let all responses of the system be assessed by the black brothers in the community. Let him whose individual actions jeopardize the community, and whose actions were without the consensus of the brothers, be liable to the judgment of the brothers.

NOTES

1. Archie Rich, "The Black Methodists' Response to Black Power" (a mimeographed paper prepared for the National Conference of Negro Methodists, Cincinnati, Ohio, February 6-9, 1968).
2. "Statement of Black Power" (reprinted here as Document 1).
3. Nathan Wright, Jr., *Black Power and Urban Unrest* (New York: Hawthorn Books, Inc., 1967), p. 60.
4. Ibid., p. 136.

17

A STATEMENT OF THE BLACK CATHOLIC
CLERGY CAUCUS

The Catholic Church in the United States, primarily a white racist institution, has addressed itself primarily to white society and is definitely a part of that society. On the contrary, we feel that her primary, though not exclusive work, should be in the area of institutional, attitudinal and societal change. Within the ghetto, the role of the Church is no longer that of spokesman and leader. Apart from a more direct spiritual role, the Church's part must now be that of supporter and learner. This is a role that white priests in the black community have not been accustomed to playing and are not psychologically prepared to play.

The Catholic Church apparently is not cognizant of changing attitudes in the black community and is not making the necessary, realistic adjustments. The present attitude of the black community demands that black people control their own affairs and make decisions for themselves. This does not mean, however, that black leadership is to be exercised only in the black community, but must function throughout the entire gamut of ecclesial society.

It is imperative that the Church recognize this change. White persons working in the black community must be educated to these changing attitudes, and must be prepared to accept and function in conjunction with the prevailing attitudes of the black community.

One of these changes must be a re-evaluation of present attitudes towards black militancy. The violence occurring in the black communities has been *categorically* condemned and has called forth a wide variety of response, from "shoot to kill" to the recommendation of the Kerner Report. Such violence has even been specified as "Negro violence," as though there were a substantial or significant difference between violence in the black community and that which has occurred consistently throughout the history of the United States and of the world. Black people are fully aware that violence has been consciously and

---

This document, drafted on April 18, 1968, was first published by the National Office of Black Catholics in its magazine of Black liturgy, *Freeing the Spirit*, vol. 1, no. 3, Summer 1972.

purposely used by America from its fight for independence to its maintenance of white supremacy. Since the black man is encouraged to fight abroad for white America's freedom and liberty, we are now asking why it is not moral for him to fight for his liberty at home. We go on record as recognizing:

1. the reality of militant protest;
2. that non-violence in the sense of black non-violence hoping for concessions after white brutality is dead;
3. that the same principles on which we justify legitimate self-defense and just warfare must be applied to violence when it represents black response to white violence;
4. the appropriateness of responsible, positive militancy against racism is the only Christian attitude against this or any other social evil.

Because of its past complicity with and active support of prevailing attitudes and institutions of America, the Church is now in an extremely weak position in the black community. In fact, the Catholic Church is rapidly dying in the black community. In many areas, there is a serious defection especially on the part of black Catholic youth. The black community no longer looks to the Catholic Church with hope. And unless the Church, by an immediate, effective and total reversing of its present practices, rejects and denounces all forms of racism within its ranks and institutions and in the society of which she is a part, she will become unacceptable in the black community.

We, **The Black Catholic Clergy Caucus**, strongly and deeply believe that there are few choices left to the Catholic Church, and unless it is to remain an enclave speaking to itself, it must begin to consult the black members of the Church, clerical, religious and lay. It must also begin to utilize the personnel resources of black Catholics in leadership and advisory positions in the whole Church and allow them to direct, for the most part, the mission of the Church in the black community. It is especially important that the financial resources channelled into the work of the Church in the black community be allocated and administered by black Catholic leadership. To this end, in charity, we demand:

1. That there be black priests in decision-making positions on the diocesan level, and above all in the black community.
2. That a more effective utilization of black priests be made. That the situation where the majority of black priests are in institutions be changed; that black priests be given a choice of assignment on the basis of inclination and talent.
3. That where no black priests belong to the diocese, efforts be made to get them in or at least consultation with black priests or black-thinking white priests be made.
4. That special efforts be made to recruit black men for the priesthood. Black priests themselves are better qualified for this recruitment at a time

when the Catholic Church is almost irrelevant to the young black men.

5. That dioceses provide centers of training for white priests intending to survive in black communities.

6. That within the framework of the United States Catholic Conference, a black-directed department be set up to deal with the Church's role in the struggle of black people for freedom.

7. That in all of these areas black religious be utilized as much as possible.

8. That black men, married as well as single, be ordained permanent deacons to aid in this work of the Church.

9. That each diocese allocate a substantial fund to be used in establishing and supporting permanent programs for black leadership training.

18

FACTORS IN THE ORIGIN AND FOCUS OF THE NATIONAL BLACK EVANGELICAL ASSOCIATION

William H. Bentley

From its inception in Los Angeles in 1963, the National Black Evangelical Association has, in the language of the streets "gone through many changes." Growing out of a deeply felt need for meaningful fellowship among Blacks of evangelical persuasion across denominational lines, NBEA soon expanded its horizons and its self-conception to include ministry. Fellowship and Ministry—these are the poles around which the Association revolves.

At first we were not certain as to whom we should direct our ministry, which seems strange in view of the statement above. Should we concentrate on our Black community exclusively, or should we attempt an "a-race" approach (which everyone said was *the* Gospel Way)? And if racial identity should play a part, a seemingly superfluous question in view of the conscious choice of our name, how could we reconcile ethnic consciousness with Christian witness? Were we any different from white Christians in whose institutions of the time we were for the most part not welcome? Such ambiguities and considerations underlay our soul searching.

But these and other uncertainties shortly received at least initial clarification when the existing racial realities within white evangelicalism confronted our expanding self-consciousness. It was then that we were convinced that our major, concentrated field of service would be, and rightly so, the community which both birthed and nurtured us—Afro-America! Later this initial dedication to reaching our people was to receive more positive reenforcement as we

William H. Bentley is author of *The Relevance of a Black Evangelical Theology for American Theology* (1981). This essay is from William H. Bentley, *National Black Evangelical Association: Evolution of a Concept of Ministry.* Chicago: published by the author, 1979, chapters 1 and 7.

progressively came to see that as a distinct people we had peculiar needs which whites as a group were not able to deal with—because of the fact of our distinctiveness.

Even a cursory glance at our programs of the first five conventions (Los Angeles, Philadelphia, Baltimore, Detroit, and Cleveland)[1] will show how pervasive was the idea among us that the "best" and "proper" methods for reaching our people—indeed all people—were those we had learned in the Bible Schools and theological seminaries of white evangelicalism. The author remembers, somewhat humorously, the reception his early dissenting from this tradition received when he daringly suggested that Black people, particularly their leaders, needed to understand their own people before they could effectively minister to them. Considering the background of the situation, perhaps such a revolutionary challenge to the exclusivity of white evangelical models should have been expected. Nevertheless, the subsequent history of the Association has shown how revolutionary that unintended challenge was.

In this respect, at least initially, we were not particularly clear in our vision, and were far from prophetic in our insights. Theological education, then as largely now,[2] was for the most part oblivious (due to its often unconscious, and therefore seldom questioned, preoccupation with its own ethnic consciousness) to the specific group needs of Afro-Americans. Since we were trained in such institutions it was virtually unavoidable that we would as unconsciously absorb the same views as those who taught us. Accordingly, there was little or no serious thought given to the development of viable strategies of an indigenous nature for reaching Black America.[3]

The closest we came to anything remotely akin to developing indigenous strategies was in a paper read at the Philadelphia Convention on "The Nature and Manifestation of Race Prejudice" (a title not original with the author), in which an attempt was made to explore the origins and contemporary development of racism within American culture in general, and within white American Christianity in particular. The paper sought to address the question of how white American religious culture has affected the nature of the Black religious experience. Today, there are many who are attempting to deal with the question,[4] but in 1964 and '65, neither Black nor white evangelicals seemed aware of the extent to which this was true. Nevertheless, there were some who had some sensitivity to the issues involved in a consideration of this valid query.

At the time, though unknown to us, a few of us were antedating many Black secularists in our rudimentary beginnings of coming to grips with the cruciality of ethnic self-acceptance. Thus, though unknown outside the parochialism of our endemic Black evangelicalism, NBEA early manifested the potential of becoming a pace-setter. Before "Black Power" became the rallying cry it later did, some Black evangelicals among us were thinking seriously in terms of group consciousness.

As indicated above, this essay on the origins of race prejudice within white American Christianity, and how this has affected both form and content of the Black religious tradition, created some small furor. But because at that time our priorities were elsewhere, the ideas expressed and explored gathered dust and were filed away in that shadowy place where all ideas go when their time has not come. Little hope was expressed that these ideas would experience a resurrection. For then, as now,[5] a searching analysis of the roots of racism in Christian context was a major no-no! It was, and is, almost as unpopular with some Blacks as with many white brethren.

Some of the reasons for this reticence were related to our philosophy of economic support. Few of us within our organization were able to believe that sufficient financial support could be obtained from other sources than the standard white institutions to which we as Black evangelicals together with those who shared our separatist stance[6] were tied. It was from these same white institutions that we drew our role models and standards of leadership. The idea that traditional Black Christianity has for the most part been functionally and very often financially independent of white Christianity never seemed to occur to us.

Here was a strange thing! We were seeking to reach people, our people, but we had little awareness of the resources to be found within our own religious tradition, resources that had been forged in the fires of affliction and had not been exhausted by the mere passage of time. We could not draw on these because we hardly recognized their existence.[7] This is a rock upon which all white-based Black organizations eventually founder. The resulting cycle of dependency is so complete that those caught in its coils are virtually unable to escape. The will to self-discovery is paralyzed and Blacks caught in this situation are doomed to look at themselves through the eyes of others. It is no wonder that appreciation for Black institutions and Black resources is so infrequent, and—even then—so inadequate. And even less frequently drawn upon! This is no blanket condemnation of white support, providing that no dehumanizing or paternalistic strings are attached to it. The history of the Black church has shown that substantial support from white Christians has played a more than respectable role in its welfare. Nevertheless, the Black church, especially the Black church in Black structures,[8] has for the most part remained financially independent in spite of its often precarious economic backing. This is a fact not sufficiently appreciated by many detractors of the Black church. Because of its independence, the Black community expects and demands that all religious interests and institutions minister effectively to community needs.

This is a major key to in-depth evangelization of Black Americans. It lies with the Black focus on Black community needs. In saying this no intent is made to deny or invalidate efforts by whites to reach Black Americans either in the past or contemporarily. But we wish to stress the point that the major efforts to accomplish the in-depth evangelization of Black Americans must be the work of Black leadership, with indigenous methods, and with the concept of total needs of the Black community in mind. Why this is so will be discussed in other places throughout the body of this essay.

The theology of James Cone,[9] and others who are in the same or similar theological bag, has had an effect, salutary or otherwise, upon the doing of theology in this country. Cone in particular is also enjoying considerable exposure across the water in a number of European theological schools.

Primarily, Black Theology has a wider currency among white theologians who are not known to be evangelical. White evangelical theologians are not exactly unaware of the existence of Black Theology, since a few Black evangelicals have had minimal input into these sacred precincts via academia,[10] but for the most part, they are far more comfortable dealing with Latin American liberation theology than with this home-grown variety. Which is one of the endemic conceptual as well as structural weaknesses of much of American theology—a chronic myopia in matters pertaining to the interaction of the American social context with the doing of theology. On the whole, therefore, there has been next to nothing done to recognize the existence of Black Theology as a viable contribution, or even a critique to American evangelical theology.[11] It is at least arguable that what we shall have to await is the go-ahead signal from Basel, Heidelberg, Cambridge, Oxford, or the Sorbonne, before conceding even its conditional existence. As Blacks, however, we need not be dependent upon the outcome of that verdict, whether it comes or not. Within NBEA, its existence and its right to existence is acknowledged. What remains to be done is to construct a Black evangelical approach to it.

Nevertheless, not even white evangelical theology can entirely and forever escape from at least an acknowledgment of Black Theology's presence. And the credit, or blame, for much of the little contact they have had with it, and probably will have with it, has come from a tiny group of Blacks, mostly centrally located within the theological discussions which take place within NBEA theology workshops.

As yet, there is no real Black evangelical Black Theology. This is so for several reasons. Very few Black evangelicals are even conversant with the work James Cone and others are doing. The names Shelby Rooks, Henry Mitchell, Gayraud Wilmore, Cecil Cone, Deotis Roberts strike no familiar chord and call forth no recognition from the majority of us. And of the few who are aware of the existence of these and others, numbers of us prematurely reject what we little understand. Still others quickly condemn James Cone, the recognized leader of the movement, as a "radical" who is attempting to institutionalize Black racism as an antidote to white racism.[12] But perhaps the most telling indictment of all is, in the eyes of a considerable number, the "brazenness" of postulating "an ethnic brand of theology." For as a group, Black evangelicals believe that theology should be color blind. Black Theology is therefore "divisive"!

When we look at the ranks of those who are at least rudimentarily aware of what is happening in the realm of Black Theology, we discover that reaction rather than action is the most familiar response. Nevertheless, there have been some scattered, sporadic, and impressionistic attempts on the part of a few to suggest elements of what a Black Theology should be.[13] *Specific* plans are now underway at the forthcoming Atlanta III Convention of NBEA, to address this very need and to get such a project at least ready for the launching pad. The project will be the joint product of Anthony Evans, doctoral student at Dallas Theological Seminary and Chairman of the Commission on Theology, this author, and perhaps several younger theologues who have already made some contributions to the development of an evangelical viewpoint.[14]

The very intense interest shown in this new aspect of NBEA ministry is an indication that we are becoming less and less dependent upon taking our first cues from our white preceptors before we ourselves decide upon the discussion of issues crucial to our experience as Blacks and Christians in this country. What Blacks need most, in the eyes of this writer, as well as a number of others of similar persuasion, is a theological interpretation and exposition of our collective experience, the Black Agenda as perceived by those of us who are committed to the Lordship of Jesus Christ and who believe that contained within the essence of the liberative Gospel of Jesus is the revealed rationale for prosecuting the total deliverance of Black people here in America.

We are, therefore, proclaiming our Declaration of Independence from uncritical dependence upon white evangelical theologians who would attempt to tell us what the content of our efforts at liberation should be. In an effort to make clear that our Declaration is not from theology per se, it will be made more and more evident that our starting point will be as much the doctrine of God and his attributes as the most staunch evangelical theological system. In fleeing from the lion we seek to make certain that we do not fall into the arms of the subjective bear.[15] We see no necessity of freeing ourselves from our own evangelicalism. We do seek to free ourselves from the *implied norms* of white theologians' exclusivisms! Simply stated, we will think for ourselves and will no longer submit, even if that "enforcement" has been the product of our own collective minds, to the compulsion to *first* seek others' opinions before we formulate our own.

As stated above, we are aware, as are traditional white theologians, that the doctrine of God is virtually determinant of the type of theology one comes up with, but we are equally aware of the fact that merely starting with the idea of God does not necessarily lead to a humane doctrine of Man! Had this been automatically so then the history of Christianity in America would have been singularly free from theologically supported and derived systems and etiquettes of racism—something which a study of such history shows was decidedly not the case.

Black Theology, then, as some of us as Black evangelicals see it, in its present form, boldly addresses itself to this very issue. Its chief affirmation, at least in the view of James Cone, its leading exponent, is that God is active in the struggles of the oppressed in a special way in order to effect their liberation. The same view comes forth, with different emphases, in the work of Deotis Roberts, Cecil W. Cone, Henry Mitchell, Shelby Rooks, and others. In these and other writings, it is made clear that God's sovereign intervention gives the struggle a transcendent dignity, and justifies the unconquerable tenacity with which Black people in this country have continued the struggle.

As biblical rationale for this principle of liberation, Cone proposes the Exodus Model. According to this model, God's intervention on the side of the oppressed hinges solely upon divine election and not through real or supposed virtues possessed by Black folk. Thus we are rendered free from the necessity of making ourselves to be qualitatively, in an absolute sense, "better" or "worse" than other ethnics, whether comprising the majority or minority population.

Cone, Mitchell, Roberts, and some others see parallels between the experience of Israel of the Old Testament, and that of Black Americans within America. But the Exodus Model is not the only one made use of by other Black theologians. For instance, Shelby Rooks (of the University of Chicago Divinity School) critiques the Exodus Model and sees it as inadequate for explaining major aspects of Black experience. Instead, he opts for what, to him, more satisfactorily accounts for our experience. To him, Blacks should be viewed as in exile (another biblical idea) and he proposes to call his model, the "Diaspora Model."[16] And there is the view of William Jones. To him, neither the Exodus Model nor the Diaspora Model have substance. If there is divine intervention at all, it is so ambiguous as to be irrelevant. To base the case on the Exodus Model gains nothing, for even in the case of Israel, it has historically proven nothing. Israel has suffered at least as much at the hands of the nations as she has experienced deliverance at God's hand. Thus Jones injects the problems of theodicy into the discussion and tentatively resolves the issue by coming up with, if not a limited God, one who is not sure on which side to intervene. In true William Jones fashion, he comes up with the idea that if Black people or any other people depend solely upon the supposed will of a God, limited or otherwise, for their deliverance, they will exhibit the same ambiguous collective experience as did the Jews, Afro-Americans, and any other oppressed and powerless group. The best, and safest, thing to do is to get on the battlefield and assist God in gaining the victory! Thus Jones' model is called the "Humanocentric,"[17] in distinction to the others, which are "theocentric."

It ought to be obvious from what has been said: the Black evangelicals are not remotely as advanced in Black theological thought as are the men whose views have been briefly and inadequately given above. It is partly in recognition of this fact that our Commission on Theology evolved. Long before the idea was accepted, the need was recognized. For if there are, and there are, substantive bases for recognition of common ground with the *idea* of a Black Theology, there are areas of concern upon which Black evangelicals, as a group, come to some differences in conclusions than some of our less than evangelical brethren come to. Thus we see our task, among other things, as a coming to grips with *both* theological traditions. Not that we expect, or even aspire, to come up with *the* truth. But we certainly hope to learn much more about the theological dimensions of our collective experience than the knowledge we thus far have in our grasp.

Within the Association itself, our interest in Black Theology grew naturally out of the Black awareness movements of the sixties. It has already been indicated that our first rudimentary contact came at the Chicago Convention of

1968. In Atlanta, despite the radical color of the Convention, there was no reference made to it.

Following Jackson, Mississippi, however, interest in it began to grow. In the same period Black writers like Howard Jones *(Shall We Overcome?),* James Earl Massey (at the time his unpublished article was in a manuscript edited by this author), William Pannell *(My Friend the Enemy),* Bobby Harrison *(When God Was Black),* Columbus Salley and Ron Behm (Behm is white and co-author with Salley of the important book *Your God Is Too White),* and the later books of Tom Skinner *(How Black Is the Gospel,* etc.) discussed aspects of it.

In addition, a conference involving both Blacks and whites was held in Boston, Massachusetts, which sought to discuss the issues raised by the Black consciousness ferment. Among the leaders who addressed themselves to this cluster of issues was Roxbury pastor, politician, and educator, Michael Haynes, Ron Potter, Carl Ellis (now a student a Westminster Theological Seminary), and others. The results of this conference, which was not held under the auspices of NBEA, were written up and became the substance of an entire issue of *Freedom Now,* which later was to be transmuted into *The Other Side.*

At the second New York Convention, there was little emphasis placed upon Black awareness per se. But of significance at that meeting was a series of off-the-cuff interviews conducted by John Alexander of *The Other Side.* The interviews involved several members of an intra-NBEA Black Caucus,[18] which became the basis of another special issue under the heading of "The New Black Evangelicals."[19] Ron Potter, one of the better informed and articulate younger Black theologues, was special editor of the issue, which featured articles by Tom Skinner, Potter, Clarence Hilliard, Randy Jones (Philadelphia pastor and one of the more advanced exponents of an economic critique of the role of evangelicalism within the American social system, etc.), and this author. It also included a major discussion of some distinctives of the Black evangelical movement, in which Wyn Wright Potter (co-chairperson of the National Black Christian Students Conference, and now a coordinator of Christian Education activities within the Office of the Black Council of the Reformed Church of America), and Debbie Scott (she has since adopted an African name — Asabi Yakini), together with others participated.

The issue likewise presented an interview with James Cone, though from another connection, and it was generally assumed that our contribution was intended to present some sort of interaction, though perhaps very basic, with the views of Cone. My article, together with the co-authored bibliographical one, was a quick sortie into the area of suggesting some principles, hermeneutical and otherwise, which could go into gathering materials for discussing a Black evangelical approach to a Black theology.

It was at the second Chicago Convention, however, where a consciously Black awareness emphasis was present, and where NBEA initiated the format of a theological workshop, so that the issues inherent in construction of such a theology could be debated. Discussants were three of our younger theological students: Anthony Evans, of Dallas Seminary, Ronald Potter, of Rutgers University, and John Skinner, at that time of Union Theological Seminary in New York. To observers, this was a major highlight of the Convention, attracting overflow crowds and productive of some very enlightening interaction between the discussants.

The format initiated here was repeated at San Francisco the following year, and this time Anthony Evans, now Chairman of the Commission on Theology, presided. In the absence of Potter, co-chairman of the Commission, Lem Tucker of Westminster Seminary, Professor Henry Mitchell of Claremont and Fuller Seminaries, and this author engaged in dialogue.

Again at Atlanta II, the format was expanded to include a paper read by Professor Noel Erskine, of Emory University and Candler School of Theology. The results of this meeting included a less strident emphasis than those that preceded this one, with all participants and observers agreeing that perhaps the meeting was the crucial one in which all ground was cleared and the laying of a foundation for a viable Black evangelical theology could commence.[20]

This rather extended treatment of the expanding role of theology, and Black Theology in particular, as it has developed within NBEA, has several purposes.

One is to show how the emergence of this activity has broadened the scope of how the entire Association conceives its mission of how to reach Black America with the Gospel. Two, it suggests that we are evolving guiding principles which are pertinent to developing indigenous strategies for the areas of missions, evangelism, Christian education, higher education, social action, children and youth ministries, community outreach, political education and involvement, and economic issues involving the collective lives of Afro-Americans. Thirdly, we are coming to be more convinced that programs of social action must be first undergirded with clear understanding of the issues involved and be capable of developing strategies, and not merely reacting, which can effectively enable us to cope with social reality and to build in spite of it.

Because as evangelicals, we have been taught—often without adequate appreciation of our own social, political, economic, and religious realities, or with insufficient understanding of our capabilities and gifts—to see ourselves as others see us, the first step toward answering the question of who we really are must come from the awareness of the frame of reference we are to locate within in order to know ourselves. In this we do not deny the correctness, within limits, of the view of ourselves others have of us. We cannot see ourselves as others see us. But the point made is that we cannot allow the *determination* of who we are to be placed into, or remain as the case may be, outside ourselves and in the hands of others, no matter who they are. The Delphian oracle long ago gave good advice: "Know thyself!"

Again, because an historical and contemporary characteristic of evangelicalism is to dichotomize too artificially "social" and "sacred"—in its extreme form we believe this to be more cultural than Gospel—we Blacks who have come to be called "evangelicals" (and so identify ourselves), having been nurtured under this world view from which the dichotomy comes, have need to be more critical of the extent to which the dichotomy is valid and actually reflective of biblical truth. The outcome of our evaluation should bring new knowledge not only of who we are, but also a deeper appreciation of the cultural realities which are indigenous to us as a distinct people.

A very important part of our cultural heritage is a tendency which may be regarded as the very opposite of the dichotomy. Unchecked, and uncritically accepted, it can lead us to that other extreme—which is just as incomplete and only partially reflective of Gospel truth. Our tendency to social perception, carried to the extreme, can lead to an equally unbiblical blurring of distinctions, where distinctions ought to and do exist. In either case we will be left with a truncated Gospel. Either it will be so severely individualistic, that it is for all practical purposes societally blind. Or, and this is the other horn of the dilemma, we can be so blinded by some elements of our cultural heritage, that we in effect identify the Gospel with our Black culture. Caring for the whole, we must not minimize care for the soul! Our escape from the dilemma consists in our critical adoption of the more realistic "Both-And!"

All this boils down to the fact that we must be anchored to the Rock even while geared to the times! Both extremes must be carefully avoided, in the interest of full truth. Both extremes express important aspects of it.

Perhaps as good a note to end this part of our exploration as any other is to call all of us, Black and white, evangelical, fundamentalist, "Bible believing," or whatever, to the Scripture found in Luke 4:18: "The Gospel IS liberation!"

NOTES

1. A complete listing of all national conventions to date, through 1979, appears in an appendix at the end of the book. Also dates and locations of future conventions will appear in specific places in the body of the history.

2. Black Theology especially in the works of James Cone, but in a very rudimentary sense also to be found in the works of a few Black evangelicals (see the Bibliography), has introduced some unwanted leaven into the theological lump. It is true that such theological leadership evangelical or otherwise, hardly trembles in its boots at the appearance of this immature upstart. Nevertheless, even in its admittedly incomplete form, the theological upstart has addressed itself to the interpretation of the entire Black American experience, something white traditional theological exponents never did. Black Theology has raised some very grave moral and ethical questions and has injected them into the establishment theological debate—questions which cannot be ignored or brushed aside with the time-serving remark that Black people are subsumed under the rubric of the universal. The rationale, however, for this particular ethnic approach is not based solely on response to the negation or ignoring of the Black ethnic experience. As noted above, its basic reason for being is to expound the Black experience in the light of the biblical revelation.

3. The sole exception consisted in some brief remarks which the author addressed to an opening session of the first Los Angeles meeting in 1963. The biblical passage Ezekiel 3 was the basis of the remarks, and through them the message of the need for empathy rather than mere sympathy was expressed.

4. We are now in the post-sixties era, when such topics are regarded by many younger Black Christians, and by some whites, as irrelevant and passe. The gains made possible by Civil Rights and Liberation activists, in spite of the large element of bombast and rhetoric associated with both movements, are so taken for granted by the present generation "which knows not struggle" that it is as though the struggle never had been.

Great effort, therefore, is required to cause the present generation, particularly those whose parents were peers to the activists, to think of racism within American culture as endemic and self-perpetuating, and therefore very much present in basically undiminished form. This is especially noteworthy, since present-day social analysis in this area places far more emphasis on the factor of class than race.

5. Resistance to in-depth analyses of racism comes from an array of sources and will not be entered into here. We are concerned to make the point that there is resistance and it is as alive and well as it was in the sixties. To date the only contemporary attempt to make such an analysis occurred a decade ago, but the majority culture did not accept the results then, and does not now. The Kerner Report was never accepted and made palatable to white America, and that is where the real roots of the problem originate. The problem is far deeper, however, than even the Kerner Report was able to demonstrate, and goes far back into the social, psychological, economic, and religious past of the nation. There are some unresolved basic antinomies enshrined in the political philosophy of the ruling documents of this country, and the ethical practices which historically have grown out of them, which keeps the racial pot boiling without ever cooking anything to mutual satisfaction. It is this author's view that such analyses must continue to be made so long as racism within American culture remains undealt with to the extent that little meaningful and measurable systemic change results. Ironically, an increasing number of Blacks of all ages (but not all classes) oppose such analyses almost as much as do many whites. Their view seems to be, "Why rub salt in old wounds?" A valid point—*if* that is all that is involved.

6. See my article in *The Evangelicals* ... "Bible Believers in the Black Community." *Black evangelicalism as a distinct phenomenon*—and *so* identified—is of very recent origin, and developed out of the same forces which reacted with a new burst of orthodoxy to the issues of the unresolved "Fundamentalist-Liberal" controversy of the late 1920s and '30s. In its earliest form, Black evangelicalism (as a distinct movement outside the traditional mainline Black church) was most influenced by the Scofield Bible and the Bible school movement, which itself was heavily influenced by elements of the Dallas Theological Seminary faculty, notably the Lewis Sperry Chafer theology. It adopted, therefore, the same stance toward the traditional Black church in Black structures, which it regarded as empty of Gospel proclamation, and the Black church within white structures—which it regarded as apostate—as white fundamentalism did toward the major white denominations. Until this day there is much in Black evangelicalism which consciously stands outside the mainstream of the Black church, which it adjudges to be apostate and therefore pathological. Black evangelicalism nevertheless as a belief system though not necessarily identifying itself by that name has historically been the position of Black Christianity and contemporarily exists in major dimensions within mainline Black denominations in both Black and white structures.

7. Special mention is made of the fact that the Black church survived the "Great Depression" years because Black people believed in their institution as having been raised up by God as a shelter in the midst of their experiences of storm and stress. Long before the days when we had a significant middle class, our congregations were made up for the most part of laborers and domestics and others of severely limited income. Still we kept our churches open with beyond sacrificial giving both of our money and ourselves. It is somewhat ironic that in contemporary Black America, when the income of our middle class has risen to the highest level in our entire history, there is a higher incidence of church closings due to inability to maintain them than there was during the leanest years of the Depression. Values and not mere financial ability have a lot to do with performance in this area. The writer is most personally and intimately familiar with Black Pentecostalism, where this phenomenon was observed by him.

8. The term is used to describe the institutional identity of ethnic Black Christianity historically and contemporarily. See "Bible Believers in the Black Community," and also the First B. Moses James Lectures (the joint product of this author and Dr. Noel Erskine of the Candler School of Theology) held at New Brunswick Theological Seminary and sponsored by the Office of the Black Council of the Reformed Church of America. The

specific contribution of this author was "An Historical Overview and Interpretation of the Black Church in America."

9. Cone is the unrivaled progenitor of contemporary expressions of Black Theology. As an accomplished academic, he has within that context continued to place before his peers theological works which have provoked both heat and light. Although others have written on the subject, he more than others has commanded the critical attention of the professional community. His first book, *Black Theology and Black Power,* was a preliminary statement of the relationship of the Black liberation struggle, then carried on almost exclusively by secularists who were hostile to the Black church, to Christian theology in a Black perspective. It also was revelatory of the historical and contemporary inability, or unwillingness, or both, of traditional white theology to deal humanely with the Black experience. Its record has shown that it had been unable to extricate itself from participation in the climate of racial oppression which the white church, for the most part, had been more than a silent partner to. His second book, *A Black Theology of Liberation,* went a step further and built on the thesis that Black Theology was God's contemporary message of deliverance to the Oppressed, actualized and paradigmed by Blacks, as the most oppressed group in America. The third book, *The Spirituals and the Blues,* dealt with the substratum of materials, or at least some of them, which are a fruitful source of Black Theology. His fourth book, *God of the Oppressed,* is his most positive statement to date, although it is likewise a medium of dealing with his accumulation of critics, Black and white. It is his most ambitious struggle to relate his theology to the doctrine of God, and to show how it derives therefrom.

10. The author has had several fairly substantive contacts with some of the leading white evangelical theologians in a professional capacity, and in each case they were unable to see any validity in the case for a separate branch of theology called "Black." To a man, their feeling was that the Black experience, indeed all experience, could well and adequately be subsumed under the rubric of traditional theology as practiced in its classical form in European and American theological seminaries. The same men were willing, however, to concede, at least for purposes of debate, some conditional validity to Latin American liberation theology.

11. See, for example, the July-August 1975 issue of *The Other Side,* and also the papers written by Randy Jones and Ron Potter which were read at the Dallas Convention of NBEA. These papers were a part of an informal discussion with Dr. John Walvoord of Dallas Theological Seminary on the possibility of a Black Theology.

12. Eldridge Cleaver in his *Soul on Fire* assumes that there is no discernible difference between Black ethnocentrism and white. Both are equally productive of negative response to outsiders. Formally, he is right, of course. Black hearts are as evil as are white ones. And yet, although there is much more to it than we can take time here to explicate, the question of who possesses and continues to possess the power in the entire society to make its definitions "stick" lifts the discussion to another level than the formal. What Blacks might do if they were in power is strictly an a priori, which, while valid, is not a final or complete answer to the question. Some Black apologists seek to make a distinction between "white racism" and "Black response." And while there is a good deal of truth there, yet the possible danger to drift off into semantics needs to likewise be guarded against. Sometimes it just might not be possible to clearly distinguish between the two.

13. Witness the ensuing debates within NBEA beginning with Chicago II and running through Atlanta II. See in addition a paper read at a ministers division meeting of Operation PUSH, included in the bibliographical listing.

14. At present Anthony Evans is scheduled to treat "The Biblical Foundation for an Evangelical Black Theology," and the author will deal with "The Contextual Basis for an Evangelical Black Theology" (the titles are subject to revision prior to Convention). It is to be hoped that some in-depth interaction will be possible with some of the sharper young thinkers such as Carl Ellis and Ron Potter, and others.

15. Dr. Francis Schaeffer expressed himself some time ago in an article in *Christianity Today* as having some concern that certain younger Black scholars were in danger of

succumbing to the wiles of Barthianism in their pursuit of the varieties of Black Theology. Some of the same fears were expressed in a dialogue which took place at a conference which featured Dr. Schaeffer and in which this author was a respondent. As it is remembered, the view was expressed by Dr. Schaeffer that reaction to the failures of traditional white evangelical theology to deal satisfactorily with racism in American society could lead younger Black scholars into the mazes of neo-orthodoxy—as though such a theology was needed to give substance to Black theological protest and formulation. The fact of the matter is, neo-orthodoxy is as white as is evangelical theology. It relates even less, in a nonacademic way, to the everyday struggles of Blacks.

16. The concept is developed in a rather well-reasoned article by Rooks which appeared in *The Black Church:* Quarterly Journal of the Black Ecumenical Commission of Massachusetts, vol. Z, no. 1. The title of the article was "Toward the Promised Land."

17. William Jones, for a time, was a member of the history department at Yale University and identifies himself as Unitarian-Universalist. Jones, an avowed humanist, sees little validity to either the Exodus Model or the Diaspora Model. Theodicy is to him the crucial determinant.

How can there be a good and just God if he allows his chosen people to suffer as much as the God of the Bible allows his people the Jews to suffer. These views and others are found in his book *Is God a White Racist?*

18. Because some felt that this Convention down-played and markedly deemphasized Black awareness in Christian context, the interview with John Alexander provided a forum for airing concerns that NBEA might be drifting from its ethnic-conscious base. We somewhat uneasily referred to our interview session as an "intra-NBEA Black Caucus."

19. The lead article in this issue (July-August 1975), probably the most important one, was written by Ron. It set the stage for a better understanding of all others. The central theme expressed by Potter was the affirmation that Blacks would think for themselves. He likewise gave a concise overview of the development of the Black evangelical movement and traces its origin to a more recent time than does this author. Theodore Moran, dean of students at Payne Theological Seminary and assistant professor of Church and Society at the same institution, should be mentioned at this point since his name was not included in the references made above. He has written a perceptive article in the issue also.

20. This is the substance of a personal communication by Tony Evans to the author. All parties to the most recent discussions agree that while the earlier sessions were hot and heavy, they were probably necessary to clear the air and lay the foundation for a more positive statement of the substance of an evangelical Black Theology. Of particularly helpful assistance was Noel Erskine. His acute and sensitive mind forced all of us to clarify our conception and articulation. Carl Ellis also made valuable contributions. Plans are being made for the production of printed essays which will be the substance of the theological conversations to be held at Atlanta III in 1979.

19

THE BASIC THEOLOGICAL POSITION
OF THE NATIONAL BAPTIST
CONVENTION, U.S.A., INC.

Joseph H. Jackson

Part I

We begin with this statement of faith: "God is a spirit; and they that worship Him must worship Him in spirit and in truth" (St. John 4:24). We do not know all the qualities of things spiritual, and we cannot analyze the spirit into component parts. However, we know that spirit cannot be weighed in scales made by human hands or measured in terms of inches or feet. Neither can spirit be defined in terms of any material substances, and the most gifted artists cannot put on canvas a true picture of what spirit is. Whatever is spirit must be approached by the power of spirit or the soul forces in man. Our concept of God is spirit, and our approach to Him must be in spirit and in truth.

Jesus revealed God as spirit and as creative force, and as life-giving and life-sustaining power; and because of His all-inclusive nature, God to us is Father.

Our acceptance of Jesus Christ as our personal Savior is based on His message from the Sermon on the Mount, His personality and life force that He sheds in the gospel writings and through the revelation of truth that comes to us in all of the epistles of the New Testament.

We are drawn to Him by His divine character and by His redemptive love and mercy, and the goodness and justice through which and by which His kingdom is built—and by His sacrificial life, death, and resurrection, all sinners are invited and made welcome into His eternal kingdom.

In the light of these facts the invitation that He extends for salvation is to all men. That is why we preach "Whosoever Will Let Him Come."

Joseph H. Jackson was, at the time, president of the National Baptist Convention, U.S.A., Inc. This statement was placed in the Record of the 91st Annual Session, National Baptist Convention, U.S.A., Inc., September 3-8, 1971.

The Need for the Universality of the Gospel

The need for the universality of the gospel grows out of the universality of the sins of all mankind.

> But now the righteousness of God without the law is manifested, being witnessed by the law and the prophets;
> Even the righteousness of God which is by faith in Jesus Christ unto all and upon all them that believe for there is no difference:
> For all have sinned and come short of the glory of God;
> Being justified freely by His grace through the redemption that is in Christ Jesus;
> Whom God hath set forth to be propitiation through faith in his blood, to declare his righteousness for the remission of sins that are passed through the forbearance of God.
> To declare, I say, at this time his righteousness: that he might be just, and the justifier of him which believeth in Jesus (Romans 3:21-26).

In the light of the truth revealed above, there are no pure races and no superior nations in the sight of God. There are no individuals who can by their wisdom, their knowledge, their rank, and their possessions win for themselves salvation or liberation from the sins that do so easily beset all the children of men.

The Universality of God's Plan of Redemption

God's knowledge of this universal imperfection of man, and God's concern for all are some of the reasons why He included all men in the plan of salvation and in the scheme of redemption. The writer of the Fourth Gospel gives to us the divine motivation for human redemption:

> For God so loved the world, that he gave his only begotten son, that whosoever believeth in him should not perish, but have everlasting life (St. John 3:16).

The mission of Jesus Christ into the world was not to condemn the world or to set one race over against another, or to liberate one race by leaving another in chains:

> For God sent not his son into the world to condemn the world, but that the world through him might be saved (St. John 3:17).

Only those who refuse Him, only those who reject Him, fall under the shadow of condemnation by their own choice and by their own acts.

The Theology That We Reject

Any theology that denies or negates the above principles falls outside of the theological tradition of the National Baptist Convention, U.S.A., Inc. Any theologian, be he black or white, that limits the redemptive effort of Jesus Christ to any race, to any color, to any nationality or any rank or group in society denies and negates the positive principles of redemption as discussed above.

Racial discrimination and any form of racial segregation cannot be supported in the light of the principles of redemption as stated above. There is no revealed truth that teaches us that God is white or black. God is a spirit. National Baptists was founded and organized by Negro Christian leaders, and they themselves refused to restrict their message to their own race and their own nationality. They have not written a creed of exclusiveness against other races or nationalities. What we say against white segregationists by the gospel of Christ we must also say against members of our own race who insist on interpreting the gospel of Christ on a strictly anti-white and pro-black foundation.

National Baptists' Theological Position and Civil Rights

Our idea of God inspires us to work for the establishment of social justice for all the citizens of the nation. We participate in the struggle for first-class citizenship under the guidance of the supreme law of the land. From the teachings of the eighth-century prophets and the message of Jesus, we believe God is on the side of the right, the just and the good. Our faith encourages us and our theological position allows us to feel a sense of obligation to help break the chains of all those who are oppressed.

Part II

An Appraisal of A Black Theology of Liberation, *by Professor James H. Cone, Associate Professor of Theology, Union Theological Seminary, New York, New York.*

Professor Cone has dedicated two hundred and forty-nine pages to his thesis that he seeks to prove, and to his conviction that he most positively and clearly shares. The author displays a wide range of acquaintance and a profound knowledge of theological thought. He has not willfully sought to leave out the great themes of Christian theology. He has included them. He has not embraced naturalism or humanism.

In the very first chapter he begins with the content of theology and speaks the truth when he says:

Christian theology is a theology of liberation (p. 1).

He embraces the sources and norms of theology and deals with revelation with clarity.

He makes no attempt to bypass the subject of God or to render man less than a creature who needs salvation.

Christ is also a conspicuous part of his moving discussion, and the Christ of his theology recognizes and gives due regard to the historical Jesus.

It is further significant that the author here relates all of the great Christian themes to a specific historic struggle.

Some Weaknesses

The outstanding weakness of this brilliant theological work on the part of Professor James H. Cone is his attempt to relate divine concern, and to reduce all of the great historic theological truths of the Christian religion, to the historic conflict between blacks and whites.

The author's thesis and his purpose both circumscribe him and render all of his basic conclusions too narrow to accommodate and to properly appreciate and appraise the universality of the Christian gospel of liberation.

For him liberation means simply the liberation of blacks from the oppression of whites. One would assume from the author's argument that if the day ever comes when blacks are totally liberated from the oppressive deeds of whites, the Kingdom of God would be at hand.

The author overlooks that aspect of liberation that has to do with the individual's victory over the temptation and the demoniac forces within man that must be conquered before he can be considered totally liberated.

With his thesis and his commitment to the revolt of blacks against whites, or the black revolution, he reduces, and maybe he is forced to reduce, revelation, Jesus Christ, and God Himself to a level of blackness, although the author admits that the only way to have Christian theology is that it must be Christ-centered. But when one needs *A Black Theology of Liberation,* one must conclude that the entire document is black-centered. But the author seems to avoid this pitfall by making or reducing both Jesus Christ and God to blackness. At one point he says:

> People who want to know who God is and what He is doing must know what black people are and what they are doing. . . . Knowing God means being on the side of the oppressed, becoming one with them and participating in the goal of liberation. We must become black with God (p. 124).

The author does not at all times use black or blackness as a symbol. Sometimes he means physical blackness. He says in another place:

> Even some black people will find this view of God hard to handle. Having been enslaved by the God of white racism so long, they will have difficulty believing that God is identified with their struggle for freedom. Becoming one of his disciples means rejecting whiteness and accepting themselves

as they are in all their physical blackness. This is what the Christian view of God means for black people (p. 125).

Some Personal Reflections

1. *A Black Theology of Liberation* can easily be interpreted as a gospel of hate of blacks against whites.

2. It could become required reading for those who wish to crusade in a violent manner against the so-called white establishment. The author says:

> Speaking for the black community, black theology says with Eldridge Cleaver "we shall have our manhood. We shall have it, or the earth will be leveled by our attempt to get it" (p. 34).

3. Professor Cone in his conclusion could well defeat all of the constructive efforts in better race relations in America, and could write off the past achievements in civil rights as of little or no value.

4. He not only polarizes blacks and whites in this country, but he freezes the polarization and leaves little or no latitude for future harmony to be achieved.

5. To assume that the total so-called black experience deals only with the confrontation with whites overlooks many other areas of that experience, part of which has accounted for the great institutions of the Negro church and other achievements by Negroes without bitterness or hatred against people of other races and groups.

If the Negro church accepts the point of view and the leadership of *A Black Theology of Liberation*, then black people will become the outstanding proponents of racial segregation in the United States of America.

20

LIBERATION MOVEMENTS: A CRITICAL ASSESSMENT AND A REAFFIRMATION

Position Paper of the
African Methodist Episcopal Church

I. Introduction

African Methodism came into being as a liberation movement and a protest against segregation and racism in the Christian Church and the world. Over one hundred eighty-nine years ago, Richard Allen and his followers were laboring to prevent Christianity in America from developing the racial stratification as evidenced today. The Episcopal Fathers reaffirmed their faith in our motto: "God our Father; Christ our Redeemer; Man our Brother," and, at the 38th Quadrennial Session of the General Conference in 1964, made the following pronouncement: "We unreservedly welcome into our fellowship without regard to race, nationality or social distinction all who will share the faith of Jesus Christ as Redeemer and Lord. . . ."

In November, 1787, the colored people belonging to the Methodist Society of Philadelphia convened together in order to take into consideration the evils under which they labored arising from the unkind treatment of their white brethren. The colored people were considered a nuisance in the house of worship and were frequently pulled off their knees while in the act of prayer and ordered to the back seats. From these and various other acts of unchristian conduct, they considered it their duty to devise a plan in order to build a house of their own in which they could worship God.

The formation of the Free African Society, organized in 1787, constituted the first serious attempt of oppressed black people in the United States of

This document is one of the Black Position Papers of the 40th Session of the General Conference of the African Methodist Episcopal Church, June 16-27, 1976, in Atlanta, Ga.

America to organize for the purpose of liberating their souls, minds and bodies from the oppressive and dehumanizing effects of chattel slavery. The Free African Societies, analogous to the cellular movement of the early church, provided the survival shelter for oppressed people in a strange and alien land. The same liberating spirit that motivated black people in and around Philadelphia, Delaware, New York and Maryland to unite in forming the African Methodist Episcopal Church was not an isolated event but was part of a universal movement of freedom and liberation which, like an idea whose time had come, could not be stopped.

In 1816 the African Methodist Episcopal Church made a formal response to the liberation movement and became a corporate entity for religious purposes. This act affirmed the self-determination process by which a people could, of their own volition, worship God under their own vine and fig tree in spirit and in truth, hold property and chart their own political and economic destiny.

II. The Black Experience in America

It is self-evident that the lack of racial justice in American society both is and has been a problem. It is a problem which has existed before the founding of this nation. It was a problem for the writers of the Constitution of the United States who legitimized the existence of slavery by providing that for purposes of taxation and congressional representation each slave would count as three-fifths of a person. Congress was prohibited from stopping the slave trade before 1808. It bound states to assist in returning fugitive slaves to their masters.

Although the Emancipation Proclamation was issued in 1863, forty years later, W. E. B. Du Bois could write in *The Souls of Black Folk,* "The problem of the twentieth century is the problem of the color line." Du Bois also noted that "the whites, North and South, [have tended] to shift the burden of the Negro problem to the Negro's shoulders and stand aside as critical and rather pessimistic spectators when, in fact, the burden belongs to the nation and the hands of none of us are clean if we bend not our energies to righting these wrongs."

The absence of racial justice is a crucial problem . . . one which lies . . . not at the periphery of American society but at its very heart. Gunnar Myrdal, in his *An American Dilemma,* claims that ". . . the treatment of the Negro is America's greatest and most conspicuous scandal." That the problem still remains is attested to in a multitude of ways, among them being the basic "conclusion" of the Kerner Commission: "Our nation is moving toward two societies, one black, one white—separate and unequal." This report, written some one hundred years later, following the assassination of Dr. Martin Luther King, Jr., makes it plain: ". . . white, moderate, responsible America is where the trouble lies. . . . White society is deeply implicated in the ghetto. White institutions created it, white institutions maintained it, and white society condones it."

The Black Experience is a constant confrontation with racism which subordinates on the basis of color, one group to another, assigning inferior status to one and superior status to the other. For the Black man in America, racism is not a word but a fact; it is a ghetto; it is poverty; it is an event—demeaning in all of its ramifications. It is economic deprivation; it is red-lining which curtails the flow of financial aid to the inner city where the Black population is located. It is benign neglect; it is police brutality; it is inferior education; it is blatant disregard for the health, welfare and safety of the Black community. It is the denial of employment opportunities.

Justice is the ultimate goal because it promotes, as no other single goal, the realization of societies, social systems and institutions which both allow and encourage individuals to realize their full potential as unique persons. This is the end of the liberation movement and to this end the African Methodist Episcopal Church is irrevocably committed.

III. The Meaning of Liberation for the Church

The White Anglo-Saxon Protestant Churches in America are deeply involved in the oppression and racism which exists in America. They have condoned the spread of racism throughout the world. Their missionary emphasis was to carry the gospel to the heathens in foreign parts. The task was enshrouded with a benevolent despotism that brought on 18th and 19th century colonialism—a handmaiden of racism and economic exploitation.

Every white pulpit in America admonished slaves to obey their masters. After the Nat Turner revolt of 1837, many church denominations which opposed slavery vacillated. Many dropped the subject altogether.

As far back as 1775, Thomas Paine denounced the slave trade and indicted the WASP Church for its complicity in the slave trade:

TO AMERICANS: That some desperate wretches should be willing to steal and enslave men by violence and murder for gain, is rather lamentable than strange. But that many civilized, nay christianized people should approve, and be concerned in the savage practice, is surprising and still persists, though it has been so often proved contrary to the light of nature, to every principle of justice and humanity. . . .

Most shocking of all is alleging the sacred scriptures to favor this wicked practice. The plea is, in a great measure, false; they had no permission to catch and enslave people who never injured them.

Such arguments ill become us, since the time of reformation came, under gospel light. All distinctions of nations, and privileges of one above others, are ceased; Christians are taught to account all men their neighbors; and love their neighbors as themselves; and do to all men as they would be done by; to do good to all men; and man-stealing is ranked with enormous crimes.

After America had achieved her liberation and became a free and independent nation, the African Methodist Episcopal Church became the voice of God and the conscience of America.

The Black Free Church reminded America that a righteous God could not smile upon their new-won freedom when blacks, stolen from their native sod, were being held in bondage. A new interpretation and theological frame of reference was established: "God our Father; Christ our Redeemer; Man our Brother." This became the cutting edge and the "balance" in which America was weighed and found wanting.

God's work of salvation in Jesus Christ is human liberation. Jesus Christ becomes the point of departure for oppressed people to analyze the meaning of liberation. The Christological implications are implicit in the prophetic tradition. Jesus applies this tradition to himself:

> The Spirit of the Lord is upon me, because he hath anointed me to preach the gospel to the poor; he hath sent me to heal the brokenhearted, to preach deliverance to the captives, and recovering of sight to the blind, to set at liberty them that are bruised. To preach the acceptable year of the Lord.

The analogy becomes clear after Jesus' resurrection. The struggle for liberation and freedom continues with a new mandate and a new promise of power. It is God's will that all oppressive forces will be done away with. This is the meaning of the Exodus and the Incarnation. It is also the meaning of the Crucifixion and the Resurrection.

The struggle for liberation addresses the "now" and the "not yet" of the Gospel. God's Kingdom is breaking in on oppression, tearing down oppressive cruelty systems.

The Church is that community that participates in Christ's liberating work in history; it can never endorse unjust laws for the sake of order. The Church must say "no" to structures of oppression.

The historical liberation of God is the defining characteristic of the Church:

a) The Church proclaims the reality of divine liberation.
b) The Church actively shares in the liberation struggle. The Church lives on the basis of the radical demands of the gospel and makes the gospel message a social, economic and political reality.
c) The Church cannot be in isolation from the concrete realities of human suffering. It must share the suffering of oppressed people, bear the reproach of its enemies and struggle to bring about a new order.

> The eschatological implications for liberation are to speak of the promise of God's Word of liberation, disclosed in his future breaking into our present and overthrowing the powers of evil that hold people in captivity. (James H. Cone, *God of the Oppressed.*)

IV. Liberation Movements in the Black Community

The liberation movement had its origin in the formation of the Black Church. Much of the post-Emancipation leadership for the liberation movement came from the Black Church.

The cruelty and violence of the post-Civil War oppression, especially below the Mason-Dixon line, encouraged and, in most instances, demanded the urban centers of the North. Uprooted and frightened, these dispossessed and powerless Black people set out in quest of the "promised land" and its new opportunities. They did not find the promised land overflowing with milk, honey and opportunities but they found New York, Chicago, Philadelphia and other similar urban centers to be desolate wildernesses of cultural, political, social and economic exile.

Unfortunately, the Black Church was not prepared to confront this resulting crisis; therefore, destiny and necessity demanded the birth of new organizations which could effectively share in the fight to liberate and empower the disfranchised Black masses. Out of this chaotic bewilderment and against this racist system called America came into being new social liberation movements. The National Association for the Advancement of Colored People (NAACP) and the National Urban League were among the first such groups to appear and, later, The Southern Christian Leadership Conference (SCLC), Congress on Racial Equality (CORE), Student Non-Violent Coordinating Committee (SNCC) and People United to Save Humanity (PUSH). Each of these movements has served and made a contribution to the liberation of Black and other oppressed peoples. Each has sought to fight and resist racist oppression and to advance the cause of liberation. Each group has worked separately as well as collectively in the interest of the mobilization and organization of the Black community for total liberation and self-determination.

The liberation movement in America during the early 1900s was advanced by the NAACP and the Urban League. Through the leadership provided by these organizations, there existed an "era of legalism" in America. Historian August Meier, in *Black Protest Thought in the Twentieth Century*, states that during the First World War the NAACP won its first two cases before the Supreme Court and enjoyed an expanded membership as a result. The NAACP pursued the legal struggle for the civil rights of Black Americans to insure their liberation while the Urban League assisted Black families in adjusting to city life. The Great Migration and the serious problems which resulted from the swelling numbers of urban dwellers presented organizations like the NAACP and the National Urban League with ever increasing responsibilities.

The era of non-violent, direct action was born during the Montgomery Bus Boycott in 1965. Our own sainted Rosa Parks, a deaconess in the African Methodist Episcopal Church, in the spirit of Allen, took a seat for justice by refusing to acquiesce to the racist dehumanization of the South. She found that the walk to the back of the bus was much farther than she had ever realized so she took the first seat she saw.

This era was characterized by a struggle for an interracial society with justice and equality as the motivating principles. The style of SCLC and Dr. Martin Luther King, Jr., SNCC and CORE was non-violent direct action as they pursued these noble objectives for what was still a disfranchised Black community. Operation PUSH, born out of Operation Breadbasket, an offspring of SCLC, has sought to move the liberation struggle into the arena of economic and political self-determination. The seeds of this struggle are vivid in the pages of history for they describe the intensity of the suffering patience of Black people. The history of this struggle is an epic in American culture characterized by sit-ins, paddy wagons, fire hoses, bombed churches, lynchings, police dogs, pray-ins, and a second march on Washington.

An historical assessment reveals that while these foregoing organizations and movements are distinctive in style, methods and orientation, yet they are inextricably one in their quest for the liberation and empowerment of the Black masses. Dr. James Cone, in his book *A Black Theology of Liberation,* states that the hand of God is "unreservedly with those who are humiliated and abused." The same has been evidenced in the liberation and accomplishments of those communal liberation groups.

V. Moral and Ethical Rationale for a Strategy of Liberation

The Church of Allen followed the Federal troops into the heart of the South, gathered together the scattered sheep of Africa who had been dispersed by the ravages of war and human exploitation, fed and clothed them and provided a means of education for over three million disfranchised, unlettered Blacks. Black bishops and preachers of African Methodism came into the South proclaiming the "gospel of liberation," declaring that the spirit of the living Christ was loose in the world—tearing down oppressive systems and ministering to the needs of the dispossessed and providing for the social, political and economic rehabilitation of our wounded race and our wounded nation.

Our quest for the liberation ethic and strategy can be realized only through radical identification with the dispossessed Black masses. This ethic of radical identification must provide for us a framework which enables us to fight with the victims of apartheid in South Africa against racist oppression. This ethic of radical identification helps us to fight for the liberation of the Black masses in Rhodesia. This ethic of radical identification was the raison d'etre of our Lord and Saviour who, like many of the Black and poor masses, proclaimed that "He had nowhere to lay His head." It was this ethic that motivated our sainted founder to minister to the sick and dying during the yellow fever epidemic. Through this dispositional ethic we reaffirm and recommit ourselves and our resources to the cause of justice, equality and freedom everywhere. We, therefore, unequivocally and unreservedly, in the spirit of Allen and Turner, oppose racism, oppression and tyranny everywhere but especially in Africa, South

America and the Caribbean. We vehemently oppose the abuses of the Federal Bureau of Investigation and the Central Intelligence Agency in their several attempts to disdain and debunk Black leaders and Black organizations in their quest and struggle for freedom in America. We call for an immediate cessation to these atrocities. We support the struggles of the oppressed in their quest for liberation. We, therefore, call upon all humankind everywhere to join in the fight to end racism and oppression now, henceforth and forever more.

This interim ethic of radical identification demands that we search for an adequate and appropriate alternative to violence — an alternative which empowers the powerless with the Christian techniques of peace for the righting of injustice and the solution of conflict. We see in the present world-wide revolution and struggles the providential hand of Almighty God pulling down all structures and cultures that dehumanize and enslave, and establishing upon the earth new structures and cultures and societies founded upon justice wherein individuals are able and encouraged to realize their full potential as unique and authentic persons to the end that we all ". . . shall beat our swords into plowshares, and our spears into pruning hooks . . . and study war no more . . . ," and to the end that the kingdoms of this world will become the kingdom of our Lord and of His Christ.

VI. Recommendations

In 1976, at the Quadrennial Session of the General Conference, the Church of Allen, founded as a liberation movement, reaffirmed its position as a liberating influence in the world and made the following recommendations:

1. That the Committee on Position Papers be authorized to study, analyze and type liberation movements world-wide as to nature, function and purpose and to make recommendations to the Council of Bishops as to which movements would most appropriately correspond with our position on liberation. (While we support liberation movements, in principle, we should primarily concern ourselves with those which are consistent with the liberation theology and which characterize the life and teachings of the African Methodist Episcopal Church.)

2. That the 40th Session of the General Conference of the African Methodist Episcopal Church direct the Council of Bishops in their next session to petition the United Nations for Non-Governmental Status.

3. That the African Methodist Episcopal Church convene other Black church bodies world-wide to address the question of Africa, its liberation and development.

4. That the 40th Session of the General Conference of the African Methodist Episcopal Church take a position in favor of the liberation and in support of liberation movements in South Africa and Rhodesia.

21

THE EPISCOPAL ADDRESS TO THE 40TH QUADRENNIAL GENERAL CONFERENCE OF THE AFRICAN METHODIST EPISCOPAL ZION CHURCH (Excerpt)

Herbert Bell Shaw

The Church and Racism

Racial hatred is an old and persistent disease in the blood stream of human society. It divided the Jew and the Samaritan, Greek and Barbarian, the Black American and the White American; and racial hatred is not a one-way-street type of infection, because it infects equally the one who harbors it as well as the one against whom it is directed; because invariably the one who is the object of racial hatred learns to hate the one who has made him a victim.

The Church's supreme consideration must be concerned with the fact that the hatred that arises between human beings for any reason, and most especially when based upon physical differences, offends heaven and shuts such people out from fellowship with God. This is the ultimate danger of all sin, and the sin of racism is so deep-seated and rampant that it should be of urgent consideration and concern within the Church. The Church should not and cannot be silent in this critical hour of mounting racism.

The voice of the Christian Church has been too weak in addressing itself to the task of solving the problem of racial hatred, for whether the Church wishes to be or not, it is still a definite part of the racial crisis. The Christian Church must speak outwardly with a fresh message of hope from God, or, by remaining silent, it will proclaim to one and all that Our God is inadequate for solving the racial problem.

This document is an excerpt from the address of Herbert Bell Shaw, former chairman of the Board of Directors of NCBC and Bishop of the First Episcopal District of the A.M.E.Z. Church. The 40th Quadrennial General Conference was held in Chicago, May 5-15, 1976.

Historically the voice of the Christian Church has been heard speaking out on matters that were thought to be important. It has been quick and ready to defend a theological heritage which has been handed down from generation to generation, for the Church dares not allow its theological heritage to become tainted. But the Church has failed to become sufficiently involved in the racial crisis, which is actually the greatest crisis to rock our nation. While the Christian Church has been only half-heartedly involved in the battle against racism, some of the leaders in other areas of the American national life have spoken out definitely and boldly on the question of racism, and have acted decisively in behalf of minority groups.

We call upon its leaders to make the Church a powerful force in solving the racial problem. The pulpits of this land must point out that hatred—the deep, angry, bitter animosity which we call racial prejudice—warps the thinking in the United States, and is a sin cancer eating at the nation's vitals and dooming the nation to failure. The acts of hatred directed towards Black people in this country are well known and of long duration, but there are depths of hatred and bitterness directed from the Black community towards white America that would shock and shake this land if they could be fully exposed.

The Church must assume that it is not too late for America to solve its racial problem, and it must begin to make its voice to be heard. It is a frightening truth that too often various agencies of the government, and some agents of commerce, have acted in closer harmony with the teachings of Jesus on justice and mercy than has the Christian Church. . . .

The Christian Church and the Third World

During many critical periods of human history, men are called upon to rise up and proclaim a new faith, establish a new religion and build a new civilization. Western civilization is rapidly declining, it is decaying from within. As it now exists it is incapable of serving as a proper vehicle of human progress. The kind of world in which we live now has rendered all present forms of organized society obsolete. This is not only true of western civilization, but of other civilizations as well. The time has come for mankind to rise up and create a new civilization.

Because of their detachment and youthful dynamism, third world people possess the kind of freedom from vested interest in both capitalistic and socialistic societies that are prerequisites for this task. Both the capitalistic and socialistic societies are so involved in the preservation of the status quo that they are blinded to the urgent need of a new civilization.

The time has come for the third world people to rise up and build a new order. The African Methodist Episcopal Zion Church represents the third world people of the Black diaspora as well as the continent of Africa. Because of its ethnic origin and social economic history, Zion Methodism is aware of its identity with the people of the third world. God is preparing to build a new heaven and a new earth. He is calling upon the third world people to lead the way. If this sounds ridiculous or as wishful thinking, I call your attention to the Scripture that says:

> Remove the diadem and take off the crown, this shall be the same; exalt him that is low, and abase him that is high. I will overturn and overturn and overturn it and it shall be no more, until he comes whose right it is; and I will give it him (Ezek. 21:26-27).

Human civilization is ordained of God as an instrument of human progress. When it no longer serves its purpose it is discarded by Divine Providence, and is replaced by a new civilization that is more relevant to the needs of the time.

In the book of Nehemiah, we see God preparing to restore a heritage, and build a new civilization. When God gets ready to build a civilization, redeem a nation, or restore a heritage the first thing He does is to find a man.

When God decided to save human nature from the flood . . . He found Noah. When He wanted to establish a new religion, He found Abraham. When He decided to liberate a people, He found Moses. When He got ready to make Israel a great nation, He found David. When God wanted to redeem mankind, He found Jesus Christ. When God's man and God's time meet, something new is the inevitable result. In Andrew Cartwright, God's man and God's time met, and Zion Methodism was planted in Africa.

Also in prophet Nehemiah, God's man and God's time met. Nehemiah was able to understand that the greatness of Israel depended upon the restoration of Jerusalem. Jerusalem was Israel's turf. It was Israel's place in the sun. The fortunes of the people of Israel were entwined with the destiny of the city of Jerusalem. The prophet understood this. The Israelites with whom he talked understood this. Therefore, they replied, "Let us rise up and build." The men of Israel who accepted the prophet's challenge were those who shared his faith.

This historic truth applies not only to Israel, but to the third world, to Black Africa and to Black men throughout the world as well. It has a peculiar application to this historic moment of world civilization. We would do well to ask ourselves, "What is the Black man's role in the world today?"

Like Israel of old the Black man has endured the affliction of slavery, exploitation, oppression and humiliation. God is moving to restore the heritage of the Black man. Africa is the Black man's Jerusalem. It is the Black man's turf. It is the symbol and focal point of his heritage. This heritage will never be restored as long as Africa is raped, exploited and oppressed. The reproach of the Black man throughout the world is directly related to the plight of Africa. The third world is made up of a multiplicity of ethnic groups and a complexity of religions and cultures. So is Africa. For this reason, we have chosen to view the plight of third world people through the African perspective.

Like Israel of old, if the Black man is to regain his lost domain, he must rebuild the walls of his Jerusalem, and establish a new civilization. He must build anew. The challenge of the Black man is to rise and build.

There is a continuity in history. The new is always built upon the foundation of the old. Therefore, the Black man must know his heritage. He must be proud of his ancient culture. He must believe that this heritage is worth restoring.

When we speak of restoring our heritage, we do not mean that we shall attempt to turn back the clock to pre-colonial days. We will use this heritage as a foundation, the fiber, out of which we shall weave a new culture. Our glorious past will serve as the foundation of this new civilization. It must be one which is based upon Black solidarity, pan-Africanism, and universal fraternity.

To believe in Blackness is not to despise whiteness. To work for Black liberation is not synonymous with white alienation. We believe that it is God's will that all men should live together in a state of harmonious mutuality and creative good will. The only guarantee of such an existence is to possess the power to protect ourselves against the demonic encroachment of those who would enslave or exploit us.

Historical Foundation

If we are to restore our heritage and build a new civilization we must first know our past history. We must know what we are and what we want to be. We must let no one else decide this for us. The African must decide for himself what his self-image is to be. This decision is crucial.

A man's self-perception is vital to what he does. His self-perception is still largely the result of his view of history. If African history is to provide the African with his self-perception and thus play an effective role in the building of an independent Africa, it has to correct the distortion and bridge the gap created by the colonial experience in the African historical tradition. African history must evolve its own identity independent of western historiography, the shackles of outside acceptability notwithstanding. (*Daedalus,* Spring 1974, p. 131.)

The Black man's history goes back beyond the horizons of dim antiquity. Africa is the cradle of humanity. Our history goes back before the Sahara was a desert and before the Semites ever swept down from the Arabian desert and from other parts of Asia.

It was in Africa that the early man developed the use of tools. This was more than a million years ago. Sixty thousand years ago the Black man discovered the use of fire. Egypt is the cradle of civilizations. The earliest of Egyptian civilizations was of Black African origin.

We must study the great empires of Ancient Africa: Ghana, Mali, Kanem-Bornu, Songhay, Benin, and many others. We must learn what made the empires great, and why they disappeared.

Men make history and history makes men. Man's historical experience determines his self-image. As we study the history of pre-colonial Africa we meet a people who had developed a strong historical tradition that contributed to a wholesome self-image. For thousands of years Black Africa had its conquerors and its heroes. It had experienced change that was gradual or rapid, peaceful and tragic, local and universal, superficial and fundamental. The African historical tradition enabled him to see and view both decay and renewal as a part of human growth and development. He saw the past, present and future linked together by the continuous flow of history. Continuity and stability were the essential ingredients in the African philosophy that enabled him to understand his historical experience. This does not mean that the African had a static view of life, but that his sense of historic continuity was keen and comprehensive.

Speaking of pre-colonial Africa, E. J. Alagoa says:

Yet in spite of his conceptualization of a prosaic recent past and a glorious remote past a sense of continuity was maintained. The living identified themselves with the founding ancestors, and each man's self-confidence derived largely from his pride in them. He faced odds and tribulation in the knowledge that they continued to care about what happened to them. The youth were taught to revere and know their ancestors. The elders who were seen as drawing closer to the ancestors were regarded as potential recruits to their ranks and deemed to possess similar powers to influence the actions and fortunes of future generations. *(Daedalus,* Spring 1974, p. 126.)

The African emphasized the solidarity and uniqueness of each community. This gave him a strength and resilience that enabled him to evolve his own brand of Christianity, Judaism and Islam. Founded upon the belief of the intercommunication of past, present and future, the concept of the extended family and reverence for ancestors, the solidarity of African society and the continuity of African tradition were secured. African empires rose and fell, conquerors came and went, there were good times and bad, but African culture continued to grow from strength to strength.

European colonization interrupted this continual flow of African tradition. It produced a traumatic effect upon African life by imposing on the African a gross distortion of its historical tradition. Having conquered through the technological superiority of their armaments, Europeans sought to maintain control over Africans, not only through technology, but also psychological defeatism. (Ibid., p. 126.)

Slavery, exploitation, racism, tribal strife were used as instruments of oppression and annihilation. The colonial masters made use of the big lie.

They declared that there was no such thing as African history and African Civilization; that the African had done nothing worthy of historical attention; that they were passive recipients and mere spectators of the march of human developments. This caused the Africans themselves to experience shock, widespread disorientation and loss of identity. This tragedy, as traumatic as it was,

was by no means totally successful, neither on the African continent nor among Africans of the diaspora. Notwithstanding, much damage has been done. The African fell behind in many phases of human development.

The walls of African culture have been torn down. The gates of African dignity have been destroyed by white European exploitation, oppression, tribal strife, and the lack of technological advancement. Our task is clear. Out of the ruins of yesterday we must build our new Jerusalem.

You see the distress we are in, how Jerusalem lieth waste and the gates thereof are burned with fire; come, let us build up the walls of Jerusalem that we be no more a reproach.

Black Africa is not entirely free. Economic servitude, technological dependence and neo-colonialism conspire to make us half slave. The nations of Black Africa must make greater strides toward economic and technological self-sufficiency. The nations of Africa are aware of these needs. "Operation Feed Yourself" in Ghana and similar projects in other African countries are attempts to free Africa from the clutches of neo-colonialism. Armed with a full knowledge of Africa's past glory, we must rise up and build. As our ancestors built civilizations in the past, so must we in the present and future.

22

WHAT BLACK CHRISTIAN NATIONALISM TEACHES AND ITS PROGRAM

Statement from the Black Christian Nationalist Church, Inc., 1976

1. Nothing is more sacred than the Liberation of Black people.

2. The dream of "integration" reflects our acceptance of the myth of Black inferiority, and serves as the basis for our continuing enslavement.

3. Even within the framework of a correct analysis, philosophy, and program projection, it is impossible to build an effective organization without loyalty, discipline, and a clearly defined chain of command.

4. Individualism is a beast within each of us. We must fight the beast within as well as the beast without.

5. Black people are separate in every way and we must use our separateness as a basis for achieving power.

6. Black people had a rich and glorious history and culture long before the white man emerged from the caves.

7. The spirituality of African people encompassed the totality of life. Politics and economics are sacred because they offer programmatic mechanisms for our struggle against white oppression.

8. Properly interpreted, the Bible is a history of God's relationship with the African Nation, Israel, and the Black Messiah, Jesus. Without a correct BCN interpretation, the Bible has served to confuse and enslave a powerless Black people who have waited in vain for deliverance here on earth, and for transportation to a mythical heaven in the sky after death.

9. The "Latter Days" foretold by the Prophets ended almost 2,000 years ago. The end was climaxed by the fall of Jerusalem and the Fort of Masada and the dispersion of the Black Nation Israel throughout the world. The prophecies from the Bible cannot be applied literally to the problems and realities of today. Biblical prophecy voiced the will of God for the African Nation Israel at a particular time and place.

Only the ignorant wait for the fulfillment of the prophecies addressed to a past which is dead and finished.

BCN is the living prophetic voice of God for African people in this day, and our prophecies will come to pass when Black people totally commit their lives to the struggle against white oppression.

10. God has historically chosen to work through groups and nations rather than through individuals. As shown in the Bible, the God of the Black Nation works through the power of the group experience to transform individuals and to bring into being a communal Black Nation.

The BCN Program

I. The Black Church must seriously work for the liberation of Black people through the realization of concrete and attainable goals here on earth as defined by the Black Christian Nationalist Movement.

II. BCN understands the vicious power reality of the white man's imperialistic, capitalistic, and individualistic society, and fights to free Black men from it by giving a revolutionary programmatic structure and direction to the Black Church by re-affirming the African origins of Christianity and the historic Blackness of the biblical Nation Israel and the Black Messiah Jesus, as the basis of our struggle for African Redemption and the Liberation of Black people everywhere.

III. Realizing that power resides in institutions and not in individuals, BCN works to establish and develop counter institutions essential to a Pan-African Communal Black Society:

1. BCN works to build a revolutionary Black Church with a new Black Theology to serve the interests of Black people.
2. BCN works to build new Black schools which can re-affirm the Black man's original African identity, build a new commitment to African communal living, and teach the skills necessary for life in a highly technical, industrial society.
3. BCN works to build a complex of urban rural communes within which Black people can receive many of the advantages of African communal living in the satisfaction of everyday needs.
4. BCN works to create and implement a new Black economics which will enable many Black people to labor within a communal environment which places top priority upon service to the Black community.
5. BCN works to create a new independent Black political structure capable of focusing maximum political power in support of the interests of the Black community as defined by BCN.
6. BCN works to establish Black hospitals and social agencies to serve the Black community.
7. BCN works to establish a Pan-African communications network uniting African people and Black Liberation movements throughout the world.

8. BCN works to support Separatist Black Liberation movements everywhere.
9. BCN works for African Redemption (the Liberation, Unification, and Industrialization of our Motherland, Africa), as the cornerstone of the BCN Position.
10. Even as we work to build a world-wide institutional base for Pan-Africanism, we commit our lives and our resources to defend and protect Black communities and institutions functioning within the framework of the BCN Position.

23

BLACK THEOLOGY AND THE BLACK CHURCH: WHERE DO WE GO FROM HERE?

James H. Cone

Since the appearance of black theology in the late 1960s, much has been written and said about the political involvement of the black church in black people's historical struggle for justice in North America. Black theologians and preachers have rejected the white church's attempt to separate love from justice and religion from politics because we are proud descendants of a black religious tradition that has always interpreted its confession of faith according to the people's commitment to the struggle for earthly freedom. Instead of turning to Reinhold Niebuhr and John Bennett for ethical guidance in those troubled times, we searched our past for insight, strength and the courage to speak and do the truth in an extreme situation of oppression. Richard Allen, James Varick, Harriet Tubman, Sojourner Truth, Henry McNeal Turner and Martin Luther King, Jr., became household names as we attempted to create new theological categories that would express our historical fight for justice.

It was in this context that the "Black Power" statement was written in July 1966 by an ad hoc National Committee of Negro Churchmen [now known as the National Conference of Black Churchmen.][1] The cry of Black Power by Willie Ricks and its political and intellectual development by Stokely Carmichael and others challenged the black church to move beyond the models of love defined in the context of white religion and theology. The black church was thus faced with a theological dilemma: either reject Black Power as a contradiction of Christian love (and thereby join the white church in its condemnation of Black Power advocates as un-American and unchristian), or accept Black Power as a socio-political expression of the truth of the gospel. These two possibilities were the only genuine alternatives before us, and we

---

This essay, first presented as a lecture for the Black Theology Project of the Theology in the Americas Conference, August 1977, is reprinted from *Cross Currents,* Summer 1977.

had to decide on whose side we would take our stand.

We knew that to define Black Power as the opposite of the Christian faith was to reject the central role that the black church has played in black people's historical struggle for freedom. Rejecting Black Power also meant that the black church would ignore its political responsibility to empower black people in their present struggle to make our children's future more humane than intended by the rulers in this society. Faced with these unavoidable consequences, it was not possible for any self-respecting church-person to desecrate the memories of our mothers and fathers in the faith by siding with white people who murdered and imprisoned black people simply because of our persistent audacity to assert our freedom. To side with white theologians and preachers who questioned the theological legitimacy of Black Power would have been similar to siding with St. George Methodist Church against Richard Allen and the Bethelites in their struggle for independence during the late 18th and early 19th centuries. We knew that we could not do that, and no amount of white theological reasoning would be allowed to blur our vision of the truth.

But to accept the second alternative and thereby locate Black Power in the Christian context was not easy. First, the acceptance of Black Power would appear to separate us from Martin Luther King, Jr., and we did not want to do that. King was our model, having creatively combined religion and politics, and black preachers and theologians respected his courage to concretize the political consequences of his confession of faith. Thus we hesitated to endorse the "Black Power" movement, since it was created in the context of the James Meredith March by Carmichael and others in order to express their dissatisfaction with King's continued emphasis on non-violence and Christian love.[2] As a result of this sharp confrontation between Carmichael and King, black theologians and preachers felt themselves caught in a terrible predicament of wanting to express their continued respect for and solidarity with King, but disagreeing with his rejection of Black Power.

Secondly, the concept of Black Power presented a problem for black theologians and preachers not only because of our loyalty to Martin Luther King, but also because many of us had been trained in white seminaries and had internalized much of white people's definition of Christianity. While the rise and growth of independent black churches suggested that black people had a different perception of the gospel than whites, yet there was no formal theological tradition to which we could turn in order to justify our definition of Black Power as an expression of the Christian gospel. Our intellectual ideas of God, Jesus, and the Church were derived from white European theologians and their textbooks. When we speak of Christianity in theological categories, using such terms as revelation, incarnation and reconciliation, we naturally turn to people like Barth, Tillich and Bultmann for guidance and direction. But these Europeans did not shape their ideas in the social context of white racism and thus could not help us out of our dilemma. But if we intended to fight on a theological and intellectual level as a way of empowering our historical and political struggle for justice, we had to create a new theological movement, one that was derived from and thus accountable to our people's fight for justice. To accept Black Power as Christian required that we thrust ourselves into our history in order to search for new ways to think and be black in this world. We felt the need to explain ourselves and to be understood from our own vantage point and not from the perspective and experiences of whites. When white liberals questioned this approach to theology, our response was very similar to the bluesman in Mississippi when told he was not singing his song correctly: "Look-a-heah, man, dis yere *mah song,* en I'll sing it howsoevah I pleases."[3]

Thus we sang our Black Power songs, knowing that the white church establishment would not smile upon our endeavors to define Christianity independently of their own definitions of the gospel. For the power of definition is a prerogative that oppressors never want to give up. Furthermore, to *say* that love is compatible with Black Power is one thing, but to demonstrate this compatibility in theology and the praxis of life is another. If the reality of a thing was no more than its verbalization in a written document, the black church since 1966 would be a model of the creative integration of theology and life, faith and the struggle for justice. But we know that the meaning of reality is found *only* in its historical embodiment in people as structured in societal arrangements. Love's meaning is not found in sermons or theological textbooks but rather in the creation of social structures that are not dehumanizing and oppressive. This insight impressed itself on our religious consciousness, and we were deeply troubled by the inadequacy of our historical obedience when measured by our faith claims. From 1966 to the present, black theologians and preachers, both in the church and on the streets, have been searching for new ways to confess and to live our faith in God so that the black church would not make religion the opiate of our people.

The term "Black Theology" was created in this social and religious context. It was initially understood as the theological arm of Black Power, and it enabled us to express our theological imagination in the struggle of freedom independently of white theologians. It was the one term that white ministers and theologians did not like, because, like Black Power in politics, black theology located the theological starting point in the black experience and not the particularity of the western theological tradition. We did not feel ourselves accountable to Aquinas, Luther or Calvin but to David Walker, Daniel Payne and W. E. B. Du Bois. The depth and passion in which we express our solidarity with the black experience over against the western tradition led some black scholars in religion to reject theology itself as alien to the black culture.[4] Others, while not rejecting theology entirely, contended that black theologians should turn primarily to African religions and philosophy in order to develop a black theology consistent with and accountable to our historical roots.[5] But all of us agreed that we were living at the beginning of a new historical moment, and this required the development of a *black* frame of reference that many called "black theology."

The consequence of our affirmation of a black theology led to the creation of black caucuses in white churches, a permanent ecumenical church body under the title of the National Conference of Black Churchmen, and the endorsement of James Forman's "Black Manifesto." In June 1969 at the Inter-denominational Theological Center in Atlanta and under the aegis of NCBC's Theological Commission, a group of black theologians met to write a policy statement on black theology. This statement, influenced by my book, *Black Theology and Black Power,* which had appeared two months earlier, defined black theology as a "theology of black liberation."[6]

Black theology, then, was not created in a vacuum and neither was it simply the intellectual enterprise of black professional theologians. Like our sermons and songs, black theology was born in the context of the black community as black people were attempting to make sense out of their struggle for freedom. In one sense, black theology is as old as when the first African refused to accept slavery as consistent with religion and as recent as when a black person intuitively recognizes that the confession of the Christian faith receives its meaning only in relation to political justice. Although black theology may be considered to have formally appeared only when the first book was published on it in 1969, informally, the reality that made the book possible was already present in the black experience and was found in our songs, prayers, and sermons. In these outpourings are expressed the black visions of truth, pre-eminently the certainty that we were created not for slavery but for freedom. Without this dream of freedom, so vividly expressed in the life, teachings, and death of Jesus, Malcolm, and Martin, there would be no black theology, and we would have no reason to be assembled in this place. We have come here today to plan our future and to map out our strategy because we have a dream that has not been realized.

To be sure, we have talked and written about this dream. Indeed, every Sunday morning black people gather in our churches, to find out where we are in relation to the actualization of our dream. The black church community really believes that where there is no vision the people perish. If people have no dreams they will accept the world as it is and will not seek to change it. To dream is to know what "is ain't suppose to be." No one in our time expressed this eschatological note more clearly than Martin Luther King, Jr. In his "March on Washington" address in 1963 he said: "I have a dream that one day my four children will live in a nation where they will not be judged by the color of their skin but by the content of their character." And the night before his death in 1968, he reiterated his eschatological vision: "I may not get there with you, but I want you to know tonight that we as a people will get to the promised land."

What visions do we have for the people in 1977? Do we still believe with Martin King that "we as a people will get to the promised land"? If so, how will we get there? Will we get there simply by preaching sermons and singing songs about it? What is the black church doing in order to actualize the dreams that it talks about? These are hard questions, and they are not intended as a put-down of the black church. I was born in the black church in Bearden, Arkansas, and began my Ministry in that church at the early age of sixteen. Everything I am as well as what I know that I ought to be was shaped in the context of the black church. Indeed, it is because I love the church that I am required, as one of its theologians and preachers, to ask: When do the black church's actions deny its faith? What are the activities in our churches that should not only be rejected as unchristian but also exposed as demonic? What are the evils in our church and community that we should commit ourselves to destroy? Bishops, pastors, and church executives do not like to disclose the wrong-doings of their respective denominations. They are like doctors, lawyers, and other professionals who seem bound to keep silent, because to speak the truth is to guarantee one's exclusion from the inner dynamics of power in the profession. But I contend that *faith* of the black church lays a claim upon all church people that transcends the social mores of a given profession. Therefore, to cover-up and to minimize the sins of the church is to guarantee its destruction as a community of faith, committed to the liberation of the oppressed. If we want the black church to live beyond our brief histories and thus to serve as the "Old Ship of Zion" that will carry the people home to freedom, then we had better examine the direction in which the ship is going. Who is the Captain of the Ship, and what are his economic and political interests? This question should not only be applied to bishops, but to pastors and theologians, deacons and stewards. Unless we are willing to apply the most severe scientific analysis to our church communities in terms of economics and politics and are willing to confess and repent of our sins in the struggle for liberation, then the black church, as we talk about it, will remain a relic of history and nothing more. God will have to raise up new instruments of freedom so that his faithfulness to liberate the poor and weak can be realized in history. We must not forget that God's Spirit will use us as her instrument only insofar as we remain agents of liberation by using our resources for the empowerment of the poor and weak. But if we, like Israel in the Old Testament, forget about our Exodus experience and the political responsibility it lays upon us to be the historical embodiment of freedom, then, again like Israel, we will become objects of God's judgment. It is very easy for us to expose the demonic and oppressive character of the white church, and I have done my share of that. But such exposure of the sins of the white church, without applying the same criticism to ourselves, is hypocritical and serves as a camouflage of our own shortcomings and sins. Either we mean what we say about liberation or we do not. If we mean it, the time has come for an inventory in terms of the authenticity of our faith as defined by the historical commitment of the black denominational churches toward liberation.

I have lectured and preached about the black church's involvement in our liberation struggle all over North America. I have told the stories of Richard Allen and James Varick, Adam Clayton Powell and Martin Luther King. I have talked about the double-meaning in the Spirituals, the passion of the sermon and prayer, the ecstasy of the shout and conversion experience in terms of an eschatological happening in the lives of people, empowering them to fight for earthly freedom. Black theology, I have contended, is a theology of liberation, because it has emerged out of and is accountable to a black church that has always been involved in our historical fight for justice. When black preachers and laypeople hear this message, they respond enthusiastically and with a sense of pride that they belong to a radical and creative tradition. But when I speak to young blacks in colleges and universities, most are surprised that such a radical black church tradition really exists. After hearing about David Walker's "Appeal" in 1829, Henry H. Garnet's "Address to the Slaves" in 1843, and Henry M. Turner's affirmation that "God is a Negro" in 1898, these young blacks are shocked. Invariably they ask, "Whatever happened to the black churches of today?" "Why don't we have the same radical spirit in our preachers and churches?" Young blacks contend that the black churches of today, with very few exceptions, are not involved in liberation but primarily concerned about how much money they raise for a new church building or the preacher's anniversary.

This critique of the black church is not limited to the young college students. Many black people view the church as a hindrance to black liberation, because black preachers and church members appear to be more concerned about their own institutional survival than the freedom of poor people in their communities. "Historically," many radical blacks say, "the black church *was* involved in the struggle but today it is not." They often turn the question back upon me, saying: "All right, granted what you say about the historical black church, but *where* is an institutional black church denomination that still embodies the vision that brought it into existence? Are you saying that the present day AME Church or AME Zion Church has the same historical commitment for justice that it had under the leadership of Allen and Payne or Rush and Varick?" Sensing that they have a point difficult to refute, these radicals then say that it is not only impossible to find a black church denomination committed to black liberation but also difficult to find a local congregation that defines its ministry in terms of the needs of the oppressed and their liberation.

Whatever we might think about the unfairness of this severe indictment, we would be foolish to ignore it. For connected with this black critique is our international image. In the African context, not to mention Asia and Latin America, the black church experiences a similar credibility problem. There is little in our theological expressions and church practice that rejects American capitalism or recognizes its oppressive character in Third World countries. The time has come for us to move beyond institutional survival in a capitalistic and racist society and begin to take more seriously our dreams about a new heaven and a new earth. Does this dream include capitalism or is it a radically new way of life more consistent with African socialism as expressed in the *Arsha Declaration* in Tanzania?[7]

Black theologians and church people must now move beyond a mere reaction to white racism in America and begin to extend our vision of a new socially constructed humanity for the whole inhabited world. We must be concerned with the quality of human life not only in the ghettos of American cities but also in Africa, Asia and Latin America. Since humanity is one, and cannot be isolated into racial and national groups, there will be no freedom for anyone until there is freedom for all. This means that we must enlarge our vision by connecting it with that of other oppressed peoples so that together all the victims of the world might take charge of their history for the creation of a new humanity. As Frantz Fanon taught us: if we wish to live up to our people's expectations, we must look beyond European and American capitalism. Indeed, "we must invent and we must make discoveries. . . . For Europe, for ourselves and for humanity, we must turn over a new leaf, we must work out new concepts, and try to set afoot a new [humanity]."[8]

New times require new concepts and methods. To dream is not enough. We must come down from the mountain top and experience the hurts and pain of the people in the valley. Our dreams need to be socially analyzed, for without scientific analysis they will vanish into the night. Furthermore, social analysis will test the nature of our commitment to the dreams we preach and sing about. This is one of the important principles we learned from Martin King and many black preachers who worked with him. Real substantial change in societal structures requires scientific analysis. King's commitment to social analysis not only characterized his involvement in the civil rights movement but also led him to take a radical stand against the war in Vietnam. Through scientific analysis, King saw the connection between the oppression of blacks in North America and the United States involvement in Vietnam. It is to his credit that he never allowed a pietistic faith in the other world to become a substitute for good judgment in this world. He not only preached sermons about the promised land but concretized his vision with a political attempt to actualize his hope.

I realize, with Merleau-Ponty, that "one does not become a revolutionary through science but through indignation."[9] Every revolution needs its Rosa Parks. This point has often been overlooked by Marxists and other sociologists who seem to think that all answers are found in scientific analysis. Mao Tse-tung responded to such an attitude with this comment: "There are people who think that Marxism is a kind of magic truth with which one can cure any disease. We should tell them that dogmas are more useless than cow dung. Dung can be used as fertilizer."[10]

But these comments do not disprove the truth of the Marxists' social analysis which focuses on economics and class and is intended as empowerment for the oppressed to radically change human social arrangements. Such an analysis will help us to understand the relation between economics and oppression not only in North America but throughout the world. Liberation is not a process limited to black-white relations in the United States; it is also something to be applied to the relations between rich and poor nations. If we are an African people, as some of the names of our churches suggest, in what way are we to understand the political meaning of that identity? In what way does the economic investment of our church resources reflect our commitment to Africa and other oppressed people in the world? For if an economic analysis of our material resources does not reveal our commitment to the process of liberation, how can we claim that the black church and its theology are concerned about the freedom of oppressed peoples? As an Argentine peasant poet said:

They say that God cares for the poor
Well this may be true or not,
But I know for a fact
That he dines with the mine-owner.[11]

Because the Christian church has supported the capitalists, many Marxists contend that "all revolutions have clashed with Christianity because *historically* Christianity has been structurally counter-revolutionary."[12] We may rightly question this assertion and appeal to the revolutionary expressions of Christianity in the black religious tradition, from Nat Turner to Martin Luther King. My concern, however, is not to debate the fine points of what constitutes revolution, but to open up the reality of the black church experience and its revolutionary potential to a world context. This means that we can learn from people in Africa, Asia and Latin America, and they can learn from us. Learning from others involves listening to creative criticism; to exclude such criticism is to isolate ourselves from world politics, and this exclusion makes our faith nothing but a reflection of our economic interests. If Jesus Christ is more than a religious expression of our economic and sexist interests, then there is no reason to resist the truth of the Marxist and feminist analyses.

I contend that black theology is not afraid of truth from any quarter. We simply reject the attempt of others to tell us what truth is without our participation in its definition. That is why dogmatic Marxists seldom succeed in the black community, especially when the dogma is filtered through a brand of white racism not unlike that of the capitalists. If our long history of struggle has taught us anything, it is that if we are to be free, we black people will have to do it. Freedom is not a gift but is a risk that must be taken. No one can tell us what liberation is and how we ought to struggle for it, as if liberation can be found in words. Liberation is a process to be located and understood only in an oppressed community struggling for freedom. If there are people in and outside our community who want to talk to us about this liberation process in global terms and from Marxist and other perspectives, we should be ready to talk. But *only* if they are prepared to listen to us and we to them will genuine dialogue take place. For I will not listen to anybody who refuses to take racism seriously, especially when they themselves have not been victims of it. And they should listen to us *only* if we are prepared to listen to them in terms of the particularity of oppression in their historical context.

Therefore, I reject dogmatic Marxism that reduces every contradiction to class analysis and thus ignores racism as a legitimate point of departure in the process of liberation. There are racist Marxists as there are racist capitalists, and we must struggle against both. But we must be careful not to reject the Marxist's social analysis simply because we do not like the vessels that the message comes in. If we do that, then it is hard to explain how we can remain Christians in view of the white vessels in which the gospel was first introduced to black people.

The world is small. Both politically and economically, our freedom is connected with the struggles of oppressed peoples throughout the world. This is the truth of Pan-Africanism as represented in the life and thought of W. E. B. Du Bois, George Padmore, and C. L. R. James. Liberation knows no color bar; the very nature of the gospel is universalism, i.e., a liberation that embraces the whole of humanity.

The need for a global perspective, which takes seriously the struggles of oppressed peoples in other parts of the world, has already been recognized in black theology, and small beginnings have been made with conferences on African and black theologies in Tanzania, New York, and Ghana. Another example of the recognition of this need is reflected in the dialogue between black theology in South Africa and North America. From the very beginning black theology has been influenced by a world perspective as defined by Henry M. Turner, Marcus Garvey, and the Pan-Africanism inaugurated in the life and work of W. E. B. Du Bois. The importance of this Pan-African perspective in black religion and theology has been cogently defended in Gayraud Wilmore's *Black Religion and Black Radicalism.* Our active involvement in the "Theology in the Americas," under whose aegis this conference is held, is an attempt to enlarge our perspective in relation to Africa, Asia, and Latin America as well as to express our solidarity with other oppressed minorities in the United States.

This global perspective in black theology enlarges our vision regarding the process of liberation. What does black theology have to say about the fact that two-thirds of humanity is poor and that this poverty arises from the exploitation of the poor nations by rich nations? The people of the United States compose 6 percent of the world's population, but we consume 40 percent of the world resources. What, then, is the implication of the black demand for justice in the United States when related to justice for all the world's victims? The dependent status we experience in relation to white people, Third World countries experience in relation to the United States? Thus, in our attempt to liberate ourselves from white people in North America, it is important to be sensitive to the complexity of the world situation and the oppressive role of the United States in it. African, Latin American, and Asian theologians, as well as sociologists and political scientists can aid us in the analysis of this complexity. In this analysis, our starting point in terms of racism is not negated but enhanced when connected with imperialism and sexism.

We must create a global vision of human liberation and include in it the distinctive contribution of the black experience. We have been struggling for nearly four hundred years! What has that experience taught us that would be useful in the creation of a new historical future for all oppressed peoples? And what can others teach us from their historical experience in the struggle for justice. This is the issue that black theology needs to address. "Theology in the Americas" provides a framework in which to address it. I hope that we will not back off from this important task but face it with courage, knowing that the future of humanity is in the hands of oppressed peoples, because God has said: "Those that hope in me shall not be put to shame" (Isa. 49:23).

NOTES

1. This statement first appeared in the *New York Times,* July 31, 1966 and is reprinted here as Document 1.

2. For an account of the rise of the concept of Black Power in the civil rights movement, see Stokely Carmichael and Charles Hamilton, *Black Power. The Politics of Liberation in America* (New York: Random House, 1967). For Martin King's viewpoint, see his *Where Do We Go from Here: Chaos or Community?* (Boston: Beacon Press, 1967).

3. Cited in Lawrence W. Levine, *Black Cultural and Black Consciousness* (New York: Oxford University Press, 1977), p. 207.

4. This is especially true of Charles Long, who has been a provocative discussant about black theology. Unfortunately, he has not written much about this viewpoint. The only article I know on this subject is his "Perspectives for a Study of Afro-American Religion in the United States," *History of Religions,* vol. 11, no. 1, August 1971.

5. The representatives of this perspective include Gayraud S. Wilmore, *Black Religion and Black Radicalism* (Garden City, N.Y.: Doubleday, 1972), and my brother, Cecil W. Cone, *Identity Crisis in Black Theology* (Nashville: AMEC, 1976).

6. This statement was issued on June 13, 1969, and is also reprinted here as Document 3.

7. See Julius Nyerere, *Ujamaa. Essays on Socialism* (Dar es Salaam: Oxford University Press, 1968).

8. Frantz Fanon, *The Wretched of the Earth* (New York: Grove Press, 1966), p. 255.

9. Cited in José Míguez Bonino, *Christians and Marxists* (Grand Rapids, Mich.: Wm. B. Eerdmans, 1976), p. 76.

10. Cited in George Padmore, *Pan-Africanism or Communism* (Garden City, N.Y.: Doubleday, Anchor Books, 1972), p. 323.

11. Cited in Míguez Bonino, *Christians and Marxists* p. 71.

12. A quotation from Giulio Girardi cited in Míguez Bonino, *Christians and Marxists,* p 71.

PART V

BLACK THEOLOGY
AND
BLACK WOMEN

INTRODUCTION

Although Black women represent more than one-half of the population in the Black community and 75 percent in the Black Church, their experience has not been visibly present in the development of Black Theology. For the most part, Black male theologians have remained conspicuously silent on feminist theology generally and Black women in particular. We have spoken of the Black religious experience as if it consisted only of our male experience with no distinctive contribution from Black women. Recently the emergence of a feminist consciousness in the Black community has made Black male theologians more sensitive to the contributions of such women as Harriet Tubman, Sojourner Truth, and Rosa Parks, but not in terms of their unique contributions as women. Do Black women, *as women,* have a distinctive contribution to make in our definition of Black religion that is as significant as we claim our Black experience is in the context of North American Christianity? Unfortunately the silence of Black male theologians on feminist issues seems to suggest a negative answer on their part. But the recent appearance of Black women theologians, with a Black and feminist consciousness, means that our silence will not go unchallenged.

There are various reasons for this silence on feminist issues among Black male theologians. Some Black male theologians are blatantly sexist and thus reflect the values of the dominant society regarding the place of women. Others regard the problem of racism as the basic injustice and say that feminism is a middle-class White woman's issue. Still others make the controversial claim that the Black woman is already liberated. This list could be extended. But whatever the reason for our silence on the unique oppression of Black women, we now must realize that our continued silence can only serve to alienate us further from our sisters. We have no other choice but to take a public stance for or against their liberation.

Since I have been involved in defining the meaning of Black theology, it may be appropriate to say a word about my theological development in relation to feminism. When I first set myself to the task of developing a Black theology of liberation during the summer of 1968, the distinctive contribution of Black women was not a part of my theological consciousness. To be sure, I was aware of the women's movement, but considered it at best secondary to the Black struggle and at worst simply a White attempt to usurp the revolutionary significance of the Black liberation struggle. It was not until I was challenged by Black and other Third World women that I became aware that the significance of feminism was not exhausted by the White women's movement.

In the Third World context, two events helped to raise my consciousness of the significance of feminism for theology and the church. The first event occurred in Asia. When I was invited by the Korean Christian Church in Japan (May 1975) to lead a discussion on the theme of "The Church Struggling for the Liberation of the People," one of the four workshops was held in Fukuoko.[1] There were approximately thirty persons present, including young and old, ministers and laypersons. I began this workshop by asking each person to comment on the question "What is it that most troubles you in the church and the society?" After several persons had commented on racism in Japan, one Korean woman, to the surprise of all present, focused on the subordinate role of women and related it to other forms of oppression. She was not a university-trained person and spoke from the depth of her lived experience. I will never forget her quiet insistence that persons who do not experience a certain form of oppression often minimize its importance in human relations. She appealed to Korean men, rightly challenging the oppressive structures of Japanese society, to let their engagement in the liberation process make them more sensitive to the distinctive oppression of Korean women. I could not help but think that the truth of her comment was applicable to the often strained relations of Black men and women.

The second event happened at the conference on liberation theology in Mexico City (October 1977) entitled "Encounter of Theologians."[2] Of the nearly thirty professional theologians invited to participate, not one was a woman. The absence of this perspective was dramatically articulated by Dora E. Valentin from Cuba, who was present in the audience only because her husband, Sergio Arce Martinez of the Evangelical Seminary, had been invited. No one could question Valentin's commitment to class analysis, but she insisted that such an analysis was inadequate without combining it with racism and sexism. She asked her Latin American brothers why none of their sisters had been invited to participate in the discussion? After a few seconds of an embarrassing silence, someone apologized for the oversight and then invited Valentin to join the discussion. But she politely refused. Again, I could not help but ask myself, how long will men from oppressed communities continue to remain indifferent to the special oppression of their sisters?

It is one thing, however, to be challenged by women from a different cultural and political context, and quite another to hear the cry of pain from women in one's own community. In the Black North American context, the theological significance of the Black woman's experience has been dramatically expressed in conferences on Black women, sponsored both by seminaries and by churches. On such occasions, both formally and informally, the issue of the role of Black women in church and society inevitably arises as a topic of discussion. In most cases, Black women contend that Black men, inside and outside the church, are insensitive to experiences of sexism in the Black community. Black women's deep disappointment with the response of Black men to their oppression cannot be dismissed as a superficial inconvenience that will soon disappear.

When I observe many Black men's reaction to sexism in our community, then I can understand the significance of Sister Anna Cooper's comment that "while our [Black] men seem thoroughly abreast of the times on every subject, when they strike the women question they drop back into sixteenth century logic."[3] Among professional theologians and preachers as well as seminary and university students, few Black men seem to care about the pain our Black sisters claim that we inflict on them with our sexist behavior. If we expect to be taken seriously about our claim to love them, must not our love express itself in our capacity to hear their cry of pain and to experience with them their mental and physical suffering?

By suffering with our sisters and struggling with them to eliminate sexism in our community, we create a deeper solidarity in our common struggle against racism. When one examines the writings of Black women and listens to their testimonies, it is clear that most make the unity and liberation of Black people their starting point in an analysis of Black feminism. A significant example is the very important anthology, *The Black Woman,* edited by Toni Cade.[4] I have chosen Frances Beale's essay, "Double Jeopardy: To Be Black and Female" (Document 24) from that volume, because of the breadth of her analysis, and also because she renders incorrect the Black male's claim that feminism is a White woman's issue, and that Black women's concern for their liberation necessarily involves them in an interracial sexual alignment in lieu of racial unity. Frances Beale states clearly the complexity of the Black woman's situation, but includes in her analysis of the Black woman's particularity a universalism that embraces all people.

If Black women's liberation is a serious issue in the society at large, what then is the role of the Black Church in this struggle? Because the Black Church has a long history of struggle against racism, it should be in the vanguard of the struggle against Black women's oppression. But unfortunately the Black Church is one of the most sexist institutions in the Black community, and Black male ministers often appeal to the Bible to justify the subordinate role defined for women. While many Black male ministers have little difficulty rejecting Paul's command to slaves to be obedient to their masters as a valid justification of Black slavery, they seem incapable of taking a similar stance in relation to Paul's comments about women. Once again the social and political interests of the interpreter seem to control his exegetical conclusions.

In order to transcend the theological limitations that are often determined by political and social interests, Black churchmen will need to listen to Black feminist voices in the church. One such voice is Theressa Hoover, whose essay, "Black Women and the Churches: Triple Jeopardy" (Document 25), is a personal account of her experience in the Black Church. She shows the limitation of the Black Church in dealing with the oppression of the Black Woman in its own household.

When I first recognized the limitation of the Black Church and Black Theology in this area, I did not know what to say about it. My silence was broken when I was asked by Black women students at Garrett-Evangelical Seminary

(October 1976) to address a Black women's conference on the theme, "New Roles in the Ministry: A Theological Appraisal." It represented the first attempt of a Black male theologian to address this issue directly. Since that time, I have tried to deepen my sensitivity and knowledge of this issue, because I firmly believe with Toni Cade that "a man cannot be politically correct and a chauvinist too."[5]

Being sensitive to Black feminism inevitably leads to the question of the relationship between feminist theology and Black Theology. While Rosemary Ruether[6] and Letty Russell[7] have touched on the relation between sexism and racism in theology, neither White feminist theologians nor Black male theologians have the experience that will enable them to do justice to this issue. Only Black feminist theologians have the experience necessary for the creation of intellectual tools that are needed in analyzing the complexity of this issue. Pauli Murray's article "Black Theology and Feminist Theology" (Document 26) indicates the need for a dialogue between Black and feminist theologians. However, before such a dialogue can take place, it is necessary to create a Black feminist theology. Jacquelyn Grant's essay, "Black Theology and the Black Woman" (Document 27), is an important contribution in this area.

While Jacquelyn Grant's perspective on Black feminist theology is derived primarily from the faith of the Christian Church, not all Black women will follow that line of thinking. Some Black women express the need to separate Black feminist theology from any dependence on White feminist and Black male theologies, on the one hand, and the Christian faith on the other. In this perspective, the distinctive experience of Black women, inside and outside the Black Church, becomes the primary norm in its analysis. Alice Walker's "In Search of Our Mothers' Gardens" (Document 28) is an important contribution for this perspective. She contends that there is something unique in Black women's spirituality that is "so intense, so deep, so *unconscious,* that they [are] themselves [often] unaware of the richness they [hold]." "Therefore we must fearlessly pull out of ourselves and look at and identify with our lives the living creativity some of our great-grandmothers were not allowed to know."

From the essays included in this part, it is clear that a variety of perspectives on Black feminist theology are in the process of development. The precise shape of these perspectives is still unclear. But what is clear is Black women's challenge to the dominant male perspective in the Black Church and its theology. I only hope that our love for the Black community is deep enough to enable us to hear and to respond to the pain of our sisters.

J.H.C.

NOTES

1. For another discussion of the Korean Christian Church in Japan, see part VI, p. 359.

2. For another reference to this event, see part VI, p. 356 below.

3. Cited in Robert Staples, *The Black Woman in America: Sex, Marriage and the Family* (Chicago: Nelson-Hall, 1973), 69.

4. See also the excellent collection of essays in Toni Cade, ed., *The Black Woman* (New York: Signet Books, 1970). Another important collection is G. Lerner, *Black Women in White America: A Documentary History* (New York: Vintage Books, 1973). For book-length treatises on the Black woman, see Joyce Ladner, *Tomorrow's Tomorrow* (Garden City, N.Y.: Doubleday, 1971); Robert Staples, *The Black Woman;* Jeanne Noble, *Beautiful, Also, Are the Souls of My Black Sisters* (Englewood Cliffs, N.J.: Prentice-Hall, 1978).

5. "On the Issue of Roles," in Cade, ed., *The Black Woman*, p. 107. My essay was published in the first edition (Wilmore & Cone 1979, 389-397) but excluded here because of the concern for length and the importance of hearing only Black women's voices in this section.

6. See Ruether's *Liberation Theology* (New York: Paulist Press, 1972); *New Woman, New Earth* (New York: Seabury Press, 1975); "Crisis in Sex and Race," in *Christianity and Crisis*, no. 6 (15 April 1975).

7. See Russell's *Human Liberation in a Feminist Perspective—A Theology* (Philadelphia: Westminster Press, 1974).

24

DOUBLE JEOPARDY:
TO BE BLACK AND FEMALE

Frances Beale

In attempting to analyze the situation of the Black woman in America, one crashes abruptly into a solid wall of grave misconceptions, outright distortions of fact, and defensive attitudes on the part of many. The system of capitalism (and its afterbirth—racism) under which we all live has attempted by many devious ways and means to destroy the humanity of all people, and particularly the humanity of Black people. This has meant an outrageous assault on every Black man, woman, and child who resides in the United States.

In keeping with its goal of destroying the Black race's will to resist its sub-jugation, capitalism found it necessary to create a situation where the Black man found it impossible to find meaningful or productive employment. More often than not, he couldn't find work of any kind. And the Black woman likewise was manipulated by the system, economically exploited and physically assaulted. She could often find work in the white man's kitchen, however, and sometimes became the sole breadwinner of the family. This predicament has led to many psychological problems on the part of both man and woman and has contributed to the turmoil that we find in the Black family structure.

Unfortunately, neither the Black man nor the Black woman understood the true nature of the forces working upon them. Many Black women tended to accept the capitalist evaluation of manhood and womanhood and believed, in fact, that Black men were shiftless and lazy, otherwise they would get a job and support their families as they ought to. Personal relationships between Black men and women were thus torn asunder and one result has been the separation of man from wife, mother from child, etc.

America has defined the roles to which each individual should subscribe. It

Frances Beale is active in several Black Women's groups. She lives in New York City. This essay was first published in *The Black Woman*, edited by Toni Cade (New York: Signet, 1970). Reprinted with permission of the publisher.

has defined "manhood" in terms of its own interests and "femininity" likewise. Therefore, an individual who has a good job, makes a lot of money, and drives a Cadillac is a real "man," and conversely, an individual who is lacking in these "qualities" is less of a man. The advertising media in this country continuously inform the American male of his need for indispensable signs of his virility — the brand of cigarettes that cowboys prefer, the whiskey that has a masculine tang, or the label of the jock strap that athletes wear.

The ideal model that is projected for a woman is to be surrounded by hypocritical homage and estranged from all real work, spending idle hours primping and preening, obsessed with conspicuous consumption, and limiting life's functions to simply a sex role. We unqualitatively reject these respective models. A woman who stays at home caring for children and the house often leads an extremely sterile existence. She must lead her entire life as a satellite to her mate. He goes out into society and brings back a little piece of the world for her. His interests and his understanding of the world become her own and she cannot develop herself as an individual having been reduced to only a biological function. This kind of woman leads a parasitic existence that can aptly be described as legalized prostitution.

Furthermore it is idle dreaming to think of Black women simply caring for their homes and children like the middle-class white model. Most Black women have to work to help house, feed, and clothe their families. Black women make up a substantial percentage of the Black working force, and this is true for the poorest Black family as well as the so-called "middle-class" family.

Black women were never afforded any such phony luxuries. Though we have been browbeaten with this white image, the reality of the degrading and dehumanizing jobs that were relegated to us quickly dissipated this mirage of womanhood. The following excerpts from a speech that Sojourner Truth made at a Women's Rights Convention in the nineteenth century show us how misleading and incomplete a life this model represents for us:

> ... Well, chilern, whar dar is so much racket dar must be something out o' kilter. I tink dat 'twixt de niggers of the Souf and de women at the Norf all a talkin' 'bout rights, de white men will be in a fix pretty soon. But what's all dis here talkin' bout? Dat man ober dar say dat women needs to be helped into carriages, and lifted ober ditches, and to have de best place every whar. Nobody ever help me into carriages, or ober mud puddles, or gives me any best places, ... and ar'nt I a woman? Look at me! Look at my arm! ... I have plowed, and planted, and gathered into barns, and no man could head me — and ar'nt I a woman? I could work as much as a man (when I could get it), and bear de lash as well — and ar'nt I a woman? I have borne five chilern and I seen 'em mos' all sold off into slavery, and when I cried out with a mother's grief, none but Jesus heard — and ar'nt I a woman?

Unfortunately, there seems to be some confusion in the Movement today as to who has been oppressing whom. Since the advent of Black power, the Black male has exerted a more prominent leadership role in our struggle for justice in this country. He sees the system for what it really is for the most part, but where he rejects its values and mores on many issues, when it comes to women, he seems to take his guidelines from the pages of the *Ladies' Home Journal.* Certain Black men are maintaining that they have been castrated by society but that Black women somehow escaped this persecution and even contributed to this emasculation.

Let me state here and now that the Black woman in America can justly be described as a "slave of a slave." By reducing the Black man in America to such abject oppression, the Black woman had no protector and was used, and is still being used in some cases, as the scapegoat for the evils that this horrendous system has perpetrated on Black men. Her physical image has been maliciously maligned; she has been sexually molested and abused by the white colonizer; she has suffered the worst kind of economic exploitation, having been forced to serve as the white woman's maid and wet nurse for white offspring while her own children were more often than not starving and neglected. It is the depth of degradation to be socially manipulated, physically raped, used to undermine your own household, and to be powerless to reverse this syndrome.

It is true that our husbands, fathers, brothers, and sons have been emasculated, lynched, and brutalized. They have suffered from the cruelest assault on mankind that the world has ever known. However, it is a gross distortion of fact to state that Black women have oppressed Black men. The capitalist system found it expedient to enslave and oppress them and proceeded to do so without consultation or the signing of any agreements with Black women.

It must also be pointed out at this time that Black women are not resentful of the rise to power of Black men. We welcome it. We see in it the eventual liberation of all Black people from this corrupt system of capitalism. Nevertheless, this does not mean that you have to negate one for the other. This kind of thinking is a product of miseducation; that it's either X or it's Y. It is fallacious reasoning that in order for the Black man to be strong, the Black woman has to be weak.

Those who are exerting their "manhood" by telling Black women to step back into a domestic, submissive role are assuming a counter-revolutionary position. Black women likewise have been abused by the system and we must begin talking about the elimination of all kinds of oppression. If we are talking about building a strong nation, capable of throwing off the yoke of capitalist oppression, then we are talking about the total involvement of every man, woman, and child, each with a highly developed political consciousness. We need our whole army out there dealing with the enemy and not half an army.

There are also some Black women who feel that there is no more productive role in life than having and raising children. This attitude often reflects the conditioning of the society in which we live and is adopted from a bourgeois white model. Some young sisters who have never had to maintain a household and accept the confining role which this entails tend to romanticize (along with the help of a few brothers) this role of housewife and mother. Black women who have had to endure this kind of function are less apt to have these utopian visions.

Those who project in an intellectual manner how great and rewarding this role will be and who feel that the most important thing that they can contribute to the Black nation is children are doing themselves a great injustice. This line of reasoning completely negates the contributions that Black women have historically made to our struggle for liberation. These Black women include Sojourner Truth, Harriet Tubman, Mary McLeod Bethune, and Fannie Lou Hamer, to name but a few.

We live in a highly industrialized society and every member of the Black nation must be as academically and technologically developed as possible. To wage a revolution, we need competent teachers, doctors, nurses, electronics experts, chemists, biologists, physicists, political scientists, and so on and so forth. Black women sitting at home reading bedtime stories to their children are just not going to make it.

Economic Exploitation of Black Women

The economic system of capitalism finds it expedient to reduce women to a state of enslavement. They oftentimes serve as a scapegoat for the evils of this system. Much in the same way that the poor white cracker of the South, who is equally victimized, looks down upon Blacks and contributes to the oppression of Blacks, so, by giving to men a false feeling of superiority (at least in their own home or in their relationships with women), the oppression of women acts as an escape valve for capitalism. Men may be cruelly exploited and subjected to all sorts of dehumanizing tactics on the part of the ruling class, but they have someone who is below them—at least they're not women.

Women also represent a surplus labor supply, the control of which is absolutely necessary to the profitable functioning of capitalism. Women are systematically exploited by the system. They are paid less for the same work that men do, and jobs that are specifically relegated to women are low-paying and without the possibility of advancement. Statistics from the Women's Bureau of the U.S. Department of Labor show that in 1967 the wage scale for white women was even below that of Black men; and the wage scale for non-white women was the lowest of all:

White Males	$6704
Non-White Males	$4277
White Females	$3991
Non-White Females	$2861

Those industries which employ mainly Black women are the most exploitive in the country. Domestic and hospital workers are good examples of this oppression; the garment workers in New York City provide us with another view of this economic slavery. The International Ladies Garment Workers Union

(ILGWU), whose overwhelming membership consists of Black and Puerto Rican women, has a leadership that is nearly all lily-white and male. This leadership has been working in collusion with the ruling class and has completely sold its soul to the corporate structure.

To add insult to injury, the ILGWU has invested heavily in business enterprises in racist, apartheid South Africa—with union funds. Not only does this bought-off leadership contribute to our continued exploitation in this country by not truly representing the best interests of its membership, but it audaciously uses funds that Black and Puerto Rican women have provided to support the economy of a vicious government that is engaged in the economic rape and murder of our Black brothers and sisters in our *Motherland* Africa.

The entire labor movement in the United States has suffered as a result of the super-exploitation of Black workers and women. The unions have historically been racist and chauvinistic. They have upheld racism in this country and have failed to fight the white skin privileges of white workers. They have failed to fight or even make an issue against the inequities in the hiring and pay of women workers. There has been virtually no struggle against either the racism of the white worker or the economic exploitation of the working woman, two factors which have consistently impeded the advancement of the real struggle against the ruling class.

This racist, chauvinistic, and manipulative use of Black workers and women, especially Black women, has been a severe cancer on the American labor scene. It therefore becomes essential for those who understand the workings of capitalism and imperialism to realize that the exploitation of Black people and women works to everyone's disadvantage and that the liberation of these two groups is a steppingstone to the liberation of all oppressed people in this country and around the world.

Bedroom Politics

I have briefly discussed the economic and psychological manipulation of Black women, but perhaps the most outlandish act of oppression in modern times is the current campaign to promote sterilization of non-white women in an attempt to maintain the population and power imbalance between the white haves and the non-white have-nots.

These tactics are but another example of the many devious schemes that the ruling-class elite attempt to perpetrate on the Black population in order to keep itself in control. It has recently come to our attention that a massive campaign for so-called "birth control" is presently being promoted not only in the underdeveloped non-white areas of the world, but also in Black communities here in the United States. However, what the authorities in charge of these programs refer to as "birth control" is in fact nothing but a method of outright surgical genocide.

The United States has been sponsoring sterilization clinics in non-white countries, especially in India, where already some three million young men and boys in and around New Delhi have been sterilized in makeshift operating rooms set up by the American Peace Corps workers. Under these circumstances, it is understandable why certain countries view the Peace Corps not as a benevolent project, not as evidence of America's concern for underdeveloped areas, but rather as a threat to their very existence. This program could more aptly be named the Death Corps.

Vasectomy, which is performed on males and takes only six or seven minutes, is a relatively simple operation. The sterilization of a woman, on the other hand, is admittedly major surgery. This operation (salpingectomy)* must be performed in a hospital under general anesthesia. This method of "birth control" is a common procedure in Puerto Rico. Puerto Rico has long been used by the colonialist exploiter, the United States, as a huge experimental laboratory for medical research before allowing certain practices to be imported and used here. When the birth-control pill was first being perfected, it was tried on Puerto Rican women and selected Black women (poor), using them as human guinea pigs, to evaluate its effect and its efficiency.

Salpingectomy has now become the commonest operation in Puerto Rico, commoner than an appendectomy or a tonsillectomy. It is so widespread that it is referred to simply as *la operación. On the island 10 percent of the women between the ages of 15 and 45 have already been sterilized.*

And now, as previously occurred with the pill, this method has been imported into the United States. These sterilization clinics are cropping up around the country in the Black and Puerto Rican communities. These so-called "maternity clinics" specifically outfitted to purge Black women or men of their reproductive possibilities are appearing more and more in hospitals and clinics across the country.

A number of organizations have been formed to popularize the idea of sterilization, such as the Association for Voluntary Sterilization and the Human Betterment (! ! ! ?) Association for Voluntary Sterilization, Inc., which has its headquarters in New York City.

Threatened with the cut-off of relief funds, some Black welfare women have been forced to accept this sterilization procedure in exchange for a continuation of welfare benefits. Black women are often afraid to permit any kind of necessary surgery because they know from bitter experience that they are more likely than not to come out of the hospital without their insides. (Both salpingectomies and hysterectomies are performed.)

We condemn this use of the Black woman as a medical testing ground for the white middle class. Reports of the ill effects, including deaths, from the use of the birth control pill only started to come to light when the white privileged class began to be affected. These outrageous Nazi-like procedures on the part of medical researchers are but another manifestation of the totally amoral and

---

*Salpingectomy: Through an abdominal incision, the surgeon cuts both fallopian tubes and ties off the separated ends, after which act there is no way for the egg to pass from the ovary to the womb.

dehumanizing brutality that the capitalist system perpetrates on Black women. The sterilization experiments carried on in concentration camps some twenty-five years ago have been denounced the world over, but no one seems to get upset by the repetition of these same racist tactics today in the United States of America—land of the free and home of the brave. This campaign is as nefarious a program as Germany's gas chambers, and in a long-term sense, as effective and with the same objective.

The rigid laws concerning abortions in this country are another vicious means of subjugation and, indirectly, of outright murder. Rich white women somehow manage to obtain these operations with little or no difficulty. It is the poor Black and Puerto Rican woman who is at the mercy of the local butcher. Statistics show us that the non-white death rate at the hands of the unqualified abortionist is substantially higher than for white women. Nearly half of the childbearing deaths in New York City are attributed to abortion alone and out of these, 79 percent are among non-whites and Puerto Rican women.

We are not saying that Black women should not practice birth control. *Black women have the right and the responsibility to determine when it is in the interest of the struggle to have children or not to have them and this right must not be relinquished to anyone.* It is also her right and responsibility to determine when it is in her own best interests to have children, how many she will have, and how far apart. The lack of the availability of safe birth-control methods, the forced sterilization practices, and the inability to obtain legal abortions are all symptoms of a decadent society that jeopardizes the health of Black women (and thereby the entire Black race) in its attempts to control the very life processes of human beings. This is a symptom of a society that believes it has the right to bring political factors into the privacy of the bedchamber. The elimination of these horrendous conditions will free Black women for full participation in the revolution, and thereafter, in the building of the new society.

Relationship to White Movement

Much has been written recently about the white women's liberation movement in the United States, and the question arises whether there are any parallels between this struggle and the movement on the part of Black women for total emancipation. While there are certain comparisons that one can make, simply because we both live under the same exploitative system, there are certain differences, some of which are quite basic.

The white women's movement is far from being monolithic. Any white group that does not have an anti-imperialist and anti-racist ideology has absolutely nothing in common with the Black woman's struggle. In fact, some groups come to the incorrect conclusion that their oppression is due simply to male chauvinism. They therefore have an extremely anti-male tone to their dissertations. Black people are engaged in a life-and-death struggle and the main emphasis of Black women must be to combat the capitalist, racist exploitation of Black people. While it is true that male chauvinism has become institutionalized in

American society, one must always look for the main enemy—the fundamental cause of the female condition.

Another major differentiation is that the white women's liberation movement is basically middle-class. Very few of these women suffer the extreme economic exploitation that most Black women are subjected to day by day. This is the factor that is most crucial for us. It is not an intellectual persecution alone; it is not an intellectual outburst for us; it is quite real. We as Black women have got to deal with the problems that the Black masses deal with, for our problems in reality are one and the same.

If the white groups do not realize that they are in fact fighting capitalism and racism, we do not have common bonds. If they do not realize that the reasons for their condition lie in the system and not simply that men get a vicarious pleasure out of "consuming their bodies for exploitative reasons" (this kind of reasoning seems to be quite prevalent in certain white women's groups), then we cannot unite with them around common grievances or even discuss these groups in a serious manner because they're completely irrelevant to the Black struggle.

The New World

The Black community and Black women especially must begin raising questions about the kind of society we wish to see established. We must note the ways in which capitalism oppresses us and then move to create institutions that will eliminate these destructive influences.

The new world that we are attempting to create must destroy oppression of any type. The value of this new system will be determined by the status of the person who was low man on the totem pole. Unless women in any enslaved nation are completely liberated, the change cannot really be called a revolution. If the Black woman has to retreat to the position she occupied before the armed struggle, the whole movement and the whole struggle will have retracted in terms of truly freeing the colonized population.

A people's revolution that engages the participation of every member of the community, including man, woman, and child, brings about a certain transformation in the participants as a result of this participation. Once you have caught a glimpse of freedom or experienced a bit of self-determination, you can't go back to old routines that were established under a racist, capitalist regime. We must begin to understand that a revolution entails not only the willingness to lay our lives on the firing line and get killed. In some ways, this is an easy commitment to make. To die for the revolution is a one-shot deal; to live for the revolution means taking on the more difficult commitment of changing our day-to-day life patterns.

This will mean changing the traditional routines that we have established as a result of living in a totally corrupting society. It means changing how you relate to your wife, your husband, your parents, and your co-workers. If we are going to liberate ourselves as a people, it must be recognized that Black women have very specific problems that have to be spoken to. We must be liberated along with the rest of the population. We cannot wait to start working on those problems until that great day in the future when the revolution somehow miraculously is accomplished.

To assign women the role of housekeeper and mother while men go forth into battle is a highly questionable doctrine for a revolutionary to maintain. Each individual must develop a high political consciousness in order to understand how this system enslaves us all and what actions we must take to bring about its total destruction. Those who consider themselves to be revolutionary must begin to deal with other revolutionaries as equals. And so far as I know, revolutionaries are not determined by sex.

Old people, young people, men and women, must take part in the struggle. To relegate women to purely supportive roles or to purely cultural considerations is dangerous doctrine to project. Unless Black men who are preparing themselves for armed struggle understand that the society which we are trying to create is one in which the oppression of all members of that society is eliminated, then the revolution will have failed in its avowed purpose.

Given the mutual commitment of Black men and Black women alike to the liberation of our people and other oppressed peoples around the world, the total involvement of each individual is necessary. A revolutionary has the responsibility not only of toppling those that are now in a position of power, but of creating new institutions that will eliminate all forms of oppression. We must begin to rewrite our understanding of traditional personal relationships between man and woman.

All the resources that the Black community can muster up must be channeled into the struggle. Black women must take an active part in bringing about the kind of society where our children, our loved ones, and each citizen can grow up and live as decent human beings, free from the pressures of racism and capitalist exploitation.

25

BLACK WOMEN AND THE CHURCHES:
TRIPLE JEOPARDY

Theressa Hoover

To be a woman, black, and active in religious institutions in the American scene is to labor under triple jeopardy.

It is a well-accepted fact that women in America, though in the majority statistically, are generally in inferior positions. Economically they are at the bottom of the ladder in terms of those receiving high-paying salaries. Politically, although they have the possibility of more voters being women, they have not yet experienced the full potential of that vote. Women constitute a very small number of the persons in political office at all levels of the nation's life. Religiously, though they comprise more than 50 percent of the churches' membership, they are by no means at the higher levels of decision-making in the churches.

It has long been an established fact in American life that color is a deterrent to high achievement; not because there is inherent inferiority but because societal conditions predetermine lower achievement. Thus, while every woman in America faces economic and political discrimination, a woman who is black has an added barrier.

Religion in American society is often espoused, even in high places, but it is not yet the warp and woof of our actions. The woman who is vitally involved with religious institutions in our society must take on responsibilities often not accepted by others.

To confront the inequities of women and the inequities of blacks, and to have the responsibilities of a dedication to the church, is triple jeopardy for a black woman. There is very little written which brings together these three

Theressa Hoover is retired Associate General Secretary, Women's Division, Board of Global Ministries of the United Methodist Church. This essay first appeared in *Sexist Religior and Women in the Church*, edited by Alice Hageman, copyright © 1974. Used by permission of Follett Publishing Company.

elements. There is little or no mention of black women in accounts of any black church or black theology and in the *Ebony* special issue on "The Negro Woman" (August 1960) she is treated in every way except in the area of religion. *The Making of Black Revolutionaries* by James Forman and *Black Women in White America* by Gerda Lerner, both published in 1972, are the only books available which give a bit more dimension to the strength and courage of black Christian women now and in the past. Any thinking person cannot help wondering why so little has been written, since women are by far the largest supporting groups in our religious institutions, and, in the black church, are the very backbone.

We know too well the debates going on in the American religious institutions about women—their role, their access to all privileges and responsibilities in the priestly hierarchy, their representation in decision-making places, and their total condition in these institutions. Apparently no one has seen the plight of American black women in the religious institutions of our society. One might conclude that where something is written about women in general in these institutions black women are included. This may be true, but it is not the total picture. Even in the predominantly all-white denominations, the black woman commonly finds herself in black local congregations. Judged by what is written in the historic black denominations the black woman is invisible.

Black Women: The Backbone of the Black Churches

Some people hallow the black church, citing evidence of the hope such churches could give their communities if they had the financial support of a larger group. Others detract from the past and belittle the future potential of the black church in the black community, claiming these churches have become little more than middle-class social clubs, out of contact with the real hurts of people in their communities. The detractors use caricatures of a black preacher riding around town in his Cadillac purchased by gifts from welfare checks or chicken dinners sold by black women of his congregation. There is probably truth in both the compliment and the caricature: the black church which properly assesses the potential of its community, and applies its resources to that potential, can be the better servant of the community. The preacher in the black church *is* more directive, authoritarian, and singular in his administration. The degree to which he uses his position selfishly marks the amount of personal privilege and reward he enjoys at the expense of a "not so well endowed" membership—the majority of which are women.

This situation has sociological and psychological explanations. In the post-slavery period, the black church was the only place in the community where economic well-being was dependent on direct black giving. In many situations the preacher had to play the roles of social worker and political and religious adviser. To perform properly he had to have enough ability to get on with the powers at city hall or in the county courthouse. In town after town—even in the Deep South—he was the only black man not referred to as "George" or "boy." He was called "Rev." or "Preacher." Such courtesy did not necessarily concede he was a man, but that he was a little more than "boy."

Many of today's major black churches have their roots in protest. Richard Allen walked out of the Methodist Episcopal Church in Philadelphia rather than accept segregation at the communion table, and the African Methodist Episcopal Church is a monument to that protest. Countless hundreds of local Methodist and Baptist congregations across the country have kept alive that protest. They were the churches that provided succor to the slave family, that also helped them accommodate to earthly travail with the promise of a better life in the hereafter. Today many criticize this role of the past. Given a similar oppressive situation, however, would we have done otherwise? During the same period some churches were the places where insurrectionists gathered to plan strategies and attacks.

In the 1960s during the civil rights struggle there were black ministers in leadership in difficult places and situations. With them were women and men who had come under the teaching of the gospel in the churches and had believed. Churches were the targets of the racists' bombs and guns. In some ways, they were targets more than any other institutions, since the schools — probably the only other places in the community which could accommodate the crowds — were the property of the Establishment. The black church was of the black community, owned by it and sustained by it, and thus it became the target of the racists. Joseph R. Washington, Jr., illustrated the point well:

> In the beginning was the black church, and the black church was with the black community, and the black church was the black community. The black church was in the beginning with the black people; all things were made through the black church, and without the black church was not anything that was made. In the black church was life, and the life was the light of the black people. The black church still shines in the darkness and the darkness has not overcome it.[1]

Lest it be thought that this is a valid description of the black church in black Southern communities only, the experience of Cicely Tyson, who grew up in New York City, should be noted:

> We were in church Sunday morning to Saturday night. It was our whole life, our social life, our religious training, everything. My mother didn't believe in movies, so I didn't go to the movies. ... But I enjoyed the church services. I sang in the choir and played the piano and the organ. Sometimes when my mother worked late at night, Nana would take my sister and my brother and me to the Baptist church. It was that kind of thing that saved us. Church became a shelter for us. A lot of kids growing up with us are not here today because of drugs or alcohol, or they died some violent death. They weren't necessarily bad kids.[2]

During the period 1948 to 1958 I traveled eleven months out of each year, all across the United States. I spent those years in and out of every major city, in countless small towns, and on the back roads in open country. Needless to say, hospitality for me in those days was always arranged for in the home of some black Methodist family. The only able-bodied, employed male I observed at home during the weekdays was the pastor. For some it was an escape into a natural or acquired laziness. For others it was an opportunity to read, study, and join with other clergymen in talking of their dilemmas, boasting of last Sunday's offerings, or strategizing about some community need.

During those ten years of travel I discovered that black women were truly the glue that held the churches together. The women worked, yet found time to be the Sunday school teachers, sing in the choir, and support the church's program in every way. The women found the time and energy to be active in the women's missionary societies and to serve as counselors or sponsors for the youth group. They were the domestics of the community and the teachers in the black schools. The latter were often either hometown girls or ones who had grown up in a town similar to the one in which they now worked and boarded with a respectable family. The church was their "home away from home," the social orbit in which they met the right people.

The minister's wife deserves special mention. She often worked outside the home, too, depending on the financial status of the church her husband served. In many cases she gave piano lessons—or did sewing for a little change if she was lucky. She was sometimes a teacher in the nearby country school. On occasion she, too, joined the long line of domestics leaving her end of town to spend part of the day at work in homes on the other side of town. She was still expected to prepare her family's meals, clean the parsonage, and do the allotted amount of church work.

In most of these communities the blacks were either Methodists or Baptists. The Methodists were a mixture. Some belonged to a primarily white denomination even though they found the local expression in black congregations. Others belonged to one of the three primarily black Methodist denominations—African Methodist Episcopal, African Methodist Episcopal Zion, or Christian Methodist Episcopal. All, however, were related to a connectional system, meaning that they had a presiding elder who was their link to other churches in the denomination and to a bishop who linked them to a still larger judicatory of the denomination. The Baptists tended to belong to a fellowship of Baptists, but each local church was autonomous. History has produced many varieties: there were progressive and independent; there were Antioch and Shiloh.

In both Baptist and Methodist churches the women were the backbone, the "glue." They were present at the midweek prayer services, the Monday afternoon women's missionary meetings, and the Sunday morning, afternoon, and evening preaching services. Rarely has there been in the black church a great distinction between men and women holding office or sharing in decision-making in the local churches.

Missions as Focus for Contact and Cooperation

In the 1950s, women in the various Methodist groups began to discover one another. While there had been a sharing of programs and other resources in many local communities, there had been no real coming-together nationally. The women of the basically white Methodist Church had a joint committee with the women of the basically black Christian Methodist Episcopal (CME) Church. The relationship was still in the realm of a "missionary project" on the part of the white denomination, for it was they who provided the staff help, the printed resources, and the money to assure leadership training for the women of the CME Church. The two groups have since moved into an era of more equitable contribution to the joint experiment. Coming together later as co-units in the World Federation of Methodist Women, they extended the fellowship to include women of the African Methodist Episcopal and the African Methodist Episcopal Zion churches.

Each of the four Methodist women's groups has a history of mission work in this country and overseas. They have supported their own programs even as they have aided the mission outreach of the denomination in which they were a part. These women's missionary groups developed out of the desire of women to be involved with the hurts, needs, and potential of women everywhere. The regular mission channels of the denominations were controlled by the clergy to the point of the deliberate exclusion of women. To give expression to the needs felt by women the women's missionary society was organized as a parallel or auxiliary group. That felt need and that exclusion from main church channels still exist. Today these groups of women are strong numerically and financially.

The nationally organized churchwomen's groups active today are: the African Methodist Episcopal Church Women's Missionary Society, the African Methodist Episcopal Zion Church Women's Home and Missionary Society, the Christian Methodist Episcopal Church Women's Missionary Council, the Women's Auxiliary of the National Baptist Convention, and the United Methodist Women's Division.

There are varying degrees of autonomy in these organizations. Each is a recognized body of the denomination which makes possible the functioning of the group at all levels of the church's life. The groups range in size from two thousand to thirty thousand local units in the United States with a combined membership in the millions.

United Methodist Women, part of a Board of Global Ministries, retains the constitutional right to enlist women as members, to provide program and educational materials, and to secure and expend funds. It is the largest remaining mainline churchwomen's group with that degree of autonomy. It has some thirty thousand local units.

Black Women and the Black Manifesto

In the late 1960s the religious institutions in America toward which the Black Manifesto was directed were in disarray. The legally achieved integration of the early sixties had been found wanting in quality and in practice. For the liberal white integrationists, the apparent move toward separatism, signaled by the Black Power movement and culminating in the Manifesto of 1969, was mind-blowing to say the least. To some, separatism represented a threat or a cop-out.

Not long after the Black Manifesto was made public I was called by the executive director of Church Women United to a conference to discuss what impact this move would have on black women in that organization. My counsel to her then, later borne out, was that it would produce no "break-off" though it might well call forth some soul searching as to the seriousness with which women honor our differences and pool our resources and resourcefulness on behalf of all.

Nevertheless, to test my counsel, Church Women United called a small consultation of black churchwomen in September, 1969, at Wainwright House, Rye, New York, to consider their role and expectations in the aftermath of the Black Manifesto. The group concluded that churchwomen—black and white—must function under the limitations of religious thought and practice. This fact alone was sufficiently limiting; there was no purpose to be served by further splintering ourselves along the lines of race.

We talked about the role women can play in the total life of the church, about the areas the church has not yet given evidence of serving, about the gap between mainline black churchwomen and their younger black sisters. Most of us represented the former category. We were the ones who attended the colleges set up by the churches to educate the recently freed slaves and had gone on to become teachers in them or staff in their national headquarters. We had little experience with overt assignment of women to second-class posts in churches, largely because we were so vitally needed if churches were even to exist. We were the ones who had been taught and had accepted a role on behalf of "our people" even if it meant foregoing a personal life exemplified in husband and children. We were the ones who, if married at all, had married "beneath us"—meaning that we had married men with less education who did manual labor. (Note the influence of white society's value system.) This was not true for the young black woman of the late 1960s.

These are some of the remarks heard at that weekend consultation:

"The young black's mistake is in not making enough of their American experience. We will never be Africans. In slavery only the strong and those with a will to live survived—those with spiritual resiliency."

"Black people once thought education was the answer; they found it wasn't. Now they think economics is the answer; we'll find it won't be, either. We have to find something else—we have to deal with the attitude of people on the top in order to solve this. As churchwomen and as black women, how can we do this?"

"Women have always taken care of everyone's problems and have been left behind. Women must be free before they can begin to make decisions."

"To accomplish a specific goal, an organized minority can bring about change. It is not necessary to have great numbers."

"Women must be accepted as persons. The black man wants to assert today his so-called masculinity, but it is really *personhood*—for both sexes."

"So far as young women versus men are concerned, let the men have their power and status; we organize the women's caucus; when the men are ready for our help, they will have to bargain for it."

Ethnic Caucuses in White Churches

Ethnic caucuses in white denominations sprang up in the aftermath of the civil rights struggle. The soil had been prepared for their advent. It took an act of national significance to release the simmering disenchantment of minority groups with their place in white denominations. What is interesting is the role and status of women within the ethnic caucuses.

Not unlike the role of women in the civil rights struggle of the sixties women in the caucuses have been assigned (and have accepted) a supportive role. Most of the decision-makers have been men, primarily clergymen. It might help to look closely at the "life and growth of caucuses" in a major mainline denomination whose membership is a replica of the nation at large. Let's take the United Methodist Church (which has 54 per cent women members) as a case study.

1. At the 1966 Special Session of General Conference of the Methodist Church, with the Evangelical United Brethren Church Conference in session across the hall, there was only one visible caucus, Methodists for Church Renewal. This caucus cut across race and sex lines, though the dominant group consisted of white male clergy.

2. At the regular Methodist General Conference in 1968 (with the Evangelical United Brethren Church holding a simultaneous Special Session), a second caucus was present, Black Methodists for Church Renewal (BMCR). At this session the union of the two denominations was consummated and, with it, the official end of the Methodist all-Negro Central Jurisdiction. In February, 1968, just two months prior to the General Conference, over two hundred black Methodists had gathered in Cincinnati, Ohio. They came from the Far West and East, where structural segregation included only the local church; from the Middle West (Illinois to Colorado, Missouri to Kentucky), where conferences had already been merged with their white counterparts; and from the Southwest and Southeast, where no noticeable change was in the offing. While it was church renewal that brought them together, it was their blackness which made the gathering imperative.

Black clergymen were by far the majority of those attending, but a real effort was made to get lay men and women. Both were there. Strategically, many of them would be voting delegates in the upcoming General Conference. The national board of directors elected before the conference closed totaled forty-four, with nine women, a number not commensurate with black women's presence or support in black churches—but an action taken without recourse to pressure by women.

One directive to the board of directors says something about the group's awareness of the black woman. They were directed to "employ an assistant director which shall be a woman, if the executive director is a man." There was not the assumption, which is so often true, that the director would be a man. Instead, it was an assurance that the leadership of the staff would reflect the talents of both male and female.

Black women and men, lay and clerical, were visible at the luncheons, after-hours caucuses, and the on-floor debate at the General Conference. As a result, our denomination created and funded a Commission on Religion and Race. When the Commission was organized and staffed, however, there were no guarantees for the participation of women, and the Commission cannot be applauded for their involvement. In fact, it is fair to say that women have been generally disregarded in its life and work. So the struggle must go on.

3. At the 1970 Special General Conference, still another caucus, youthful United Methodists, secured the right to self-determination.

4. At the 1972 General Conference the youth caucus was the only caucus that included women in the warp and woof of its proceedings and decision-making. Black Methodists for Church Renewal, barely visible and still masculine and clerical, saw the rise of a women's caucus in its own ranks before it got the message that "coalition around common interests" was not only desirable but imperative.

The newest caucus—the women's caucus—was a great new fact. Black women were among its members and took active roles. Representatives of the BMCR women's caucus were a bridge so that BMCR, the women's caucus, and the Youth-Young Adult Caucus formed a working coalition to achieve common goals. As a result a Commission on the Status and Role of Women was created and funded, though not to the desired degree. The Commission has organized with a black woman as its chairperson. The effort brought together still another interesting phenomenon—the joint effort of young, unorganized women with the older, organized women's group in the denomination.

Judith Hole and Ellen Levine in their book *Rebirth of Feminism* say:

> Feminist activities within the Christian community most often fall into three categories: (1) challenging the theological view of women; (2) challenging the religious laws and/or customs which bar women from ordination; (3) demanding that the professional status and salaries of women in the church be upgraded.[3]

These categories may apply to the total feminist movement in the churches, but do not yet reflect the view of many black women. First, the economic necessity of the black woman's efforts on behalf of her church has not pressured her to the point of accepting the prevailing theological view of women. When she gets a little release from other church pressures, she will look beyond her local church and realize that such theological views and practices are operative both in her exclusion from doctrinal decision-making and in her absence from national representation.

Second, in the predominantly black churches women are not excluded from ordination by law, though they may be in practice. Third, most of the black denominations are not financially capable of maintaining even a minimal professional staff (outside the clerical hierarchy). Where there is staff, women already know the necessity of insisting on comparable salaries.

Most of the women in such staff positions—not unlike those in their more wealthy sister churches—tend to be related to the women's missionary groups and/or the church's educational agencies. Most of the national presidents receive a nominal cash stipend for the administrative work they do in the absence of a staff. The other most likely staff position is as the editor of the women's paper or the women's column in the denominational paper.

In 1967 the national Woman's Division (the Methodist Church) held a consultation of Negro women. The focus was on Negro women in merged situations. From the findings I have excerpted the following expectations the women brought: "What can be done in situations where there has been desegregation but no integration? How can we somehow deflate the superiority complex in the white woman and help to eliminate the inferiority complex in the nonwhite? What can we do to recognize good judgment, and respect it, in the noneducated woman?"

In 1968 a survey was made of Methodist leadership in merged structures.[4] Interpretive comments based on the response, elicited through a questionnaire distributed across the organization, speak to the dilemma of black leadership in white churches.

This inquiry (or survey) was planned as a broad-based, though focused, review of progress made toward integrating hitherto racially separated structures. It was not designed as a statistical inquiry. Generalizations made by the research team were:

1. It was not found that enlightenment regarding other ethnic groups is a product of geographical location.

2. It was not demonstrated that size of locality determines the nature and extent of "progress" toward successful integration.

3. It was not manifest that membership in any particular ethnic group controls or determines readiness for either "merger" or "integration."

"Merger" was an area of misconception. A number of replies indicate that this was commonly thought of as the process through which the racial or ethnic minorities were to give up their identities.

"Integrated merger" was a concept employed by a few who saw the previously separated groups as coming together in one "mix," to which each would contribute and for which each would yield some of its former prerogatives, comforts, and complacencies.

At this writing only one of the jurisdictional women's groups out of the five regional jurisdictions has a black president; two have black vice-presidents.

In February 1972, a National Black Women's Conference was called by Mrs. Elizabeth M. Scott, president of Black Women's Association. It met in Pittsburgh. In its section on "Role of Black Woman in the Community," there are conclusions and suggestions for actions that at least make some acknowledgement of the black woman in her church. One reads: "The church must be a meeting place for different people of the community, a place to listen to the problems of the community, a place for planning better opportunities for the people of the community." In its action section there are two references to black women as church women. "We, the black churchwomen, must move our churches to serve as a meeting place to provide the opportunity for volunteers, e.g., tutoring, detection of learning deficiencies, supervision, planning skills, leadership." And the following: "Black women must get on policy making boards (both secular and sacred) in the community and serve in executive positions. ..."

Black Women—Strengthened by Faith

The black churchwoman must come to the point of challenging both her sisters in other denominations and the clerical-male hierarchy in her own. In many ways she has been the most oppressed and the least vocal. She has given the most and, in my judgment, gotten the least. She has shown tremendous faithfulness to the spirit of her church. Her foresight, ingenuity, and "stick-to-itiveness" have kept many black churches open, many black preachers fed, many parsonages livable.

She has borne her children in less than desirable conditions, managed her household often in the absence of a husband. She has gathered unto herself the children of the community, she has washed them, combed their hair, fed them and told them Bible stories—in short, she has been their missionary, their substitute mother, their teacher. Many leaders of the present-day black church owe their commitment to the early influence of just such a black woman.

You may have heard of the Church of the Black Madonna in Detroit, Michigan. While I do not know how it came to be so named, I would guess that it is not to be confused with the usual "pedestal placing" of woman—above the fray, protected, adorned, and excluded! I choose to see it as homage to black women—their numbers, their strength, their faith, their sustaining and prophetic role in the black church.

In James Forman's book, referred to earlier, there is a chapter on "Strong Black Women." Forman speaks to the heart that women bring to the black church, indeed to the entire religious community, in references to women in the Albany, Georgia, protest of the 1960s.

> The strength of the women overwhelmed me. Here they were in jail, but their spirits seemed to rise each minute. They were yelling at the jailer, cursing, singing, ready to fight if someone came to their cell to mistreat them. Images of other strong black women resisting slavery and servitude flooded my mind. I thought of Georgia Mae Turner and Lucretia Collins and the young girls in the cell block next to me now as the modern-day Harriet Tubmans, Sojourner Truths, and all those proud black women who did not allow slavery to break their spirits. ... As I thought about

the women protesting their arrest, I knew that the black liberation movement would escalate, for too many young people were involved. Most of the women in the cells were very young, one of them only fourteen.[5]

With such a heritage of strength and faith, black women in the churches today must continue strong in character and in faith. They must reach other sisters and brothers with a sense of the commonality of their struggles on behalf of black people, and ultimately all humanity. They must continue to work within the "walls" of the church, challenging theological pacesetters and church bureaucrats; they also must continue to push outward the church "walls" so it may truly serve the black community. They must be ever aware of their infinite worth, their godliness in the midst of creatureliness, and their having been freed from the triple barriers of *sex, race,* and *church* into a community of believers.

NOTES

1. Joseph R. Washington, Jr., "How Black Is Black Religion?" in *Question a Black Theology,* eds. James J. Gardiner, S.A., and J. Deotis Roberts, Sr. (Philadelphia: Pilgrim Press, 1970), p. 28.

2. Cicely Tyson, *The New York Times,* October 1, 1972.

3. Judith Hole and Ellen Levine, *Rebirth of Feminism* (New York: Quadrangle Books, 1971), p. 377.

4. A survey within Woman's Societies of Christian Service and Wesleyan Service Guilds (the Methodist Church) by Research and Action, Inc., New York City, 1968.

5. James Forman, *The Making of Black Revolutionaries* (New York: Macmillan Co., 1972), p. 200.

26

BLACK THEOLOGY AND FEMINIST THEOLOGY: A COMPARATIVE VIEW

Pauli Murray

Since the 1960s, contemporary theologians within the Christian tradition have responded to movements around the globe toward liberation of oppressed peoples with a growing body of literature variously called theology of liberation, political theology, theology of hope, or theology of revolution. Their common theme is the relation between Christian theology and social action. While much of this writing has come from Europe and Latin America, black theology and feminist theology are native to the United States and have emerged out of parallel movements for black liberation and women's liberation in this country. The purpose of this essay is to examine briefly the relationship between these two theologies, their common perspectives, their points of tension, and their potential to act as effective forces for liberation within the context of the Christian message.

Theologies of liberation are specific; they are usually written out of the concrete situations and experiences of particular groups. Black theology focuses upon the black experience under white racism; feminist theology is concerned with the revolt of woman against male-chauvinist structures of society; Third World theologies develop out of the struggle for national liberation. Their common purpose is to commit Christians to radical political and social change, and to transform society in order to create a new and more humane world. This task is seen as the heart of the Gospel message. Gustavo Gutiérrez, a leading Latin American theologian, defines the purpose and method of this theological undertaking as follows:

The late Pauli Murray was a priest in the Episcopal Church and a former Professor of Law and Politics at Brandeis University. She held a J.S.D. degree from Yale Law School and a M.Div. degree from General Theological Seminary. This essay first appeared in the *Anglican Theological Review* 60, no. 1 (January 1978). Used by permission.

The theology of liberation attempts to reflect on the experience and meaning of the faith based on the commitment to abolish injustice and to build a new society; this theology must be verified by the practice of that commitment, by active, effective participation in the struggle which the exploited classes have undertaken against their oppressors. Liberation from every form of exploitation, the possibility of a more human and more dignified life, the creation of a new man—all pass through this struggle.[1]

These theologies are also strategic and contextual. They do not attempt to construct an overarching systematic theology. Their method is inductive based upon *praxis*, which Letty M. Russell describes as "action that is concurrent with reflection or analysis and leads to new questions, actions and reflections. ... The direction of thought flows, not 'downward' from 'theological experts' but also upward and outward from the collective experience of action and ministry."[2]

Gutiérrez, writing out of the Latin American experience, frankly acknowledges the influence of Marxist thought, "focusing upon praxis and geared to the transformation of the world." Pointing to the confrontation between contemporary theology and Marxism, he says, "it is to a large extent due to Marxism's influence that theological thought, searching for its own sources, has begun to reflect on the meaning of the transformation of this world and the action of man in history."[3] John C. Bennett sees Gutiérrez as a Marxist in his acceptance of the class struggle as a present reality and the source of revolutionary dynamism. He also notes that Gutiérrez sees the need for revolutionary violence in Latin America if the institutionalized violence of the established order is to be overcome.[4]

While these points of contact with Marxism appear in a Third World context, Marxist liberationist principles cannot be said to be a dominant influence in theologies of liberation. Bennett observes that Gutiérrez' basic theological method is a critical reflection on experience, always in the light of the normative sources of the Christian faith, and believes that he uses Marxism quite freely to illumine his situation in much the same way as Reinhold Niebuhr did in his *Moral Man and Immoral Society* in 1932.[5]

Among writers on black theology, James H. Cone has found Marxist analysis useful in his argument that theological ideas arise out of the social context of existence. However, he thinks that while Marxism may be helpful in providing a theoretical framework with respect to economic oppression any analysis which fails to deal with racism is inadequate.[6] Among feminists, Letty M. Russell acknowledges that groups involved in the struggle for liberation may use various ideologies as "conceptual tools for change," but holds that for Christians, "all ideologies must be subject to constant critique in the light of the gospel."[7]

It is apparent, however, that the theology of liberation goes beyond a particular theological tradition and draws upon many fields of knowledge to illuminate the human situation. Rosemary Ruether argues forcefully for a multidisciplinary integration of human sciences as the necessary foundation for a theology of liberation adequate to the present human condition. She contends that "in order to rise to the task of sketching the horizon of human liberation in its fully redemptive context," the theologian today must be willing to become "the generalist *par excellence* seeing as his context and data the whole range of human science and the whole history of human cultures of self-symbolization."[8]

Liberation theologies, according to Russell, share at least three common perspectives: biblical promises of God's liberation in the Old and New Testaments; viewing the world as history and therefore as a process of change; and strong emphasis upon salvation as a social or communal event which has its beginnings in the here and now.[9] The image of "Christ the Liberator" is part of the ideology of liberation theology and is intended to express the notion that salvation in Christ includes political and social as well as individual spiritual salvation. Christ the Savior liberates man from sin, which is the ultimate root of all injustice and oppression; the struggle for a just society is seen as a significant part of salvation history. In Gutiérrez' analysis, liberation and salvation are inseparably connected. He asserts that the term *liberation* has three distinct levels of meaning: (1) socio-political liberation; (2) a historical process of humanization and self-realization; and (3) liberation from sin and admission to communion with God. The work of Christ as the Liberator embraces all three levels of meaning which are part of an all-embracing process of salvation.[10]

Similarly, liberation theology points to the corporate nature of sin. Sin is not regarded as merely a private and individual transgression which can be cured by individual repentance, leaving unchallenged the social order in which we live. Rather, it is seen as a social, historical fact and is evident in oppressive institutional structures, in human exploitation, and in the domination of peoples, races, and classes.[11] Rosemary Ruether equates corporate evil with St. Paul's reference to "Powers and Principalities." She declares:

> The individualistic concept of sin ignores this social-cosmic dimension of evil. A concentration on individualistic repentance has led, in Christianity, to a petty and privatistic concept of sin which involves the person in obsessive compunction about individual (mostly sexual) immorality, while having no ethical handle at all on the great structures of evil which we raise up corporately to blot out the face of God's creation.[12]

Sin builds up corporate structures of alienation and oppression which man, individually, cannot overcome; salvation from corporate evil, therefore, requires participation in those political processes which seek to destroy injustice and misery. Conversion to Christ, whose saving work is seen as radical liberation from all forms of enslavement and alienation, implies conversion to the neighbor, or as Gutiérrez puts it, "the oppressed person, the exploited class, the despised race, the dominated country." "To place oneself in the perspective of the Kingdom means to participate in the struggle for the liberation of those oppressed by others."[13]

Theology of liberation also calls for a redefinition of the task of the Church in the world. Gutiérrez asserts that salvation is not limited to the action of the Church but is a reality which occurs in history and, therefore, the Church must cease looking upon itself as the exclusive place of salvation and orient itself to a new and radical service to the people. As a sacramental community and a sign of the liberation of humanity and history, the Church in its concrete existence should be a place of liberation and should signify in its own internal structure the salvation whose fulfillment it announces. True renewal of the Church must be on the basis of an effective awareness of the world and a commitment to it; "the Church must be the visible sign of the presence of the Lord within the aspiration for liberation and the struggle for a more human and just society. Only in this way will the message of love which the Church bears be made credible and efficacious."[14]

This method of doing theology is avowedly experimental, but Russell contends that this experiment in liberation is not done only on man's initiative. "It is a way of participating in the humanity of God; joining God's experiment in being together with us, so that we might be together with one another." She points out that while liberation theology looks toward the eschatological future, "the expectation of the full restoration of the groaning universe," it offers hope in the present. "It is *now* that liberation and new humanity have begun. It is now that we must risk the praxis of freedom so that God's will is done on *earth* as it is in heaven!"[15]

As we examine black theology and feminist theology in the light of these general perspectives, we will discover considerable variations in approach and emphasis. We will also find that perhaps the greatest danger to the effectiveness of specific theologies is a tendency to compete with one another in defining a particular form of oppression as the "source of all evil," and thus losing sight of the goal of universal liberation and salvation.[16]

I. Background of Racism and Sexism in the United States

Racism and sexism illustrate corporate evils which are built into the structures of the United States. There are striking similarities in their origins, ideologies, and practices. Race and sex are comparable to the extent that they form large permanent classes identifiable by indelible physical characteristics which fix one's status at birth. Blanche Crozier, a lawyer writing in 1935, pointed out that no other kind of class is as susceptible to implications of innate inferiority. "Only permanent and natural classes are open to those deep, traditional implications which become attached to classes regardless of the actual qualities of the members of the class."[17]

Feminist writers increasingly call attention to the oppression of women as the oldest form of subjugation in human history and suggest that it has served as a model for other kinds of oppression. Gunnar Myrdal's study of the racial problem in the United States, published in 1944, supports this view. He observed that the Negro problem and the women's problem in this country revealed parallels which were not accidental but were rooted in the paternalistic order of preindustrial society.

> In the earlier common law, women and children were placed under the jurisdiction of the paternal power. When a legal status had to be found for the imported Negro servants in the seventeenth century, the nearest and most natural analogy was the status of women and children. The ninth commandment — linking together women, servants, mules and other property — could be invoked as well as a great number of other passages of Holy Scripture.[18]

Thus, although tremendous differences existed between white women and black slaves in actual status and in their relations with the dominant class, the paternalistic idea placed the slave "beside women and children in the power of the *paterfamilias.*"[19]

In the American South during the period before the Civil War, "woman was elevated as an ornament and looked upon with pride, while the Negro slave became increasingly a chattel and a ward." Nevertheless, defenders of slavery exploited paternalistic ideology and the inferior status of women in their arguments. George Fitzhugh asserted in *Sociology of the South*, published in 1854, "Wives and apprentices are slaves; not in theory only, but often in fact." He found moral support for slavery in the "instance of the Patriarch Abraham. His wives and his children, his men servants and his maid servants, his camels and his cattle, were all equally his property."[20] Another typical defense called attention to the fact that "the general good requires us to deprive the whole female sex of the right to self-government. They have no voice in the formation of the laws which dispose of their persons and properties."[21]

Women, like Negro slaves, were deprived of the right to vote, legal rights over their property and custody of their children, educational opportunities, and were virtually excluded from participation in government, business, and the professions. After emancipation and well into the twentieth century, similar ideologies were used to rationalize continued subordination of blacks and women — smaller brains, less intellectual capacity, weaker moral fiber, "the woman's place," the "Negro's place," the "contented woman," the "contented Negro," and so on.

These historical similarities have persisted into the present. Both groups continue to experience in varying degrees economic and social exploitation, limited access to educational and professional opportunities, and under-representation at the higher policy levels of the major institutions which shape and control society, all of which contribute to dependency and powerlessness. Members of both groups have internalized negative images projected upon them by the dominant class and absorbed attitudes of inadequacy and self-contempt. Historically, the Christian Church has been deeply implicated in perpetuating the alienation of both groups, and the strong patriarchal tradition in the Church has been especially damaging with respect to women. The context out of which black theology and feminist theology arise, then, is what Ruether characterizes as "the overarching system of racist elite patriarchalism."[22]

II. Black Theology and Feminist Theology Compared

For purposes of comparison, we will rely primarily upon the work of three academic theologians in each of the two fields.[23] Attempts to generalize are hazardous; significant differences in perspective and formulation appear among the writers within each field as well as between the two groups. Strong differences occur in how they perceive God in relation to their struggle and in how they relate to other movements for liberation.

Mary Daly and James H. Cone are ultraradical in their respective analyses and probably stand farthest apart in their theological perspectives. Michael Berenbaum has referred to them as "theologians of survival." He says their suffering has become for them a root experience which now alters their conception of God.[24] Cone places himself within the Gospel tradition, but uses language at times which is so sweeping as to seem foreign to Christian doctrine. A typical example: "Black theology refuses to accept a God who is not identified totally with the goals of the black community. If God is not for us and against white people, then he is a murderer, and we had better kill him."[25] Daly's analysis of sexism has led her, in her own words, to "a dramatic/traumatic change of consciousness from 'radical Catholic' to postchristian feminist" and to reject entirely patriarchal symbols of God.[26]

Black theologians have not successfully resolved the dilemma of specific theologies, that of maintaining a universal perspective within the context of particularization. In their understandable preoccupation with the phenomenon of white racism, they tend to forego a sharpened analysis which would reveal its interrelatedness with other structures of oppression and human exploitation. When Cone defines black theology as a theology of liberation because it believes that "the liberation of black people *is* God's liberation,"[27] he gives the impression that black people only are the instrument of salvation. J. Deotis Roberts disavows any duty of the black theologian to speak on behalf of other minorities although he has great empathy for them and would encourage them to speak for themselves. He argues: "The white oppressor must be confronted by the scandal of particularity. He must not be allowed the escape hatch of universality."[28] The weakness of Roberts' approach is not that he sees his primary task as an analysis of racism but that he appears to overlook the fact that an effective understanding of the black experience in the United States requires knowledge of what Ruether calls the "interstructuring" of racism with sexism and class exploitation. His general tone, however, is more restrained than that of Cone. He defines black theology as liberation theology in more traditional terms.

Liberation is revolutionary — for blacks it points to *what ought to be.* Black Christians desire radical and rapid social change. . . . We believe that the

Christian faith is avowedly revolutionary and, therefore, it may speak to this need with great force.[29]

The point of departure for Ruether and Russell, on the other hand, is the universal human condition to which they speak from a feminist perspective. Ruether keeps in mind the need "to bring together the full picture" of the "history of aberrant spirituality, expressed in self-alienation, world alienation, and various kinds of social alienations in sexism, anti-Semitism, racism, alienation between classes, and finally colonialist imperialism."[30] Russell defines feminist theology as liberation theology "because it is concerned with the liberation of all people to become full participants in human society."[31]

Daly is closer to Roberts in her suspicion that "universalism" is used as a device to deflect attention from sexual caste. "One frequently hears 'But isn't the real problem human liberation?' The difficulty with this approach is that the words may be 'true,' but when used to avoid the specific problems of sexism they are radically untruthful."[32] While Daly gives priority to feminist liberation, she also claims for it a universal goal. The purpose of her work *Beyond God the Father*

is to show that the women's revolution, insofar as it is true to its own essential dynamics, is an ontological, spiritual revolution, pointing beyond the idolatries of a sexist society and sparking creative action in and toward transcendence. The becoming of women implies universal becoming. It has everything to do with the search for ultimate meaning and reality, which some would call God.[33]

On the crucial questions of violence and reconciliation in the context of black-white confrontation in America, Cone's position is radically different from that of his colleagues in black theology. Cone appears to embrace revolutionary violence and argues that no one can be nonviolent in an unjust society.[34] Roberts rejects violence not only because he believes it is inconsistent with the Christian ethic but also because he thinks it is pragmatically and psychologically bad for blacks.

The workability of violence as a means to a better position for blacks is in question. As one who has seen the stark face of racial violence in several major cities and observed up close the tragic aftermath for blacks (even at the hands of their own soul brothers), I have yet to be convinced of the pragmatic test of violence.[35]

Major J. Jones, whose work *Christian Ethics for Black Theology* examines the ethical implications of strategies for liberation, raises a number of questions about violence as a means of self-defense in the struggle for liberation. He poses the alternative of nonviolence as both a theology and a method of social action, and points to the thought of Dr. Martin Luther King, Jr.

For [King], nonviolence was not a capitulation to weakness and fear; rather nonviolence demanded that difficult kind of steadfastness which can endure indignation with dignity. For King, nonviolence always attempted to reconcile and establish a relationship rather than humiliate the opponent. For him nonviolence was always directed against the evil rather than against the person responsible for the evil.[36]

Roberts' perspective includes an abiding concern for reconciliation. He asserts that "liberation and reconciliation are the two main poles of black theology," and that "authentic existence for blacks and whites can only be realized finally in reconciliation as equals in the body of Christ." He believes there can be no liberation without reconciliation and no reconciliation without liberation, and says that the only Christian way in race relations is a liberating experience for white oppressor as well as black oppressed.[37] Jones also holds this view and believes that the black man "cannot find the way to liberation and a larger freedom for himself without also finding the way to liberation and freedom for his white brother."[38]

Cone is sharply critical of Roberts' view that black theology must work at the task of intercommunication between blacks and whites so that white Christians may be led to understand and work with blacks for liberation and reconciliation on an interracial basis. For Cone, "All talk about reconciliation with white oppressors, with mutual dialogue about its meaning, has no place in black power or Black Theology." He thinks such talk opens the door "not only for white people to be oppressors and Christians *at the same time*, but also for them to participate in black liberation and to set the *terms* of our reconciliation with them." He projects the black struggle as a closed circle to which white people may be admitted only by repentance and conversion on terms defined by black people.[39]

Both black theology and feminist theology express the goal of *wholeness* of the human being, of authentic selfhood, self-esteem, and dignity. They deal with questions of identity, the retrieval of lost history, the destruction of self-depreciation, and liberating self-affirmation. Letty Russell refers to this process as *conscientization*, a term borrowed from Latin American theology, through which people come to a self-awareness that helps them to shape their own personal and social history and learn their own potential for action in shaping the world.[40]

A crucial task for both theologies is what Russell calls "the search for a usable past."[41] Black theology sees its task as one of reclaiming a people from humiliation and achieving black consciousness, black pride, and black self-determination. Cone relates black theology to an identity crisis.

There is more at stake in the struggle for survival than mere physical existence. You have to be *black* with a knowledge of the history of this country to know what America means to black people. You also have to know what it means to be a nonperson, a nothing, a person with no past to know what Black Power is all about. Survival as a person means not only food and shelter, but also belonging to a community that remembers and understands the meaning of its past. Black consciousness is an attempt to recover a past deliberately destroyed by slave masters, an attempt to revive old survival symbols and create new ones.[42]

For Roberts the task of black theology is to provide an understanding of black self-awareness and black pride and "at the same time, to give a helpful interpretation of the Christian faith to those who honestly seek to be their true black selves and Christians at the same time."[43] In seeking continuity of tradition with the African past, he finds linkages between the African world view and black religious tradition in the United States which he thinks are worthy of further exploration. He also argues that American blacks, being neither fully African nor fully American, but in a real sense participating in both worlds, "may yet be the most important bridge to humanize relations between the West and the Third World."[44] From the feminist perspective, Ruether sees the first stage of women's liberation as the process of raising consciousness, of exorcising debasing self-images which women have internalized. This "involves the exploration of the history of sexism and the reconstruction of its ideology in order to loosen its hold on the self and to permit the gradual growth of self-definition over against a world defined in male terms."[45] Russell observes that almost all existing historical records have been preserved by men who defined women's roles and functions for them and that for women as a group, awareness of their own history and struggles is frequently nonexistent. She notes that the attempt on the part of women "to recreate a usable past as *her-story* and not just *history* is part of a widespread development in the modern world," and sees it as a necessary effort in order for women to shape their future as partners in society.[46]

Both groups are also engaged in a critical reexamination of biblical tradition as well as Christian theology and anthropology. Roberts and Ruether call attention to the dualistic strain in Christianity absorbed from the Platonic view of the split in human existence between body and soul, which they find antagonistic to the principle of wholeness in human relations.[47] Ruether relates it explicitly to the subjugation of women. She finds that this dualistic view which Christianity inherited from classical civilization repressed the possibility of the liberation of women — a possibility clearly revealed in the teaching and action of Jesus and in the early Christian community — by "equating soul-body dualism with male-female dualism, and thus reestablishing the subordination of women in a new form."[48] She also shows how religious tradition has facilitated this subjugation.

Traditional theological images of God as father have been the sanctification of sexism and hierarchalism precisely by defining this relationship of God as father to humanity in a domination-subordination model and by allowing ruling class males to identify themselves with this divine fatherhood in such a way as to establish themselves in the same kind of hierarchical relationship to women and lower classes.[49]

This analysis has implications for both blacks and women in their attempts to express images of God which will be meaningful to them in their struggle. Black theologians, however, seem to have no difficulty with patriarchal symbolism. For Cone and Roberts, at least, the concern is racial. Both reject a "white Americanized Christ" and have substituted the symbol of a Black Christ. According to Cone,

> To say that Christ is black means that black people are God's poor people whom Christ has come to liberate. . . . To say that Christ is black means that God, in his infinite wisdom and mercy, not only takes color seriously, he takes it upon himself and discloses his will to make us whole—new creatures born in the divine blackness and redeemed through the blood of the Black Christ. . . . The "blackness of Christ," therefore, is not simply a statement about skin color, but rather the transcendent affirmation that God has not ever, no not ever, left the oppressed alone in the struggle.[50]

Roberts wrestles with the implications of such particularism and offers the following explanation:

> In one sense Christ must be said to be universal and therefore colorless. Only in a symbolic or mythical sense, then, must we understand the black Messiah in the context of the black religious experience. . . . In other words the universal Christ is particularized for the black Christian in the black experience of the black Messiah, but the black Messiah is at the same time universalized in the Christ of the Gospels who meets all men in their situation. The *black Messiah* liberates the black man. The universal Christ *reconciles* the black man with the rest of mankind.[51]

Ruether's comment on this symbolism is that since God is the God of all men, each in his own particular culture, "the Gospel rightfully comes to the black man in the form of a Black Messiah . . . in the sense of that historical contextualism, which gives to each people a salvation that encounters their situation."[52]

Jones, however, seems less certain about the usefulness of such imagery in the long run. He concedes that "when the oppressed is no longer willing to accept or adopt the God of his oppressor, especially his explicit or implicit color as it is expressed in art and literature, then the process of liberation has already begun." He also suggests that it is a sign of maturity when an oppressed people are no longer willing to adopt without question a religion or God who accepts the idea of inequality for any part of the human family. But he wonders "what this altering of God's color will do for the black man. Will it make him, as a mature religious person, any more responsible with the use of his newly acquired black power than the white man was with his white power? Will the black man, with his black God, be a better man than the white man was with his white God?" He observes that those who advocate black awareness and separation as a means to achieve the ultimate realization of black self-identity often ignore the fact that the humanity of man is much deeper than color.

> The deeper question is whether it is possible for God to acquire color without becoming identified with that which is too narrow to be fully representative of the total human family, much less that which is Divine. . . . This is the inherent danger in representing God in any human conception, either concrete or abstract.[53]

The question of theological symbolism arises in a more intensified form for women confronted with the weight of Judaeo-Christian tradition filled with imagery of an exclusively male, patriarchal God. Religion, as Ruether points out, "is undoubtedly the single most important shaper and enforcer of the image and role of women in society."[54] Joan Arnold Romero accurately describes how women are beginning to respond.

> In much the same way as blacks have experienced the white Jesus in a white church preaching an alienating message, a number of women, too, are becoming conscious of the alienation from a masculine God, a masculine Church, and a masculine theology. For women the situation has in many ways been worse, for they form the bulk of the population of the Church, while in the structures of authority as represented both theologically and institutionally, it is men who have had the role of representing God to the people.[55]

The negative impact upon women of the "maleness" of God-language cannot be regarded lightly. In her study of sexist ideologies, Ruether points to language as the prime reflection of the power of the ruling group to define reality in its own terms and demote oppressed groups into invisibility. "Women, more than any other group, are overwhelmed by a linguistic form that excludes them from visible existence."[56] Nelle Morton has dramatized this issue by using reversed terminology. She asks what image is invoked in the reader:

> When one enrolls in a seminar on "The Doctrine of Woman" [and] the professor intends at least to deal with men also. When one sings of the Motherhood of God and the Sisterhood of Woman, one breathes a prayer that all men as well as women will come to experience true sisterhood.[57]

Daly speaks of liberation as retrieving the power to name.

> To exist humanly is to name the self, the world, and God. The "method" of the evolving spiritual consciousness of women is nothing less than this

beginning to speak humanly—a reclaiming of the right to name. The liberation of language is rooted in the liberation of ourselves.[58]

She introduces the phrase "sisterhood of man," explaining:

What "sisterhood of man" does is to give a generic weight to "sisterhood" which the term has never before been called upon to bear. At the same time it emasculates the pseudo-genetic "man." The expression, then, raises the problem of a sexually oppressive world and it signals other possibilities.[59]

Similarly, she speaks of "the death of God the Father in the rising woman-consciousness and the consequent breakthrough to conscious, communal participation in God the Verb."[60]

Thus, while a black theologian may find the Old Testament symbolism of the Chosen People "important for the unity of purpose among black people and the feeling that their group life has lasting salvific significance,"[61] a feminist theologian may look upon the Old Testament as "a man's 'book,' where women appear for the most part simply as adjuncts of men, significant only in the context of men's activities."[62] While Roberts finds the symbol of the black Christ "related to the affirmation of blackness and the antidote of self-hatred,"[63] Daly finds the patriarchal implications of Christology so overwhelming and "the functioning of the Christ image in Christianity to legitimate sexual hierarchy" so blatant that she would move beyond what she terms "Christolatry" to the "Second Coming of Women," the "new arrival of the female presence, once strong and powerful, but enchained since the dawn of patriarchy."[64]

The images "Black Messiah" and the "Second Coming of Women" are irreconcilable symbols to one who shares both the black experience and the experience of being a woman. Ruether thinks it impossible for the black movement to respond to Daly's sort of feminist theology because of her heavy stress on marological symbols as symbols of feminine superiority and her judgmental symbol of castration. Ruether believes these symbols "are totally encapsulated in white racism through which black women and black men have been victimized" and, instead of being liberating, "such symbols seem simply expressions of white sexual pathology conducting business as usual."[65] Both the racial and the sexual symbols point to the danger of exclusivism.

Russell seeks to avoid both extremes. She believes that Christian women can see in Jesus one who helped both men and women to understand their total personhood, and that to think of Christ first in terms of his racial origin or his male sex "is to revert again to *biological determinism* which affirms that the most important thing about a person is her or his race or sex. The most important affirmation of ourselves and of Jesus is that we want to be accepted as subjects and persons, within whom biological differentiation is a secondary aspect."[66]

III. Areas of Tension

Although certain historical similarities and common motifs would suggest a basis for fruitful dialogue between black theology and feminist theology, so far this has not happened. Ruether has been deeply concerned about the tensions between the two groups. In a thoughtful analysis she has observed that although these are the two most important theologies of liberation to emerge in the United States, "an undeclared war is brewing between them." She notes that both groups are potential victims of typical efforts on the part of a ruling class to divide and rule.[67] She points to the historical parallel in the nineteenth century when women leaders who supported abolition of slavery became alienated after the Civil War as they saw their own concerns shunted aside by white male legislators who extended suffrage to black males only, and warns this can happen again in this century unless women and blacks can find ways to avoid the trap. The symptoms are already evident.

> Black caucuses, appearing a year or two earlier than women's caucuses, have generally denied reciprocal solidarity with the women's movement. . . . In the black power and black nationalist movements that arose in the latter half of the 1960s the negative reactions toward women's liberation have come from many black males themselves. Far from being open to the question of female oppression, the model of black liberation has appeared to be modeled after the super-male chauvinist traditions.[68]

Analyzing the roots of this clash, Ruether focuses upon the results of plantation slavery in the American South which depended not only upon a debasing racist anthropology but also upon the destruction of black family life, sexual exploitation of the black woman, and suppression of the rights of the black male as husband, father, and householder. Postbellum white racism was a system which combined social and economic deprivation of the black group with direct terrorization of the black family, especially directed against the black male. Today, Ruether says, "the memory of that terrorization still forms the ultimate point of reference for black liberation." She notes that the movement for black liberation "has been overwhelmingly male-oriented in style and leadership."[69]

Differences in status and outlook contribute to misunderstandings and tensions. Blacks have been set apart through rigidly enforced segregation buttressed by institutionalized violence. Their apartness and the pervasiveness of their humiliation gave rise to a high degree of solidarity against racial oppression, the development of parallel institutions, notably the black Church, and to recurring periods of intense cultural nationalism. Thus, black theologians speak of a quest for a distinctive "peoplehood."

Women's status is more ambiguous. Ruether notes that sociologically, women are a caste within every class and race. As women, they share a common condition of dependency, secondary existence, domestic labor, sexual exploitation, and the projection of their role in procreation into a total definition of their existence. But this common condition is expressed in profoundly different forms, she says, as women are divided against each other by class and race.[70] In sum, women are distributed throughout every segment of the population and share the particular advantages or disadvantages of the race or class to which they belong. It is difficult for a black person to see a white upper-class woman as "oppressed." Her concerns seem trivial beside the stark struggle of existence. For many blacks, she represents the white "oppressor." Black males, especially, express the fear that the women's movement is a diversionary tactic to deflect attention from the more urgent struggle for black liberation.

Ruether suggests that racism and sexism should not be looked upon as exactly parallel but as "interstructural elements within the overarching system of white male domination." As she sees it,

> this interstructuring of oppression by sex, race, and also class creates intermediate tensions and alienations—between white women and black women, between black men and white women, and even between black men and black women. Each group tends to suppress the experience of its racial and sexual counterparts. The black movement talks as though "blacks" mean black males. In doing so it conceals the tensions between black males and black females. The women's movement fails to integrate the experience of black and poor women, and so fails to see that much of what it means by female experience is confined to those women within the dominant class and race.[71]

She is critical of a tendency among radical feminists to make a monolithic analysis of sexism as the ultimate evil and believes it essential that the women's movement reach out and include in its struggle the interstructuring of sexism with all other kinds of oppression as well as recognize the pluralism of women's movements in the context of different groupings. Otherwise, she thinks, the women's movement will tend to remain a women's movement of the white upper class that can be misused to consolidate the power of that class against the poor and nonwhite of both sexes. She also believes that only as autonomous women's movements develop in the context of various kinds of race, ethnic, and class oppression will the missing links in the structure of oppression become visible.[72]

Black theology presently suffers from a similar tendency toward monolithic analysis. It reveals little understanding of the problems of black women as women and almost totally ignores feminist theology. Black women are torn between their loyalty to their racial community and growing consciousness of the need to struggle against sexism. Although they are now beginning to form their own feminist networks, there is a dearth of black women theologians— due in large part to the strong patriarchal tradition of the black Church—who can bring to bear their influence upon the development of black theology. The interlocking factors of racism and sexism within the black experience await analysis.

IV. Possibilities and Limitations

One can make only tentative assessments of theologies still in their embryonic stages, but it would seem that black theology and feminist theology have the potential to develop as strong forces for the renewal of Christian dynamism in the United States. They speak prophetically to the Church, confronting it with its own contradictions. Ruether says bluntly that the Church has allowed itself to become the cultural guardian of the symbols of domination and subjugation and this role is apostasy to the mission of the Church. The Church must exorcise these demonic symbols within its structure and must recover its own revolutionary heritage as liberating force in the world.

> The gospel of the Church must again come to be the recognized social mandate of human history, not the means of setting up a new regime of domination or, on the other hand, of withdrawing into a private world of individual "salvation."[73]

For those who, by birth or circumstance, are necessarily involved in the struggle against racism, sexism, or both, these theologies present many liberating ideas, offer hope and a vision of new humanity. In doing so they help to give deeper meanings to the Christian faith and its relevance to their struggle.

On the other hand, as we have seen, there are certain limiting factors which seem to arise out of efforts to particularize the theology of liberation within different contexts. Carried to the extreme, particularization can stifle self-criticism, lead to isolation and ultimately frustration. It can develop into a myopia and obscure the vision of the wholeness of humanity which liberation theologians seek. We have already made reference to this danger in discussing the tensions between the black movement and the feminist movement. Here we call attention to the tendency to identify without qualification the suffering of a particular group with righteousness and redemption. This tendency appears in Third World theology[74] and is particularly strong in Cone's writings. He uses language which identifies "whiteness" with all that is evil and "blackness" with authentic personhood. His identification of blacks with ultimate righteousness is central to his theological perspective. A striking example is his assertion that "[t]he divine election of the oppressed means that black people are given the power of judgment over the high and mighty whites."[75]

Cone has drawn sharp criticism from his black colleagues for his extreme views. Jones wonders "whether Cone's God is big enough for the liberation struggle," and says "the black Christian can never dismiss the fact that the white oppressor is also God's child in need of a redemption of another kind."[76] Roberts is also concerned that blacks not fall into the danger of exchanging physical oppression for the bondage of race hate on the part of blacks themselves. Blacks should "be aware that their own togetherness is shot through with the possibility of exploitation of one another." Roberts warns that sin as self-centeredness is a disease which infects the black community as well as the white community. "Even the black church has not escaped the blight of self-centeredness."[77]

Ruether finds that liberation theologies which stress "the role of the 'oppressed community' as the primary locus of the power for repentance and judgment" have adopted this model from the literature of apocalypticism. This model has inherent limitations, she believes. The initial effort of self-affirmation on the part of an oppressed group becomes distorted at the point where all evil is projected upon an alien group, "so that judgment is merely a rejection of that 'other' group of persons, and salvation is simply self-affirmation *per se*" without regard for the humanity of the oppressors. She is convinced that all theologies of liberation will abort both their power to liberate themselves and their possibilities as a liberating force for their oppressors "unless they finally go beyond the apocalyptic sectarian model of the oppressor and the oppressed" and "rise to a perspective that affirms a universal humanity as the ground of their own self-identity, and also to a power of self-criticism."[78]

To a great extent, the writings of Ruether and Russell, who stand within the Christian tradition, reveal an awareness of the need for broad social analysis, a sensitivity to other forms of oppression, a willingness to engage in dialogue with black theology, and to overcome the tensions. Despite the limitations of feminist analysis to which Ruether has referred, feminist theology indicates an inclusive approach and a capacity for self-critical reflection which, if taken seriously, can be a powerful force for humanizing the entire spectrum of liberation movements. As Ruether points out, no other definable group has such a broad range of historical tasks. "The woman's story must encompass the entire scope of the human condition. Moreover the issue of sexism crosses and includes every field of specialization."[79] Women, through coalitions on issues of common concern, can begin to transcend barriers of race, class, and nationality. They can provide a basis for intercommunication and interpenetration of all social structures and act as leaven within all groups.

Black theology has much to gain by recognizing this dynamic potential as a resource which can be tapped to strengthen rather than compete with the black liberation movement. It offers a vital link to broader insights and larger perspectives. It also offers the possibility of effective cooperation, especially at points where race, sex, and class intersect. Such interchange and cooperation within the Christian context make it possible to experience moments of liberation and reconciliation, however fleeting and fragmentary, in the course of the struggle. These glimpses of the "new creation" and the "new human being" provide the hope which is the wellspring of any meaningful theology of liberation in our time.

NOTES

1. Gustavo Gutiérrez, *A Theology of Liberation,* tr. and ed. Caridad Inda and John Eagleson (Maryknoll N.Y.: Orbis Books, 1973), p. 307.

2. Letty M. Russell, *Human Liberation in a Feminist Perspective—A Theology* (Philadelphia: Westminster Press, 1974), p. 55. The Oxford Universal Dictionary defines *praxis* as action, practice. Gutiérrez writes of "the importance of concrete behavior, of deeds, of action, of praxis in the Christian life." In liberation theology the term seems to carry the meaning *action-reflection* in a continuing process.

3. Gutiérrez, *Theology of Liberation*, p. 9.

4. John C. Bennett, *The Radical Imperative* (Philadelphia: Westminster Press, 1975), p. 136.

5. Bennett, *Radical Imperative*, p. 134. Gutiérrez writes, "Our purpose is not to elaborate an ideology to justify postures already taken. . . . It is rather to let ourselves be judged by the Word of the Lord, to think through our faith, to strengthen our love, and to give reason for our hope from within a commitment which seeks to become more radical, total and efficacious. It is to reconsider the great themes of Christian life within this radically changed perspective and with regard to the new questions posed by the commitment." *Theology of Liberation*, p. ix.

6. James H. Cone, *God of the Oppressed* (New York: Seabury Press, 1975), pp. 42-43, 155-156. J. Deotis Roberts says that "Black political theology is not cast in the mold of the Marxist-Christian dialogue." *A Black Political Theology* (Philadelphia: Westminster Press, 1974), p. 218.

7. Russell, *Human Liberation*, p. 60.

8. Rosemary Radford Ruether, *Liberation Theology* (New York: Paulist Press, 1972), pp. 2-3.

9. Russell, *Human Liberation*, pp. 56-62. God is portrayed in both the Old Testament and New Testament as the Liberator, the one who sets people free. God is not the liberator of one small nation or group, but of all humankind, pp. 56-57.

10. Gutiérrez, *Theology of Liberation*, pp. 175-178.

11. Gutiérrez, *Theology of Liberation*, ch. 9.

12. Ruether, *Liberation Theology*, p. 8.

13. Gutiérrez, *Theology of Liberation*, pp. 203-205. See also Frederick Herzog, *Liberation Theology* (New York: Seabury Press, 1972), passim.

14. Gutiérrez, *Theology of Liberation*, pp. 256-261, 262.

15. Russell, *Human Liberation*, pp. 183-185.

16. "In order to qualify as true liberation movements, *black liberation* from the oppressors and *women's liberation* from the traditionally fixed set of feminine roles should regard themselves as steps on the road toward a *human liberation of all people*, becoming free in conformity with the authentic humanity of the Son of Man . . . The time may have come to divest ourselves of the Ideological fixations of our own peculiar concerns and to seek concrete cooperation with other liberation movements. It is impossible to eliminate racism without putting an end to economic exploitation by one part of the human family of their brothers and sisters. True human rights for women is a utopia as long as we refuse to eliminate racism and a competitive society." Elisabeth Moltmann-Wendel and Jürgen Moltmann, Foreword to *Human Liberation*, by Russell, pp. 13-14, 15.

17. Blanche Crozier, "Constitutionality of Discrimination Based on Sex," *Boston University Law Review* 15 (1935):723, 727-728.

18. Gunnar Myrdal, *An American Dilemma* (New York: Harper & Bros., 1944), Appendix 5, "A Parallel to the Negro Problem," pp. 1073-1078, 1073.

19. Myrdal, *American Dilemma*, p. 1073.

20. Cited and quoted in Myrdal, *American Dilemma*, pp. 1073-1074.

21. Charles Hodge, "The Bible Argument on Slavery" (1860) cited and quoted in Myrdal, *American Dilemma*, p. 1074.

22. Rosemary Ruether, *New Woman/New Earth. Sexist Ideologies and Human Liberation* (New York: Seabury Press, 1975), p. 116.

23. The writers selected for black theology are: James H. Cone (Union Theological Seminary); J. Deotis Roberts (Howard University School of Religion); and Major J. Jones (Gammon Theological Seminary in Atlanta). The writers on feminist theology are: Mary Daly (Boston College); Letty M. Russell (Yale Divinity School); and Rosemary Radford

Ruether (Garrett Theological Seminary). The three black theologians are Protestant. Daly and Ruether are products of the Roman Catholic tradition, Letty Russell is an ordained Presbyterian minister.

24. Michael Berenbaum, "Women, Blacks, and Jews: Theologians of Survival," *Religion in Life. A Christian Quarterly of Opinion and Discussion* 45 (Spring 1976): 106-118.

25. James H. Cone, *A Black Theology of Liberation* (Philadelphia: J. B. Lippincott Co., 1970), pp. 59-60.

26. Mary Daly, *The Church and the Second Sex, With a New Feminist Post-Christian Introduction by the Author* (New York: Harper Colophon Books, 1975), p. 5. See also Mary Daly, *Beyond God the Father: Toward a Philosophy of Women's Liberation* (Boston: Beacon Press, 1973).

27. Cone, *Black Theology of Liberation,* p. 23.

28. Roberts, *Black Political Theology,* p. 16.

29. J. Deotis Roberts, *Liberation and Reconciliation. A Black Theology* (Philadelphia: Westminster Press, 1971), p. 27. Cf. Major J. Jones, *Black Awareness: A Theology of Hope* (Nashville: Abingdon Press, 1971), passim.

30. Ruether, *Liberation Theology,* p. 21.

31. Russell, *Human Liberation,* p. 20.

32. Daly, *Beyond God the Father,* pp. 4-5.

33. Daly, *Beyond God the Father,* p. 6.

34. James H. Cone, *Black Theology and Black Power* (New York: Seabury Press, 1969), pp. 138ff; and *God of the Oppressed,* pp. 217ff.

35. Roberts, *Liberation and Reconciliation,* p. 189.

36. Major J. Jones, *Christian Ethics for Black Theology* (Nashville: Abingdon Press, 1974), p. 142.

37. Roberts, *Liberation and Reconciliation,* pp. 25, 26; and *Black Political Theology,* p. 222.

38. Jones, *Christian Ethics,* p. 195.

39. Cone, *God of the Oppressed,* pp. 239, 241, 242. See footnote 75 *infra.*

40. Russell, *Human Liberation,* p. 66. Cf. Paulo Freire, *Pedagogy of the Oppressed* (New York: Seabury Press, 1973), passim.

41. Russell, *Human Liberation,* ch. 3.

42. Cone, *Black Theology of Liberation,* p. 37.

43. Roberts, *Liberation and Reconciliation,* p. 14.

44. Roberts, *Black Political Theology,* pp. 53, 55-56, 74ff.

45. Ruether, *New Woman/New Earth,* p. 29.

46. Russell, *Human Liberation,* p. 81.

47. Roberts, *Black Political Theology,* pp. 75, 84-85.

48. Ruether, *Liberation Theology,* p. 99.

49. Ruether, *New Woman/New Earth,* p. 65.

50. Cone, *God of the Oppressed,* pp. 136-137.

51. Roberts, *Liberation and Reconciliation,* pp. 139-140.

52. Ruether, *Liberation Theology,* p. 133.

53. Jones, *Black Awareness,* pp. 115, 116.

54. Rosemary R. Ruether, ed. *Religion and Sexism* (New York: Simon & Schuster, 1974), p. 9.

55. Joan Arnold Romero, "The Protestant Principle: A Woman's-Eye View of Barth and Tillich," in *Religion and Sexism,* ed. Ruether, p. 319.

56. Ruether, *New Woman/New Earth,* p. xiii.

57. Nelle Morton, "Preaching the Word," in *Sexist Religion and Women in the Church,* ed. Alice L. Hageman (New York: Association Press, 1974), p. 29.

58. Daly, *Beyond God the Father,* p. 8.

59. Daly, *Beyond God the Father,* p. 9.

60. Daly, *Beyond God the Father,* p. 12.

61. Roberts, *Liberation and Reconciliation,* p. 58

62. Phyllis Bird, "Images of Women in the Old Testament," in *Religion and Sexism,* ed. Ruether, p. 41.

63. Roberts, *Black Political Theology*, p. 137.

64. Daly, *Beyond God the Father*, pp. 79, 96.

65. Ruether, *New Woman/New Earth*, p. 121.

66. Russell, *Human Liberation*, pp. 138-139.

67. Ruether, *New Woman/New Earth*, p. 115.

68. Ruether, *New Woman/New Earth*, p. 116.

69. Ruether, *New Woman/New Earth*, pp. 117-121.

70. Ruether, *New Woman/New Earth*, p. 125.

71. Ruether, *New Woman/New Earth*, p. 116. For a discussion of the analogous position of race and sex in the process of social control and of social change, and of the differences, see William H. Chafe, *Women and Equality* (New York: Oxford University Press, 1977), chaps. 3, 4.

72. Ruether, *New Woman/New Earth*, pp. 121-125, 131-132.

73. Ruether, *New Woman/New Earth*, p. 82.

74. "The future of history belongs to the poor and exploited. True liberation will be the work of the oppressed themselves; in them, the Lord saves history." Gutiérrez, *Theology of Liberation*, p. 208.

75. Cone, *God of the Oppressed*, p. 225. "When the whites undergo the true experience of conversion wherein they die to whiteness and are reborn anew in order to struggle *against* white oppression and *for* the liberation of the oppressed, there is a place for them in the black struggle of freedom. Here reconciliation becomes God's gift of blackness through the oppressed of the land. But it must be made absolutely clear that the black community decides both the *authenticity* of white conversion and also the place these converts will play in the black struggle of freedom. The converts can have nothing to say about the validity of their conversion experience or what is best for the community or their place in it, *except* as permitted by the oppressed community itself." Ibid., p. 242.

76. Jones, *Christian Ethics*, pp. 69-74.

77. Roberts, *Liberation and Reconciliation*, pp. 112-113.

78. Ruether, *Liberation Theology*, pp. 10-16. Elsewhere Ruether speaks of "the tendency of both the black movement and the women's movement to ignore the structures of oppression within their own groups and to attempt to reduce 'oppression' to a single-factored analysis. . . . To recognize structures of oppression within our own group would break up this model of ultimate righteousness and projection of guilt upon the 'others.' It would force us to deal with ourselves, not as simply oppressed or oppressors, but as people who are sometimes one and sometimes the other in different contexts. A more mature and chastened analysis of the capacities of human beings for good and evil would flow from this perception. The floodgates of righteous anger must then be tempered by critical self-knowledge." *New Woman/New Earth*, p. 132.

79. Ruether, *New Woman/New Earth*, p. 12.

27

BLACK THEOLOGY AND
THE BLACK WOMAN

Jacquelyn Grant

Liberation theologies have arisen out of the contexts of the liberation struggles of Black Americans, Latin Americans, American women, Black South Africans and Asians. These theologies represent a departure from traditional
Christian theology. As a collective critique, liberation theologies raise serious
questions about the normative use of Scripture, tradition and experience in
Christian theology. Liberation theologians assert that the reigning theologies of
the West have been used to legitimate the established order. Those to whom
the church has entrusted the task of interpreting the meaning of God's activity
in the world have been too content to represent the ruling classes. For this
reason, say the liberation theologians, theology has generally not spoken to
those who are oppressed by the political establishment.

Ironically, the criticism that liberation theology makes against classical theology has been turned against liberation theology itself. Just as most European
and American theologians have acquiesced in the oppression of the West, for
which they have been taken to task by liberation theologians, some liberation
theologians have acquiesced in one or more oppressive aspects of the liberation
struggle itself. Where racism is rejected, sexism has been embraced. Where
classism is called into question, racism and sexism have been tolerated. And
where sexism is repudiated racism and classism are often ignored.

Although there is a certain validity to the argument that any one analysis —
race, class or sex — is not sufficiently universal to embrace the needs of all
oppressed peoples, these particular analyses, nonetheless, have all been well
presented and are crucial for a comprehensive and authentic liberation theol-

Jacquelyn Grant is an Associate Professor of Theology at the Interdenominational Theological
Center in Atlanta and author of the influential text *White Women's Christ and Black Women's
Jesus: Feminist Christology and Womanist Response* (1989). This essay originally appeared in
the first edition of this book (Wilmore & Cone 1979).

ogy. In order for liberation theology to be faithful to itself it must hear the critique coming to it from the perspective of the Black woman — perhaps the most oppressed of all the oppressed.

I am concerned in this essay with how the experience of the Black woman calls into question certain assumptions in liberation theology in general, and Black Theology in particular. In the Latin American context this has already been done by women such as Beatriz Melano Couch and Consuelo Urquiza. A few Latin American theologians have begun to respond. Beatriz Couch, for example, accepts the starting point of Latin American theologians, but criticizes them for their exclusivism with respect to race and sex. She says:

> ... we in Latin America stress the importance of the starting point, the praxis, and the use of social science to analyze our political, historical situation. In this I am in full agreement with my male colleagues ... with one qualitative difference. I stress the need to give importance to the different cultural forms that express oppression; to the ideology that divides people not only according to class, but to race and sex. Racism and sexism are oppressive ideologies which deserve a specific treatment in the theology of liberation.[1]

More recently, Consuelo Urquiza called for the unification of Hispanic-American women in struggling against their oppression in the church and society. In commenting on the contradiction in the Pauline Epistles which undergird the oppression of the Hispanic-American woman, Urquiza said: "At the present time all Christians will agree with Paul in the first part of [Galatians 3:28] about freedom and slavery that there should not be slaves. . . . However, the next part of this verse . . . has been ignored and the equality between man and woman is not accepted. They would rather skip that line and go to the epistle to Timothy [2:9-15]."[2] Women theologians of Latin background are beginning to do theology and to sensitize other women to the necessity of participating in decisions which affect their lives and the life of their communities. Latin American theology will gain from these inputs which women are making to the theological process.

Third World and Black women[3] in the United States will soon collaborate in an attack on another aspect of Liberation Theology — Feminist Theology. Black and Third World women have begun to articulate their differences and similarities with the Feminist Movement, which is dominated by White American women who until now have been the chief authors of Feminist Theology. It is my contention that the theological perspectives of Black and Third World women should reflect these differences and similarities with Feminist Theology. It is my purpose, however, to look critically at Black Theology as a Black woman in an effort to determine how adequate is its conception of liberation for the total Black community. Pauli Murray and Theressa Hoover have in their own ways challenged Black Theology. Because their articles appear in this section

(Documents 26 and 25), it is unnecessary for me to explain their point of view. They have spoken for themselves.

I want to begin with the question: "Where are Black women in Black Theology?" They are, in fact, invisible in Black Theology and we need to know why this is the case. Because the Black church experience and Black experience in general are important sources for doing Black Theology, we need to look at the Black woman in relation to both in order to understand the way Black Theology has applied its conception of liberation. Finally, in view of the status of the Black woman vis-à-vis Black Theology, the Black Church and the Black experience, a challenge needs to be presented to Black Theology. This is how I propose to discuss this important question.

The Invisibility of Black Women in Black Theology

In examining Black Theology it is necessary to make one of two assumptions: (1) either Black women have no place in the enterprise, or (2) Black men are capable of speaking for us. Both of these assumptions are false and need to be discarded. They arise out of a male-dominated culture which restricts women to certain areas of the society. In such a culture, men are given the warrant to speak for women on all matters of significance. It is no accident that all of the recognized Black theologians are men. This is what might be expected given the status and power accorded the discipline of theology. Professional theology is done by those who are highly trained. It requires, moreover, mastery of that power most accepted in the definition of manhood, the power or ability to "reason." This is supposedly what opens the door to participation in logical, philosophical debates and discussions presupposing rigorous intellectual training, for most of history, outside the "woman's sphere." Whereas the nature of men has been defined in terms of reason and the intellect, that of women has to do with intuition and emotionalism. Women were limited to matters related to the home while men carried out the more important work, involving use of the rational faculties.[4] These distinctions were not as clear in the slave community.[5] Slaves and women were thought to share the characteristics of emotionality and irrationality. As we move further away from the slave culture, however, a dualism between Black men and women increasingly emerges. This means that Black males have gradually increased their power and participation in the male-dominated society, while Black females have continued to endure the stereotypes and oppressions of an earlier period.

When sexual dualism has fully run its course in the Black community (and I believe that it has), it will not be difficult to see why Black women are invisible in Black Theology. Just as White women formerly had no place in White Theology—except as the receptors of White men's theological interpretations—Black women have had no place in the development of Black Theology. By self-appointment, or by the sinecure of a male-dominated society, Black men have deemed it proper to speak for the entire Black community, male and female.

In a sense, Black men's acceptance of the patriarchal model is logical and to be expected. Black male slaves were unable to reap the benefits of patriarchy. Before emancipation they were not given the opportunity to serve as protector and provider for Black women and children, as White men were able to do for their women and children. Much of what was considered "manhood" had to do with how well one could perform these functions. It seems only natural that the post-emancipation Black men would view as primary importance the reclaiming of their property—their women and their children. Moreover, it is natural that Black men would claim their "natural" right to the "man's world." But it should be emphasized that this is logical and natural only if one has accepted without question the terms and values of patriarchy—the concept of male control and supremacy.

Black men must ask themselves a difficult question. How can a White society characterized by Black enslavement, colonialism, and imperialism provide the normative conception of women for Black society? How can the sphere of the woman, as defined by White men, be free from the evils and oppressions that are found in the White society? The important point is that in matters relative to the relationship between the sexes, Black men have accepted without question the patriarchal structures of the White society as normative for the Black community. How can a Black minister preach in a way which advocates St. Paul's dictum concerning women while ignoring or repudiating his dictum concerning slaves? Many Black women are enraged as they listen to "liberated" Black men speak about the "place of women" in words and phrases similar to those of the very White oppressors they condemn.

Black women have been invisible in theology because theological scholarship has not been a part of the woman's sphere. The first of the above two assumptions results, therefore, from the historical orientation of the dominant culture. The second follows from the first. If women have no place in theology it becomes the natural prerogative of men to monopolize theological concerns, including those relating specifically to women. Inasmuch as Black men have accepted the sexual dualisms of the dominant culture they presume to speak for Black women.

Before finally dismissing the two assumptions a pertinent question should be raised. Does the absence of Black women in the circles producing Black Theology necessarily mean that the resultant theology cannot be in the best interest of Black women? The answer is obvious. Feminist theologians during the past few years have shown how theology done by men in male-dominated cultures has served to undergird patriarchal structures in society.[6] If Black men have accepted those structures, is there any reason to believe that the theology written by Black men would be any more liberating of Black women than White Theology was for White women? It would seem that in view of the oppression that Black people have suffered Black men would be particularly sensitive to the oppression of others.[7]

James Cone has stated that the task of Black Theology "is to analyze the nature of the gospel of Jesus Christ in the light of oppressed Black people so they will see the gospel as inseparable from their humiliated condition, bestowing on them the necessary power to break the chains of oppression. This means that it is a theology of and for the Black community, seeking to interpret the religious dimensions of the forces of liberation in that community."[8] What are the forces of liberation in the Black community and the Black Church? Are they to be exclusively defined by the struggle against racism? My answer to that question is No. There are oppressive realities in the Black community which are related to, but independent of, the fact of racism. Sexism is one such reality. Black men seek to liberate themselves from racial stereotypes and the conditions of oppression without giving due attention to the stereotypes and oppressions against women which parallel those against Blacks. Blacks fight to be free of the stereotype that all Blacks are dirty and ugly, or that Black represents evil and darkness.[9] The slogan "Black is Beautiful" was a counterattack on these stereotypes. The parallel for women is the history of women as "unclean" especially during menstruation and after childbirth. Because the model of beauty in the White male-dominated society is the "long-haired blonde," with all that goes along with that mystique, Black women have an additional problem with the Western idea of "ugliness," particularly as they encounter Black men who have adopted this White model of beauty. Similarly, the Christian teaching that woman is responsible for the fall of *mankind* and is, therefore, the source of evil has had a detrimental effect in the experience of Black women.

Like all oppressed peoples the self-image of Blacks has suffered damage. In addition they have not been in control of their own destiny. It is the goal of the Black liberation struggle to change radically the socioeconomic and political conditions of Black people by inculcating self-love, self-control, self-reliance, and political power. The concepts of self-love, self-control, self-reliance, and political participation certainly have broad significance for Black women, even though they were taught that, by virtue of their sex, they had to be completely dependent on *man*; yet while their historical situation reflected the need for dependence, the powerlessness of Black men made it necessary for them to seek those values for themselves.

Racism and sexism are interrelated just as all forms of oppression are interrelated. Sexism, however, has a reality and significance of its own because it represents that peculiar form of oppression suffered by Black women at the hands of Black men. It is important to examine this reality of sexism as it operated in both the Black community and the Black Church. We will consider first the Black Church and secondly the Black community to determine to what extent Black Theology has measured up to its defined task with respect to the liberation of Black women.[10]

The Black Church and the Black Woman

I can agree with Karl Barth as he describes the peculiar function of theology as the church's "subjecting herself to a self-test." "She [the church] faces herself with the question of truth, i.e., she measures her action, her language about God, against her existence as a Church."[11]

On the one hand, Black Theology must continue to criticize classical theology and the White Church. But on the other hand, Black Theology must subject the Black Church to a "self-test." The task of the church according to James Cone is threefold: (1) "It proclaims the reality of divine liberation. . . . It is not possible to receive the good news of freedom and also keep it to ourselves; it must be told to the whole world. . . ." (2) "It actively shares in the liberation struggle." (3) It "is a visible manifestation that the gospel is a reality. . . . If it [the church] lives according to the old order (as it usually has), then no one will believe its message."[12] It is clear that Black Theology must ask whether or not the Black Church is faithful to this task. Moreover, the language of the Black Church about God must be consistent with its action.[13] These requirements of the church's faithfulness in the struggle for liberation have not been met as far as the issue of women is concerned.

If the liberation of women is not proclaimed, the church's proclamation cannot be about divine liberation. If the church does not share in the liberation struggle of Black women, its liberation struggle is not authentic. If women are oppressed, the church cannot possibly be "a visible manifestation that the gospel is a reality"—for the gospel cannot be real in that context. One can see the contradictions between the church's language or proclamation of liberation and its action by looking both at the status of Black women in the church as laity and Black women in the ordained ministry of the church.

It is often said that women are the "backbone" of the church. On the surface this may appear to be a compliment, especially when one considers the function of the backbone in the human anatomy. Theressa Hoover prefers to use the term "glue" to describe the function of women in the Black Church. In any case, the telling portion of the word backbone is "back." It has become apparent to me that most of the ministers who use this term have reference to location rather than function. What they really mean is that women are in the background and should be kept there. They are merely support workers. This is borne out by my observation that in many churches women are consistently given responsibilities in the kitchen, while men are elected or appointed to the important boards and leadership positions. While decisions and policies may be discussed in the kitchen, they are certainly not made there. Recently I conducted a study in one conference of the African Methodist Episcopal Church which indicated that women are accorded greater participation on the decision-making boards of smaller rather than larger churches.[14] This political maneuver helps to keep women "in their place" in the denomination as well as in the local congregations. The conspiracy to keep women relegated to the background is also aided by the continuous psychological and political strategizing that keeps women from realizing their own potential power in the church. Not only are they rewarded for performance in "backbone" or supportive positions, but they are penalized for trying to move from the backbone to the head position—the leadership of the church. It is by considering the distinction between prescribed support positions and the policy-making, leadership positions that the oppression of Black women in the Black Church can be seen more clearly.

For the most part, men have monopolized the ministry as a profession. The ministry of women as fully ordained clergypersons has always been controversial. The Black church fathers were unable to see the injustices of their own practices, even when they paralleled the injustices in the White Church against which they rebelled.

In the early nineteenth century, the Rev. Richard Allen perceived that it was unjust for Blacks, free and slaves, to be relegated to the balcony and restricted to a special time to pray and kneel at the communion table; for this he should be praised. Yet because of his acceptance of the patriarchal system Allen was unable to see the injustice in relegating women to one area of the church—the pews—by withholding ordination from women as he did in the case of Mrs. Jarena Lee.[15] Lee recorded Allen's response when she informed him of her call to "go preach the Gospel":

> He replied by asking in what sphere I wished to move in? I said, among the Methodists. He then replied, that a Mrs. Cook, a Methodist lady, had also some time before requested the same privilege; who it was believed, had done much good in the way of *exhortation*, and *holding prayer meetings;* and who had been permitted to do so by the *verbal license* of the preacher in charge at the time. But as to women preaching, he said that our Discipline knew nothing at all about it—that *it did not call* for women preachers.[16]

Because of this response Jarena Lee's preaching ministry was delayed for eight years. She was not unaware of the sexist injustice in Allen's response.

> Oh how careful ought we be, lest through our by-laws of church government and discipline, we bring into disrepute even the word of life. For as unseemly as it may appear nowadays for a woman to preach, it should be remembered that nothing is impossible with God. And why should it be thought impossible, heterodox, or improper for a woman to preach, seeing the Saviour died for the woman as well as the man?[17]

Another "colored minister of the gospel," Elizabeth, was greatly troubled over her call to preach, or more accurately, over the response of men to her call to preach. She said:

> I often felt that I was unfit to assemble with the congregation with whom I had gathered. . . . I felt that I was despised on account of this gracious calling, and was looked upon as a speckled bird by the ministers to whom I looked for instruction . . . some [of the ministers] would cry out, "you are an enthusiast," and others said, "the Discipline did not allow of any such division of work."[18]

Sometime later when questioned about her authority to preach against slavery and her ordination status, she responded that she preached "not by the commission of men's hands: if the Lord had ordained me, I needed nothing better."[19] With this commitment to God rather than to a male-dominated church structure she led a fruitful ministry.

Mrs. Amanda Berry Smith, like Mrs. Jarena Lee, had to conduct her ministry outside the structure of the A.M.E. Church. Smith described herself as a "plain Christian woman" with "no money" and "no prominence."[20] But she was intrigued with the idea of attending the General Conference of 1872 in Nashville, Tennessee. Her inquiry into the cost of going to Nashville brought the following comments from some of the A.M.E. brethren:

> "I tell you, Sister, it will cost money to go down there; and if you ain't got plenty of it, it's no use to go"; . . . another said:
> "What does she want to go for?"
> "Woman preacher; they want to be ordained," was the reply.
> "I mean to fight that thing," said the other.
> "Yes, indeed, so will I," said another.[21]

The oppression of women in the ministry took many forms. In addition to not being granted ordination, the authenticity of "the call" of women was frequently put to the test. Lee, Elizabeth, and Smith spoke of the many souls they had brought to Christ through their preaching and singing in local Black congregations, as well as in White and mixed congregations. It was not until Bishop Richard Allen heard Jarena Lee preach that he was convinced that she was of the Spirit. He, however, still refused to ordain her. The "brethren," including some bishops of the 1872 General Conference of the A.M.E. Church were convinced that Amanda Berry Smith was blessed with the Spirit of God after hearing her sing at a session held at Fisk University. Smith tells us that ". . . the Spirit of the Lord seemed to fall on all the people. The preachers got happy. . . ." This experience brought invitations for her to preach at several churches, but it did not bring an appointment to a local congregation as pastor or the right of ordination. She summed up the experience in this way: ". . . after that many of my brethren believed in me, especially as the question of ordination of women never was mooted in the Conference."[22]

Several Black denominations have since begun to ordain women.[23] But this matter of women preachers having the extra burden of proving their call to an extent not required of men still prevails in the Black Church today. A study in which I participated at Union Theological Seminary in New York City bears this out. Interviews with Black ministers of different denominations revealed that their prejudices against women, and especially women in the ministry, resulted in unfair expectations and unjust treatment of women ministers whom they encountered.[24]

It is the unfair expectations placed upon women and blatant discrimination that keeps them in the pew "and out of the pulpit." This matter of keeping women in the pew has been carried to ridiculous extremes. At the 1971 Annual Convocation of the National Conference of Black Churchmen,[25] held at the Liberty Baptist Church in Chicago, I was slightly amused when, as I approached the pulpit to place my cassette tape recorder near the speaker, Walter Fauntroy, as several brothers had already done, I was stopped by a man who informed me that I could not enter the pulpit area. When I asked why not, he directed me to the pastor who told me that women were not permitted in the pulpit, but that he would have a man place the recorder there for me. Although I could not believe that explanation a serious one, I agreed to have a man place it on the pulpit for me and returned to my seat in the sanctuary for the continuation of the convocation. The seriousness of the pastor's statement became clear to me later at that meeting when Mary Jane Patterson, a Presbyterian Church executive, was refused the right to speak from the pulpit.[26] This was clearly a case of sex discrimination in a Black church — keeping women "in the pew" and "out of the pulpit."

As far as the issue of women is concerned it is obvious that the Black Church described by C. Eric Lincoln has not fared much better than the Negro Church of E. Franklin Frazier.[27] The failure of the Black Church and Black Theology to proclaim explicitly the liberation of Black women indicates that they cannot claim to be agents of divine liberation. If the theology, like the church, has no word for Black women, its conception of liberation is inauthentic.

The Black Experience and the Black Woman

For the most part, Black church*men* have not dealt with the oppression of Black women in either the Black Church or the Black community. Frederick Douglass was one notable exception in the 19th century. His active advocacy for women's rights was a demonstration against the contradiction between preaching "justice for all" and practicing the continued oppression of women. He, therefore, "dared not claim a right [for himself] which he would not concede to women."[28] These words describe the convictions of a man who was active both in the church and in the larger Black community. This is significant because there is usually a direct relationship between what goes on in the Black Church and the Black secular community.

The status of Black women in the community parallels that of Black women in the church. Black Theology considers the Black experience to be the context out of which its questions about God and human existence are formulated. This is assumed to be the context in which God's revelation is received and interpreted. Only from the perspective of the poor and the oppressed can theology be adequately done. Arising out of the Black Power Movement of the 1960s, Black Theology purports to take seriously the experience of the larger community's struggle for liberation. But if this is, indeed, the case, Black Theology must function in the secular community in the same way as it should function in the church community. It must serve as a "self-test" to see whether the rhetoric or proclamation of the Black community's struggle for liberation is consistent with its practices. How does the "self-test" principle operate among the poor and the oppressed? Certainly Black Theology has spoken to some of the forms of oppression which exist within the community of the oppressed. Many of the injustices it has attacked are the same as those which gave rise to the prophets of the Old Testament. But the fact that Black Theology does not include sexism specifically as one of those injustices is all too evident. It suggests that the theologians do not understand sexism to be one of the oppressive realities of the Black community. Silence on this specific issue can only mean conformity with the status quo. The most prominent Black theologian, James Cone, has recently broken this silence.

> The Black church, like all other churches, is a male dominated church. The difficulty that Black male ministers have in supporting the equality of women in the church and society stems partly from the lack of a clear liberation-criterion rooted in the gospel and in the present struggles of oppressed peoples. . . . It is truly amazing that many black male ministers, young and old, can hear the message of liberation in the gospel when related to racism but remain deaf to a similar message in the context of sexism.[29]

It is difficult to understand how Black men manage to exclude the liberation of Black women from their interpretation of the liberating gospel. Any correct analysis of the poor and oppressed would reveal some interesting and inescapable facts about the situation of women within oppressed groups. Without succumbing to the long and fruitless debate of "who is more oppressed than whom?" I want to make some pointed suggestions to Black male theologians.

It would not be very difficult to argue that since Black women are the poorest of the poor, the most oppressed of the oppressed, their experience provides a most fruitful context for doing Black Theology. The research of Jacquelyne Jackson attests to the extreme deprivation of Black women. Jackson supports her claim with statistical data that "in comparison with black males and white males and females, black women yet constitute the most disadvantaged group in the US, as evidenced especially by their largely unenviable educational, occupational, employment and income levels, and availability of marital partners."[30] In other words, in spite of the "quite insignificant" educational advantage that Black women have over Black men, they have "had the greatest access to the worst jobs at the lowest earnings."[31] It is important to emphasize this fact in order to elevate to its rightful level of concern the condition of Black women, not only in the world at large, but in the Black community and the Black Church. It is my contention that if Black Theology speaks of the Black community as if the special problems of Black women do not exist, it is no different from the White Theology it claims to reject precisely because of its inability to take account of the existence of Black people in its theological formulations.

It is instructive to note that the experience of Black women working in the Black Power movement further accented the problem of the oppression of women in the Black community. Because of their invisibility in the leadership of the movement they, like women of the church, provided the "support" segment of the movement. They filled the streets when numbers were needed for demonstrations. They stuffed the envelopes in the offices and performed other menial tasks. Kathleen Cleaver, in a *Black Scholar* interview, revealed some of the problems in the movement which caused her to become involved in women's liberation issues. While underscoring the crucial role played by women as Black Power activists, Kathleen Cleaver, nonetheless, acknowledged the presence of sex discrimination.

I viewed myself as assisting everything that was done. . . . The form of assistance that women give in political movements to men is just as crucial as the leadership that men give to those movements. And this is something that is never recognized and never dealt with. *Because women are always relegated to assistance* and this is where I became interested in the liberation of women. Conflicts, constant conflicts came up, conflicts that would rise as a result of the fact that I was married to a member of the Central Committee and I was also an officer in the Party. Things that I would have suggested myself would be implemented. But if I suggested them the suggestion might be rejected. If they were suggested by a man the suggestion would be implemented.

It seemed throughout the history of my working with the Party, I always had to struggle with this. The suggestion itself was never viewed objectively. *The fact that the suggestion came from a woman gave it some lesser value.* And it seemed that it had something to do with the egos of the men involved. I know that the first demonstration that we had at the courthouse for Huey Newton I was very instrumental in organizing; the first time we went out on the soundtrucks, I was on the soundtrucks; the first leaflet we put out, I wrote; the first demonstration, I made up the pamphlets. And the members of that demonstration for the most part were women. I've noticed that throughout my dealings in the black movement in the United States, that the *most anxious, the most eager, the most active, the most quick to understand the problem and quick to move are women.*[32]

Cleaver exposed the fact that even when leadership was given to women sexism lurked in the wings. As executive secretary of the Student Nonviolent Coordinating Committee (SNCC), Ruby Doris Robinson was described as the "heart beat of SNCC." Yet there were "the constant conflicts, the constant struggles that she was subjected to because she was a woman."[33]

Notwithstanding all the evidence to the contrary, some might want to argue that the central problem of Black women is related to their race and not their sex. Such an argument then presumes that the problem cannot be resolved apart from the Black struggle. I contend that as long as the Black struggle refuses to recognize and deal with its sexism, the idea that women will receive justice from that struggle alone will never work. It will not work because Black women will no longer allow Black men to ignore their unique problems and needs in the name of some distorted view of the "liberation of the total community." I would bring to the minds of the proponents of this argument the words of President Sekou Toure as he wrote about the role of African women in the revolution. He said, "if African women cannot possibly conduct their struggle in isolation from the struggle that our people wage for African liberation, African freedom, conversely, is not effective unless it brings about the liberation of African women."[34] Black men who have an investment in the patriarchal structure of White America and who intend to do Christian theology have yet to realize that if Jesus is liberator of the oppressed, all of the oppressed must be liberated. Perhaps the proponents of the argument that the cause of Black women must be subsumed under a larger cause should look to South African theologians Sabelo Ntwasa and Basil Moore. They affirm that "Black Theology, as it struggles to formulate a theology of liberation relevant to South Africa, cannot afford to perpetuate any form of domination, not even male domination. If its liberation is not human enough to include the liberation of women, it will not be liberation."[35]

A Challenge to Black Theology

My central argument is this: Black Theology cannot continue to treat Black women as if they were invisible creatures who are on the outside looking into the Black experience, the Black Church, and the Black theological enterprise. It will have to deal with the community of believers in all aspects as integral parts of the whole community. Black Theology, therefore, must speak to the bishops who hide behind the statement "Women don't want women pastors." It must speak to the pastors who say, "My church isn't ready for women preachers yet." It must teach the seminarians who feel that "women have no place in seminary." It must address the women in the church and community who are content and complacent with their oppression. It must challenge the educators who would reeducate the people on every issue except the issue of the dignity and equality of women.

Black women represent more than 50 percent of the Black community and more than 70 percent of the Black Church. How then can an authentic theology of liberation arise out of these communities without specifically addressing the liberation of the women in both places? Does the fact that certain questions are raised by Black women make them any less Black concerns? If, as I contend, the liberation of Black men and women is inseparable, then a radical split cannot be made between racism and sexism. Black women are oppressed by racism *and* sexism. It is therefore necessary that Black men and women be actively involved in combating both evils.

Only as Black women in greater numbers make their way from the background to the forefront will the true strength of the Black community be fully realized. There is already a heritage of strong Black women and men upon which a stronger nation can be built. There is a tradition which declares that God is at work in the experience of the Black woman. This tradition, in the context of the total Black experience, can provide data for the development of a wholistic Black Theology. Such a theology will repudiate the God of classical theology who is presented as an absolute Patriarch, a deserting father who created Black men and women and then "walked out" in the face of responsibility. Such a theology will look at the meaning of the total Jesus Christ Event; it will consider not only how God through Jesus Christ is related to the oppressed men, but to women as well. Such a theology will "allow" God through the Holy Spirit to work through persons without regard to race, sex, or class. This theology will exercise its prophetic function, and serve as a "self-test" in a church characterized by the sins of racism, sexism, and other forms of oppression. Until Black women theologians are fully participating in the theological enterprise, it is important to keep Black male theologians and Black leaders cognizant of their dereliction. They must be made aware of the fact that Black women are needed not only as Christian educators, but as theologians and church leaders. It is only when Black women and men share jointly the leadership in theology and in the church and community that the Black nation will become strong and liberated. Only then will there be the possibility that Black Theology can become a theology of divine liberation.

One final word for those who argue that the issues of racism and sexism are too complicated and should not be confused. I agree that the issues should not be "confused." But the elimination of both racism and sexism is so crucial for the liberation of Black persons that we cannot shrink from facing them together. Sojourner Truth tells us why this is so. In 1867 she spoke out on the issue of suffrage and what she said at that time is still relevant to us as we deal with the liberation of Black women today.

> I feel that if I have to answer for the deeds done in my body just as much as a man, I have a right to have just as much as a man. There is a great stir about colored men getting their rights, but not a word about the colored women; and if colored men get their rights, and not colored women theirs, you see the colored men will be masters over the women, and it will be just as bad as it was before. So I am for keeping the thing going while things are stirring: because if we wait till it is still, it will take a great while to get it going again. . . .[36]

Black women have to keep the issue of sexism "going" in the Black community, in the Black Church, and in Black Theology until it has been eliminated. To do otherwise means that they will be pushed aside until eternity. Therefore, with Sojourner Truth, I'm for "keeping things going while things are stirring. . . ."

NOTES

1. Beatriz Melano Couch, remarks on the feminist panel of Theology in the Americas Conference in Detroit in August 1975, printed in *Theology in the Americas*, ed. Sergio

Torres and John Eagleson (Maryknoll, N.Y.: Orbis Books, 1976), p. 375.

2. Consuelo Urquiza, "A Message from a Hispanic-American Woman," *The Fifth Commission: A Monitor for Third World Concerns* IV (June-July 1978), insert. The Fifth Commission is a commission of the National Council of the Churches of Christ in the USA (NCC), 475 Riverside Drive, New York, N.Y.

3. I agree with the Fifth Commission that "the Third World is not a geographical entity, but rather the world of oppressed peoples in their struggle for liberation." In this sense, Black women are included in the term "Third World." However, in order to accent the peculiar identity, problems, and needs of Black women in the First World or the Third World contexts, I choose to make the distinction between Black and other Third World women.

4. For a discussion of sexual dualisms in our society, see Rosemary Ruether, *New Woman/New Earth* (New York: Seabury Press, 1975), chap 1; and *Liberation Theology* (New York: Paulist Press, 1972), pp. 16ff. Also for a discussion of sexual (social) dualisms as related to the brain hemispheres, see Sheila Collins, *A Different Heaven and Earth* (Valley Forge: Judson Press, 1974), pp. 169-170.

5. Angela Davis, "Reflections on the Black Woman's Role in the Community of Slaves," *The Black Scholar*, vol. 4, no. 3 (December 1971), pp. 3-15. I do take issue with Davis's point however. The Black community may have experienced "equality in inequality," but this was forced on them from the dominant or enslaving community. She does not deal with the inequality within the community itself.

6. See Sheila Collins, op. cit., Rosemary Ruether, op. cit., Letty Russell, *Human Liberation in the Feminist Perspective* (Philadelphia: Westminster Press, 1974); and Mary Daly, *Beyond God the Father* (Boston: Beacon Press, 1973).

7. Surely the factor of race would be absent, but one would have to do an in-depth analysis to determine the possible effect on the status of Black women.

8. James Cone, *A Black Theology of Liberation* (Philadelphia: J.B. Lippincott, 1970), p. 23.

9. Eulalio Baltazar discusses color symbolism (white is good; black is evil) as a reflection of racism in the White Theology which perpetuates it. *The Dark Center: A Process Theology of Blackness* (New York: Paulist Press, 1973).

10. One may want to argue that Black Theology is not concerned with sexism but with racism. I will argue in this essay that such a theology could speak only half the truth, if truth at all.

11. Karl Barth, *Church Dogmatics*, vol 1, part 1, p. 2.

12. Cone, op. cit., pp. 230-232.

13. James Cone and Albert Cleage do make this observation of the contemporary Black Church and its response to the struggles against racism. See Cleage, *The Black Messiah* (New York: Sheed and Ward, 1969), passim; and Cone, op. cit., passim.

14. A study that I conducted in the Philadelphia Conference of the African Methodist Episcopal Church, May 1976. It also included sporadic samplings of churches in other conferences in the First Episcopal District. As for example, a church of 1,660 members (500 men and 1,160 women) had a trustee board of 8 men and 1 woman and a steward board of 13 men and 6 women. A church of 100 members (35 men and 65 women) had a trustee board of 5 men and 4 women and a steward board of 5 men and 4 women.

15. Jarena Lee, *The Life and Religious Experience of Jarena Lee: A Colored Lady Giving an Account to Her Call to Preach the Gospel* (Philadelphia, 1836), printed in Dorothy Porter, ed., *Early Negro Writing 1760-1837* (Boston: Beacon Press, 1971), pp. 494-514.

16. Ibid., p. 503 (italics added). Carol George in *Segregated Sabbaths* (New York: Oxford University Press, 1973), presents a very positive picture of the relationship between Jarena Lee and Bishop Richard Allen. She feels that by the time Lee approached Allen, he had "modified his views on woman's rights" (p. 129). She contends that since Allen was free from the Methodist Church he was able to "determine his own policy" with respect to women under the auspices of the A.M.E. Church. It should be noted that Bishop Allen accepted the Rev. Jarena Lee as a woman preacher and not as an ordained preacher with full rights and privileges thereof. Even Carol George admitted

that Lee traveled with Bishop Allen only "as an unofficial member of their delegation to conference sessions in New York and Baltimore," "to attend," not to participate in them. I agree that this does represent progress in Bishop Allen's view as compared to Lee's first approach; on the second approach, he was at least encouraging. Then he began "to promote her interests" (p. 129)—but he did not ordain her.

17. Ibid.

18. "Elizabeth: A Colored Minister of the Gospel," printed in Bert James Loewenberg and Ruth Bogin, eds., *Black Women in Nineteenth-Century American Life* (University Park, Pa.: The Pennsylvania State University Press, 1976), p. 132. The denomination of Elizabeth is not known to this writer. Her parents were Methodists, but she was separated from her parents at the age of eleven. However, the master from which she gained her freedom was Presbyterian. Her autobiography was published by the Philadelphia Quakers.

19. Ibid., p. 133.

20. Amanda Berry Smith, *An Autobiography. The Story of the Lord's Dealings with Mrs. Amanda Berry Smith, the Colored Evangelist* (Chicago, 1893); printed in Loewenberg and Bogin, op. cit., p. 157.

21. Ibid.

22. Ibid., p. 159.

23. The African Methodist Episcopal Church started ordaining women in 1948, according to the Rev. William P. Foley of Bridgestreet A.M.E. Church in Brooklyn, New York. The first ordained woman was Martha J. Keys.

The African Methodist Episcopal Zion Church ordained women as early as 1884. At that time Mrs. Julia A. Foote was ordained Deacon in the New York Annual Conference. In 1894 Mrs. Mary J. Small was ordained Deacon and in 1898, she was ordained Elder. See David Henry Bradley, Sr., *A History of the A.M.E. Zion Church*, vol. (part) II, 1872-1968 (Nashville: The Parthenon Press, 1970), pp. 384, 393.

The Christian Methodist Episcopal Church enacted legislation to ordain women in the 1970 General Conference. Since then approximately 75 women have been ordained. See the Rev. N. Charles Thomas, general secretary of the C.M.E. Church and director of the Department of Ministry, Memphis, Tennessee.

Many Baptist churches still do not ordain women. Some churches in the Pentecostal tradition do not ordain women. However, in some other Pentecostal churches, women are founders, pastors, elders, and bishops.

In the case of the A.M.E.Z. Church, where women were ordained as early as 1884, the important question would be, what happened to the women who were ordained? In addition all of these churches (except for those which do give leadership to women) should answer the following questions: Have women been assigned to pastor "class A" churches? Have women been appointed as presiding elders? (There is currently one woman presiding elder in the A.M.E. Church.) Have women been elected to serve as bishop of any of these churches? Have women served as presidents of conventions?

24. Yolande Herron, Jacquelyn Grant, Gwendolyn Johnson, and Samuel Roberts, "Black Women and the Field Education Experience at Union Theological Seminary: Problems and Prospects" (New York: Union Theological Seminary, May 1978).

25. This organization continues to call itself the National Conference of Black Churchmen despite the protests of women members.

26. NCBC has since made the decision to examine the policies of its host institutions (churches) to avoid the reoccurrence of such incidents.

27. E. Franklin Frazier, *The Negro Church in America*; C. Eric Lincoln, *The Black Church Since Frazier* (New York: Schoeken Books, 1971), passim.

28. Printed in Philip S. Foner, ed., *Frederick Douglass on Women's Rights* (Westport, Conn.: Greenwood Press), p. 51.

29. Cone, "Black Ecumenism and the Liberation Struggle," delivered at Yale University, February 16-17, 1978, and Quinn Chapel A.M.E. Church, May 22, 1978. In two other recent papers he has voiced concern on women's issues, relating them to the larger question of liberation. These papers are: "New Roles in the Ministry: A Theological

Appraisal" and "Black Theology and the Black Church: Where Do We Go from Here?" Both papers appear in this volume.

30. Jacquelyne Jackson, "But Where Are the Men?" *The Black Scholar*, op. cit., p. 30.

31. Ibid., p. 32.

32. Kathleen Cleaver was interviewed by Sister Julia Herve. Ibid., pp. 55-56.

33. Ibid., p. 55.

34. Sedkou Toure, "The Role of Women in the Revolution," *The Black Scholar*, vol. 6, no. 6 (March 1975), p. 32.

35. Sabelo Ntwasa and Basil Moore, "The Concept of God in Black Theology," in *The Challenge of Black Theology in South Africa*, ed. Basil Moore (Atlanta, Ga.: John Knox Press, 1974), pp. 25-26.

36. Sojourner Truth, "Keeping the Things Going While Things Are Stirring," printed in Miriam Schneir, ed., *Feminism: The Essential Historical Writings* (New York: Random House, 1972), pp. 129-130.

28

IN SEARCH OF OUR
MOTHERS' GARDENS

Alice Walker

*I described her own nature and temperament. Told how they needed a
larger life for their expression. . . . I pointed out that in lieu of proper
channels, her emotions had overflowed into paths that dissipated them.
I talked, beautifully I thought, about an art that would be born, an art
that would open the way for women the likes of her. I asked her to hope,
and build up an inner life against the coming of that day. . . . I sang,
with a strange quiver in my voice, a promise song.*

> "Avey," Jean Toomer, *Cane*
> The poet speaking to a prostitute
> who falls asleep while he's talking—

When the poet Jean Toomer walked through the South in the early twenties,
he discovered a curious thing: Black women whose spirituality was so intense,
so deep, so unconscious that they were themselves unaware of the richness they
held. They stumbled blindly through their lives: creatures so abused and mutilated in body, so dimmed and confused by pain, that they considered themselves
unworthy even of hope. In the selfless abstractions their bodies became to the
men who used them, they became more than "sexual objects," more even than
mere women: they became Saints. Instead of being perceived as whole persons,
their bodies became shrines: what was thought to be their minds became tem-
ples suitable for worship. These crazy "Saints" stared out at the world, wildly,
like lunatics—or quietly, like suicides; and the "God" that was in their gaze
was as mute as a great stone.

Who were these "Saints"? These crazy, loony, pitiful women?

Some of them, without a doubt, were our mothers and grandmothers.

Alice Walker, poet and novelist, is the author of many books, the most recent of which is
Possessing the Secret of Joy (Harcourt, Brace, Jovanovich, 1992). This essay originally appeared
in *Ms.* 2, no. 11 (May 1974). Reprinted with permission.

In the still heat of the Post-Reconstruction South, this is how they seemed to Jean Toomer: exquisite butterflies trapped in an evil honey, toiling away their lives in an era, a century, that did not acknowledge them, except as "the *mule* of the world." They dreamed dreams that no one knew—not even themselves; in any coherent fashion—and saw visions no one could understand. They wandered or sat about the countryside crooning lullabies to ghosts, and drawing the mother of Christ in charcoal on courthouse walls.

They forced their minds to desert their bodies and their striving spirits sought to rise, like frail whirlwinds from the hard red clay. And when those frail whirlwinds fell, in scattered particles, upon the ground, no one mourned. Instead, men lit candles to celebrate the emptiness that remained as people do who enter a beautiful but vacant space to resurrect a God.

Our mothers and grandmothers, some of them: moving to music not yet written. And they waited.

They waited for a day when the unknown thing that was in them would be made known; but guessed, somehow in their darkness, that on the day of their revelation they would be long dead. Therefore to Toomer they walked, and even ran, in slow motion. For they were going nowhere immediate, and the future was not yet within their grasp. And men took our mothers and grandmothers, "but got no pleasure from it." So complex was their passion and their calm.

To Toomer, they lay vacant and fallow as autumn fields, with harvest time never in sight: and he saw them enter loveless marriages, without joy; and become prostitutes, without resistance; and become mothers of children, without fulfillment.

For these grandmothers and mothers of ours were not "Saints," but Artists; driven to a numb and bleeding madness by the springs of creativity in them for which there was no release. They were Creators, who lived lives of spiritual waste, because they were so rich in spirituality—which is the basis of Art—that the strain of enduring their unused and unwanted talent drove them insane. Throwing away this spirituality was their pathetic attempt to lighten the soul to a weight their work-worn, sexually abused bodies could bear.

What did it mean for a Black woman to be an artist in our grandmothers' time? In our great-grandmothers' day? It is a question with an answer cruel enough to stop the blood.

Did you have a genius of a great-great-grandmother who died under some ignorant and depraved white overseer's lash? Or was she required to bake biscuits for a lazy backwater tramp, when she cried out in her soul to paint watercolors of sunsets, or the rain falling on the green and peaceful pasturelands? Or was her body broken and forced to bear children (who were more often than not sold away from her)—eight, ten, fifteen, twenty children—when her one joy was the thought of modeling heroic figures of Rebellion, in stone or clay?

How was the creativity of the Black woman kept alive, year after year and century after century, when for most of the years Black people have been in

America, it was a punishable crime for a Black person to read or write? And the freedom to paint, to sculpt, to expand the mind with action, did not exist. Consider, if you can bear to imagine it, what might have been the result if singing, too, had been forbidden by law. Listen to the voices of Bessie Smith, Billie Holiday, Nina Simone, Roberta Flack, and Aretha Franklin, among others, and imagine those voices muzzled for life. Then you may begin to comprehend the lives of our "crazy," "Sainted" mothers and grandmothers. The agony of the lives of women who might have been Poets, Novelists, Essayists, and Short Story Writers (over a period of centuries), who died with their real gifts stifled within them.

And, if this were the end of the story, we would have cause to cry out in my paraphrase of Okot p'Bitek's great poem:

> O, my clanswomen
> Let us all cry together!
> Come,
> Let us mourn the death of our mother,
> The death of a Queen
> The ash that was produced
> By a great fire!
> O this homestead is utterly dead
> Close the gates
> With *lacari* thorns,
> For our mother
> The creator of the Stool is lost!
> And all the young women
> Have perished in the wilderness!

But this is not the end of the story, for all the young women—our mothers and grandmothers, *ourselves*—have not perished in the wilderness. And if we ask ourselves why, and search for and find the answer, we will know beyond all efforts to erase it from our minds, just exactly who, and of what, we Black American women are.

One example, perhaps the most pathetic, most misunderstood one, can provide a backdrop for our mothers' work: Phillis Wheatley, a slave in the 1700s.

Virginia Woolf, in her book, *A Room of One's Own,* wrote that in order for a woman to write fiction she must have two things, certainly: a room of her own (with key and lock) and enough money to support herself.

What then are we to make of Phillis Wheatley, a slave, who owned not even herself? This sickly, frail, Black girl who required a servant of her own at times—her health was so precarious—and who, had she been white, would have been easily considered the intellectual superior of all the women and most of the men in the society of her day.

Virginia Woolf wrote further, speaking of course not of our Phillis, that "any woman born with a great gift in the sixteenth century [insert *eighteenth century,* insert *Black woman,* insert *born or made a slave*] would certainly have gone crazed, shot herself, or ended her days in some lonely cottage outside the village, half witch, half wizard [insert *Saint*], feared and mocked at. For it needs little skill and psychology to be sure that a highly gifted girl who had tried to use her gift for poetry would have been so thwarted and hindered by contrary instincts [add *chains, guns, the lash, the ownership of one's body by someone else, submission to an alien religion*], that she must have lost her health and sanity to a certainty."

The key words, as they relate to Phillis, are "contrary instincts." For when we read the poetry of Phillis Wheatley—as when we read the novels of Nella Larsen or the oddly false-sounding autobiography of that freest of all Black women writers, Zora Hurston—evidence of "contrary instincts" is everywhere. Her loyalties were completely divided, as was, without question, her mind.

But how could this be otherwise? Captured at seven, a slave of wealthy, doting whites who instilled in her the "savagery" of the Africa they "rescued" her from . . . one wonders if she was even able to remember her homeland as she had known it, or as it really was.

Yet, because she did try to use her gift for poetry in a world that made her a slave, she was "so thwarted and hindered by . . . contrary instincts, that she . . . lost her health. . . ." In the last years of her brief life, burdened not only with the need to express her gift but also with a penniless, friendless "freedom" and several small children for whom she was forced to do strenuous work to feed, she lost her health, certainly. Suffering from malnutrition and neglect and who knows what mental agonies, Phillis Wheatley died.

So torn by "contrary instincts" was Black, kidnapped, enslaved Phillis that her description of "the Goddess"—as she poetically called the Liberty she did not have—is ironically, cruelly humorous. And, in fact, has held Phillis up to ridicule for more than a century. It is usually read prior to hanging Phillis's memory as that of a fool. She wrote:

> The Goddess comes, she moves divinely fair,
> Olive and laurel binds her *golden* hair:
> Wherever shines this native of the skies,
> Unnumber'd charms and recent graces rise.
> (Emphasis added.)

It is obvious that Phillis, the slave, combed the "Goddess's" hair every morning; prior, perhaps, to bringing in the milk, or fixing her mistress's lunch. She took her imagery from the one thing she saw elevated above all others.

With the benefit of hindsight we ask, "How could she?"

But at last, Phillis, we understand. No more snickering when your stiff, struggling, ambivalent lines are forced on us. We know now that you were not an idiot or a traitor; only a sickly little Black girl, snatched from your home and country and made a slave; a woman who still struggled to sing the song that was your gift, although in a land of barbarians who praised you for your bewildered tongue. It is not so much what you sang, as that you kept alive, in so many of our ancestors, *the notion of song.*

Black women are called, in the folklore that so aptly identifies one's status in society, "the mule of the world," because we have been handed the burdens that everyone else—*everyone* else—refused to carry. We have also been called "Matriarchs," "Superwomen," and "Mean and Evil Bitches." Not to mention "Castraters" and "Sapphire's Mama." When we have pleaded for understanding, our character has been distorted; when we have asked for simple caring, we have been handed empty inspirational appellations, then stuck in the farthest corner. When we have asked for love, we have been given children. In short, even our plainer gifts, our labors of fidelity and love, have been knocked down our throats. To be an artist and a Black woman, even today, lowers our status in many respects, rather than raises it: and yet, artists we will be.

Therefore we must fearlessly pull out of ourselves and look at and identify with our lives the living creativity some of our great-grandmothers were not allowed to know. I stress *some* of them because it is well known that the majority of our great-grandmothers knew, even without "knowing" it, the reality of their spirituality, even if they didn't recognize it beyond what happened in the singing at church—and they never had any intention of giving it up.

How they did it: those millions of Black women who were not Phillis Wheatley, or Lucy Terry or Frances Harper or Zora Hurston or Nella Larsen or Bessie Smith—nor Elizabeth Catlett, nor Katherine Dunham, either—bring me to the title of this essay, "In Search of Our Mothers' Gardens," which is a personal account that is yet shared, in its theme and its meaning, by all of us. I found, while thinking about the far-reaching world of the creative Black woman, that often the truest answer to a question that really matters can be found very close. So I was not surprised when my own mother popped into my mind.

In the late 1920s my mother ran away from home to marry my father. Marriage, if not running away, was expected of 17-year-old girls. By the time she was 20, she had two children and was pregnant with a third. Five children later, I was born. And this is how I came to know my mother: she seemed a large, soft, loving-eyed woman who was rarely impatient in our home. Her quick, violent temper was on view only a few times a year, when she battled with the white landlord who had the misfortune to suggest to her that her children did not need to go to school.

She made all the clothes we wore, even my brothers' overalls. She made all the towels and sheets we used. She spent the summers canning vegetables and fruits. She spent the winter evenings making quilts enough to cover all our beds.

During the "working" day, she labored beside—not behind—my father in the fields. Her day began before sunup, and did not end until late at night. There was never a moment for her to sit down, undisturbed, to unravel her own private thoughts; never a time free from interruption—by work or the noisy inquiries of her many children. And yet, it is to my mother—and all our mothers who were not famous—that I went in search of the secret of what has fed that muzzled and often mutilated, but vibrant, creative spirit that the Black woman has inherited, and that pops out in wild and unlikely places to this day.

But when, you will ask, did my overworked mother have time to know or care about feeding the creative spirit?

The answer is so simple that many of us have spent years discovering it. We have constantly looked high, when we should have looked high—and low.

For example: in the Smithsonian Institution in Washington, D.C., there hangs a quilt unlike any other in the world. In fanciful, inspired, and yet simple and identifiable figures, it portrays the story of the Crucifixion. It is considered rare, beyond price. Though it follows no known pattern of quiltmaking, and though it is made of bits and pieces of worthless rags, it is obviously the work of a person of powerful imagination and deep spiritual feeling. Below this quilt I saw a note that says it was made by "an anonymous Black woman in Alabama, a hundred years ago."

If we could locate this "anonymous" Black woman from Alabama, she would turn out to be one of our grandmothers—an artist who left her mark in the only materials she could afford, and in the only medium her position in society allowed her to use.

As Virginia Woolf wrote further, in *A Room of One's Own.*

> Yet genius of a sort must have existed among women as it must have existed among the working class. [Change this to *slaves* and *the wives and daughters of sharecroppers.*] Now and again an Emily Bronte or a Robert Burns [change this to a *Zora Hurston* or a *Richard Wright*] blazes out and proves its presence. But certainly it never got itself on to paper. When, however, one reads of a witch being dunked, of a woman possessed by devils [or *Sainthood*], of a wise woman selling herbs [our rootworkers], or even a very remarkable man who had a mother, then I think we are on the track of a lost novelist, a suppressed poet, of some mute and inglorious Jane Austen. . . . Indeed, I would venture to guess that Anon, who wrote so many poems without signing them, was often a woman. . . .

And so our mothers and grandmothers have, more often than not anonymously, handed on the creative spark, the seed of the flower they themselves never hoped to see: or like a sealed letter they could not plainly read.

And so it is, certainly, with my own mother. Unlike "Ma" Rainey's songs, which retained their creator's name even while blasting forth from Bessie Smith's mouth, no song or poem will bear my mother's name. Yet so many of the stories that I write, that we all write, are my mother's stories. Only recently did I fully realize this: that through years of listening to my mother's stories of her life, I have absorbed not only the stories themselves, but something of the manner in which she spoke, something of the urgency that involves the knowledge that her stories—like her life—must be recorded. It is probably for this reason that so much of what I have written is about characters whose counterparts in real life are so much older than I am.

But the telling of these stories, which came from my mother's lips as naturally as breathing, was not the only way my mother showed herself as an artist. For stories, too, were subject to being distracted, to dying without conclusion. Dinners must be started, and cotton must be gathered before the big rains. The artist that was and is my mother showed itself to me only after many years. This is what I finally noticed:

Like Mem, a character in *The Third Life of Grange Copeland,* my mother adorned with flowers whatever shabby house we were forced to live in. And not just your typical straggly country stand of zinnias, either. She planted ambitious gardens—and still does—with over 50 different varieties of plants that bloom profusely from early March until late November. Before she left home for the fields, she watered her flowers, chopped up the grass, and laid out new beds. When she returned from the fields she might divide clumps of bulbs, dig a cold pit, uproot and replant roses, or prune branches from her taller bushes or trees—until night came and it was too dark to see.

Whatever she planted grew as if by magic, and her fame as a grower of flowers spread over three counties. Because of her creativity with her flowers, even my memories of poverty are seen through a screen of blooms— sunflowers, petunias, roses, dahlias, forsythia, spirea, delphiniums, verbena . . . and on and on.

And I remember people coming to my mother's yard to be given cuttings from her flowers; I hear again the praise showered on her because whatever rocky soil she landed on, she turned into a garden. A garden so brilliant with colors, so original in its design, so magnificent with life and creativity, that to this day people drive by our house in Georgia—perfect strangers and imperfect strangers—and ask to stand or walk among my mother's art.

I notice that it is only when my mother is working in her flowers that she is radiant, almost to the point of being invisible—except as Creator: hand and eye. She is involved in work her soul must have. Ordering the universe in the image of her personal conception of Beauty.

Her face, as she prepares the Art that is her gift, is a legacy of respect she leaves to me, for all that illuminates and cherishes life. She had handed down respect for the possibilities—and the will to grasp them.

For her, so hindered and intruded upon in so many ways, being an artist has still been a daily part of her life. This ability to hold on, even in very simple ways, is work Black women have done for a very long time.

This poem is not enough, but it is something, for the woman who literally covered the holes in our walls with sunflowers:

> They were women then
> My mama's generation
> Husky of voice—Stout of
> Step
> With fists as well as
> Hands

How they battered down
Doors
And ironed
Starched white
Shirts
How they led
Armies
Headragged Generals
Across mined
Fields
Booby-trapped
Ditches
To discover books
Desks
A place for us
How they knew what we
Must know
Without knowing a page
Of it
Themselves.

Guided by my heritage of a love of beauty and a respect for strength — in search of my mother's garden, I found my own.

And perhaps in Africa over 200 years ago, there was just such a mother; perhaps she painted vivid and daring decorations in oranges and yellows and greens on the walls of her hut; perhaps she sang — in a voice like Roberta Flack's *sweetly* over the compounds of her village; perhaps she wove the most stunning mats or told the most ingenious stories of all the village storytellers. Perhaps she was herself a poet — though only her daughter's name is signed to the poems that we know.

Perhaps Phillis Wheatley's mother was also an artist.

Perhaps in more than Phillis Wheatley's biological life is her mother's signature made clear.

PART VI

BLACK THEOLOGY
AND
THIRD WORLD THEOLOGIES

INTRODUCTION

Black theologians' dialogue with other Third World theologians has been limited. Aside from the historical independent Black churches' mission in Africa, the Caribbean, and their very limited work with the Black community in Britain, the North American Black Christian's encounter with poor Christians in other countries is almost nonexistent. The reason for this is obvious. Poor people seldom have the economic and political resources to enable them to come together for conversation regarding their common plight.

One of the unhappy results of this situation is that what poor people in one country know about poor people in another country is usually limited to what their oppressors permit them to know. Because what we think we know about each other has been communicated to us by a common White capitalist oppressor (through the news media and White missionaries), we often share the stereotypes of each other that have been created by oppressors in order to control us more effectively. "Divide and rule" is the motto of all oppressors and they have successfully applied it in politics and theology. While most oppressed groups can easily recognize stereotypes applied to themselves, they often thoughtlessly accept similar contemptuous stereotypes applied to other oppressed groups. Consequently, when representatives of oppressed groups do meet, usually in ecumenical settings controlled by White Christians from Europe and North America, their conversations are often poisoned by misunderstanding, distrust, and contempt.

The antidote is *independent* dialogue among the poor. An indispensable aspect of the process of liberation is the people's responsibility to seize control of their history so that their identity as a people can be defined by themselves. When a people engage themselves in this process of historical self-definition, they also begin to reject all the stereotypes about their community created by their oppressors. The rise of Third World theologies (in Africa, Asia, Latin America, and the Caribbean) and theologies of the poor in rich countries is a theological witness to a global liberation process of self-definition. The distinguishing mark in all these theologies of the poor is the opportunity for the poor to define themselves and to reject all definitions about their communities created and promoted by their oppressors. Such theologies open new possibilities for transcending petty differences and establishing an effective coalition against the common enemy. But, of course, theologians of the poor have themselves been caught in networks of mutual misunderstanding. Failing on some crucial occasions to seize control of our talks, we have found ourselves manipulated by our oppressors.

When the meaning of the poor is placed in a global context, with Africa, Asia, Latin America, and the Caribbean as focal points, the complexity of the problem is enhanced. There is, of course, the cultural barrier, with language being a major problem to surmount, especially in Asia and Africa. Even if poor people could manage to travel to each other's setting, how are they going to talk with each other if they do not know each other's language? Language is not simply a technical tool but is the mirror that reflects a people's culture. Without the proper sensitivity to a people's cultural definition of themselves, it is not possible to talk with them. Culture is the source of a people's spiritual empowerment. Without the spiritual resources that are mediated through culture, there is no way for a people to sustain itself in the midst of extreme forms of economic and political oppression. That is why it is important to recognize that an economic and political analysis of a people's oppression is not enough. Culture is also important. If oppressed groups are going to converse with each other and thereby establish an effective coalition, it will be necessary to show a mutual respect for each other's cultural identity.

I think that Black theologians' dialogue with other oppressed peoples should begin with people in Africa and its diaspora and then move to other oppressed minorities in North America. Our cultural continuity with Black people in Africa, the Caribbean, and Latin America should enable us to talk with each other about common hopes and dreams in politics and economics. A similar political and economic oppression of racial minorities in the United States should enable Black people to share their cultural identities with each other so as to achieve a mutual recognition of the value of each culture in a common historical project of liberation. On the basis of Black people's solidarity with other oppressed minorities in the United States, they would be in a better position to create a coalition with oppressed people in other parts of the world.

Unfortunately there has not been much formal dialogue between Black theologians and other minorities in the United States: Chicanos, Asian Americans, Puerto Ricans, and Native Americans. To be sure, there have been informal conversations between individual theologians but no planned conversations such as might be arranged through the National Conference of Black Churchmen or the Society for the Study of Black Religion. This fact makes it especially important to note the one instance of dialogue between Black theologians and theologians of other United States minorities. The occasion was the Theology in the Americas Conference in Detroit (1975), which was planned and dominated by White North Americans. The dialogue between minorities was definitely *not* planned. Rather, it was the result of the reaction of United States minority delegates against some White North Americans who tried to dominate the conference by verbally expressing their solidarity with oppressed people in Latin America. If these White North American so-called liberation theologians had not been able to establish a genuine solidarity with oppressed people in their own country, what right had they to address the oppressed of other lands?

As Jean-Paul Sartre puts it: "The only way of helping the enslaved out there is to take sides with those who are here." We wanted to caution our Latin American brothers and sisters about North American White theologians' solidarity with suffering humanity, which usually extends no further than a conference speech on behalf of the poor. As a result, North American minorities formed a caucus within the conference and issued a brief statement (Wilmore & Cone 1979, 529–530). Following the Detroit conference, various projects were created under the auspices of Theology in the Americas, representing the various minority groups in the United States. At present, dialogue between minorities is beginning to take place but no written documents have emerged from these conversations.

The remainder of this introductory essay will be devoted to Black theologians' dialogue with African, Latin American, and Asian theologians.

Black Theology and African Theology

Black theologians' dialogue with African theologians began when the board of directors of the National Conference of Black Churchmen decided in May 1969 to take steps that would enhance relations between the two groups. NCBC representatives went to the All-Africa Conference of Churches (AACC) in Abidjan, Ivory Coast, in September 1969. Numerous meetings together followed this conference as well as the creation of NCBC of a Pan-African Skills Project devoted to the recruitment of "technically skilled Afro-Americans who have a sense of commitment toward the development of truly independent, progressive African nations. . . ."[1] Because of the effectiveness of this project in Tanzania, some church people in that country grew eager to hold a consultation with the National Conference of Black Churchmen. The first formal consultation between Black theologians and African theologians (about forty participants equally divided) occurred in Dar es Salaam, August 22-28, 1971, under the joint sponsorship of the Tanzanian Council of Churches and the newly established African Commission of NCBC.

The papers and other documents prepared for this conference were published under the title *Black Faith and Black Solidarity*. An excellent discussion of this dialogue between Africans and Black Americans is found in Cornish Rogers's *Christian Century* article, "Pan-Africanism and the Black Church: A Search for Solidarity."[2] The major issues discussed were economic development, education, and theology. These issues were perceived and discussed in relation to each other. As we expected, there were both agreement and disagreement reflected in our discussions, but all of us firmly agreed on the necessity for independent dialogue among ourselves. On the subject of "Black Theology and African Theology," a great deal of discussion happened around a paper jointly written by Gayraud Wilmore and me (see Document 29). This paper identified *liberation* and *Africanization* as the respective chief themes of the two theologies. These two themes, liberation and Africanization, have remained at the center of our discussions, with Black Theology emphasizing politics and African Theology focusing on culture. Neither theology has denied the importance of the other's emphasis, and that alone has enabled us to learn from each other's experiences of oppression.

One of the participants at the Dar es Salaam consultation was Charles S. Spivey, Jr., a Black American who was then working with the World Council of Churches Program to Combat Racism. At his suggestion and with support from the Program to Combat Racism, a second consultation was held at Union Theological Seminary, New York (June 7–9, 1973), under the sponsorship of the All-Africa Conference of Churches and the Society for the Study of Black Religion. There were twelve Black Americans and six Africans in attendance. Unlike the Dar es Salaam consultation (which covered a wide range of subjects and included persons from many backgrounds and fields of study), the Union consultation included only professional theologians, and they limited their concern to African and Black religions, with special reference to Christian theological expressions in Africa and North America. The explicit purpose was to explore the meaning of African and Black theologies as they are articulated in seminaries and universities and preached in churches on both continents.

We decided to limit the Union consultation to a small group discussion because we felt that we were not ready for carefully structured papers. We needed to sit down and talk about our political and religious situations and the theological responsibility we perceived in them. No one denied the influence of the situation on theological formulation. But how much should a particular sociopolitical situation define theological expression? Rather than try to answer this question in the abstract, we talked about its concrete implications for Africa and North America. Our conversation lasted for three days, touching on themes ranging from Jesus and violence to the idea of sacrifice in the Old Testament and African Traditional Religions.

We became convinced of the worth of our discussion and decided to meet again in Ghana to probe more deeply some of the questions raised at the Union consultation. However, before our next meeting in Ghana, John Mbiti, who was present at the Union consultation, published an article entitled "An African Views American Black Theology" *(Worldview,* August 1974). In this article (see Document 30), he makes a sharp distinction between African Theology and Black Theology, identifying the latter with bitterness, anger, and hatred and the former with "joy in the experience of the Christian faith." Needless to say, many North American Black theologians were deeply disturbed by Mbiti's analysis, because they felt that it did not represent fairly their theological perspectives.

John Mbiti's article also disturbed South African Black theologians. For the Ghana consultation (December 29–31, 1974), Desmond Tutu wrote a paper entitled "Black Theology/African Theology—Soul Mates or Antagonists?" (see Document 31). It was obviously written as a reply to Mbiti's *Worldview* article and caused a great deal of discussion in Ghana. Unfortunately, neither Mbiti nor Tutu was present at the Ghana meeting, which also included other papers.[3] By the time we met in Ghana, we were beginning to move beyond a certain politeness toward each other to a discussion of serious differences. Again the critical difference focused at the point of Africanization and liberation, but this difference could not be defined simply *between* African and Black Americans but also *among* Africans and *among* Black Americans. The consultation ended with the realization that our conversations must continue.

Our next consultation occurred in Accra, Ghana (December 17–23, 1977) in connection with the Pan-African Conference of Third World Theologians, sponsored by the Ecumenical Association of Third World Theologians. There were about 100 participants from Africa, Latin America, and Asia, with the largest number from Africa. A small number of Black Americans were invited, including Wilmore and me.[4] I had been asked by Africans who planned this conference to present a paper on "A Black American Perspective on the Future of African Theology" (Document 32). I took the occasion to respond to Mbiti's *Worldview* article and to try to move the dialogue between African and Black theologians to a deeper level by placing it in the larger context of the Third World. The account of the conference, as well as the reactions to my presentation, is found in Wilmore's *Christian Century* article, "Theological Ferment in the Third World."[5]

The discussion following my presentation was provocative and intense. As expected, not everyone agreed with my analysis and emphasis, but the paper created a context for discussing seriously our agreements and disagreements. Our agreement is reflected in the Communiqué coming out of this conference (Wilmore & Cone 1979, 503–509).

There have been many other discussions between Africans and Black theologians in Africa, the Caribbean, and North America. The Society for the Study of Black Religion held one of its annual meetings in Kingston, Jamaica (November 1976), and heard papers on various themes in relation to Black religion in Jamaica and the United States. Also a Seminar on Liberation Theology was held in the Caribbean at St. Andrew's Theological College, San Fernando, Trinidad, under the sponsorship of the Caribbean Conference of Churches, in which I was invited to make presentations on Black Theology (December 8–11, 1976).[6] African and Black theologians have also met each other in the context of the World Council of Churches and its Bossey Institute in Celigny near Geneva, Switzerland, but none of these proceedings has been published.

The influence of North American Black Theology on Black Theology in South Africa has been pointed out many times.[7] Black theologians from both continents have met each other in the context of dialogues on Black and African theologies, and other ecumenical contexts in Africa, Europe, and North America. But we have not been able to get together for a conference among ourselves. I was invited to a conference in South Africa on the theme "The Role of the Black Clergy in South Africa Today," in August 1976. I applied for my visa and, to my surprise, received it in July. But before I could reach South Africa, F. D. Tothill, the South African Consul-General in Geneva, informed me by telephone (at the World Council of Churches) of the following, and later hand-delivered the same message, which read:

> Inasmuch as the Chief Magistrate of Pretoria has declined to give his permission for the holding of the Hammanskraal seminar, scheduled for 9 to 13 August 1976, the Department of the Interior desired you to be informed that your visa to visit South Africa, which was issued solely for the purpose of enabling you to attend the seminar, is no longer valid and should be regarded as withdrawn. If you should in any event decide to come to South Africa, it would unfortunately not be possible to admit you.

I found out later that the meeting was held as scheduled, and the reason for the withdrawal of my visa was obviously related to my theological perspective. I certainly hope that the dialogue between South African Black theologians and North American Black theologians can take place soon on the subject of their mutual interest in Black Theology. There are obvious similarities and some differences that need to be explored.

Black Theology and Latin American Liberation Theology

The first encounter of Black Theology with Latin American Liberation Theology took place at a symposium in Geneva at the World Council of Churches in May 1973 (Document 33).[8] This event was not for the purpose of discussions between these theologians but, rather, to introduce them both on the agenda of the WCC, whose theological focus was so decidedly European. Therefore the dialogue was essentially between traditional European theologians and Black and Latin theologians. Only in a small part of the symposium, and in the context of speaking to Europeans, did we raise the question about our mutual relations. In connection with our mutual condemnation of European theology, we began to ask about the differences and similarities among Black theologians and Latin American theologians. The matter was touched on in a comment by Paulo Freire and then addressed pointedly by Hugo Assmann, who suggested that we needed to discuss among ourselves the issues of *color* and *class*. My response touched on the issue he raised, but the presence of the Europeans prevented its exploration. I am including this brief exchange in this volume because it represents the beginning of fruitful dialogue, and the issues raised here (especially by Assmann) have remained central in our conversations.

The next occasion for dialogue occurred at the Detroit Conference on Theology in the Americas: 1975.[9] The conference began with presentations from Latin American theologians, José Míguez Bonino, Juan L. Segundo, Javier Iguiñiz, Enrique Dussel, José P. Miranda, Leonardo Boff, Hugo Assmann, and Beatriz M. Couch. Gustavo Gutiérrez arrived later in the week and also made a statement. The first day was devoted to an explication of Latin American Liberation Theology and its relation to social analysis as defined by Marxism.

The class contradiction was emphasized by Latin theologians. Some persons felt that Latin theologians were too antagonistic toward any other contradiction (i.e., race and sex). Since the conference was held in the midst of an oppressed Black community in Detroit at the White Roman Catholic Sacred Heart Seminary, which obviously had little relation to the Black community, many Black theologians strongly resented the Latin theologians' dogmatic position on class, as if Black people have no creative contribution to make in the liberation process.

Even before the Detroit conference, the tension between Black Theology and Latin American Liberation Theology began to take place early in the planning process when Black theologians were first invited to the conference about nine months before its occurrence. The announced statement of the conference read:

> The intention of the planners of the "Theology in the Americas: 1975" conference is to invite a group of Latin American theologians, representing the theology of liberation, to dialogue with North American theologians concerning the context and methodology of this new theological current. It is hoped that such a dialogue would help both groups: the Latin Americans to understand the complex reality of the U.S.; the North American theologians to initiate a process of evaluation of the American reality from the viewpoint of the poor and the oppressed.

When Black theologians were confronted with this plan, we protested the assumption that North American theologians do not do theology from the perspective of the poor. This assumption is true *only* if by North American theologians one means White theologians exclusively, which is apparently what some persons had in mind. Thus Black theologians and other minorities felt that the invitation to them was more of an afterthought. Some expressed their opinions sharply to Sergio Torres, the chief organizer and executive secretary of the Theology in the Americas. Black theologians contended that if Latin Americans are really interested in a global understanding of the theological enterprise as it relates to the liberation of victims, then why not talk with the victims in other countries and not with the oppressors, especially since the expressed assumption of Liberation Theology in Latin America is directly connected with what Hugo Assmann has called "the epistemological privilege of the poor."[10] This controversy inspired the coalition statement (Wilmore & Cone 1979, 529–530).

Prior to the presentation of the coalition statement Herbert O. Edwards presented a paper on "Black Theology and Liberation Theology" (Wilmore & Cone 1979, 516–528), which was followed by a panel of Black theologians for the purpose of answering questions on Black Theology. Both the paper and the panel discussion created heated exchanges between Latin and Black participants and led to a private meeting between the two groups. The exchanges in this meeting were even more heated, the differences centering on the significance of color and class in social analysis. Most Black theologians felt that Latin theologians were completely insensitive to racism, and many Latin Americans contended that we needed to be awakened to the global oppression of international capitalism. But all of us left this Detroit meeting understanding each other better and with the resolution to continue our dialogue.

Because of the sensitivity of Sergio Torres to the concerns of oppressed minorities in the United States, Theology in the Americas has radically redirected its concerns toward the oppressed in North America, with projects representing each group.[11] The Black Theology Project held its first major event in Atlanta, Georgia (August 1977).[12] The influence of Latin American Liberation Theology was openly affirmed and the significance of class in the struggle for liberation was strongly emphasized.

The following October (1977) Latin American theologians held a conference in Mexico City on the Encounter of Theologians, and invited me as a representative of Black Theology. Other theologies were represented by Harvey Cox, Jürgen Moltmann, and David Griffin. At this meeting, it was clear that we had come a long way since Geneva 1973 and thus expressed our willingness to listen and learn from each other in a common struggle for liberation. The same openness was expressed in our meeting together in the context of the Pan-African Conference of Third World Theologians at Ghana in December 1977.[13] Gustavo Gutiérrez, Sergio Torres, Gayraud Wilmore, George Thomas, other Blacks and Latin Americans, and I worked smoothly together with Africans and Asians. The experience of a common struggle became a reality for us all. While we still recognized our differences in emphasis, the experience of working together on a common project tended to bring all of us closer together rather than to separate us as had happened in earlier meetings.

I think that the most significant and fruitful dialogue between Latin and Black theologians occurred in Matanzas, Cuba, February 25 to March 2, 1979. This conference focused on the theme of "Evangelization and Politics" and was sponsored by the Evangelical Theological Seminary of Matanzas and the Christian Peace Conference for Latin America and the Caribbean. Seventy-eight theologians from Christian Churches of Europe, Asia, Africa, the United States, the Caribbean, and Latin America dialogued on the general theme of "Evangelization and Politics."

The focus of my paper, "Evangelization and Politics: A Black Perspective" (Wilmore & Cone 1979, 531–542), addressed Black Theology's interpretation of this general theme as defined in the context of its dialogue with Latin American theologians. The response was provocative, and the discussion continued in a group session under the heading of "Evangelization, Racism, and Sexism." For the first time the question of racism was faced head-on by Latin American liberation theologians. The progress we have made on this issue since 1973 is reflected in the "Final Document" (Wilmore & Cone 1979, 543–551) emerging from our conversations.

Our ability to move the dialogue to a much deeper level was undoubtedly due to a large extent to our presence in Cuba and to the significant role that Cuban theologians played in our discussions. Cuban theologians have developed a slightly different methodological approach to both theology and race, an approach open, if not similar, to Black theologians. They take the Bible seriously as the point of departure for doing theology, and their approach to the Scripture clearly shows the continued influence of Karl Barth. Sergio Arce, perhaps the most influential theologian in Cuba, has referred to Barth as the greatest theologian of all time, a judgment that no Latin American liberation theologian is likely to make.

Cuban theologians also take the race question seriously, and this is due to the fact that Black people are taken seriously in the context of the larger society. The Cuban Revolution affected deeply the relations between Blacks and Whites, and the positive consequences are found in the openness of Cuban people to face head-on the race question in their society. I met no Cuban people who attempted to minimize the sickness of racism or who attempted to reduce it to a category under the class issue.

Because other Latin American liberation theologians look to Cuba as a concrete symbol to which their sociological and theological analyses refer, they are naturally open to hearing what Cubans have to say, even on the question of race. And Cubans have much to say on that subject which supported many of the concerns of Black theologians. I think Black and Cuban theologians have much to learn from each other, because our respective histories have prepared us for an openness for genuine dialogue.

However, even before our meeting in Cuba, the impact of Latin and Black theologians' dialogue since 1973 was reflected in the document emerging from the Third General Conference of the Latin American Episcopate in Puebla, for they spoke of having seen the "faces of Indians" and of "Afro-Americans who live marginalized and in sub-human conditions and can be considered to be the poor among the poor." A special session on Puebla was held at the Cuba conference, and it enabled us to deal openly with racism, sexism, and classism.

Most Latin American liberation theologians now take seriously the issue of race, and this new-found theological consciousness is beginning to appear in their public writings and speeches. I have been informed that the forthcoming Latin American Conference of the Ecumenical Association of Third World Theologians (February 1980 in Brazil) plans to take seriously the issue of race. (How could it be avoided in Brazil, where more Blacks live than in the United States?) As a preparation for the Brazil Conference, a pre-conference meeting will be held in order to focus directly on the special problems of Indians and Blacks in Latin America.

An account of the dialogue between Latin and Black theologians would not be complete without a special reference to the contributions of Sergio Torres of Chile and Gustavo Gutiérrez of Peru. The former deserves much credit for the breakdown of the tension between Latin and Black theologians. He has helped to keep us together with his patience and his leadership in creating contexts for dialogue. In addition to Torres, Gustavo Gutiérrez has made an important contribution to our dialogue in his teaching at Union Theological Seminary and his lecturing in the United States. We taught a joint course on the theme of "Theology from the Reversal of History." This course enabled us both to understand each other better, which has been reflected in an enlargement of our theological perspectives. His openness to the importance of racism and popular religion is genuine. With a similar openness from other Latin theologians and with more Black theologians becoming open to the significance of the Marxist class analysis in theology, I am sure that we can mutually enrich each other's theology and thereby help to create a common Christian theology that will take seriously oppression in its global manifestations.

The essay "Black Theology and Marxist Thought" by Cornel West is an important contribution for our dialogue (Document 34). He has not only shown the importance of both class and race analyses in uncovering the structures of domination but has also demonstrated the weakness of either emphasis without an appropriate stress on the other. According to West, the Latin Americans are correct in their contention that "class position contributes more than racial status to the basic form of powerlessness in America." Therefore, without the focus on class as the primary contradiction, no analysis can claim to be adequate. However, on the other hand, West contends that Black theologians are correct with their emphasis on race and culture (even though it is not the primary contradiction), because without culture no oppressed people can be expected to participate creatively in their own struggle for freedom. His essay moves the debate to a deeper level and thus enables both Latin American and Black theologians to learn from each other's historical struggles for freedom.

Some of the similarities and differences have already become clear.

1. We have already mentioned the emphasis on class and color. This means that Marxism as a tool of analysis is more important for Latin American theologians. However, some Black theologians are beginning to introduce Marxism into Black Theology, while others remain resistant to it. The same is true of Latin theologians in relation to the importance of racism. It is clear from our dialogue that some Latin theologians are open to the problem of racism. In fact, we pointed out to them that there are more Blacks and Indians in Latin America than in North America, and that they should therefore be suspicious of their silence on racism. With the exception of Gutiérrez (part Indian), why is it that there are no people of color among the theologians of liberation in Latin America? Some Latin theologians understood the significance of this question and others did not.

2. Latin American Liberation Theology is recent in origin, and it is often connected with the revolutionary struggle of the Colombian priest Camilo Torres, who said: "I discovered Christianity as a life centered totally on love of neighbor. . . . It was later that I understood that in Colombia you can't bring about this love simply by beneficence. There was needed a whole change of political, economic, and social structures. These changes demanded revolution. That love was intimately bound up with revolution." There was little involvement of the church in radical change or of theologians interpreting the gospel in the context of revolution before the 1960s in Latin America.

The opposite is the case with Black Theology in North America. Black Theology interprets itself in the context of Nat Turner, Henry Highland Garnet, and the independent Black Church movement. It views itself as part of the realization of a revolutionary past in the context of the Black Church. Therefore, Black theologians do not regard God-talk to be as alien to the liberation struggle as do some Latin Americans. In view of their church history, Latin Americans are suspicious of any talk that seems to usurp the human responsibility to transform the world.

3. Most of the representatives of Black Theology are Protestant, and most of the Latin American representatives of Liberation Theology are Roman Catholic. Although we have not discussed too much the significance of this difference, it perhaps does explain some of our sensitivities in theology.

4. Both theologies agree that the content of Christian theology is liberation and that it is inseparably connected with the struggle of the victims. But the methodology of its explication is different in both theologies. Latin American Liberation Theology begins with Marxism and the analysis of social reality and then moves to the Bible for secondary support. Black Theology begins with the Bible and the culture of Blacks extending back to Africa. The Exodus, prophets, and Jesus as interpreted by Black History and culture are central for Black Theology, and it gets only secondary support from social philosophy. It is obvious that both approaches can learn from each other.

Black Theology and Asian Theology

If Black Theology's dialogue with African Theology and Latin American Liberation Theology has been limited, the dialogue with Asian Theology has been almost nonexistent. To my knowledge we have not had a formal face-to-face dialogue, and there has been very little informal conversation between us. In such ecumenical contexts as the World Council of Churches, especially in the Faith and Order Commission, we have met each other, but have seldom talked about our theologies.[14] In the absence of formal dialogues, my comments must be limited to personal reflections on the possibility of dialogue in the future.

My first contact with Asia occurred in May 1975 when I was invited by the Korean Christian Church in Japan (KCCJ) in cooperation with the Japan North American Commission on Cooperative Mission to initiate a three-year leadership training program for church laity. There was also an opportunity to visit several Japanese universities and churches and to visit with struggling Christians in South Korea. During my three-week visit in Asia, I was impressed by the historical commitment of Korean Christians in Japan and South Korea to struggle against injustice and oppression. For Koreans in Japan, oppression was expressed in the racism of the Japanese who created societal structures that excluded them. That was why the KCCJ chose as the theme of its four workshops "The Church Struggling for the Liberation of the People." They asked me to speak on this theme in the light of the role of the Christian faith and the church in Black people's struggle for freedom in the United States. My living together with Korean Christians in Japan, listening to their stories of pain and suffering in a racist Japanese society, enabled me to see the close relation between the Black struggle in the United States and the Korean struggle in Japan. For Koreans, also, the church is an important instrument in the struggle for justice, and the gospel it preaches becomes the Word which empowers the people to take charge of their history.

It is significant that Asian theologians in the context of the Christian Conference of Asia have chosen to focus their distinctive theological reflections on *suffering* and *hope*.[15] This is certainly an accurate way to define the mood of Korean Christians in Japan. They experience racial suffering and discrimination in life and work.[16] This suffering arises because the Koreans have *chosen* to struggle (refusing the option of assimilation into Japanese culture). Having the option but refusing it gives the Korean struggle a certain strength, integrity, and freedom—qualities which can make a deep impression on movements of oppressed people throughout the world. I pointed out to the Korean Christians the importance of the option that they had freely chosen. Black people in the United States do not have the choice of assimilation because we cannot escape our blackness in a White society. Thus we are *forced* to struggle or accept the place defined for us by White society. But Koreans could assimilate; they could deny their identity and become Japanese because the physical differences are not clearly visible. I was deeply impressed by their refusal to assimilate, and they grounded it in their faith in the God of the Exodus and Jesus Christ. I was encouraged by their expressions of hope in the midst of suffering. On several occasions in church worship, they expressed their hope with such songs as "Were you there when they crucified my Lord" and "Lord, I want to be a Christian in my heart." When I first heard these songs, they were sung, of course, in the Korean language but I recognized the melody and turned to my interpreter (Dr. In Ha Lee) for a translation. Suddenly the cultural and language barriers were temporarily broken and we were one in spirit and the struggle of freedom. I realized that the spirit and meaning of Black Theology was already present among Koreans in song. But from their own experiences of hope in struggle, the Korean people are creating a Liberation Theology, grounded in the universal hope that God has not left the little ones alone in the fight for justice. Therefore when they tell their stories of suffering, they are not expressions of despair but of their faith that God is still keeping the divine promise to liberate the oppressed from the shackles of bondage. I left Koreans in Japan with the knowledge that we have much to learn and share with each other in the struggle of freedom.

In contrast to Koreans in Japan, Japanese Christians reminded me very much of the White Christians whom I have met so often in the United States and Europe. With rare exceptions, the theologians I met at their universities seemed more concerned with the dialogue with European-American theologians of the West than addressing the oppression of Koreans or of the poor generally. The lay people and ministers of the Japanese churches seemed especially bothered when the gospel was identified with the liberation of the poor. In fact, I could easily distinguish between the composition of my audience in terms of Korean or Japanese people by the kind of reaction they gave to my analysis of the gospel in terms of liberation. Koreans without exception heard the message of liberation as good news. In presenting this message in sermons, talks, and discussions to Koreans in Tokyo, Nagoya, Osaka, Kyoto, and Fukuoka, I experienced no resistance but was received gladly. By contrast, most Japanese audiences had difficulty with my interpretation of the gospel as liberation and asked all of the questions I had already been so accustomed to hearing from White people in the United States. Once again, I realized that one's social location in a given society will determine, at least partly, one's theological interest. From Japan I flew to South Korea. I will never forget that experience. Again the theme of suffering and hope is appropriate. In South Korea, the suffering is obviously political and is directly connected with South Korean Christians who have refused to accept the oppression of the poor as consistent with the gospel. Their theological stand is found in the "Theological Declaration of Korean Christians of 1973"[17] and it has been compared with the "Barmen Declaration" of 1934. I have read it in the light of several NCBC statements included in this volume.

During my brief stay, I encountered Christians whose friends and loved ones had been put in jail because of their resistance to the Park dictatorship. I met many others who had been in jail for similar reasons and others who expected to be arrested soon. The government had made it clear that anyone attending my lectures would be subject to arrest. I met university and seminary professors who had been fired and others who expected to be released soon. In the context of such blatant expressions of political oppression and with little leverage for resistance without the risk of imprisonment and death, how could people still struggle when the odds seemed so much against them? Again I thought of the struggles of my people in Mississippi, Arkansas, and Alabama, and in Harlem and Watts. It is hope in the midst of suffering that sustains people for struggle. When people no longer hope, suffering destroys them. To hope is to know that one's humanity cannot be defined by oppression. This knowledge is God's gift to the weak so that they will be led to struggle for the realization of their hopes and dreams.

In reading the documents on suffering and hope published by the Christian Conference of Asia, it is clear that Black theologians have much to learn from Asian Theology. That Asians have something to learn from Black theologians has already been demonstrated by their openness to Black Theology.[18] Gayraud Wilmore (with Choan-Seng Song) delivered the Cook Memorial Lectures, which were published by the Christian Conference of Asia under the title *Asians and Blacks*. While the lectures do not deal with a proposed dialogue between Asians and Blacks, they do lay the foundation for such a dialogue. And in a recent publication, Song has made an initial step in this direction when he writes on the theme of "The Black Experience of the Exodus" (Wilmore & Cone 1979, 568–583).

My first opportunity to dialogue with a cross-section of Asian theologians occurred at the Asian Theological Conference, sponsored by the Ecumenical Association of Third World Theologians which was held at Wennappuwa, Sri Lanka, January 7–20, 1979. I found out more about the Asian reality and the theology arising from it than I could ever learn by reading textbooks on the subject. This conference affected me deeply, and I am still struggling to assimilate its impact upon my theological consciousness. I believe that this conference lays a foundation for the formal beginning of Black Theology's dialogue with Asian Theology (Wilmore & Cone 1979, 584–601).

As a concluding comment for this introductory essay, what can be said about the distinctive elements of Black Theology's dialogue with other Third World theologies? With reference to African Theology, our concerns have focused almost exclusively on *Africanization* and *liberation,* as well as how we can bridge the gap created by colonization and slavery. There have been some tensions, but they are clearly of a different sort in character and depth when compared with our relation to European-American theologians or even Latin American theologians. Our common racial origin has undoubtedly contributed to the ease with which our dialogues have taken place.

More tensions have occurred between Black and Latin theologians than with theologians from either Africa or Asia. This is unquestionably due to the issues of *race* and *class* and *which* should define our priority. Since Black theologians have said so little about class, it is easy for Latin Americans to conclude that they must be capitalists, and thus indifferent to the global context of oppression. This is the opinion of many Latin theologians. Since, on the other hand, Latin theologians have said so little about color and have no Blacks among their theologians, it is easy for Black Americans to conclude that they are racists. Many Black theologians share this opinion. I am hopeful that this account of the growth of our dialogue will help to create less tensions and more fruitful conversations.

Because Black theologians' dialogue with Asian Theology has been so limited, the tensions present between Blacks and Latins or even between U.S. Blacks and Africans are not found in our dialogue with Asians. Because there has been little historical contact between us, there is hardly any reason to be suspicious of each other. Asians are certainly open to the issue of racism, as the Final Statement of the Asian Theological Conference clearly indicates. I was on the writing committee that produced the statement and experienced first-hand the openness of Asian theologians to Black Theology. This openness is found not only in what the Final Statement says about racism but especially in what it says about theology and culture and their mutual relation. Black theologians have much to learn from Asians on the relation of religion and culture to the struggle for political freedom. A symbolic expression of Asia's openness to the Black reality happened to me in Ratmalana, Sri Lanka, when I met a young Buddhist industrial worker. She did not know English very well, and I did not know her language. We were frustrated because of this language barrier. But we knew that we had a commonality, and she managed to express it by putting her arm next to mine, saying: "Same color, same struggle!" This phrase symbolized the fruitful dialogue that is certain to occur among Asians and Blacks in the future.

The importance of the international context of Black Theology is clearly emphasized in an essay, "The New Context of Black Theology in the United States," by Gayraud Wilmore published in the *Occasional Bulletin of Missionary Research* (Wilmore & Cone 1979, 602–608). Whether Black theologians like it or not, it is no longer possible to limit one's theological concern to White racism in North America or to the ecclesiastical issues arising out of Black church politics. Racism is an international phenomenon, and it is connected with class-ism, sexism, and imperialism. Therefore our analysis of it in North America must reflect the global perspective of human oppression. I believe that the future of Black Theology will be determined by Black theologians' ability to reflect this international awareness in their theological practice in the Black Church and community. When Black theologians and church people are able to articulate in word and practice the international dimension of human oppres-sion, the Third World poor and those who have expressed their solidarity with them will perceive that the Black struggle in North America is not an isolated, bourgeois Black attempt to gain a larger share of the capitalistic pie. Our struggle is global and is connected with Black and poor people throughout the world. We are a Third World people in the First World, and thus our fight for justice is in solidarity with the poor of this earth. If what I am saying is true, then we Black theologians must begin to relate the particularity of our concern about racism to Africa, Asia, Latin America, and the poor wherever they may be found. I only hope that we Black theologians can implement this interna-tional concern in the Black church and community, for the realization of Black humanity in North America is intimately connected with the humanization of all peoples.

J.H.C.

NOTES

1. *Black Faith and Black Solidarity,* ed. Priscilla Massie (New York: Friendship Press, 1973), p. 134.

2. November 17, 1971, pp. 1345-1347.

3. The essays, with an Introduction by Charles S. Rooks, Jr., and Summary Reports by G. S. Wilmore and J. N. K. Nugambi, are published in *The Journal of Religious Thought,* vol. 32, no 2, (Fall-Winter 1975). See also James Cone, "Black and African Theologies: A Consultation," in *Christianity and Crisis,* vol. 35, no. 3 (March 3, 1975); G. S. Wilmore, "To Speak with One Voice?: The Ghana Consultation on African and Black Theology," *Christian Century,* February 19, 1975.

4. The first conference of the Ecumenical Association of Third World Theologians was held in Dar es Salaam, Tanzania (August 1976). See *The Emergent Gospel,* ed. S. Torres and V. Fabella (Maryknoll, N.Y.: Orbis Books, 1978).

5. *Christian Century,* February 17, 1978.

6. Black theologians' dialogue with theologians in the Caribbean is at its beginning stage on the subject of theology. While our social, economic, and political situations are similar, there are important differences. These differences will necessitate a different theological approach, and Caribbean theologians are already in the process of developing such a theology. See, for example, Idris Hamid, *In Search of New Perspectives* (Barbados:

CADEC); "Theology and Caribbean Development," in David I. Mitchell, ed., *With Eyes Wide Open* (Barbados: CADEC, 1973); Idris Hamid, ed., *Troubling of the Waters* (Trinidad: Rahaman Printery Limited, 1973); Idris Hamid, ed., *Out of the Depths* (Trinidad: Rahaman Printery Limited, 1977); K. Davis, ed., *Moving into Freedom* (Bridgetown, Barbados: Cedar Press, 1977); Leonard Barrett, *Soul-Force* (Garden City, N.Y.: Doubleday, 1974); Leonard Barrett, *The Rastafarians* (Boston: Beacon Press, 1977).

7. See Basil Moore, ed., *The Challenge of Black Theology in South Africa* (Atlanta: John Knox Press, 1974); Alan Boesak, *Farewell to Innocence: A Socio-Ethical Study on Black Theology and Black Power* (Maryknoll, N.Y: Orbis Books, 1977); David J. Bosch, "Currents and Crosscurrents in South African Black Theology," *Journal of Religion in Africa*, vol. 6, no. I (Leiden: Brill, 1974), which is also reprinted in Wilmore & Cone 1979, 220–237.

8. The papers and proceedings of this symposium were published in *Risk,* vol. 9, no. 29 (1973).

9. The papers and proceedings of the conference were published under the title *Theology in the Americas,* eds. S. Torres and J. Eagleson (Maryknoll, N.Y.: Orbis Books, 1976).

10. "Statement by Hugo Assmann," in ibid., pp. 299-303.

11. Theology in the Americas is a five-year program for doing theology (1975-1980) that has divided itself into affinity groups. According to its brochure "the affinity groups, organized around a specifically felt injustice, create *a project* within the Theology in the Americas program. The projects grapple theologically and analytically with the particular oppression of each group. While focusing on its own context of exploitation, each affinity group seeks to enrich and be enriched by the action reflection process of the others so that a holistic U.S. theology might develop from the perspective of the society's poor and powerless." The projects include: The Black Project, The Hispanic Project, The Women's Project, Quest for Liberation in the White Church, The Task Force of Professional Theologians, Labor and Church Dialogue, Asian-Americans in the U.S. Context, and Land: Native Americans and Red Theology. This approach is far more creative and responsible than the earlier one, which tended to exclude oppressed United States minorities. This major change in focus is undoubtedly due to the united voices of United States minorities in rejecting White domination, together with the capacity of Sergio Torres and others to hear them.

12. See the "Message to the Black Church and Community" (Wilmore & Cone 1979, 345–349) and James Cone's "Black Theology and the Black Church: Where Do We Go From Here?" Document 23 of this volume. See also 'The Atlanta Statement: Some Background and Commentary," by Shawn Copeland in *Cross Currents,* vol. 27, no. 2 (Summer 1977), pp. 144-146.

13. It is significant to note that during the first meeting of the Ecumenical Association of Third World Theologians in Dar es Salaam, Tanzania (August 1976) only *one* Black North American was present (the Rev. C. T. Vivian). But largely due to the protests of Africans, a significant number were invited to their second meeting in Ghana and are now a part of this important association. Sergio Torres reported the tensions regarding exclusion of North American Blacks with this comment: "One point was discussed at length in Dar es Salaam. Some of the participants felt that North American blacks did not belong to the Third World, so they should not be included in the process. However, the Africans claimed that for them, there was only one black world, whether in Africa, in North America, or in the Caribbean. The future will show whether this statement proves true or not" *(The Emergent Gospel,* eds. S. Torres and V. Fabella [Maryknoll, N.Y.: Orbis Books, 1978], p. x; this book is an account of the conference). Although not explicitly stated by Torres, most Black North Americans contend that it was primarily the Latin Americans who attempted to exclude us, and that such an attempt was motivated by our heated discussions on racism versus class oppression. This conclusion is partly supported by D. S. Amalorpavadass's account of the conference. On the "areas of disagreement," he writes: "The Latin Americans were the whole time harping on socio-economic political dimensions as the major or only reality, and applied rigorously

the Marxian tool of analysis. All the other realities were so insignificant for them that they could be integrated into the economic-political domination or its consequences. This was questioned strongly by Asians and Africans though they agreed with the analysis and results of socio-economic-political reality" ("News and Comments: Ecumenical Dialogue of Third World Theologians," *Indian Theological Studies,* vol. 14, no. 4, December 1977). The difficulty of Black theologians with Latin Americans was precisely at this point. Most Black theologians have never questioned the importance of class analysis and did not do so with Latin Americans. Our conflicts emerged when Latin Americans reduced to insignificance the issue of race. That our exclusion from the Dar es Salaam Conference is related to a difference on class and race also seems supported by Sergio Torres's definition of the Third World: "The concept of Third World is, in the first place, not limited to geographical space. It is not enough to live in Africa or Asia to share what we understand by theology of the Third World. There are people who live in Hong Kong or Bolivia who do not identify ideologically with the Third World. Their hearts, their interests, their futures are linked with the dominant classes of the world. ... It is not enough for [theologians] to live in or come from poor countries for their theology to differ basically from the theology of the rich countries. Herein lies the originality of this book and the emergent theology it represents. It proposes to develop scientifically a theology that speaks with the voice of the poor and the marginated in history" *(Emergent Gospel,* p. ix). If what Sergio Torres says here represented the consciousness of the participants, why then should there be such a lengthy discussion on the inclusion or exclusion of Black North Americans. The only issue (on the basis of the above description of the Third World) should be whether Black North Americans or any people represent "the poor and the marginated in history."

14. One significant context for dialogue has been the Ecumenical Institute Bossey Colloquiums with African and Asian theologians, in which a small number of Black North Americans have been present. There have been three colloquiums, two of which have been published. See John S. Mbiti, ed., *African and Asian Contributions to Contemporary Theology* (Geneva: World Council of Churches, 1976); J. S. Mbiti, ed., *Confessing Christ in Different Cultures* (Geneva: World Council of Churches, 1977). All of these proceedings are expected to be made available in print.

15. See especially *Asia Focus,* no. 661 (January 1977), ed. Yap Kim Hoa, on the theme "Asian Theological Reflections on Suffering and Hope," Christian Conference of Asia, Singapore; *Towards a Theology of People: I,* published by Urban Rural Mission and Christian Conference of Asia, 1977; *Testimony Amid Asian Suffering,* ed. T. K. Thomas, CCA, 1977, *Jesus Christ in Asian Suffering and Hope,* ed. J. M. Colaco (Madras: The Christian Literature Society, 1977), *Christian Action in the Asian Struggle* (Singapore: CCA, 1973).

16. See "Race and Minority Issues in Theological Perspective" by In Ha Lee in *Towards a Theology of People: I.* See also the report of the Consultation on Minority Issues in Japan and Mission Strategy, May 6-10, 1974, Kyoto, Japan, *IDOC,* no. 65, September 1974.

17. This Declaration is included in *Towards a Theology of People: I,* pp. 28-32; it is also included in the important publication *Documents on the Struggle for Democracy in Korea,* ed. The Emergency Christian Conference on Korean Problems (Tokyo: Shinkyo Shuppansha, 1975), pp. 37-43. It is also found in Kim Chi Ha, *The Gold Crowned Jesus and Other Writings* (Maryknoll, N.Y.: Orbis Books, 1978). See also the excellent article by Y. Kim, "Christian Koinonia in the Struggle and Aspirations of the People of Korea," in *Asia Focus,* January 1977.

18. I found this openness to be clearly present among Korean theologians in Japan and South Korea. The famous poet Kim Chi Ha, who is currently in prison on charges of subversion, referred to Black Theology in his "Declaration of Conscience," and Steve Moon of Hankuk Theological Seminary calls for a dialogue of Korean Theology with Black Theologies of Liberation and Latin American Theologies of Liberation. (See Y. Kim's reference to Moon's "Theology of Liberation and Korean Christianity" in his "Christian Koinonia in the Struggle and Aspirations of the People of Korea," in *Asia Focus,* January 1977, p. 46.)

29

BLACK THEOLOGY AND AFRICAN THEOLOGY: CONSIDERATIONS FOR DIALOGUE, CRITIQUE, AND INTEGRATION

James H. Cone and Gayraud S. Wilmore

A young Ghanaian scholar of the University of Ghana at Legon remarked recently: "You Afro-Americans are very concerned about Africa these days. As we say in Ghana: *'Akwaaba'* — 'You are welcome.' You are, after all, our brothers and sisters and we have missed you. But why do you speak of Black Theology? Why don't you call the theology you are doing today an *African Theology?*"

That question uncovers a historic anomaly which points to a vast and largely unexplored wilderness of other questions about political, social, and intellectual developments on both sides of the Atlantic between peoples of African descent who, in one way or another, received the message about Jesus Christ from the hands of White men. We cannot hope in this consultation to reconnoitre the full expanse of this overgrown and almost trackless wilderness. But upon its rough terrain lay the most difficult problems and promising opportunities of our encounter and we cannot hope to find one another unless we make a beginning of blazing some trails and erecting some guideposts along the way.

I

H. R. Mackintosh begins his well-known book *Types of Modern Theology* with a discussion of what he understands to be important differences between German and Anglo-Saxon styles of theological scholarship. For many years these

This essay was first published in *Pro Veritate*, January 15 and February 15, 1972 under the title "The Future and ... African Theology." Later this article was published in *Black Faith and Black Solidarity*, edited by Priscilla Massie (New York: Friendship Press, 1973). Reprinted with permission of the publisher.

two races dominated the theological scene, with the ponderous scholarship of Teutonic philosophers and theologians holding, perhaps, a slight edge. But neither German nor British theologians have occupied the field exclusively. Over the past two centuries or more we have had a French Catholic theology, a Swedish Lutheran theology, an American evangelical theology or "Fundamentalism," and more recently that peculiarly American "God-is-dead" theology. Since the end of the Second World War theological thinking in India has been stamped with a British-influenced, but distinctive Indian or Ceylonese flavor by such men as D. T. Niles and M. M. Thomas. Dutch Catholic theologians have led certain nationalistic developments within contemporary Roman Catholicism and a politically self-conscious Latin American theology is emerging among both Protestant and Roman Catholic churchmen in Brazil, Chile, Colombia, and elsewhere south of the Rio Grande.

With all these distinctive emphases and schools of thought centering around particular national or regional identities, why has it seemed so outlandish and so threatening to some of our White Christian friends to find Afro-Americans talking about *Black* Theology and Africans beginning to shape *African* Theology? Does it not have to do with the residual influence of the age-old assumption that African culture and intellectuality is and always has been inferior to that of Europe and the accepted adage of American liberals that "the Negro is nothing but a chocolate-covered White American"?

What we are experiencing among Black people in the United States, the Caribbean, and Africa is an outright rejection of both of these assumptions and a new consciousness of racial, national, and cultural identity which asserts a certain discontinuity with Euro-American values and perceives Black people to have, by virtue of historical circumstances if not innate characteristics, a distinctive and independent contribution to make to world civilization. This assumption is, by no means, something new. Long before Africa had extricated itself from European colonial domination or the slogan "Black Power" was bandied about on the civil rights march through Mississippi, Black preachers in Africa and in the United States were proclaiming the prophecy of Psalm 68:31: "Princes shall come out of Egypt; Ethiopia shall soon stretch out her hands unto God."

Our fathers fervently believed that God had a grand and glorious plan for Black people and that the redemption of the African race—both in Africa and in the diaspora—would begin an outpouring upon the world of gifts of inestimable worth from a despised and rejected race. Whatever our poets, writers, and statesmen have said about the sources of African nationalism and Pan-Africanism, it was from religious men in Africa and the United States—from Paul Cuffee, Daniel Coker, Bishop Turner, Mangena Mokone, James M. Dwane, John Chilembwe, Edward Blyden, and a host of others—that the religious vision of Africa's great destiny first arose and the initial call went out for the elevation and solidarity, under God, of all peoples of African descent.

These were the first Black or African Christian theologians south of the Sahara and in the New World and all that we have today that can be termed

Black Theology or African Theology, all that we can justly interpret as Black Consciousness or Pan-Africanism, had its origin in their thoughts and actions. It remains for young scholars on both sides of the Atlantic to reopen the neglected pages of history and trace the development of African nationalism and Black Power back through these men of faith who believed that God had revealed something for the Black race beyond that which it had received from Europe and Africa and that in good time he would bring it to fulfillment for the benefit of all mankind.

Black consciousness did not come into being with Stokely Carmichael or Leopold Senghor. It began with the plunder of Africa by the Portuguese, the Dutch, and the English. It began with the slave ships, the auction blocks, and the insurrections. It began with the experience of and resistance to White domination and it was shaped and honed and given its most profound statement by the preaching of the gospel by Black men to Black men in the cotton fields of the South, on the plantations of the Caribbean, among the freedmen of Philadelphia and New York, in Cape Colony and Nyasaland. All along, it was more than simply color consciousness. It was the consciousness of God's liberation. It was the consciousness that White was not always right and Black always wrong. It was saying Yes to what the White man regarded as evil, and No to his definition of good. It was, as Delany would say, *thanking* God for making us *Black* men and women and believing that implicit in what he had led us through was a gift and a blessing which the White world could neither give nor take away.

II

Despite their common relationship to the experience of Black suffering, the preaching of the gospel of liberation and resistance to White political and ecclesiastical domination, what we are calling Black Theology in the United States and African Theology in Africa have, since the independence of most of sub-Saharan Africa and the rise of the Black Power movement in the 1960s, proceeded along somewhat different lines. The Black experience in Africa and the Black experience in the United States and the Caribbean have not been the same. In the United States it has been a minority experience, separated, for the most part, from the ownership of land, from a discrete tribal language and culture, and from a living, historical memory. In Africa it has been a majority experience which has never been wholly disjoined from the land, the tribe, and the ancestors. White oppression in Africa did not show the same face as it did in the United States. Even where Direct Rule was administered, as in the French and Portuguese colonies, and under brutally repressive systems, such as the former Belgian Congo and the Republic of South Africa, there was for the White man always the pervasive, overwhelming reality of the vast and alien land and the conspicuousness of an indigenous people who had latent power to resist foreign acculturation and swallow up the transplanted White civilization in the bowels of blackness. Africa and the African people had to be reckoned with—their existence was bound to be acknowledged and respected, if grudgingly.

Such was not the case in the Americas. The Black man had never been known as anything but a slave, a species without an authentic racial or national identity, a beast of burden. While his power to rise up and overthrow his masters was recognized, that possibility decreased each passing year as the total White majority increased and the controls were tightened. Thus the peculiar form of White oppression and racism which developed in the United States did not simply exploit the Black man, it denied his right to exist except by sufferance of the White man. Christian America has known a virulent disease of hatred against the Black man and against blackness as a symbol of the very evil the White man knew to be in his own heart. In both Africa and America, "dark skin came to symbolize the voluntary and stubborn abandonment of a race in sin" (Roger Bastide), but in Calvinistic, Protestant America that symbolic association became rooted in a pathological hatred and fear of what Laurens van der Post has called "the dark brother within."

Blackness, for the White American, has been something that needed to be expunged from reality, blotted out before the face of God. There was, therefore, an ontological basis for White racism in America and a corresponding ontological ground for Black pride and the Black man's struggle against a latent but frighteningly real possibility of genocide. This is why it is correct to say that the Black American's struggle is against the threat of nonbeing, the ever present possibility of the inability to affirm one's own existence. The structure of White society in America attempts to make "Black being" into "nonbeing" or "nothingness." Black Power, therefore, whatever else it may be, is a humanizing force by which we Black Americans have attempted to affirm our being over against the White power which seeks to dehumanize us.

Without understanding this difference between White racism in the United States and White racism in colonial Africa, one cannot understand why there has to be a Black Theology or the differences between Black Theology in America and African Theology in Africa.

III

What does Black consciousness in America have to do with theology? This question forces us to consider the relationship between Black self-identity and the biblical faith. White American theology has never inquired into this relationship because it has pursued the theological task from the perspective of the oppressor rather than the oppressed. White religious thinkers have been blind to the theological significance of Black presence in America and no White American theologian or church historian has bothered to discover what Black religious thinkers have been saying for almost two hundred years.

The theological perspective that defines God as unquestionably identified with the liberation of the oppressed from earthly bondage arises out of the biblical view of divine revelation. According to the Bible, the knowledge of God is neither mystical communion nor abstract rational thought. Rather, it is recognizing divine activity in human history through faith. The biblical God is the God who is involved in the historical process for the purpose of human liberation. To know him is to know what he is doing in historical events as they relate to the liberation of the oppressed. Faith is the divine-human encounter in the historical situation of oppression, wherein the enslaved community recognizes that its deliverance from bondage is the Divine himself at work in history. To know God, therefore, is to know the actuality of oppression and the certainty of liberation.

The liberation theme stands at the center of the Hebrew view of God in the Old Testament. Throughout Israelite history, God is known as the one who acts in history for the purpose of Israel's liberation from oppression. This is the meaning of the Exodus, the Covenant at Sinai, the conquest and settlement of Palestine, the United Kingdom and its division, and the rise of the great prophets and the emancipation from Babylonian captivity. This is also why salvation in the Old Testament basically refers to "victory in battle" (I Sam. 14:45). "He who needs salvation," writes F. J. Taylor, "is one who has been threatened or oppressed, and his salvation consists in deliverance from danger and tyranny or rescue from imminent peril (I Sam. 4:3; 7:8; 9:16). To save another is to communicate to him one's prevailing strength (Job 26:2), to give him the power to maintain the necessary sovereign rule in guiding the course of human history, setting right that which is unrighteous, liberating the oppressed."

In the New Testament the same theme is carried forward by the appearance of Jesus Christ the Incarnation of God, born of common parentage under highly suspicious circumstances, in a lowly stable, during the Roman occupation of Palestine. This Jesus takes upon himself the oppressed condition, so that all men may be what God created them to be. He is the Liberator par excellence, who reveals not only who God is and what he is doing, but also who we are and what we are called to do about human degradation and oppression. It is not possible to encounter Jesus Christ and acquiesce in oppression—either of oneself or of others. Human captivity of every sort is ruled out by the coming of Jesus. That is why Paul writes, "For freedom, Christ has set us free" (Gal. 5:1). The free man in Christ is the man who rebels against false authorities by reducing them to their proper status. The Christian gospel is the good news of liberation.

If the gospel is preeminently the gospel of the liberation of the oppressed, then the theological assessment of divine presence in America must begin with the Black condition as its point of departure. It is only through an analysis of God as he is revealed in the struggle for Black liberation that we can come to know the God who made himself known through Jesus Christ.

The presence of Black people in America, then, is the symbolic presence of God and his righteousness for *all* the oppressed of the land. To practice theology is to take the radical Black perspective wherein all religious and nonreligious forms of thought are redefined in the light of the liberation of the oppressed. This is what we call "Black Theology."

Black Theology, therefore, is that theology which arises out of the need to articulate the religious significance of Black presence in a hostile White world. It is Black people reflecting on the Black experience under the guidance of the Holy Spirit, attempting to redefine the relevance of the Christian gospel for their lives. It is a mood, a feeling that grips the soul of a people when they realize that the world is not what God wills it to be—with respect to the defining reality of their lives—Black subjugation under White oppression. To practice theology from the perspective of Black Theology means casting one's intellectual and emotional faculties with the lot of the oppressed so that they may hear the gospel in terms of the cause and cure of their humiliation.

In the words of the official statement on Black Theology of the National Conference of Black Churchmen:

> Black Theology is a theology of black liberation. It seeks to plumb the black condition in the light of God's revelation in Jesus Christ, so that the black community can see that the gospel is commensurate with the achievement of black humanity. Black theology is a theology of "blackness." It is the affirmation of black humanity that emancipates black people from white racism, thus providing authentic freedom for both white and black people. It affirms the humanity of white people in that it says No to the encroachment of white oppression.

As we have seen, the seminal Black Theology was the theology that secretly taught that God wanted Black people to be free. Our greatest fighters for freedom were religious leaders—Denmark Vesey, Nat Turner, David Walker, Henry Highland Garnet, and others. Our spirituals and slave songs echoed a theology of liberation and laid the groundwork for a faith that reflected the essential meaning of the biblical revelation in a way that broke radically with conventional White Christianity. As the young Black professor Sterling Stuckey, of the University of Massachusetts, writes:

> There was theological tension here, loudly proclaimed, a tension which emanated from and was perpetuated by American slavery and race prejudice. This dimension of ambiguity must be kept in mind, if for no other reason than to place in bolder relief the possibility that a great many slaves and free Afro-Americans could have interpreted Christianity in a way quite different from white Christians.

Today some Black theologians are seeking the original source of this unique form of Christianity in the New World, not only in the experience of the slaves and freedmen, but even further back—in the traditional religions of Nigeria, Dahomey, Ghana, and other areas of Africa from which our ancestors came. Until very recently, and in some cases (such as in the Sea Islands off the coast of South Carolina) survivals of African religiosity could be found in Black religion in the United States. For example: the deep sense of the pervasive reality of the spirit world; the blotting out of the line between the sacred and the profane; the practical use of religion in all of daily life; reverence for the ancestors and their presence with us; the corporateness of social life; locating evil in the consequences of an act rather than in the act itself; and using drums, singing, and dancing in the worship of God.

The search for a Black Theology takes us not only into the survivals of African religions and the syncretistic religion of the slaves yearning for freedom, but also into the Black experience in the Black ghetto today. Black theologians cannot ignore the words of Langston Hughes about the living religion of the Black poor:

> But then there are the low-down folks, the so-called common element, and they are the majority—may the Lord be praised! The people who have their nip of gin on Saturday nights and are not too important to themselves or the community, or too well fed, or too learned to watch the lazy world go round. They live on 7th Street in Washington, or State Street in Chicago and they do not particularly care whether they are like white folks or anybody else. Their joy runs, bang! into ecstasy. Their religion soars to a shout. Work maybe a little today, rest a little tomorrow. Play awhile. Sing awhile. O, let's dance! These common people are not afraid of spirituals, as for a long time their more intellectual brethren were, and jazz is their child. They furnish a wealth of colorful, distinctive material for any artist because they still hold their own individuality in the face of American standardization.

It is from this reservoir of Black culture—of which religion has always been an inseparable part—that Black Theology seeks the genius of what Professor Joseph Washington called "Negro Folk Religion—the religion of protest and relief." It was this Folk Religion that Marcus Garvey, Elijah Muhammad, Malcolm X, Maulana Ron Karenga, and Albert Cleage tapped when they began to build their Black nationalist movements. It was this same Folk Religion which came into its own in the Southern civil rights movement under Martin Luther King, Jr., and has found its most profound expression in the Black Power and Black Theology movements of the 1960s and 1970s. In the final analysis, Black Theology is concerned with the ultimate questions which arise from the Black folk of the ghetto—from their suffering, their joy, their perception of themselves and of American reality. Black Theology is saying that the God who spoke to us out of our African past and out of the religion of the slaves, is speaking to us today in the accents of the contemporary Black community—and his message is Liberation.

IV

It is clear that there are areas of convergence and dissimilarity between what we are calling Black Theology in the United States and what is termed African

Theology in Africa. Both of these theologies are rooted in the experience of Black people who received a highly attenuated form of Christianity from the White churches of Europe and America. Both are, in part, religious reactions to White ecclesiastical domination and political and economic oppression. Both are in quest for a base in the authentic milieu of an indigenous people—in one case, in the environment of the postcolonial African state; in the other, in the environment of the contemporary Afro-American ghetto. In both instances we are dealing with self-conscious African or Afro-American churches (or the Black constituencies of White controlled European or American churches and missionary societies) which are emerging from a period of emulating White standards and are seeking a distinctive style of life and relevance to the culture of the people to whom they minister. But in terms of theological renewal there are important differences that we must consider—differences which are inevitable in light of the different situations in which these churches exist, but which may be used to enrich the life of each other.

It would be presumptuous for the authors of this paper to attempt to commend what follows here as an accurate interpretation of African Theology. That task belongs to African theologians themselves. What we will present is what some African theologians are saying and what, rightly or wrongly, is communicated to us about the theological program implicit in the work now in process.

Professor Idowu of Nigeria, in one of his first published works on indigenization, describes the "shock of recognition" he experienced when he first realized that the Christ he worshiped as an African had been presented to him in the context of a language and culture not his own, and that he had assumed that it was impossible to understand Christ and Christianity in any other way. Idowu was only one of several African theologians for whom it has become increasingly and disturbingly clear that the Church in Africa could not attain selfhood and maturity until it possessed a knowledge of Jesus Christ in African terms and could communicate that knowledge in the languages and thought-forms of Africa. For many years it had been assumed that God did not come to Africa until the first European missionaries landed on these shores and that, lying in the darkness of a primitive and pagan faith, Africa had nothing to offer as a cultural or spiritual basis for the gospel.

In his *African Ideas of God,* Edwin Smith reports his conversation with Emil Ludwig, an eminent biographer, in which he told Ludwig about the progress of Christian missions in Africa, how the Africans were being taught about the Christian God. Ludwig was perplexed. "How," he exclaimed, "can the untutored African conceive God? . . . How can this be? . . . Deity is a philosophical concept which savages are incapable of framing." Thus have the traditional religions of Africa and African spirituality, as such, been regarded by both Africans and Europeans in the not distant past. We understand that one of the first tasks of African Theology is to put an end to this nonsense, for which White missionaries and anthropologists must bear no little responsibility, and begin a reconstruction of the Christian faith in Africa which takes seriously the fact that God had revealed himself in the traditional religions and that by a selective process African theologians can use this revelatory content to throw light on the message and meaning of Jesus Christ. Thus the consultation of African theologians held in Ibadan in 1965 could conclude:

> We recognize the radical quality of God's self-revelation in Jesus Christ; and yet it is because of this revelation we can discern what is truly of God in our pre-Christian heritage: this knowledge of God is not totally discontinuous with our people's previous traditional knowledge of him.

In the now standard work by Kwesi Dickson and Paul Ellingworth, *Biblical Revelation and African Beliefs* (London: Lutterworth Press, 1969; Maryknoll, N.Y.: Orbis Books), Idowu, Mbiti, Kibongi, Adegbola, and other distinguished African theologians deal with such themes as the African image of man, concepts of God and the spirit world, priesthood, sacrifice, and ideas of morality in such a way as to demonstrate the linkages between African and Christian religious knowledge. This cataloguing of African beliefs and comparing them with similar beliefs in biblical religion, particularly in the Old Testament, was evidently an early stage in the development of African theological thinking and indicates the extent to which African theologians, most of whom were educated in European and American seminaries, have sought, first of all, a deepening of Christian orthodoxy by bringing to it insights and discernments which lie outside the Judeo-Christian tradition. In an unpublished paper presented at the 1969 AACC [All Africa Conference of Churches] meeting in Abidjan, Professor Dickson of Ghana clarifies the significance of this tendency in the theological work being done in Africa:

> Of course, whatever help that may come from sources outside the Judeo-Christian traditions are most likely to lie within the realm of the explicatory rather than the foundational; nevertheless, it could fill out a hitherto western expression of Christian theological concepts. One might hazard the example that the doctrine of Justification by Faith, which is the most missionary of doctrines, is usually expounded in terms of the salvation of the individual, to the exclusion of all ideas of corporate salvation, through the body of Christ. ... We have only to allude to the metaphors of the Body and the Vine and its Branches to show that the African sense of corporateness ... could be a reminder that the traditional western interpretation of the doctrine of Justification does not preempt the implications of that doctrine.

According to Dickson this approach to the African theological task is complemented by a second line of approach, which is represented by the work of Professor Mbiti, who, "recognizing the essential limitation of certain aspects of African thought by comparison with Christian teachings ... suggests that Christian views should be imported into African thought to the enrichment of the latter." In this he refers to Mbiti's comment that the African cyclical view of history must be invaded by the Christian concept of the *eschaton* because, while Africa has an eschatology, it has no teleology and it is in this area that Christian eschatology can contribute to natural revelation in Africa.

With the publication of *African Religions and Philosophy* (New York: Praeger, 1969) Professor Mbiti of Uganda became widely acknowledged as the leading scholar of religion in Africa and his recent published works lay down some of the new directions for an indigenous African theology. As indicated by the above reference to African eschatology, Mbiti's work on the concept of Time in African religions has major significance for a fuller understanding of traditional values and how Christian theology, properly integrated with what he calls "transfused Religion" in the culture, can help shape the future of modern Africa. Thus, having exonerated African traditional religions from the charge of "primitivism" and given them the dignity they deserve, African Theology seems now to be taking up the task of bringing to traditionalism the insights of the Christian faith which are able to renovate the total life and culture of the new African nations.

In a lecture delivered at St. Paul's Theological College in Kenya, Mbiti said: "I believe that this is one of the most exciting principles in the whole relationship between Christianity and Traditional Religions. It calls for a theological articulation of the fulfillment not only as an academic exercise, but to guide the church in its life, work and mission in Africa. . . . The Lord God may have spoken Hebrew to the children of Israel: He now speaks the Christ-language. This is the language of the Gospel; and the Gospel comes to fulfill, not to destroy."

From the perspective of many of the younger Afro-American theologians, the "Africanization" of theology in Africa seems more academic, more bound to orthodoxy and more conservative than Black Theology in the United States and the Caribbean. It is, however, among the burgeoning phenomena of African Independent or "spiritual" churches that one sees another side of this picture, with increasing significance for African Theology. Thousands of Independent Churches now exist in all parts of Africa alongside the older churches; and their evangelistic fervor, their appeal to the poor and uneducated masses, and their utilization of traditional elements in music and liturgy give them a vitality and relevance to African Christianity which cannot be ignored by African theologians. The problem that African Theology has in helping to relate Christianity to the new social and political realities cannot be solved without reference to the spiritual churches. The influence of these churches, as they become more institutionalized and led by trained clergy, is inestimable. Because of the role that they now and will increasingly play in the urbanization process, family life, social education and action, etc., they offer to African theologians the same exciting prospects for the indigenization of theology and the renewal of the church that the Black Consciousness churches of the ghettos offer to Black theologians in the United States. It is clear that the AACC is prepared to make a more energetic approach to the African Independent Churches, and at Abidjan it was proposed that a secretariat be set up for that purpose, with broad implications for theological study, dialogue, and collaboration, as well as affiliation.

We conclude this part of the paper with reference to the significant fact that at Abidjan the discussion of African Theology was held in the section dealing with the topic "Working with Christ in the Cultural Revolution." The group recognized that since African Theology was in an early stage of development, an exhaustive definition was impossible. An attempt was, however, made and seems to gather up all of the emphases, nuances, and problems we have noted in this brief discussion:

> By African Theology we mean a theology which is based on the Biblical Faith and speaks to the African "soul" (or is relevant to Africa). It is expressed in categories of thought which arise out of the philosophy of the African people. This does not mean that it is narrow in outlook. To speak of African theology involves formulating clearly a Christian attitude to other religions. It must be pointed out that the emphasis is basically on *Christian* theology, which could be expressed through African thinking and culture.

V

One of the peculiar features of our present situation is that Black Theology is reaching out to African Theology, but the reverse is not necessarily true. In a sense Black American theologians are more isolated, more suspect of heretical inclinations, and more embattled than African theologians. Therefore we are in greater need of dialogue and collaboration with those with whom we believe we have something in common. This is so not only because of forces within the American churches which define the canons of theological respectability, but also because, paradoxically, Black people in the United States are probably the most religious *and* the most secular of all American ethnic minorities (with the possible exception of the Jews). It is not an exaggeration to say that the hostility of the present generation of young Blacks outside the church to what they understood to be the subservience of Black Christianity to the status quo, played an important part in forcing Black Theology and Black churchmen generally into a more independent and militant posture vis-à-vis White Christianity. On the other hand, African theologians and the African churches, because of the recent paternalistic relationship in which they stood to European churches, enjoy a certain popularity among White Christians outside Africa, both Protestants and Roman Catholics, and feel less insecure about their status within the ecumenical Church.

This does not mean that African theologians feel no need to "reason together" with their Afro-American brethren. Quite the contrary, for many of them recognize a certain tokenism in ecumenical circles, and some of the same pressures we feel from our young people are experienced increasingly by African churchmen. It does mean that in the nature of the situation Afro-American theologians are and will be taking the initiative for dialogue. Black Theology needs African legitimation, for strategic reasons if for no other. But the situation is a delicate one. No one should expect African Theology, as yet so tentative in its disengagement from the categories of Western thought, to permit itself to fall into what could become the suffocating embrace of another style of theological reflection — even that of black brothers from across the sea. There is an amiability and gentleness about African religion, which is not true today about religion in Black America. In any dialogue between Black Theology and African Theology, care needs to be taken that the aggressiveness and "hard-nosedness" of Black Theology does not mount such an assault on African religious sensibilities that the situation turns out to be one side shouting and the other closing its ears in pained indifference. On the other hand, African Theology cannot be so impressed with its good reputation in WCC circles, and so convinced that theological reflection is something that properly takes place in a setting resembling a sequestered English vicarage, that it cannot bring itself to converse with its tough, boisterous counterpart from the urban ghettos of America. We must talk to one another, for we have much to talk about. But we must hear one another with sympathy and understanding.

Dialogue first requires getting acquainted, but any dialogue between Black Theology and African Theology should, in due course, lead to mutually constructive critique and correction. The criterion of judgment is, of course, the Word of God and the testimony of the Holy Spirit. But there is also the action of God in history and the discernment of faithful men of how God is moving in their world to plant and build, and to root out and tear down. "Now we see through a glass darkly" and neither the church in Africa nor the church in Black America has the full truth about what God is saying today to people of African descent and what he is doing in the world to make them fulfill their calling among the races of mankind.

African Theology is concerned with Africanization. Black Theology is concerned with liberation. But Africanization must also involve liberation from centuries of poverty, humiliation, and exploitation. A truly African Theology cannot escape the requirement of helping the indigenous churches to become relevant to the social and political ills of Africa, which are not unrelated to Euro-American imperialism and racism. Similarly, liberation has to do with more than political oppression and social justice. It is Jesus Christ who is the Liberator; the justified man is also liberated from "the lust of the flesh and the pride of life." The liberated man is no longer under the unqualified power of sin and the Devil. How can these two theologies correct the excesses and deficiencies of one another? What can African Theology learn from Black Theology about the demonic power of White racism in the world today and what God is doing about it? What can Black Theology learn from African Theology about faithfulness to the Word of God in a situation of rapid secularization out of a traditional ethos, about Christian morality and the devotional life? What can the older churches of Africa learn from the Black churches of the United States about the assimilation of quasi-Christian ideologies and secular cults which can help them in rapprochement with the Independent Churches? What can the Black churches of America learn from the African churches about reconciliation between tribal groups and between Black and White in a multiracial society? Does African Theology depend too much upon the modalities of European theology in discriminating between what traditional religion offers as "preparation for the gospel" and what it does not? Is Black Theology so obsessed with concepts of negritude, "Black Consciousness," and revolution that it is in danger of becoming so localized and so self-interested that it loses the universal message of love, peace, and redemption for the whole world?

These are a few of the critical questions which will arise in any serious and candid encounter between Black Theology and African Theology. There are many more that can be instructive to both sides if we believe that mutual critique and reformation, under the judgment and the grace of God, are the true functions of theological reflection.

To what end will this long-frustrated and belated encounter between African and Afro-American theologians lead our churches in Africa and the United States? The answer to that question is not given to us today. We can only say that there exists between us a mysterious bond of blood brotherhood, a common past and a common experience of suffering and subjugation which God can use to his own good purposes as we come closer together in faith and life. The old Black theologians (and we have used that term broadly to encompass all reflective Christian churchmen) used to talk about the destiny of the Black race and how the sons of Ham would be a blessing to the world. Surely Fanon and others have taught us that the star of Euro-American civilization is in decline and a new humanity must arise and point the way to a future of justice and equality for all peoples. In these days of revolutionary Black Power and African Socialism those themes are being sounded again. It is not racist madness to believe that Africa shall again have one of the greatest civilizations the world has known and that long-separated brethren, weary of bruising their fists upon doors that will not fully open, will come home by the millions to contribute to and share in the building of that greatness. It is not too much to believe that God wills to use the churches of Africa and Black America to give the sublimity and spiritual depth to that historical process that will make it minister to the humanization and redemption of the world. If some future integration of the truths and insights of Black Theology and African Theology can accelerate the fulfillment of that lofty vision of our destiny, then we need to be about the task that has brought us together.

The young theologian at Legon wanted to know why we cannot speak of an *African* Theology which encompasses the theological work we are doing on both sides of the Atlantic. That felicitous possibility is not available to us today, but by meeting and critically examining one another's views and working together in the world, that day may come. Let the Church say, "Amen."

30

AN AFRICAN VIEWS
AMERICAN BLACK THEOLOGY

John Mbiti

Black Theology is a painful phenomenon in the history of the Church. Painful not because of what it says—although it certainly does not deal in soft phrases—but because it has emerged in an America that, since the arrival of the Pilgrims in the seventeenth century, has claimed to be a Christian country. Black Theology is a judgment on American Christianity in particular and Christianity in general. Ideally there would be no reason for Black Theology. It was forced into existence by the particularities of American history.

Black Theology as an academic concern can be dated from July 31, 1966, when the National Conference of Black Churchmen issued a statement asking for power and freedom from the leaders of America, for power and love from white churchmen, for power and justice from Negro citizens, and for power and truth from the American mass media [see Document 1]. Three years later the Black Manifesto [see Document 2] demanded, inter alia, reparations to Negroes by the white churches because of the latter's complicity in the exploitation of Negroes (blacks, as they now prefer to call themselves). In the same year Professor James H. Cone published *Black Theology and Black Power,* which marked the formal inauguration of Black Theology as a serious academic concern with which the whole of Christian theology must reckon. Other publications appeared earlier, but Cone's is the one that formally incorporated Black Theology into the stream of Christian theology at large.

The roots of Black Theology must in fact be traced to a much earlier period of American history, the arrival of the first African slaves in the seventeenth century. The subsequent history of Americans of African origin—of exploitation, segregation and general injustice—is the raw material of what we now call

John Mbiti is a leading African Theologian, author of the influential book, *African Religions and Philosophy* (1969). This essay first appeared in *Worldview* 17 (August 1974). Used by permission of the author.

Black Theology. Insofar as Black Theology is a response to this history of humiliation and oppression it is a severe judgment and an embarrassment to Christianity, especially in America. Black Theology was born from pain and communicates pain and sorrow to those who study it. It is a cry of protest against conditions that have persisted for nearly four hundred years in a land which otherwise takes pride in being free and Christian, or at least in having Christian institutions.

One would hope that theology arises out of spontaneous joy in being a Christian, responding to life and ideas as one redeemed. Black Theology, however, is full of sorrow, bitterness, anger and hatred. Little wonder Black Theology is asking for what black Americans should have had from the start— freedom, justice, a fair share in the riches of their country, equal opportunities in social, economic and political life. The wonder is that it has taken all these years for the anger of Black Theology to surface. It draws from the peculiar history of the Negroes in America: from the "Black Experience," which is "a life of humiliation and suffering . . . existence in a system of white racism"; from the Black History of "the way Black people were brought to this land and the way they have been treated in this land"; from Black Culture with its "creative forms of expressions as one reflects on the history, endures the pain, and experiences the joy"; and in a more general way from the Scriptures, Christian tradition and African religious heritage (see Cone's *A Black Theology of Liberation* and Gayraud S. Wilmore's *Black Religion and Black Radicalism*). Professor Cone defines Black Theology as "that theology which arises out of the need to articulate the significance of Black presence in a hostile white world. . . . Black Theology is revolutionary in its perspective. It believes that Black people will be liberated from oppression" ("Black Consciousness and the Black Church" in *Christianity and Crisis,* November 2 and 16, 1970).

The main concerns of Black Theology are directly related to the circumstances that brought it into being. One such concern is "blackness" itself. It wants to see "blackness" in everything. It speaks of a Black God, Black Church, Black Liberation, Black this and Black that. While some theologians, notably James Cone, try to give a wider ontological meaning to "blackness," it is nevertheless a color terminology arising out of the color consciousness of American society. Indeed Professor Cone goes so far as to say that "white theology is not Christian theology." In reading Black Theology one becomes sated by color consciousness. It is necessary to remind oneself that racial color is not a theological concept in the Scriptures. A few black theologians are becoming aware of the dangers in excessive emphasis upon color. Professor Miles J. Jones has written (*The Christian Century*, September 16, 1970): "Color is merely a vehicle; experience is the concern. . . . Changing our concept of Christ's color is no acceptable substitute for interpreting our experience as black people in what God did and is doing through the Christ. Moreover, such 'coloring' is dangerously idolatrous. We need not color God or the Christ black in order to appreciate blackness as an instrument of the Divine."

Nonetheless, for Black Theology blackness has become an ideology embracing much of the life and thinking of Negroes in America, whether their skin color is black, dark brown, light brown, khaki or coffee, or even if they have a remote African ancestry and most of their biological heritage is actually French, English, Scottish, American Indian or other. All are "black."

Next to blackness the main concern of Black Theology is liberation. It is also, of course, the concern of Black Power and of the Negro community as a whole. Black Theology simply provides a theological dimension to the concept of liberation, a dimension for which there is a great deal of biblical support. Black Theology speaks of liberation in all spheres of the Negro's experience in America—social, economic, political, ecclesiastical, educational and cultural. Black Theology is a response to an American past and to an American present. It is a highly politicized theology designed to shape, advance and protect a popular ideology within the American scene. Without the American history of slavery, racism and domination by whites (pinks) over blacks (browns) and without the present realities of an America shaken by the Vietnam war, student protest, the civil rights movement and continued poverty among large numbers of whites and Negroes there could be no Black Theology.

Black Theology's preoccupation with liberation is brought out powerfully in James Cone's *Black Theology and Black Power*. "Black Power and Christianity have this in common: the liberation of man!" "Jesus' work is essentially one of liberation"; "Black rebellion is a manifestation of God himself actively involved in the present-day affairs of men for the purpose of liberating people"; and so forth. His subsequent book, *A Black Theology of Liberation,* opens with the assertion that "Christian theology is a theology of liberation," and that "liberation [is] the content of theology."

On the question of liberation there is a near absolute unanimity among the theologians of Black Theology. They find ample grounds for it in the Old Testament, in the story of the Exodus and the history of Israel, and in the life and work of Jesus Christ. As a theology of the oppressed, every concern in Black Theology has some bearing on the question of liberation. What I view as an excessive preoccupation with liberation may well be the chief limitation of Black Theology. When the immediate concerns of liberation are realized, it is not at all clear where Black Theology is supposed to go. Black Theology is deeply "eschatological," yet its eschatological hopes are not clearly defined. There is no clue as to when one arrives at the paradise of "liberation." One gets the feeling that Black Theology has created a semi-mythological urgency for liberation that it must at all costs keep alive. As a result it seems that Black Theology is avoiding other major theological issues not directly related to "liberation."

Black Theology presents Jesus Christ variously as the liberator, the Black Messiah, the Black Christ, and so on. We are told that Negroes are tired of a Jesus seen through the eyes of white or pink Americans. The Negroes in the Black Power movement are said to cry: " 'Give us no pink, two-faced Jesus who counsels love for you and flaming death for the children of Vietnam. Give us no bloodsucking savior who condemns brick-throwing rioters and praises dive-bombing killers. That Christ stinks. We want no black men to follow in *his steps* ..." (see "Black Power and the American Christ" by V. Harding in *The Christian Century,* January 4, 1967). So in Black Theology Jesus has to be "the liberator par excellence" who sets free the oppressed and identifies himself with the poor; there is no salvation apart from identification with this Black Christ. Some see the Negroes as the Old Testament children of Israel, enslaved, delivered, led to the Promised Land, promised the Messiah and finally welcoming the Black Messiah who leads them to the Kingdom of God. The most explicit statement along these lines is *The Black Messiah* by Albert B. Cleage, Jr. (New York, 1968). Similar sentiments are variously expressed in the Negro Spirituals and, undoubtedly, from many a pulpit in Negro churches.

A further theme in Black Theology is that "God himself must be known only as he reveals himself in his blackness. The blackness of God, and everything implied by it in a racist society, is the heart of Black Theology's doctrine of God. There is no place in Black Theology for a colorless God in a society when people suffer precisely because of their color. . . . The blackness of God means that God has made the oppressed condition his own condition . . . [and] that the essence of the nature of God is to be found in the concept of liberation. . . . It is Black Theology's emphasis on the blackness of God that distinguishes it sharply from contemporary white views of God" (James H. Cone in *A Black Theology of Liberation).* Cone declares categorically, "We must become black with God!"

Of course Black Theology addresses itself also to other themes, such as the Church, the Community, the Bible, the World, Man, Violence and Ethics. But the treatment of these topics is subservient to the overriding emphasis on blackness and liberation as they relate to Jesus Christ and God. At least this is my impression of Black Theology as I have tried to read it sympathetically and have discussed it extensively with such leading Black Theologians as James Cone of Union Theological Seminary in New York, Charles Long of the Divinity School at Chicago, Preston Williams of Harvard, Vincent Harding and George Thomas at Atlanta, Gayraud Wilmore of Boston University and many others. A number of questions keep coming up as one views Black Theology from the perspective of an African theologian. It is impossible to offer anything but provisional comments, for I am still digesting Black Theology and admiring it as a specifically American phenomenon. I admire the boldness with which it is presented. I admire the commitment Black Theologians have shown to this theological movement. I admire the zeal, the enthusiasm, even the joviality with which these Americans are going about their work. I understand the reasons for their bitterness, their anger, their hatred, all of which come through in their Black Theology. Standing as I do at a distance, I am impressed with this sudden eruption of theological liveliness in America. Black Theology has been made necessary by the American past and present; the wonder is that it did not erupt sooner. It is long overdue.

But Black Theology cannot and will not become African Theology. Black Theology and African Theology emerge from quite different historical and contemporary situations. To a limited extent the situation in Southern Africa is similar to that which produced Black Theology in America. African peoples in Southern Africa are oppressed, exploited and unjustly governed by minority regimes; they have been robbed of their land and dignity and are denied even a minimum of human rights. For them Black Theology strikes a responsive chord and perhaps offers some hope, if that be any consolation. In Southern Africa Black Theology deserves a hearing, though it is impossible to see how that hearing could be translated into practical action. But even in Southern Africa the people want and need liberation, not a theology of liberation. America can afford to talk loud about liberation, for people are free enough to do that in America. But in Southern Africa people are not even free enough to talk about the theology of liberation. Thus when *Essays on Black Theology* (edited by Mokgethi Motlhabi) was published in Johannesburg in 1972, the government banned it before it reached the bookstores. (The same work has since been republished, edited by B. Moore, in London under the title *Black Theology: The South African Voice*). This book, however, is no more than an echo of American Black Theology; it even includes a contribution by James Cone. But the fact that it was banned so readily clearly indicates that Black Theology has a measure of relevance in Southern Africa.

Apart from Southern Africa the concerns of Black Theology differ considerably from those of African Theology. The latter grows out of our joy in the experience of the Christian faith, whereas Black Theology emerges from the pains of oppression. African Theology is not so restricted in its concerns, nor does it have any ideology to propagate. Black Theology hardly knows the situation of Christian living in Africa, and therefore its direct relevance for Africa is either nonexistent or only accidental. Of course there is no reason why Black Theology should have meaning for Africa; it is not aimed at speaking for or about Africa. As an African one has an academic interest in Black Theology, just as one is interested in the "water buffalo theology" of Southeast Asia or the theology of hope advocated by Jürgen Moltmann. But to try and push much more than the academic relevance of Black Theology for the African scene is to do injustice to both sides. In America and Europe, and to a lesser extent in Africa, there is an obvious temptation to make a connection that should not be made.

It would seem healthier if Black Theology and African Theology were each left to its own internal and external forces to grow in a natural way without artificial pressure and engineering. African Theology is concerned with many more issues, including all the classical theological themes, plus localized topics, such as religious dialogue between Christianity and African Religion and between Christianity and Islam. Relations between Christianity and African culture, between Church and State, together with innumerable pastoral and liturgical problems, give African Theology a very full agenda for the years ahead. African Theology is not something that can be done in a decade or covered in one volume. It is a living phenomenon that will continue as long as the Church exists in our continent. African Theology has no interest in coloring

God or Christ black, no interest in reading liberation into every text, no interest in telling people to think or act "black." These are interests of Black Theology across the Atlantic, and they are admirable on the American scene.

Similarly, African theologians have no business trying to tell other Christians how to solve their theological problems, or what theology to use for their situations. We (I) wish only for dialogue, fellowship, sharing of ideas and insights, and learning from one another as equal partners in the universal Body of Christ, even if we Africans may still speak the theological language of Christianity with a stammering voice, since most of us are so new to it. We appreciate what others are saying according to their peculiar circumstances and the inspiration of the Holy Spirit, but what they say reaches us only in whispers because they are speaking primarily to themselves and for themselves, just as we speak first and foremost to ourselves and for ourselves. We must recognize simultaneously our indebtedness to one another as fellow Christians and the dangers of encroaching upon one another's theological territories.

Black Theology and African Theology have each a variety of theological concerns, talents and opportunities. Insofar as each contributes something new and old to Christian theology as such, it will serve its immediate communities and also serve the universal Church.

31

BLACK THEOLOGY/AFRICAN THEOLOGY — SOUL MATES OR ANTAGONISTS?

Desmond M. Tutu

This consultation being held at this time at the University of Ghana, Accra, between black American theologians and churchmen and their African counterparts is a welcome sequel to a similar consultation on African and Black Theology which was held in New York in June, 1973, under the auspices of the All Africa Conference of Churches and the Society for the Study of Black Religion. But already in August, 1971, a meeting between a similar group of black Americans and East Africans had taken place sponsored by the National Conference of Black Churchmen and the Council of Churches of Tanzania in Dar es Salaam. The papers delivered at that first consultation are available in paperback.[1]

I have referred to these past occasions because the series of consultations reflects a noteworthy phenomenon — a new and deep desire for black men to find each other, to know one another as brothers and sisters because we belong to one another. We are bound together by close bonds on three levels at least.

We are united willy nilly by our blackness (of all shades). Now some may feel squeamish about this apparently excessive awareness of our skin color. But are we not in fact so bound? If anyone of us assembled here today goes into a situation where racial discrimination is practiced would he ever escape the humiliation and indignity that are heaped on us simply because he was black no matter whether he was native to that situation or not? Our blackness is an intractable ontological surd. You cannot will it away. It is a brute fact of existence and it conditions that existence as surely as being male or female, only more so. But would we have it otherwise? For it is not a lamentable fact. No, far from it. It is not a lamentable fact because I believe that it affords us the

Desmond M. Tutu, a leading South African theologian, is a Nobel Laureate and Archbishop of Capetown. This essay first appeared in the *Journal of Religious Thought* 32, no. 1 (Fall-Winter 1975).

glorious privilege and opportunity to further the gospel of love, forgiveness and reconciliation—the gospel of Jesus Christ in a way that is possible to no other group, as I hope to show later.

The second level of unity between us is this. All of us are bound to mother Africa by invisible but tenacious bonds. She has nurtured the deepest things in us as blacks. All of us have roots that go deep in the warm soil of Africa; so that no matter how long and traumatic our separation from our ancestral home has been, there are things we are often unable to articulate, but which we feel in our very bones, things which make us, who are different from others who have not suckled the breasts of our mother, Africa. Don't most of us, for instance, find the classical arguments for the existence of God just an interesting cerebral game because Africa taught us long ago that life without belief in a supreme divine being was just too absurd to contemplate? And don't most of us thrill as we approach the awesomeness of the transcendent when many other of our contemporaries find even the word God an embarrassment? How do you explain our shared sense of the corporateness of life, of our rejection of hellenistic dichotomies in our insistence that life, material and spiritual, secular and sacred, that it is all of a piece? Many characteristics of our music, our religion, our culture and so on, today in Africa and America can be explained adequately only by reference to a common heritage and common source in the past. We cannot deny too that most of us have had an identical history of exploitation through colonialism and neo-colonialism, that when we were first evangelized often we came through the process having learned to despise things black and African because these were usually condemned by others. The worst crime that can be laid at the door of the white man (who, it must be said, has done many a worthwhile and praiseworthy thing for which we are always thankful) is not our economic, social and political exploitation, however reprehensible that might be; no, it is that his policy succeeded in filling most of us with a self-disgust and self-hatred. This has been the most violent form of colonialism, our spiritual and mental enslavement when we have suffered from what can only be called a religious or spiritual schizophrenia. What I said in an unpublished paper, titled "Whither African Theology?" of the African is largely true too of the black American.

> Up to fairly recently, the African Christian has suffered from a form of religious schizophrenia. With part of himself he has been compelled first to pay lip service to Christianity as understood, expressed and preached by the white man. But with an ever greater part of himself, a part he has been ashamed to acknowledge openly and which he has struggled to repress, he has felt that his Africanness has been violated. The white man's largely cerebral religion was hardly touching the depths of his African soul; he was being given answers, and often splendid answers to questions he had not asked.

Speaking about this split in the African soul, J. C. Thomas writes:

The African in fact seems to find himself living at two levels in every aspect of his life. First, there is the western influence on him from two different quarters: there is the influence inherited from the period of colonial rule; but also the inevitable influence of post colonial industrialization and education. Secondly, there is the influence of his traditional culture and upbringing that gives many Africans the sense that they have a unique culture of their own which gives them an identity as Africans. Yet it appears inevitable that in some areas traditional culture will be abandoned if African states are to become self-sufficient economically and so free of dependence on foreign aid and trade.[2]

The third level of unity comes through our baptism and through our membership in the Body of Christ which makes us all His ambassadors and partakers in the ministry of reconciliation. As a consequence of our imperatives of the Gospel and being constrained by the love of God in Jesus Christ, we cannot but be concerned to declare the whole counsel of God as much to the white man as to our own black communities. We are compelled to help the white man to correct many of the distortions that have happened to the gospel to the detriment of all. To paraphrase what Manas Buthelezi from South Africa once said: God will say to the blackmen: "Where were you when the white man did this to my Gospel?" We are together involved in a common task and we are engaged in a single quest. After this preamble let us return to the subject of this paper.

Black Theology/African Theology—Are They Compatible?

Are black theology and African theology related or are they quite distinct and even incompatible entities? John Mbiti, an outstanding theologian, is quite clear in his own mind about the answer to the question. In a recent article, Mbiti has this to say:[3] "But Black Theology cannot and will not become African Theology." He can be so categorical because, to quote from the article again: "the concerns of Black Theology differ considerably from those of African Theology. The latter grows out of our joy and experience of the Christian faith, whereas Black Theology emerges from the pains of oppression." He seems to imply at an earlier point without being explicit that black theology is perhaps not quite Christian: "One would hope that theology arises out of spontaneous joy in being a Christian responding to life and ideas as one redeemed. Black Theology, however, is full of sorrow, bitterness, anger and hatred."[4] But is this borne out by a study of the history of Christian doctrine? Most New Testament commentators appear to agree that the Epistle to the Galatians was written when Paul was very angry and yet in the Galatians he develops the theology of justification by faith. And what would we make of the theology that occurs in the Christian Apocalypse of St. John the Divine? There was no oppression, no anger and not even hatred of the oppressor, and yet this book has found its way, admittedly after a long struggle, into the Christian canon. Professor Mbiti is unhappy with Black Theology, mainly because it is concerned too much with blackness and liberation. To quote again:

> Of course Black Theology addresses itself also to other themes, such as the Church, the Community, the Bible, the World, Man, Violence and Ethics. But the treatment of these topics is subservient to the overriding emphasis on blackness and liberation as they relate to Jesus Christ and God.[5]

Another African, this time a young theologian, J. Ndwiga Mugambi, writes concerning liberation and theology as follows:

> Liberation is the objective task of a contemporary African Christian theology. It is not just one of the issues, but rather, all issues are aimed at liberating Africans from all forces that hinder them from living fully as human beings.
> In the African context, and in the Bible, SALVATION as theological concept cannot be complete without LIBERATION as a social/political concept.[6]

I will have something to say on this issue later. I contend that there are very close similarities between African Theology and Black Theology:

(a) Both to my way of thinking have arisen as reactions against an unacceptable state of affairs. Most people would agree that the most potent impetus for the development of an African Christian theology has come because Christianity came swathed in Western garb. Most Western missionaries in the early days found it difficult if not virtually impossible to distinguish between the Christian faith and Western civilization. No less a person than Robert Moffat could say:

> Satan has employed his agency with fatal success, in erasing every vestige of religious impression from the minds of the Bechuana, Hottentots and Bushmen; leaving them without a single ray to guide them from the dark and drab futurity, or a single link to unite them to the skies.[7]

And if this was how you felt then it was logical to pursue a policy of the root and branch condemnation of things African, which had to be supplanted by their obviously superior Western counterpart. It was as if Robertson Smith had never written as he did in his *Religion of the Semites:*

> No positive religion that has moved man has been able to start with a *tabula rasa* to express itself as if religion was beginning for the first time; in form if not in substance, the new system must be in contact along the line with the old ideas and practices which it finds in possession. A new scheme of faith can find a hearing only by appealing to a religious instinct

and susceptibility that already exists in its audience and it cannot reach these without taking account of the traditional forms in which religious feeling is embodied, and without speaking a language which men accustomed to these forms can understand.

The African religious consciousness and Weltanschauung were not acknowledged as possessing much validity or value. Much the same comment could be made of the Black American experience. The blacks in America had their humanity defined in the terms of the white man. To be really human he had to see himself and be seen as a chocolate-colored white man. His humanity was stunted. It is against this deplorable condition that both African and Black Theology have reacted. They stake the claim for the personhood and humanity of the African and Afro-American, for anything less than this is blasphemy against God who created us as we are in His own image, not to be carbon copies of others of His creatures no matter how advanced or prosperous they might conceive themselves to be. Some might feel ashamed that the most serious enterprise in which they have engaged should be characterized as a reaction rather than resulting from their own initiative. But there is no need for such a negative response. Much of the development of Christian dogma may be shown to resemble the oscillations of a pendulum. When Hegelian idealism was the philosophy of the day, Christian theology, not remaining unaffected, moved very far in the direction of immanentism. Against this trend a reaction set in exemplified by the stress on transcendence as in the theology of Karl Barth. In its turn, this emphasis on transcendence provoked the reaction that spoke about "a beyond in our midst" as in John Robinson's *Honest to God*. Perhaps today we are beginning to discern a tentative groping towards a renewed sense of awe and mystery. And this would be as yet another reaction.

More positively we could say that African theology and Black Theology are an assertion that we should take the Incarnation seriously. Christianity to be truly African must be incarnated in Africa. It must speak in tones that strike a responsive chord in the African breast and must convict the African of his peculiar African sinfulness. It must not provide him with answers to questions he has never asked. It must speak out of and to his own context. Christ came to fulfill, not to destroy. Christianity should be seen as fulfilling the highest and best in the spiritual and religious aspirations of the black and yet stand in judgement of all that diminishes him and makes him less than what God intended him to be.

African and Black theology provide a sharp critique of the way in which theology has been done mostly in the North Atlantic world. Westerners usually call for an ecumenical, a universal theology which they often identify with their brand of theologizing. Now this is thoroughly erroneous. Western theology is no more universal than other brands of theology can ever hope to be. For theology can never properly claim a universality which rightly belongs only to the eternal Gospel of Jesus Christ. Theology is a human activity possessing the limitations and the particularities of those who are theologizing. It can speak relevantly only when it speaks to a particular historically and spatio-temporally conditioned Christian community: and it must have the humility to accept the scandal of its particularity as well as its transcience. Theology is not eternal nor can it ever hope to be perfect. There is no final theology. Of course the true insights of each theology must have universal relevance, but theology gets distorted if it sets out from the very beginning to speak or attempt to speak universally. Christ is the Universal Man only because He is first and foremost a real and therefore a particular Man. There must therefore of necessity be a diversity of theologies and our unity arises because ultimately we all are reflecting on the one divine activity to set man free from all that enslaves him. There must be a plurality of theologies because we don't all apprehend the transcendent in exactly the same way nor can we be expected to express our experience in the same way. On this point, Maurice Wiles writes:

> Theology today is inductive and empirical in approach. It is the ever changing struggle to give expression to man's response to God. It is always inadequate and provisional. Variety is to be welcomed because no one approach can ever do justice to the transcendent reality of God; our partial expressions need to be complemented by the different apprehensions of those whose traditions are other than our own. There are no fixed criteria for the determination of theological truth and error. We ought therefore to be ready to tolerate a considerable measure even of what seems to us to be error, for we cannot be certain that it is we who are right. On this view a wide range of theological difference (even including what we regard as error) is not in itself a barrier to unity.[8]

African theology has given the lie to the belief that worthwhile religion in Africa had to await the advent of the white man. Similar to African history, African theology has done a wonderful service in rehabilitating the African religious consciousness. Both African and Black theology have been firm repudiations of the tacit claim that white is right, white is best. In their own ways these theologies are giving the black man a proper pride in things black and African. Only thus can we ever be able to make our distinctive contributions to the kingdom of God. We must love and serve God in our own way. We cannot do it as honorary whites. And so Black and African theology have contributed to those exhilarating movements of our day, Black and African consciousness. Both say we must provide our source for theologizing. They seek to be effective instruments in bringing about change not merely as academic exercises. I may be wrong, but at these levels, I see remarkable similarities between African theology and Black Theology and I contend that they have a great deal to learn from one another and to give to each other. But there are obvious differences.

(b) There must be differences because the two theologies arise in a sense from different contexts. African theology on the whole can probably afford to be a little more leisurely (I am not convinced of this) because Africa by and large is politically independent (but is it really free?). There is not the same kind of oppression which is the result of white racism except in Southern Africa (soon it may only be South Africa the way things seem to be developing in the sub-continent, and God let the day soon come when all of Africa will be truly free). Black Theology arises in context of black suffering at the hands of rampant white racism. And consequently Black Theology is much concerned to make sense theologically out of the black experience whose main ingredient is the suffering in and the light of God's revelation of Himself in the man, Jesus Christ. It is concerned with the significance of black existence, with liberation, with a meaning of reconciliation, with humanization, with forgiveness. It is much more aggressive and abrasive in its assertions because of a burning and evangelistic zeal necessary to convert the black man out of the stupor of his subservience and obsequiousness to acceptance of the thrilling but demanding responsibility of full human personhood—to make him reach out to the glorious liberty of the sons of God. It burns to awake the white man to the degradation into which he has fallen by dehumanizing the black man and so is concerned for the liberation of the oppressor equally with that of the oppressed. I am not quite sure that I understand what Professor Mbiti in the article I have referred to means when he says that people in Southern Africa "want and need liberation, not a theology of liberation." Could we not say the same thing about a theology of hope, that what people want is hope, not a theology of hope?

Black Theology is more thoroughly and explicitly political than African theology is. It cannot be lulled into complacency by a doctrine of pie in the sky which is reprehensible travesty of the gospel of the Incarnation. It has an existential urgency which African theology has so far appeared to lack. African theology has tended to be more placid; to be interested still too much with what I call anthropological concerns. This has been its most important achievement in the quest for indigenization.

Conclusion

I myself believe I am an exponent of Black Theology coming as I do from South Africa. I also believe I am an exponent of African theology coming as I do from Africa. I contend that Black Theology is like the inner and smaller circle in a series of concentric circles. I would not care to cross swords with such a formidable person as John Mbiti, but I and others from South Africa *do* Black Theology, which is for us, at this point, African theology.

But I fear that African theology has failed to produce a sufficiently sharp cutting-edge. It has indeed performed a good job by addressing the split in the African soul and yet it has by and large failed to speak meaningfully in the face of a plethora of contemporary problems which assail the modern African. It has seemed to advocate disengagement from the hectic business of life because very little has been offered that is pertinent, say, about the theology of power in the face of the epidemic of coups and military rule, about development, about poverty and disease and other equally urgent present-day issues. I believe this is where the abrasive Black Theology may have a few lessons for African theology. It may help to recall African theology to its vocation to be concerned for the poor and the oppressed, about men's need for liberation from all kinds of bondage to enter into an authentic personhood which is constantly undermined by a pathological religiosity and by political authority which has whittled away much personal freedom without too much opposition from the church. In short, African theology will have to recover its prophetic calling. It can happen only when a radical spiritual decolonization occurs within each exponent of African theology. Too many of us have been brainwashed effectively to think that the Westerners' value system and categories are of universal validity. We are too much concerned to maintain standards which Cambridge or Harvard or Montpelier have set even when these are utterly inappropriate for our situations. We are still too docile and look to the metropolis for approval to do our theology, for instance, in a way that would meet with the approval of the West. We are still too much concerned to play the game according to the white man's rules when he often is the referee as well. Why should we feel that something is amiss if our theology is too dramatic for verbalization but can express itself adequately only in the joyous song and movement of Africa's dance in the liturgy? Let us develop our insights about the corporateness of human existence in the face of excessive Western individualism, about the wholeness of the person when others are concerned for hellenistic dichotomies of soul and body, about the reality of the spiritual when others are made desolate with the poverty of the material. Let African theology enthuse about the awesomeness of the transcendent when others are embarrassed to speak about the king, high and lifted up, whose train fills the temple. It is only when African theology is true to itself that it will go on to speak relevantly to the contemporary African— surely its primary task—and also, incidentally, make its valuable contribution to the rich Christian heritage which belongs to all of us.

NOTES

1. *Black Faith and Black Solidarity. Pan Africanism and Faith in Christ,* ed. Priscilla Massie (New York: Friendship Press, 1973).
2. "What Is African Theology?" *Ghana Bulletin of Theology,* vol. 4, no. 4 (June 1973), p. 15.
3. "An African Views American Black Theology," *Worldview,* vol. 17, no. 8 (August 1974), p. 43; see also Document 30, above, for reprint of Mbiti article.
4. Mbiti, op. cit.
5. Ibid.
6. *World Student Christian Federation Dossier,* no. 5 (June 1974), pp. 41-42.
7. E. W. Smith, *African Ideas of God* (London: Edinburgh House, 1966), p. 83.
8. "Theology and Unity," *Theology,* vol. 77, no. 643 (January 1974), p. 4.

32

A BLACK AMERICAN PERSPECTIVE
ON THE FUTURE OF AFRICAN THEOLOGY

James H. Cone

Because I am a Black North American, whose theological consciousness was shaped in the historical context of the civil rights movement of the 1950s[1] and the subsequent rise of Black Power during the 1960s,[2] it is difficult for me to speak about the future of African Theology without relating it to the social and political context of Black people's struggle for freedom in the United States of America. The effect of this social reality upon my theological perspective could blind me to the uniqueness of the African situation. The concern to accent the distinctiveness of the African context has led many African theologians to separate African Theology not only from traditional European theology but also from American Black Theology. In an article entitled "An African Views American Black Theology," John Mbiti is emphatic on this issue.

> . . . the concerns of Black Theology differ considerably from those of African Theology. [African Theology] grows out of our joy in the experience of the Christian faith, whereas Black Theology emerges from the pains of oppression. African Theology is not so restricted in its concerns, nor does it have an ideology to propagate. Black Theology hardly knows the situation of Christian living in Africa, and therefore its direct relevance for Africa is either nonexistent or only accidental.[3]

In order to appreciate the seriousness and depth of Mbiti's concern, it is necessary to point out that his perspective is not based upon a superficial encounter with Black Theology. On the contrary, Mbiti made these remarks *after* he and I had had many conversations on the subject in the context of our

---

This paper was presented at the Pan-African Conference of Third World Theologians, held December 17-24, 1977, in Accra, Ghana.

jointly taught year-long course on African and Black theologies at Union Theological Seminary.[4] Nevertheless, it seems to me that he misrepresented Black
Theology.[5] More important, however, was Mbiti's contention that African and
Black American theologians should have no more than an indirect or accidental
interest in each other. This perspective on African Theology not only makes
substantive dialogue difficult but also excludes Black American theologians
from a creative participation in the future development of African Theology.

John Mbiti is not alone in making a sharp distinction between Black Theology and African Theology. Similar views are found in the writings of Harry
Sawyerr,[6] E. W. Fashole-Luke,[7] and (to a lesser extent) Kwesi Dickson.[8] While
there are significant exceptions to this perspective among theologians in
Southern Africa and also among certain African church-people associated with
the All-Africa Conference of Churches,[9] these exceptions do not remove the
risks inherent in any attempt by a North American to speak about the future
of African Theology. For there is much truth in the widespread belief that the
future of African Theology belongs to Africans alone.

There is a second difficulty in approaching this topic, in addition to existential and intellectual sensitivities of African theologians. That other problem is
the existential conflict inherent in my double identity as American *and* African.
This identity conflict is widespread among Black Americans, and it is a prominent theme in Black literature and theology. This theme is found in Ralph
Ellison's *Invisible Man* and in James Baldwin's claim that "nobody knows my
name." In a theological context, Cecil Cone has addressed this problem in his
book entitled *The Identity Crisis in Black Theology*.[10] But one of the earliest and
most classic statements on this problem is found in the writings of W. E. B. Du
Bois:

> It is a peculiar sensation, this double-consciousness, this sense of always
> looking at one's self through the eyes of others, of measuring one's soul
> by the tape of a world that looks on in amused contempt and pity. One
> ever feels his twoness—an American, a Negro; two souls, two thoughts,
> two unreconciled strivings; two warring ideals in one dark body, whose
> dogged strength alone keeps it from being torn asunder.[11]

The significance of the problem of Black identity in the context of African
Theology may be clarified by asking: How can I speak about the future of
African Theology when my Black identity is so inextricably tied to North America? Aside from the technicality of my genetic origin and its relation to the
African continent, what right do I have to participate in the future development
of African Theology? Unless these questions are honestly faced, then the relations between African Theology and Black Theology will remain superficial.
The purpose of this essay is to attempt to move our dialogue beyond the phase
of theological politeness to a serious encounter of each other's historical
options. What is the relation between our different historical contexts and our
common faith in God's power to make us all one in Jesus Christ? How do we

translate the universal claim of our faith into a common historical practice? These are the issues that define the focus of this paper.

In order to protect against a possible misunderstanding of my concern, an additional word of clarification is necessary. If by African Theology we mean an interpretation of the Christian gospel in the light of the political and cultural situation in Africa, then it is obvious that the future of this enterprise belongs primarily to Africans alone. Persons who have little or no knowledge of Africa or whose theological consciousness was shaped elsewhere should not expect to play a decisive role in the future development of theology on the African continent. This point is applicable not only to White Europeans but to Black Americans as well. I want to emphasize this point, because my disagreement with Mbiti and other African theologians who separate radically African Theology and Black Theology does not mean that I believe that Black Americans should play a major role in the formulation of the meaning of African Theology. My contention is that Black and African theologies are not as different as has been suggested and that their common concerns require a dialogue that is important to both. I want to suggest two reasons why we ought to engage in a substantive dialogue, and then use the third section of this paper to say a word about the future of African Theology.

I

The history of American Blacks cannot be completely separated from the history of Africa. Therefore, whatever may be said about the significant distinctions between Africans and Black people of the American diaspora there was once a time when these distinctions did not exist. The significance of this point extends beyond a mere academic interest in historical origins. The recognition of the interrelation of our histories is also important for assessing our present realities and the shaping of our future hopes and dreams. Whether we live in Africa or the Americas, there is some sense in which the Black World is one, and this oneness lays the foundation and establishes our need for serious dialogue. Marcus Garvey expressed this point in his ill-fated "back to Africa" movement. With a similar philosophical ideal but a radically different political vision, W. E. B. Du Bois, George Padmore, and Kwame Nkrumah expressed the unity of the Black World in their development of Pan-Africanism. But we do not need to accept Garveyism or the Pan-African philosophy of Du Bois in order to realize that the future of Africa and Black people in the Americas is inextricably bound together. International economic and political arrangements require a certain kind of African and Black nationalism if we are to liberate ourselves from European and White American domination. This economic and political domination, sharply enhanced and defined by racism, will not cease simply through an appeal to reason or the religious piety of those who hold us in captivity. Oppression ceases only when the victims accumulate enough power to stop it.

The oneness that I refer to is made possible by a common historical option available to both Africans and Black Americans in their different social contexts. Each of us can make a choice that establishes our solidarity with the liberation of the Black World from European and American domination. This domination is not only revealed in the particularity of American White racism or European colonialism in Africa, but also in Euro-American imperialism in Asia, Latin America, and the Caribbean. World history has been written by "white hands" (to borrow a graphic expression from Leonardo Boff), and the time has come to recover the memory of the victims of this world. The need to reinterpret history and theology in the light of the hopes and struggles of the oppressed peoples of the world establishes not only a oneness between Africans and Black Americans, but also makes possible our common solidarity with the liberation of the poor in Asia and Latin America. This global perspective requires that we enlarge the oneness of the Black World to include our solidarity with the world's poor. It was this assumption that defined the "Final Statement" of the Ecumenical Dialogue of Third World Theologians that met in Tanzania (August 1976),[12] and it continues to shape our dialogue in Ghana. To be sure, we must recognize that we live in quite different historical and contemporary situations, which will naturally influence certain emphases in our theologies. But we should guard against the tendency of allowing our various particularities to blind us to the significance of our commonality. It is a oneness grounded in a common historical option for the poor and against societal structures that oppress them. This "poor perspective" (to use an apt phrase from Gustavo Gutiérrez) makes us one and establishes the possibility of our mutual sharing in the creation of one humanity.

II

The possibility of substantive dialogue between African Theology and other Third World theologies is created not only on the basis of our common historical option, but also on the basis of our common faith in Jesus Christ. Because we confess Jesus as Lord, we are required to work out the meaning of that confession in a common historical project. Faith and practice belong together. If we are one in Christ Jesus, then this oneness should be seen in our struggle together to create societal structures that bear witness to our vision of humanity. If our common confession of faith is in no way related to a common historical commitment, how do we know that what we call the universal Church is not the figment of our theological imagination? I contend that the unity of the Church can only be found in a common historical commitment.

Anyone acquainted with my theological perspective knows that I have placed much emphasis on the social context of theology. And I have no intention of relinquishing this point in this paper. But it is important to recognize the limitation of our particularity so that we will not ignore the universal claims that the gospel lays upon all of us. Whether Christians live in Africa, Asia, Latin America, or Europe, we have been called by God to bear witness to the gospel of Jesus to all peoples. Therefore, we must ask not only what does the gospel mean for me in Africa or North America, but also for Christians in the whole inhabited world. And our explication of the gospel must be universal enough to include the material conditions in which people are forced to live. There is only one history, one Creator, and one Lord and Savior Jesus Christ. It is the centrality of this faith claim that brings us together and requires us to have dialogue with each other about its meaning in society. Our cultural limitations do not render us silent but open us up to share with others our perspective about the historical possibility for the creation of a new humanity.

What is the universal dimension of the gospel that transcends culture and thus lays a claim upon all Christians no matter what situation they find themselves in?[13] This is the question that every theology must seek to answer. Because our various theologies are so decidedly determined by our historical option in a given context, different answers have been given to this question. Because dominant European and American theologies have chosen an option that establishes their solidarity with western imperialism and capitalism, they usually define the universality of the gospel in terms that do not challenge the White western monopoly of the world's resources. There have been many debates in traditional theology about the precise content of the essence of the gospel, but seldom has the debate included political and economic realities that separate the rich nations from the poor ones. This is not an accident, and our meeting together in Ghana means that we recognize the danger of defining the universal aspect of the gospel in the light of western culture.

We meet here today because we are in search for other theological options than the ones found in traditional theology. I believe that we will find our common vision of the gospel through a serious encounter of the biblical message as defined by our common historical commitment in our various social contexts. We must be prepared to listen to each other, and to learn what it means to be historically involved in the realization of the gospel. Our dialogue is only beginning, and it is thus too early to expect unanimous agreement on various issues. But if we take seriously our common faith in the crucified Christ, as encountered in the struggle for freedom, then I believe that God's Spirit will break down the barriers that separate us. For Christian "unity only becomes a reality to the extent that we partake of Christ [who] is hidden in those who suffer."[14] It is within this ecumenical context that I will venture to say a word about the future of African Theology.

III

The future of African Theology is found in its creative interpretation of the gospel for the African situation and in relation to the theologies of the poor throughout the world. This emphasis does not exclude the legitimacy of African Theology's concern with indigenization and selfhood[15] in its attempt to relate the biblical message to the African cultural and religious situation. But selfhood and indigenization should not be limited to cultural changes alone. There is a *political* ingredient in the gospel that cannot be ignored if one is to remain faithful to biblical revelation. The recognition of this political ingredient in the gospel is clearly implied in the All-Africa Conference of Churches' call for a moratorium and in its continued support of the liberation movements in Southern Africa. It is within this context that we should understand Canon Burgess Carr's highly publicized distinction between the "selective violence employed by the Liberation Movement" and the " 'collective vengeance' perpetrated by the South African, Rhodesian and Portuguese regimes in Africa. Thus, any outright rejection of violence is an untenable alternative for African Christians."[16] These words caused a great deal of unrest. He drew a radical theological conclusion from the liberation struggles of African people, and the churches of Africa and Europe are still trying to assimilate its significance.

> If for no other reason, we must give our unequivocal support to the Liberation Movements because they have helped the Church to rediscover a new and radical appreciation of the cross. In accepting the violence of the cross, God, in Jesus Christ, sanctified violence into a redemptive instrument for bringing into being a fuller human life.[17]

Burgess Carr is not alone among African theologians and church people who define liberation as a common theme in the gospel. "Liberation," writes Jesse Mugambi, "is the objective task of contemporary African Christian Theology. It is not just one of the issues, but rather, all issues are aimed at liberating Africans from all forces that hinder them from living fully as a human being." According to Mugambi, the idea of liberation is inherent in the concept of salvation. "In the African context, and in the Bible, *salvation* as a theological concept cannot be complete without *liberation* as a social/political concept."[18] A similar point is also made by Eliewaha Mshana: "Africanization must involve liberation from centuries of poverty, humiliation and exploitation. A truly African Theology cannot escape the requirement of helping the indigenous churches to become relevant to the spiritual, social, and political ills of Africa."[19] Kofi Appiah-Kubi also includes liberation as an important ingredient of African Theology. He not only uses liberation as an important christological theme in Africa,[20] but locates liberation in his definition of African Theology. African Theology, he contends, "should be a liberating theology, liberating us from the chains of social, economic, political and even at times traditional and cultural dominations and oppressions."[21]

No African theologians, however, have expressed the theme of liberation more dramatically than South African theologians. Desmond Tutu[22] and Manas Buthelezi[23] are prominent examples of this new theological perspective emerging from behind the apartheid walls of the Republic of South Africa. Both have challenged African theologians to take seriously the political ingredient of the gospel as related to the contemporary problems of Africa. Desmond Tutu is emphatic:

> . . . African theology has failed to produce a sufficiently sharp cutting edge. . . . It has seemed to advocate disengagement from the hectic busi-

ness of life because very little has been offered that is pertinent, say, about the theology of power in the face of the epidemic of coups and military rule, about development, about poverty and disease and other equally urgent present-day issues. I believe this is where the abrasive Black Theology may have a few lessons for African theology. It may help to recall African theology to its vocation to be concerned for the poor and the oppressed, about [people's] need for liberation from all kinds of bondage to enter into an authentic personhood which is constantly undermined by pathological religiosity and by political authority which has whittled away much personal freedom without too much opposition from the church.[24]

These are strong words and they remind us all of the prophetic calling of the Church and theology.

Additional examples of this African perspective in theology are found in a collection of essays entitled *Essays on Black Theology*. This book was banned by the Republic of South Africa and was later published in Britain under the title *Black Theology: The South African Voice*.[25] More recently Allan Boesak has added his contribution to South African Black Theology with his publication of *Farewell to Innocence*.[26] The central theme among these new theological voices from South Africa is their focus on liberation in relation to politics and blackness. They insist that blackness is an important ingredient in their view of African Theology.

Unfortunately, John Mbiti and Edward Fashole-Luke have been very critical of this South African Black Theology as being too narrowly focused on blackness, liberation, and politics. Both contend that Christian theology must transcend race and politics.[27] I believe that their criticisms are misplaced because the theme of liberation, as interpreted by the particularity of the African economic and political situation, provides the most creative direction for the future development of African Theology. If God came to us in the human presence of Jesus, then no theology can transcend the material conditions of humanity and still retain its Christian identity. Jesus did not die on the cross in order to transcend human suffering, but rather, so that it might be overcome. Therefore, any theology whose distinctive perspective is defined by Jesus is required to find its creative expression in the practice of overcoming suffering.

The need for African Theology to focus on politics and liberation arises not only out of a christological necessity. It is also a necessity that arises out of the ecumenical context of contemporary theology. By locating the definition of African Theology in the context of the political and economic conditions of Africa, African theologians can easily separate their theological enterprise from the prefabricated theologies of Europe and establish their solidarity with other Third World theologies. This point is suggested by Canon Burgess Carr.

The forthrightness of Black Theology and the theology of liberation canvassed today presents a dual challenge to our Christian style of life. In a

profound way, it challenges the preoccupation with African Theology to
advance beyond academic phenomenological analysis to a deeper appropriation of the ethical sanctions inherent in our traditional religious experience. It also forces Christians to come to grips with the radical character
of the gospel of Jesus as an ideological framework for their engagement
in the struggle for cultural authenticity, human development, justice and
reconciliation.[28]

If Black Theology's focus on liberation is its challenge to African Theology,
what then is the challenge of African Theology to Black Theology, Latin American Liberation Theology, and theology in Asia? Unless the challenge is mutual,
then there is no way for substantive dialogue to take place. I believe that African
Theology's challenge to us is found by rejecting prefabricated theology, liturgies,
and traditions and focusing the theological task on the selfhood of the Church
and the incarnation of Christianity in the life and thought of Africa. African
theologians challenge all Christians in the Third World to take seriously popular
religion and unestablished expressions of Christianity. Perhaps more than any
other Third World theological expression, African Theology takes seriously the
symbols and beliefs of the people whom all liberation theologians claim to
represent. If liberation theology in any form is to represent the hopes and
dreams of the poor, must not that representation be found in its creative appropriation of the language and culture of the people? If the poor we claim to
represent do not recognize themselves in our theologies, how then will they
know that we speak for them? From their earliest attempt to create an African
Theology, African theologians are agreed that their theology must take seriously
three sources: the Bible, African traditional religion, and the African Independent Churches. The appropriation of these sources structurally locates the
theological task among the poor people of Africa. Until recently Latin American Liberation Theology has tended to overlook the importance of this cultural
ingredient in theology. The same is true to some extent of American Black
Theology and perhaps, to a lesser degree, of theology in Asia.[29]

The relation between indigenization and liberation does not have to be
antagonistic. In fact, we need both emphases. Without the indigenization of
theology, liberation theology's claim to be derived from and accountable to
oppressed peoples is a farce. Indigenization opens the door for the people's
creative participation in the interpretation of the gospel for their life situation.
But indigenization without liberation limits a given theological expression to
the particularity of its cultural context. It fails to recognize the universal dimension of the gospel and the global context of theology. It is simply not enough
to indigenize Christianity or to Africanize theology. The people also want to
be liberated from racism, sexism, and classism. If theology is to be truly indi-
genized, its indigenization must include in it a social analysis that takes seriously
the human struggles against race, sex, and class oppression. I contend therefore
that indigenization and liberation belong together. The future of African Theology, and all Third World theologies, is found in the attempt to interpret the

Christian gospel in the historical context of the people's struggle to liberate themselves from all forms of human oppression.

NOTES

1. The beginning of the contemporary civil rights movement of American Blacks is usually identified with the bus boycott in Montgomery, Alabama, led by Martin Luther King, Jr., in December 1955. For an account of this event, see Martin Luther King, Jr., *Stride Toward Freedom* (New York: Harper & Row, 1958). For more information about the later development of this movement in the 1960s and Martin King's reaction to the rise of Black Power, see his *Why We Can't Wait* (New York: Harper & Row, 1963) and *Where Do We Go From Here: Chaos or Community* (New York: Harper & Row, 1967).

2. For an account of the rise of Black Power, see Stokely Carmichael and Charles Hamilton, *Black Power: The Politics of Black Liberation* (New York: Random House, 1967).

3. John Mbiti, "An African Views American Black Theology," reprinted in this volume (quotation found on p. 383).

4. John Mbiti was the Harry Emerson Fosdick Visiting Professor at Union Theological Seminary, New York, during the academic year 1972-1973.

5. I was especially disturbed by Mbiti's assertion that "Black Theology . . . is full of sorrow, bitterness, anger and hatred." I know of no Black American theologian who would accept this description of Black Theology.

6. See his "What Is African Theology?" *Africa Theological Journal,* no. 4, August 1971.

7. See his "The Quest for African Christian Theology," *The Journal of Religious Thought,* vol. 32, no. 2 (Fall-Winter 1975). This issue is devoted to essays presented at the Consultation on African and Black Theology, Accra, Ghana, December 1974. See also an earlier article in which Fashole-Luke questions the possibility of the development of an African Theology, "An African Indigenous Theology: Fact or Fiction?" *The Sierra Leone Bulletin of Religion,* 1969.

8. While Kwesi Dickson is not as emphatic about the distinction between Black and African Theology, as suggested by Mbiti, Sawyerr, and Fashole-Luke, the sharp separation of African Theology from Black Theology is clearly implied in his writings. See his contribution at the Ghana Consultation, "African Theology: Origin, Methodology and Content," *The Journal of Religious Thought,* Fall-Winter 1975. See also his "Towards a Theologia Africana," in M. E. Glasswell and E. W. Fashole-Luke, eds., *New Testament Christianity for Africa and the World* (London: S.P.C.K., 1974); "The Old Testament and African Theology," *The Ghana Bulletin of Theology,* vol. 4, no. 4 (June 1973); "The African Theological Task" in *The Emergent Gospel* edited by Sergio Torres and Virginia Fabella (Maryknoll, N.Y.: Orbis Books, 1978).

9. A partial account of these exceptions is treated in the third section of this paper.

10. Nashville: AMEC, 1975.

11. *The Souls of Black Folk* (Greenwich, Conn.: Fawcett, 1961). Originally published in 1903, pp. 16-17.

12. See *The Emergent Gospel,* ed. S. Torres and V. Fabella, pp. 259ff.

13. This question involves the problem of ideology in theological discourse. I have discussed the implications of this problem in my *God of the Oppressed* (New York: Seabury Press, 1975).

14. Rubem Alves, "Protestantism in Latin America: Its Ideological Function and Utopian Possibilities," *The Ecumenical Review,* January 1970, p. 15.

15. The themes of selfhood and indigenization are very prominent in African Theology. On indigenization, see the important book by Bolaji Idowu, *Towards an Indigenous Church* (London: Oxford University Press, 1965); Kwesi Dickson and Paul Ellingworth, eds., *Biblical Revelation and African Beliefs* (London: Lutterworth Press; Maryknoll, New York: Orbis Books, 1969). On the theme of selfhood, see Kwesi Dickson, "African The-

ology: Origin, Methodology and Content," *The Journal of Religious Thought; The Struggle Continues,* official report, Third Assembly of the All-Africa Conference of Churches, Lusaka, May 1974. This theme is also found in the report of the First Assembly of the AACC in Kampala, 1963. See *Drumbeats from Kampala* (London: Lutterworth Press, 1963).

16. "The Engagement of Lusaka," in *The Struggle Continues,* p. 78.

17. Ibid., p. 78.

18. "Liberation and Theology," in WSCF Dossier no. 5, June 1974, pp. 41-42.

19. "The Challenge of Black Theology and African Theology," *Africa Theological Journal,* no. 5, 1972.

20. See his "Jesus Christ—Some Christological Aspects from African Perspectives," in *African and Asian Contributions to Contemporary Theology,* ed. John Mbiti (Celigny: WCC Ecumenical Institute, Bossey, 1977).

21. "Why African Theology?" *AACC Bulletin,* vol. 7, no. 4 (July-August 1974), p. 6.

22. See his contribution at the Ghana Consultation on African and Black Theology, "Black Theology/African Theology—Soul Mates or Antagonists?" (reprinted above, Document 31); see also his "Black Theology," *Frontier,* Summer 1974; "African and Black Theologies," an interview in the *AACC Bulletin,* vol. 7, no. 4 (July-August 1974).

23. See his contribution "Toward Indigenous Theology in South Africa," in *The Emergent Gospel;* see also his important essay "An African Theology or a Black Theology," in *Essays on Black Theology,* ed. George Mokgethi Motlhabi (Johannesburg, 1972). Other essays by Buthelezi include "Apartheid in the Church Is Damnable Heresy," *AACC Bulletin,* vol. 9, no. 2; "Daring to Live for Christ," in *Mission Trends No. 3: Third World Theologies,* ed. G. H. Anderson and T. F. Stransky (New York: Paulist Press, 1976).

24. "Black Theology/African Theology—Soul Mates or Antagonists?" see above, Document 31.

25. Edited by Basil Moore (London: Hurst, 1973). This book was later published in the United States by John Knox Press under the title *The Challenge of Black Theology in South Africa.* The original book, *Essays on Black Theology,* was edited by Mokgethi Motlhabi.

26. Maryknoll, N.Y.: Orbis Books, 1977.

27. See John Mbiti, "African Theology," *Worldview,* August 1973, pp. 37f.; see also his "Some Current Concerns of African Theology," *The Expository Times,* March 1976, p. 166. See E. W. Fashole-Luke, "The Quest for an African Christian Theology," *The Journal of Religious Thought,* pp. 87f. Fashole-Luke writes: "In the Republic of South Africa, African Theology is equated with Black Theology and the emphasis on Blackness indicates the ethnic implications of the task; considerable attention is given there to the exposition of the Gospel in terms of liberation from political, social and economic injustice, and the creation of a new sense of dignity and equality in the face of white oppression and discrimination. It is surely at this critical point that African theologians are challenged by the Gospel to raise African Christian theologies above the level of ethnic or racial categories and emphasis, so that Christians everywhere will see that Christianity is greater and richer than any of its cultural manifestations, and that the Gospel of liberation is for the oppressed and oppressor alike" (ibid., pp. 87-88).

28. "The Engagement of Lusaka," p. 78.

29. African Theology's concern to use the thought forms for the people is not a slogan. The extensive research that African theologians have done on indigenous African religions and unestablished forms of Christianity does not have its counterpart among Latin American liberation theologians or even among Black theologians in the United States. John Mbiti has been one of the most prolific in this area. His books include *New Testament Eschatology in an African Battleground* (London: Oxford University Press, 1971); *African Religions and Philosophy* (London: Heinemann, 1969); *Concepts of God in Africa* (London: S.P.C.K., 1970). Some of his articles that are particularly appropriate in this discussion are "The Growing Respectability of African Traditional Religion," *Lutheran World,* Geneva, vol. 49, no. 236 (October 1970); "The Ways and Means of Communicating the Gospel," in C. G. Baëta, ed., *Christianity in Tropical Africa* (London, 1968).

Other African theologians' work in this area include Harry Sawyerr, *Creative Evangelism: Towards a New Christian Encounter with Africa* (London: Lutterworth Press, 1968); *God: Ancestor or Creator* (London: Longmans, 1970); Bolaji Idowu, *Olódùmaré* (London: Longmans, 1962); *African Traditional Religion: A Definition* (Maryknoll, N.Y.: Orbis Books, 1973).

33

BLACK THEOLOGY AND LATIN AMERICAN
LIBERATION THEOLOGY

Excerpts from a Symposium of the World Council
of Churches

Paulo Freire. * In this meeting I have again seen something which has become clear to me from my experiences in Europe and the United States. First of all, we who call ourselves educated and civilized people, the academics, the intellectuals—and I mean *we,* I don't want to exclude myself—we are so alienated, so domesticated, so ideologically conditioned in our existential and intellectual experience that we have created a terrible dichotomy between manual and intellectual work. Education, instead of being an act of knowing, is an act of transference of knowledge. We think knowledge is something we can possess. We divide the world into those who know and those who do not know . . . those who work manually and those who do not. In this way, instead of touching the reality, we touch the concepts. And the concepts become empty and lose their dialectical relationship with the facts.

We come to a meeting like this previously conditioned ideologically by this false concept of knowledge. And so instead of trying to look at the complete context in which we live and experience, we come looking for answers and prescriptions and transference of knowledge. That is my first observation.

My second observation is a challenge. There is a dialectical relationship between thinking and acting. We think and act in context: no language without context; no text without context. I look at my friend James Cone, whom I admire, as a Third World man—it does not matter that he was born in the United States—it's an accident. He is a Third World man because he was born

---

This symposium, from which this statement is excerpted, was held in May 1973, at the Geneva headquarters of the World Council of Churches, and the material was later published in *Risk,* vol. 9, no. 2 (1973).

*Paulo Freire, a staff member of the Office of Education, World Council of Churches, is the author of *Pedagogy of the Oppressed.*

in the world of dependence — of exploitation — within the First World. So our way of thinking is absolutely conditioned by our existential experience in your context. This does not mean that because I am a Latin American I cannot use Marx because Marx was a German. No. But I am conditioned not only by my physical context but by the ideology which is being developed in my concrete situation. Many times we say something and the question is not tongue but language. We can speak the same tongue using a different language, and many times we cannot understand.

For example, one of the participants could not at first understand when I said that the oppressors hate the flowers. He said, "It's a myth about the oppressors." No, it is not a myth, and by using the word *myth* he is using a different language. There is no time to begin the process of unveiling ourselves so that we can become equals, to discover ways to improve our communication by analyzing some texts within our contexts.

Another thing that I have perceived on different occasions in Europe is that when we are explaining our position the Europeans are really curious to understand what we are trying to do, what we are trying to say. But there is a background of ideology which means that behind much curiosity there is a certain paternalistic attitude. For example, many Europeans listen to us in the same style in which some parents — not good parents — listen to their children. *"Oh, yes, let's listen to what little John can tell us."* It is not conscious, it is because of your historical experience: you have commanded the world, you have imposed on Africa, Latin America and Asia your way of thinking, your technology, your values, your civilization, your goods, your humanism . . . and so on.

I would like to die like I am now, without systematizing things. I love to live, to exist, to love the flowers, but when people whose experience has been developed in the culture of silence — the culture of dependent people, oppressed people — come to talk within the spoken culture there is a tendency towards estrangement. You are very curious about what we are saying, but because of your ideological background you see our wish to say something as an attempt to impose our point of view on you. No, my friends, we are not trying to impose anything on you. We don't really want to receive anything from you. We want to exchange some things with you. It is not impossible to have dialogue. I was told in the United States: "Now the Latin Americans are trying to colonize us." I said, "No, we did not come here to impose our point of view, but we have something to say." This is what we are trying to do here.

It is a myth that Europeans have to teach the ignorant people of Africa and Latin America how to be civilized: the myth of the superiority of whites vis-à-vis blacks. This myth is reinforced by white science, which says that blacks are inferior. It is myth, it is not science; it is ideology and not science; it is the myth of the superiority of the colonizers vis-à-vis the colonized. It is a myth which is fundamental to the preservation of exploitation. Take, for example, the myth of the superiority of language. The language of the colonizers is language; the language of the colonized is dialect. The cultural productions of the colonizers are art; the cultural productions of the colonized are folklore. This is ideology, not science. The myth of the *conciliation des inconciliables* is the same myth. A Brazilian philosopher said, "Myth is the attribution of absolute value to something which is relative."

A last word. If you ask me if I think we have wasted our time here, I would say, "No, I learned a lot of things here. I was challenged." It was not the intention of the symposium to arrive at final conclusions or to define Black Theology or the Theology of Liberation. The intention was to provoke a step towards dialogue, and I think it has been achieved.

Hugo Assmann. * I would like to say something to the representatives of Black Theology. My biggest mistake in the first days of the symposium was that I was speaking to the participants and not to my friends who represent Black Theology. In my group there was a problem. . . . It was a dialogue between Latin American Theology of Liberation and European questions and problems. I would like to enter into dialogue with Black Theology. Let me say openly, though, that a very positive aspect of this symposium has been the experience of "incommunication" between us, because this "incommunication" is a dialectic part of our communication—the starting point. It would be terrible to remain in "incommunication" with Black Theology.

I ask myself: What is Latin American Theology of Liberation? Is it a new theology for the Western part of Latin America? In the name of what part of Latin America can we theologians of the Theology of Liberation in Latin America speak? In the name of Latin Americans? In the name of the Western part of Latin America? An important element of the Latin American reality is Western.

There is another problem: the non-Western part of Latin America—the Brazilian Africans, the people of the Caribbean Islands, the mysterious Mexicans. In Latin America there are whole countries where up to 80% of the people do not speak Spanish. Travelling in Latin America, I have had the experience of terrible "incommunication" with these people.

Until now the Latin American Theology of Liberation has used mostly Western and European theories and this poses a great question. We are trying now in Christian revolutionary groups to find a new communicative language. The Christians for Socialism movement in Chile is attempting to reinterpret in Marxist popular language the history, the revolution, the struggles and the processes of the proletarian movement in Chile. This strikes a somewhat false note, I must say, in an effort to communicate with Black Theology. It is false, because *who* is making this effort of communication in a popular language, a popular translation? Western people—Latin Americans, but Western people. There is another language—a grass-roots language. They have a language; we don't want to give them one. Perhaps it is impossible to wait until they "say their word,"

---

*Hugo Assmann, Brazilian theologian and author of *Theology for a Nomad Church,* is now serving as Professor of Communications at the University in San José, Costa Rica.

as Freire says. It is necessary to have a dialectic relationship between our Western, colonized, dependent language and their language. Both ISAL and the Christians for Socialism are trying to make them speak *their* language, not translations of our versions.

I am a Marxist and I can't see the reality of Latin America in any other category. But what is Marxism in Latin America? What would a Marx born in Latin America be like. A Quechua Christ? An Aymara Christ? Until now I have had very little communication with black people in the United States because when as a Westernized Latin American I read books and articles about the problem of black people in the United States, I am tempted to introduce Western Marxism. What must I do in order to have a better dialogue with you?

Perhaps we have something to give you—our experiences, our struggle, our difficulties in our theology of liberation—but we have much to learn from you. This is not an attempt at Christian reconciliation, it's a Latin American problem. In my country [Brazil], for example, there is a serious lack of communication between black people and half-black people. I think that when we make progress in this direction with people in Latin America, we will find another language, a different language, a third language. Also, if there is more communication with Black Theology and theologies from other countries of the Third World, there will be less "incommunication" between us.

In my opening address I was sometimes aggressive because, as a Westernized Latin American, I don't feel at ease with my color, my "gringo" face, my German origin. I don't feel happy with the fact that my theological dissertation was written in German. I have a psychological necessity to say to you in Western language that I am not Western. We Latin Americans are still in the early stages of our search for a Latin American identity. If you look in my library you will find books by German authors, French authors, Italian authors, Marx, Moltmann, etc. There is something false in this. ... Something which is not Latin American. I would like to say to my friends in Black Theology: I don't know how this dialogue with you can be improved, but it is more important than European theology for us Latin Americans. I don't want to destroy the connection with you. But I do want to reach a state of tension with you—a third kind of tension which is found more and more in the Third World.

In my group it was said that the contradictions of the world are not between the United States and Moscow, or between Europe and the United States—the fundamental contradiction is between the rich world and the oppressed world. I think a lot of things will be different when we come to an alliance with our real friends—the people of the Third World. In the United States and Europe, there are people of the Third World—the poor and oppressed world. If I believe as a Marxist in the necessity of the conflict in history, can it change the world? If I believe that the class struggle is really necessary in order to change the world, can it change the world?

People who are not the allies of the Third World are our enemies, and we will struggle against them. This class struggle inside the churches will be the biggest opportunity to transform the Church.

James Cone. In the last four days, one important issue has emerged, and it has to do with what I have called the social context of theological language. That phrase is related to my conviction that thinking, or thought, can never be separated from our socio-political existence. If one is a slave, then one's thinking about God will have a different character than if one is a slave master. This conviction has been illustrated again in this conference, and in one way, the relation between thought and social existence is the source of our communication with each other.

I have sensed this both as a black person from the United States trying to speak to Europeans, and also in the relationship between Black Theology and Latin American Theology. How do we communicate when we live in different worlds?

The question arises from the very moment of our presentations. What is Black Theology? Or, again, what is Liberation Theology in Latin America? The Europeans want to understand. When I am in America, white people want to understand. They want to know what we are talking about. What do we mean when we say: God is black? What do we mean when we say: Jesus is black? The more the question is explained, the more you realize that communication is not possible ... because we live in two worlds: the world of the oppressed and the world of the oppressors; the world of the black and the world of the white. These separate worlds, in part, define our language, our communication. This issue is illustrated by the way in which liberation theology in Latin America takes *class* as its point of departure and people in the black world take *color* as a point of departure for theological analysis. One of the reasons for the separate starting points is the separate ways in which people make an *entrée* into their language about God, politics, economics, etc., because of the historical context in which they live; and language and symbols—whether they be about politics or God or religion—are created in this historical context.

As long as we live in a world in which we may be defined as the oppressed and the oppressors, I do not believe that communication is possible. I do not believe that the oppressed and the oppressors can communicate at levels where it really makes a difference, because they have different realities to which the symbols and the language refer. I am pleased to hear you describe your world in order to see how that world is radically different from mine.

I will stop at this point because I sense on your faces an anxious desire to respond to the four of us—not only in terms of what we have said here but in terms of what we have said in our groups. If I wanted to be an oppressor, I would talk until one o'clock. But I will stop, in a gracious attempt to be—quote—"a Christian."

34

BLACK THEOLOGY
AND MARXIST THOUGHT*

Cornel West

Black theologians and Marxist thinkers are strangers. They steer clear of one another, each content to express concerns to their respective audiences. Needless to say, their concerns overlap. Both focus on the plight of the exploited, oppressed and degraded peoples of the world, their relative power-lessness and possible empowerment. I believe this common focus warrants a serious dialogue between Black theologians and Marxist thinkers. This dialogue should not be a mere academic chat that separates religionists and secularists, theists and atheists. Instead it ought to be an earnest encounter that specifies clearly the different sources of their praxis of faith, yet accents the possibility of mutually arrived-at political action.

The aim of this encounter is to change the world, not each other's faith; to put both groups on the offensive for structural social change, not put Black Christians on the defensive; and to enhance the quality of life of the dispos-sessed, not expose the empty Marxist meaning of death. In short, Black theo-logians and Marxist thinkers must preserve their own existential and intellectual integrity and explore the possibility of promoting fundamental social amelio-ration together.

Black theology and Marxist thought are not monolithic bodies of thought; each contains different perspectives, distinct viewpoints and diverse conclu-sions. Therefore it is necessary to identify the particular claims put forward by Black Theology and Marxist thought, those claims that distinguish both as dis-cernible schools of thought. Black Theology claims that (1) the historical expe-

*I would like to extend my gratitude to my close colleagues at Union Theological Seminary, Professors James Cone and James Washington, for our provocative and fruitful discussions and conversations which bear directly on the subject matter of this essay. *C.W.*

Cornel West is professor of Religion and director of the Afro-American studies program at Princeton University.

rience of Black people and the readings of the biblical texts that emerge from there are the centers around which reflection about God evolves; and that (2) this reflection is related, in some way, to the liberation of Black people, to the creation of a more abundant life definable in existential, economic, social and political terms.

Marxist thought contains two specific elements: a theory of history and an understanding of capitalism. Both are inextricably interlinked, but it may be helpful to characterize them separately.

The *Marxist theory of history* claims: (1) The history of human societies is the history of their transitional stages. (2) The transitional stages of human societies are discernible owing to their systems of production, or their organizational arrangements in which people produce goods and services for their survival. (3) Conflict within systems of production of human societies ultimately results in fundamental social change, or transitions from one historical stage to another. (4) Conflict within systems of production of human societies consists of cleavages between social classes (in those systems of production). (5) Social classes are historically transient, rooted in a particular set of socioeconomic conditions. (6) Therefore, the history of all hitherto existing society is the history of class struggles.

The *Marxist theory of capitalist society* claims: Capitalism is a historically transient system of production which requires human beings to produce commodities for the purpose of maximizing surplus value (profits). This production presupposes a fundamental social relation between the purchasers and sellers of a particular commodity, namely the labor-power (time, skill and expertise) of producers. This crucial commodity is bought by capitalists who own the land, instruments and capital necessary for production; it is sold by producers, whose labor-power is needed for production. The aim of the former is to maximize profits; that of the latter, to insure their own survival.

I shall claim that Black Theology and Marxist thought share three characteristics. (1) Both adhere to a similar methodology, the same way of approaching their respective subject matter and arriving at conclusions. (2) Both link some notion of liberation to the future socioeconomic conditions of the downtrodden. (3) And this is most important, both attempt to put forward trenchant critiques of liberal capitalist America. I will try to show that these three traits provide a springboard for a meaningful dialogue between Black theologians and Marxist thinkers and possibly spearhead a unifying effort for structural social change in liberal capitalist America.

Dialectical Methodology: Unmasking Falsehoods

Black theologians have either consciously or unconsciously employed a dialectical methodology in approaching their subject matter. This methodology consists of a three-step procedure of negation, preservation, and transformation; their subject matter, of White interpretations of the Christian gospel and their own circumstances. Dialectical methodology is critical in character and hermeneutic in content.¹ For Black theologians it is highly critical of dogmatic viewpoints of the gospel, questioning whether certain unjustifiable prejudgments are operative. It is hermeneutic in that it is concerned with unearthing assumptions of particular interpretations and presenting an understanding of the gospel that extends and expands its ever unfolding truth.

Black theologians have, for the most part, been compelled to adopt a dialectical methodology. They have refused to accept what has been given to them by White theologians: they have claimed that all reflection about God by Whites must be digested, decoded and deciphered. The first theological formulations by Afro-Americans based on biblical texts tried to come to terms with their White owners' viewpoints and their own servitude. Since its inception, Black theologians have been forced to reduce White deception and distortion of the gospel and make the Christian story meaningful in light of their oppressive conditions.

Black theological reflection begins by negating White interpretations of the gospel, continues by preserving its own perceived truths of the biblical texts, and ends by transforming past understandings of the gospel into new and novel ones. These three steps embody an awareness of the social context of theologizing, the need to accent the historical experience of Black people and the insights of the Bible, and the ever evolving task of recovering, regaining and repeating the gospel.

Black theologians underscore the importance of the social context of theological reflection.² Their dialectical methodology makes them sensitive to the hidden agendas of theological formulations they negate, agendas often guided by social interests. Their penchant for revealing distortions leads them to adopt a sociology of knowledge-approach that stresses the way in which particular viewpoints endorse and encourage ulterior aims.

An interpretation of the Black historical experience and the readings of the biblical texts that emerge out of this experience constitute the raw ingredients for the second step of Black theological reflection. By trying to understand the plight of Black people in light of the Bible, Black theologians claim to preserve the biblical truth that God sides with the oppressed and acts on their behalf.³ Subsequently, the Black historical experience and the biblical texts form a symbiotic relationship, each illuminating the other.

Since Black theologians believe in the living presence of God and the work of the Holy Spirit, they acknowledge the constant unfolding process of the gospel. Paradoxically, the gospel is unchanging, yet it is deepened by embracing and encompassing new human realities and experiences. The gospel must speak to every age. Therefore it must be recovered and repeated, often sounding different, but, in substance, remaining the same. For Black theologians, it sounds different because it addresses various contexts of oppression; it remains the same because it is essentially a gospel of liberation.

Marxist thinkers, like Black theologians, employ a dialectical methodology in approaching their subject matter. But they do so consciously and their subject matter is bourgeois theories about capitalist society. The primary theoretical task of Marxist thinkers is to uncover the systematic misunderstanding of capitalist society by bourgeois thinkers; to show how this misunderstanding, whether deliberate or not, supports and sanctions exploitation and oppression in this society; and to put forward the correct understanding of this society in order to change it.

Marxist social theory is first and foremost a critique of inadequate theories of capitalist society and subsequently a critique of capitalist society itself. The subtitle of Marx's magnum opus, *Capital*, is "A Critique of Political Economy," not "A Critique of Capitalism." This work takes bourgeois economists to task for perpetuating falsehoods, and results in revealing the internal dynamics of capitalism and their inhumane consequences. For Marx, a correct understanding of capitalist society is possible only by overcoming present mystifications of it; and this correct understanding is requisite for a propitious political praxis.

Marxist thought stresses the conflict-laden unfolding of history, the conflict-producing nature of social processes. Therefore it is not surprising that Marxist thinkers employ a dialectical methodology, a methodology deeply suspicious of stasis and stability, and highly skeptical of equilibrium and equipoise. This methodology, like that of Black theologians, is critical in character and hermeneutic in content. It is critical of perspectives presented by bourgeois social scientists, questioning whether certain ideological biases are operative. It is hermeneutic in that it is obsessed with discovering correct understanding underneath wrong interpretations, disclosing latent truths behind manifest distortions. For Marx, to be scientific is to be dialectical and to be dialectical is to unmask, unearth, bring to light.[4]

This conception of science, derived from Hegel, attempts to discern the hidden kernel of an evolving truth becoming manifest by bursting through a visible husk. The husk, once a hidden kernel, dissolves, leaving its indelible imprint upon the new emerging kernel. This idea of inquiry highlights the moments of negation, preservation and transformation. By presenting his theory of history and society from this perspective, Marx provided the most powerful and penetrating social criticism in modern times. Dialectical methodology enabled him to create a whole mode of inquiry distinctively his own, though often appearing hermetic and rigid to the untutored and fanatic.

Despite the similar procedure Black theologians and Marxist thinkers share, there has been little discussion about it between them. This is so primarily because a dialectical methodology is implicit, undeveloped and often unnoticed in Black Theology. This failure to examine the methodological stance embodied in Black theological reflection obscures its similarity with that of Marxist thought.

Liberation: Its Constitutive Elements

Black theologians all agree that Black liberation has something to do with ameliorating the socioeconomic conditions of Black people. But it is not clear what this amelioration amounts to. There is little discussion in their writings about what the liberating society will look like. The notion and process of liberation is often mentioned, but, surprisingly, one is hard put to find a sketch of what liberation would actually mean in the everyday lives of Black people, what power they would possess, and what resources they would have access to.

There are two main reasons for this neglect among Black theologians. First, a dialectical methodology discourages discussions about the ideal society and simply what ought to be. Instead, it encourages criticizing and overcoming existing society, negating and opposing what is.

The second reason, the one with which we shall be concerned in this section, is the failure of Black theologians to talk specifically about the way in which the existing system of production and social structure relates to Black oppression and exploitation. Without focusing on this relation, it becomes extremely difficult to present an idea of liberation with socioeconomic content. In short, the lack of a clear-cut social theory prevents the emergence of any substantive political program or social vision.

Except for the latest writings of James Cone, Black theologians remain uncritical of America's imperialist presence in Third World countries, its capitalist system of production, and its grossly unequal distribution of wealth. Therefore we may assume they find this acceptable. If this is so, then the political and socioeconomic components of Black liberation amount to racial equality before the law; equal opportunities in employment, education and business; and economic parity with Whites in median income.

Surely this situation would be better than the current dismal one. But it hardly can be viewed as Black liberation. It roughly equates liberation with American middle-class status, leaving the unequal distribution of wealth relatively untouched and the capitalist system of production, along with its imperialist ventures, intact. Liberation would consist of including Black people within the mainstream of liberal capitalist America. If this is the social vision of Black theologians, they should drop the meretricious and flamboyant term "liberation" and adopt the more accurate and sober word "inclusion."

Marxist thought, like Black Theology, does not elaborate on the ideal society. As we noted earlier, a dialectical methodology does not permit this elaboration. But the brief sketch Marxist thinkers provide requires a particular system of production and political arrangement: namely, participatory democracy in each. Human liberation occurs only when people participate substantively in the decision-making processes in the major institutions that regulate their lives. Democratic control over the institutions in the productive and political processes in order for them to satisfy human needs and protect personal liberties of the populace constitutes human liberation.

Marxist thinkers are able to present this sketch of human liberation primarily because they stress what people must liberate themselves *from*. They suggest what liberation is for only after understanding the internal dynamics of the society people must be liberated from. Without this clear-cut social theory about what *is*, it is difficult to say anything significant about what *can be*. The possibility of liberation is found only within the depths of the actuality of oppression. Without an adequate social theory, this possibility is precluded.

Social Criticism: Class, Race, and Culture

Black Theology puts forward a vehement, often vociferous, critique of liberal capitalist America. One of its most attractive and alluring characteristics is its theological indictment of racist American society. An undisputable claim of Black Theology is America's unfair treatment of Black people. What is less apparent is the way in which Black theologians understand the internal dynamics of liberal capitalist America, how it functions, why it operates the way it does, who possesses substantive power, and where it is headed. As noted earlier, Black theologians do not utilize a social theory that relates the oppression of Black people to the overall make-up of America's system of production, foreign policy, political arrangement, and cultural practices.

Black theologians hardly mention the wealth, power, and influence of multinational corporations that monopolize production in the marketplace and prosper partially owing to their dependence on public support in the form of government subsidies, free technological equipment, lucrative contracts and sometimes even direct-transfer payments. Black theologians do not stress the way in which corporate interests and the government intermesh, usually resulting in policies favorable to the former. Black theologians fail to highlight the fact that in liberal capitalist America one-half of 1 percent own 22 percent of the wealth, 1 percent own 33 percent of the wealth, the lower 61 percent own only 7 percent of the wealth, and the bottom 45 percent own only 2 percent of the wealth.[5] Lastly, Black theologians do not emphasize sufficiently the way in which the racist interpretations of the gospel they reject encourage and support the capitalist system of production, its grossly unequal distribution of wealth and its closely connected political arrangements.

Instead of focusing on these matters, Black theologians draw attention to the racist practices in American society. Since these practices constitute the most visible and vicious form of oppression in America, Black theologians justifiably do so. Like the Black Power proponents of the sixties, they call for the empowerment of Black people, the need for Black people to gain significant control over their lives. But neither Black Power proponents nor Black theologians have made it sufficiently clear as to what constitutes this Black control, the real power to direct institutions such that Black people can live free of excessive exploitation and oppression. The tendency is to assume that middle-class status is equivalent to such control, that a well-paying job amounts to such power. And surely this assumption is fallacious.

The important point here is not that racist practices should be stressed less by Black theologians, for such practices deeply affect Black people and shape their perceptions of American society. What is crucial is that these practices must be linked to the role they play in buttressing the current mode of production, concealing the unequal distribution of wealth, and portraying the lethargy of the political system. Black theologians are correct to relate racist practices to degrees of Black powerlessness, but they obscure this relation by failing to provide a lucid definition of what power is in American society. Subsequently, they often fall into the trap of assuming power in American society to be synonymous with receiving high wages.

Marxist social criticism can be quite helpful at this point. For Marx, power in modern industrial society consists of a group's participation in the decision-making processes of the major institutions that affect their destinies. Since institutions of production, such as multinational corporations, play an important role in people's lives, these institutions should be significantly accountable to the populace. In short, they should be democratically controlled by the citizenry; people should participate in their decision-making processes. Only collective control over the major institutions of society constitutes genuine power on behalf of the people.

For Marx, power in modern industrial society is closely related to a group's say over what happens to products produced in the work situation, to a group's input into decisions that direct the production flow of goods and services. The most powerful group in society has the most say and input into decisions over this production flow; the least powerful group does not participate at all in such decisions. In liberal capitalist America, the former consists of multiple corporate owners who dictate policies concerning the mass production of a variety of products produced by white- and blue-collar workers who receive wages in return. The latter consists of the so-called underclass, the perennially unemployed, who are totally removed from the work situation, precluded from any kind of input affecting the production flow, including negotiation and strikes available to white- and blue-collar workers.

Racist practices intensify the degree of powerlessness among Black people. This is illustrated by the high rates of Black unemployment, the heavy Black concentration in low-paying jobs, and inferior housing, education, police protection and health care. But it is important to note that this powerlessness differs from that of white- and blue-collar workers in degree, not in kind. In human terms, this difference is immense, incalculable; in structural terms, this difference is negligible, trifling. In other words, most Americans are, to a significant degree, powerless. They have no substantive control over their lives, little participation in the decision-making process of the major institutions that regulate their lives. Among Afro-Americans, this powerlessness is exacerbated, creating an apparent qualitative difference in oppression.

This contrast of the social criticism of Black theologians and Marxist thinkers raises the age-old question as to whether class position or racial status is the major determinant of Black oppression in America. This question should be formulated in the following way: Does class position or racial status contribute more to the fundamental form of powerlessness in America?

Racial status contributes greatly to Black oppression. But Black middle-class people are essentially well-paid white- or blue-collar workers who have little control over their lives primarily owing to their class position, not racial status.

This is so because the same limited control is held by White middle-class people, despite the fact that a higher percentage of whites are well-paid white- and blue-collar workers than Blacks. Significant degrees of powerlessness pertain to most Americans and this could be so only if class position determines such powerlessness. Therefore, class position contributes more than racial status to the basic form of powerlessness in America.

I am suggesting that the more Black theologians discard or overlook Marxist social criticism, the further they distance themselves from the fundamental determinant of Black oppression and any effective strategy to alleviate it.[6] This distancing also obscures the direct relation of Black oppression in America to Black and Brown oppression in Third World countries. The most powerful group in America, those multiple corporate owners who dictate crucial corporate policies over a variety of production flows, is intimately and inextricably linked (through their highly paid American and Third World white-collar workers and grossly underpaid Third World blue-collar workers) to the economies and governments of Third World countries, including the most repressive ones. Marxist social criticism permits this relation to come to light in an extremely clear and convincing way.

The social criticism of Black theologians reflects the peculiar phenomenon of American liberal and radical criticism. This criticism rarely has viewed class position as a major determinant of oppression primarily owing to America's lack of a feudal past, the heterogeneity of its population, the many and disparate regions of its geography, and the ever increasing levels of productivity and growth. These facts make it difficult to see class divisions; indeed, along with other forms of oppression, they make it almost impossible to see the divisions. But, like protons leaving vapor trails in a cloud chamber, one is forced to posit these class divisions in light of the overwhelming evidence for their existence. Only class divisions can explain the gross disparity between rich and poor, the immense benefits accruing to the former and the depravity of the latter.

Region, sex, age, ethnicity, and race often have been considered the only worthy candidates as determinants of oppression. This has been so primarily because American liberal and radical criticism usually has presupposed the existing system of production, assumed class divisions and attempted to include only marginal groups in the mainstream of liberal capitalist America. This criticism has fostered a petit-bourgeois viewpoint that clamors for a bigger piece of the ever growing American pie, rarely asking fundamental questions such as why it never gets recut more equally or how it gets baked in the first place. In short, this criticism remains silent about class divisions, the crucial role they play in maintaining the unequal distribution of goods and services, and how they undergird discrimination against regions, impose ceilings on upward social mobility and foster racism, sexism and ageism. With the exception of the most recent writings of James Cone, contemporary Black theologians suffer from this general myopia of American liberal and radical criticism.

Despite this shortsightedness, Black theologians have performed an important service for Marxist thinkers, namely emphasizing the ways in which culture and religion resist oppression. They have been admirably sensitive to the Black cultural buffers against oppression, especially the Black religious sources of struggle and strength, vitality and vigor. They also have stressed the indispensable contribution the Black churches have made toward the survival, dignity and self-worth of Black people.

Contrary to Marxist thinkers, Black theologians recognize that cultural and religious attitudes, values, and sensibilities have a life and logic of their own, not fully accountable in terms of a class analysis. Subsequently, racist practices are not reducible to a mere clever and successful strategy of divide-and-conquer promoted by the ruling class to prevent proletarian unity. Rather, racism is an integral element within the very fabric of American culture and society. It is embedded in the country's first collective self-definition; enunciated in its subsequent laws; and imbued in its dominant way of life.

The orthodox Marxist analysis of culture and religion that simply relates racist practices to misconceived material interests is only partially true, hence deceptive and misleading. These practices are fully comprehensible only if one conceives of culture, not as a mere hoax played by the ruling class on workers, but as the tradition that informs one's conception of tradition, as social practices that shape one's idea of social practice.

The major objection to the orthodox Marxist analysis of culture and religion is not that it is wrong, but that it is too narrow, rigid and dogmatic. It views popular culture and religion only as instruments of domination, vehicles of pacification. It sees only their negative and repressive elements. On this view, only enlightenment, reason, or clarity imposed from the outside can break through the cultural layers of popular false consciousness.[7] Therefore, the orthodox Marxist analysis refuses to acknowledge the positive, liberating aspects of popular culture and religion, and their potential for fostering structural social change.

This issue is at the heart of the heated debate over the adequacy of a Marxist analysis between Black theologians and Latin American liberation theologians. The latter tend to adopt the orthodox Marxist view, paying little attention to the positive, liberating aspects of popular culture and religion.[8] They display a contempt for popular culture and religion, a kind of tacit condescension that reeks of paternalism and elitism. They often speak of the poor possessing a privileged access to truth and reality, but rarely do they take seriously the prevailing beliefs, values or outlooks of the poor. Instead, Latin American liberation theologians stress the discontinuity and radical rupture of progressive consciousness with popular culture and religion, suggesting a desire to wipe the cultural slate clean and begin anew.

To the contrary, Black theologians recognize the positive and negative elements, the liberating and repressive possibilities, of popular culture and religion. To no one's surprise, they devote much attention to the armors of survival, forms of reaction, and products of response created by Black people in order to preserve their dignity and self-respect.[9] Black theologians view themselves as working within a tradition of political struggle and cultural and religious resistance to oppression. They emphasize their continuity with this tradition.

It is possible to account for this important difference between Black theologians and Latin American liberation theologians by appealing to the different histories of the particular countries about which they theorize. But there is possibly a deeper reason for this disagreement. It relates directly to the composition of the two groups of theologians.

For the most part, Latin American liberation theologians belong to the dominant cultural group in their respective countries. As intellectuals educated in either European schools or Europeanized Latin American universities and seminaries, they adopt cosmopolitan habits and outlooks.[10] Like their theoretical master, Karl Marx, a true cosmopolitan far removed from his indigenous Jewish culture, they tend to see popular culture and religion as provincial and parochial. It is something to be shed and ultimately discarded, replaced by something qualitatively different and better. They do not seem to have encountered frequently situations in which they were forced to rely on their own indigenous cultural and religious resources in an alien and hostile environment. So their own experiences often limit their capacity to see the existential richness and radical potential of popular culture and religion.

In contrast to this, Black theologians belong to the degraded cultural group in the United States. As intellectuals trained in American colleges, universities and seminaries, they have first-hand experiences of cultural condescension, arrogance and haughtiness. They know what it is like to be a part of a culture considered to be provincial and parochial. Hence they view Black culture and religion as something to be preserved and promoted, improved and enhanced, not erased and replaced. In short, Black theologians acknowledge their personal debts to Black culture and religion, and incorporate its fecundity and fertility in their understanding of American society.

Latin American liberation theologians and Black theologians can learn from each other on this matter. The former must be more sensitive to the complexities and ambiguities of popular culture and religion; the latter should more closely relate their view of Black culture and religion to a sophisticated notion of power in liberal capitalist America. And both can learn from the most penetrating Marxist theorist of culture in this century, Antonio Gramsci.[11]

Gramsci provides a valuable framework in which to understand culture, its autonomous activity and status, while preserving its indirect yet crucial link with power in society. Unlike the Latin American liberation theologians he does not downplay the importance of popular culture; unlike the Black theologians, he does not minimize the significance of class. Instead, he views the systems of production and culture in a symbiotic relationship with one another, each containing intense tension, struggle and even warfare. Class struggle is not simply the battle between capitalists and proletariat, owners and producers, in the work situation. It also takes the form of cultural and religious conflict over which attitudes, values and beliefs will dominate the thought and behavior of people. For Gramsci, this incessant conflict is crucial. It contains the key to structural social change; it is the springboard for a revolutionary political praxis.

According to Gramsci, no state and society can be sustained by force alone. It must put forward convincing and persuasive reasons, arguments, ideologies or propaganda for its continued existence. A state and society require not only military protection, but also principled legitimation. This legitimation takes place in the cultural and religious spheres, in those arenas where the immediacy of everyday life is felt, outlooks are formed, and self-images adopted.

Gramsci deepens Marx's understanding of the legitimation process by replacing the notion of ideology with his central concept of hegemony. For Marx, ideology is the set of formal ideas and beliefs promoted by the ruling class for the purpose of preserving its privileged position in society; for Gramsci, hegemony is the set of formal ideas and beliefs and informal modes of behavior, habits, manners, sensibilities and outlooks that support and sanction the existing order.

In Gramsci's view, culture is both tradition and current practices. Tradition is understood, not as the mere remnants of the past or the lingering, inert elements in the present but, rather, as active formative and transformative modalities of a society. Current practices are viewed as actualizations of particular modalities, creating new habits, sensibilities and world-views against the pressures and limits of the dominant ones.

A hegemonic culture subtly and effectively encourages people to identify themselves with the habits, sensibilities, and world-views supportive of the status quo and the class interests that dominate it. It is a culture successful in persuading people to "consent" to their oppression and exploitation. A hegemonic culture survives and thrives as long as it convinces people to adopt its preferred formative modality, its favored socialization process. It begins to crumble when people start to opt for a transformative modality, a socialization process that opposes the dominant one. The latter constitutes a counter-hegemonic culture, the deeply embedded oppositional elements within a society. It is these elements that the hegemonic culture seeks to contain and control.

Based on the insights of Gramsci, along with those of the distinguished English cultural critic Raymond Williams, I shall present a theoretical framework that may be quite serviceable to Black theologians, Latin American liberation theologians, and Marxist thinkers.[12] Cultural processes can be understood in light of four categories: hegemonic, pre-hegemonic, neo-hegemonic, and counter-hegemonic.

Hegemonic culture is to be viewed as the effectively operative dominant world-views, sensibilities, and habits that sanction the established order. Pre-hegemonic culture consists of those residual elements of the past which continue to shape and mold thought and behavior in the present; it often criticizes hegemonic culture, harking back to a golden age in the pristine past. Neo-hegemonic culture constitutes a new phase of hegemonic culture; it postures as an oppositional force, but, in substance, is a new manifestation of people's allegiance and loyalty to the status quo. Counter-hegemonic culture represents genuine opposition to hegemonic culture; it fosters an alternative set of habits, sensibilities, and world-views that cannot possibly be realized within the perimeters of the established order.

This framework presupposes three major points. First, it accents the equivocal character of culture and religion, their capacity to be instruments of freedom or domination, vehicles of liberation or pacification. Second, it focuses on the ideological function of culture and religion, the necessity of their being either forces for freedom or forces for domination, for liberation or for pacification. Third, it views the struggle between these two forces as open-ended. The only guarantee of freedom rests upon the contingencies of human practice; the only assurance of liberation relies on the transformative modalities of a society. No matter how wide the scope of hegemonic culture may be, it never encompasses or exhausts all human practice or every transformative modality in a society. Human struggle is always a possibility in any society and culture.

In order to clarify further my four categories, I shall identify them crudely with particular elements in contemporary American society. Hegemonic culture can be seen as the prevailing Horatio Alger mystique, the widespread hopes and dreams for social upward mobility among Americans. This mystique nourishes the values, outlooks, and lifestyles of achievement careerism, leisurism, and consumerism that pervade American culture. Pre-hegemonic culture is negligible owing to the country's peculiar inception, namely, that it was "born liberal." Subsequently, American conservatives and reactionaries find themselves in the ironic position of quarreling with liberals by defending early versions of liberalism. Neo-hegemonic culture is best illustrated by the countercultural movement of the sixties, specifically the protests of White middle-class youth (spin-offs of the Black political struggles) which, with few exceptions, was effectively absorbed by the mainstream of liberal capitalist America. The continuous creation of a counter-hegemonic culture is manifest in the multifarious, though disparate, radical grass-roots organizations; elements of the socialist feminist groups; and aspects of Afro-American culture and religion.

A present challenge confronting Black theologians is to discover and discern what aspects of Afro-American culture and religion can contribute to a counter-hegemonic culture in American society. They may find Gramsci's conception of organic intellectuals helpful on this matter.[13] Gramsci views organic intellectuals as leaders and thinkers directly tied to a particular cultural group primarily by means of institutional affiliations. Organic intellectuals combine theory and action, and relate popular culture and religion to structural social change.

Black religious leadership can make an enormous contribution to a counter-hegemonic culture and structural social change in American society. Black preachers and pastors are in charge of the most numerous and continuous gatherings of Black people, those who are the worst victims of liberal capitalist America and whose churches are financially, culturally and politically independent of corporate influence.[14] This freedom of Black preachers and pastors, unlike that of most Black professionals, is immense. They are the leaders of the only major institutions in the Black community that are not accountable to the status quo. Needless to say, many abuse this freedom. But what is important to note is that the contribution of Black religious leaders can be prodigious, as exemplified by the great luminaries of the past, including Nat Turner, Martin Delany, Martin Luther King, Jr., and Malcolm X.

An Alliance of Black Theology and Marxist Thought: The Case of Reverend George Washington Woodbey

The best example of a Black religious thinker and leader who combined the insights of Black theological reflection and Marxist social theory was the Rev. George Washington Woodbey.[15] He devoted his life to promoting structural social change and creating a counter-hegemonic culture in liberal capitalist America.

Rev. Mr. Woodbey was a Baptist preacher, for many years pastor of Mt. Zion Baptist Church in San Diego, California, and a major socialist leader in the first few decades of this century. He was uncompromising in his religious faith, unyielding in his confidence in the radical potential of Black culture and religion, and unrelenting in his devotion to fundamental social change. Widely known in California during his day as "The Great Negro Socialist Orator," Woodbey delivered poignant yet incisive lectures across the country, including his famous reply to Booker T. Washington's "Capitalist Argument for the Negro." Woodbey also wrote books such as *The Bible and Socialism: A Conversation between Two Preachers* (1904) and *The Distribution of Wealth* (1910), and such essays as "Why the Negro Should Vote the Socialist Ticket" (1908) and "Why the Socialists Must Reach the Churches with Their Message" (1915).[16]

Woodbey's most influential work, *What to Do and How to Do It or Socialism vs. Capitalism* (1903) was translated into three languages. It was often compared to Robert Blatchford's *Merrie England,* the most widely read Socialist educational publication at the turn of the century.

Woodbey's important work consists of a conversation between himself and his mother, taking place after a long separation. She begins with the question, "Have you given up the Bible and the ministry and gone into politics?" He replies that he became a Socialist precisely because of his strict adherence to principles put forward in the Bible. She then points out that many of his comrades do not believe in God or in biblical truths. He reminds her that other political parties, such as the Republican and Democratic parties, have their equal portion of nonbelievers. He assures her that he does not fully agree with some of his comrades on religious matters, but since Socialism is "a scheme for bettering things here first," he can be a Socialist without giving up his religious beliefs. He then states that, under Socialism, religious freedom will be guaranteed.

Later on, the mother asks, "Like all other women, I want to know where are we to come in?" He answers that it is in the interest of "the women, more than the men, if possible, to be Socialists because they suffer more from capitalism than anyone else." Under Socialism, each woman will receive her own income and be an equal shareholder in the industries of the country. Under these conditions, there will be no need for a woman to "sell herself through a so-called marriage to someone she did not love, in order to get a living"; instead, she could marry for genuine love. In capitalist society, a working man is a slave, "and his wife is the slave of a slave." Therefore liberation of both would enhance the position of women more than that of men. This conversation ends with the mother's conversion to Socialism, and she comments,

> Well, you have convinced me that I am about as much a slave now as I was in the south, and I am ready to accept any way out of this drudgery.

Rev. Mr. Woodbey was the only Black delegate to the Socialist Party conventions of 1904 and 1908. In the latter convention, he was nominated as Eugene Debs's running mate in the presidential election of 1908. He was once described as "the greatest living negro in America. . . . his style is simple and his logic invincible. He knows the race question, and one of his most popular lectures relates to the settlement of this vexed question under Socialism."

Jailed frequently, hospitalized more than once owing to police brutality, barely escaping murder during the famous 1912 Free Speech fight in San Diego, Rev. Mr. Woodbey was a devoted Christian who sacrificed greatly for fostering a counter-hegemonic culture and promoting structural social change in liberal capitalist America. He was a man of inexorable Christian faith, anchored deep in the best of Black culture and religion, and of intransigent Socialist conviction. His life and writings best exemplify the point at which Black theologians and Marxist thinkers are no longer strangers.

NOTES

1. Dialectical methodology is a complex procedure useful for grasping, comprehending, interpreting, explaining or predicting phenomena. Aside from the foundation laid by Plato, this procedure was first fully developed by Hegel and deepened by Marx. Hegel's most succinct discussions of this approach can be found in his *Logic* (Part 1, *Encyclopedia of Philosophical Sciences),* trans. William Wallace (Oxford, 1975), no. 81, pp. 115-119, and *The Phenomenology of Mind,* trans. B. Baillie (New York, 1967), pp. 80ff. For Marx's brief formal presentation of this approach as it relates to his social theory, see *The Grundrisse,* trans. Martin Nicolaus (New York, 1973), pp. 83-111.

2. The most explicit and extensive treatment of this matter by a Black theologian is found in James Cone's *God of the Oppressed* (New York, 1975), chap. 3, pp. 39-61.

3. The most sophisticated dialogue among Black theologians has focused on the status of this biblical truth. William Jones has claimed that Black theologians do not provide sufficient empirical evidence to warrant this truth. He suggests that Black theologians have not taken seriously the possibility of a malevolent deity. For Jones, an acceptable Black Theology must deal adequately with the problem of theodicy. James Cone has responded to Jones's argument by claiming that Jesus' victory over suffering and death constitutes the necessary and sufficient evidence for the belief that God sides with the oppressed and acts on their behalf. In short, Cone holds that empirical evidence is never a reliable basis of a biblical truth; the problem of theodicy is never solved in a theoretical manner, only defeated by one's faith in Jesus Christ. For Jones's incisive and insightful discussion, see *Is God a White Racist* (Garden City, N.Y., 1973). For Cone's reply, see his *God of the Oppressed,* op. cit., pp. 187-194.

4. This conception of science pervades Marx's mature writings. For example, he states, "But all science would be superfluous if the outward appearance and the essence

of things directly coincided." *Capital,* ed. Friedrich Engels (New York, 1967), vol. 3, p. 817. Notice also the demystifying aim of theory in the first few paragraphs of the famous section 4, entitled, "The Fetishism of Commodities and the Secret Thereof" of chap. 1 in *Capital,* vol. 1, pp. 71ff.

5. These figures come from the nearest thing to an official survey on the maldistribution of wealth in America, conducted by the Federal Reserve Board in 1962. As one of its authors, Herman Miller, noted, "the figures were so striking as to obviate the need to search for trends." For further exposition and elaboration on this study, see "The Other Economy: America's Working Poor," Gus Tyler, *The New Leader* (Special Issue), May 8, 1978, pp. 20-24.

6. I have tried to give persuasive reasons as to why this is so for any viewpoint which overlooks class oppression, in my paper, "Institutional Racism, Liberalism, and Self-Determination" (to be published in the Fall 1979 issue of *The Journal of Religious Ethics*).

7. This point illustrates the undeniable link of the orthodox Marxist view to the Enlightenment. More specifically, it portrays the inherent elitism and paternalism of such a view. We need only recall Lenin's well-known claim (in *What Is to Be Done?*) that the working class can achieve only trade-union consciousness on its own, thereby requiring a vanguard party to elevate it to revolutionary consciousness. For Lenin, this party brings enlightenment to the benighted proletariat.

8. This view is illustrated clearly in an essay by José Míguez Bonino, a leading Latin American liberation theologian, entitled "Popular Piety in Latin America," in which he states, "From a theological as well as a political perspective the popular piety that used to exist and that still predominates in Latin America can only be considered as a profoundly alienated and alienating piety, a manifestation of an enslaved consciousness and, at the same time, a ready instrument for the continuation and consolidation of oppression. The intent to transform the mobilizing power of that piety to goals of transformation without radically altering the very content of the religious consciousness seems psychologically impossible and theologically unacceptable." This essay appeared in *Cristianismo y Sociedad* (Buenos Aires), no. 47 (first issue, 1976), pp. 31-38, trans. James and Margaret Goff. Gustavo Gutiérrez, another prominent Latin American liberation theologian, understands popular culture and religion in a more subtle and sophisticated way. I base this judgment on my cordial and provocative discussions with him during his visiting professorship at Union Theological Seminary in the fall of 1977. It seems to me his own cultural roots and his serious study of cultural Marxist thinkers, especially Antonio Gramsci and Jose Carlos Mariategui (the father of Latin American Marxism) principally account for his sensitivity to popular culture and religion.

9. This serious concern of Black theologians and religious scholars is exemplified best by Charles H. Long's highly suggestive essay, "Perspectives for a Study of Afro-American Religion in the United States," *History of Religions*, vol. 2, no. 1 (August 1977), pp. 54-66, Gayraud S. Wilmore's solid study, *Black Religion and Black Radicalism* (Garden City, N.Y., 1972), esp. pp. 298-306, and James Cone's speculative work, *The Spirituals and the Blues* (New York, 1972). The "armors, forms, and products" of Afro-American culture I have in mind here are the spirituals, blues, gospels, jazz, folktales and sermons. What is not sufficiently emphasized by Black theologians, religious scholars or cultural critics is the radical potential embedded within the style of these art-forms. The most important aspect of them is not what is conveyed, but *how* this "what" is conveyed. It is this "how" which bears the imprint of struggle and constitutes the distinctive imposition of order on chaos by Black people. It is this "how," or style, that contains the real message or genuine content of these works of art. To my knowledge, only the essays of Ralph Ellison and Albert Murray explore this frontier of Afro-American art-forms.

10. This point is best illustrated by the words of Hugo Assmann, one of the most radical Latin American theologians. "In my opening address I was sometimes aggressive because, as a Westernized Latin American, I don't feel at ease with my color, my 'gringo' face, my German origin. I don't feel happy with the fact that my theological dissertation was written in German. I have a psychological necessity to say to you in Western language that I am not Western. We Latin Americans are still in the early stages of our search

for a Latin American identity. If you look in my library you will find books by German authors, French authors, Italian authors, Marx, Moltmann, etc. There is something false in this, . . . something which is not Latin American." This quote is from the publication *Risk,* which is based on the Symposium on Black Theology and Latin American Theology of Liberation, May 1973, at the Ecumenical Center in Geneva, Switzerland, p. 62; see Document 33 above.

11. It is not surprising that Gramsci comes from a degraded cultural region in Italy, namely Sardinia, and had intense experiences of ostracism owing to his hunchback, poor health and short height (he was barely five feet tall). A sample of his writings can be found in *Selections from the Prison Notebooks*, trans. and ed. Quintin Hoare and Geoffrey Nowell Smith (New York, 1971).

12. The book by Raymond Williams I have in mind is his *Marxism and Literature* (London, 1977), esp. chap. 2, pp. 75-141.

13. Gramsci discusses this conception in his seminal essay, "The Intellectuals," *Selections from the Prison Notebooks*, op. cit., pp. 5-23. Although he completely misunderstands the nature of the radical potential of Afro-American culture and Afro-American intellectuals, this does not harm his theoretical formulation of the notion of organic intellectuals.

14. I should add that this also holds to an important degree for White poor and Hispanic Pentecostal churches.

15. My information about this fascinating Black preacher comes directly from Philip Foner's timely essay, "Reverend George Washington Woodbey: Early Twentieth-Century California Black Socialist," *The Journal of Negro History*, vol. 61, no. 2 (April 1976). For Foner's treatment of Woodbey along with other Black Socialist preachers in the United States, including the Reverends George W. Slater, Jr., S. C. Garrison and George Frazier Miller, see his monumental work, *American Social Black Americans: From the Age of Jackson to World War II* (Westport, Conn., 1977), chap. 7, pp. 151-181.

16. It is interesting to note that the first book mentioned here was dedicated to "the Preachers and Members of the Churches, and all others who are interested in knowing what the Bible teaches on the question at issue between the Socialists and the Capitalists, by one who began preaching twenty-nine years ago, and still continues."

EPILOGUE:
AN INTERPRETATION OF THE
DEBATE AMONG BLACK THEOLOGIANS

James H. Cone

The purpose of this bibliographical essay is to evaluate the literature of Black Theology in the light of the internal debates of Black theologians among themselves in the academy and in the church. (The context for the latter was located in the Theological Commission of the National Conference of Black Churchmen and the former in the Society for the Study of Black Religion.) Few outside persons realize how seriously and vigorously the various theological perspectives in the Black community have been debated, and the effect these debates have had in defining the issues to which Black theologians have addressed themselves in their writings. To be sure, there has been much discussion about the imperialistic and racist character of Euro-American theology and the need to develop an alternative Black liberation theology. But because we generally agree on that point, we have seldom debated it among ourselves. Our discussions have involved much more than simply reacting to the racism of White theologians and church people. More important has been our concern to develop a Black theological perspective that takes seriously the *total* needs of the Black community, here and abroad. Needless to say, we have not been in total agreement about our needs, and our differences are partly reflected in the published writings on Black Theology.

The place to begin is with Joseph R. Washington, Jr., *Black Religion: The Negro and Christianity in the United States.* Before the publication of this book in 1964, most interpreters viewed Black religion as an aspect of North American Protestantism as defined by the traditions of the Reformation and contrasted with Catholicism and Judaism.[1] Washington was one of the first scholars to challenge this thesis and insisted that Black religion was a distinctive phenomenon in North American religious life. However, he viewed that distinction negatively. He contended that the unique quality of Black religion, namely, its emphasis on the quest for freedom, justice and equality in this world, prevented Blacks from developing a genuine Christian theology. Indeed, Washington ques-

---

This essay was originally published in the first edition of this book (Wilmore & Cone 1979).

tioned whether the Black religious community itself was a genuine *Christian* community (i.e., a church), since the distinctive identity of a Christian community in North America would involve participation in the Western theological tradition. According to Washington:

> Concern with the ultimate in the Christian faith and what God requires of those who are called to live responsibly in His world may easily be less than primary for a segregated minority without a theology. It is evident that a crass materialism pervades Negro congregations, overlaid with a few theological generalizations, a terminology, and a feeling for religion which when analyzed may now be more this-worldly than other-worldly. But a firm theological basis for a responsible perspective is missing, and Negro congregations are finally forced to seek purpose from the twin stimuli of social dictates and class values.[2]

Washington located the problem almost exclusively at the point of the lack of a theology in Black religious communities. In a bold assertion, which did not win him many admirers among religiously oriented Blacks, he wrote:

> Negro congregations are not churches but religious societies — religion can choose to worship whatever gods are pleasing. But a church without a theology, the interpretation of a response to the will of God for the faithful, is a contradiction in terms.[3]

The only solution to this problem in Black religious societies is for the White church to integrate them into the mainstream of American religion.

Although seldom referred to in Black scholars' critiques of Washington's book, one of its chief purposes was to criticize the White churches for excluding Black religious societies from the mainstream of American Protestantism. But his assault on the authenticity of the Black Church was so grave that no Black theologian could afford to ignore his interpretation. What precisely was at stake in Washington's interpretation of Black religion?

By defining Black religion as an instrument of social protest and excluding it as a genuine historical manifestation of Christianity, Washington undermined the connection between the Christian faith and political struggle as found in the history of the Black Church. The discipline of Black theology was developed partly to correct this distortion.[4] In view of the continuity of the secular and sacred in our African heritage and the biblical location of God's revelation in history, many of us believed that it would be a serious mistake to sever the connection between theology and politics. If we were going to protect the Black community from Washington's promotion of this widely held White thesis that the Black Church had no theology, then we needed to give some intellectual structure to the implicit Black Theology that we claimed was already present in the history of the Black Church.

The issues at stake were not simply intellectual or theoretical. They involved the identity and survival of the Black community. If it is true that the Black Church has no theology, because it has not produced professional theologians like Karl Barth or Paul Tillich, then are not White theologians and preachers correct in their almost universal tendency to separate Christianity from the political struggle of an oppressed people for freedom? If there is an inseparable connection between the Christian confession of faith and the struggle of poor people for justice, as the songs and sermons of Black Christians had suggested, then there was the need to demonstrate that connection in formal theological discourse.

The so-called riots in the cities, the cry of Black Power (Spring 1966), and James Forman's "Black Manifesto" (Spring 1969) made the situation even more acute. In response to White theologians and church people who demanded that their Black constituency denounce Black Power as unchristian, an ad hoc group of Black church people wrote a statement entitled "Black Power,"[5] which, to the surprise of the White church establishment, provided a theological defense of this emotionally charged phrase. But as Black church people themselves realized, they could not afford for the Black perspective on religion and politics to be limited to a "Black Power" statement or to other topical statements, such as those later produced by the National Conference of Black Churchmen. Such statements are too severely limited by the particularity of the historical events that occasioned them and by the lack of a clear theological structure upon which they were based. What was needed was the development of a theological methodology derived from and accountable to the Black community in the struggle for freedom.

Some of the vacuum was filled with the publication of Albert Cleage's *The Black Messiah* (Sheed and Ward, 1968). Cleage also insisted on the uniqueness of Black religion. But unlike Washington he gloried in it, claiming that Black Christianity is the only true expression of the religion of the Old Testament Israel and the New Testament Jesus, both of whom were African in their origins. Cleage's concern was to provide a Black nationalist interpretation of biblical religion and the Black Church, so that young Black Power advocates could view the church as an important agent in our struggle for justice and freedom. But Cleage's book did not have much impact in the Black church community, because it was seriously limited by its rhetorical and sermonic style, the historical and theological problems associated with his use of the terms "Black Nation" and "Black Messiah," and the absence of an ecumenical vision in his theological perspective. If Black Theology were to have any impact beyond the particularity of the American Black community, then there was a need to broaden the dialogue to include the ecumenical church. If we were going to liberate the Black church community from a mental enslavement to White definitions of the Christian gospel, then there was the need to challenge White North American theology in a larger world context.

My *Black Theology and Black Power* (Seabury, 1969) was the first book to be published on the subject of Black Theology. Its central thesis was that Black Power, contrary to dominant White theological opinion, is an authentic historical embodiment of the Christian faith in our time. This was so because Christianity is essentially a religion of liberation. Any theology, therefore, that takes this religion as its starting point must also be accountable to an oppressed community in its struggle for freedom. It was in this theological and political context that the task of Black Theology was defined as that of analyzing "black [people's] condition in the light of God's revelation in Jesus Christ with the purpose of creating a new understanding of black dignity among black people, and providing the necessary soul in that people to destroy white racism."[6]

The publication of *Black Theology and Black Power* caused a great deal of unrest in the White theological and church community. Immediately following its April 1969 appearance in seminary and college bookstores, James Forman presented the Black Manifesto at Riverside Church in New York (May 4) and NCBC's Theological Commission, in its first public statement on "Black Theology" (June 13, 1969), endorsed both Forman's concept of reparations and my view of Black Theology as liberation theology.[7] Black theologians and church people were determined not to let the White church and theological establishment escape the intellectual and political impact of Black Theology.

The following year, in *A Black Theology of Liberation* (Lippincott, 1970), I developed further the theological structure already present in *Black Theology and Black Power*, taking the theme of liberation as the organizing principle for my theological program. With the publication of this book, it was clear to some persons that Black Theology would not pass too quickly from the scene, and that what was needed was more discussion among Black theologians about the scope of their task, so that it would not be merely a reaction against errors of White theology.

My first two books on Black Theology defined several issues around which the subsequent debates among Black theologians would occur; especially (1) liberation, reconciliation, and violence; (2) Black religion and Black Theology; and (3) Black Theology and Black suffering.

1. Liberation, Reconciliation, and Violence

With the publication of J. Deotis Roberts's *Liberation and Reconciliation: A Black Theology* (Westminster, 1971), the assumption that all Black theologians agreed with my perspective on Black Theology was laid to rest. There is little doubt that Roberts was writing in response to my earlier works, and our previous discussions in the Theological Commission of NCBC and the Society for the Study of Black Religion had already prepared me for his book on Black Theology.

Roberts did not deny that liberation is as important as I would claim. Indeed he would insist with me that liberation precedes reconciliation. "Liberation," he writes, "is a proper precondition for reconciliation in the area of race relations."[8] Roberts's difficulty with my perspective is that I, according to him, have overlooked reconciliation. A Christian perspective must include both liberation *and* reconciliation. "Christians are called to be agents of liberation. We have been able to love and forgive. . . . The assertion that all are 'one in Christ Jesus' must henceforth mean that all slave-master, servant-boss, inferior-superior frames of reference between blacks and whites have been abolished."⁹ For Roberts, this means that we should begin to act as if these relations do not exist by being always open to the reconciling love in Christ Jesus. He therefore insists that Black people "must hold up at all times the possibility for black-white interracial fellowship and cooperation."¹⁰

In order to understand the debate between Roberts and me on this issue, it is necessary to note that there is a significant difference in what the terms "liberation" and "reconciliation" mean for both persons and the social context that defines them. Contrary to Roberts's implications, it is not true that I have overlooked love and reconciliation. In *Black Theology and Black Power,* there is a discussion of "Christian Love and Black Power" (pp. 47-56), and also a section on "Reconciliation" in the last chapter (pp. 143-152). The problem is that his view of love and reconciliation is different from mine, and it would have been more accurate if he had pointed that out rather than suggest that I have omitted them. I reject any view of love and reconciliation that would imply that oppressed people ought to be passive in the face of the oppressor's brutality. The weight of my perspective on love and reconciliation is located therefore at the point of guarding against any interpretation of the gospel that would render Black people powerless when confronted with White violence. I still do not see any reason why Black theologians should assure White oppressors that we want to be reconciled with them while they are brutalizing our communities.

Roberts obviously has a different concern, even though he also rejects any theology that supports Black passivity in the context of injustice. Indeed it is here that I am often confused regarding the emphasis of Roberts's theological perspective. Sometimes he seems to advocate seeking reconciliation with Whites while the latter are still in power, but at other times he explicitly makes liberation a precondition of reconciliation. How is it possible to say that "liberation is a proper precondition of reconciliation" and then also say that

> a black theology that takes reconciliation seriously must work at the task of intercommunication between blacks and whites under the assumption that for those who are open to the truth, there may be communication from the inside out, but at the same time there may be communication from the outside in. In the latter sense, white Christians may be led to understand and work with blacks for liberation and reconciliation on an interracial basis.¹¹

If liberation comes before reconciliation, then that assumption seems to negate the view that White oppressors can participate creatively in the liberation of the oppressed Blacks. Sociologically and theologically, I do not think that there is any reason to believe that oppressors can participate in the liberation of the people they hold in bondage.

Roberts takes up similar themes in a later book, *A Black Political Theology*

(Westminster, 1974). But the discussion does not appear to be any further advanced than that found in his earlier book. It seems that part of our differences on this issue is related to the different political periods in which our theological consciousness was developed. Roberts belongs to the "integration period," and I belong to the era of "Black Power." This difference in the social and political formation of our theological perspectives affects how we treat the themes of love, reconciliation, and violence. Roberts seems to make the integration of Black people into White society the primary goal of his theological endeavors, and I do not regard that as a desirable goal. I believe that Black theologians need to move beyond "civil rights" (i.e., integration of Black people into a capitalistic, oppressive White society) to a political commitment that seeks to restructure society along the lines of creative socialism.[12]

A similar point can be made also about Major Jones, whose two books on the subject of Black Theology should be mentioned, even though they have not been discussed as much as they perhaps deserve. In fact, the third volume to appear on Black Theology was Jones's *Black Awareness: A Theology of Hope* (Abingdon, 1971). He was undoubtedly borrowing from the current popularity of Jürgen Moltmann's theology of hope, and the lack of an original approach to the theme probably accounted for the absence of much serious discussion of this book in the Black theological and church community. In 1974 Jones published a second book under the title of *Christian Ethics for Black Theology* (Abingdon).

It is clear that, in both books, Jones is addressing himself to what he regards as inadequacies in my theological program. Like Roberts, he questions my view of love, reconciliation, and violence. There is no need to discuss the details of Jones's argument, because they are not significantly different from Roberts's, especially at the point of his theological perspective reflecting the "integration period" rather than the "Black Power" era. Again, like Roberts, he appears to be more concerned with presenting a theological perspective acceptable to the White church establishment than about the Black community he claims to represent.

2. Black Religion and Black Theology

No issue has generated more discussion among Black theologians than the twin questions of "What is the essence of Black religion, and what is its relation to the development of a Black Theology?" I have learned much from these discussions and regard them as having made a critical difference in the development of my theological perspective. Even a superficial reading of my writings on Black Theology will reveal a significant difference in my first two books and the last two, *The Spirituals and the Blues* (Seabury, 1972) and *God of the Oppressed* (Seabury, 1975). What precisely is at stake in the discussion, and who are some of the chief participants?

The issue of the relation between Black religion and Black Theology was first sharply defined by Charles Long, and he received much oral support from the late Carlton Lee. This debate has been subsequently taken up by Gayraud S. Wilmore (*Black Religion and Black Radicalism,* Doubleday, 1972) and my brother, Cecil Cone (*Identity Crisis in Black Theology,* AMEC, 1975).

The debate itself is not easy to describe. The issues are complex, and the participants do not agree on the theological consequences of their assumptions, even though there is general agreement on the limitation of my theological perspective. The place to begin is with Charles Long, whose viewpoint is perhaps the most influential, despite his failure to publish a long-awaited book on the subject. He has written, however, an important article, "Perspectives for a Study of Afro-American Religion in the United States" (1971),[13] that emerged out of the context of our discussions. A similar article appeared under the title "Structural Similarities and Dissimilarities in Black and African Theologies" (1975).[14]

Charles Long was one of the first persons to raise the question about the legitimacy of a Black Theology, and he did it at a time when most Black scholars took Black Theology for granted. Long did not share Joseph Washington's reduction of Black religion to the quest for freedom and equality, and he also rejected my tendency to identify Black Theology with Black Power based on a theological program whose christological structure was derived from the Western theological tradition.[15] Whether the political liberation theme was treated negatively (Washington) or positively (Cone), neither view is adequate for describing the essence of Black religion. Long is a provocative and persuasive discussant, and has won many adherents to his viewpoint, which was largely directed against my theological program.

Long's concern is to make a sharp contrast between Europe and Africa, with the latter serving as the decisive ingredient in the definition of Black religion. While being keenly aware of the scholarly difficulties in deciding the question about the persistence of African cultural elements in the North American Black communities, he is convinced that there is "a characteristic mode of orienting and perceiving reality.[16] There are the "image of Africa" and "the involuntary presence and orientation as a religious meaning."[17] Here Long introduces what he calls the "historical and present experiences of opacity,"[18] the meaning of which is not altogether clear, but definitely related to "the otherness of Blackness."

This Black reality took us down, down, way down yonder where we saw only another deeper Blackness, down where prayer is hardly more than a moan, down there where life and death seem equitable. We descended into hell, into the deepest bowels of despair, and we were becoming blacker all the time. We cried like a Job or we laughed to keep from crying and we wanted to curse God and die.[19]

According to Long, this is the reality that any serious student of Black religion cannot ignore, and it is not reducible to Christianity. Indeed this experience of blackness as Other cannot be analyzed theologically, because it is an African way of experiencing the world.

Long's radical departure on Black religion led him to question the legitimacy of a Black Theology, because theology itself is a Western theological construct, especially useful as a language of domination. Referring to Paul Tillich's Christology, Long writes: "Now Tillich's theology is a theology that presupposes the 'will to power' of modern Western civilization and it is addressed to those who have been imbued with the cultural form of inordinate and unrestrained use of power."[20] Those who are the victims of this power are the colonized and oppressed peoples.

The practical implication of Long's theoretical analysis was not entirely clear, and that partly accounts for the limitation of its influence in the Black Church and theological community. The Black community confronts a situation of oppression, and it must choose political options that will enlist participation in the struggle to transform the world. A simple call to a return to our African cultural heritage is not enough. What is the political import in our return to African culture? There is no clear answer in any of Long's published writings. While I do not minimize the need for culture if a people are going to survive in an alien society, cultural survival alone is not enough. We must survive politically with dignity by creating a social theory that will help us to transform the world according to our peoplehood.

An important contribution of Charles Long's scholarship has been its emphasis on Africa, the Caribbean, and Latin America. Thus in the early development of Black Theology, a Third World element was present. We began to realize that we could not develop a Black Theology in isolation from Blacks in other parts of the world. This global perspective that began with Africa and its diaspora would be extended to other Third World peoples.[21]

Gayraud Wilmore and Cecil Cone represent perspectives on Black religion similar to Charles Long's, but unlike Long, neither rejects theology itself. When the question is asked, "What is the proper subject matter of Black Theology?," their answer is, "Black religion." Cone and Wilmore agree with Joseph Washington in his contention that Black religion is unique and therefore cannot be subsumed under the categories of Protestant, Catholic, and Jew. They differ with Washington when the latter defines this uniqueness in terms of politics alone, instead of faith. Like Charles Long, they do not think that Black religion is reducible to political struggle even when it is related to Christianity. While Black religion has elements of Christianity and political resistance in it, neither of these elements can be elevated to the exclusion of the other. Their critique of my theological program begins precisely at this point. They claim that I have proposed a Black Theology that is based on White Western theological doctrine and the politics of Black Power, neither of which can really explain the complex phenomena of Black religion.

Since there are differences between Cone and Wilmore, it is necessary to look briefly at each theological proposal separately. The weight of Wilmore's critique is that I have simply blackened White Theology, failing to develop a unique Black Theology based on Black religion. "Is Black theology simply the blackenization of the whole spectrum of traditional Christian theology, with particular emphasis on the liberation of the oppressed, or does it find in the experience of the oppression of black people, as *black,* a single religiosity, identified not only as Christianity, but with other religions as well?"[22] While J. Deotis Roberts and Major Jones claim that I am too exclusive and not universal enough to include White people, Wilmore claims that I am too universal and not exclusive enough. Wilmore says that I am too oriented toward Christian categories as defined by White theology and have not paid sufficient attention to the complete uniqueness of Black religion.

Cecil Cone's perspective is similar to Wilmore's. He contends that since Black religion is unique and should be the foundation of Black Theology, the error of Black theologians has been their failure to recognize this uniqueness (Roberts and me) or of having located it in the wrong place (Washington). The failure to use Black religion as the foundation of Black Theology has produced an identity crisis in this discipline. This identity crisis is located at two points. First, the tools which Black theologians use to do Black Theology are derived from White seminaries and are therefore inadequate for understanding Black religion and thus for developing a Black Theology. Second, while Black religion is related to Black Power, it is not identical with it or with any political program.

According to Cecil Cone, these two chief characteristics of Black Theology have produced an identity crisis, because they separate Black Theology from the essence of Black religion. The essence of Black religion is found in its distinctive origin in Africa with the focus on the Almighty Sovereign God. Both Wilmore and Cecil Cone agree with Melville Herskovits in his debate with E. Franklin Frazier on the issue of African survivals.[23] Both also contend that Black religion in North America is not reducible to Christian doctrine. And Cecil Cone, with Charles Long, would add that it is not identical with the politics of Black Power.

Wilmore is interested in a definition of Black Theology that will speak to Black "street people," the non-Christian, and the cult-oriented religions of the Americas, the Caribbean, and Africa. Therefore his list of sources for Black Theology includes the following: (1) "the existing Black community, where the tradition of Black folk religion is still extant and continues to stand over and against the institutional church ... "; (2) "the writings and addresses of the Black preacher and the public men of the past ... "; and (3) "the traditional religions of Africa."[24] There is no reference to Scripture or Jesus Christ in the sources. Because of Wilmore's failure to use the Scripture and Jesus Christ as theological sources, his approach to Black Theology will be more acceptable among non-Christian Blacks (especially nationalists) than among Black Christians in the institutional Church, for whom Jesus Christ is the most important religious symbol.

Cecil Cone's perspective is closer to the Black institutional Church than Wilmore's. Wilmore is a member of the predominantly White Presbyterian Church and has spent much of his time making that church and other White churches take seriously the political demands of Black nationalists and other radical Black non-Christians.[25] Cecil Cone, on the other hand, wants to rehabilitate the institutional Black Church, because he believes it to be the primary instrument of Black liberation. Therefore he is critical of Black Theology's allegiance to Black Power, while Wilmore is not. Both are critical of Black Theology's dependence on White theological categories, but for different reasons. Wilmore wants a Black Theology that is accountable to the non-Christian Blacks, and Cecil Cone is concerned about the absolute integrity of the Black institutional Church.

As I suggested earlier, I have learned much from this discussion on Black religion and Black Theology, because there is a basic truth in the critiques of Long, Cone, and Wilmore. I have endeavored to incorporate this basic truth into *The Spirituals and the Blues* (1972) and *God of the Oppressed* (1975). If the struggle of the victims is the only context for the development of a genuine Christian theology, then should not theology itself reflect in its speech the language of the people about whom it claims to speak? This is the critical issue. When this assumption is applied to Black Theology, I think that Black religion or the Black religious experience must become one of the important ingredients in the development of a Black Theology. In his critical interpretations of Joseph Washington, J. Deotis Roberts, and my theological viewpoint, Cecil Cone has demonstrated the limitations of our perspectives at this point, even though he overstated his case and tended to be too superficial in his analysis of Black religion.

However, my concession on the importance of Black religion does not mean that I agree with their various interpretations of Black religion or the theological programs they seek to develop. Aside from the historical problems in the recovery of our African past, which only Charles Long seems to realize, all three appear to be unaware of the theological import of their historical suggestions. Long even makes the absurd contention that there can be no Black Theology based on Black religion. If he expects this point to be taken seriously, he will need to develop it much less in his sermonic oral style and much more comprehensively and systematically.

Cecil Cone and Gayraud Wilmore have a similar theological problem. While they do not reject the possibility of a Black Theology, both fail to say what Black Theology would look like if their suggestions about Black religion were taken seriously. There are several important questions which they need to answer. Is there anything in Black Theology that criticizes Black religion? If not, what is there in Black Theology that will prevent it from becoming ideology? It is interesting that neither raises this question. If Black religion is the *only* source for Black Theology, and if Black religion is identical with the *only* possible interpretation of the Bible for Black people, then what is the universality implied in the particularity of Black religion? Without this universalism, I do not see how we can make any Christian or human claims about Black religion. (The Christian identity of Black religion seems still to be important for Cecil Cone, and its human outreach is significant for Wilmore.) To be

Christian and human means developing a perspective on life that includes all peoples.

Both Cecil Cone and Gayraud Wilmore's books end where I think they need to begin. They only devote a few pages to the future directions of Black Theology, and neither has proceeded to develop Black Theology according to their suggestions. Wilmore claims to be a social ethicist and Cecil Cone is deeply involved in the life of the institution he seeks to rehabilitate (African Methodist Episcopal Church). It would appear that Cecil Cone's existential involvement in the A.M.E. Church prevents his creative criticism of Black religion and thereby limits his theological imagination. The same is true of Wilmore in his concern for Black nationalists, especially non-Christians. But my question to both is this: What is the critical principle that should be used in the theological assessment of the Black Church or Black nationalism? This is the hard question which both appear to avoid but which desperately needs to be addressed. I have tried to answer this question by appealing to the biblical Christ who is present in the Black experience but not limited to it.[26]

Cecil Cone appears to equate the testimonies of Black people's experiences of God and Jesus with the biblical portrayal of them, without even asking whether the two (Bible and Black experience) are identical. If it makes no difference what the Scripture says and the only thing that matters is what Black religion says, then he should say that. He should not only assert it but be prepared to make a reasonable theological argument on its behalf. This same point is applicable to Wilmore in relation to Black nationalism. We Black theologians should not only be prepared to answer what a certain *segment* of the Black community thinks about the ultimate, but also the question, "What is the truth as applied to humanity?" I do not believe that we should limit our analysis of the truth to a certain ethnic manifestation of it in the Black community. This means that our development of a Black Theology must start with the particularity of the Black experience but cannot be limited to it. Therefore, we should create a perspective on Black Theology that invites other oppressed peoples to share with us in the search for the truth that defines us all. We must not allow Black Theology to reduce itself to an ethnic particularism.

As I suggested in an earlier comment about Charles Long, I am bothered by the lack of political vision inherent in Cecil Cone's analysis of Black religion. His analysis of Black religion is so "spiritual" and thus separated from politics that what he says about Black religion appears to be no different from conservative White evangelical Protestantism. What is the difference between Black religion and White evangelical Protestantism if the former must be radically distinguished from politics? Again it is revealing that Cecil Cone does not raise this question. It is a question that needs to be answered because most interpreters who appeal to the distinctiveness of Black religion and also insist on its *Christian* identity locate the uniqueness at the point of Black religion's focus on politics. The other possibility is to insist on Black religion's uniqueness but reject its primary Christian identity, a perspective represented by Long and Wilmore. But Cecil Cone appears to insist on Black religion's uniqueness with-

out connecting it with politics or denying its primary Christian identity. Since
he simply asserts his views about Black religion and Christianity without asking
critical questions that seem to contradict his viewpoint, his analysis is often
more confusing than clarifying.

We Black theologians cannot afford to ignore our political responsibility. For
example, when the Black Church becomes politically conservative and defends
that conservatism with a theological terminology similar to White evangelical
Protestantism, what is the task of Black Theology? When Black Church preachers, bishops, and church executives begin to define the Black Church in the
light of their own personal interests, is there anything in Cecil Cone's perspective on Black Theology that could critique them? When Black nationalists
become so narrow in their view of Black reality, is there anything in Wilmore's
perspective on Black Theology that could stand in judgment upon them? Of
all the things we may say about our needs in Black Theology, we cannot ignore
the need for creative criticism of Black religion and the Black Church, lest both
become instruments of Black enslavement.

3. Black Theology and Black Suffering

Another important discussion among Black theologians has centered around
the writings of William Jones, and it has focused on the problem of Black
suffering generally and theodicy in particular. Although Roy Morrison has not
written extensively on this issue, he also shares Jones's concern.[27] Both approach
the themes in Black Theology from the perspective of philosophers of religion
with no particular commitment to the Christian faith or the Black Church. I
will limit my comments to Jones because he has been the most active and
provocative discussant and also the most widely published.

In his book, *Is God a White Racist?* (1973), Jones uses Albert Camus and
Jean-Paul Sartre in order to raise the problem of suffering in a fashion similar
to what is found in the history of Western theology. If God is good and all-
powerful, why is there so much evil? He takes this philosophical understanding
of the problem and applies it to the writings of Albert Cleage, J. Deotis Roberts,
Joseph Washington, Major Jones, and myself. He presents an argument from
a Black humanist perspective, and no Black theologian should ignore the
cogency of his analysis. Since Jones first raised this issue in an article in the
Harvard Theological Review, it has received much discussion among Black theologians.

It is important to note that Jones claims to make an *internal* critique of Black
theologians' various programs of Black Theology in the light of their own
assumptions about the liberating activity of God in the world. He contends that
in view of what Black theologians claim about God and Black people *and* the
continued presence of Black suffering, each of their versions of Black Theology
has an internal logical contradiction that cannot be tolerated. His critique of
my perspective can be stated in this manner: If God is the liberator of Black
victims, as you claim he delivered Israel from Egypt, where then is the empirical

evidence that warrants that assertion of faith? If I claim that there is no empirical evidence, then Jones would say that that assertion contradicts what I say about God's liberating action in history. If God is involved in history, then there should be some empirical evidence of that involvement. Where then is the proof of your assertion that God is the God of oppressed Blacks, liberating them from bondage? Without an exaltation-liberation event, there is no basis for the theological claim.

The substance of my response to Jones is found in *God of the Oppressed,* chapter 8, "Divine Liberation and Black Suffering." I will not rehearse the details of my argument here, but the main point is that the Christ-event is the exaltation-liberation event to which Christians turn in order to answer the question that Jones raises. Because Jones does not refer to my Christology as the internal answer to the theodicy question in Black Theology, his claim to be doing only internal criticism is questionable.

However, as an *external* critique from the vantage point of Black humanism, Jones's analysis remains as a challenge to Black theological proposals and will continue to require the serious attention of Black theologians. We cannot remain satisfied with an easy *internal* solution, because what we say about God and suffering should be publicly defensible outside the confessional contexts from which they emerge. If we do not test the credibility of our theological judgments in a public arena, without resource to confessional narrowness, then we should not complain if what we say about God is ignored by those outside of our confession of faith. It is because Christians claim to have a universal message that they are required to speak its truth in a language publicly accessible to all. What then do Christians have to say about the continued presence of evil when we claim that God is both all-good and all-powerful? The historical character of divine revelation makes this question critically important.

I do not think that there is a definitive answer to the problem of suffering. Every generation of Christians must continue to try to give a response to the question of how one can believe in God in the context of human suffering. Two points can be made.

First, suffering is the source of faith. That is, without human suffering, there would be no need for the Christian gospel in particular or religion generally. Ludwig Feuerbach was right: "Thought is preceded by suffering." There would be no need for a Christian doctrine of salvation if there were no evil in the world. Therefore the gospel is the Christian answer to human misery.

Second, while the Christian faith arises out of suffering, suffering is the most serious contradiction of faith. This is the paradox. If the gospel of God is the answer to human misery, why do people still continue to suffer? There is no easy answer to this question.

I think that the only appropriate Christian and human answer is located at the point of what it causes people to do who are victimized by oppression. There is no way to answer to everyone's satisfaction the question of the objective status of God in relation to suffering, but we can ask about the political implications of our theological and philosophical claims. The problem with Jones's analysis and with many other philosophical treatments of suffering is that they are unlikely to engage the victims of injustice in the fight against those who enslave them. Jones's analysis can easily lead to despair, whereas belief in the presence of God in an oppressed community *can* lead to the empowerment of that community to struggle even though the odds may be against them. The task of Black Theology is to make sure that Black faith remains critical of itself so that Black religion can continue to function as a creative revolutionary challenge to the structures of injustice. If Jones can provide an interpretation of humanity and divinity that captures the imagination of poor people and enlists them in the struggle against oppression, at a deeper level than found in Black religion, then I would support his theological program. But I do not think that such an alternative is found in Black humanism.

NOTES

1. See Will Herberg, *Protestant, Catholic, and Jew* (Garden City, N.Y.: Doubleday, Anchor Books, 1960).
2. *Black Religion: The Negro and Christianity in the United States* (Boston: Beacon Press, 1964), p. 141.
3. Ibid., pp. 142-143.
4. A similar comment on the use of Black Theology in relation to Washington's interpretation of Black religion is found in Gayraud S. Wilmore, "Black Theology: It's Significance for Christian Mission Today," *International Review of Mission*, vol. 63, no. 250 (April 1974).
5. See Document 2 of Wilmore & Cone 1979.
6. *Black Theology and Black Power* (New York: Seabury Press, 1969), p. 117.
7. James Forman's "Black Manifesto" and NCBC's first "Black Theology" statement are found in this volume as Documents 2 and 3 respectively.
8. *Liberation and Reconciliation: A Black Theology* (Philadelphia: Westminster Press, 1971), p. 117.
9. Ibid., p. 72.
10. Ibid.
11. Ibid., p. 23.
12. For more information of my critique of Roberts, see my *God of the Oppressed* (New York: Seabury, 1975), chap. 10. See also our reviews of each other's books in the *Journal of the Interdenominational Theological Center*, vol. 3, no. 1 (Fall 1975).
13. *History of Religion*, vol. 11, no. 1 (August 1971).
14. *The Journal of Religious Thought*, vol. 32, no. 2 (Fall-Winter 1975). Other articles that make a similar point are "Civil Rights—Civil Religion: Visible People and Invisible Religion," in R.E. Richey and D.G. Jones, *American Civil Religion* (New York: Harper Forum Books, 1974); "The Oppressive Elements in Religion and the Religions of the Oppressed," *Harvard Theological Review*, vol. 69, no. 3-4 (1976).
15. See his references to Washington and me in "Perspectives for a Study of Afro-American Religion in the United States." His critique of Washington and me is directly influenced by his dialogue with Carlton L. Lee. See the latter's review of Joseph Washington's "Black Religion" in *The Christian Scholar*, Fall 1965. See also Jerome Long's review in *Foundation*, October 1964.
16. "Structural Similarities and Dissimilarities in Black and African Theologies," p. 10.
17. Ibid., p. 13.
18. Ibid., p. 21.
19. Ibid.
20. Ibid., p. 19.

21. On the issue of the Third World, note the gradual development of this concern for Third World people in the various statements of the National Conference of Black Churchmen. In "Black Power" and "Racism and the Elections" (both issued in 1966), there is no reference to the Third World. But in "A Message to the Churches from Oakland" (1969, Document 11 of Wilmore & Cone, 1979), there are specific references to the Third World (especially Africa and the Caribbean), a condemnation of racism, capitalism, and imperialism. This same concern is continued in its subsequent statements to its most recent Atlanta statement: "Message to the Black Church and Community" (1977, Document 34 of Wilmore & Cone, 1979).

22. *Black Religion and Black Radicalism* (Garden City, N.Y.: Doubleday, 1972), p. 296.

23. See Melville Herskovits, *Myth of the Negro Past* (Boston: Beacon, 1969); E. Franklin Frazier, *The Negro Church in America* (New York: Schocken, 1962).

24. Wilmore, *Black Religion and Black Radicalism*, pp. 298, 300.

25. Before Wilmore's recent tenure as the Martin Luther King, Jr., Professor at Boston University and now Colgate Rochester/Bexley Hall/Crozer, he was the Chairperson of the Division of Church and Race of the United Presbyterian Church in the United States of America. On the issues of getting his church in particular and the White church generally to respond creatively to the Black struggle of freedom in the 1960s and 1970s, few persons made a greater contribution than Wilmore. His challenge to his church involved support for Angela Davis, for James Forman's "Black Manifesto," and for Black Theology. See his "Reparations: Don't Get Hung Up on a Word," *Theology Today*, vol. 26, no. 3 (October 1969), and an early essay introducing Black Theology entitled "Stalking the Wild Black Theologian," in *Social Progress*, vol. 60, no. 1 (October 1969).

26. I have discussed this issue directly in *A Black Theology of Liberation* (Philadelphia: Lippincott, 1970), chap. 2; and in *God of the Oppressed*, chap. 2.

27. William Jones's earliest article on this theme appeared in the *Harvard Theological Review*, vol. 64, no. 4 (October 1971): "Theodicy and Methodology in Black Theology: A Critique of Washington, Cone and Cleage" and is reprinted above as Document 11. See also Roy D. Morrison II, "Black Philosophy: An Instrument for Cultural and Religious Liberation," *Journal of Religious Thought*, vol. 33, no. 1 (Spring-Summer 1976).

ANNOTATED BIBLIOGRAPHY
OF BLACK THEOLOGY
1966-1979

Mark L. Chapman

The emergence of Black Power in the late 1960s produced a theological revolution in the African American religious community. A great number of articles and books rolled off the printing presses seeking to articulate a new self-consciously Black perspective on the Christian faith. The articles and books selected in this bibliography are representative of the range and diversity of this explosion in Black theological reflection. Needless to say there are many important works not included in this bibliography, but the articles and books listed below are among the most significant attempts to write a Black theology of liberation. In the selection and annotations of the works cited, I have attempted to demonstrate the diversity of perspectives that characterized nascent Black theology. At no point in its development has Black theology been a monolithic enterprise. While a commitment to Black liberation is seen in all of the writings cited below, special attention has been given to highlight the issues that Black theologians have debated among themselves. This bibliography also operates on the claim that articles are a better source for studying the early formation and development of Black theology than full length books. The articles provide an excellent introduction to the issues surrounding the emergence and systematic development of Black theology. It is hoped that the reader will find this annotated bibliography useful in the study of Black theology.

Articles Published 1966-1979

Cleage, Albert B., Jr. "The Black Messiah and the Black Revolution." In *Quest For A Black Theology,* edited by J. Deotis Roberts and James J. Gardiner, 1–21. Philadelphia: Pilgrim Press, 1971.

This essay analyzes the negative impact of integration on the minds of Blacks who believed they must renounce their African heritage in order to be accepted by White society. The author argues that although Blacks accepted a slave Christianity

---

Mark L. Chapman is instructor of Afro-American Studies at Fordham University.

from their masters and made it into an instrument of survival, the Black Church must now respond to the needs of the Black revolution. The author's major claim is that White distortions of Christianity must be discarded in order to show Blacks that the original Christian faith (Jesus the Black Messiah sent to rebuild the Black nation of Israel) is consistent with the goals of the Black revolution.

Cone, Cecil W. "Toward a New Introduction to Christian Theology: Telling the Story." *Journal of the Interdenominational Theological Center* 3 (Spring 1976): 17–27.

This article examines the biblical story of salvation and deliverance as the foundation for Christian theology. The author argues that Western theology from Justin Martyr to Martin Luther has failed to emphasize the biblical story of God's revelation in the Exodus as the starting point for theology. The author concludes that Black theology is an authentic expression of Christianity because it takes seriously the biblical story in its theological discourse.

Cone, James H. "Christianity and Black Power." In *Is Anybody Listening to Black America?,* edited by C. Eric Lincoln, 3–9. New York: Seabury Press, 1968.

This seminal essay represents the author's first attempt to relate the Christian gospel to the message of Black Power. The author argues that the goals of Black Power are consistent with the Christian message of freedom and liberation. On the basis of this observation, the author claims that Black Power is not alien to Christianity, but rather is Christ's central message to twentieth-century America. This very important essay was the foundation for the author's book *Black Theology and Black Power* (1969).

Cone, James H. "Black Consciousness and the Black Church." *Christianity and Crisis* 30 (2 and 16 November 1970): 244–250.

This article examines the impact of the Black consciousness movement on the Black Church. The author argues that as Blacks began to better understand the sources of their victimization, they expressed a renewed determination to glorify Blackness and resist White oppression. The author discusses the roots of Black consciousness in Black history, and concludes by examining the relationship between biblical faith and Black liberation and the role of the church in the Black freedom struggle.

Cone, James H. "Theological Reflections on Reconciliation." *Christianity and Crisis* 32 (22 January 1973): 303–308.

In this article the author discusses the Christian doctrine of reconciliation in relation to the theme of liberation. The author's central claim is that according to the Bible, divine liberation is always the precondition of reconciliation. The author is critical of interpretations of reconciliation that dehistoricize the work of Christ and separates it from God's liberation acts in history. The author concludes that in the context of race relations, reconciliation means fighting against the structures of oppression and putting an end to white-skin privilege.

Cone, James H. "Black Theology on Revolution, Violence, and Reconciliation." *Union Seminary Quarterly Review* 31 (Fall 1975): 5–14.

This article seeks to answer the question "How is Christianity related to the

Black revolution in America?" The author discusses the role of Western Christianity as a supporter of the status quo and argues that the true content of the gospel is liberation. The author argues that the problem of violence is not what Blacks do in resisting their oppression, but what the structures of White society do to perpetuate the victimization of Black people. The author concludes that there can be no reconciliation between Blacks and Whites as long as Blacks are oppressed by the social, political, and economic structures of White society.

Cone, James H. "Black Theology and the Black College Student." *Journal of Afro-American Issues* 4 (Summer-Fall 1976): 420–431.

This important article examines the diminishing respect for Christianity among African-American college and university students. The author discusses his participation as chair of the religion workshop at the first annual convention of the Congress of African People in Atlanta (1970), and his response to the charge that Christianity is "the White man's religion." The author argues that while Black Christianity has often failed to live up to the faith it affirms, it has been a liberating force in the Black freedom struggle from slavery to the present, and therefore cannot be discarded.

Cone, James H. "Sanctification, Liberation, and Black Worship." *Theology Today* 35 (July 1978): 139–152.

In this important article the author interprets the spiritual foundations of Black worship. The author first discusses the role of the Holy Spirit in the Black religious experience, and then identifies six principal components of Black worship: preaching, singing, shouting, conversion, prayer, and testimony. The author goes on to discuss each element separately, and concludes that Black worship and Black spirituality have been indispensable ingredients in the historic Black liberation struggle.

Edwards, Herbert O. "Black Theology: Retrospect and Prospect." *Journal of Religious Thought* 32 (Fall-Winter 1975): 46–59.

This article is an evaluation of Black theology in light of three tasks the author believes every new theological movement must accomplish: prove the inadequacy of previous and existing theologies for the present crisis; demonstrate its own adequacy for the present moment; and establish its continuity with normative expressions of the faith. The author argues that Black theology addresses all of these tasks, but that its value and acceptance by the Black Church has not been fully determined.

Garber, Paul R. "Black Theology: The Latter Day Legacy of Martin Luther King, Jr." *Journal of the Interdenominational Theological Center* 2 (Spring 1975): 100–113.

This important article examines the impact of King's life and message on the emergence of Black theology. The author argues that while Black theologians such as James Cone may not be overt disciples of King, King's commitment to Black liberation is his central legacy to Black theology. The author concludes with a brief discussion of the diversity of perspectives in Black theology. This article serves as a necessary corrective for those who think that King and Black theology have nothing in common.

Harding, Vincent. "Black Power and the American Christ." In *Black Theology: A Documentary History, 1966–1979*. Edited by Gayraud S. Wilmore and James H.

Cone. Maryknoll: Orbis Books, 1979: 35–42. First appeared in *Christian Century* (4 January 1967).

This article is a critique of American Christianity from the perspective of Black Power. The author interprets Black Power as a response to the hypocrisy of American Christianity, and suggests that God is using the Black Power movement to speak a word of judgment on the White Church in the United States. This important article helps to explain why many young Black Power advocates repudiated Christianity in the late 1960s.

Harding, Vincent. "The Religion of Black Power." In *The Religious Situation: 1968*, edited by D. R. Cutler. Boston: Beacon Press, 1968.

This very important article represents one of the first attempts to analyze the religious elements of the Black Power movement. The author discusses the essential ingredients of Black Power ideology and illuminates the religious issues they point to. The author interprets the mood of Black Power by explicating its understanding of love, messianism, resurrection, Black leadership, self-defense, and the nature and purpose of power. The author then provides a critique of Martin Luther King, Jr.'s argument against violence as a means of social change and his response to the emergence of Black Power. The author concludes that Black Power is a serious religious option for African Americans seeking to express their spirituality.

Johnson, Joseph A. "The Need for a Black Christian Theology." *Journal of the Interdenominational Theological Center* 2 (Fall 1974): 19–29.

This article examines the emergence of Black theology as a response to the inability of classical Euro-American theologies to relate the Christian gospel to the Black experience. The author discusses the acceptance of Christianity by African slaves, and notes that liberation has always been at the core of Black Christian faith. The author concludes with an interpretation of the role of Christology in the Black religious experience.

Jones, Major J. "Black Awareness: Theological Implications of the Concept." *Religion In Life* 38 (Autumn 1969): 389–403.

This article examines the emergence of Black awareness and its implications for theology. The author discusses the Black search for self-identity and applauds the positive benefits of the Black awareness movement. However, the author raises questions about the validity of some theological appropriations of the concept that distort the universal nature of Judeo-Christian faith. This article lays the foundation for the author's book *Black Awareness: A Theology of Hope* (1971).

Jones, William R. "Theodicy: The Controlling Category for Black Theology." *Journal of Religious Thought* 30 (Spring-Summer 1973): 28–38.

In this article the author discusses the role of theodicy in Black theology. The author argues that because Black theology presents itself as a theology of liberation, it must make theodicy its central category. The author believes that Black theologians must be able to point to definitive exaltation-liberation events in order to demonstrate that perpetual Black suffering is not the will of God. The author concludes that Black theology must essentially become an extended theodicy.

Jones, William R. "Toward an Interim Assessment of Black Theology." *The Christian Century* 89 (May 3, 1972): 513–517.

This article proposes a set of interpretive principles for appraising Black theology. The author argues that Black theology must be understood as a strategy of Black liberation that is also concerned to legitimate its existence as authentic Christian theology. The author notes that Black theology is not monolithic, and that internal critique is an important stage in its development. The author concludes that Black theology is still in the formative stages of development and deserves the support of the church universal.

Long, Charles H. "Perspectives for a Study of Afro-American Religion in the United States." *History of Religions* 11 (August 1971): 54–66.

In this important article the author provides an interpretation of Black religion from the perspective of an historian of religions. The author argues that most studies of Black religion adopt either a social-scientific or theological-apologetic perspective. The author seeks to move beyond these limited traditions by proposing three interrelated perspectives for the study of Black religion: Africa as historical reality and a religious image; the involuntary presence of the Black community in the United States; and the experience and symbol of God in the Black religious experience. The author interprets spirituals, folklore, and proverbs in his attempt to prove that an interpretation of religious consciousness is more fruitful for the study of Afro-American religion than a purely existential analysis.

Long, Charles H. "Structural Similarities and Dissimilarities in Black and African Theologies." *Journal of Religious Thought* 32 (Fall-Winter 1975): 9–24

Drawing on the foundation of his 1971 essay cited above, this article examines the relation between Black theology in the United States and African theology. The author analyzes the image of land; the image and historical reality of Africa; and the use of biblical motifs in Black and African theologies. The author discusses these issues in relation to the symbol of "opaque," and concludes that the experience of Blackness and its impact on religious consciousness is a common thread linking Black and African theologies.

McKinney, Richard I. "Reflections on the Concept of 'Black Theology.' " *Journal of Religious Thought* 26 (Summer Supplement 1969): 10–14.

This article is representative of the misgivings most pre-Black Power African American religious thinkers had concerning the emergence of Black theology. The author argues that Black theology jeopardizes the universal nature of the Christian faith; is designed to further polarize Blacks and Whites; and is essentially a substitution of one racism for another. Although the author is extremely skeptical about the viability of a Black theology, he does note that the concept would be acceptable if it avoided the pitfalls mentioned above.

Mitchell, Henry H. "Black Power and the Christian Church." *Foundations* (April-July 1968): 99–109.

This article presents one of the earliest theological responses to the challenge of Black Power. The author calls for an examination of the uniqueness of Black religious culture as a source for Black theological reflections. The author concludes that the distinctiveness of Black religious culture is not only a rich source for the development of a new Black theological tradition, but also contains insights for the White Church as well.

Roberts, J. Deotis. "The Black Caucus and the Failure of Christian Theology." *Journal of Religious Thought* 26 (Summer Supplement 1969): 15–25.

In this article the author critiques American Christianity for failing to respond theologically to the racial crisis. The author discusses the need to make Christian theology relevant to the problem of racism, and examines the emergence of Black caucuses in White denominations as a response to the Black Power movement. The author calls for the development of a Black theology that makes the eternal message of the gospel relevant to Black consciousness and Black pride; and that addresses the reality of life in the ghetto proclaiming the Christian message of hope and deliverance.

Roberts, J. Deotis. "Black Consciousness in Theological Perspective." In *Quest For a Black Theology*, edited by J. Deotis Roberts and James J. Gardiner. Philadelphia: Pilgrim Press, 1971.

This essay examines the emergence of Black consciousness and its implications for the development of a Black theology. The author discusses the urgent need for more Black theologians to reflect on the meaning of the Christian faith in light of the Black experience. The author concludes by suggesting an agenda for the constructive phase of Black theology that includes: the providence of God, the nature of power, the issue of theodicy, and the reality of sin in both its personal and social dimensions.

Roberts, J. Deotis. "Black Liberation Theism." *Journal of Religious Thought* 33 (Spring-Summer 1976): 25–35.

This article is a critique of the religious humanism of William Jones and the christocentric theism of James Cone. The author believes that the position of Jones seems limited to a select few of the Black middle class, and that Cone's christocentrism limits the possibilities for dialogue with Blacks who are committed to liberation but not Christianity. The author proposes his own position of Black liberation theism as a mediating perspective between Jones and Cone.

Rooks, Charles Shelby. "Toward the Promised Land: An Analysis of the Religious Experience of Black Americans." *The Black Church* (journal of the Black Ecumenical Commission of Massachusetts) 2 (1972): 1–48.

This important essay examines the development of Black theology and its significance for shaping the ministry of the Black Church. The author argues that the image of the African diaspora based on the biblical story of the Babylonian Exile offers more immediate parallels to the contemporary situation of Blacks than does the image of the Exodus frequently used by Black theologians. The author concludes with a discussion of the role of the minister and the church in the African American Christian community.

Williams, Preston N. "The Ethical Aspects of the Black Church—Black Theology Phenomenon." *Journal of Religious Thought* 26 (Summer Supplement 1969): 34–45.

This article is an interpretation of the emergence of Black theology from the perspective of a social ethicist. The author examines the ethical implications of the 1966 NCBC Black Power statement and relates it to the problem of race relations in America. The author concludes with a discussion of the prophetic role of Black theology as a critic of White society and the White Church.

Williams, Preston N. "James Cone and the Problem of a Black Ethic." *Harvard Theological Review* 65 (1972): 483–494.

This article is an interpretation of the theological ethics implicit in James Cone's first two books, *Black Theology and Black Power* (1969) and *A Black Theology of Liberation* (1971). The author argues that Cone's unqualified acceptance of the Black revolution compromises a commitment to a universal Christian ethic. The author proposes an alternative ethic that emphasizes the need for Blacks to take responsibility for their own actions and to hold White America accountable to the promises of the Constitution. The author urges Cone to adopt an ethic that is based on rational debate and free choice rather than on a passionate defense of the gut emotions in the Black community.

Williams, Robert C. "Moral Suasion and Militant Aggression in the Theological Perspective of Black Religion." *Journal of Religious Thought* 30 (Fall-Winter 1973–74): 27–50.

In this important article the author examines the strategies of moral suasion and militant aggression in Black history, and relates them to the theological perspectives of James Cone and Albert Cleage respectively. The author argues that Cone's theology basically adopts the moral suasion strategy practiced by Frederick Douglass, W. E. B. Du Bois, and Martin Luther King, Jr.; while Cleage utilizes the militant aggression strategy practiced by Henry Highland Garnett, Marcus Garvey, and Malcolm X. The author concludes that although these perspectives are valid interpretations of the Black religious experience, they do not make use of sufficient folkloristic, historical, and sociological source materials.

Wilmore, Gayraud S. "Report of the Theological Commission Project of the National Conference of Negro Churchmen — Fall 1968." In *Christian Faith in Black and White*, edited by Warner Traynham, 83–90. Wakefield, Mass: Parameter Press, 1973.

This very important document traces the activity of the NCNC in its first two years of existence and summarizes the work of the group's theological commission, which was chaired by the author. In the summer of 1968 the commission solicited the responses of twenty scholars of the Black Church and theologians to a series of questions regarding key themes that would later occupy the thoughts of Black theologians. The questions and responses provide an excellent introduction to the emergence of Black theology.

Wilmore, Gayraud S. "Martin Luther King, Jr. — 20th-Century Prophet." In *Asians and Blacks*, edited by Kyaw Than, 64–75. Bangkok, Thailand: East Asia Christian Conference, 1972.

This important essay analyzes the life and ministry of Martin Luther King, Jr., in relation to Malcolm X. The author examines the impact of King's ministry on the Black Church in the 1950s and 1960s, and then discusses the life and thought of Malcolm X. The author argues that the ministries of Martin and Malcolm complemented each other and must therefore be evaluated together. The author interprets both men as the product of Black folk religion, and concludes that one cannot grasp the religious foundations of the Black revolution without understanding the manner in which Martin and Malcolm challenged and supported each other.

Wilmore, Gayraud S. "Black Theology: Its Significance for Christian Mission Today." *International Review of Mission* 63 (April 1974): 211–231.

This important article provides a thorough discussion of the origin and development of Black theology in the United States. The author argues that Black theology arose to correct the false claim made by Joseph R. Washington in *Black Religion* (1964) that Black churches had no theology and therefore were not Christian. The author then discusses four major issues in the development of Black theology: the meaning of authority, Blackness, liberation and reconciliation, and the mission of the church. The author concludes that Black theology's emphasis on liberation as the core of the gospel has important implications for the church universal.

Wilmore, Gayraud S. "The New Context of Black Theology in the United States." In *Mission Trends No. 4: Liberation Theologies*, edited by G. H. Anderson and T. F. Stransky, 113–122. New York: Paulist Press.

This article examines the strengths and weaknesses of nascent Black theology. The author believes that the participation of Black theologians at the 1975 Detroit Conference of Theology in the Americas helped to create a new context for Black theology that takes seriously other ethnic theologies including Native American, Asian American, and Hispanic voices. The author concludes that an openness to other theologies should not detract from the need for each ethnic group to do its own contextual theology.

Wright, Leon E. "Black Theology or Black Experience." *Journal of Religious Thought* 26 (Summer Supplement 1969): 46–56.

This article is an interpretation of the theme of suffering and oppression in the Black experience. The author believes that the Black experience of suffering is representative of universal human suffering, and is thus a viable point of departure for Christian theology in general. However, the author makes an important distinction between Christian theological reflection on the Black experience of suffering and the notion of "Black theology," which appears to him to be simply a reaction to White racism.

Books Published 1966–1979

Boesak, Allan A. *Farewell to Innocence: A Socio-Ethical Study on Black Theology and Black Power.* Maryknoll, N.Y.: Orbis Books, 1977.

This text represents one of the first book-length attempts to write a Black theology from a South African perspective. The author draws on the insights of Black theologians in the United States in his discussion of the Black Messiah; the impact of Black Power and Black consciousness on an interpretation of the gospel; and the question of ideology in Black theology. The author also seeks to develop a Black ethic that is suitable for the Black liberation struggle in South Africa. This book is a very important work in the history of Black theology in South Africa.

Bruce, Calvin E. and William R. Jones, eds. *Black Theology II: Essays on the Formation and Outreach of Contemporary Black Theology.* Lewisburg, Pa.: Bucknell University Press, 1978.

This book is a collection of essays that seeks to address the future direction of Black theology. The editors believe that these essays represent the constructive, second phase of Black theology that moves beyond "the rage stage" of works done by James Cone, Albert Cleage, and others. The authors examine the relation between political and spiritual liberation; the mission of the church and its theologians; and Black theology's dialogue with White male and feminist theology.

Cleage, Albert B., Jr. *The Black Messiah.* New York: Sheed and Ward, 1968.

This important text is a collection of sermons by the founder of the Shrine of the Black Madonna in Detroit. These messages attempt to relate Christianity to the Black revolution that swept across the nation in the late 1960s. The author's central claim is that Jesus was a Black revolutionary zealot whose primary goal was to free the Black nation of Israel from Roman oppression. This book along with Cone's *Black Theology and Black Power* (1969) are the two most important texts in the history of the Black theology movement.

Cleage, Albert B., Jr. *Black Christian Nationalism: New Directions for the Black Church.* New York: Morrow, 1972.

This book is a manifesto of the Black Christian Nationalist Movement founded by the author. The author argues that Black people constitute a nation within American society and that Black Christian Nationalism is a program designed to support the Black liberation struggle. The reader should note the influence of Malcolm X and the Nation of Islam on the author's articulation of the nature and program of Black Christian Nationalism.

Cone, Cecil W. *The Identity Crisis in Black Theology.* Nashville: The African Methodist Episcopal Church, 1975.

This book is an analysis of the problem of identity in the development of Black theology. The author critiques the theologies of Joseph R. Washington, James Cone, and J. Deotis Roberts pointing to the tensions inherent in their perspectives. The author argues that their desire to be accepted by the White theological establishment on the one hand and their commitment to the ideology of Black Power on the other, have produced an identity crisis in their work. The author concludes that the Black religious experience of conversion is the only viable point of departure for Black theology.

Cone, James H. *Black Theology and Black Power.* New York: Seabury Press, 1969; Reprint; 20th-Anniversary Edition, Harper & Row, 1989.

This seminal text is the author's first book on Black theology. The central thesis is that goal and message of Black Power is consistent with the gospel of Jesus Christ. The author understands liberation to be the core of the Christian faith, and issues a scathing critique of American theology and the White church for their role in the perpetuation of Black oppression. The author argues that the task of Black theology is to apply the freeing power of the gospel to Black people under White oppression. The classic text is the most important book in the history of Black theology in particular and North American liberation theology in general.

Cone, James H. *A Black Theology of Liberation.* Philadelphia: Lippincott, 1970. Reprint 1986; 20th-Anniversary ed., 1990, Maryknoll, N.Y.: Orbis Books.

This book further develops the theme of liberation as the content of Christian theology. The author develops a systematic Black theology of the classical Christian doctrines (God, humanity, Christology, ecclesiology, and eschatology) drawing on the sources of Black history, Black culture, the Bible, and revelation. Like the author's first book, this text is written in the passionate, provocative style that has characterized his theology.

Cone, James H. *The Spirituals and the Blues*. New York: Seabury Press, 1972. Reprint 1991, Maryknoll, N.Y.: Orbis Books.

This book examines the theological and sociological implications of the spirituals and the blues as expressions of Black culture. The author analyzes previous interpretations of the spirituals and discusses the experience of slavery that gave rise to them. The author interprets the themes of God, Jesus Christ, suffering, and heaven in the spirituals, and concludes with a discussion of the blues as "secular spirituals." This book should be read as the author's first response to critics who charged that he overlooked Black cultural sources in his first two books.

Cone, James H. *God of the Oppressed*. New York: Seabury Press, 1975.

This text represents the author's second book-length attempt to make wider use of Black cultural sources in shaping his theology. The author interprets the theological significance of the Black experience as reflected in sermons, songs, proverbs, and folktales as an example of his thesis that all theology is conditioned by the social and historical contexts of a particular people. This work is a classic text in Black theology and provides important insights into the issues that have fueled the debate among Black theologians.

Gardiner, James J. and J. Deotis Roberts. *Quest for a Black Theology*. Philadelphia: Pilgrim Press, 1971.

This book is the product of an important conference on Black theology and the Black Church held at Georgetown University on May 2-3, 1969. The essays in this volume are representative of the earliest attempts to develop a Black theology in the wake of the Black Power movement. The contributors include Albert Cleage, J. Deotis Roberts, Joseph Washington, Walter Yates, Preston Williams, and Joseph A. Johnson.

Johnson, Joseph A., Jr. *The Soul of the Black Preacher*. Philadelphia: Pilgrim Press, 1971.

This book is a collection of sermons and lectures delivered by the author, a bishop in the Christian Methodist Episcopal Church. The author interprets the significance of Jesus in the African American religious experience and relates it to the Black liberation struggle. The author defends Black theology as a much needed expression of authentic Christian faith in Jesus, the Liberator of the oppressed.

Jones, Major J. *Black Awareness: A Theology of Hope*. Nashville: Abingdon Press, 1971.

This text is the author's first book-length attempt to develop a Black theology based on the Black awareness movement and Jürgen Moltmann's theology of hope. The author analyzes the history of the Black Church and discusses the significance of Black awareness for the development of a theology of hope for the Black community. The author concludes with an interpretation of the concept of God in the Black community and expresses misgivings about the theology of James Cone, where God is understood to be solely on the side of oppressed Blacks.

Jones, Major J. *Black Christian Ethics*. Nashville: Abingdon Press, 1974.

This book is the product of the author's belief that Black theology lacks an adequate ethical base. The author examines the biblical roots of Christian ethics and argues that Black theologians such as James Cone have failed to fully adhere to these binding ethical principles. The author believes that Cone's ethical program is too confined to those passages of Scripture that fit the themes of Black political liberation. The author goes on to propose an adequate Christian ethical strategy for Black liberation that is consistent with the biblical ethical position.

Jones, William R. *Is God a White Racist? A Preamble to Black Theology*. Garden City, N.Y.: Anchor Books/Doubleday, 1973.

In this book the author seeks to establish the need for a viable theodicy that invalidates the claim of divine racism. The author critiques the theodicies of Albert Cleage, James Cone, J. Deotis Roberts, Major Jones, and Joseph Washington for their failure to reconcile the inordinate amount of Black suffering with the presupposed benevolence of God. The author proposes the position of humanocentric theism as the most suitable theological perspective that addresses the problem of Black suffering.

Lincoln, C. Eric. *The Black Church Since Frazier*. Published with E. Franklin Frazier's *The Negro Church in America* in one volume. New York: Schocken Books, 1974.

This short book provides an important analysis of the impact of Black Power on the theology and ministry of the Black Church. The author argues that the "Negro" church the noted sociologist E. Franklin Frazier wrote about in the early 1960s died in the midst of the Black Power movement; and that a new "Black" church emerged to meet the needs of a new generation. The author discusses the emergence of Black theology in the context of the civil rights and Black Power movements thus providing a useful introduction to the study of the discipline.

Lincoln, C. Eric. *The Black Experience in Religion*. Garden City, N.Y.: Anchor Books/ Doubleday, 1974.

This book is a collection of important essays (some of which are cited in this bibliography) on the Black religious experience published in the late 1960s and early 1970s. The book is divided into five chapters: Black Religion and the Black Church; Black Preachers, Black Preaching, and Black Theology; Black Religion and Black Protest; Black Cults and Sects; and Black Religion in Africa and the Caribbean. This text is a valuable resource for studying the impact of Black Power on Black religion.

Lucas, Lawrence E. *Black Priest/White Church: Catholics and Racism*. New York: Random House, 1970.

This book chronicles the experiences of a Black priest from Harlem whose major claim is that the Catholic Church accommodates itself to the racist systems and attitudes of American society. The book reflects the impact of Malcolm X's nationalist philosophy and the militancy of the Black Power movement on Black Catholics who sought to make the Catholic Church more relevant to the concerns of the Black community. The author concludes by sharing his reasons for remaining in the church, namely, to work within it in order to transform it into a community that works for the liberation of Black and oppressed peoples. This book is an important example of nascent Black theology from a Catholic perspective.

Massie, Priscilla, ed. *Black Faith and Black Solidarity: Pan-Africanism and Faith in Christ*. New York: Friendship Press, 1973.

This book is a collection of the papers presented at the 1971 consultation of Black and African theologians and church leaders at Dar es Salaam, Tanzania. The consultation (sponsored by the Tanzanian Council of Churches and the National Committee of Black Churchmen) addressed the theme "The Role of the Church as a Medium for Social Change," and was an important event in the ongoing dialogue between Black and African theologians.

Mitchell, Henry H. *Black Preaching*. New York: Lippincott, 1970.

This book provides an analysis of the distinctiveness of Black culture and its impact on Black preaching. After sketching the history of Black preaching, the author gives what has become the authoritative interpretation of the style, content, and technique of Black preaching. The author analyzes the use of story telling, Black English, types of delivery, and the role of celebration in Black preaching. The author concludes with a chapter suggesting a theology of Black preaching that seeks to interpret some of the theological assumptions that underlie this unique art form.

Mitchell, Henry H. *Black Belief*. New York: Harper & Row, 1975.

This book examines the continuity between African religious beliefs and those of African Americans. The author discusses the African roots of Black religion and culture as the source of a distinctive theology that is only recently being celebrated. The author discusses the doctrines of God and the Holy Spirit in Africa and among African Americans, and demonstrates the African retentions in Black religious culture.

Moore, Basil, ed. *The Challenge of Black Theology in South Africa*. Atlanta: John Knox Press, 1974.

This important text is a collection of the very first essays published on Black theology in South Africa. The book (originally published by the University Christian Movement in South Africa in 1972) was immediately banned by the South African Government, which viewed it as a threat to national security. All of the essays are groundbreaking attempts to reinterpret the gospel in light of Black oppression in South Africa. Some of the contributors include Steve Biko, Basil Moore, Bonganjalo Goba, Manas Buthelezi, James Cone, and Mokgethi Motlhabi.

Moyd, Olin P. *Redemption in Black Theology*. Valley Forge, Pa.: Judson Press, 1979.

In this book the author argues that redemption is a more inclusive term than liberation for describing the central motif of the Black religious experience. Redemption is understood as liberation from oppression and the formation of a community in covenantal relationship with God. Like Cecil Cone's *Identity Crisis in Black Theology* (1975), this work should be read as a critique of the exclusive focus on political liberation as a point of departure for Black theology.

Oglesby, Enoch H. *Ethics and Theology from the Other Side: Sounds of Moral Struggle*. New York: University Press of America, 1979.

This book is an analysis of the ethical content of Black religion and the role it plays in the African-American struggle for justice. The author examines slave religion; the Black Church; the moral and political philosophies of Booker T. Washington, W. E. B. Du Bois, and Marcus Garvey; the development of Black Power in the 1960s; and devotes a chapter to the liberation ethics of Martin Luther King, Jr. The author concludes that Black theology must emphasize the need for Blacks to take moral responsibility for their own welfare instead of focusing exclusively on their social and political victimization.

Raboteau, Albert J. *Slave Religion: The "Invisible Institution" in the Antebellum South*. New York: Oxford University Press, 1978.

This book is perhaps the most important historical study on the role of religion among African-American slaves. The author discusses the impact of African Traditional Religions on the slaves; the evangelization and conversion of African slaves to Christianity; and the distinctive nature of religion in the slave quarters. The book is an invaluable resource for the construction of a Black theology based on the religious experience of African-American slaves.

Roberts, J. Deotis. *Liberation and Reconciliation: A Black Theology*. Philadelphia: Westminster Press, 1971.

This text (the author's first book on Black theology) establishes the claim that the doctrine of reconciliation must be considered alongside liberation in any Black theological position that seeks to be authentically Christian. Like Major Jones, the author believes that the theology of James Cone lacks an adequate ethical base and overlooks the important doctrine of reconciliation. The author discusses the concepts of Blacks as the chosen people, God, Christology, and eschatology in light of the biblical notion of reconciliation. The author concludes by rejecting both integration and separatism in favor of a truly interracial community between equals.

Roberts, J. Deotis. *A Black Political Theology*. Philadelphia: Westminster Press, 1974.

This text is the author's second book attempting to develop a systematic Black theology. The author believes that the existing political theologies in Europe and Latin America provide important insights for Black theologians as they seek to interpret the Christian faith within the highly political context of racist America. The author seeks to establish the ethical foundations of Black theology; discusses Black theology as political theology; and articulates a systematic theology in dialogue with Albert Cleage, James Cone, and others. This book continues the debate over the place of reconciliation in Black theology.

Washington, Joseph R. *Black Religion: The Negro and Christianity in the United States*. Boston: Beacon Press, 1964.

This controversial book is one of the most important texts in the history of Black theology. The author's central thesis is that Black churches are not authentically Christian because they lack a doctrinal understanding of the Christian faith, and care more about social protest than theology. The author argues that the Black Church has no theology and consequently is an expression of folk religion—a fifth major religion in American culture alongside Judaism, Protestantism, Roman Catholicism, and secularism. The author concludes that Black churches must integrate into White churches in order to be a part of the authentic Christian tradition. The emergence of Black theology was, in part, a response to the author's claim that the Black Church had no theology.

Washington, Joseph R. *The Politics of God*. Boston: Beacon Press, 1967.

In this book the author reverses his optimistic views about the viability of integration for the Black Church, and exposes the limits of reason in dealing with the problem of racism. The author discusses the racist and demonic character of White folk religion and calls on the Black Church to make full use of its institutional power in the struggle to change White society.

Wilmore, Gayraud S. *Black Religion and Black Radicalism*. Garden City, N.Y.: Doubleday and Co., 1972. Second edition, 1983, Orbis Books.

This important text is an historical-theological interpretation of the African American religious experience. The author examines the theme of radicalism in Black religion characterizing it as a perspective that emphasizes a revalorization of the image of Africa, independence from White control, and acceptance of protest as a theological prerequisite to liberation. The author's central thesis is that the twentieth-century witnesses the deradicalization of Black religion and the dechristianization of Black radicalism. The author identifies the prophetic ministries of Martin Luther King, Jr., and Malcolm X, and the emergence of radical Black theology as examples of the necessary reunion that must take place between Black religion and Black radicalism.

Wright, Nathan, Jr. *Black Power and Urban Unrest: Creative Possibilities*. New York: Hawthorn Books, 1967.

This important book represents one of the very first responses by a Black clergyman to the emergence of Black Power. The author interprets the significance of the July 1966 NCNC statement on "Black Power," and then discusses the creative use of Black Power in relation to economics, education, Black leadership, and the churches of America. The author concludes that the creative use of Black Power will foster unity among Black people for the good of the entire nation as a whole. Chapter 9 of the book, "A Religious Opportunity," appears in the first edition of Wilmore and Cone, *Black Theology: A Documentary History 1966–1979* (Maryknoll, N.Y.: Orbis Books, 1979).

INDEX

Aaron, 67
Abortion, 290
Abraham, 67, 157, 160, 167, 259, 308
Africa, 259-62
African Ideas of God, 373
African Methodist Episcopal Church, 221, 250, 295, 328
African Methodist Episcopal Zion Church, 221, 257
African Religions and Philosophy, 375
Africanization, 351, 353, 375, 377
Agyeman, Jaramogi Abebe. *See* Albert Cleage
Alagoa, E. J., 261
Alexander, John, 239
All Africa Conference of Churches (AACC), 374-75, 385, 394, 398
Allen, Earl, 17, 34
Allen, Richard, 75, 134, 250, 255, 266, 270, 295, 329-30
Altizer, Thomas J., 72
Alves, Rubem, 201
American Academy of Religion, 6
American Dilemma, 251
Amos, 163, 194
Appiah-Kubi, Kofi, 398
Arce Martinez, Sergio, 280
Arius, 73
Armstrong, George D., 74
Asians and Blacks, 361, 447
Assmann, Hugo, 354-55, 406-7
Athanasius, 73
Austen, Jane, 344
Baille, John , 185
Baldwin, James, 106-7, 119, 120, 394
Baptists, 96, 220, 245, 296
Baraka, Imamu Amiri, 133
Baraka, LeRoi Jones Amir, 118
Baroni, Geno, 8
Barr, James, 179, 182
Barth, Karl, 3, 71, 81-83, 118, 156-57, 327, 357, 389, 427

Bastide, Roger, 369
Beale, Frances, 281, 284
Behm, Ron, 239
Bennett, John C., 5, 305
Bennett, Lerone, 116
Bennett, Robert A., 4, 157, 177
Bentley, William H., 233
Berenbaum, Michael, 309
Berger, Peter, 34, 159
Berton, Pierre, 73
Bethune, Mary McLeod, 287
Betz, Otto, 180
Beyond God the Father, 310
Bible, in Black theology, 184-89
Bible and Socialism: A Conversation between Two Preachers, 421
Bible in the Modern World, 179
Biblical Revelation and African Beliefs, 374
Biblical Theology in Crisis, 179
Black Awareness: A Theology of Hope, 178, 430, 450
Black Belief, 452
Black Christian Ethics, 451
Black Christian Nationalism: New Directions for the Black Church, 449
Black Christian Nationalist (BCN) Church, 263
Black Church in the African American Experience, 217
Black Church Since Frazier, 451
Black consciousness, 4
Black Economic Development Conference (BEDC), 128, 221
Black Experience in Religion, 451
Black Faith and Black Solidarity: Pan-Africanism and Faith in Christ, 351, 366, 452
Black Manifesto, 8, 16, 17, 27, 125, 138, 297, 427
Black Messiah, 90, 118, 127, 178, 382, 427, 449

Black Methodists for Church Renewal (BMCR), 299-300

Black Mood, 116

Black Political Theology, 178, 185, 430, 453

Black power, 4, 15-16, 18, 19, 23, 40-43, 74, 90, 106, 108-9, 225, 266, 427; and American theology, 79-84; and community, 43-46; and M. L. King, 61-64; and white church, 66

Black Power and Urban Unrest: Creative Possibilities, 454

Black Preaching, 452

Black Priest/White Church: Catholics and Racism, 451

Black Protest Thoughts in the Twentieth Century, 254

Black Religion: The Negro and Christianity in the United States, 89, 118, 228, 425, 448, 453

Black Religion and Black Radicalism, 91, 125, 274, 380, 454

Black Theology: A Documentary History, 1966-1979, 444, 454

Black Theology: The South African Voice, 383, 399

Black Theology II: Essays on the Formation and Outreach of Contemporary Black Theology, 448

Black Theology and Black Power, 17-18, 90, 118, 128, 156, 269, 379, 381, 427-28, 447, 449

Black Theology of Liberation, 90, 131, 135, 177, 185, 221, 247-49, 255, 380-82, 428, 447, 449

Black Woman, 281, 284

Black women, 294-98, 302; exploitation of, 287-88

Black Women in White America, 294

Blackness, 217, 220, 226, 248, 380-82, 385

Blatchford, Robert, 421

Blyden, Edward, 134, 367

Boesak, Allan, 157, 399, 448

Boff, Leonardo, 354, 396

Bonhoeffer, Dietrich, 68, 78

Boumédienne, Hanari, 107

Brazil, 407

Bronte, Emily, 344

Brown, H. Rap, 49, 64

Brown, James, 112, 116

Bruce, Calvin E., 448

Brunner, Emil, 118, 210

Bultmann, Rudolf, 170-71, 186, 188, 204, 208, 209

Bunche, Ralph, 219

Burns, Robert, 344

Buthelezi, Manas, 387, 398

Cade, Toni, 281-82, 284

Calvin, John, 184

Camus, Albert, 72, 108, 436

Canon, 184

Capital, 412

Capitalism, 7, 27, 29, 284, 286, 356, 410

Cardonnel, J., 201

Carmichael, Stokely, 42, 44, 46, 50, 52, 55, 57, 66, 108, 126, 205, 266-67, 368

Carr, Burgess, 398-400

Carter, Jimmy, 7

Catlett, Elizabeth, 343

Cartwright, Andrew, 259

Casalis, Georges, 5

Casserley, J. V. L., 131

Castro, Emilio, 66

Catholic Clergy Caucus, Black, 220, 230

Catholicism and Blacks, 99

Caucuses, ethnic, 299-302

Central Intelligence Agency (CIA), 28, 256

Cesaire, Aime, 116

Chapman, Mark L., 9, 441

Chauvinism, male, 290

Childs, Brevard, 179, 181-83, 189

Chilembwe, John, 367

Choice, 119

Christian Doctrine of Slavery, 74

Christian Ethics for Black Theology, 310, 430

Christian Faith in Black and White, 447

Christianity, 67

Christians for Socialism, 406-7

Church, 67-71, 103, 122, 226; Black, 217-222; and Black woman, 327-31; local, 227-29

Civil rights, 20-21

Civil War, 218

Classism, 355-56, 358, 362, 418

Cleage, Albert B., Jr., 17, 59, 89-90, 101, 117, 118, 127-28, 141, 178, 221, 372, 382, 427, 436, 441, 449

Cleaver, Eldridge, 39, 120, 249

Cleaver, Kathleen, 333
Cleveland, James, 116
Coker, Daniel, 367
Collins, Lucretia, 302
Colonialism, 261, 386
Colorlessness, 112
Comfort, Mark, 34
Communitarianism, 60
Community, 41, 43-46, 55
Cone, Cecil W., 236-37, 394, 431-35, 442, 449
Cone, James H., 5, 8-9, 17-18, 66, 90, 106, 116, 117, 118, 128-29, 131, 135, 141, 156-57, 177, 185-89, 199, 220-22, 235-36, 239, 243n9, 247-49, 253, 255, 266, 305, 309-11, 313, 318, 326, 328, 332, 351, 353, 356, 366, 379, 381, 383, 393, 404, 408, 413, 416, 425, 429-30, 442-43, 447, 449-50; theodicy, 146-49
Congregation and church, 98
Congress on Racial Equality (CORE), 254-55
Conscience, 55-56
Cooper, Anna, 281
Copher, Charles B., 4, 156
Couch, Beatriz Melano, 324, 354
Covenant, 161-62
Cox, Harvey, 69, 71, 356
Criticism, social, 414-20
Cross, 57
Crozier, Blanche, 307
Cuba, 280, 356-57
Cuffee, Paul, 367
Cullen, Countee, 104
Cullman, Oscar, 69
Culture, 350, 352, 419; Black, 227; four categories, 419-20
Cunningham, Devon, 90
Daly, Mary, 309-10, 314-15
David, 164, 259
David, Angela, 6
Debs, Eugene, 422
Deep River, 190
Definition, 108
Delaney, Martin, 134, 421
Dentan, Robert, 179-80
Diakonia, 69-70
Diaspora, 238
Dickson, Kwesi, 374, 394
Distribution of Wealth, 421

Divino Afflante Spiritu, 184
Douglass, Frederick, 331
Drake, St. Clair, 104
Du Bois, W. E. B., 51, 107, 116, 134, 206, 251, 268, 274, 394-95
Dunham, Katherine, 343
Dussel, Enrique, 354
Dwane, James M., 367
Eason, Vaughn, 221
Ebeling, Gerhard, 181
Edwards, O. Herbert, 25, 355, 443
Eichrodt, Walter, 180, 182, 189
Ekklesia, 68
Eliade, Mircea, 136
Elizabeth (slave), 329-30
Ellingworth, Paul, 374
Ellis, Carl, 239
Ellison, Ralph, 394
Erasmus, 118
Erskine, Noel, 240
Essays on Black Theology, 383, 399
Esther, 190
Ethics, 95
Ethics and Theology from the Other Side: Sounds of Moral Struggle, 453
Evans, Anthony, 237, 239-40
Exodus, 67, 150, 160-61, 238
Experience, 115
Ezekiel, 166
Fair, Ronald, 48
Faith, 62-63, 270
Fanon, Frantz, 119, 135, 205, 272, 378
Farewell to Innocence: A Socio-Ethical Study on Black Theology and Black Power, 399, 448
Farmer, Herbert, 185
Fashole-Luke, Edward W., 394, 399
Fauntroy, Walter, 331
Federal Bureau of Investigation (FBI), 256
Felder, Cain Hope, 157
Feuerbach, Ludwig, 437
Fitzhugh, George, 308
Flack, Roberta, 341, 346
Forman, James, 16, 32, 91, 128, 221, 294, 302, 427-28
Fox, George, 76
Franklin, Aretha, 341
Frazier, E. Franklin, 126, 228, 331, 451
Freedom, 38, 94, 109, 173, 195
Freire, Paulo, 354, 404-6, 407

Frustration, 102
Fuchs, Ernst, 211
Galatians, Epistle, 387
Garber, Paul R., 443
Gardiner, James J., 450
Garnet, Henry H., 271, 359, 371
Garvey, Marcus, 47-49, 104, 274, 372, 395
Germany, 407
Ghana, 352, 356, 385
God, 56, 67, 99-100, 160-61, 194, 246-47, 370; absence of, 50, 72; Black, 382
God of the Oppressed, 177-78, 185, 253, 430, 450
God Who Acts: Biblical Theology as Recital, 181
Gollwitzer, Helmut, 5
Graham, Billy, 208
Gramsci, Antonio, 418-20
Grant, Jacquelyn, 282, 323
Griffin, David, 356
Gutiérrez, Gustavo, 304-5, 356-57, 396
Hageman, Alice, 293
Hamer, Fannie Lou, 34, 287
Hamilton, Charles, 66
Harding, Vincent, 18, 34, 40, 116, 126-27, 179, 207, 382, 443-44
Harper, Frances, 343
Hare, Nathan, 49
Harris, Patricia, 7
Harrison, Bobby, 239
Hasel, Gerhard, 182, 188
Haselden, Kyle, 72-74, 76, 207
Haynes, Michael, 239
Hedgeman, Anna Arnold, 17, 25
Hegel, Friedrich, 412
Hermeneutics, 173-74, 178, 187
Herod, 198
Herzog, Frederick, 5
Hilliard, Clarence, 239
History, 410; biblical, 110-11; Black, 106-8, 109
Hitler, Adolf, 82
Hodgson, Peter C., 5
Hole, Judith, 300
Holiday, Billie, 341
Honest to God, 389
Hoover, Theressa, 281, 293, 324, 328
Hope, 360-61
Hordern, William, 70
Hosea, 163, 195

How Black Is the Gospel, 239
Hughes, Langston, 133, 372
Hurston, Zora, 342-44
Identity Crisis in Black Theology, 394, 449, 453
Ideology, 29
Idowu, Bolaj, 373-74
Iguiñiz, Javier, 354
Imago Dei, 150
Imari, Brother, 133
Imperialism, 29
Incarnation, 114, 389
Independent churches, African, 375, 400
Integration, 21, 44, 45, 120
International Black Appeal (IBA), 323
Interpretation, biblical, 181-82
Interpreter's Dictionary of the Bible, 180
Interreligious Foundation for Community Organization (IFCO), 6, 8, 16, 128, 221
Invisible Man, 394
Isaac, 160, 167
Is Anybody Listening to Black America?, 442
Is God a White Racist? A Preamble to Black Theology, 91, 178, 436, 451
Isaiah, 164, 169, 194
Islam, 104
Israel, 67-68, 101, 127, 160-67, 194, 263
Jackson, Jacquelyne, 332
Jackson, Joseph H., 6, 117, 220, 245
Jacob, 160, 167
James, C. L. R., 274
Japan, 280, 359-61
Jeremiah, 164, 166
Jeremias, Joachim, 172
Jesus, 2, 45, 47, 59, 68, 99, 101, 111, 122, 168-71, 209, 259, 264, 352, 370, 381-82; Black, 70-71; Liberator, 203-4
Jewish synagogues, 30-31, 33
John, 211, 387
John the Baptist, 168-69
Johnson, Joseph A., Jr., 15, 158, 203, 444, 450
Johnson, Lyndon, 6
Jones, Howard, 239
Jones, Major J., 178, 310-11, 313, 318, 430, 436, 444, 450-51
Jones, Miles J., 380

Jones, Randy, 239
Jones, William R., 91, 118, 141, 178, 238, 436-38, 444-45, 448, 451
Joseph, 209
Justice, 166
Karenga, Maulana Ron, 44, 46, 50, 52, 54-56, 58-59, 63, 91, 133, 205, 372
Keith, George, 76
Kerygma, 69
Kierkegaard, Soren, 213
Killens, John Oliver, 41-42, 48, 53, 56
King, Martin Luther, Jr., 1, 3, 4, 15, 41, 77, 90, 126, 133, 200, 205, 251, 255, 266-67, 269-70, 272-73, 310, 372, 421; and Black power, 61-64
Knox, John, 209
Kohler, Ludwig, 181
Koinonia, 69, 71
Korea, 280, 359-61
Kuitert, H. M., 195
Larsen, Nella, 342-43
Lee, Carleton, 134, 430
Lee, In Ha, 360
Lee, Jarena, 329-30
Lehmann, Paul, 117
Lerner, Gerda, 294
Lester, Julius, 43, 44, 46, 51
Levine, Ellen, 300
Lewis, C. S., 190
Lewis, G. P., 70
Liberation, 28, 109, 117, 119, 142, 171, 252-53, 264, 306, 351, 353, 372, 381, 388, 398, 428-30; Black, 111-12, 265; constitutive elements, 412-13; movements, 250-56
Liberation and Reconciliation: A Black Theology, 91, 178, 428, 453
Lincoln, C. Eric, 126, 217, 219-20, 331, 451
Loescher, Frank, 73, 77
Long, Charles, 3, 136, 179, 382, 430-34
Long, Huey, 148
Love, 21, 41; Black, 42; of enemy, 43
Lovell, John, Jr., 156
Lucas, Lawrence E., 5, 451
Luckman, Thomas, 159
Ludwig, Emil, 373
Luke, 167, 172, 208, 211-12
Luther, Martin, 118, 184
Mackintosh, H. R., 366
MacQuarrie, John, 114

Making of Black Revolutionaries, 294
Mamiga, Lawrence, 217
Mannheim, Karl, 159
Mao Tse-tung, 272
Mark, 167, 208, 211
Marshall, Calvin, 5, 221
Marx, Karl, 412, 418-19
Marxism, 9, 128, 222, 272-73, 305, 355, 358-59, 405, 407
Massey, James Earl, 239
Massie, Priscilla, 452
Matthew, 167, 171-72, 208, 211
Marty, Martin E., 89
Mary, 209
Mass media, 24
Mbiti, John, 352, 374-75, 379, 387-88, 391, 393-95, 399
McCall, Emmanuel L., 219
McKinney, Richard I., 445
Meredith, James, 267
Merger, 301
Merrie England, 421
Messiah, Black, 101-5, 104, 196-97, 254, 263
Messianism, 47-48
Methodists, 75, 96, 220, 224, 226, 250, 255, 296-97, 299-300 329
Methodology, dialectical, 410-12
Micah, 164
Míguez Bonino, José, 354
Miranda, Jose, 354
Mission Trends No. 4: Liberation vs. Theologies, 448
Missions, 296-97
Mitchell, Henry H., 129, 135, 236-37, 240, 445, 452
Moffat, Robert, 388
Mokone, Mangena, 367
Moltmann, Jürgen, 120, 141, 356, 383, 430
Moore, Basil, 334, 383
Moore, Howard, 28, 34
Moral Man and Immoral Society, 305
Morrison, Roy, 436
Morton, Nelle, 314-15
Moyd, Olin P., 452
Moses, 67, 187, 190, 259
Motlhabi, Mokgethi, 383
Mozley, J. K., 209
Mshana, Eliewaha, 398
Mugambi, Jesse, 388, 398

Muhammad, Elijah, 372
Murray, Pauli, 282, 304, 324
My Friend Is the Enemy, 239
Myrdal, Gunnar, 77, 251, 307
Nation of Islam, 58
National Association for the Advancement of Colored People, 254
National Black Economic Development Conference, 27, 30, 32, 33, 34
National Black Evangelical Association, 220, 233
National Committee of Black Churchmen. *See* National Conference of Black Christians
National Committee of Negro Churchmen. *See* National Conference of Black Christians
National Committee of Black Christians (NCBC), 5-7, 17, 19, 27, 37, 91, 129-30, 138, 221, 266, 269, 351, 371, 379, 425, 427
National Council of Churches, 17
Nationalists, Black, 27
Negritude, 116
Negro Church in America, 228, 451
Negro Spiritual Speaks of Life and Death, 190
Nehemiah, 259
Newton, Huey, 333
Niagara Movement, 51
Niebuhr, H. Richard, 76, 117
Niebuhr, Reinhold, 305
Niles, D. T., 367
Nixon, Richard M., 5-6
Nkrumah, Kwame, 395
Noah, 259
Ntwasa, Sabelo, 334
Nyerere, Julius K., 8
Oglesby, Enoch H., 453
Old and New in Interpretation, 179
Old Testament and Modern Study, 179
Old Testament Theology, 181
Oppression, 142
Otherworldly vs. this-worldly distinction, 22
Padmore, George, 274, 395
Paine, Thomas, 252
Pan-Africanism, 274, 351, 395
Paneloux, Father, 150
Pannell, William, 239
Parks, Rosa, 254, 272, 279

Patterson, Mary Jane, 331
Paul, St., 78, 102, 203-4, 210, 281, 306, 324, 326, 370, 387
Payne, Daniel, 268
Payton, Benjamin F., 16, 25
P'Bitek, Okot, 341
Peace Corps, 289
People United to Save Humanity (PUSH), 254-55
Plague, 150
Pluralism, 93
Poinsett, Alex, 90
Political element of Gospel, 398
Politics of God, 126, 454
Porteous, Norman, 179
Potter, Ronald, 239
Potter, Wyn Wright, 239
Poverty, 172, 397
Powell, Adam Clayton, Jr., 133, 270
Power, 55, 57, 61
Preaching, 69
Preface to Old Testament Theology, 179
Protestantism, 93-94, 96-97
Qahal, 67
Quakers, 76-77
Quest for a Black Theology, 450
Quietism, 150
Qumran, 184
Raboteau, Albert J., 453
Racism, 27, 29-30, 57, 69, 71, 73, 106, 121, 218, 224-25, 256, 257-58, 307, 317, 356-57, 362; divine, 142-43; origins of, 234-35; tolerated by the Church, 78
Rainey, "Ma," 344
Rebirth of Feminism, 300
Reconciliation, 22, 71, 118, 120, 311, 428-30
Redemption in Black Theology, 452
Reflections on the Psalms, 190
Reist, Benjamin, 5
Relevance of a Black Evangelical Theology for American Theology, 232
Religion, 58-60, 293; Black, 40, 92, 372
Religion of the Semites, 388
Reparations (owed to Black citizens), 31, 130
Resurrection, Black, 49-54
Revelation, 114, 160; social context of, in Old Testament, 160-66; social context of, in New Testament, 167-73

Revolution, 28, 35
Rhodesia, 255-56
Ricks, Willie, 266
Roberts, J. Deotis, 5, 91, 114, 129, 177-78, 179, 185, 236-37, 309-15, 318, 428-30, 436, 446, 450, 453
Robinson, John, 389
Robinson, Ruby Doris, 333
Rogers, Cornish, 351
Romero, Joan Arnold, 314
Rooks, Charles Shelby, 236-38, 446
Room of One's Own, 341, 344
Ross, Fred A., 74
Rowley, H. H., 179
Rubenstein, Richard, 141-42
Ruether, Rosemary, 282, 305-6, 309-10, 312-19
Russell, Letty M., 282, 305-7, 310-11, 319
Sacrifice, 352
Salley, Columbus, 239
Sallman, Warner, 90
Solomon, 197
Salpingectomy, 289
Salvation, 110, 370, 388
Sanders, James, 179, 183, 189
Sarah, 157
Sartre, Jean-Paul, 351, 436
Satan, 170
Saunders, Stanley, 45
Sawyerr, Harry, 394
Scandal, 171, 186
Scott, Debbie, 239
Scott, Elizabeth M., 301
Segregation, 21
Segundo, Juan L., 354
Self-defense, 53-54
Self-esteem, 41
Senghor, Leopold, 116, 368
Sexism, 307, 317, 332, 335
Sexist Religion and Women in the Church, 293
Shaw, Herbert Bell, 25, 221, 257
Simone, Nina, 341
Sin, 121, 151, 306
Skinner, John, 240
Skinner, Tom, 239
Slave Religion: The "Invisible Institution" in the Antebellum South, 453
Slavery, 74, 107, 218, 251-52, 316, 325; tolerated by the Church, 75-78

Slavery Ordained by God, 74
Small, Adam, 193
Smith, Amanda Berry, 330
Smith, Bessie, 341, 343-44
Smith, Edwin, 373
Smith, Robertson, 388
Socialism, 271, 378, 421-22
Society for the Study of Black Religion (SSBR), 1, 4, 7, 8, 352-53, 385, 425
Sociology of the South, 308
Song, Choan-Seng, 361
Soul, 116
Soul of the Black Preacher, 158, 203, 450
Souls of Black Folk, 251
South Africa, 29, 157, 200, 255, 288, 353, 383, 391, 398
Southern Christian Leadership Conference (SCLC), 15, 125, 254-55
Speiser, E. A., 183
Spirituals and the Blues, 190, 430, 450
Spivey, Charles S., Jr., 352
Stark, Werner, 159
Stendahl, Krister, 178, 180
Sterilization, 288-90
Stevens, Thaddeus, 22
Stuckey, Sterling, 371
Student Non-Violent Coordinating Committee (SNCC), 28, 51, 52, 55, 254, 333
Suffering, 142, 144-46, 360
Tanzania, 351
Taylor, F. J., 110, 370
Temple, William, 114
Terry, Lucy, 343
Theodicy, 141-42, 178, 238
Theology, 80, 111, 114, 174
Theology, African, 8, 373-76, 382-83; future, 393-400
Theology, American, 81
Theology, biblical, 180-82; and Black theology, 177, 184-86, 189-90
Theology, Black, 4, 17, 37-39, 106, 109, 114, 130, 132, 199, 206, 220, 236-38, 268-69, 324, 371-72; and African theology, 351-54, 366-78; and American theology, 379-84; and Asian theology, 359-63; and the Bible, 155-58; and Black women, 279-82, 323-35; and feminist theology, 304-19, 324; and Latin American theology, 354-59, 404-8; and Marxism, 409-22;

methodology, 141-43; sources of, 110-12, 133-38; in the theological curriculum, 189-90

Theology, eventful, 3

Theology, feminist, and Black theology, 304-19

Theology, liberation, 5, 8, 236, 304-7, 323-24

Theology, Third World, 7, 304, 318

Theology, western, 389

Theology, white, 205-6, 380

Theology, womanist, 6-7

Theology in the Americas (TIA), 8, 266, 274, 350-51, 354-56, 364n11

Theology of the Historical Traditions of Israel, 181

Theology of the Prophetic Traditions of Israel, 181

Third Life of Grange Copeland, 345

Third World, 258-60, 280

Thomas, George, 356, 382

Thomas, J. C., 386

Thomas, M. M., 367

Thurman, Howard, 190

Tillich, Paul, 81, 111, 185

Timothy, 324

Toomer, Jean, 339-40

Torah and Canon, 183

Torres, Camilo, 358

Torres, Sergio, 355-57

Tothill, F. D., 353

Toure, Sekou, 334

Tradition, 174

Tripp, Luke, 34

Troubling Biblical Waters: Race, Class, and Family, 157

Truth, Sojourner, 266, 279, 285, 287, 335

Tubman, Harriet, 266, 279, 287

Tucker, Lem, 240

Turner, Georgia Mae, 302

Turner, Henry M., 133, 271, 274

Turner, Nat, 76, 134, 252, 273, 359, 371, 421

Tutu, Desmond M., 352, 385

Types of Modern Theology, 366

Tyson, Cicely, 295

Unemployment, 21

Urban League, 254

Urquiza, Consuelo, 324

Valentin, Dora E., 280

Van der Post, Lawrens, 369

Varick, James, 266, 270

Vesey, Denmark, 371

Violence, 35, 352, 398; Black, 230

Von Rad, Gerhard, 181-82, 188-89

Vorster, Balthazar J., 8

Vos, M. C., 198

Walker, Alice, 282, 339

Walker, David, 268, 271, 371

Walker, Lucius, 16-17, 34

Washington, Booker T., 421

Washington, Joseph R., Jr., 83, 89, 92, 116, 125-26, 141, 228, 295, 372, 425-27, 436, 453-54; theodicy, 144-46

Watts, Leon, 221

West, Cornel, 9, 358, 409

What to Do and How to Do It or Socialism vs. Capitalism, 421

Wheatley, Phillis, 341-43, 346

When God Was Black, 239

Where Do We Go From Here?, 61

White Christians, 30-31, 33

White Women's Christ and Black Women's Jesus: Feminist Christology and Womanist Response, 323

Wieser, Thomas, 70

Wiles, Maurice, 390

Williams, Preston N., 129, 382, 446-47

Williams, Raymond, 419

Williams, Robert C., 447

Wilmore, Gayraud S., 26, 91, 125, 179, 236, 274, 351, 353, 356, 361, 363, 366, 380, 382, 431-35, 447-48, 454

Women and socialism, 421-22

Woodbey, George Washington, 421-22

Woolf, Virginia, 341, 344

World Council of Churches (WCC), 354, 377

Wright, G. E., 181

Wright, Leon E., 133, 448

Wright, Nathan, 26, 50-51, 56-57, 127, 454

Wright, R. R., 89

Wright, Richard, 120, 344

X, Malcolm, 1, 3, 4, 48-49, 90, 107, 205, 269, 372, 421

Yakini, Asabi. *See* Debbie Scott

Yevette, Samuel, 119

Young, Andrew, 7, 8

Your God Is Too White, 239

Zacchaeus, 38, 130